THE RISE OF MODERN AMERICA

1865–1951

THE MACMILLAN COMPANY
NEW YORK · BOSTON · CHICAGO · DALLAS
ATLANTA · SAN FRANCISCO

MACMILLAN AND CO., Limited
LONDON · BOMBAY · CALCUTTA · MADRAS
MELBOURNE

THE MACMILLAN COMPANY
OF CANADA, Limited
TORONTO

The Secretariat Building of the United Nations in New York

The Rise of

MODERN AMERICA

⋆ *1865-1951* ⋆

BY

Arthur Meier Schlesinger

Francis Lee Higginson Professor of History
at Harvard University

A fourth edition of *Political and Social Growth of the American People, 1865–1940;* in former editions entitled *Political and Social Growth of the United States, 1852–1933* and *Political and Social History of the United States, 1829–1925.*

NEW YORK · THE MACMILLAN COMPANY

PREFACE

EVERYONE recognizes the importance of a knowledge of the past for a better understanding of the present. In this sense, as Croce has observed, all history is contemporaneous. That reason for reading and studying United States history is as compelling as ever, but it has recently been reinforced by a new and equally vital one: the need to interpret America's ideals to other peoples. Americans have always moved freely over the face of the United States; now, with the nation obliged to shoulder global responsibilities, they are moving almost as freely over the face of the earth. If they are ill informed about their country's history, they cannot properly represent its great traditions or help make America's influence count everywhere for peace, human rights and economic improvement. In the words of Secretary of State Dean Acheson,

Democracy is a dynamic idea in the world. Many millions of persons look to this country for leadership in applying both the moral and practical idea of democracy to the problems which we and they face. It is our responsibility to demonstrate the unlimited creative possibilities of the democratic process for "better standards of life in larger freedom," in the language of the United Nations Charter.

This book traces the rise of modern America from a nation just emerging from a struggle for internal unity to a nation devoting its thought and strength to achieving world unity. In between these two milestones the people completed the settling of the continent, healed the sectional wounds left over from the Civil War, built up the country industrially, established new concepts of social justice, fought two gigantic wars and contributed significantly to the world's culture. In the course of these developments the line between 'domestic' and 'foreign' affairs has grown increasingly dim until in the aging twentieth century it has become almost a distinction without a difference. Today the intelligent citizen must be informed about Ethiopia and Manchuria, Iran and Israel, India and Pakistan, French Indo-China and Korea, as well as about his own land, since what goes on in far corners of the globe may immediately affect his own welfare and happiness.

This volume is the fourth edition of a work, first appearing in 1925, which bridged the years from 1829 to the time of publication. The second edition (1933) began with 1852 and the third (1941) with 1865, and continued to the dates of publication. Despite the tremendous piling up of history in the last decade I have resisted the temptation to shift the starting point still later. The transition to America's modern period came with the close of the Civil War, and the movements and problems that have arisen since then form an indispensable background for comprehending current situations at home and abroad. By judicious compression of the less important happenings in earlier years I have sought to give the entire narrative coherence, balance and perspective while leaving room for an ample consideration of the most recent events. As in the case of each previous revision, this one is largely rewritten.

My indebtedness to fellow historians is only partially indicated by the chapter bibliographies and the comprehensive list of books at the end of the volume. Similar citations could not be made to articles in scholarly journals for lack of space. I am under obligation to Professor Charles I. Foster of the North Carolina State College of Agriculture and Engineering for suggestions as to this revision; to my wife Elizabeth Bancroft Schlesinger and my son and colleague Arthur M. Schlesinger, Jr., for critical comments on some of the chapters; and to Professor Donald Born of Boston University for assistance in reading proof. In particular, I have leaned upon my secretary Elizabeth F. Hoxie who stood constant guard over the writing, helped see the manuscript through the press and compiled the index.

A. M. S.

Cambridge, Massachusetts
August 1, 1951

CONTENTS

PART TWO. DEMOCRACY AND EMPIRE

PART THREE. THE SEARCH FOR SECURITY

ILLUSTRATIONS

The 39-Story Secretariat Building of the United Nations with
the 7-Story UN Library in the Foreground   *Frontispiece*

Situated east of First Avenue between 42d and 48th Streets, New
York City, overlooking the East River. John D. Rockefeller, Jr.,
gave the original tract, New York City added other land, and the
United States Congress in 1948 advanced a loan of $65,000,000
for construction and equipment. Work on the site began in 1946,
and the buildings were completed in 1951. "When I look up at
the gleaming glass walls of the striking United Nations Building,"
wrote a refugee from Transylvania in the *New York Times,* Dec.
25, 1950, "I find it natural that it rose in this country and in this
city, at whose shores the whole world lies like the sea. Those countless millions, white and colored, the voices of a hundred nations,
singing as Americans the rousing chorus of freedom, and stretching
willing hands to help the world—those millions reveal the one great
goal: peace among men, and love driving out hate." Courtesy of
Brown Brothers.

xi

The Adams Memorial (1891) by Augustus Saint-Gaudens

Erected at the grave of Mrs. Henry Adams in Rock Creek Ceme-
tery, Washington, D. C., the inscrutable figure has been variously
called "The Peace of God," "Grief" and "Death." Courtesy of
Brown Brothers.

The Democratic Donkey

Said to have been invented by Thomas Nast in this cartoon. From
Harper's Weekly, Jan. 15, 1870. (For the Republican elephant,
which he also created, see page 81.)

A Populist View of How Wall Street Manipulated the Mind
of the Average Businessman

From William H. Harvey, *Coin's Financial School* (Chicago, 1894),
26.

"The Croquet Scene"

Painted in 1869 by Winslow Homer, better known for his seascapes.
Courtesy of the owner, William Sumner Appleton of Boston, and
the Fogg Art Museum. "One prime feature of the new game," says
How to Play Croquet, a Pocket Manual (rev. ed., Boston, 1878),
4, "is that it is an outdoor sport in which ladies and gentlemen,
boys and girls, may alike engage."

Bicycling on Riverside Drive, New York, 1895

Drawn by W. A. Rogers for *Harper's Weekly,* June 15, 1895.

An Eastern View of Free Silver

W. A. Rogers, the artist, titles the picture: "A Perilous Situation."
He sees the laborer and the farmer as the chief victims of the "silver
demagogues and Populists." From *Harper's Weekly,* April 27, 1895.
For a different interpretation of the situation, see the cartoon on
page 161.

"The Real British Lion"

An anti-imperialist view of Britain at the time of the Venezuelan
boundary dispute. Drawn by T. Powers and reproduced in the *Literary Digest,* Dec. 28, 1895, from the *New York Evening World.*
Compare this picture with the one on page 199. By 1898 Uncle Sam
himself was reaching out for world dominion.

The United States as a World Power

This cartoon, drawn by Walt McDougall for the *New York Eve-
ning Journal* and reproduced in the *American Monthly Review of
Reviews* for Sept., 1898, bore the legend: "Now, will he let go?
If you think he will let go you don't know him."

MAPS

PART I

NEW FOUNDATIONS OF AMERICAN
SOCIETY

*The whole basis of American life was transformed in
the generation after the Civil War. The South, at last
emancipated from slavery, suffered a painful rebirth. The
Great West, filling in its vacant spaces, emerged as a force
in national affairs. The East changed rapidly, almost fear-
somely, toward an urban and industrial order. These developments deeply affected all aspects of American government and society and influenced foreign relations as well.
At the end of the century a contemporary of Abraham
Lincoln could scarcely have recognized the new nation that
had arisen.*

CHAPTER I

THE FRUITS OF THE CIVIL WAR

THE REUNITED STATES

I T is the peculiar nature of war that in solving old problems it creates
new ones. The Civil War, which tragically set the American people
at each others' throats for so long, was no exception. On the one
hand, it settled the question of state sovereignty in favor of national
supremacy and in doing so banished Negro slavery, the underlying
cause of the struggle. The triumphant North, assured of a peaceful
and undivided country as well as a universal system of free labor,
could now turn freely to developing the nation's material resources
without fear that the Southern slavocracy would block its efforts.
On the other hand, the country was confronted with the problem of
integrating the South once more into the national life. Not only must
means be devised to return the eleven states to their earlier place in
the Union, but the conquered people must accept a repugnant conception of race relations and learn again to cherish the nation they
had tried to destroy.

Still other difficulties flowed from the war. The country was saddled
with an unprecedented debt of $2,750,000,000 and a huge mass of
depreciated paper money, creating uncertainty in the business world
and calling for suitable action by the government. Politically a new
factor appeared in the presence of several million ex-soldiers in the
electorate, whose support was eagerly sought by the politicians in
both geographic sections. The Republicans, as the party which had
guided the North to victory, lost no opportunity in the years ahead
to remind the voters that the Democrats had once espoused secession
and disloyalty, and in every presidential election but one through the
rest of the century they emphasized their own rectitude by naming as
their candidate a former officer of the Union army. As a further and
more concrete bid for the old-soldier vote they saw to it that Congress,
starting in 1862, granted pensions to the veterans on increasingly
generous terms until by 1900 the total amount had come to over
$2,500,000,000—nearly as much as the original war debt.

3

Though the government faced varied problems at the war's close, the first and most pressing one was that of the South. Inflamed by two generations of sectional controversy ending in four years of bloodshed, neither the victors nor the vanquished were in a fit mood to tackle the delicate task of mending the torn fabric of the Union. The ex-Confederate people, beaten in battle and broken in spirit, had also experienced the principal ravages of the war. The Northern foe had laid waste such thriving centers as Richmond, Columbia, Atlanta, Mobile and Vicksburg. Charleston, a Yankee visitor reported, was "a city of ruins, of desolation, of vacant houses, of widowed women, of rotting wharves." Transportation facilities had suffered. "Bridges were burnt," wrote an observer, "rails were torn up and twisted for miles and miles." Nor had the rural districts escaped. The South Carolina back country "looked for miles like a broad black streak of ruin and desolation—the fences all gone, lonesome smoke stacks, surrounded by dark heaps of ashes and cinders, marking the spots where human habitations had stood." Even in regions where the invaders had not penetrated, plantations had fallen into neglect and land values declined almost to the vanishing point. Added to these direct consequences of the fighting were the permanent costs of defeat: the derangement of the only labor system the South had ever known and the wiping out of private wealth through the confiscation of $2,000,000,000 or more in slave property and the collapse of Confederate bonds and currency.

Some persons, embittered and hopeless, fled the scene. At least eight thousand Southerners sought to rebuild their shattered fortunes in Canada, Mexico and other Latin American countries, especially Brazil where Negro slavery proved an attraction. But most stayed on, facing the future with whatever courage they could muster. Such men found a spokesman in the revered Robert E. Lee who urged the Southern people to "unite in honest efforts to obliterate the effects of the war and to restore the blessings of peace." Lee himself spent the five remaining years of his life as president of Washington College (afterward renamed Washington and Lee), where he helped educate the rising generation of Virginians in a new loyalty to the Union.

The South's immediate fate, however, hung on the decision of the North. But opinion in these twenty-five commonwealths was divided. Some men believed that the South had learned its lesson and there need be no fear of future misdoing. They favored forgiveness of the past and the prompt return of the seceded states upon the least onerous terms. This was what both President Lincoln and his successor Andrew Johnson strove to bring about with the support of Northern Democrats and conservative Republicans in Congress. But others regarded the attempt to dismember the Union as a fiendish act calling for stern retribution. Untouched by Lincoln's sentiment of "malice toward none, with charity for all," men like Thaddeus Stevens, Charles Sumner and Benjamin Wade demanded the surgeon's knife. Through creating conditions favorable to the growth of the Republican party in the Southern states they also counted on extending its power. They emphasized their belief in extreme measures by assuming the name of Radical Republicans or Radicals.

This clash of views supplies the key to the illogical, confused and protracted piece of statecraft known as Southern Reconstruction. The framers of the Constitution, content with making a Union which they expected to endure, had not thought it necessary to prescribe how to remake it; but even if they had, men were lacking in Washington after Lincoln's untimely death to direct the process with wisdom and skill. At no other crisis in American history has the quality of statesmanship been so poor, and at no time has the need been greater. The Southern question was actually threefold in character. As a humanitarian venture it involved looking after the four million former slaves until they found their feet in freedom. As a governmental problem it meant reviving the normal political life of the South and reattaching the states to the federal system. As an economic undertaking it implied assistance in combating the chaos into which agriculture and trade had fallen.

Unhappily, action could not be postponed until wartime passions cooled. Partisan prejudice, sectional spleen and motives of revenge colored the conduct of both victor and vanquished, with the result that no well-considered plan could be devised. Negro welfare began as an enterprise of private philanthropy and ended as a football for politicians. Political reconstruction early excited fierce differences within the majority party and, as the months passed, increasingly antagonized the more co-operative elements in Dixie. As for economic recovery, neither Congress nor the executive branch gave it serious thought, leaving the stricken people to muddle through as best they could.

STRIFE OVER THE SOUTHERN QUESTION

While the war was still going on, tentative steps had been taken both to aid the Negroes and to hasten the political reorganization of states where possible. From the early months of the fighting, when slaves began fleeing into the Union lines in the border states, the American Missionary Society and other Northern groups, assisted by British benevolent societies, ministered to their needs. They not only gave emergency relief—food, clothing and medical care—but they also set up schools to teach the 'three R's' and they provided religious instruction. As the federal armies occupied additional territory, however, the task became too great for private initiative, and Congress in March, 1865, anticipating the ratification of the Thirteenth Amendment abolishing slavery, created the Freedmen's Bureau.

Authorized to continue for one year after the war, this body under Major General Oliver O. Howard established branches throughout the South, co-ordinated and supplemented the activities of the private agencies, protected the civil rights of the freedmen in unfriendly communities and supervised labor contracts to ensure fair treatment by the former master class. The undertaking could hardly have been more difficult, for apart from the resentful attitude of the whites, who regarded the blacks as a hopelessly inferior breed of human beings, the Negroes themselves had yet to learn the distinction between freedom and idleness. Besides, the Bureau officials were inexperienced and often overzealous on behalf of their charges. Nevertheless the Freedmen's Bureau rendered a notable service at a critical time. Its chief failure lay in doing so little to partition abandoned plantations among the displaced persons. This had been authorized by the law, the tenant to pay a small rental with the right of purchase after three years, but both practical and legal difficulties stood in the way. On the other hand, the agency in its eventual four and a half years accomplished most of its aims. Among other things, it issued 15,500,000 rations to the needy, gave medical aid to nearly half a million, set up about fifty hospitals and spent more than $5,000,000 on schools.

In reinstating loyal governments in the South, President Lincoln took the lead. Designated by the Constitution as commander in chief of the army and navy and endowed with the pardoning power, he considered that he, rather than Congress, should decide when and how to terminate the military occupation. In line with his desire to restore normal conditions as fast as possible, he proceeded to set up new regimes wherever he could find a substantial nucleus of well-disposed citizens. First, he recognized as legal the makeshift government of Virginia, which had been improvised in 1861 to authorize the separation of West Virginia. Then in 1862 and 1863, when Tennessee, Louisiana and Arkansas passed under federal control, he appointed temporary military governors, and in a proclamation of December 8, 1863, he announced the terms upon which these and any other states could institute civil governments. The essential condition was that a tenth of the voters of 1860 in a state (excluding certain classes of citizens such as prominent Confederate officials) should swear to uphold the Constitution and to abide by the measures against slavery. Under this 'ten-per-cent plan' Tennessee, Louisiana and Arkansas held conventions and established governments during 1864. Though these, in Lincoln's homely phrase, were but "as the egg to the fowl," he believed that "we shall sooner have the fowl by hatching the egg than by smashing it."

Congress, though dominated by the President's own party, observed these proceedings with mounting concern. The Radical Republicans contended that the Constitution put Congress, not Lincoln, in the driver's seat, since Congress alone had the power to judge of the elections and qualifications of its members. Moreover, they thought his terms quite too soft to discourage treasonable movements in the future. While the lines were not as sharply drawn as they soon would be, the two houses refused to admit the members from Virginia and the ten-per-cent states and in July, 1864, laid down their own specifications in the Wade-Davis bill. This measure, among other things, imposed a far more drastic disfranchisement and required that a majority of the whites, not a mere tenth, qualify as voters. The President by a pocket veto stopped the bill from becoming a law, but he diplomatically recommended it nevertheless as "one very proper plan for the loyal people of any state choosing to adopt it."

This action is an augury of how he might have dealt with Congress when the return of peace made reconstruction the paramount issue. But hardly had Lee surrendered than an assassin's bullet ended Lincoln's life on April 14, 1865, while he was attending a Washington theater, and this calamity brought to the White House a man ill fitted to assume the reins at so critical a moment. Andrew Johnson's rise from humble origins had been even more remarkable than that of

Lincoln himself. Starting as a tailor's apprentice in a Tennessee mountain hamlet and unable to read or write until taught by his wife, he had fought his way upward by sheer pluck and native ability. Against tremendous odds and the scorn of the planter aristocracy he had won election to high state offices, the national House of Representatives and, shortly before the war, to the United States Senate. Thickset, swarthy, somber of visage, he possessed Andrew Jackson's attributes of pugnacity, self-confidence and an immovable loyalty to duty as he conceived it. He had stoutly resisted the secession of Tennessee, and his choice as Lincoln's running mate in 1864 was a sop to the War Democrats to support the ticket. Long experience in public life wore off some of his rough edges, revealing sterling traits of intellectual honesty and moral courage. Unfortunately the situation before him called also for tact, patience and political skill, and these were alien to his nature. To handicap him further, he entered office without an assured following in either the North or the South and without the personal prestige which would have been Lincoln's for having saved the Union.

While horror over the assassination was still at its height, Johnson offered rewards for the capture of Jefferson Davis and five other Southern leaders as instigators of the deed; and the Radicals, misled by this ill-considered action, hailed him as one of their own and spoke of Lincoln's murder as a "godsend to the country." Even the pastor of St. George's Church in New York declared that Divine Providence had "introduced a ruler whose stern experience of Southern wickedness will cut off all pleas of leniency to the base destroyers of their country."

But the new President disappointed such hopes, for on sober second thought he accepted the fundamentals of Lincoln's magnanimous policy. He approved the four state governments already formed (Virginia, Tennessee, Louisiana and Arkansas), retained his predecessor's cabinet [1] and hurried the reconstruction of the other seven commonwealths, though demanding a somewhat wider disfranchisement than had Lincoln. In addition, he urged the conventions when they met to disavow both secession and the state debts contracted in fighting the

[1] Consisting of William H. Seward of New York, Secretary of State; Hugh McCulloch of Indiana, Secretary of the Treasury; Edwin M. Stanton of Ohio, Secretary of War; Gideon Welles of Connecticut, Secretary of the Navy; J. P. Usher of Indiana, Secretary of the Interior; William Dennison of Ohio, Postmaster-General; and James Speed of Kentucky, Attorney-General.

Union, and asked that their legislatures upon assembling ratify the pending Thirteenth Amendment. When Congress convened on December 4, 1865, for the first time under the new executive, regular civil administrations were functioning in all the former Confederate states but Texas, which completed its handiwork the following April. Two weeks after the session began, the Thirteenth Amendment became a part of the Constitution. It carried Lincoln's wartime Emancipation Proclamation to its logical conclusion and rendered impossible the future revival of slavery.

The executive had proposed, but the legislative must dispose. Many people both in and out of Congress felt that the White House had proceeded overhastily. In particular, the Radical members stormed at the failure to fortify the freedmen with the suffrage. As a matter of fact, Johnson, like Lincoln before him, would have welcomed action by the Southern states to enfranchise educated Negroes and those who had fought in the Union army, but neither considered the vast bulk of the race ready for the responsibility.[1] But men like Senator Charles Sumner of Massachusetts regarded the ballot as an inherent democratic right, while others like his colleague in the House, Thaddeus Stevens of Pennsylvania, saw in it a means of building up a strong Republican party in the South. Indeed, unless the Negro were given the vote, the Southern Democrats would actually gain from losing the war, since they would increase their membership in Congress and the electoral college through the lapsing of the constitutional provision requiring that only three fifths of the slaves be counted for representation. A black electorate would, in Republican eyes, help offset the white electorate.

Further misgivings with the President's program arose from the willful course of the people in the reorganized states. Prominent ex-Confederates such as Jefferson Davis's Vice-President Alexander H. Stephens, just chosen Senator from Georgia, were again entering politics, while the new legislatures were adopting 'black codes' which to

[1] Even so ardent an abolitionist as William Lloyd Garrison disapproved action by Congress to force Negro suffrage upon the South, as also did Harriet Beecher Stowe, whom Lincoln called "the little woman who wrote the book that made this great war." The Negro historian Carter G. Woodson asserted in 1922, "Had there been a close coöperation among the best whites in the South and a gradual incorporation of the intelligent freedmen into the electorate, many of the mistakes made would have been obviated." The only Northern commonwealths in which Negroes could vote in 1865 were New York and five of the New England states, but the Radicals never deemed consistency a virtue.

Northerners seemed singularly like the old slave codes. This legislation sought chiefly to impose restraints which might discourage idleness, vagrancy and race friction. Thus, while granting freedmen basic rights like making contracts and acquiring property, it usually inflicted special penalties for breaking labor contracts, excluded the testimony of blacks in cases involving whites and forbade them to bear arms without a license. Mississippi and Georgia went so far as to subject idle Negroes to a fine which, if unpaid, must be worked out in the service of an employer. However reasonable in the eyes of the former master class, such regulations appeared to the Radicals a brazen effort to undo one of the principal results of the war.

This was the situation confronting Congress when it set about to formulate its own program of reconstruction. The Republican majority contained conservative and middle-of-the-road elements along with the Radical contingent. If President Johnson had known how to conciliate the middle-of-the-roaders with minor concessions, he might have been able to preserve the main features of his plan with the backing of the conservatives and the Democratic minority. But the insolence of the Radicals stung him beyond endurance, arousing all his combativeness and dogmatism. As a result, many of his potential allies were driven into league with Stevens and Sumner, iron-willed, imperious men who for the next two years carried everything their own way.

The two houses, after appointing a Joint Committee on Reconstruction to consider the terms of admitting the Southern members, turned to the problem of safeguarding the emancipated race against the black codes. Their first move, the Freedmen's Bureau bill in February, 1866, extended indefinitely that agency's life, enlarged its powers and expressly authorized it to invoke military aid. The President promptly rejected the measure as unconstitutional in peacetime, and in an intemperate speech he classed Sumner and Stevens with Jefferson Davis as traitors to the American system of government. Never again, however, was Johnson able to balk the lawmakers. In April Congress passed over his veto the Civil Rights Act, which conferred the duty of protecting the Negro against the black codes upon the federal courts instead of the Bureau, together with the right to call on the troops if necessary. Three months later Congress retrieved its earlier defeat by prolonging the existence of the Freedmen's Bureau.

Meanwhile the Joint Committee on Reconstruction had been taking evidence on Southern conditions, and at the end of April, 1866, it reported its conclusions in the form of a proposed change of the Constitution. With some modification at the hands of Congress this eventually became the Fourteenth Amendment. It dealt with every important phase of the Southern question. The first section embedded the principles of the Civil Rights Act in the basic law, thereby setting at rest all questions of its constitutionality. The second sought to bring about Negro suffrage by giving states the option of enfranchising all their male adult citizens or suffering a proportionate loss of representation in Congress. The third, inspired by the wish to delay the return of Southern leaders into politics, barred from office, until pardoned by Congress, every supporter of the Confederacy who had held a federal or state position before the war. The fourth section declared that the war debt of the South should never be paid nor that of the Union repudiated, and that former masters should never receive compensation for their slaves. In June the amendment went to the legislatures for ratification. As Johnson did not fail to point out, Southern governments regarded as unfit for membership in Congress were nonetheless deemed competent to assist in altering the Constitution. Tennessee quickly acceded and five days later, on July 24, Congress declared her entitled to representation. The other ten states rejected the amendment by thumping majorities.

Since both Congress and the executive had now put forward their proposals for Southern reconstruction, the fall elections of 1866 gave the people a chance to choose between them. The President's adherents sought to attract the moderates of both parties, but these promising efforts were unwittingly defeated by Johnson himself when he made a 'swing round the circle,' delivering blustering impromptu speeches in principal cities of the East and Midwest. His cause suffered further from a bloody race riot in New Orleans on July 30, which convinced many voters of the South's implacable hostility to the freedmen. Both sides strove to capture the soldier vote by assembling conventions of the veterans—efforts that may be said to mark the formal entry of the old-soldier influence into postwar politics. The Radicals gained a smashing victory, electing more than two thirds of each branch of Congress. If the President had stayed quietly in Washington, the outcome might have been different. As it was, the Radicals acclaimed the result as a popular mandate to treat the South as harshly as they pleased.

THE TRIUMPH OF THE RADICALS

When Congress met shortly after the election the Radicals proceeded to put their ideas into effect. Thaddeus Stevens drove through the House a bill imposing military rule for an indefinite period on the ten remaining commonwealths, but the Senate provided for its discontinuance whenever the people of a state agreed to Negro suffrage. The plan as worked out along these lines in legislation of March and July, 1867, rested on the assumption that no lawful governments existed in the South. The states were to be grouped in five districts under generals who should preserve order and retain or supplant civil officials as they saw fit. A state would recover membership in Congress when a constitutional convention, elected by both races (excluding unpardoned rebels), provided for Negro suffrage, when the newly elected legislature ratified the Fourteenth Amendment, and when a sufficient number of other ratifications placed the amendment in the United States Constitution.

Meanwhile the feeling between the President and Congress had grown constantly more vindictive. Johnson vainly vetoed the reconstruction legislation as unwise and unconstitutional, and the Radicals, for their part, set about to hamper and humiliate him at every turn. In the Tenure of Office Act of March, 1867, Congress, reversing all previous practice in this matter, declared that if the President discharged any officeholder without the Senate's consent he would commit a "high misdemeanor"—one of the offenses named in the Constitution for impeaching and removing the President himself. As a special protection for cabinet officers against dismissal, the act stated that, unless the Senate concurred, they were entitled to serve "during the term of the President by whom they may have been appointed and for one month thereafter." This provision was designed particularly to safeguard Secretary of War Edwin M. Stanton who had long been secretly in league with the Radicals. On February 21, 1868, Johnson made the move for which they had been hoping, when he fired Stanton without consulting the Senate. Three days later the House amid intense excitement voted to impeach the President for "high crimes and misdemeanors." If they could get rid of him, his successor, under the law as it then was, would be Benjamin Wade of Ohio, the president pro tem of the Senate and a confirmed Radical. They would thus kill two birds with one stone.

The trial, beginning on March 30, lasted two months. In accordance with the Constitution the Senate acted as the court under the Chief Justice of the Supreme Court (Salmon P. Chase) as presiding officer. The principal accusation involved the "high misdemeanor" of violating the Tenure of Office Act, but it was readily shown that this was not so, since Stanton, a Lincoln appointee, had served nearly three years after the term of the President who had named him. The Radicals then strove to oust the chief executive on purely political grounds. Throughout the North feeling ran high, with sentiment strong against Johnson. Even the Methodist General Conference, then in session in Chicago, set aside an hour of prayer that the Senators might be directed to do their "high duty." When the crucial vote came on May 16, the Senate stood 35 to 19 for conviction, only one vote short of the necessary two thirds. Seven Republicans manfully joined the Democratic minority to make this result possible. To posterity it is clear that Johnson had done nothing to merit removal. As Senator Lyman Trumbull said before casting his ballot for acquittal, "Once set the example of impeaching a President for what, when the excitement of the hour shall have subsided, will be regarded as insufficient causes . . . and no future President will be safe who happens to differ with a majority of the House and two thirds of the Senate on any measure deemed by them important."

While these stormy scenes were being enacted in Washington, Congress's program of Southern reconstruction had gone into effect. Johnson, notwithstanding his deep-seated objections, scrupulously observed the letter of the law. The district commanders he appointed sought to co-operate with the local authorities, but when this proved impossible, they did not hesitate to remove governors, as in Louisiana, Texas, Georgia and Mississippi, or to substitute military tribunals for the civil courts. In due course they set in motion the machinery for holding constitutional conventions. In six of the ten states ex-slaves made up a majority of the registered voters. These constituent assemblies were the most extraordinary in American history. Each contained Negro members, though only in South Carolina did they outnumber the whites and there the *Charleston Daily News* considered them, despite their political inexperience, "the best men in the convention." Another and more influential element consisted of 'Carpetbaggers,' Northern newcomers, mostly seeking spoils, who were popularly alleged to have carried all their belongings to the South in carpetbags, the usual hand luggage of the times. Allied with them was a small number of 'Scalawags,' Southern whites who for various reasons had forsaken their neighbors to espouse the Radical cause. The bulk of the Negro members counted for little except as pawns in the hands of white or black leaders.

During the late winter and spring of 1868 the conventions concluded their labors in every state but Texas. Surprisingly enough, the constitutions formed under these unpromising conditions contained many excellent provisions, notably for setting up free public schools, reforming local government and abolishing property qualifications for voting. All of them also guaranteed the civil and political equality of the freedmen, and some carried the principle of disfranchising ex-Confederates beyond any previous limits.

To the old master class these frames of government seemed to upset the natural order of society. Proclaiming themselves the defenders of 'Caucasian civilization' against 'African barbarism,' they did their utmost to prevent ratification at the polls, but the odds proved too heavy. Only in Mississippi, where the white-disfranchisement clause was exceptionally harsh, did a majority of those voting reject the instrument. Elsewhere—in Arkansas, the Carolinas, Georgia, Alabama, Florida and Louisiana—the constitutions were approved, and

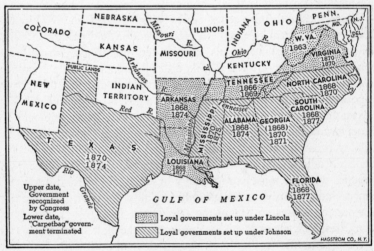

The Progress of Congressional Reconstruction, 1866–1877

the newly installed legislatures promptly ratified the Fourteenth Amendment. Though the amendment did not become a part of the federal Constitution until the next month, Congress in June, 1868, authorized the readmission of the seven states on the "fundamental" condition that they forever retain Negro suffrage. As Virginia and Texas had not yet completed the process of adopting constitutions, these two commonwealths along with Mississippi continued under military occupation. An important reason for hurrying action in the the other seven states was the desire to have their electoral support in the impending presidential election.

While Johnson's fate still hung in the balance before the Senate, the Radicals, calling themselves the National Union Republican party, met in Chicago on May 20, 1868, and unanimously nominated General Ulysses S. Grant as the head of their ticket, with Schuyler Colfax of Indiana, Speaker of the House, in the second place. The Radicals, afraid to put up one of their own number, were frankly hiding behind Grant's military fame. His political affiliations, so far as he had ever had any, had been Democratic until shortly before the impeachment trial when a quarrel with Johnson turned him toward the Radicals. The platform praised Congressional reconstruction and, anticipating the stand of the Democrats, pledged payment of the national debt in gold.

The Democrats faced a far harder problem, that of survival. Once the dominant party but now discredited by Southern secession and Northern Copperheadism, they must make a new start: atone for past offenses and develop fresh issues and fresh leaders. Assembling in New York on July 4 they strove to do this. Their platform pronounced the questions of slavery and secession "settled for all time," termed Radical reconstruction "unconstitutional" and "revolutionary" and, in a bid for new support, championed the 'Ohio Idea' of redeeming war bonds in greenbacks unless the law specifically called for "coin" (gold). This would mean that the investor would be paid off in the same depreciated money he had spent for the bonds. But the Eastern delegates felt otherwise, and on the twenty-second ballot they persuaded the convention to offset the financial 'heresy' by nominating for President a 'sound-money' man, Governor Horatio Seymour of New York. Francis P. Blair, Jr., of Missouri was picked for Vice-President. It would have been logical to back President Johnson for a second term, but the party was unwilling to carry the onus of his unpopularity and, much to his disappointment, he received little support.

The campaign was hotly contested. In the Midwest the slogan, 'The same currency for the bondholder and the ploughholder,' proved popular, but in the East the Democrats stood divided on the issue, while the Republicans largely contented themselves with insisting upon the 'treasonable' character of their opponents—an election device that was soon to be known as 'waving the bloody shirt.' Though both platforms promised pensions to Union veterans, naturally the Republican pledge was looked upon as the better bet. Grant won with 214 electoral votes to 80 for Seymour, but his victory was not so overwhelming as this indicates, since he polled only 53 per cent of the popular ballots (3,013,000) to 47 per cent (2,703,000). Except for the Negro vote in the seven newly reorganized states he would not have received a popular majority.

The new President was purely a product of the war. A West Point graduate, he had left the army in 1854 rather than stand trial on a charge of drunkenness. After failing at various occupations he was clerking for $800 a year in his father's leather store at Galena, Illinois, when the war broke out. This short, slouchy, taciturn man knew neither the theory nor the practice of politics; he had scarcely visited a state capital unless to capture it. Yet no executive ever took over the reins with greater assurance. "The responsibilities of the position I feel," he said in his brief inaugural address, "but accept them without fear." As chief magistrate he appeared to regard the office as a reward for his military services rather than as a solemn public trust. Unfortunately, too, he customarily turned for advice to men with selfish and often corrupt motives. No one could question his personal honor, however, and despite his shortcomings as President most people continued to venerate him as the 'Hero of Appomattox.'

Congress moved at once to dispose of the two issues raised by the campaign: the financial question and the completion of reconstruction. It settled the first on March 18, 1869, by formally pledging payment of the public debt in coin. As for the Southern problem, the Radicals, taught by the recent election how important Negro support was for party success, proposed a Fifteenth Amendment providing that the vote must never be denied "on account of race, color, or previous condition of servitude." This amendment rendered mandatory what the Fourteenth had left optional. Congress then required ratification by the still unreconstructed states of Virginia, Mississippi and Texas, and in the first three months of 1870 they were declared entitled to representation. Even so, the process was not yet finished, for Congress in December, 1869, incensed with Georgia for expelling all Negro members from its legislature, returned it to military rule until it, too, should ratify the Fifteenth Amendment. Upon compliance Georgia regained membership the following July. The Fifteenth Amendment had gone into effect nearly four months before.

THE SOUTHERN COUNTEROFFENSIVE

Though all the ex-Confederate states were now back in Congress, the Radicals had no thought of allowing them free rein. With good reason they feared the continuing resentment of the prewar ruling elements. The forcible remaking of Southern political and economic relations had wrenched the traditional life in ways that the upholders of white supremacy could only regard as monstrous and intolerable. Even as punishment for rebellion it smacked to them of petty spite. Nor was their exasperation lessened by the behavior of the ex-slaves. Though the rank and file went quietly about their tasks, delusions of grandeur dazzled others who, abetted by mulatto and white leaders from the North, strove to stir the freedmen to self-assertiveness. Organized in secret oath-bound societies known as Union Leagues, they often employed violence against former masters and others, waylaying them and burning houses and barns. All the latent Southern dread of a bloody race conflict revived. The whites were at first driven to anger, then to genuine alarm.

In politics the fruits of the new dispensation appeared in the actions of the state governments installed after martial rule was withdrawn. These regimes were dominated by Carpetbaggers. In the seven commonwealths reconstructed in 1868 they furnished four of the governors and ten of the United States Senators. Every legislature also contained a substantial group of Negroes, South Carolina's a majority. As James S. Pike, a Northern journalist, described the lawmakers of Calhoun's state, "The Speaker is black, the Clerk is black, the doorkeepers are black, the little pages are black, the chairman of the Ways and Means is black. . . . Every one esteems himself as good as his neighbor, and puts in his oar, apparently as often for love of riot and confusion as for anything else." But, he added acutely, "underneath all this shocking burlesque upon legislative proceedings" lay "something very real to this uncouth and untutored multitude. . . . Seven years ago these men were raising corn and cotton under the whip of the overseer. Today they are raising points of order and questions of privilege."

The new rulers seldom had large property interests; in Alabama the taxes paid by the legislators totaled less than a hundred dollars. Since the burden of taxation would fall upon the hated aristocracy, lawmakers saw no reason for staying their hand. Besides, there was real need of heavy expenditures for repairing roads, bridges and public buildings and for establishing free schools. The mounting costs, however, resulted mainly from other reasons: the irresponsible character of those in power, their ignorance of the rudiments of finance and, most of all, downright corruption and fraud. By 1872 the increased indebtedness of the eleven commonwealths stood at about $132,000,-000, much of it due to loans and guarantees to wildcat railroad enterprises. The orgy rose highest in Louisiana and South Carolina. In the latter state a free restaurant and bar was maintained for the lawmakers, and among the articles purchased as "legislative supplies" were hams, perfumes, suspenders, bonnets, champagne and a coffin.

Southern whites, trained to different civic standards, stood aghast at the social and political chaos. How could their proud civilization be saved from 'Africanization'? From Congress no relief was to be expected, and the Supreme Court in three cases in 1867 had turned a deaf ear to their pleas. They therefore resorted to that form of secret resistance which minority groups in other countries have adopted in similar moments of despair. The Ku Klux Klan, the best known of such organizations, started innocently in 1866 at Pulaski, near Nashville, Tennessee, as a means of providing diversion for local youths bored after the excitements of army life. When they observed that their weird nocturnal ceremonies aroused the superstitious dread of the Negroes, they quickly took advantage of this fact. Clad in ghostly manner and riding white-sheeted horses with muffled hoofs, they would visit the homes of unruly blacks and obnoxious whites at dead of night and warn them to behave or flee.

The Pulaski idea spread like wildfire, causing similar groups or "dens" to spring up elsewhere in Tennessee and nearby states. A secret meeting at Nashville in May, 1867, united the dens under the name of the Invisible Empire of the South, with officers bearing awe-inspiring titles. As time went on, the use of violence increased. Sometimes the midnight riders maimed their victims or killed them. Criminal bands, too, found it useful to don the disguise for purposes of loot or private vengeance. The situation was already out of hand when in March, 1869, the top men of the order decreed its disbandment. But this only worsened matters, for many of the dens refused to obey, and the withdrawal of the more responsible members gave the turbulent elements free sway. Through a misapprehension of the true facts, Northerners applied the term 'Ku Klux' to all terrorist movements in the South. In reality, scores of others existed, notably the powerful Knights of the White Camelia who operated in the states from Texas to the Carolinas under nominal control of a supreme council at New Orleans.

Northern Radicals saw in this lawlessness not evidence of their own blundering, but added proof of the South's impenitence. Benjamin Butler of Massachusetts, rising in the House of Representatives to demand stern measures of reprisal, brandished before the members a nightshirt stained with the blood of a Mississippi Carpetbagger. This gave rise to the expression 'waving the bloody shirt' and suggests the temper in which Congress dealt with the disorders. A series of Force Acts in 1870 and early 1871 empowered President Grant to break up the underground organizations and assure the Negroes their full rights under the Fourteenth and Fifteenth Amendments. For these purposes he might use armed force, suspend the writ of habeas corpus and appoint commissioners to supervise Congressional elections. Soon hundreds of men were haled before the federal courts, troops reappeared in many parts of the South, and for a while in the autumn of 1871 the privilege of habeas corpus was denied in nine South Carolina counties. As a result 'Ku Kluxing' virtually ceased early in 1872. It is a sufficient commentary upon the zeal of the Radicals that most of the basic provisions of these laws were afterward held unconstitutional by the Supreme Court.

In spite of this fresh intervention by the federal authorities steady strides were made toward the re-establishment of white rule. Tennessee, the first state to be reconstructed, cast off the Carpetbag yoke as early as 1869. Though the Force Acts threatened to halt progress elsewhere, the resourceful whites learned that a mere suggestion of violence served to scare the Negroes from the polls without affording evidence upon which a court could act. In 1870 and 1871 the Carpetbag regimes toppled in North Carolina, Virginia and Georgia. In 1872 Congress unwittingly aided the cause by restoring the right of office-holding to nearly a hundred thousand of those disqualified by the Fourteenth Amendment, thus restoring many of the South's ablest citizens to active public life. Meanwhile the Scalawags, wearying of their unnatural alliance with ex-slaves and Northern adventurers, began to vote with their white neighbors. Aided by these circumstances, Alabama, Arkansas, Texas and Mississippi were 'redeemed' in 1874 and 1875.

Only the presence of federal bayonets prolonged the Carpetbaggers' hold on the remaining commonwealths: Florida, South Carolina and Louisiana. The frantic struggle of the contending elements in these states to get the upper hand had grave consequences in the presidential campaign of 1876, for their electoral votes were thrown into dispute and thereby the outcome of the national election. The seating of the Democratic candidate, Samuel J. Tilden, would have ensured the withdrawal of the troops, but, as it happened, his rival's elevation had the same effect, since Rutherford B. Hayes belonged to that wing of the Republican party which had grown desperately tired of meddling in the South's affairs. Even before he took office the Carpetbag government fell in Florida, and when the soldiers were recalled from the other two states early in 1877, they too lapsed into white control.

In this tortuous fashion Reconstruction dragged to a close. For a decade, more or less, the Radical Republicans had denied to the Southern people the essentials of self-government, causing them to experience what Americans had never before known: military rule in time of peace. Northern influences, moreover, had degraded traditional political standards, and by loading premature duties upon the ex-slave had retarded his growth in civic responsibility. Southerners who had endured the nightmare could not easily forgive or forget. Not only did the ordeal make it harder to love the Union again, but it arrayed the mass of whites against the Republican party as an alien and 'nigger' party, hardening the ex-Confederate states into a Democratic 'Solid South,' which generally included also the border slave states.

Yet this is not the whole story. Much of the legislation of the Carpetbag regimes was the most progressive the South had yet known, as the native whites themselves recognized by continuing it after returning to power. As for the financial excesses, these, however deplorable, had less effect than might have been expected, since all the

states but Mississippi and Texas repudiated most of the bonded indebtedness—to the amount of $138,000,000—including in some
instances honestly incurred prewar obligations. As a national undertaking, moreover, it is to be remembered that the Reconstruction
process took the place of what in an international war would have
been the terms of peace. The South, having surrendered uncondi-
tionally, lay wholly at the mercy of its conqueror; yet few, if any,
countries had ever dealt so generously with vanquished minorities.
The Radicals executed no one for a political offense, confiscated
almost no enemy land, and within seven years after Appomattox restored the right of officeholding to all but four or five hundred of the
recent foe. Even Jefferson Davis, though never actually pardoned,
was left to his own devices after two years' detention as a state
prisoner. It was the considered opinion of James Bryce in his great
work *The American Commonwealth* that "there was never a civil war
or rebellion . . . followed by so few severities."

ECONOMIC RECOVERY IN THE SOUTH

Not only the political but the economic fabric of the South had to
be refashioned as a result of the war. A semifeudal order of society
resting upon slavery had to be made over into a modern system resting
upon free labor. Impoverished by the conflict, the big planters nevertheless tried to re-establish agriculture on its former large-scale basis.
But the obstacles proved insuperable, for they had to operate upon
borrowed capital, and they were hampered further by the rigors of
Carpetbag taxation as well as by the waywardness of their Negro
labor. Salvation seemed possible only through a breakup of the great
estates.

Accordingly the plan was widely adopted of disposing of small
tracts to Negroes and poor whites. These folk, unable to pay cash for
the land, usually became share-croppers, receiving tools, animals and
seed from the landlords in return for a third or a half of what they
raised. From 1860 to 1880 the number of farm holdings in Dixie
more than doubled, reaching a total of 1,500,000, with 300,000 added
in the next decade. To some extent this increase came from the cultivation of new land. As farms grew in number, the average holding
shrank in size—from 335 acres at the beginning of the war to 153 in
1880 and 139 in 1890. Southern agriculture began to take on the appearance of the Northern small-farm system. But there were signifi-

cant differences. The bulk of the farmers were tenants living in dire poverty, and often the landlord, through his control over them, managed a whole group of farms as a unit, thus preserving most of the advantages of prewar operation. Moreover, the tenants were constantly driven to borrow from local moneylenders at heavy rates of interest in anticipation of their harvest. This "lazy descent into hell," as Ben Tillman of South Carolina called it, plunged many into a bog of debt-peonage from which escape was heartbreakingly difficult.

Yet, in the long run, the subdivision of the great plantations made possible an independent economic footing for both Negroes and poor whites, the two classes which had been the chief victims of the slavery system. Under the share-crop arrangement any tenant might, and many did, save money and eventually purchase their holdings. But the scheme more immediately benefited the small yeoman farmers, whose larger financial resources enabled them to buy the choicer lands without waiting. It was this group who, as the old gentry retired from the countryside to the towns, were to seize the reins of political power and in the 1880's give Southern public life a distinctly plebeian cast. The agricultural reconstruction of the South involved the emancipation of the white masses in as real a sense as the Thirteenth Amendment had that of the Negroes.

The effects on production were no less impressive. Already by 1870 the average cotton yield per acre was greater than in prewar days, and before the close of the seventies both the cotton and tobacco crops exceeded the totals in 1860. Though the South continued to lag behind the North in agricultural methods, more farmers than ever before conserved the soil by crop rotation and the use of fertilizers. Cotton continued to be the mainstay, partly because of the insistence of moneylenders who knew it was always marketable. Nevertheless diversification increased, and in time the combined value of these other crops—tobacco, rice, sugar, fruits, vegetables, wheat, hay—surpassed that of cotton. Moreover, the quickened spirit of enterprise made men vision the possibility of developing manufactures. "If we have lost the victory on the field of fight," declared a South Carolina editor in 1881, "we can win it back in the work shop, in the factory, in an improved agriculture and horticulture, in our mines and in our schoolhouses." The industrializing trend of the eighties and nineties, however, formed part of an economic revolution that was transforming the whole nation, and will be considered in that connection.

THE DIPLOMATIC AFTERMATH

The close of the war left the North with accounts to settle with France and England as well as with the South. Napoleon III, in violation of the Monroe Doctrine, had engineered the overturn of the Mexican Republic in 1861, when America's hands were tied at home, and had established in its stead a regime under the Austrian Archduke Maximilian as puppet emperor supported by French bayonets; but realizing that the return of peace freed the Union army for action across the border, he recalled his forces early in 1867, and the situation promptly righted itself. Britain had offended by observing benevolent neutrality toward the Confederacy, and this problem proved harder to solve. The first attempt, the Johnson-Clarendon Convention in January, 1869, failed almost unanimously of Senate ratification because the pact did not specifically provide for defraying the damages inflicted on American commerce by the *Alabama* and other English-built Southern raiders. In an impassioned speech Senator Sumner, besides asking $15,000,000 for direct reparations, demanded over $2,000,000,000 more as indirect costs due largely to the effect of Britain's recognition of Confederate belligerency in prolonging the war. By running up the bill he hoped to induce England to cede Canada.

Sumner's extreme demands temporarily chilled British ardor for a settlement, but at this point a new factor entered the situation. Some Irish-Americans, organized in a secret Fenian Brotherhood, had formed in 1865 an Irish Republic-in-exile in New York, and in 1866 and again in 1870 they conducted raids into Canada in a quixotic attempt to seize it as a hostage for Erin's independence. The United States government displayed little zeal in restraining these activities, and the lesson was not lost on Great Britain. As mistress of many subject peoples she saw the importance of strict neutral conduct by other nations when her own sovereign authority was challenged.

In the Treaty of Washington in 1871 the two countries undertook to dispose of all existing questions at issue. After adjusting certain differences as to the fisheries and the use of waters of common concern to Canada and the United States, they referred the more contentious matters to arbitral commissions. A boundary dispute with Canada over the San Juan Islands in the channel dividing British Columbia from the state of Washington was submitted to the German Emperor, who afterward decided for the United States. In like manner the claims of British citizens for damages suffered from the North's prosecution of the Civil War went to a tribunal, which eventually made an award of nearly $2,000,000. As to the *Alabama* claims, the chief source of dissension, the British inserted in the treaty a frank expression of "regret" for what had happened and agreed that more rigorous rules should govern both the court of arbitration and the future observance of neutrality. Meeting in Geneva, the court, composed of members from Switzerland, Italy, Brazil, England and America, excluded Sumner's demands for indirect damages and in September, 1872, granted direct reparations of $15,500,000. The outcome was a signal triumph for the cause of international peace and good will. Two great nations had found a better method than the sword for settling their quarrels.

Still another consequence of the war was the acquisition of Alaska from Russia. Ever since 1861, when the Czar liberated the serfs, the Northern people had felt a sympathetic bond with Russia, and this was strengthened two years later by the appearance of her fleets in American waters at a time when the United States feared Anglo-French intervention on behalf of the South. Johnson's Secretary of State, William H. Seward, leaped at Russia's offer to sell the territory. The United States would thereby not only pay a supposed debt of gratitude, but oust another foreign power from North America as well as save Alaska from the clutches of England, long entrenched in Canada. The distant region was little known to the public—one wag proposed calling it "Walrussia" to honor both its most numerous denizens and the mother land—but the Senate in 1867 resoundingly ratified the treaty. As the future was to disclose, the United States for the modest sum of $7,200,000 had unwittingly made a noble purchase.

This acquisition and Sumner's eagerness for Canada represented in part a revival of the old sentiment of 'Manifest Destiny,' now shorn of its overtones of proslavery aggression. It fitted in with the heightened postwar nationalism and found in Secretary Seward a zealous champion. In 1867 he negotiated a treaty to buy two of the Danish West Indies (now the Virgin Islands) for $7,500,000, only to see it killed in the Senate. Three years later President Grant had no better luck when he submitted another project of Seward's, the annexation of the Dominican Republic. In the absence of special reasons and with the Great West still unoccupied, no real case existed for additional territory, and the Senate, moreover, was unwilling to take on a new problem of race relations in the West Indies while the one in the Southern states remained unsolved. American expansion into the Caribbean had to await more favorable circumstances. By odd chance the only semitropical outpost acquired in these years lay on the other side of the globe: the tiny, uninhabited Midway Islands, twelve hundred miles northwest of Hawaii, which a navy captain occupied in 1867. The average citizen remained unaware of their existence until shocked into knowledge by the Japanese attempt to capture them in World War II.

FULLER ACCOUNTS

New Foundations of American Society. For large-scale treatments spanning the years from 1865 to the close of the century, see Oberholtzer, *History of the United States;* Rhodes, *History of the United States;* and the later volumes of the co-operative works: Hart, ed., *The American Nation;* Johnson, ed., *Chronicles of America Series;* and Schlesinger and Fox, eds., *History of American Life,* the last of which stresses social and intellectual development. Johnson and Malone, eds., *Dictionary of American Biography,* offers succinct sketches of both major and minor figures, with bibliographical references to more extensive accounts. Of the pictorial surveys the more valuable compilations include Adams, *Album of American History;* Butterfield, *The American Past;* Gabriel, *Pageant of America;* Kouwenhoven, *Adventures of America;* Partridge and Bettmann, *As We Were;* and Rogers and Allen, *The American Procession.* Paullin, ed., *Atlas of the Historical Geography of the United States,* is the most complete work of its kind.

Southern Reconstruction. Besides Oberholtzer and Rhodes, cited in the preceding section, the subject is treated at length in Dunning, *Reconstruction, Political and Economic;* Henry, *Story of Reconstruction;* and Schouler, *History of the United States,* VII; and, more concisely, in Franklin, *From Slavery to Freedom;* Randall, *Civil War and Reconstruction;* and Simkins, *South Old and New.* The constitutional issues are discussed in Hockett, *Constitutional History,* II; Lewis, *American Political Thought;* Swisher, *American Constitutional Development;* and Warren, *Supreme Court in United States History,* II. DeWitt, *Impeachment and Trial of Andrew Johnson,* and Milton, *Age of Hate,* deal mainly with Johnson's role; Peirce, *Freedmen's Bureau,* with relief work among the Negroes; Horn, *Invisible Empire,* with the Ku Klux Klan and related movements; and Coleman, *Election of 1868,* with the Grant-Seymour campaign. Woodward, *Reunion and Reaction,* discusses the ending of Reconstruction in the last three Southern states. The principal biographies include Winston, *Johnson;* Current, *Stevens;* Haynes, *Sumner;* and Hesseltine, *Grant.*

Economic Recovery in the South. Bruce, *Rise of the New South,* Nevins, *Emergence of Modern America,* Shannon, *Farmer's Last Frontier,* and Thompson, *New South,* sketch the main developments, while Hammond, *Cotton In-*

dustry, Scott, *Repudiation of State Debts,* and Wesley, *Negro Labor,* treat particular phases.

The Diplomatic Aftermath. The short discussions in Bailey, *Diplomatic History,* and Bemis, *Diplomatic History,* can be supplemented by extended treatments of special aspects, such as Perkins, *Monroe Doctrine, 1826–1867* (on the Maximilian incident); Shippee, *Canadian American Relations* (which is also good on the Fenians); Goldwin Smith, *Treaty of Washington;* Thomas, *Russo-American Relations;* Farrar, *Annexation of Russian America;* Smith, *Republican Expansionists of the Early Reconstruction Era;* Tansill, *Purchase of the Danish West Indies* and his *United States and Santo Domingo.* For the part played by Grant's Secretary of State, consult Nevins, *Hamilton Fish.*

CHAPTER II

THE FRUITS OF PEACE

THE ECONOMIC REVOLUTION

WHAT the war did to remake the pattern of Southern life, other factors, only incidentally related to it, did to remake the pattern of national life. While the smoke still lingered over the battlefields and the Carpetbaggers ran their reckless course, mute forces were ushering in an Economic Revolution which brought changes so sudden and far-reaching that ever since the country has been trying to adjust itself to them. Like so many other developments in United States history, this one had its roots abroad—in eighteenth-century England where about the time of the War for Independence power-driven machinery began replacing human muscle in the making of textiles and other products. As fast as circumstances permitted, enterprising Americans adopted the improved methods, and early in the nineteenth century they added a new and vitally important feature, the principle of standardized or interchangeable parts. The device was applied to the manufacture of guns, plows, sewing machines and a few other articles, and from it was to arise the modern system of mass production. By the time of the Civil War mill districts had sprung up in New England and the Middle Atlantic states and to some extent gained a footing in the Midwest and Upper South. The mass of people, however, worked at other occupations, mainly farming.

Prewar industry was on a small scale, based usually on limited capital and supplying restricted markets. About two hundred companies in the 1850's made mowers and reapers, nearly a thousand turned out cotton goods, and after petroleum was found in western Pennsylvania in 1859, numerous little concerns took over the refining of that product. Slaughtering was perhaps the most decentralized business of all. Every town had at least one slaughterhouse, New York more than two hundred. The street now famed as Fifth Avenue was often choked with dusty cattle creeping toward great enclosures where today stand hotels, apartment houses and fine retail stores.

Mining and transportation were hardly more advanced. Though the discovery of the Comstock Lode in Nevada shortly before the war suggested the unplumbed underground wealth, so little had been done with America's mineral resources that large amounts of copper and coal were still imported. Nor had railway development passed much beyond its infancy. The lines were seldom longer than a few hundred miles, and wheezy engines hauled soot-covered passengers along a single track of iron rails in jerky, unheated, dimly lit cars.

Nevertheless the foundations of future achievement were already laid when the Civil War greatly stepped up the rate of progress. Military needs, currency inflation and the wartime protective tariffs stimulated nearly every branch of industry and trade, most notably perhaps the production of leather and woolen goods and ready-to-wear clothing. Pittsburgh, lying in an area rich in coal, petroleum and natural gas, moved rapidly ahead in iron manufactures, while Chicago as America's principal inland rail center assumed the lead in meat packing and certain other fields. A potent factor in the North's advance was the absence of Southerners from Congress for nearly a decade after 1861. Probably the Northern industrial and agrarian classes did not deliberately block the South's return to accomplish their ends, but there can be no doubt that they seized the opportunity to enact essential legislation which Southern opposition had earlier prevented. From these years date the conversion of high protection into a peacetime policy, the lavish subsidizing of transcontinental railway projects and the expanding of agriculture by free homesteads.

Spurred by these developments, the Economic Revolution reached full momentum in the years that followed. To men seeking money or the power that money gives, nothing under heaven seemed impossible, and the Republican-controlled federal government, sometimes by acting and sometimes by not acting, seconded their efforts. Many things of a more fundamental character also aided their success, notably brilliant business leadership, technological genius, abundant capital (much of it from abroad), the country's unmatched natural resources, the wide application of the principle of mass production and a copious supply of cheap labor. To these factors should be added, in the words of the 1900 census report, America's good fortune in being the biggest area in the world "unrestricted by customs, excises, or national prejudice," containing a people whose high standard of living gave them "a larger consuming capacity than that of any other nation."

Within a few short decades the United States evolved from a country employing simple methods of tillage and importing the bulk of its manufactures into an industrial country with an export trade in farm and factory products that reached the outer fringes of the globe. In the language of Edward Atkinson in 1891, "There has never been in the history of civilization a period, or a place, or a section of the earth in which science and invention have worked such progress or have created such opportunity for material welfare as in these United States in the period which has elapsed since the end of the civil war." "In short," as David A. Wells, another economist, put it, "to one whose present memory and life-experiences do not extend over a period of time more extensive than what is represented by a generation, the recital of the economic experiences and industrial conditions of the generation next preceding is very much akin to a recurrence to ancient history."

So swift and momentous a change could not take place without disrupting established ways of life and forcing profound readjustments. Never before had American society suffered such a severe attack of 'growing pains.' The political issues due to the Civil War were soon submerged by these newer interests. Southern Reconstruction touched only part of the Union; the reconstruction resulting from the Economic Revolution affected the whole. In the quarter of a century after Appomattox the machine extended its sway over all industry, the rise of the modern city disturbed the ancient balance of national life, the rift between capital and labor ominously widened, and a host of mechanical conveniences added greatly to the comfort of the average man. The social, political and intellectual consequences of the Economic Revolution form the central themes of American history since the Civil War. Industrial monopoly, the money question, the tariff, political corruption, immigration, labor and agrarian unrest, the turn to imperialism—such questions, new in kind or degree, illustrate the diversity and gravity of the problems. In the long run, the nation had to decide whether governmental institutions and practices, devised in the eighteenth century for a few million people living under rural conditions with easy means of livelihood, could be adapted to the needs of a teeming population fast becoming urban and industrialized.

The far-reaching character of the transformation can best be understood by examining its effects on the different sections of the country.

OCCUPYING THE LAST FRONTIER

In 1865 the settled area of the United States still lay largely to the east of a line running north through central Texas along the further limits of the states just beyond the Mississippi and including the eastern parts of Kansas and Nebraska. Even in the older regions considerable land remained vacant, while to the westward stretched the untenanted prairies till they merged in the gray, sagebrush plains extending to the foothills of the Rockies. For nearly a thousand miles the mountains then interposed their bulk, with more plains and deserts on the Pacific side ending in well-watered valleys and the shore of the ocean. Populated districts adjoined San Francisco and San Diego, with others in the Willamette and Columbia Valleys. Except for such scattered places, and notably the Mormon commonwealth in Utah, this immense domain was inhabited mostly by wild buffaloes and still wilder Indians. It took twenty-one days for the stagecoach line, inaugurated in 1858, to make the dangerous journey from St. Joseph on the Missouri to the West Coast, and ten days for the pony express, established two years later, to carry the mail. The American of 1865 looked upon this imperial expanse as a well-nigh inexhaustible reserve which would provide farms and natural resources for untold generations. Yet within a quarter of a century practically all the country was carved into states and territories, and what was regarded as the last of the arable lands had passed from the government into private hands. Never before had so far-flung a frontier been so quickly overrun by civilization.

Three factors speeded the process. One, the Homestead Act of 1862, granted free farms of 160 acres to citizens who would occupy and improve the land for five years. The original statute was supplemented in the 1870's by others making it possible for settlers to obtain additional acreage that was unwooded or arid.[1] This legislation had a

[1] The Timber Culture Act of 1873 (in effect until 1891) authorized a grant of 160 acres on condition that a part be planted with trees. The Desert Land Law of 1877 provided for selling 640 acres at $1.25 an acre to anyone who would undertake their irrigation. In addition, an act of 1878 enabled settlers to buy at $2.50 an acre tracts of 160 acres valuable chiefly for stone and timber. A further 160 acres might be secured under the Pre-emption Law of 1841 (repealed in 1891) at $1.25 an acre. By the Homestead Act and these other enactments an individual might conceivably acquire a holding of 1280 acres or two square miles. Much fraud developed in the actual operation.

double purpose: to hasten the development of the nation's neglected resources, and to serve as a form of federal work relief for persons who found the going too hard at home. It would doubtless have been wiser if the government had also extended credit to tide the occupants over the first trying years and if it had provided guidance in farming to the inexperienced, but such action would have been too far in advance of the times. Though many gave up before completing the five-year period, by 1900 possibly 400,000 families, totaling 2,000,-000 men, women and children, had received homesteads and held on to them.

The two other influences promoting settlement were the construction of the transcontinental railways and the taming of the redskins. A steam line to the Pacific had long been agitated, but sectional rivalries in the 1850's had prevented agreement as to its location. In 1862 Congress decided on a central route, following generally the path of the pony express, and entrusted the undertaking to two companies. The Union Pacific was to build westward from Council Bluffs on the Missouri River, and the Central Pacific, a California corporation, eastward from Sacramento, with the meeting point undetermined. To finance their operations the law, as amended in 1864, offered each company a free right of way through the public domain together with twenty alternate square miles of land for each mile of track laid and a loan in government bonds of $16,000, $32,000 or $48,000 a mile according as the roadbed traversed plain, plateau or mountain. Actual work on the lines, begun in 1866, proceeded under construction companies controlled by the leading stockholders of the roads concerned, an arrangement which led to shameless profiteering. The Crédit Mobilier, which acted for the Union Pacific, received, according to a Congressional inquiry, a total of $73,000,000 for work that cost less than $50,000,000. Greedy for the federal subsidies, each group tried to outdo the other in the trackage laid. The results were often hasty and wasteful construction and a failure to follow the natural and shortest route.

In the west, Chinese coolies in basket hats and flapping trousers served as the pick-and-shovel men, competing with the Irish paddies and ex-soldiers who were rushing the tracks toward them across the plains of Nebraska and Wyoming. All were guarded by scouts against hostile Indians and had to be ready in a twinkling to drop their tools for rifles and revolvers. The engineering difficulties sometimes were appalling. In traversing the Sierra Nevadas frequent tunnels and rock-cuttings were necessary, or long, high trestles had to be flung over ravines and gorges. To make matters worse, the men lacked steam shovels, steam derricks and other modern appliances; the road was almost literally handmade. The nation's imagination was deeply stirred as the work neared completion, and on May 10, 1869, when the two tracks met near Ogden, Utah, the 'wedding of the rails' was signalized with great pomp and circumstance. By means of the transcontinental telegraph, which had been constructed with federal help eight years before, the whole country listened to the blows of the silver sledge as it drove gold spikes into the connecting rails. New York amid booming cannon held thanksgiving services in Trinity Church, Philadelphia rang the old Liberty Bell, and Chicago celebrated with a seven-mile

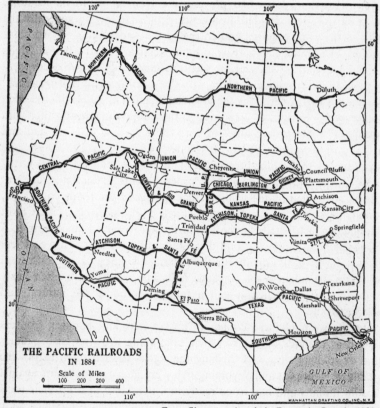

THE PACIFIC RAILROADS
IN 1884
Scale of Miles
0   100   200   300   400

From Shannon, *America's Economic Growth*, 1951

procession. The Union Pacific had built 1086 miles, the Central Pacific 689. The two oceans, hitherto sundered by a month's arduous travel, now lay within a week of each other.

The zeal for transcontinental roads did not spend itself with this first line. Even before it was finished, Congress had authorized the building of three others, one to the north of the original route and two to the south. Though these enterprises lacked the Union Pacific's advantage of government loans, they received even larger land subsidies. By 1884 these railways—the Northern Pacific, the Santa Fé (Atchison, Topeka and Santa Fé) and the Southern Pacific—were all in operation. In addition, a fifth line, the Canadian Pacific, which paralleled their tracks beyond the international border, often carried American pioneers. The rival companies left nothing undone to promote settlement, for established communities meant larger revenues from passenger and freight traffic and from the sale of railroad lands. They scattered boom literature and set up agencies in the Eastern states and in Europe. They offered low passenger rates to settlers and sometimes hauled them free. "Without the railroad," declared a Dakotan in the eighties with understandable exaggeration, "it would have required a century to accomplish what has been done in five years under its powerful influence." The federal government also benefited, since in return for its favors the roads were required to carry mail, as well as United States officials and soldiers, at reduced charges.

Meanwhile progress had been made in allaying the Indian peril. The story is hardly one to excite pride in the vaunted American spirit of fair play, but it amply illustrates the inexorable character of the conflict between two civilizations, the one dynamic and acquisitive, the other static and content with simple wants. In 1860 about 225,000 Indians were scattered through the Western country. In return for annual government rations of food, munitions and clothing, the bulk of them had agreed to live on reservations, keep the peace and allow migration along their trails. But as settlers penetrated the region these solemn treaty stipulations proved mere scraps of paper. Land-hungry or gôld-crazy, the newcomers viewed the redskin as a bar to the introduction of their 'superior' way of life, and whenever it suited their purpose, they seized his lands without further ado. In the end, the 'Great White Father' in Washington acquiesced, removing the tribes to less desirable tracts. "Many, if not most, of our Indian wars,"

President Hayes told Congress in 1877, "have had their origin in broken promises and acts of injustice on our part."

A further cause of friction was the destruction of the buffalo herds, the red man's mainstay of existence. From the buffalo or bison he secured food, clothing, bowstrings and harness, and from the sale of skins his principal source of cash. Perhaps thirteen million of these great shaggy beasts were roving the plains in the 1860's. The men building the railroads subsisted in large part on the meat supplied by scouts, such as William F. Cody who won his nickname of 'Buffalo Bill' from having shot down in eighteen months 4280 of the ungainly creatures. The worst slaughter, however, came from persons who killed wantonly for the sake of what they called sport, leaving the carcasses for coyotes and buzzards, and from bands of professional hunters who sold the hides to Eastern leather dealers. By 1878 the huge southern herd was wiped out, and with the constructing of the Northern Pacific a few years later, a like fate befell the smaller northern herd. By the 1890's less than a hundred buffaloes survived in the entire West.

Almost incessant conflict raged between the two races in the quarter of a century after 1862. Stung to reprisals by white encroachments or the actions of unprincipled government agents, the redskins would suddenly take to the warpath, burning, scalping and slaying. Savagery, unhappily, was not always on the one side, for probably most Western soldiers shared General Sheridan's sentiment: "The only good Indians I ever saw were dead." Never before had the United States waged such extensive frontier hostilities. One of the most tragic incidents was 'Custer's last stand,' when that audacious leader and some 260 soldiers were massacred on the banks of the Little Big Horn in southern Montana in 1876 by more than 2500 Sioux and Cheyenne. A list of the engagements between 1868 and 1882 alone fills over a hundred pages. One never knew when out of the vast treeless expanse murderous bands would swoop down on isolated settlements. Success for the whites depended upon eternal vigilance, instant preparedness and dauntless daring. Fortunately many of the commanders, like Nelson A. Miles, George Crook, Ranald S. Mackenzie, Philip H. Sheridan and George A. Custer, had been seasoned for the task in the Civil War. Every mile of Western railroad increased the white man's advantage, while the vanishing of the buffalo left the red man little choice but to accept confinement in government reservations. As the eighties drew to a close, the Indian problem had become less a military one than one of assimilating the tribesmen to American civilization. The protracted warfare, however, had made the Great West safe for the more advanced race and placed the best lands at its disposal.

The news of valuable metals in the mountain regions started the first great influx of population. The Comstock Lode in Nevada, which yielded $145,000,000 worth of gold and silver in little more than a decade, was but the most fabulous of these strikes. In the same year as its discovery, 1859, prospectors located gold in Colorado, precipitating a stampede of perhaps a hundred thousand persons for 'Pike's Peak or Bust!' Some set out on foot, shouldering packs; others pulled flimsy handcarts laden with meager supplies; still others went on horseback or in canvas-covered wagons. Subsequent years saw the opening of rich mineral deposits of various kinds in other areas: eastern Washington and Oregon, western Montana, Idaho, New Mexico and Arizona.

In the wake of these finds boom towns sprang up like mushrooms in a lush soil. Of Virginia City, Montana, a resident later wrote, "This human hive, numbering at least ten thousand people, was the product of ninety days. Into it were crowded all the elements of a rough and active civilization. . . . Gold was abundant, and every possible device was employed by the gamblers, the traders, the vile men and women that had come with the miners to the locality, to obtain it. . . . Not a day or night passed which did not yield its full fruition of vice, quarrels, wounds, or murders." Such conditions represented only a passing phase, difficult to control because of remoteness from the seats of constituted authority. In many cases the more substantial citizens took the law into their own hands, forming bands of vigilantes to depose the badman and the desperado. Most of the adventurers failed to 'strike it rich' or to gain anything at all save experience, but many nevertheless stayed on, finding an unexpected source of livelihood in ranching or agriculture. Despite the stupendous mineral discoveries, the new country itself benefited little, for the lion's share of the profits went to California mining corporations and Eastern stock speculators.

Meanwhile almost as powerful a magnet was drawing settlers into the plains country east of the Rockies. That vast stretch of grassland had halted the westward trek of farmers, who knew not how to cope with the dry climate, sparse vegetation and unfamiliar soils. Since Spanish days cattle raising had been a major occupation in Texas, and after the war enterprising men took advantage of the fact that if the tough, wiry longhorns were driven north across the unfenced public domain, grazing as they went, they would arrive at the railway shipping points in Kansas fatter than when they started. Soon the 'Long Drive' became a regular event, with an estimated average of half a million making the journey annually between 1870 and 1890. At the terminal points 'cow towns' grew up, rivaling the mining camps in their gaudy, turbulent life. If Dodge City on the newly built Santa Fé had special claims to being the 'Bibulous Babylon of the Frontier,' the other places also had their 'boot-hill' cemeteries for burying drovers killed in drunken brawls. At the same time the cattle industry spread into the Northern Great Plains, thanks to the demand of mining towns for fresh beef and to the facilities afforded by the rail lines for marketing meat in the East by means of the newly devised refrigerator cars. Before long, great herds dotted Colorado, Wyoming, Montana, Kansas, Nebraska and Dakota, while Western towns took up the slaughter and dressing of meat. "Cotton was once crowned king," exulted a frontier editor, "but grass is now."

Life on the open range was stirring and colorful, with the cowboy, later celebrated in song and story, as the central figure. "We led a free and hardy life, with horse and with rifle," wrote Theodore Roosevelt in fond memory of his own experiences in Dakota. "We worked under the scorching mid-summer sun, when the wide plains shimmered and wavered in the heat; and we knew the freezing misery of riding night guard round the cattle in the late fall roundup." But, he went on, "we felt the beat of hardy life in our veins and ours was the glory of work and the joy of living." The huge profits of the 'cattle kings' stemmed from the benevolent neglect of the government. After branding the animals the cowboys allowed them to roam at will over the public domain and then, at the spring roundup, collected them for the drive to market. Cattle, costing relatively little, raised in vast numbers, fed on free pasturage and requiring few men to tend them, could be sold in several years for five or six times the initial outlay. Peace did not always dwell on the ranges. Petty wars often raged over water rights, the illicit changing of brands and cattle stealing. Sometimes, to vary the routine, the stockmen made common cause against the sheepherders, who soon appeared to appropriate their share of free land and free grass.

By the late eighties, however, the halcyon days of the cattlemen were over. Not far behind the cowman creaked the covered wagon of the 'nester' or farmer, bringing his womenfolk and children, his draft horses, milch cows and pigs. Under the Homestead Act he staked off his claim, fenced it with barbed wire and, protected by the government, ousted the ranchmen from lands illegally held. Other developments also injured the industry. State quarantine measures against the spread of cattle diseases impeded the movement of herds using the Long Drive, the criss-crossing of railroad lines chopped up the open range, and the immense profits led to overstocking and declining prices. Money had poured into the business not only from Chicago, New York and other Eastern points, but also from Europe, notably Great Britain and Germany. As the crowning disaster, the bitter winters from 1885 to 1887 killed countless animals. Hastened by these circumstances, the romantic cattle kingdom steadily gave way to settled communities and prosaic fields of wheat, corn and oats. "It was right and necessary that this life should pass," declared Roosevelt in retrospect, "for the safety of our country lies in its being made the country of the small home-maker." In order to survive, the stock grower had to adopt new ways—own his grazing grounds, provide winter feed and breed better cattle. Actually, the enclosure of land led to no decline of the business, for the total number of beef cattle in the United States nearly doubled between 1880 and 1900.

The influx of farmers into the West quickened the agricultural revolution that was overspreading the United States. In the single decade from 1870 to 1880 an area as large as the British Isles and Sweden was brought under cultivation, and the next score of years added an even greater domain. California and Florida featured citrus fruits, Wisconsin took the lead in dairy products, while wheat was the main reliance in Minnesota, Illinois, Ohio and Kansas, and corn in Iowa, where it went to market either as grain or in the converted form of hogs. Between 1860 and 1880 the production of wheat and corn doubled, only to double again by the end of the century. By 1880 the United States had become the greatest wheat-exporting country in the world. The recurrent crop surpluses provided one of the mainsprings of agrarian unrest in these years.

The enormous output, however, was due to better farming methods as well as to more farms. With nearly every husbandman a landowner, mechanical power was necessary to offset the shortage of hired hands. Improvement followed upon improvement, invention upon invention, causing many a homestead to be mortgaged to obtain the labor-saving implements. As early as the 1850's steam engines began to be used in threshing. Windmills suitable for parched regions appeared on the market soon after the Civil War. The twine binder, invented in 1878 by John F. Appleby of Wisconsin, greatly stimulated wheat growing by increasing the speed of harvesting. While these and other technological devices were making the farmer more efficient, the federal government in 1862 aided the cause by establishing the Department of Agriculture and passing the Morrill Act, which offered each state a generous land grant to endow a college devoted chiefly to agriculture and the mechanic arts. With the more than eleven million acres so distributed—an area twice the size of Massachusetts —the states either enlarged old institutions or founded new ones. In 1887 Congress went even further in the Hatch Act by subsidizing state experiment stations for agricultural research. Soon important discoveries helped to improve soil fertility, animal breeding and methods of combating both insect pests and the diseases of plants and animals. America led the world in transforming a traditional folk exercise into an applied science.

The various influences furthering westward migration hastened the organization of the frontier country into self-governing communities. The amazing increase of population prompted the saying that you couldn't tell the truth about the Great West without lying. From 1870 to 1890 Idaho grew sixfold, Montana and Wyoming sevenfold, Colorado tenfold, Washington fifteenfold. The areas known as New Mexico and Utah, though thinly settled, had early obtained territorial status as a by-product of the Compromise of 1850, and similar governments were set up in the next few years in Washington, Kansas and Nebraska, and in the sixties in nearly all the rest of the region. Only so-called Indian Territory, lying immediately north of Texas, continued under purely Indian control. In most of these instances statehood ensued. Kansas was admitted in 1861, and Nevada somewhat prematurely three years later, thanks to Lincoln's need of support in Congress. Nebraska followed in 1867, Colorado in 1876, and six more states in 1889–1890: the Dakotas, Montana, Washington, Idaho and Wyoming. Utah, one of the most populous, was denied statehood until the Mormon Church in 1896 finally satisfied Congress that the national laws against polygamy were being enforced. Only New Mexico and Arizona failed to attain the goal.

Meanwhile, pressure to open additional lands to settlers brought about the curtailment of Indian Territory, the last considerable remnant of the red man's once continental domain. On April 22, 1889, the President at Congress's bidding admitted homesteaders to the Oklahoma district, an unoccupied tract of nearly three thousand square miles in the heart of the Territory. Hordes of 'boomers,' many of whom had been straining at the leash for weeks, awaited the signal to cross the borders. At high noon a bugle sounded, the soldiers stood aside, and the motley throng—on horses, in wagons, some on Santa Fé trains—raced to stake their claims. By nightfall Oklahoma City and Guthrie, tented communities of ten or twelve thousand, had sprung into being, while over the countryside flickering campfires told of farm homes in the making. With sixty thousand settlers in the district before the year's end, Congress in 1890 created the Territory of Oklahoma out of an irregular area in the western part of Indian Territory plus 'No Man's Land,' a narrow rectangular strip adjoining the northernmost wedge of Texas. As additional tracts of Indian land were opened from time to time, similar though less spectacular scenes were enacted, and the population continued to mount. As with New Mexico and Arizona, however, statehood was delayed until the twentieth century.

Though public lands still remained for occupancy, the unbroken frontier was gone by 1890 and the best sites had been transferred to private owners. From earliest times the existence of untapped natural resources open to all had served as an insurance policy of national prosperity. By draining off the restless souls from the older parts of the country the West had also acted as an exhaust valve of social discontent. The rugged individualism and incurable optimism which pioneer life engendered became part of the American habit of mind. Thus a great historic force, shaping the national character from the first days of colonization, was slowing to a halt. Yet there occurred no sudden shock to the social and economic structure. Much scattered good land still awaited the settler, since only a thin film of population covered most of the Great West. The years ahead would, moreover, reveal unsuspected vistas for husbandry as Americans learned the secret of dry farming and the federal authorities reclaimed countless acres through irrigation and drainage. Actually, more land was taken up for homestead and grazing purposes in the generation after 1890 than in the one before. Furthermore, an abundance of privately owned cheap land was available apart from the free government tracts, while across the international border lay an immense untenanted zone to which in the years 1900–1920 went over a million settlers willing to throw in their lot with Canada. But most important of all was the prospect of employment and wealth afforded by the growth of urban centers and the rise of new industries. Even while men were still crowding westward, the city was vying with the "lure of the sunset regions"; later it became the major attraction. If the townward drift meant turning American thought and energy in a different direction, at least it provided equally challenging opportunities for individual initiative, enterprise and achievement.

INDUSTRY OVERTAKES AGRICULTURE

While the agricultural revolution wrought its marvels, the revolution in manufacturing, mining, transportation and communication was accomplishing even more astonishing results. Though the Great West contributed to these developments, the activity centered in the older parts of the country. The years after the Civil War, according to the United States Industrial Commission in 1902, saw "probably the most rapid change in the methods of industry observable at any time in history." The value of manufactures rose from less than two billion dollars in 1860 to almost five and a half in 1880. Though in 1880 farming was still the chief source of national wealth, manufacturing took the lead before 1890, and by the century's close it overtopped the value of agricultural products by more than two to one. The rate of advance in particular industries was even greater. By 1894 the United States, which had been the fourth manufacturing nation in the world in 1860, had become the first, its output exceeding the combined total of Great Britain and Germany, its nearest competitors.

The major progress took place in the North Atlantic states, where many sections became thoroughly industrialized. Southern New England excelled in textiles, boots and shoes and the finer grades of paper; Pennsylvania, in tanning and iron and steel products; New Jersey, in silks; and eastern and southern New York, in the bewildering variety and total value of its wares. At the same time factories spread into the Midwest in such numbers as to shift the center of manufactures in the nation from western Pennsylvania in 1860 to northeastern Ohio (near Canton) in 1890. This newer part of America specialized in farm implements, railway supplies, building materials, furniture and prepared foods and drinks. Chicago, presiding over a far-flung network of transportation facilities, possessed nearly eight hundred woodworking establishments, machine shops and metal works by 1880, besides more than a hundred breweries and distilleries.

During these years, too, manufacturing invaded Dixie on a considerable scale, being attracted by abundant raw materials, cheap water power and the absence of unions and of factory legislation. The cry, 'Bring the mills to the cotton,' awakened the seaboard South to the possibilities, and in the 1880's the fall line of the rivers became dotted with plants built by the meager savings of the people nearby and operated by underpaid poor whites—men, women and children. By 1900 nearly half of America's cotton mills were to be found there. Iron manufactures made comparable progress, thanks to the discovery of great beds of ore near deposits of coal and limestone, as if Nature purposely had associated the necessary ingredients for refining the crude metal. During the eighties fifty new blast furnaces were erected in the Birmingham district of Alabama, in Tennessee and Virginia. Tobacco manufactures constituted another achievement. Union soldiers sampling the smoking tobacco made in Durham, North Carolina, wrote back for more, and this originated a business in which Durham by 1884 led the world. Cottonseed mills, canneries and vehicle and furniture factories represented other important undertakings. The prime movers in this tardy industrialization were usually of the old yeoman strain rather than of the prewar gentry, and Yankee capital played little part until toward the close of the century when the certainty of profits had been clearly demonstrated. An observer in 1889 scarcely needed to point out that "the nonsense that it is beneath the dignity of any man or woman to work for a living is pretty much eliminated from the Southern mind."

The revolution in manufacturing rested everywhere upon the exploitation of immense fields of coal and iron, the two minerals indispensable to modern industrial society. Large coal beds were uncovered along the Appalachians as well as in Ohio, Indiana and Illinois. With improved transportation facilities and the increasing use of machinery, the nation's production rose tenfold from 1860 to 1890. The yield of iron ore in western Pennsylvania also advanced with giant strides, and in the 1880's great ranges in the Lake Superior region began to be developed. Besides being extremely rich and pure, these deposits, lying near the surface, could be mined with labor-saving machines. From 1860 to 1890 the country's output of pig iron multiplied eleven-fold. At the same time the manufacture of iron and steel products was speeded by new methods of smelting, notably the Bessemer process, which removed carbon impurities by forcing a cold blast through the molten metal, and the Siemens-Martin or open-hearth process, which utilized inferior grades of ore.

The revolution in mining extended also to petroleum, the newest source of subsurface wealth, which underwent an even more spectacular development. Thanks to the use of pipe lines and tank cars and the increasing demand for oil and its derivatives, the output grew ninety times between 1860 and 1890. Still other treasures of the earth originated in the Great West. In the eighties copper mines were opened in Arizona and Montana, rivaling those of Michigan. Large-scale silver mining was based on the great finds in Nevada, Colorado and elsewhere. From a value of $157,000 in 1860, the yield reached $36,000,000 in 1873, with an even bigger return in the years to follow. Gold production, on the other hand, steadily declined from 1872 to 1893. The contrasting fortunes of the two precious metals were to have important consequences in national politics.

Meanwhile the transportation revolution spun a web of rails that radiated to every part of the land. Besides the transcontinental roads, lines multiplied in the older districts of the North and pushed southward to spur the industrialization of Dixie. From 1860 to 1890 the miles of track increased from 31,000 to 164,000. Moreover, improvements of service attended this expansion. Iron rails were replaced as quickly as possible with steel to ensure both greater safety and heavier carrying capacity, and double tracks afforded further safety. In 1864 the ingenious sleeping cars of George M. Pullman—rhapsodized by one contemporary as "gorgeous traveling hotels"—rendered train journeys more comfortable, and four years later the inventor added the Pullman diner. In 1872 George Westinghouse's automatic air brake eliminated the jolting due to the loose coupling of the cars, by enabling the engineer to set the brakes simultaneously in all parts of the train. As more and more short roads were linked into through lines and a standard gauge of track was adopted, longer continuous

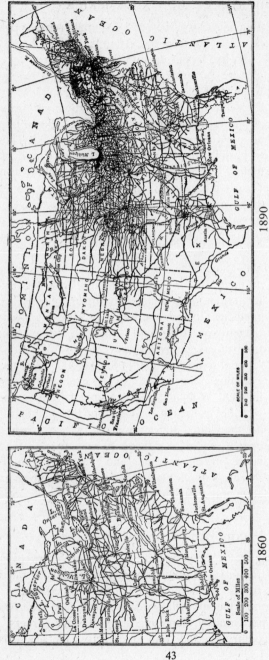

1890

1860

The Revolution in Rail Transportation, 1860–1890

In these thirty years the railway attained an importance greater than in any other country. "It is the locomotive," wrote William Barrows in *The United States of Yesterday and of To-morrow* (1887), "which has hauled up the United States to the front in the procession of the nations."

43

travel resulted. The passenger who before 1870 might have to change trains half a dozen times between the Atlantic Seaboard and the Mississippi now seldom had to put up with the inconvenience.

No less profound were the strides in communication, a revolution based on new applications of electricity, whose possibilities were just beginning to be glimpsed. After several unsuccessful trials the principle of the telegraph was turned to account in the first cable to Europe in 1866, an epochal engineering feat due to Cyrus W. Field. Thomas A. Edison, the most prolific contributor of electrical inventions, took out nearly eight hundred patents between 1868 and 1900, mostly in this field. One of his early discoveries, quadruplex telegraphy in 1874, allowed four messages, two in each direction, to be sent simultaneously over the same wire, thus effecting a tremendous saving in line construction. Two years later Professor Alexander Graham Bell of Boston University devised the telephone as a by-product of his efforts to teach the deaf to talk. Though this new marvel in its crude form was hardly more than an interesting toy—the London *Times* wrote it off as the "latest American humbug"—Edison and others quickly helped to develop it into an efficient instrument. Leroy B. Firman's invention of a multiple switchboard in 1879 greatly enlarged the telephone's usefulness and assured its commercial success. From 1880 to 1890 the number of subscribers rose from 50,000 to 250,000. At the same time long-distance communication was constantly extended. As presidential candidate in 1896 William McKinley talked from his home in Canton, Ohio, with his campaign managers in thirty-eight states. At the century's close the United States possessed twice as many telephones as all Europe. It would be difficult to overestimate the importance of the advances in transportation and communication. They not only furthered business development, but they also helped break down regional isolation and contributed in countless ways to national unity.

THE GROWTH OF CITIES

The city, growing by leaps and bounds, constituted the nerve center of the rising industrial order. Within its borders were concentrated all the new economic forces: the surplus capital, the business brains, the gaunt smoky factories, the sprawling railroad yards, the white-collar middle class, the portentously increasing army of wage earners. Recruited from the countryside and from lands across the sea, villages sprang into towns and towns into cities almost overnight. Urban communities, said a contemporary, "start like Jonah's gourd, but grow and endure like the oaks of Bashan, and promise to live like the cedars of Lebanon." With only one out of every six people in localities of 8000 or over in 1860 the proportion rose to one out of three in 1900. "We cannot all live in cities, yet nearly all seem determined to do so," lamented the *New York Tribune* in 1867, adding that with "millions of acres" awaiting cultivation "hundreds of thousands reject this and rush into the cities." Considerably more than half of the urban-moving throng gravitated to places of 25,000 and upward.

The effect on the agricultural sections of the East and Midwest was startling. While the cities of Maine, Vermont, Massachusetts, Rhode Island, New York, Maryland and Illinois gained 2,500,000 inhabitants in the 1880's, their rural districts lost 200,000. The drain of humanity from northern New England left mute witnesses in deserted hill villages and abandoned farms. "The crumbling ruins of the foundations only are left to mark the site," mourned one observer, or perhaps "the tottering well sweep and perennial lilac bush still stand as mementoes of once happy homes." In the nation as a whole two fifths of all the townships declined. This was due partly to the attraction of free homesteads, but the phenomenon was so widespread—and, indeed, as true of Europe as of the United States—as to indicate the far stronger pull of the city.

The reasons for the urban advance on both sides of the water were much the same: the superior opportunities afforded by cities, the waning profits of agriculture, and the expanding railways which, while making cities easier to reach, also simplified the problem of feeding dense numbers. By 1890 London and Paris had doubled in population since mid-century, Berlin more than quadrupled. American cities achieved a comparable growth. New York-Brooklyn (consolidated into a single municipality in 1898) rose from a little more than a million in 1860 to two and a half million in 1890, about the size of Paris; and Chicago and Philadelphia with more than a million each in 1890 outranked all but five European cities. In these three decades, moreover, Baltimore doubled in population, Kansas City and Detroit grew fourfold, San Francisco and Memphis fivefold, Cleveland sixfold, Los Angeles twentyfold, while certain places like Minneapolis and Omaha, which had been mere hamlets when the Civil War began, increased fifty times or more. "The youngest of the nations," wrote

Samuel L. Loomis in 1887, "has already more large cities than any except Great Britain and Germany." Though the majority of towns were smaller, they strove to copy the enterprise and ways of the bigger ones. In Josiah Strong's phrase, the city was "the mighty heart of the

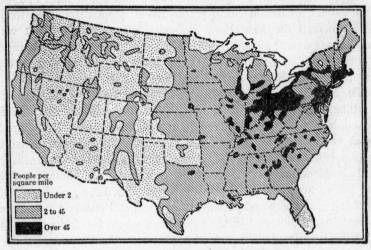

Distribution of Population in 1890

body politic, sending its streams of life pulsating to the very finger-tips of the land." As a center of wealth and economic power, moreover, it molded business institutions and transportation facilities to suit its own needs and ambitions, thus aggravating the farmers' troubles during these years.

Earlier, most American cities had been hardly more than overgrown villages; now, as populations thickened, they matured into modern municipalities. Though coming of age later than European cities, they quickly surpassed the Old World in meeting new needs, notably for rapid transit and lighting. Shortly after the Civil War, New York and Philadelphia, following the prior example of Boston and Chicago as well as foreign precedents, replaced volunteer fire fighters with full-paid departments. The demand for swift conveyance, no longer satisfied by horse-drawn cars, led to a variety of solutions. New York in 1870 introduced steam-propelled trains on elevated rails high above the streets; San Francisco in 1873 installed the cable car, which ran

IMPEACHMENT TRIAL OF PRESIDENT JOHNSON
See page 13.

COMPLETION OF THE PACIFIC RAILROAD, 1869

BROOKLYN BRIDGE, 1883

TWO GREAT ENGINEERING ACHIEVEMENTS

See pages 32 and 47.

by grappling onto an endless steel rope moving in a slotted trench between the tracks; Richmond, Virginia, in 1888 inaugurated the even more successful electric trolley car; and Boston in 1895 undertook America's first subway. Meanwhile Greater New York, divided by the East River, supplanted the slow-moving ferry in 1883 with Brooklyn Bridge, the longest suspension bridge in the world, built by Washington A. Roebling over a period of thirteen years. As a further aid to traffic, city streets, hitherto ill-paved if paved at all, began to be surfaced with asphalt or brick.

At the same time better means of lighting dispelled much of the darkness of night as well as some of its dangers. In 1878 Charles F. Brush of Cleveland, improving upon efforts abroad, devised a practical system of outdoor arc lamps, and two years later Thomas A. Edison patented the first successful incandescent bulb for indoors. Better gas illumination resulted from Thaddeus S. C. Lowe's discovery in 1873 of how to manufacture water gas. Serious attention was also given for the first time to sewage and garbage disposal, and from 1860 to 1890 the number of waterworks increased nearly thirteenfold. Though some places were quicker than others to adopt the improvements, urban life everywhere assumed a new aspect, causing towns on the advancing frontier to flaunt conveniences and comforts that the largest centers had lacked a generation before.

Pride in these achievements led to the holding of two great international expositions, one in 1876 at Philadelphia to celebrate the centennial of American independence and the other in 1893 at Chicago to commemorate (a year late) the four-hundredth anniversary of Columbus's discovery. These occasions afforded a welcome opportunity to show the world that in the arts and technology of modern life the United States challenged comparison with the best Europe could offer. At the Philadelphia exhibition Machinery Hall particularly entranced the visitors, who, in this building as well as elsewhere on the grounds, could see a thousand articles being manufactured before their eyes. Chicago, without neglecting mechanical accomplishments, accented the progress in cultural and artistic fields. That the second and finer of these expositions took place in the great midland metropolis dramatized the westward march of urbanism and awakened Easterners to the new significance of the interior country in the nation's life. Of the nearly fifteen million who attended the two fairs many had never been farther than a buggy's ride from home, and the impressions they carried away quickened the spread of better standards of taste and of living to all parts of the land.

The rise of the city, however, had less pleasing aspects. Urban life in undress revealed only too plainly the ill effects of hasty growth and bad civic practices. The larger places presented stark contrasts of riches and squalor, New York reminding one English visitor of "a lady in ball costume, with diamonds in her ears, and her toes out at her boots." In the slums huddled the newly arrived immigrants, living amid conditions that made for diseased minds as well as diseased bodies. Organized crime, long characteristic of frontier communities, now shifted to the cities, attracted by the concentration of wealth and the inadequacy of police protection. It may not be without significance that the last great frontier villainy, the James Boys' attempted robbery of the bank at Northfield, Minnesota, in 1876, was followed two years later by the first large-scale urban criminal exploit, the looting of New York's Manhattan Savings Institution of nearly $3,000,000 by 'Western George' Leslie and his gang.

The increase of lawlessness was due in no small degree to the collusion of municipal officials with wrongdoers. During these years the boss and the machine, working hand in glove with the most vicious elements of the community, rose to political dominance. As in national affairs, predatory men found opportunities for illicit gain in lax law enforcement and particularly in battening on the expanding public utilities. "Where the carcass is," Francis Parkman bitterly observed, "the vultures gather together." Contracts for street paving, sewer construction and the like provided one source of graft, but more profitable were the franchises granted to private individuals and companies for supplying water, light and rapid transit, usually with few or no safeguards for the public. One of the sensations of Grant's first term was the exposure of the Tweed Ring in New York, whose members, controlling the district attorney, the courts, the police and most of the newspapers, stole at least $30,000,000 in thirty months through fraudulent bond issues, the sale of franchises and other corrupt means. Though 'Boss' William M. Tweed was himself finally haled to justice, most of his confederates escaped, and later years found New York again plagued with Tammany misrule.

Other places fared hardly better: Philadelphia with its Gas Ring, Minneapolis under the corrupt 'Doc' Alonzo Ames, San Francisco

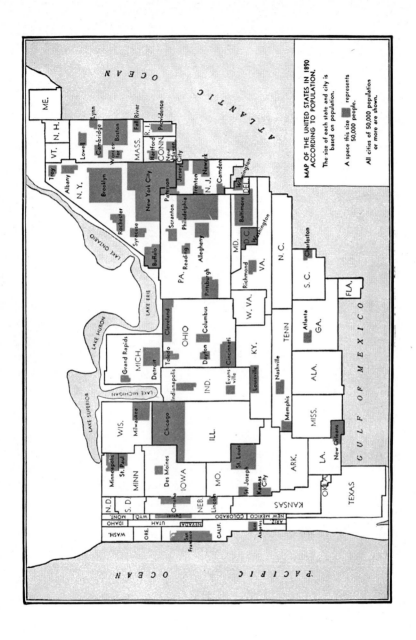

MAP OF THE UNITED STATES IN 1890
ACCORDING TO POPULATION.

The size of each state and city is based on population.

A space this size ▪ represents 50,000 people.

All cities of 50,000 population or more are shown.

under 'Blind Boss' Buckley. "There is not a city with a population exceeding 200,000," declared James Bryce in 1888, "where the poison germs have not sprung into a vigorous life; and in some of the smaller ones, down to 70,000, it needs no microscope to note the results of their growth." He called municipal government "the one conspicuous failure of the United States." The American people, having developed their political institutions under simple rural conditions, had not yet learned to govern cramped populations. Fortunately, as will be seen later, this did not prevent urban communities from exerting a fructifying influence on cultural life.

FULLER ACCOUNTS

The Economic Revolution. The larger aspects are concisely presented in the standard surveys of American economic development such as Faulkner, *American Economic History;* Kirkland, *History of American Economic Life;* Shannon, *America's Economic Growth;* and Wright, *Economic History.*

Occupying the Last Frontier. The latest and best over-all account appears in the concluding chapters of Billington, *Westward Expansion,* whose bibliography itemizes the plethora of special studies. For particular areas, see Briggs, *Frontiers of the Northwest;* Dick, *Sod-house Frontier* and *Vanguards of the Frontier;* Richardson and Rister, *Greater Southwest;* Webb, *Great Plains;* and Winther, *Great Northwest.* For the workings of land legislation, turn to Hibbard, *History of Public Land Policies,* and Robbins, *Our Landed Heritage.* Riegel, *Story of the Western Railroads,* illuminates that subject, with more intensive treatments available in Hedges, *Henry Villard and the Railways of the Northwest;* Marshall, *Santa Fé;* Overton, *Burlington West;* and Sabin, *Building the Pacific Railway.* Border warfare is delineated in Paxson, *Last American Frontier,* and Wellman, *Death on Horseback,* with Branch telling of *The Hunting of the Buffalo.* The story of mining is related in Lyman, *Saga of the Comstock Lode;* Trimble, *Mining Advance into the Inland Empire;* and Rickard, *History of American Mining,* a technical treatment. Notable among the works on the cattle kingdom are Dale, *Range Cattle Industry;* Dobie, *Longhorns;* Osgood, *Day of the Cattleman;* Pelzer, *Cattlemen's Frontier;* Rister, *Southern Plainsmen;* Streeter, *Prairie Trails & Cow Towns;* and Wellman, *Trampling Herd.* For the agricultural revolution, consult Shannon, *Farmer's Last Frontier,* and for the government's promotion of agricultural education, Ross, *Democracy's College.* Gittinger, *Formation of the State of Oklahoma,* describes the white penetration of Indian Territory.

Industry Overtakes Agriculture. Clark, *History of Manufactures,* is an encyclopedic work, while Armes, *Story of Coal and Iron in Alabama,* Mitchell, *Rise of Cotton Mills,* and Robert, *Story of Tobacco,* trace major aspects of Dixie's manufacturing advance. Among other histories of separate industries are Clemen, *American Livestock and Meat Industry;* Cole, *American Wool Manufacture;* Copeland, *Cotton Manufacturing Industry;* Giddens, *Birth of the*

Oil Industry and *Early Days of Oil* (the latter a pictorial commentary); Kuhl-man, *Flour-milling Industry;* Smith, *Story of Iron and Steel;* and Woodworth, *American Tool Making and Interchangeable Manufacturing.* General accounts of technological progress include Burlingame, *Engines of Democracy,* and Kaempffert, ed., *Popular History of American Invention,* with Casson, *History of the Telephone,* Husband, *Story of the Pullman Car,* and Martin and Coles, eds., *Story of Electricity,* filling in many details, and with Dyer and Martin, *Edison,* Mackenzie, *Bell,* and Prout, *Westinghouse,* singling out leading inventors.

The Growth of Cities. Schlesinger, *Rise of the City,* explores many phases, while Weber, *Growth of Cities,* emphasizes the world setting. Kirkland, *Men, Cities, and Transportation,* and Wilson, *Hill Country of Northern New England,* present contrasting pictures of the situation in New England. Schuyler, *Roeblings,* gives the story of Brooklyn Bridge, and Lynch, *"Boss" Tweed,* Patton, *Battle for Municipal Reform,* and Zink, *City Bosses,* throw light upon municipal politics.

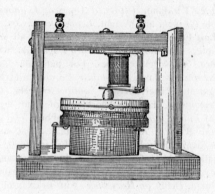

CHAPTER III

THE REBIRTH OF PARTIES

OFFICIAL LAXITY AND ECONOMIC MUDDLE

WHILE Ulysses S. Grant was still in the White House the Economic Revolution began to recast political standards and practices. Ambitious men, worshiping the Almighty Dollar, demanded special privileges of the government and cared not what means they used to gain their ends. Unfortunately the times favored their designs, for the country was suffering a moral relapse from the idealism of the struggle to preserve the Union, and the great prosperity continuing from the war tended to drug the public into indifference toward official wrongdoing. To Francis Parkman in 1869 it seemed that nearly everybody had come to regard material achievement, with "the resulting fine houses, fine clothes and sumptuous fare," as the "sum and substance of progress and civilization." In particular, Senator Henry Wilson of Massachusetts, ancient foe of the Southern slavocracy, named "the power of wealth, individual and associated," as "the new danger threatening us with its portentous and increasing dimensions," while another early Republican, Indiana's George W. Julian, charged the "railway power" with "sapping and mining its way through the consciences" of those in political authority. As though to confirm such views, a Congressional committee reported in 1873, "The country is fast becoming filled with gigantic corporations wielding and controlling immense aggregations of money and thereby commanding great influence and power." Tweedism in the cities and Carpetbaggery in the Southern states were symptomatic of conditions equally strong in national affairs.

President Grant possessed neither the experience nor the will to stem the tide. As a man who had himself striven vainly against poverty he, too, deemed financial success the "sum and substance of progress and civilization" and hence observed the new tendencies with complacency. Though his personal integrity was unimpeachable, he and members of his family received loans from the banks of Jay Cooke at a time when the Northern Pacific and other of Cooke's enterprises were seeking government favors. Grant, moreover, openly consorted with Jim Fisk, an unscrupulous stock manipulator, and accepted costly gifts from persons whose motives were dubious, if not corrupt. Nor, with a few exceptions, did Grant's cabinet offset his own short-comings. The ablest member was Hamilton Fish of New York, his second appointee as Secretary of State, who won merited fame for negotiating the Treaty of Washington which settled the *Alabama* claims, and who in other respects proved a tower of strength. To the Treasury he named Alexander T. Stewart, a New York merchant and one of America's richest men, and when Stewart was found to be ineligible under an old law disqualifying anyone engaged in "trade or commerce," he was replaced with George S. Boutwell, a Massachu-setts politician with no special fitness for the place. Of the remaining officers only Jacob D. Cox of Ohio, Secretary of the Interior, and E. Rockwood Hoar of Massachusetts, Attorney-General, had the quali-fications usually expected.[1]

Grant's selections for lesser positions showed his uncritical accept-ance of the spoils system. The *Nation*, a New York journal inde-pendent of parties, accused him of making not only "bad appoint-ments but probably some of the worst ever made by a civilized Christian government." In 1870 the President, egged on by his inti-mates, got rid of Attorney-General Hoar and Secretary of the Interior Cox because of their unwelcome zeal in resisting spoilsmen. James A. Garfield, a stout Republican, called Cox's removal "a clear case of surrender on the part of the President to the political vermin which infest the government." Alarmed by the deterioration of government personnel, the better elements in the party pressed for a system of basing appointments on competitive examinations, such as existed in England, France and Prussia. In March, 1871, Congress finally took the step, probably with an eye on the approaching presidential elec-tion, and Grant applied the rules, beginning in 1872, to the federal offices in Washington and New York. He soon chafed under the re-strictions, however, and to his great relief Congress in 1873 ended the plan by withholding further appropriations. Effective civil-service reform had to await a change of political climate.

[1] Besides the three named above, the original cabinet consisted of Elihu Washburne of Illinois, Secretary of State, who served only a few months; John A. Rawlins of Illinois, Secretary of War; Adolph E. Borie of Pennsylvania, Secretary of the Navy; and John A. J. Creswell of Maryland, Postmaster-General.

The drift of public affairs reflected the rise of a new generation of political leaders. The giants of the Civil War era were fast passing away, Stevens dying in 1868, Stanton in 1869, Seward in 1872, Chase in 1873, Sumner (from whom Grant became estranged as early as 1870) in 1874, Johnson in 1875. Their places were taken by men of smaller stature and of dissimilar interests and aims. In Henry Adams's opinion, "No period so thoroughly ordinary had been known in American politics since Christopher Columbus first disturbed the balance of American society." It is likely that the men of creative vision and administrative capacity—the natural leaders of the time—felt the challenge of the rising capitalist order and willingly left governmental matters to those who they knew would do their bidding. At any rate, the men who now seized the reins in Congress—Roscoe Conkling of New York, James A. Garfield of Ohio, James G. Blaine of Maine, Samuel J. Randall and William D. ('Pig-Iron') Kelley of Pennsylvania, and their like—hastened the exploitation of the nation's resources through lavish subsidies, charter grants and tariffs, and were often themselves personally interested as stockholders or lawyers in corporate enterprises which they could affect by their votes as legislators.

One of the urgent problems facing the government was to reorganize the national finances on a peace basis. These efforts, initiated under President Johnson, included the conversion of the war debt into bonds at lower interest rates, a steady reduction of internal-revenue duties, and a lessening of the income tax (until in 1872 it was abolished). Proposals to lower import duties, however, aroused the ire of the manufacturing interests suckled by the wartime tariff: they wanted more rather than less protection. Beginning in 1866, swarms of lobbyists descended upon Washington ready to do battle at a moment's notice for the industries they represented. John L. Hayes, agent of the newly formed National Association of Wool Manufacturers, worked a miracle by bringing together the wool-growing and wool-manufacturing groups in a combined demand for steeper rates. Though no Republican national platform had yet advocated tariff protection apart from a passing mention in 1860, Congress raised the duties on wool and woolens in 1867, on copper in 1869, and on steel rails, nickel and marble in 1870. The Republicans, however, had reckoned without their farming constituencies, who cried out at the resulting rise of prices. So strong were Western objections that Congress felt obliged to make a gesture toward tariff reduction, but the act of 1870 failed to allay the discontent, since the decreases chiefly affected tea, coffee, spices and a few other items in which no domestic manufacturing interest was involved. As the presidential election drew closer, the party chieftains, deeming discretion the better part of valor, went further. In May and June, 1872, Congress imposed a horizontal cut of 10 per cent on the principal imported manufactures. The concession proved only temporary, however, for the deficit in revenue occasioned by the Panic of 1873 caused the protective duties to be restored in 1875. At this point they were permitted to remain until the general revision of 1883.

Though the major shortcomings of the administration were still undisclosed, certain elements in Grant's following were already beginning to distinguish between the wartime man of iron and the peacetime man of clay. As early as 1870 an insurgent faction in Missouri, led by United States Senator Carl Schurz, carried the state elections with Democratic support. The Liberal Republicans, as they called themselves, favored a more generous treatment of their fellow Missourians who had sided with the South during the war and, in addition, demanded civil-service reform and a lower tariff. The incident was like a spark to a powder train. As similar bolts occurred elsewhere, the movement assumed national proportions. Unfortunately the leaders were more agreed upon what they did not want than on what they did. The Liberal Republican convention in Cincinnati on May 1, 1872, contained diverse ingredients—tariff protectionists as well as reductionists, along with civil-service reformers, foes of federal intervention in the South and disgruntled politicians nursing personal grudges—with the result that the gathering quickly degenerated into what the Republicans gleefully termed the 'Convention of Cranks.' The platform, after arraigning the Grant regime, declared for civil-service reform and home rule in the South, but because of admitted "irreconcilable differences" it took no stand on the tariff. For President the convention on the sixth ballot made the preposterous mistake of naming Horace Greeley of the *New York Tribune,* a rabid protectionist who was further known to the Democrats for having once said, "All Democrats may not be rascals, but all rascals are Democrats." Governor B. Gratz Brown of Missouri was given the second place.

Though it was a bitter pill to swallow, the Democrats upon convening saw nothing better to do than to endorse the ticket. The Republicans in Philadelphia on June 5 unanimously renominated Grant, associating with him Senator Henry Wilson of Massachusetts. Their platform, after justifying the party's Southern policy, pledged tariff protection and paid sanctimonious respects to civil-service reform. Republican spellbinders, vigorously waving the bloody shirt, told the people that Grant's defeat would mean pensions for the ex-rebels, if not the South's peaceable secession. The outcome was never in doubt. Many Democrats stayed at home rather than stultify themselves by voting for Greeley. Yet even a stronger candidate could hardly have succeeded, for the average Republican still saw Grant with his martial laurels, and the Carpetbag regimes dominating seven Southern states gave him solid support. Indicative of the new trend of politics, the great business and financial interests contributed generously to the Republican efforts, Jay Cooke alone subscribing over $50,000. Grant mustered 286 electoral votes to 62 and a popular majority of almost 56 per cent (3,600,000 votes) to 44 per cent (2,835,000). The Republicans also swept both houses of Congress. Greeley died a broken-hearted man a few weeks later. In the history of the Republican party the contest was notable as signalizing the adoption of tariff protection as an official article of faith. The campaign also marked the entry of labor into national politics in the guise of the feebly supported and short-lived Labor Reform party. No presidential race since has been without one or more minor parties devoted to the welfare of urban or rural workers.

The luster of the victory soon dimmed, however, as the administration found itself beset on the one hand by economic depression and on the other by political scandals. An inflated currency and illimitable credit had caused untold capital to pour into factories, mills and railroads until their capacity far outstripped existing needs. In the decade after the Union Pacific's incorporation over a billion was sunk in rail construction alone. Only the future growth of the country could make many of these enterprises profitable, and meanwhile indebtedness piled up beyond ability to pay. Moreover, a good deal of the speculation was sheer dishonesty foisted on the gullible by rascals. Mark Twain and Charles Dudley Warner, calling these years *The Gilded Age*, portrayed the unquenchable optimism by having one of their characters boast, "I wasn't worth a cent two years ago, and now I owe a million dollars." Even the farmers felt the contagion, mortgaging their lands to excess for implements and additional acreage.

Much of the business expansion had been financed from abroad; and a panic in Vienna in May, 1873, spreading to other European money centers, caused a large part of this support to be withdrawn. American bankers, already overburdened, were unable to carry the added load. In September came the crash, precipitated by the failure of Jay Cooke whose banking firm, the greatest in the United States, had invested too heavily in the projected Northern Pacific Railroad. A frenzy of fear gripped the business world, the government stood helpless before the storm, and the foundations of credit began to crumble. Banks and business houses toppled, eighty-nine railroads defaulted on their bonds, and the industrial regions were stricken as by a paralysis. In all, more than five thousand concerns failed during the Panic year with an aggregate loss of about $228,500,000. Nearly three million wage earners were rendered idle, and the Western and Southern farmers, their crops a drug on the market, found themselves unable to meet their mortgage payments.

DEPRESSION POLITICS

Five years were to follow the Panic of 1873 before normal conditions returned—years all the more trying because of revelations of the graft and dishonor that corroded the administration. According to George F. Hoar, Republican Senator from Massachusetts, corruption "never got so dangerous a hold upon the forces of the Government, or upon a great political party." Early in 1873 a Congressional committee disclosed that the outgoing Vice-President Schuyler Colfax and a number of Congressmen, including James A. Garfield and 'Pig-Iron' Kelley, had accepted gifts of stock from the Crédit Mobilier, which dreaded a government investigation because of financial irregularities in constructing the Union Pacific. The go-between, Congressman Oakes Ames, an officer of the company, had told his business associates he would place the securities where they would "protect us" and "do the most good." The House, adopting the committee's view that most of the members had acted without "any corrupt motive," contented itself with censuring Ames and one other Representative. Next to be exposed were two cabinet officers: Postmaster-General Creswell, who had authorized payment of nearly $500,000 for services which the recipient himself later estimated to be worth only $176,000; and William A. Richardson, who had abused his authority as Secretary of the Treasury to divert unearned commissions of an undetermined amount into the pockets of a Massachusetts politician. In the Creswell case Congress suspended the payment before harm was done, but Richardson in May, 1874, hurriedly resigned to avert a vote of censure.

The public, racked by the hard times but as yet unaware how far the moral poison had spread, turned on the party in the fall elections, giving the Democrats their first victory since before the war. While the Senate remained under administration control, the House changed from two-thirds Republican to three-fifths Democratic, a fact which would give Republican chieftains sleepless nights when the time came to count the returns of the next presidential contest. Besides, the Democrats captured twenty-three states out of thirty-five, including New York where Samuel J. Tilden, a leader in the assault on the Tweed Ring, won the governorship on a platform of political reform. But this stinging rebuke came too late to undo the damage. In 1875 Benjamin H. Bristow, Richardson's successor in the Treasury, uncovered a Whisky Ring of distillers and revenue officers who since 1870 had been cheating the government of millions in taxes. Even Grant's private secretary, Orville E. Babcock, was implicated, and escaped punishment only through the President's unwise intervention. Then in March, 1876, Secretary of War William W. Belknap hastily resigned to avoid impeachment for having received an annual bribe since 1870 from an officeholder anxious to escape removal.

A few weeks later came a scandal involving one of the most promising of the younger Republican leaders, James G. Blaine. The investigation showed that while Speaker of the House he had sold bonds for a land-grant railway, and that afterward the Union Pacific and certain other corporations had relieved him of a large block of the securities at a sum far above their market value. By a trick Blaine got possession of the incriminating evidence, the so-called Mulligan letters, and though he refused to allow them to be examined, he made a brilliant speech in the House, which, if it left the skeptical unsatisfied, at least convinced orthodox Republicans of his innocence. But Blaine's penalty was to be a heavy one, for his connection with this affair was to prevent him from ever attaining the goal of his ambitions, the White House.

Meanwhile the business depression continued to spread its black wings over the nation. In the industrial centers hordes of the jobless crowded the bread lines, and speakers on soapboxes entreated the government to find employment for the idle. When private charities exhausted their funds, the municipal authorities in New York, Chicago, Boston and other places provided food and, in some instances, work relief in the form of wood chopping and street construction. Immigrants departed for Europe by the tens of thousands, while many native wage earners turned hobo, wandering aimlessly through the country—pathetic caricatures of the restless, hardy pioneers who had subdued the wilderness. Criminality increased, and the violence attending the railroad strikes of 1877 (described later) gave additional evidence of the unrest and despair. These grim years lent impetus to many a scheme of social and economic redemption: the labor movement, consumers' and producers' co-operatives, 'free silver,' socialism, the 'single tax' and the like. They rendered clamorous the demands for railway regulation and greenback inflation.

The Midwestern farmers led the fight against the railroads. Already smarting from low crop prices as well as the excessive charges of middlemen for tools and other supplies, they considered the costs of transporting their produce to market inexcusably high. The rail companies, in fact, did often fix extortionate rates and even discriminated against some communities and shippers in favor of others. In 1867 a secret order called the Patrons of Husbandry and popularly the Grange had appeared in the rural sections to foster a pleasanter social life among the isolated inhabitants. The movement to curb the railroads is always associated with this organization, though the Grange was avowedly nonpolitical and grew but slowly until the hard times after 1873 suddenly swelled its membership to two and a half million. From the first, however, it provided a common meeting ground for farmers, and as it increased in strength, it played an important, if indirect, part in politics. Inspired by "Farmers' Declarations of Independence" against the "Slave-Power of Monopoly," political parties sprang up in the prairie states and bent the legislatures to their will. Acts were passed to regulate railroad rates either by direct legislative mandate or through commissions created for the purpose. After Illinois and Minnesota acted in 1870 and 1871, Ohio and Michigan followed in the Panic year, and Iowa, Wisconsin and Missouri in the next two years.

These laws were based upon the then novel doctrine that railways should be regarded as public-service enterprises, not as private businesses for the sole enrichment of stockholders. Some of the acts were

too hastily framed or tinged with a spirit of vengeance, but the fury
of the rail magnates was directed less against the specific provisions
than against the constitutionality of any control at all by the states.
The so-called Granger cases, decided in 1877, settled the constitutional
point. In Munn *v.* Illinois, the Supreme Court declared that a legislature had ample authority to regulate businesses "clothed with a
public interest." [1] "Property," asserted the judges, "does become
clothed with a public interest when used in a manner to make it of
public consequence. . . . When, therefore, one devotes his property
to a use in which the public has an interest, he, in effect, grants to
the public an interest in that use, and must submit it to be controlled
by the public for the common good, to the extent of the interest he
has thus created." In Peik *v.* Chicago and Northwestern Railway, the
tribunal dismissed a further objection by declaring that in the absence
of federal action states could even fix railroad rates that might incidentally affect interstate charges.

Not content with success on this front, the farmers strove to combat
the evil of high middlemen's profits. Local Granges founded co-
operative creameries, grain elevators and general stores, and in Iowa
the state organization set up factories for making plows and harvesters.
As another means of cutting costs the farmers sometimes pooled their
funds in order to buy direct from manufacturers at wholesale prices.
But by 1876 most of these undertakings had ceased because of inadequate support, poor business management or the ruthless practices
of competitors. Yet the activity was not without result. Besides serving
a warning on middlemen, it prompted the establishment of Chicago's
original mail-order house, which undercut prices in rural communities
and enabled the people to buy at better advantage. As the 1870's
drew toward a close, this first farmers' uprising subsided.

Meanwhile an increasing number of agrarian leaders had turned
to currency inflation as a remedy for their ills. Since the early 1860's
the only money in circulation had been depreciated greenbacks which
the government had issued to finance the war but declined to redeem
at face value in gold. When peace came, the business classes in the
East demanded the withdrawal of this 'cheap money,' or at least of
enough of it to restore its parity with gold. As a result, Congress in

---

[1] Though this case directly involved an Illinois law regulating grain warehouses,
the principle applied equally to railway regulation and was so construed by the
court in the Peik and other decisions.

1866 authorized a gradual reduction of the greenbacks, but Western objections halted the process two years later after $44,000,000 had been retired and the amount stood at $356,000,000. Farmers saw in this deflation the major cause of low crop prices. Besides, with so many farms under mortgage, they felt it wrong to have to repay the loans in money that had become harder to get, or, to put it differently, had increased in value. If dollars worth 65 cents in gold appreciated to 95 or 100 cents in gold, the debtor could not be convinced that he was not in effect paying back more than he had borrowed and more than his creditor had a right to. Hence members of the 'debtor class' began to insist that the government retain the wartime currency permanently.

During the Panic of 1873 the administration as an emergency measure reissued $26,000,000 worth of the greenbacks that had been recalled. This action only whetted the demand, and in April, 1874, Congress passed a bill to increase the total volume to $400,000,000. Though an act of his own party, President Grant, yielding to Eastern business pressure, vetoed it. When the fall elections guaranteed the Democrats control of the next House, the Republicans made use of their remaining months to enact a plan for the resumption of specie payments. Far from drastic, this act of January 14, 1875, sought to appease both the greenback notions of the West and the gold-standard sentiment of the East. It provided that the government, beginning with 1879, stand ready to exchange gold dollars for greenback dollars, and that meanwhile it should retire more of the greenbacks and accumulate a sufficient gold reserve to assure full specie value of those left in circulation. This reserve was subsequently set at $100,-000,000, and Congress decided in 1878 to keep $346,681,016 of greenbacks as a permanent part of the monetary system. The plan proved entirely feasible, for, as it happened, the time fixed for resumption coincided with the return of prosperity.

The passage of this act incensed the small but noisy group of extreme greenbackers. They subscribed to the doctrine that money derived its value solely from the stamp or fiat of the government, not from its intrinsic value or the fact that it was exchangeable for gold. Forming the National Greenback party in May, 1875, they presented candidates in the next three presidential elections. Their platform called for a legal-tender currency redeemable only in low-interest United States bonds. Though winning some followers in the Midwest and in Eastern labor centers, and polling a million votes in the Congressional elections of 1878, the party never came near casting an electoral vote. It gradually succumbed to the rising tide of sentiment for unlimited silver coinage.

The mass of people, satisfied for the moment with Congress's disposition of the money question, were thinking of other things as the campaign of 1876 got under way. To head off a third term for President Grant, two thirds of the Republicans in the House joined the Democratic majority in December, 1875, in decrying "any departure from this time-honored tradition." At the Republican convention in Cincinnati on June 14, 1876, Blaine was at first the favorite for the nomination, but he faced the implacable opposition of both the reform elements and the powerful Roscoe Conkling, who cherished a personal grudge against him. The prize went on the seventh ballot to Rutherford B. Hayes whose only asset, according to Henry Adams, was in being "obnoxious to no one," but whose solid worth had nevertheless won him a high military commission during the war, and afterward three terms as governor of Ohio. William A. Wheeler of New York was named for Vice-President. In the hope of diverting attention from the party's record of corruption, the platform bristled with bloody-shirt allusions and, as four years before, declared for tariff protection and civil-service reform. Two weeks later in St. Louis the Democrats decided on the second ballot for Samuel J. Tilden. As New York's governor Tilden had destroyed the Canal Ring which had looted many millions of state funds through public-works contracts; and this feat, together with his earlier activities against the Tweed Ring, had gained him national renown as a reformer. Moreover, as a wealthy corporation lawyer he enjoyed the confidence of many conservative Easterners. The second place went to Thomas A. Hendricks of Indiana. The crucial issue, declared the Democratic platform, was reform—financial, tariff and governmental—a duty which could not safely be entrusted to a party "honey-combed with incapacity, waste, and fraud."

In the campaign the Democrats hammered away at the crying need for reform and strove to capitalize upon the popular discontent due to the persisting depression. To offset these tactics the Republicans concentrated on reviving wartime passions. In the wry comment of James Russell Lowell, himself a Hayes adherent, "the worst element of the Republican party has got hold of the canvass." On the morning after the election Tilden's victory was conceded almost universally by the press, but the Republican national headquarters stoutly maintained the contrary. Within a few days it developed that, with 185 electoral votes necessary for success, Tilden had unquestioned right to 184, including the usually decisive states of New York, New Jersey, Connecticut and Indiana, while Hayes without argument had 165. Twenty votes—one from Oregon, seven from South Carolina, four from Florida and eight from Louisiana—were in doubt. Tilden's popular majority was 4,285,000 (49.9 per cent) to Hayes's 4,034,000 (47.9 per cent), and the Democrats also carried the new House of Representatives.

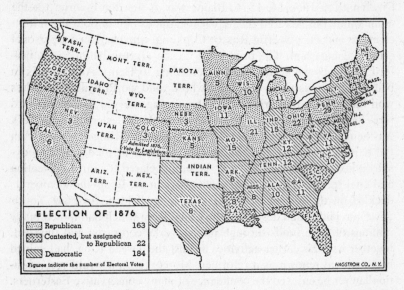

The trouble in Oregon involved the question whether a Republican elector who was found to be disqualified by the constitutional provision forbidding federal officeholders to act in that capacity should be replaced by someone chosen by his two Republican colleagues, as the state law said, or by the highest Democratic candidate for elector, as the Democratic governor contended. In the three Southern states the issue went deeper. There the native whites, engaged in a final desperate effort to dislodge the Carpetbaggers, had in countless instances frightened Negroes from the polls; but the top election machinery was controlled by the Carpetbaggers, who doctored the results to their own advantage. The worst conditions prevailed in

Louisiana, where the state election board refused to add a Democratic member as required by law, offered at one stage to sell out to Tilden for $1,000,000 and ended up by rejecting Democratic votes wholesale in order to create a majority for Hayes.[1]

From each of the four states contradictory sets of returns went to Congress. Unfortunately the Constitution makes no clear provision for such a contingency, and since the Senate and the House were controlled by opposite parties, compromise proved necessary. A law of January 29, 1877, created an electoral commission of five Senators, five Representatives and five members of the Supreme Court, the fifth Justice to be chosen by the four named in the statute. The commission's decisions on disputed returns were to be final unless rejected by both branches of Congress. It was understood that seven members of the commission would be from each party, and it was intended that the unnamed Justice be David Davis, a political independent. But Davis's unexpected election as Senator from Illinois brought about the appointment of a third Republican Justice, Joseph P. Bradley, the least objectionable to the Democrats of the remaining members of the bench. The commission sat throughout the month of February, with inauguration day drawing perilously near. Tense excitement pervaded the country, the bad economic conditions aroused fears of violence, and Grant strengthened the military forces about Washington. Bent on averting the possibility of another civil war, forty-two ex-Confederates in the House took a solemn pledge to oppose all attempts to prevent the electoral count. On all crucial points the commission divided along party lines, favoring the Hayes electors by eight to seven.[2] Just two days before the inauguration the outcome was announced. The disappointment of the Democrats is indescribable, but with angry mutterings they yielded grudging acquiescence. In the peaceful acceptance of Hayes's election the supremacy of the law won one of the greatest victories in the history of free government.

[1] President Grant believed that Tilden was entitled to Louisiana and hence to election. James Ford Rhodes takes the same view. But another historian, Paul L. Haworth, while conceding "grossly partisan and illegal acts," holds that "in an absolutely fair and free election the state would have gone Republican by five to ten thousand." The members of the election board all subsequently received lucrative appointments from the Hayes administration.

[2] It is known that Justice Bradley, who held the balance of power in the commission, decided originally in favor of the Tilden returns from Florida, but was talked out of it by his wife and two Republican friends, who insisted that a Democratic victory would spell national disaster.

THE BATTLE FOR POLITICAL REFORM

The narrowness of Hayes's victory dismayed the practical politicians and gave a strategic advantage to those Republicans and independents who wished to purify the party. Such persons, alarmed by the ominous creaking of the governmental machinery in inept or unscrupulous hands, feared lest the theory of democracy be defeated by the practice. They saw the remedy in civil-service reform, prompt punishment of faithless officials and the abolition of campaign assessments on officeholders. Chief among the leaders were Carl Schurz, one of the founders of the short-lived Liberal Republican party, Edwin L. Godkin, the Irish-born editor of the *Nation,* and George W. Curtis of *Harper's Weekly.* The reformers' rejection of party discipline, their insistence that parties be instruments for the public good rather than ends in themselves, enraged the professional politician who, in Roscoe Conkling's words, castigated them as "guerrillas—the men who deploy between the lines, and forage now on the one side and then on the other." But their example helped to fashion a tradition of independent voting at a period when the fetish of party regularity was probably stronger than at any other time in American history.

In the new President the reformers found an ally. Though Hayes entered office under a cloud, he earnestly tried to live up to the maxim, announced in his inaugural address, that "he serves his party best who serves his country best." A simple, dignified man, conscientious and hard-working but without personal magnetism, he gathered about him able advisers, including William M. Evarts of New York as Secretary of State and John Sherman of Ohio as head of the Treasury. To the horror of Senator Conkling and the old Grant clique, Hayes confided the Interior Department to the 'guerrilla' Schurz and the Post Office Department to a Democrat and ex-rebel, David M. Key of Tennessee.[1] They found equally unpalatable other of the President's early acts, such as his refusal to lend further military support to the Carpetbag governments and, particularly, his determination to curb the spoils system. Soon they came to refer to him as merely a 'half-breed' Republican in contrast to their own 'stalwart' Republicanism.

---

[1] The other members of the cabinet were George W. McCrary of Iowa, Secretary of War; Richard W. Thompson of Indiana, Secretary of the Navy; and Charles Devens of Massachusetts, Attorney-General.

The names, Halfbreed and Stalwart, clung to the two wings of the party through this regime and the next.

As part of Hayes's plan to improve administrative standards, Schurz placed his department on a merit basis, and certain other department heads took similar action with less enthusiasm. Against unremitting opposition from Conkling and his fellow Stalwarts, the President also applied the reform to the federal offices in New York City. There an investigating committee had found incompetence and graft in the country's principal customhouse, and Hayes—who, having declared against a second term, had no fear of political reprisals— ousted Chester A. Arthur, the collector, and Alonzo B. Cornell, the naval officer, the men who ruled the Republican party in that state. The Senate at 'Lord Roscoe's' instigation declined for two months to confirm their successors. Hayes's devotion to the cause undoubtedly won popular favor for civil-service reform and helped hasten its final accomplishment.

Though the President's most relentless foes were in his own party, the Democrats lost no occasion to remind the public of the circumstances of his gaining office. By keeping the matter alive they hoped to sweep the country in 1880 in a dramatic campaign of vindication. In the summer of 1878 a House Democratic committee, after examining over two hundred witnesses as to conditions in Louisiana and Florida in 1876, decided by a strict party vote that Tilden had been rightfully elected. The effect was dulled, however, by the enterprise of a Senate Republican committee in unearthing a batch of cipher telegrams that had been sent or received by Democratic leaders during the heat of the contest. These revealed efforts to bribe the Florida and South Carolina election boards. Thanks to someone's foresight, Republican telegrams sent at the same time could nowhere be found. Although Tilden was not personally implicated, his party found itself somewhat in the position of the pot calling the kettle black: it could hardly expect to cash in on the "political crime" as an issue in the next presidential campaign. Nevertheless, in the fall elections of 1878 the Democrats captured both branches of Congress.

In the hope of warding off further disaster for themselves and the party, Conkling and his Stalwart cronies set about to engineer a comeback for Grant in the approaching presidential election. When the Republicans met in Chicago on June 2, 1880, a 'Grant phalanx' of 306 of the 755 delegates voted doggedly for the ex-President throughout the balloting. Though blocking Blaine, who stood next in the running, they lost out on the thirty-second ballot to a 'dark horse,' James A. Garfield, ex-soldier, moderate Halfbreed and long-time Congressman from Ohio. The best they could do was to obtain the vice-presidential nomination for Chester A. Arthur, the recently discharged New York customs collector. The platform blended self-praise with abuse of the Democrats, eulogized the protective-tariff system and, however reluctantly, endorsed Hayes's civil-service policy. The Democrats had their own troubles, since Tilden had eliminated himself because of ill health and the powerful opposition of Tammany in his own state. At Cincinnati on June 22 the party on the third ballot chose General Winfield S. Hancock of Pennsylvania, with William H. English, a wealthy Indiana banker, as his teammate. Hancock's nomination was designed to refute the customary Republican charge of disloyalty as well as to profit from the popularity of a faithful war veteran. The platform, while demanding civil-service reform and a tariff for revenue only, proclaimed the "great fraud of 1876–77" as the issue that "precedes and dwarfs every other."

In the electioneering, though, the "great fraud" created little interest, and this despite the fact that Garfield had been on the electoral commission that seated Hayes. Nor did the efforts to discredit him for his connection with the Crédit Mobilier succeed any better. The people, rejoicing over the return of good times after six years of depression, accepted John Sherman's view that "Providence has been on the side of the Republican party." To make assurance doubly sure, however, the Republicans again stirred the devil's brew of sectional animosities, while dismissing Hancock as "a good man weighing two hundred and fifty pounds." Hancock's chief utterance was a repudiation of the Democratic tariff plank on the ground that the tariff was a "local issue." Garfield won by an electoral majority of 214 to 155, though polling only 48.3 per cent (4,449,000) of the popular ballots to his opponent's 48.23 per cent (4,442,000). His party also captured the House and the Senate.

The new President promptly revealed his political leanings within the party by naming James G. Blaine Secretary of State and making further appointments to the cabinet and other posts which horrified the Stalwarts.[1] When Garfield nominated William H. Robertson,

[1] The remaining members of the cabinet were William Windom of Minnesota, Secretary of the Treasury; Robert T. Lincoln of Illinois, Secretary of War; William

Conkling's bitterest foe in his own state, for New York customs collector, 'Lord Roscoe' declared open war on the administration. Unable to prevent confirmation, he and his colleague Thomas C. Platt resigned from the Senate and asked the legislature to vindicate them by re-election. Though Vice-President Arthur went to Albany to lend his aid, both were defeated after fifty-six ballots, much to their chagrin and the country's mirth. Conkling retired permanently to private life, 'Me Too' Platt to temporary eclipse. Meanwhile Garfield's Postmaster-General, Thomas L. James, exposed a hive of corruption in the postal service, which had mulcted the government of about $4,000,000 in five years. One of the accused, Thomas W. Brady, a Grant appointee, struck back at the administration by publishing a letter of Garfield's which showed that in his campaign he had encouraged the practice of assessing officeholders. The trials involving the 'Star Route frauds' dragged on until 1884 when the major culprits managed on technical grounds to escape prison. Some good nevertheless resulted, since the ring was dispersed and public attention called anew to the need for better-qualified officials.

While still struggling with problems of patronage, President Garfield was shot in a Washington railway station by a crazed office seeker on July 2, 1881, only four months after his inauguration. At the time, the Vice-President was at the New York capital lobbying for Conkling and Platt; and when Garfield after a gallant fight died on September 19, many people shared the consternation of the man who exclaimed, "Chet Arthur President of the United States! Good God!" Handsome, affable, debonair, the new executive was best known as a machine politician; yet in the White House he displayed unexpected courage and sagacity and, to the dismay of his former associates, he greatly advanced the cause of reform. Though reorganizing the cabinet, he left most of Garfield's other appointees undisturbed, including Robertson whose choice as customs collector had caused Conkling's resignation.[1] As further evidence of his change of heart, Arthur in 1882

H. Hunt of Louisiana, Secretary of the Navy; Wayne McVeagh of Pennsylvania, Attorney-General; Thomas L. James of New York, Postmaster-General; and Samuel J. Kirkwood of Iowa, Secretary of the Interior.

[1] The new cabinet consisted of Frederick T. Frelinghuysen of New Jersey, Secretary of State; Charles J. Folger of New York, Secretary of the Treasury; William E. Chandler of New Hampshire, Secretary of the Navy; Benjamin H. Brewster of Pennsylvania, Attorney-General; Timothy O. Howe of Wisconsin, Postmaster-General; and Henry M. Teller of Colorado, Secretary of the Interior. Secretary of War Lincoln, son of the martyred President, was the only holdover.

vetoed a bill for $19,000,000 passed by his own party for river and harbor improvements in five hundred localities. This pioneer 'pork-barrel' measure had too many friends, however, and Congress overrode his veto.

Most surprising of all, he attacked two bulwarks of past Republican success: the spoils system and the protective tariff. Garfield's murder by an aggrieved job hunter gave tragic force to the arguments for civil-service reform that had been mooted since the Civil War, and Arthur soon after assuming his duties urged Congress to take the step. But the lawmakers, loath to give up an accustomed perquisite, failed to respond until the people in the fall elections of 1882 sent a Democratic majority to the House. The Democrats also swept thirteen of the sixteen states in which governors were chosen, including New York where Grover Cleveland, an ardent civil-service reformer, won by an unprecedented plurality. Though Republican factionalism was partly responsible for the reverses, the party's failure to safeguard the government service was a prime contributing factor. The outgoing Republican Congress, fearing a more drastic law when the Democrats came in, now hastened to adopt the legislation while time permitted. The Pendleton Act in January, 1883, provided for a bipartisan Civil Service Commission to administer a system of competitive examinations as a test of fitness for federal appointment. It also forbade a government official to solicit campaign contributions from office-holders and protected them against removal if they failed to pay. The plan went into effect at once only in the executive departments in Washington, the customhouses and the larger post offices, but the President was authorized to extend the classified list, as it was called, to other groups at his discretion.

True, the statute left much to be desired. The rules affected merely future appointments and, at first, fewer than fourteen thousand positions, leaving nearly nine tenths of the total still subject to partisan politics. Nevertheless the law has rightly been termed the "Magna Charta of civil-service reform," for through the flexible provision Arthur and his successors were enabled to apply the merit system to ever greater numbers of employees, with the principal gains coming in the twentieth century. While devotion to the public weal sanctioned this course, self-interest also played a part, for an outgoing administration, acting on the principle that 'to the vanquished belong the spoils,' often increased the classified list to protect the faithful from dismissal by the victorious opposition. The Pendleton Act failed principally in not putting an effective end to the practice of levying party assessments on officeholders. Incidentally, the federal example strengthened the hands of local civil-service reformers and, beginning with Massachusetts and New York in 1884, promoted the spread of the merit system to other states and many municipalities.

Arthur's interest in tariff reform grew out of the fact that in 1881 a surplus began piling up in the Treasury at the rate of more than $100,000,000 a year. This excess of income over outgo inflicted needless taxes on the people at the same time that it decreased the volume of money available for business development. Moreover, it tempted Congress to wasteful spending, such as the pork-barrel act in 1882 and the lavish outlays for pensions, for by using up the surplus the Republicans hoped to avoid lowering the tariff of 1875, which was the real source of the trouble. The President, nevertheless, urged Congress to relieve "industry and enterprise from the pressure of unnecessary taxation," and in May, 1882, the lawmaking branch grudgingly provided for a tariff commission to recommend a revision "just to all interests." The commission, headed by John L. Hayes of the National Association of Wool Manufacturers, consisted wholly of protectionists, yet it approved reductions averaging from 20 to 25 per cent. At once the lobbyists wheeled into action, including Hayes himself who in his private capacity now fought the proposals he had earlier endorsed. In Congress they found potent allies in Senators Justin S. Morrill of Vermont and Nelson W. Aldrich of Rhode Island and in Representatives William McKinley of Ohio and Pennsylvania's 'Pig-Iron' Kelley. As finally enacted the tariff of 1883 left the protective system virtually unchanged. While internal-revenue duties were substantially sliced, the decreases in import duties averaged less than 5 per cent, and these concerned manufactures little affected by foreign competition.

THE EMERGENCE OF GROVER CLEVELAND

President Arthur hoped for the Republican nomination in 1884, but he had lost his former Stalwart support without winning the full confidence of the Halfbreeds. In Chicago on June 3 the convention chose the perennial aspirant James G. Blaine on the fourth ballot over the protests of younger delegates like Theodore Roosevelt and Henry Cabot Lodge. As he lacked the usual recommendation of war service,

General John A. Logan of Illinois was picked for the second place. To the reform wing of the party Blaine's candidacy meant a reversal of all the progress toward good government that had been made since Grant left office. A conference of Independent Republicans denounced his selection and called upon the Democrats to do better. Meeting in Chicago on July 8, the Democrats rose to the occasion, naming Grover Cleveland on the second ballot and adding Thomas A. Hendricks, Tilden's running mate in 1876, in a feeble effort to resurrect the old 'fraud' issue. Cleveland's nomination admirably met the requirements of the situation. With none of the qualities of the dashing political cavalier or the wiles of the professional intriguer, he had shown aggressive devotion to clean government first as mayor of Buffalo and afterward in the governor's chair. In appearance he was rather unimpressive, weighing over two hundred pounds and being clean-shaven when most statesmen affected beards. "We love him most for the enemies he has made," said General Edward S. Bragg in seconding his nomination. The Independents at a later gathering endorsed Cleveland as an exemplar "of political courage and honesty and of administrative reform," while stigmatizing Blaine as "a representative of men, methods, and conduct which the public conscience condemns."

The two platforms offered no real points of contrast. Even as regards the tariff both pledged revision without harm to domestic manufactures. Accordingly the contest turned upon the pervasive influence of party loyalty and the personal fitness of the nominees. Cleveland's Republican supporters, scorned by the regulars as 'Mugwumps' and captained by such men as Schurz and Godkin, stumped the North, proclaiming Cleveland's precept, "Public office is a public trust," as the paramount question. To their aid came additional Mulligan letters, giving fresh cogency to charges of Blaine's illicit dealings with corporations seeking government favors. The force of the attack seemed likely to be nullified, however, when the bachelor Cleveland, accused of being the father of a seven-year-old son, replied in a manner that apparently admitted his culpability. At once clergymen carried the 'moral issue' into the pulpit. A middle-class people, deeply imbued with rigid notions of chastity, faced the bitter choice between a candidate of loose private morals and one of loose public morals. Blaine—the first nominee since Greeley in 1872 to tour the country—employed his magnificent oratorical powers in waving the bloody shirt, while his campaign managers tried heroically to wean Irish Catholic voters from their traditional Democratic allegiance because his mother was of that faith. But the Democrats had the better of the argument when the Reverend Samuel D. Burchard introduced Blaine at a New York ministers' gathering a few days before the election as the leader of the party opposed to "rum, Romanism and rebellion"—a remark which Democratic newspapers promptly attributed to Blaine himself. Both sides received generous donations from the moneyed interests, though the Republicans fared better as the surer investment.

The contest proved so close that three days passed before the outcome was definitely known. Cleveland received 219 electoral votes to 182 for Blaine and 48.9 per cent (4,911,000) of the popular ballots to 48.3 per cent (4,848,000). The Democrats carried the usually doubtful states of New Jersey, Connecticut and Indiana by a few thousand each and the pivotal state of New York by but 1149 out of a total poll of over a million. Had Cleveland lost New York's 36 electoral votes, or had he lost New Jersey and either of the other two states, Blaine would have triumphed. Many things helped tip the scale: the lukewarmness of the Stalwarts toward Blaine, Republican defections in New York to the Prohibition party, Burchard's injudicious remark, a brief business recession, and the participation of many new voters grown to manhood since the war. But, in last analysis, the major credit belonged to the Mugwumps, who wielded their greatest influence in those states where the Republicans could least afford losses. The Democrats also won the House of Representatives.

Cleveland's election, the first Democratic victory since Buchanan, indicated less the strength of his party than a rebuke to reactionary Republicanism. Countless voters who had confidence in the man disliked and distrusted his heterogeneous following. For twenty years the Democrats, itching for power, had relied upon opportunism rather than principles. To Cleveland fell the choice—as long before it had to Andrew Jackson—of letting the party continue rudderless and adrift or of seizing the helm and steering a bold course. Happily, he was well situated to undertake the latter role. A newcomer in the national arena, he was unhampered by political entanglements. Moreover, his phlegmatic temperament rendered him impervious to either flattery or threats. Unfamiliar with the tariff and other national problems before taking office, he worked at his job as had no other President. Night after night he would spend in his study only to be back at his desk early the next morning. But when once he formed his conclusions they became his inflexible guide. The key to his political thinking appeared in his inaugural address. "The people," he said, "demand reform in the administration of the government and the application of business principles to public affairs." Like the more progressive members of the opposition party, he was interested mainly in administrative efficiency, being little conscious of those profound influences which were breeding labor unrest and social friction. The opportunity of the Democrats either for good or ill was limited, however, for the Senate remained Republican throughout Cleveland's term. The new policies therefore seldom fruited in legislation, but were expressed rather in presidential recommendations, executive orders and veto messages.

Cleveland's cabinet, headed by Thomas F. Bayard of Delaware, compared favorably with those of his Republican predecessors and included two members from the Deep South: Augustus H. Garland of Arkansas, the Attorney-General, and Lucius Q. C. Lamar of Mississippi, Secretary of the Interior.[1] In applying the merit plan to the civil service the President met stubborn resistance within his own party, notably from Arthur P. Gorman in the Senate and Samuel J. Randall in the House, who openly flouted the 'Goody Two-Shoes' reform. Hence he had to move cautiously to avert factional wrangling which might defeat his other policies. As far as he could, he stilled the "everlasting clatter for offices" with appointments in the unclassified service, while quietly putting twelve thousand more positions under the examination system and extending the competitive principle to include promotions as well as first appointments.

In a further endeavor to extend "business principles to public affairs" Cleveland moved vigorously to stamp out laxness and fraud in the granting of pensions. Particularly culpable was Congress's practice of passing special acts to take care of persons who could not pass the scrutiny of the Pension Bureau. After painstaking study he killed two hundred and thirty-three such bills. One applicant, who

---

[1] The other members were Daniel Manning of New York, Secretary of the Treasury; William C. Whitney of New York, Secretary of the Navy; William C. Endicott of Massachusetts, Secretary of War; and William F. Vilas of Wisconsin, Postmaster-General. Bayard, Garland and Lamar were Senators at the time of their appointment.

alleged "long and faithful service," had actually spent most of the time in prison as a deserter. Another claimant, a veteran's widow, asked recompense for her husband's death at the hands of a neighbor who was shooting at an owl. In 1887 Congress sought to rebuke Cleveland by passing a general pension measure to compensate ex-soldiers of as little as ninety days' service if they found themselves unable to make a living. This he rejected on the ground that the pension list would become a refuge for impostors instead of a "roll of honor." Nevertheless he accepted far more private pension bills than he denied, and in his four years the annual outlay rose from $56,000,000 to $81,000,000. His determination to keep expenditures within reasonable bounds was further shown by vetoes in 1887 of an extravagant rivers-and-harbors bill and of an appropriation for distributing seed grain to drought-stricken Texas farmers. Notwithstanding that the amount in the latter instance was only $10,000, he maintained that "though the people support the government, the government should not support the people." In all his vetoes he was reproving a Democratic House as well as a Republican Senate.

Inevitably Cleveland's interest in "the application of business principles to public affairs" caused him to pay increasing attention to the tariff. Though the Democrats had been a low-tariff party before the Civil War, their attitude in more recent years had been inconsistent and confused. Indeed, some of the leaders like Pennsylvania's Samuel J. Randall, who voted for the 1883 tariff, were ardent protectionists. When William R. Morrison, acting for the Democratic majority in the House, drew up a bill in 1884 cutting most of the duties horizontally by 20 per cent, forty-one Randall Democrats teamed up with the Republican minority to defeat it. Even the platform on which Cleveland entered office betrayed protectionist influences, promising a revision that would not "injure any domestic industries." Nevertheless, a rising sentiment among the members from the agricultural West and South favored a genuine lowering of duties. Cleveland was little given to abstract theories and at no time did he espouse the extreme doctrine known as 'free trade.' Confronted, however, by the large annual surplus revenue which the act of 1883 had failed to remove, he studied the problem assiduously and resolved to attack the evil at its source. From a rather vague recommendation of tariff reduction in his message of 1885, he became more definite in 1886 and finally in December, 1887, he defied all precedent and startled the country by devoting his entire annual message to the subject. Branding the 1883 law as the inequitable source of unnecessary taxation, he declared that the surplus would breed business stagnation. He charged the protective system with enhancing living costs for the masses in order to give "immense profits" to the manufacturing class. As a remedy he proposed a "readjustment" of rates to eliminate the "hardships and dangers" without, however, "imperiling the existence of our manufacturing interests." He excluded theoretical considerations as irrelevant, for, he added in a phrase quick to catch the public ear, "It is a *condition* which confronts us, not a theory." Cleveland's thunderbolt cleared the air. The Mills bill incorporating his ideas passed the House in July, 1888, with only four Democrats dissenting. Since the Senate was Republican, further action awaited the outcome of the presidential election.

Cleveland had already been renominated by acclamation in St. Louis the month before, with Allen G. Thurman of Ohio as his running mate. The platform devoted most space to commending the President's tariff program. The Republicans lacked an outstanding candidate, since Blaine declined to allow his name to be considered. Meeting in Chicago on June 19, they finally chose on the eighth ballot ex-Senator Benjamin Harrison of Indiana, a war veteran, strong protectionist and grandson of William Henry Harrison, with Levi P. Morton of New York for Vice-President. The platform resounded with praise of the "American system of protection," promised pension increases from the "overflowing treasury" and declared for wiping out the surplus by repealing internal-revenue taxes. The campaign was the first in American history to turn mainly on the tariff. The Philadelphia merchant John Wanamaker, seasoned in raising money for the Y. M. C. A., now took over the task for the Republicans. "If you were confronted with from one to three years of general depression by a change in our revenue and protective methods," he asked businessmen, "what would you pay to be insured for a better year?" Funds rolled in to the tune of $3,000,000, the largest sum hitherto expended by any party in a presidential race. In the closing weeks of the canvass many industrialists frightened their workers with the specter of unemployment in the event of a Democratic victory.

Neither side, however, forgot the influence of the Irish vote in the election of 1884, and both platforms feelingly, if prematurely, congratulated the Irish-Americans upon the approach of 'home rule' in Erin. This time the advantage lay with the Republicans, for Democratic tariff reform was promptly represented as a surrender to English manufacturing interests. They made the most of a letter of the British Minister in Washington advising a supposed former fellow countryman to support Cleveland; and a campaign poster displayed the Democratic ticket under the Union Jack and the Republican under the Stars and Stripes, with the sentiment, falsely ascribed to the London *Times:* "The only time England can use an Irishman is when he emigrates to America and votes for free trade." Next to the tariff, Cleveland's pension vetoes provoked unrestrained attack. Moreover, he received but half-hearted backing from the professional politicians in his own party, and in New York there is reason to believe that Tammany threw its support to his rival. Harrison garnered an electoral majority of 233 to 168 through winning the large states by small pluralities, but Cleveland overtopped him in the popular returns with nearly 48.7 per cent (5,538,000 votes) to 47.8 per cent (5,440,000). Except for Hayes in 1876 and perhaps John Quincy Adams in 1824, Harrison has been the only presidential candidate to succeed with a smaller popular support than that of his leading opponent. His party also carried both branches of Congress. The buying of votes by Republicans in Indiana, Connecticut, West Virginia and certain other close states had been so notorious as to make the campaign of 1888 probably the most corrupt in United States history. One outcome was a widespread movement to adopt the Australian ballot system of secret voting and official ballots. Within ten years all the states but four had in some form gone over to the plan.

THE TRIUMPH OF PROTECTIONISM

The new President's chief claim to distinction had consisted in long and faithful service to his party. A stocky, bearded man of gentle disposition, he shrank from leadership. His reserved manner tended to repel even political friends, giving point to the saying: 'Harrison sweats ice water.' From the outset he leaned heavily upon the higher-ups in the Republican organization: Blaine, who had helped obtain his nomination; Speaker Thomas B. Reed of Maine, whose iron rule of the new House won him the nickname of 'Czar'; and, for a time, large-state bosses like Senators Tom Platt of New York and Matt

Quay of Pennsylvania. Harrison put Blaine at the head of his cabinet, and rewarded Wanamaker with the office of Postmaster-General.[1] In dispensing patronage he allowed the spoilsmen almost unobstructed sway in the unclassified service. J. S. Clarkson of Iowa, Assistant Post-master-General, won the title of 'headsman' by replacing thirty-one thousand fourth-class postmasters in a single year before he himself was beheaded. Like Grant, Harrison also gave many jobs to relatives. On the other hand, after waiting two years, he extended the merit system to new classes of offices. His greatest service to the cause, however, was the appointment to the Civil Service Commission of Theodore Roosevelt, whose aggressive championship of the reform made his name a source of terror to politicians in both parties during his six-year tenure.

The government, now under sole Republican control, quickly grappled with the problem of the surplus. One way was to use up as much as possible of the current income. James ('Corporal') Tanner of New York, upon becoming head of the Pension Bureau, is said to have cried, "God help the surplus revenue!" In the six months he was allowed to remain, he drummed up new claimants, reopened rejected cases and boosted existing allowances. In June, 1890, the general pension bill, which Cleveland had vetoed, was repassed by Congress. During Harrison's regime the annual cost of pensions rose from $81,000,000 to $135,000,000. Congress disposed of more of the surplus by larger appropriations for the navy.

The Republican leaders knew that such methods dealt with effects rather than causes, but they were resolved not to lessen the tariff unless they could do so without lessening protection. Under William McKinley, head of the House Ways and Means Committee, an answer was found. A son and grandson of Ohio iron manufacturers, he had long held the protective system in almost religious awe. As he described his measure, "Enveloped in it are my country's highest development and greatest prosperity; out of it come the greatest gains to the people, the greatest comforts to the masses, the widest encouragement for manly aspirations." The McKinley Tariff of 1890 lifted the general level of duties from 38 per cent to nearly 50, yet, through

[1] The other members were William Windom of Minnesota, Secretary of the Treasury; Redfield Proctor of Vermont, Secretary of War; William H. H. Miller of Indiana, Attorney-General; Benjamin F. Tracy of New York, Secretary of the Navy; John W. Noble of Missouri, Secretary of the Interior; and Jeremiah M. Rusk of Wisconsin, Secretary of Agriculture (a cabinet office created in 1889).

ingenious arrangements, produced a smaller financial return. Thus, by removing the duty on raw sugar $50,000,000 was cut from the surplus revenue, while a compensatory bounty of two cents a pound to domestic sugar growers took away $10,000,000 more. In other cases the rates were fixed so high as virtually to exclude foreign imports. Another reduction came from lowering the internal taxes on tobacco and alcohol. In two further respects the McKinley Act introduced novelties. Steeper duties on agricultural products were intended to convince the farmer that he was sharing in the benefits of protection as well as the manufacturer. A second feature, that of reciprocity, was inserted at the urgency of Secretary of State Blaine, who pointed out that the original bill disregarded the possibilities of commerce with Latin America. As a result, certain articles commonly imported from those countries, such as molasses, tea, coffee and hides, were placed on the free list, with the proviso that the President might impose duties on them in the case of any nation which levied "unjust or unreasonable" duties on United States products.[1]

The high rates prescribed by the new tariff were quickly reflected in retail prices, causing widespread discontent. The fall elections of 1890, coming about a month after the act went into effect, inflicted a crushing defeat on the Republicans, McKinley himself failing to regain his seat. In the new House the Democrats obtained nearly a three-fourths majority. The law, however, met the expectations of its framers in drying up the source of superabundant revenue. The provisions for revenue reduction, together with Congress's lavish expenditures, rapidly wiped out the surplus, and in Harrison's last months a deficit appeared.

Though Harrison's renomination was regarded without enthusiasm by the Republicans, the party, not daring to disown a President of its own making, chose him on the first vote at Minneapolis on June 7, along with the New York editor, Whitelaw Reid. On the foremost question of the day the platform roundly reaffirmed the "American doctrine of protection." Cleveland, who had been quietly practicing law in New York City since his retirement, was named on the first ballot by the Democrats. The convention, meeting in Chicago on June 21, added Adlai E. Stevenson of Illinois to the ticket. The plat-

[1] Under this provision agreements were effected with ten countries, and the President reimposed duties against three others. These agreements came to an end with the Democratic tariff of 1894.

form as first drawn up repeated the 1888 pledge for a reduction of duties without injury to domestic industries, but the radical wing induced the delegates to substitute a declaration that any duties, except for revenue only, were unconstitutional. As four years before, the storm center of the campaign was the tariff. Cleveland in accepting the nomination quietly disposed of the doctrinaire tariff utterance by asserting, "We need not base our attack upon questions of constitutional permission." Once more the Republicans collected the sinews of war from the great industrialists who, to play safe, also gave to the Democrats. A violent labor disturbance arising from wage reductions in the Carnegie steel works at Homestead, Pennsylvania, aided Cleveland's cause, since it apparently disproved the vaunted connection between high pay and high duties in the case of an exceptionally protected industry.

Cleveland scored a decisive victory, polling 277 votes in the electoral college to 145 for Harrison and 46 per cent of the popular ballots (5,557,000) as compared with less than 43 per cent (5,176,000). The Democrats also won both houses of Congress. The remaining 22 electoral votes went to a third contender, James B. Weaver of Iowa, candidate of the People's party. The spectacular rise of this group denoted the emergence of factors and forces with which the old parties had failed to reckon. The story of the Populists, however, can be better understood in connection with the later discussion of the growing demand for silver inflation.

Cleveland returned to the White House, heartened by the people's endorsement of tariff reform and their confidence in his own unflinching integrity. Moreover, for the first time in nearly a third of a century his party controlled both the legislative and executive branches, and he might therefore hope to write his policies into law. Appearances, however, proved deceptive. Cleveland's second term was cut across by currents and countercurrents of social and political discord: business depression, labor conflict, agrarian unrest. These multiplying difficulties aroused all the President's fighting qualities; but what had formerly been deemed sturdiness of character now sometimes looked like mere stubbornness, while his independence of public opinion often seemed indifference to the public welfare. Time, however, has softened such judgments and has revealed him, whatever his limitations, as a fearless and high-minded executive.

In recognition of the low-tariff elements in the two parties, Cleve-

ART GALLERY, PHILADELPHIA CENTENNIAL, 1876

PALACE OF FINE ARTS, CHICAGO WORLD'S FAIR, 1893

ARCHITECTURAL ADVANCE

See page 47.

CAPTAIN CLEVELAND HAS TROUBLE WITH HIS CREW

See page 78.

land appointed Walter Q. Gresham, an Illinois Republican, Secretary of State and John G. Carlisle, a Kentucky Democrat, head of the Treasury.[1] As in his first administration, he appeased the hunger for spoils with offices not in the classified list, but during the four years he more than doubled the number under the merit system, bringing the total to about 82,000 out of some 200,000. Work on a new tariff bill proceeded under William L. Wilson of West Virginia, chairman of the Ways and Means Committee. In contrast to the object of the McKinley Act, his purpose was to increase the revenue and decrease protection. The Wilson bill, adopted by the House in February, 1894, embodied certain principles which, broadly speaking, were to guide later Democratic efforts at tariff revision. Basic raw materials in manufacturing and construction—wool, sugar, lumber, iron ore and the like—were put on the free list. As this enabled industrialists to cut production costs, protective duties on manufactures were generally reduced. In order to offset losses in revenue, new internal taxes were placed on domestic liquors, tobacco and other luxuries and, for the first time since Civil War days, an income tax was adopted. This last provision—a two-per-cent levy on incomes above $4000—was the price the Democrats paid for Populist support of the bill, and was championed as a means of shifting some of the tax burden to those best able to pay.

Once more lobbyists swooped down upon Washington, determined to repair in the Senate the mischief wrought by the House. Their path was eased by the willingness of Democratic members from the industrial sections to join the Republicans in obtaining rates beneficial to their constituents. Personal gain also played a part. Senator Quay, for example, admitted to an investigating committee that he had speculated in sugar stock for a rise while the sugar duties were under consideration. With Gorman of Maryland directing the proceedings, six hundred and thirty-four amendments were attached to the House bill, altering it both in principle and detail. The most important items, including sugar, were taken from the free list, and protective duties generally increased. Only the income tax and the internal-revenue

[1] The other members were Daniel S. Lamont of New York, Secretary of War; Richard Olney of Massachusetts, Attorney-General; Wilson S. Bissell of New York, Postmaster-General; Hilary A. Herbert of Alabama, Secretary of the Navy; Hoke Smith of Georgia, Secretary of the Interior; and J. Sterling Morton of Nebraska, Secretary of Agriculture. On Gresham's death in June, 1895, Olney became Secretary of State, and Judson Harmon of Ohio, Attorney-General.

duties remained without material change. After stubborn opposition the House finally accepted the Gorman version; and in August, 1894, the President, assailing the Senate's "party perfidy and party dishonor," allowed the measure to become law without his signature. The Wilson-Gorman Act lowered the general scale of duties to only about 40 per cent. Another blow was yet to fall. In 1895 the Supreme Court by a vote of five to four knocked out the income-tax provision, thereby reversing an earlier unanimous decision in 1881. The majority held that a tax on incomes was a "direct" tax and hence subject to the constitutional limitation of being apportioned among the states according to population.[1]

This series of mishaps, along with the hard times precipitated by the Panic of 1893, helped discredit the Wilson-Gorman Act with the public. Though protection was only a minor issue in the next presidential election, McKinley when he entered office in March, 1897, summoned Congress in special session to revise the tariff according to the Republican formula. The outcome was the Dingley Act of 1897, a thoroughgoing measure which raised the customs wall to the highest point it had yet reached, an average of 57 per cent. After a decade of almost ceaseless contention victory thus rested with the ultraprotectionists. The remarkable prosperity which shortly burst upon the country was hailed by the Republicans as vindicating their most extravagant claims for the system. For ten years the tariff disappeared from public controversy.

FULLER ACCOUNTS

Official Laxity and Economic Muddle. Political development to the end of the century may be followed in Binkley, *American Political Parties;* Josephson, *The Politicos,* a survey with cynical overtones; Oberholtzer, *History,* II–V; Rhodes, *History,* VI–VIII; Stanwood, *History of the Presidency,* I; and three volumes of the *American Nation Series:* Dunning, *Reconstruction, Political and Economic,* Sparks, *National Development,* and Dewey, *National Problems.* For a rating of the Presidents by fifty-five historians and students of government, see Schlesinger, *Paths to the Present,* chap. v. Leading biographies for the period include Hesseltine, *Grant;* Chidsey, *Gentleman from New York* (Conkling); Muzzey, *Blaine;* Fuess, *Schurz;* Ogden, *Godkin;* Williams, *Hayes;* Flick, *Tilden;* Smith, *Garfield;* Howe, *Arthur;* Nevins, *Cleveland;* and Olcott, *McKinley.* Dewey, *Financial History,* presents the essential facts concisely.

---

[1] Pollock *v.* Farmers' Loan and Trust Company. All later federal income taxation had to await the adoption of the Sixteenth Amendment in 1913, since distribution of population does not determine the relative concentration of wealth.

Ferliger deals with *David A. Wells and the American Revenue System, 1865–1870;* Ross with *The Liberal Republican Movement;* and Burton, *Financial Crises,* and Larson, *Jay Cooke,* with the Panic of 1873.

Depression Politics. Among the relevant studies are Feder, *Unemployment Relief;* Buck, *Granger Movement* and his *Agrarian Crusade;* Mitchell, *History of Greenbacks;* Barrett, *Greenbacks and Resumption of Specie Payments;* and Haworth, *Hayes-Tilden Disputed Presidential Election.*

The Battle for Political Reform. Of particular note are Fish, *Civil Service and Patronage,* and Sageser, *First Two Decades of the Pendleton Act.*

The Emergence of Grover Cleveland. Thomas discusses *The Return of the Democratic Party to Power in 1884,* while special accounts include Oliver, *History of Civil War Pensions;* Stanwood, *American Tariff Controversies;* Tarbell, *Tariff in Our Times;* and Taussig, *Tariff History,* an economist's analysis.

The Triumph of Protectionism. Besides the works on the tariff just cited, see Knoles, *Presidential Campaign and Election of 1892.*

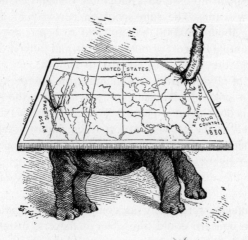

CHAPTER IV

THE CONSOLIDATING MOVEMENT

THE NATURE OF THE PROCESS

As tariffs climbed upward and the Economic Revolution moved into higher gear, the output of mills and mines multiplied, the expanding railways whisked the products to every part of the land, and high-pressure salesmanship assured a mounting demand by educating the public to new wants. The sum spent on newspaper advertising increased from about $40,000,000 in 1880 to nearly $96,000,000 in 1900, not counting the cost of outdoor signs and billboards. "America is daubed from one end of the country to the other with huge white-paint notices of favorite articles of manufacture," wrote one observer, while another spoke of advertising as "playing upon the brain of man as a musician does upon a piano." To supply the waxing domestic market as well as the growing export trade, industry turned toward large-scale methods, toward concentration in bigger units and fewer hands. By the eighties organization on an interstate or national basis had become the distinguishing mark of most fields of capitalistic enterprise.

The advantages were many as compared with small-scale business. A large concern could hire abler managers, install up-to-date machinery, buy raw materials in quantity and therefore more cheaply, effect economies in marketing and finance, and withstand more easily labor's demands for higher pay and better conditions. If the business approached a monopoly, the owners were also in a position to restrict production and raise prices. A big plant, moreover, could make profitable use of wastes and by-products. As the newspaper humorist "Mr. Dooley" (Finley Peter Dunne) said of one of the mammoth Chicago packing houses, "A cow goes lowin' softly in to Armours an' comes out glue, gelatine, fertylizer, celooloid, joolry, sofy cushions, hair restorer, washin' sody, soap, lithrachoor an' bed springs so quick that while aft she's still cow, for'ard she may be anything fr'm buttons to pannyma hats." [1] With such advantages captains of industry could appease the clamor of investors for higher returns and, when they wished, the public's demand for lower prices.

In this age of dinosaurs the corporation tended to replace individual ownership and the partnership, the forms of business organization typical of earlier America. Through the sale of stock a corporation could tap a wide reservoir of capital. The investor was attracted not only by the hope of unusual dividends, but also by the knowledge that in case of the company's failure he was liable only to the extent of his stock, instead of for the full indebtedness as was any single member of a partnership. The corporation enjoyed the further advantage of being able to plan its activities beyond the lifetime of particular individuals. Moreover, if it wished to hide excessive profits from the public, it could 'water' its stock by giving additional shares to its stockholders. Thus a concern earning 12 per cent might cut the nominal rate to 6 per cent by doubling its stock. In such case the board of directors could, with a specious show of sincerity, combat the demands both of consumers for cheaper prices and of wage earners for better pay. The practice also enabled unprincipled financiers to fleece investors unaware of the diminished value of the stock. One expert estimated in 1883 that more than a quarter of the railroad capitalization represented water.

The actual process of absorption and consolidation was directed by men who, because of their boldness, creative energy and relentless driving power, embodied many of the mythical elements of folk heroes. By common consent they were termed 'steel kings,' 'coal barons,' 'railway magnates,' 'Napoleons of finance.' They constituted, as Henry Clews, the Wall Street banker, said, "the modern nobility," a class who in his opinion far outshone the "English parchment nobility." Among the leaders were Cornelius Vanderbilt, J. Edgar Thomson, Jay Gould, James J. Hill and Edward H. Harriman in the railroad field; John D. Rockefeller, Henry H. Rogers and Henry M. Flagler in the oil industry; Andrew Carnegie, Henry C. Frick and Charles M. Schwab in steel; Philip D. Armour, Nelson Morris and Gustavus F. Swift in meat packing; and Jay Cooke and J. Pierpont

---

[1] Actually, Mr. Dooley's fiction hardly exceeded the fact, for the by-products included glue, gelatine, fertilizer, soap, leather, felt, knife handles, combs, buttons, brushes, pepsin, albumen, oils, oleomargarine, candles, glycerine, isinglass, lard, tennis strings, hairpins, umbrella handles, dice, perfume-bottle caps and artificial teeth.

Morgan in banking and finance. Arising in most cases from obscure origins, and unhindered by moral scruples, they were fired by a passionate will to succeed. They conceived of themselves as above the law though always willing to hide behind it. "Law!" roared Cornelius Vanderbilt. "What do I care about the law? Hain't I got the power?" Some were builders with far-reaching plans; others, wreckers with no plans at all. The story of their activities is a singular blend of the heroic and splendid with the sordid and sinister.

Without exception they waved the banner of free enterprise. This implied, first and foremost, their belief in the traditional American gospel of individualism or laissez faire, that is, the right to be let alone. But they proclaimed the doctrine with tongue in cheek, for, while decrying governmental intervention to their hurt, they demanded it whenever it would help—in the form, for example, of tariff protection, subsidies and gifts of natural resources. Moreover they hymned the glories of free enterprise at the same time that they strove to destroy the free enterprise of everyone but themselves. They spoke the language of individualism that was a legacy of pioneer days when the doors of opportunity swung wide for all. Only gradually did the public come to realize that with the changed conditions unbridled liberty for the few spelled economic servitude for the many. Yet the best of these men were inspired by the conviction that they were building a better and greater America, that the wealth they amassed would indirectly benefit all ranks of society. Some indeed, like Rockefeller, who taught Baptist Bible classes in Cleveland, and Hill, who gave $1,000,000 to a Catholic seminary in St. Paul, identified their work with religion itself.

In the more industrialized nations abroad similar consolidating tendencies were at work. In England, the birthplace of the steam railway, the roads had started uniting much earlier than in America, but, in the absence of a protective tariff, industrial combinations made relatively little progress. In Germany, after the political unification in 1870 and under a protective system, great corporations came to dominate economic life. As in the United States, both of these governments intervened to curb the consolidations when they began to injure the public interest. England commenced regulating the railroads in the 1840's, and in 1873 established a supervisory commission. A German law of 1884 outlawed stock watering, forbade other loose practices of corporations and required publicity of their transactions.

Railways, however, presented no problem in that country because they were generally owned and operated by the government.

RAILROAD AMALGAMATION

Though mergers of railroads in America had not been unknown before the Civil War, the era of rapid and extensive consolidation came afterward. Cornelius Vanderbilt, who had made $10,000,000 mostly in the steamboat business, was one of the first to vision the possibilities. Selling his vessels in 1865, he set about to develop a continuous rail route from New York City to the heart of the Middle West. Starting with a line to Albany, he added the New York Central in 1867 to connect with Buffalo and in 1873 bought control of the Lake Shore & Michigan Southern to reach Chicago. When he died four years later at the age of eighty-three, he had acquired over $100,-000,000, the first great modern fortune. Much of it came from the unscrupulous manipulation of railway stocks and from methods of competition akin to the ethics of the jungle. Meanwhile the Pennsylvania Railroad under J. Edgar Thomson outgrew its line from Philadelphia to Pittsburgh, gaining entry to Chicago and St. Louis in 1869 and forging links with New York City two years later. Its business methods, however, were a welcome contrast to Vanderbilt's. By 1875 three other trunk lines had been completed between the Atlantic and Lake Michigan: the Erie, the Baltimore and Ohio, and the Grand Trunk. Similar mergers took place in the Mississippi Valley. Three through lines joined Chicago and St. Louis by 1870, and others were subsequently established. In the South comparable tendencies were at work.

It is doubtful whether enough business existed as yet to support all these railroads. In the furious strife for traffic certain practices resulted that harmed both the roads and the public. Thus in 1869, and again from 1874 to 1876, the lines between Chicago and the Atlantic Seaboard carried their rate wars to the point of slashing charges below operating costs. Another scheme was to manipulate rates in ways that favored some cities over others. The lower charges were designed to undercut competing roads; the higher ones, to recoup losses where the company had a monopoly. As a result it actually cost less to ship goods from Chicago to New York than to points a few hundred miles east of Chicago. This 'long-and-short-haul' device aroused much indignation, especially among small-town and rural folk, who were its chief victims. Equally objectionable was the plan of discriminating against small shippers by granting secret rebates to competitors who provided a larger freight traffic. When the companies themselves owned other businesses, such as coal mining, they nearly always dealt unfairly with independent concerns in those fields. Fearing hostile legislation because of their practices, the railroads sought to influence public opinion by furnishing free passes to government officials, judges, politicians, newspaper editors and preachers.

The roads found the cutthroat rivalry so disastrous that from time to time competing lines tried to escape the evils by treaty. Rate agreements were formed to fix uniform charges, only to break down sooner or later for want of mutual confidence. Pooling, a more ingenious device, suited the conditions better. By this plan rival companies divided the freight business according to some ratio, or placed the total earnings in a common fund for distribution as prearranged. The first notable pool, that organized in 1870 by the Northwestern, the Rock Island and the Burlington, all running between Chicago and Omaha, lasted fourteen years. Each line retained about half its receipts on the through traffic, leaving the remainder to be shared equally. Rail companies elsewhere often made similar arrangements, the duration usually depending upon the willingness of erstwhile competitors to trust one another.

Popular resentment at railroad practices deepened as the years went on. While the movement for state regulation culminating in the Granger laws had a good effect, especially for short hauls, the transportation problem was by its very nature interstate in character, calling for national action. The Eastern businessman as well as the Western farmer had a stake in bringing this about, for, as the New York Board of Trade pointed out in 1879, even that great metropolis depended upon the uncertain favor of railroads for its prosperity or ruin. In 1874 and again in 1878 the House passed a bill to regulate rates, and in 1885 both branches acted but without being able to agree upon the same measure. A Supreme Court decision in October, 1886, brought matters to a head. In the Wabash case the judges, shifting ground from the Peik decision of nine years before, forbade individual states to exercise any control over commerce passing beyond their borders, that being the exclusive function of Congress. The Interstate Commerce Act of 1887 prohibited unreasonable charges, special rates, pools, rebates and the long-and-short-haul discrimination, and pro-

vided for an Interstate Commerce Commission to guard against violations. The Commission, though denounced by the rail interests as
'state socialism,' was only a fact-finding body with no coercive powers:
it could not fix rates or enforce its orders. If a railroad refused to
comply, the Commission must bring suit in a federal court.

This first experiment in national supervision of transportation
proved in most respects a disappointment. In sixteen cases brought
before the Supreme Court between 1887 and 1905 the roads won
fifteen. Justice Samuel F. Miller, criticizing the majority's attitude,
explained, "It is vain to contend with judges who have been at the
bar the advocates for forty years of railroad companies and all the
forms of associated capital." Accordingly the lines were for the most
part able to continue their illegal ways, though they had to pay greater
attention than before to external appearances. For example, since
pooling was banned, they achieved much the same result by means of
traffic associations, which regulated rates and punished violations.
The Interstate Commerce Commission after a decade of experience
declared the situation "intolerable both from the standpoint of the
public and the commission." When the Supreme Court in 1897 in a
case involving the Trans-Missouri Freight Association held by a
five-to-four vote that traffic associations were illegal, a new consolidating movement began which led to the merging of many hitherto
independent roads.

Notwithstanding the continuing expansion of mileage the number
of rail companies shrank from 1500 to about 800 in the last two
decades of the century. By 1900 more than half of the nation's track-
age centered in six major financial groups, the Vanderbilt, Morgan,
Harriman and Pennsylvania interests with approximately 20,000
miles each, the Gould group with 16,000 and the Hill interests with
5000. The unifying trend was not without its benefits, however.
Thanks to the economies inherent in large-scale undertakings, freight
rates, which in 1860 had rarely fallen below two cents per ton-mile,
averaged three quarters of a cent in 1900. Though the Interstate
Commerce Act had pretty much missed its aim, nevertheless the
principle of national regulation was established, and a somewhat better
adjustment of transportation charges was secured. Moreover, official
machinery for railway control now existed, which Congress might
strengthen and enlarge whenever public opinion should demand.

INDUSTRIAL CONCENTRATION

The movement for the consolidation of manufacturing ran a similar course. Following the Civil War, industrial concerns, unhampered by legal restraints, grew rapidly in size and, like the railroads, fought desperately to absorb or destroy their competitors. This phase in turn gave way to widespread attempts by the greater ones to stabilize their industries through price agreements, pools and other schemes for restricting output and lifting prices. Finally, with public opinion at full tilt against 'Big Business,' both states and nation intervened with legislation. The centralizing trend, while more powerful in some branches than others, left untouched few of basic importance.

The story of the Standard Oil Company, one of the earliest and strongest combinations, illustrates the process of concentration in other fields as well. In 1865 John D. Rockefeller, a young Clevelander who had made a small fortune out of army contracts and a produce concern, entered the oil-refining business. First absorbing his local competitors, he proceeded in 1870 with the help of capitalists in Cleveland and New York to organize the million-dollar Standard Oil Company of Ohio, which controlled 4 per cent of all the oil processed in the United States. Now began a career of conquest Napoleonic in daring, scope and execution. In the ensuing years Rockefeller and his associates acquired the biggest companies in New York, Philadelphia and Baltimore. The Standard next achieved mastery of the industry in Pittsburgh and western Pennsylvania. Within a decade 90 per cent of the nation's refining business had passed into its hands.

Many elements, good and evil, made possible this brilliant feat. Not least was the remarkable group of men surrounding Rockefeller —Henry M. Flagler, Henry H. Rogers, John D. Archbold and others —who strained every nerve to plan, plot and fight for the Standard and exacted equal devotion from their underlings. Another factor was the superior efficiency attained through large-scale operation. The Standard not only set up factories to make its own barrels and produce its own acids, but it acquired tank cars and built pipe lines to transport the crude oil. It also created its own selling agencies, and it saved storage charges by erecting large tanks at strategic points. In addition to its main product, kerosene or coal oil for lamps, it utilized and popularized many by-products such as lubricating oils, gasoline, paraffin and vaseline. Its success was further assured by unfair methods of competition, ranging all the way from secret rebates on rail shipments (a favor which it enjoyed for thirty years or more) to the bribery and blackmail of public officials. Of its tactics in one state an observer remarked, "The Standard has done everything with the Pennsylvania legislature except to refine it." When other means failed, it crushed competitors with price-slashing campaigns, followed by price increases to make up for the losses when the object was achieved.

By 1882 the Rockefeller group owned fourteen companies outright and a majority interest in twenty-six others. Earlier, price agreements and pooling arrangements had helped secure harmony of operation, but now, with so vast an empire to manage, the Standard undertook a novel form of organization: the industrial trust. It was an old legal device fitted to new conditions. Adopted in 1879 and revised in 1882, the plan provided for a secret union of the various concerns under nine trustees to whom was confided a controlling amount of the stock of the individual companies and who thus exercised centralized direction. The original holders, in return for their stock, received $70,000,000 in trust certificates, which entitled them to their proportionate share of the joint earnings. Functioning without a charter, the trust could do pretty much as it pleased. So successful did the scheme prove that it prompted the formation of trusts in other businesses, such as cottonseed oil, lead, whisky and sugar.

Meanwhile the outcry against Big Business was reaching a climax. The gains to the public from the improved quality and generally lower prices of commodities were obscured by the brutal practices of throttling competition, corrupting government officials, extorting excessive profits, watering stock and curbing labor unions. The idea of monopolies had always been abhorrent to Americans. Now, under the reign of laissez faire, not only the comforts but the necessities of life—"from meat to tombstones," said Henry Demarest Lloyd—were drifting into the maw of the moneyed interests. We find, he wrote in *Wealth against Commonwealth* (1894), "that competition has killed competition, that corporations are grown greater than the State and have bred individuals greater than themselves, and that the naked issue of our time is with property becoming master instead of servant." President Cleveland, too, spoke out, declaring in his annual message of December, 1888, that "aggregated capital" had in many instances "trampled to death" the ordinary citizen "beneath an iron heel." As an omen of the mounting storm an Anti-Monopoly party appeared in the campaign of 1884, though with slight success. Four years later the two old parties for the first time condemned trusts and monopolies, thanks to pressure from the farming regions where the aroused people were urging similar action on their state legislatures. In 1889 and 1890 fifteen commonwealths, mostly in the West and South, banned conspiracies or agreements restricting competition. Before the movement spent its force, all but New Jersey, Delaware and West Virginia followed suit. These laws had little effect, however, since a corporation chartered in one of the three delinquent states had a constitutional right to do business in any other state.

Recognizing the need of supplementary legislation, Congress in July, 1890, adopted the Sherman Antitrust Act. It declared illegal "every contract, combination in the form of trust or otherwise, or conspiracy, in restraint of trade or commerce among the several States, or with foreign nations." Passed in response to an imperious popular demand, the law, according to Orville H. Platt, Republican Senator from Connecticut, was not intended so much to break up trusts as to tide the Republican party over the next election. It was drafted with such haste that the purport of its apparently simple and direct language was for many years the subject of impassioned controversy. The words might signify that all extensive businesses were unlawful, since the economies of large-scale management necessarily enabled them to undercut competitors. If this were the true import, then the act aimed to prevent the benefits of industrial concentration as well as its evils. But others contended that the phrase "restraint of trade," of old usage in the common law, had a technical legal meaning. If this were so, acts in restraint of trade, when reasonable and fair, would not be affected. Still other ambiguities lurked in the statute. Were railway combinations outlawed as well as other kinds? Were labor organizations prohibited along with capitalistic combinations? These and similar questions had ultimately to be decided by the judiciary.

The Supreme Court in these early years leaned toward an interpretation which made the Sherman Act apply equally to reasonable and unreasonable restraints of trade. The judges also defined the phrase "trade or commerce" as narrowly as possible. When the government sought to dissolve the Sugar Trust, which controlled nearly all the sugar refining in the country, the tribunal in United States *v.* E. C. Knight Company (1895) denied the plea by drawing a tenuous distinction between the manufacture of products within a state, which lay beyond the federal government's reach, and the transportation of the same products to other states. Under the circumstances the executive department put little energy into enforcing the statute. Only seven suits were instituted under Harrison, eight under Cleveland and three under McKinley, and some of these were directed against labor combinations. It was left for later administrations to discover how to sharpen the edge of the law.

With the Sherman Act hardly more than an empty threat, it is not surprising that the centralizing trend proceeded with increased impetus. Up to 1890 only 24 industrial combinations had been formed with a total book capital of $436,000,000, but in the century's last decade 157 were added with a capitalization of $3,150,000,000. The years 1898–1901 were particularly prolific, ushering in an era of superconsolidation signalized by the formation of the United States Steel Corporation (1901), the first billion-dollar amalgamation. This leviathan combined 228 companies located in 127 towns and cities in 18 states and controlled nearly 70 per cent of the iron and steel production. Similarly, the Amalgamated Copper Company, organized in 1899, controlled 60 per cent of the output of that metal.

By this time, however, the particular type of organization known properly as the trust was a thing of the past. Two decisions in state courts were responsible, one in New York in 1890 against a unit of the Sugar Trust and the other in Ohio in 1892 against the Standard Oil Trust. But the word itself continued in popular parlance to denote any form of Big Business that approached a monopoly. In deference to these decisions great capitalistic combinations now assumed a different framework. Some changed into single huge corporations. Others became holding companies, which united corporations in the same branch of industry by securing a controlling share of their stock. To many people the holding company seemed the old trust doing business under a different name and with better legal protection. Indeed, the shifts in structure had no perceptible effect on efficiency of operation or on earnings. As a trust from 1882 to 1891 the Standard, for example, never made less than $8,000,000 a year; under a system of interlocking directorates from 1892 to 1896 the individual corporations totaled from $19,000,000 to $34,000,000; and as a holding company the annual profits from 1899 to 1905 ranged from $34,000,000 to $57,000,000.

The centripetal tendency in manufacturing and transportation was symptomatic of a similar movement in almost every other important economic sphere. As the century drew to a close, the telephone, telegraph and express businesses passed into the hands of a few corporations, and in banking and finance the Morgan and Rockefeller groups wielded such immense power that it was virtually impossible to launch a large commercial enterprise without their participation or approval. In many instances they actually dictated the policies of industrial corporations, life-insurance companies, railroads, public-utility companies and the like. Thus the country was confronted with the spectacle of combinations and monopolies forming on nearly every hand. Thoughtful men began to wonder how long democratic institutions could withstand the strain.

THE RISE OF ORGANIZED LABOR

If the public at large awoke but slowly to a sense of the peril, the wage earners, more patently affected, had long since taken up the gage of battle with the economic overlords. As industry under the impact of the Economic Revolution changed over to large-scale methods and impersonal corporate control, the rift between those who worked and those who paid for work steadily widened. Once, the laboring man had been a self-respecting craftsman, often master of his own tiny shop; now, he began to find himself a mere tender of a machine, his conditions of employment fixed by managers representing absentee owners. When stockholders insisted on higher dividends or employers engaged in price-cutting campaigns, his wages were the first to suffer. His earnings were further affected by the increasing presence of underpaid women and children in the mills and factories and by the multiplying immigrants willing to work for a pittance. Moreover, he toiled in a gloomy, ill-ventilated structure amid dangerous unguarded machinery, and the workday, which in many branches had fallen to ten hours in the short-lived labor movement of the 1830's, tended to grow longer rather than shorter.

An aggrieved class in the United States usually turns to the ballot for relief, but to the workingman the prospect was not encouraging in an era when government and people were enchained by the doctrine of laissez faire. Though some optimistic souls did try to launch labor

parties from time to time, the shrewder leaders, mindful of the successes gained by capital through collective efforts, devoted their energies to promoting similar combinations among their own kind. The
opportunity was challenging, for the number employed in factories,
mines and rail transportation rose from about one and a third million
in 1860 to more than four and a quarter million in 1890, a rate of
increase far outstripping that of the population.

The great business prosperity in the North during the Civil War
had revived the earlier labor movement, with the result that by 1865
local unions existed in many crafts, city trade assemblies were
numerous, and national unions had increased from five to eighteen,
with more to follow. In 1866 William H. Sylvis of the Iron Molders'
Union undertook to federate the country's labor organizations in an
over-all body called the National Labor Union. As its constitution
explained, "Heretofore the highest form labor organizations have
taken is the national union of some of the trades. Between these organizations, however, there was no sympathy or systematic connection,
no co-operative effort, no working for the attainment of a common
end." The National Labor Union, which also took in various political-
reform groups, sought to unite all these bodies behind a program
featuring the eight-hour day, better pay, arbitration as a substitute
for strikes and, with particular emphasis, business undertakings in
which the workers should supply the capital and share the profits.
Such co-operatives as were tried, however, including the stove foun-
dries run by Sylvis's own union, failed either from mismanagement,
inadequate funds or unfair competition. The National Labor Union
held seven annual congresses, the last one for the purpose of launching
a labor party. But internal strife rent the organization, and the crash
of 1873 dealt the finishing blow.

The five lean years that followed had a blighting effect on the
whole labor world. Most unions discontinued, and the total membership dropped from some 300,000 in 1873 to less than 50,000 in 1878,
with only eight or nine national unions surviving. One of the organizations, however, served as the channel for a second and more successful
effort to combine the working class on a nation-wide basis. This was
the Noble Order of the Knights of Labor, founded in 1869 by a group
of Philadelphia garment cutters. Unlike the National Labor Union, it
aimed to join all workers, skilled and unskilled and regardless of task,
in one big union, in the belief that the mechanization of industry was

reducing all to the same level and providing a sounder framework for common action than craft unions. Until 1881 it existed in secret from fear of reprisals by employers. It remained small until 1879 when the return of good times hoisted the membership to a peak of 700,000 in 1886, recruited mainly from the unskilled. The Knights strove for such objectives as the eight-hour day, fairer wages, industrial arbitration and the abolition of child labor. Under Terence V. Powderly, who became head of the order in 1879, it also fostered co-operatives. More than a hundred and thirty-five were begun, chiefly in the mining, cooperage and shoe industries, where the pay was exceptionally low, but these enterprises encountered the same difficulties and met the same fate as those of the National Labor Union. Nor did the efforts to promote arbitration get very far, for most employers were hostile. Meanwhile the sudden expansion of membership drew into the organization many socialists, radicals and other jangling elements, and the Knights became embroiled in an increasing number of strikes, boycotts and other disturbances. The disastrous failure of some important railway strikes in 1886 cast further discredit on the order, hurling it into a decline as rapid as its rise.

Another reason for its collapse was the emergence of a rival aggregation rooted in the older craft principle of organization. Started in 1881 by disgruntled Knights, it adopted its present name, the American Federation of Labor, in 1886 when it reorganized on a broader basis. Modeled upon the British Trades Union Congress, the AFL was a league of self-governing labor bodies supervised by a central board of elected officials. Its core consisted of national unions, but it also included city trade assemblies, state federations, and local unions lacking national affiliations. Embracing only skilled workers, the organization through its federal structure left scope for the special interests of particular groups and at the same time united them against the competition of the unskilled. The central officials confined their activities to strengthening and extending the union movement, acting in an advisory capacity during industrial conflicts and lobbying for favorable legislation. The Federation shunned co-operatives, but otherwise its goals resembled those of the Knights, including the eight-hour day, the prohibition of child labor and the improvement of working conditions in factories and mines.

From the outset the dominant figure was Samuel Gompers, the Federation's president almost continuously until his death in 1924.

Born of Jewish parentage in a London tenement, he had made a name for himself by organizing the Cigarmakers' Union of New York so effectively that it issued from the depression years stronger than when it entered. Distrustful of intellectuals and theorists, he consistently fought all attempts to commit the Federation either to the socialist program of displacing the capitalist system or to the experiment of a separate political party. In day and out he preached the gospel of collective bargaining. The AFL's membership rose from 150,000 in 1886 to 200,000 in 1890 and to 550,000 in 1900. One important group of unions, the four Railway Brotherhoods (engineers, conductors, firemen and brakemen), remained outside, feeling that the advantages afforded by their strategic position in the American economy would be weakened by uniting with the Federation, though they were generally willing to make common cause with it. Its chief handicap lay in the fact that as an organization of the skilled it represented only the favored few of labor, excluding perhaps 90 per cent of the whole. Its hope of success rested on its effectiveness as a militant and compact minority.

CAPITAL AND LABOR

With both labor and capital mobilized for defense and aggression the stage was set for a trial of strength. The issues most in contention were wages, the length of the workday and the right to organize unions; but behind such specific differences lay a fundamental clash of viewpoint. Labor asserted its inalienable right to a voice in determining working conditions and demanded a larger share of the employers' profits so that it might improve its standard of living. In short, the workers insisted that their earnings keep pace with the increase of the wealth they helped create. To the employer, however, labor's contribution was but one of many factors in industry, hardly comparable to the part played by financial resources, technology, managerial talent and business enterprise. Wages, he maintained with laissez-faire zeal, should be governed by the 'iron law' of supply and demand, not by humane considerations or notions of fancied right.

With attitudes so irreconcilable protracted strife was inevitable. Neither side was blameless, since each in varying degree was actuated by irresponsibility, lawlessness and bad faith. It took labor many years to live down the criminal activities of the 'Molly Maguires,' a secret organization in the Pennsylvania anthracite region, whose career of terrorism was finally ended in 1876 by the execution and imprisonment of the ringleaders; it was not till long afterward that a part of the violence was discovered to have been instigated by the owners themselves, who wanted a pretext for breaking up the organization. Neither party envisaged the conflicts as other than private wars in which the public had no stake. Only gradually did the American people come to realize that, whichever side won a strike, the community lost because of the interruption of business, the enhanced prices and the added costs of police protection and of charity.

The first great struggle stemmed from a succession of wage reductions on the Pennsylvania, New York Central and Baltimore & Ohio railroads during the hard times following the Panic of 1873. In late July, 1877, rioting and turbulence convulsed rail centers all the way from Baltimore to St. Louis and San Francisco. Ten or more states found it necessary to call out the militia, and President Hayes at the instance of governors or United States marshals sent regular troops into six of them. In Pittsburgh the contest resembled a pitched battle. The local guardsmen called to arms fraternized with the men, and when a militia detachment from Philadelphia killed seventeen demonstrators and bystanders, a frenzied mob besieged the soldiers for twelve hours in a roundhouse. Patrols of citizens finally restored order. Meanwhile about 1600 cars, 126 locomotives and most of the railway shops and supplies had been destroyed at an estimated loss of $5,000,000. Here as elsewhere the strike failed.

If the return of prosperity in 1879 did not end the tension between employer and employee, at least strikes could be won more easily by the men while the good times lasted, for owners could offset higher costs with higher prices. In all, nearly 24,000 work stoppages took place from 1881 to 1900, idling about 128,000 plants and over 6,600,000 workers at a total loss to employers and employees of $450,000,000 and an untold cost to the public. A business recession in the mid-eighties produced twice as many disorders as in any previous two-year period, causing the years 1885–1886 to be known as the 'Great Upheaval.' Three involved the Gould railways in the Southwest. The first, in March, 1885, ended in restoring a 10-per-cent wage cut; six months later a second strike, caused by discrimination against members of the Knights of Labor, also brought victory to the men; but the third and greatest concluded in their utter rout. Started in protest against the firing of a Knight, this conflagration raged during March and April, 1886, in all parts of the Gould system, laying off nearly 9000 workers in five states and territories. The same year the American Federation of Labor sponsored a general strike for May 1 for an eight-hour day. The mere threat enabled 150,000 to get a shorter day (eight or nine hours), while of the 190,000 who actually quit work, 42,000 won their point. But most of the gains were later lost through the activities of employers' associations formed to fight unions. The demand was renewed in 1888, however, when the building trades obtained permanently reduced hours.

The next historic disturbance broke out in Homestead, Pennsylvania, where the employees of the Carnegie Steel Company struck in July, 1892, because of wage reductions and the company's refusal to recognize their union. When three hundred armed Pinkerton detectives were hired to guard the plant, a fierce battle resulted in ten deaths and the injury of over sixty. After a few days of quiet the governor was induced to send in eight thousand militiamen, who proceeded to break the strike. The defeat prevented organized labor from unionizing the steel industry for many years. Meanwhile, far off in Idaho, repeated wage cuts due to the falling price of silver goaded the miners of the Cœur d'Alene district to bloody hostilities. When the management imported strikebreakers, the men seized the mining property and drove the 'scabs' out of the region. Then President Harrison sent in troops at the governor's request, martial law was declared, and the uprising failed. This affair proved the forerunner of intermittent disorders that ravaged Cœur d'Alene for years.

The nation-wide unemployment and distress bred by the Panic of 1893 plunged labor into another welter of struggles whose violence made thoughtful citizens tremble for the stability of the social order. The strikers in 1894 totaled 690,000, surpassing the mark set in 1886. The gravest outbreak occurred in Chicago, where the Pullman Palace Car Company, though possessing a $4,000,000 surplus and not reducing the salaries of officers and managers, had slashed the pay of the rank and file. Their cause was at once taken up by the American Railway Union, recently organized by Eugene V. Debs to fuse all rail workers in a single group. This body is an early example of the vertical or industrial union which was to lead forty years later to the rise of the CIO. After vainly demanding that the company submit the dispute to arbitration, the American Railway Union ordered its 150,000 members to cease handling Pullman cars on all roads. In the last week of June the walkout spread to twenty-three lines in twenty-seven states and territories, a battle front covering two thirds of the United States.

The vortex of the storm, however, was Chicago. There, until the United States government stepped in, the principal antagonists were the General Managers' Association, representing the rail companies, and Debs's Railway Union. Governor John P. Altgeld, feeling he had the situation well in hand, declined to ask for federal troops, but President Cleveland intervened on his own authority. On July 2 the government secured from a federal court a blanket injunction forbidding Debs and "all other persons whomsoever" to interfere in any manner, direct or indirect, with the operation of the railways. The next day two thousand soldiers were dispatched to Chicago. Though the Constitution specifies that the governor or legislature should apply for federal protection against "domestic violence," Cleveland found warrant for his intervention in the obligation to safeguard the mails, protect interstate commerce and uphold the processes of the federal courts. After the military arrived—not before—widespread rioting began, with mobs and gangs of hoboes and criminals looting, burning and killing. On July 10 Debs and three associates were indicted on the charge of conspiracy in restraint of trade under the Sherman Antitrust Act. Released on bail, they were rearrested a week later on a fresh charge, contempt of court, that is, violation of the judicial injunction of July 2. The government's vigorous course broke the back of the disturbance, bringing its complete collapse a few weeks later. The damages, direct and indirect, to property and business in the whole country were reckoned at $80,000,000.

Other than as a great labor insurrection, the Pullman strike is epochal because of the legal conceptions and practices arising from it. The employment of United States troops without the state's consent was a much criticized but impressive assertion of national power. The application of the Sherman Antitrust Act to unions—later upheld by the courts—threw unexpected light on that law. Perhaps most significant of all was the part played by the judiciary in using the injunction as a weapon in industrial warfare. Though this was not the first time it had been so applied, the sweeping character of the injunction in the Pullman strike caused profound concern among the friends of labor. The Court's action was denounced as unjust because it ranged the might of the government on the side of management, and illegal because it imposed penalties not provided by statute and without trial by jury. Opposition to 'government by injunction' became a cardinal issue of the American Federation of Labor, resulting finally in legislation under President Wilson to restrict it.

The tumult and lawlessness attending this thirty years' war should not be allowed to hide the constructive forces which were breeding saner relations. As trade-unions grew in strength and improved in leadership, they were slower to resort to coercion and violence. Amidst the "confused alarms of struggle and flight" they gradually learned lessons of self-control and responsible action in the economic sphere not unlike the lessons in political self-government which the colonists had learned through the town meeting and the provincial assembly. Enlightened employers, for their part, betrayed greater readiness to meet their demands. In the better-organized industries the practice developed of settling differences through joint conferences instead of the ordeal by battle, with the arrangements embodied in trade agreements. If adjustment by common consent proved impossible, the alternative still existed of arbitration by outside parties.

Some employers strove to improve relations by removing sources of friction before trouble arose, after a plan familiar in European industrial countries. The Baltimore and Ohio Railroad, for example, joined with its employees in 1880 to establish a fund for disability and death benefits, and four years later it provided for old-age pensions. Another scheme, also known abroad, allowed workers to participate in a company's earnings over and above their regular wages. The Pillsbury Flour Mills in Minneapolis, which adopted profit sharing in 1882, was the largest corporation in the world using the plan. Within ten years more than a hundred American concerns followed suit. By these and kindred methods it was hoped to spur the employee to his best endeavors and make him feel more genuinely a part of the business. Some companies also founded 'model towns' for employees; but from the standpoint of labor this smacked of feudal paternalism, and perhaps in most cases the real motive was less to raise living standards than to head off the formation of trade-unions. The residents, moreover, were often exploited by unreasonable charges for rent, food, water and heat. Dissatisfaction with conditions in the company-owned town of Pullman, near Chicago, contributed to the ill feeling which produced the 1894 explosion.

The unions found more acceptable the gains arising from legislation. Under labor pressure the government departed bit by bit from extreme laissez faire, though the concessions fell far short of the thorough-going steps taken by England and Germany during these years. In 1868 Congress fixed an eight-hour day for laborers in federal employ, and various legislatures also acted presently for a shorter workday; but for one reason or another these statutes failed, being unenforced or unenforceable. In 1879 Massachusetts put teeth into its ten-hour law for women and children, and as other industrial states fell into line, the evil of child labor declined a third during the 1880's, only to rise again, however, in the next decade as cotton mills multiplied in the South. During the eighties, too, acts began to be passed for guarding dangerous machinery, assuring better sanitary conditions in factories, and providing for government inspection.

The Great Upheaval elicited in 1886 the first presidential message devoted solely to labor when Cleveland proposed a national commission to help in settling industrial controversies of an interstate character. Congress, unwilling to go so far, responded with a law in 1888 for the voluntary arbitration of railroad disputes on condition that neither party be bound by the outcome. Not until ten years later did it declare that, once a question was submitted to arbitration, the decision should be final. Meanwhile fifteen states had adopted the milder procedure in cases falling exclusively within their limits. These as well as other measures for labor welfare usually left much to be desired, while even adequate laws were seldom adequately administered. Least progress of all greeted the efforts to legislate a shorter workday for men, who were viewed as in a different category from women and children. When such acts were passed, the courts held them unconstitutional, save in especially hazardous occupations, on the ground that they violated the individual's freedom of contract. As late as 1900 seven out of ten industrial wage earners still labored ten hours or more each day. In particular fields the conditions were appalling. The steel industry generally maintained a twelve-hour day for seven days a week, trainmen commonly worked seventy hours a week, and the hours in the textile mills varied from sixty to eighty-four.

ECONOMIC PANACEAS

Notwithstanding the disastrous effects of the Economic Revolution on their status the bulk of the workers had no sympathy with the idea of a class war. Deeming their difficulties temporary and curable, they were wage-conscious rather than class-conscious. Like the discontented farmers, they desired more of the fruits of the capitalist system, not its overthrow. Their philosophy was well summed up by Adolph Strasser, president of the Cigarmakers' Union, before a Senate committee in 1885: "We have no ultimate ends. We are going on from day to day. We are fighting only for immediate objects—objects than can be realized in a few years." It was this attitude that gave rise to the saying that the American workingman was a capitalist without money. The same psychology pervaded the labor parties which sprang up from election to election to enjoy a brief moment of life. However roundly they might flay the industrial system as a "prolific womb" spawning "the two great classes, tramps and millionaires," they in fact wanted merely to remove specific abuses, such as the long workday, bad factory conditions, immigrant competition, the growth of monopolies and the dearth of circulating medium. Polling but a handful of votes, they nevertheless through incessant agitation helped educate the public to the need of remedial action. There were, however, some splinter groups impatient with reform by installments. Through the labor world stalked Marxian socialists from Germany, French refugees who had taken part in the Paris Commune of 1871, and Russian nihilists. Rankling from Old World wrongs and deriding the bourgeois aspirations of American labor, they saw in the stark extremes of wealth and want confirmation of their belief that the United States was going the way of Europe.

The first socialist parties appeared in New York, Philadelphia, Chicago, St. Louis, Milwaukee and other large cities shortly after the Civil War, making their chief bid to citizens of German stock. In 1877, under goad of the depression, the various groups combined nationally in the Socialist Labor party. Its purpose was not to reform but to revolutionize the industrial order. Blaming the plight of the masses on the concentration of economic power in private hands, it proposed to turn over all the basic means of production and distribution—large-scale industries, railways, telephones and the like—to the government to run in democratic association with the employees. For some years the Socialist Laborites shunned ordinary political activities, seeking rather to worm their way into control of the Knights of Labor or the AFL. At last presenting a presidential ticket in 1892, they mustered but 22,000 votes and, in the next election, but 34,000.

The party was too foreign in make-up to attract wide support. To offset this deficiency a rival organization, the Socialist party (first named the Social Democratic party), was formed, which in 1900 won for its candidate, Eugene V. Debs, nearly 95,000 votes. Debs well represented the new influence in the movement. Born in Indiana, a friend of the poet James Whitcomb Riley and American to the core, he had become converted to the doctrine of the class struggle while brooding over the relations of capital and labor when in jail during the Pullman strike. Four times more he was to be the standard-bearer, but neither his party nor the older socialist body ever succeeded in gaining an electoral vote.

Another imported ideology also made its appeal. Anarchism, as it was called, would replace all political government with loosely federated groups, each owning its means of production and exchanging its commodities with the others. To bring about this idealistic society, where everybody acted voluntarily and no one could coerce anyone else, most of the leaders advocated the use of terrorism and force. This repelled many who might otherwise have been attracted, and the cause never had more than five or six thousand converts, mostly among Chicago Germans. People generally remained ignorant of its existence until May 1, 1886, when during a mass meeting in Haymarket Square, Chicago, at which some anarchists had protested against the shooting of strikers by the police, an unknown hand hurled a bomb that killed a policeman and wounded many bystanders. The fighting that ensued caused ten more deaths, including six policemen. In a burst of popular rage eight anarchists (six of them foreign-born) were promptly haled to court. Although the trial did not reveal the bomb thrower's identity or even prove that the act had been incited by the accused, the jury found them all guilty. Four were hanged, one took his own life, and the rest were sent to prison. William Dean Howells, asserting Anglo-American principles of justice, vigorously denounced the punishing of men "because of their frantic opinions, for a crime which they were not shown to have committed"; and in 1893 Governor Altgeld braved the fury of mob hysteria by releasing the three survivors. But, however unjust the conviction, anarchism received a blow from which it never recovered. The attempt of the Russian-born Alexander Berkman during the Homestead strike of 1892 to kill Henry C. Frick, head of the Carnegie Steel Company, intensified the popular aversion, and President McKinley's assassination at the hands of another anarchist brought about a law of 1903 barring anarchists from admission to the country.

The philosophy of discontent also produced native projects for a perfect society. Between 1875 and 1900 nearly eighty novelists indulged such fantasies in books less significant as literature than as expressing the widespread yearning to escape the chaos and miseries of the Economic Revolution. Though these utopias bore a close resemblance to socialism or communism, the authors did not use the terms and in most cases seem to have hit upon their ideas from their own reflection. They further revealed their American inspiration by picturing the consummation as coming peacefully through education and the ballot. These writings appealed particularly to members of the middle class. The most notable, Edward Bellamy's *Looking Backward, 2000–1887* (1888), visioned a society in which the gigantic trust development of the later nineteenth century had culminated in all industry being nationalized by the people for the common good. Under a system of universal service everyone must work, hence everyone had leisure. All received the same pay, not because they did equal amounts but because they put forth the same effort. Poverty was unknown, hospitals took the place of prisons, and man's creative energies were freed for unparalleled cultural and technological achievement. Among other inventions Bellamy foretold the radio and television. The book sold four hundred thousand copies within ten years in the United States alone, while his dream of "Nationalism" brought into being a hundred and sixty-five Nationalist Clubs in twenty-seven states. No political party resulted, however, and the adherents, avoiding the foreign-flavored Socialist Labor party, worked generally with the Populists.

Less comprehensive but quite as unacceptable to most people was another native solution, the single tax, which Henry George set forth in *Progress and Poverty* (1879). A self-taught economist, he had been shocked while living in California by the evils growing from the concentration of land ownership, and a visit to New York City had shown the same evils in exaggerated form. Unaware that others had held similar ideas, he maintained that every human being had as inalienable a right to land as to air and water; to deny it was to deny an essential principle of democracy. George therefore proposed a tax on land so adjusted as to take away the gain ("unearned increment") arising from advantages of location and the growth of the community. The ordinary kind of tax—on values created by the owner's enterprise—was nothing less than "a fine upon improvement." His formula, he argued, would make it unprofitable to let real estate lie idle; it would reduce the size of large holdings, thus multiplying the number of landowners; it would "abolish poverty, give remunerative employment to whoever wishes it," and "carry civilization to yet nobler heights." So considerable would be the revenue that no other taxes would be needed, to the great advantage of business and industry. Moreover, the government, rolling in funds, could take over the railroads and telegraphs and embark on a vast variety of social services such as public baths, playgrounds and theaters.

The single tax interested city folk rather than farmers, who hoped to profit from rising land values, and by the same token it interested intellectuals and industrial workers rather than the well-to-do; but the appeal was limited in any event. Yet George polled a surprising vote in his unsuccessful race for mayor of New York in 1886, and the single tax formed the cornerstone of the United Labor party, which offered candidates two years later in the presidential election. Over two million copies of *Progress and Poverty* were sold by 1905. In England, and notably in Australia, the idea exerted greater influence than in the United States, where its chief importance in the long run lay in directing attention to more rational methods of local taxation.

The more extreme plans of social redemption presumed a degree of human suffering and despair which, save at certain moments and in certain spots, did not exist in America. There could be no class struggle in the Marxian sense where the lot of the poor was not hereditary. "The poverty of the frontier," as James G. Blaine said, ". . . . is but the beginning of wealth, and has the boundless possibilities of the future always opening before it." The poverty of the city was no less a temporary state. Though the rich were growing richer and the poor had never been so numerous, the middle class was increasing faster than either, constantly enlarging itself by accessions from below and serving as a balance wheel in the social structure. Hence the proposed panaceas had relatively few customers. On the other hand, the ferment of new ideas helped leaven the thinking of many who had grown too complacent, or too acquiescent in things as they were. President Cleveland himself showed the effects when he told Congress in December, 1888, that "the communism of combined wealth and capital, the outgrowth of overweening cupidity and selfishness, which insidiously undermines the justice and integrity of free institutions, is not less dangerous than the communism of oppressed poverty and toil, which, exasperated by injustice and discontent, attacks with wild disorder the citadel of rule." Not a few leaders of the progressive movement in the early twentieth century received their initial impulse from youthful reading of Bellamy, the socialist writers or Henry George.

FULLER ACCOUNTS

The Nature of the Process. Besides the general textbooks of American economic history, Cochran and Miller, *Age of Enterprise,* Edwards, *Evolution of Finance Capitalism,* and Tarbell, *Nationalizing of Business,* describe the consolidating movement, while Dorfman, *Economic Mind in American Civilization,* III, and Hofstadter, *Social Darwinism,* reveal the underlying conflict of principles, and Presbrey sets forth *The History and Development of Advertising.* The personal factor is brought out in Corey, *Morgan;* Harvey, *Frick;* Hendrick, *Carnegie;* Hirsch, *Whitney;* Kennan, *Harriman;* Lane, *Commodore Vanderbilt;* Leech and Carroll, *Armour;* Nevins, *Rockefeller;* Pyle, *Hill;* and Winkler, *Du Pont Dynasty.* For a less favorable view, turn to Josephson, *Robber Barons,* and Myers, *History of Great American Fortunes.*

Railroad Amalgamation. Moody, *Railroad Builders,* and Riegel, *Story of Western Railways,* sketch the history of leading roads, and Haney, *Congressional History of Railways,* gives the legislative background of the Interstate Commerce Act. Technical aspects are emphasized in Daggett, *Railroad Reorganization;* Jones, *Principles of Railway Transportation;* and Ripley, *Railroads: Rates and Regulation.*

Industrial Concentration. Hendrick, *Age of Big Business,* and Moody, *Masters of Capital,* offer popular accounts. Moody, *Truth about the Trusts,* is a statistical survey of capitalized industry and finance at the apex of the consolidation movement. For particular industries, see Berglund, *United States Steel Corporation;* Clemen, *American Livestock and Meat Industry;* Coon, *American Tel. & Tel.;* Copeland, *Cotton Manufacturing Industry;* Jones, *Anthracite Coal Combination;* Kuhlmann, *Flour-Milling Industry;* Mussey, *Combination in the Mining Industry;* and Tarbell, *Standard Oil Company.*

The Rise of Organized Labor. The fullest treatment is Commons and others, *History of Labour,* II; shorter ones include Dulles, *Labor in America,* and Ware, *Labor Movement.* Among important special studies are Lorwin, *American Federation of Labor;* McCaleb, *Brotherhood of Railroad Trainmen;* Robbins, *Railway Conductors;* and Robinson, *Amalgamated Association of Iron, Steel and Tin Workers.* Wolman, *Growth of American Trade Unions,* consists mainly of statistics.

Capital and Labor. Besides the foregoing accounts, Yellen, *American Labor Struggles,* reviews the major uprisings, as does also Berman, *Labor Disputes and the President,* from a particular angle. Peterson, *Strikes in the United*

States, is primarily statistical. Monographic works include Allen, *Great Southwest Strike;* Coleman, *Labor Disturbances in Pennsylvania* (the Molly Maguires); and Lindsey, *Pullman Strike.*

Economic Panaceas. Fine, *Labor and Farmer Parties,* Hesseltine, *Rise and Fall of Third Parties,* and Stedmans, *Discontent at the Polls,* touch on labor's political adventures. For the more radical proposals, see Hillquit, *History of Socialism;* Schuster, *Native American Anarchism;* Taylor, *Economic Novel in America,* and Parrington, Jr., *American Dreams* (the literary utopias); Morgan, *Bellamy;* and Young, *Single Tax Movement.* David explores *The History of the Haymarket Affair,* and Ginger, *Bending Cross,* is the latest life of Eugene V. Debs.

CHAPTER V

THE NEW HUMANITARIANISM

SOCIAL UPLIFT IN THE CITIES

UNLIKE the would-be abolishers of the capitalist system, the typical reformer in the years after the Civil War believed it possible to cure the disease without killing the patient. Belonging to the middle class, he nevertheless gave his blessing to the labor movement, though he was sometimes shocked by its excesses. He devoted his own energies, however, to helping folk who could not help themselves. The interest in social betterment was in part a resurgence of the humanitarian zeal of the 1830's and 1840's, which the pressures of the sectional struggle had funneled into a single channel. Ex-abolitionists, spurning the thought that to the victor belongs repose, now gladly shouldered new tasks. Thus William Lloyd Garrison, discontinuing the *Liberator* upon ratification of the Thirteenth Amendment, joined his erstwhile comrade at arms Wendell Phillips in agitating such causes as woman suffrage, Indian welfare, Negro education and prohibition. Phillips even ran for governor of Massachusetts in 1870 on the Labor Reform ticket. The thinning ranks of these aging crusaders were swelled by a host of younger recruits who grieved at man's inhumanity to man as exhibited in the feverishly growing cities. To their hands fell the continuing leadership. In coping with urban maladjustments they commonly turned for guidance to England where reformers had earlier begun to grapple with the same problems.

For many years before the Civil War the state and even some local governments had maintained almshouses, orphanages, homes for inebriates, insane asylums and institutions for the deaf, dumb and blind. Most cities possessed, in addition, a considerable array of private benevolent societies. The difficulty was that these bodies, whether public or private, were too often run by incompetents; and in so far as they dealt with the problem of poverty, they contented themselves with methods of indiscriminate almsgiving that tended to foster permanent pauperism. They did not see that their real function

107

should be to enable the poor to make a fresh start. In 1864 Massachusetts pointed the way toward a more constructive program by setting up a State Board of Charities to supervise and systematize the work of the tax-supported relief agencies. Before the end of the century over half the Union had taken like action. Meanwhile, in 1877, the Reverend S. Humphreys Gurteen, who before coming to America had worked with the London Charity Organization Society, persuaded the private philanthropic groups in Buffalo to effect a similar arrangement. The plan involved not only a co-ordination of activities but also the rehabilitating of the needy. Other places followed the example until the century's close saw kindred organizations, under various names, in a hundred and thirty-eight cities. Henceforth the system of 'associated charities' became normal in all sizable towns.

Even more significant perhaps was the migration of colonies of social workers into slum districts. There, living amid conditions of squalor and vice, they offered opportunities for instruction and recreation to all ages—kindergartens, boys' clubs, gymnasiums, classes in arts and crafts, and the like—on the principle that a fence at the top of a precipice was better than an ambulance at the bottom. The movement was deeply indebted to the example of London's Toynbee Hall, which many of the pioneer American settlement workers had visited, and the effort appealed particularly to the idealism of young college men and women. From 1886 to 1900 more than a hundred social settlements were planted in American cities, the most famous being Hull-House, founded in Chicago in 1889 by Jane Addams and Ellen G. Starr. Among the other early leaders were Lillian D. Wald of the Henry Street Settlement and Stanton Coit of the Neighborhood Guild, both in New York; Robert A. Woods of the South End Settlement, Boston; and Mary E. McDowell of the University of Chicago Settlement.

Essential to any program of aiding the handicapped was better housing. The tenement population of America's chief city rose from 21,000 in 1879 to 1,500,000 in 1900. One New York district of thirty-two acres averaged 986 persons in 1894 as compared with 760 per acre in the most congested part of Bombay and 485 in the densest section of Prague, Europe's worst slum area. In these dilapidated, ill-ventilated, filth-soaked structures the death rate was three times as great as in the city at large. Jacob A. Riis, a police reporter on the *New York Sun,* led in agitating for reform. His book, *How the Other*

Half Lives (1890), vividly portrayed the horrors of slum existence, the conditions making for disease, vice and crime, and awakened many persons to facts they had not suspected or had not cared to know. Between 1865 and 1900 the legislature made four attempts to regulate the building of tenements; but because of the greed of landlords, faulty laws or lax enforcement, the situation actually became worse. Nor was the state of affairs much better in Philadelphia, Boston, Cincinnati and other big places.

Directly or indirectly, all such endeavors had a vital bearing upon the welfare of the rising generation. As cities walled in an ever larger proportion of America's future citizens, society for the first time felt obliged to give energetic attention to what Kate Douglas Wiggin called "children's rights." The steps initially taken were halting but grew firmer as the years passed. The law at first allowed no interference between parent and child; and when a mother was haled before a New York municipal judge in 1874 for mistreating her seven-year-old stepdaughter, the Society for the Prevention of Cruelty to Animals brought the action on the ground that for the purposes of the case Mary Ellen too should be considered an animal. In that dingy courtroom was born the Society for the Prevention of Cruelty to Children, the first of its kind in the world. It quickly developed branches in other communities, and everywhere the members strove for more humane laws and better opportunities for the young. The crop of child-labor legislation in the North during the eighties owed much to their efforts. Meanwhile an aroused public conscience sought to restore to youth a part of its heritage of outdoor play. In 1877 a minister at Sherman, Pennsylvania, devised the scheme of 'country week' for city waifs during the stifling hot season, a plan eagerly taken up by charitable agencies in leading towns and supported by the 'fresh-air funds' of newspapers. A little later, in 1885, a Boston group tried the experiment of providing sand plots for poor children. From this small beginning rose the playground movement, which spread to twenty-one communities by 1900 and was in after years to prevail in nearly all cities.

Attempts were also made to deal more intelligently with juvenile delinquency, a problem rendered urgent by the fact that one out of every twenty prisoners in 1880 was under twenty-one years of age. Deeply influenced by European example and notably by the Irish penal system, reformers such as Enoch C. Wines and Zebulon R.

Brockway contended that the primary purpose of imprisonment, especially in the case of the young, should be to regenerate rather than to punish the offender. Make him good, they said in effect, and make him good for something. In 1877 the New York State Reformatory, opening at Elmira under Brockway's direction, put the conception into effect. The youthful inmates, freed from the customary association with confirmed criminals, were encouraged to shorten their stay through good conduct and by demonstrating a capacity for self-improvement; then, conditionally released, they continued under official supervision long enough to show that their reformation was genuine. These two principles—the indeterminate sentence and the parole system—worked so successfully that other Northern and Western states introduced the Elmira plan and before the end of the century applied some of its features to older prisoners.

Urban congestion forced public authorities to tackle also the problem of communicable diseases. Since colonial times recurrent scourges had taken their toll of townsfolk, but never before had they had such crowded populations on which to feed. In the late 1860's Louisiana and Massachusetts set up state boards of health, and thirteen other commonwealths did likewise before 1878. Then came a terrible yellow-fever epidemic in 1878–1879 which blazed a trail of death through the South, nearly depopulating Memphis. Twelve more commonwealths fell into line before 1882, with the rest presently following. To the aid of these state boards and their municipal counterparts came certain momentous medical discoveries. In the 1870's and 1880's Louis Pasteur, Robert Koch and other European scientists established the germ theory of disease, and in 1889 Theobald Smith, an American, showed by his studies of Texas fever, a cattle disease, that germs might be transmitted by insects. As Austin Flint, a medical authority, summed it up in 1888, "What has been accomplished within the past ten years as regards knowledge of the causes, prevention, and treatment of disease far transcends what would have been regarded a quarter of a century ago as the wildest and most impossible speculation."

This new knowledge provided for the first time an intelligent basis for preventive medicine. Health officers now could quickly identify and more effectively control communicable disorders. Quarantine methods were extended to other ills than the traditional ones of smallpox and yellow fever; port cities were shielded against imported epi-

THE TRUST PROBLEM ACCORDING TO THOMAS NAST
See page 89.

BURNING THE PITTSBURGH ROUNDHOUSE, 1877

MOBBING PINKERTON DETECTIVES AT HOMESTEAD, 1892

EMBATTLED INDUSTRY
See pages 97–98.

demics like cholera and typhus; and special hospitals began to be provided for the isolation and treatment of contagious cases. At the same time the multiplication of public waterworks and drainage systems, earlier mentioned, greatly aided the cause. The results, even at this pioneer stage of the science, were marked, particularly in populous centers. The average expectation of life at birth, which was less than forty years in 1855, reached nearly fifty in 1900. In the century's last decade the nation's death rate fell almost 10 per cent, thanks largely to diminishing mortality from tuberculosis, diphtheria and children's diseases. It was fortunate for America that when her urban age dawned medical advances made it possible to protect huddled populations from the pestilences which for so many centuries had ravaged European and Asian cities.

THE TEMPERANCE MOVEMENT

Urban growth also gave fresh urgency to the liquor problem. The gains for state-wide prohibition in the 1850's had been mostly lost during the Civil War. Army service had helped promote the drink habit, while the United States government itself lent the traffic a certain respectability by turning to it for the first time as a productive source of revenue. At the war's close only Maine and Massachusetts remained 'dry,' and the latter soon fell by the wayside. In the years that followed, liquor manufacturing became one of the country's leading businesses, the capital investment rising from $67,-000,000 in 1870 to $269,000,000 in 1890. With so vast a financial stake, producers and retailers entered politics both to advance their interests and to resist attempts at hostile legislation, whether heavier taxation or prohibition. As early as 1867 the United States Brewers' Association resolved to "sustain no candidate, of whatever party, in any election, who is in any way disposed toward the total abstinence cause." It has already been seen how the whisky distillers in Grant's time reached corrupt hands into the very precincts of the White House. The major parties avoided taking a national stand on the temperance question, fearing either to risk a new and uncertain issue or to lose campaign funds from the liquor magnates.

The cities were the principal battlements of the 'wet' interests. There the traffic employed countless persons at every stage of the manufacture, distribution and sale; there the teeming immigrants saw no reason to forgo cherished folk customs in a land of freedom; there, too, the saloon with its free lunch and rough sociability provided a sort of poor man's club. New York in 1890 possessed seventy-five hundred saloons, or one to every two hundred persons, while smaller places like Albany, Cincinnati and San Francisco had an even greater number proportionately. By contrast, dry sentiment predominated in the farming regions. The churches most deeply rooted in rural villages and towns—the Methodist, Baptist and Presbyterian—crusaded tirelessly against 'King Alcohol' and lent driving force to such bodies as the Prohibition party, founded in 1869, and the Women's Christian Temperance Union, which arose in 1874.

The Prohibitionists demanded legal suppression of the traffic and advocated woman suffrage as the swiftest means to that end. Though never winning an electoral vote, they outrivaled other minor parties by managing at least to keep alive, and by doing so they carried on a continuing propaganda for the cause. Of greater importance was the W.C.T.U. which under Frances E. Willard became the spearhead of the movement. It waged relentless war against the foe on every front, inducing most of the legislatures to require 'scientific temperance instruction' in the schools, and fighting everywhere for the restriction or destruction of the liquor business. Even in the cities the temperance elements gained adherents, notably among persons who, unmoved by emotional appeals, turned against the saloon power as the invariable ally of corruption, criminality and political reaction. Here and there, too, employers saw the advantages of a sober laboring force, especially on the railroads, while the Catholic Church, influential with immigrant workers, consistently encouraged habits of moderation or total abstinence. In 1895 a new and aggressive body, the Anti-Saloon League of America, was formed to co-ordinate the various organized efforts for prohibition.

The actual tide of battle swayed back and forth, with the saloonless area expanding or contracting as victory was won now by the one side, now by the other. Temperance enjoyed its chief successes in the rural sections. During the eighties, for example, three states— Iowa and the Dakotas—ranged themselves beside the four states of Maine, New Hampshire, Vermont and Kansas which were dry at the decade's start. Other ways of combating the traffic were also tried. On the principle of divide-and-conquer, the drys made notable progress in the rural districts of the Midwest and the South through local option, that is, prohibitory enactments adopted by local popular vote.

Elsewhere, in the hope of making the calling unprofitable, saloons were required to operate under high licenses of from $500 to $1000 a year. One state, South Carolina, experimented from 1893 to 1907 with exclusive government liquor stores in order to eliminate completely the private-profit motive. But whatever the system of restriction, enforcement always proved a stumblingblock. If alcoholic beverages could not be legally sold, 'bootleggers' were apt to ply a brisk trade. Even in Maine, oldest of the dry states, the federal authorities collected taxes from a hundred and sixty-one Portland liquor dealers in 1893. Partly because of lax administration of repressive regulations and still more because of increased consumption in the cities, the per-capita use of intoxicants by the American people nearly trebled from 1860 to 1900. The most optimistic drys hardly dreamed that within another generation their cause would find lodgment, however briefly, in the federal Constitution.

WOMAN'S EXPANDING SPHERE

The prominence of women in the temperance and social-settlement movements and other humane enterprises attested their changing role in society. The impact of events had jarred them loose from the traditional seclusion of the home, obliging them whether they would or not to take increasing part in the world beyond domestic walls. Thus the Economic Revolution caused more and more women to find jobs as factory hands, sweatshop workers, telephone operators, typists, clerks and helpers in offices and shops. Between 1870 and 1900 the number in remunerative occupations rose from 1,800,000 to 5,300,000.

Meanwhile the portals of higher education swung open for an ever larger proportion of middle-class girls. Starting in the East with Vassar in 1865 and Wellesley and Smith a decade later, women's colleges began to offer instruction equal to that of the better men's institutions. More typical of the West was coeducation which, though dating from before the war, now became widespread. In many quarters, however, there was a dubious shaking of heads. In the opinion of Dr. Edward H. Clarke, author of *Sex in Education* (1873), "Identical education of the two sexes is a crime before God and humanity, that physiology protests against, and that experience weeps over." Nevertheless, between 1865 and 1874 at least fourteen state universities, all but three of them in the Middle or Far West, opened their courses to girls. Among them was Michigan, which in 1870 admitted women after having practiced sex discrimination for nearly three decades. The president of the university solemnly assured an inquiring English-woman after ten years of the new system that "none of the ladies had found the curriculum too heavy for their physical endurance." By 1880 the number of mixed colleges had grown from twenty-odd at the close of the war to a hundred and fifty-four. In another twenty years seven out of ten colleges and universities were coeducational.

As higher education reached an ever widening circle of women, they began increasingly to enter the professions. The displacement of men as schoolteachers occurred so rapidly that in 1900 two out of every three were women. They also moved swiftly into social work and nursing. In law, theology and medicine, however, their path proved thornier because of the reluctance of professional schools to admit them. Yet by the close of the century there were over 1000 women lawyers in the United States, nearly as many dentists, more than 3000 ministers and almost 7500 doctors and surgeons. As authors and journalists they also occupied an important place and in Emily Dickinson provided the most gifted poet of these years. Meanwhile middle-class housewives in the cities, finding time for broader interests as a result of new household conveniences, organized women's clubs. After 1868, with the founding of the first two influential ones—the Sorosis in New York and Boston's New England Women's Club—the number grew so quickly and spread so far that in 1889 they joined together nationally in the General Federation of Women's Clubs. Such groups, as the years wore on, devoted less attention to art, literature and cultural subjects and more to civic and social problems, some becoming centers of agitation for women's rights and equal suffrage.

As a consequence of the inexorable drift of events, the most glaring of the old common-law discriminations against the sex—already beginning to crumble before the Civil War—continued to fall in state after state. Throughout most of the Union the legislatures gave married women the right to own and control property, retain their earnings, make contracts, sue and be sued. In 1900 only a handful of commonwealths still expressly designated the husband as head of the family and made the wife subject to him. Even in the more enlightened states, however, smaller civil disabilities remained far into the twentieth century. Not until 1949, for example, did women obtain the right of jury service in Massachusetts.

Progress toward universal suffrage was more difficult, for it encountered the inertia and prejudice not only of most men but usually also of their wives, sisters and daughters. Such folk argued that the feminine mind was unfitted to understand affairs of state, that in the effort woman would lose her charm, and that political differences would disrupt the home. In the excited words of the Reverend Horace Bushnell, author of *Women's Suffrage; the Reform against Nature* (1869), the proposal was "an attempt to make trumpets out of flutes, and sun-flowers out of violets." On the other side were arrayed such forceful figures as Elizabeth Cady Stanton, Susan B. Anthony, Lucy Stone (who refused to take her husband's name of Blackwell), Anna Howard Shaw and Carrie Chapman Catt. They held that each sex had a distinctive contribution to make to public affairs, and that failure to accept the logic of woman's altered status was an effort to "put the bird back into the egg." As Wendell Phillips expressed it, "One of two things is true: either woman is like man— and if she is, then a ballot based on brains belongs to her as well as to him; or she is different, and then man does not know how to vote for her as well as she herself does."

As in the case of temperance, the earlier interest in equal suffrage had been shoved into the background by the Civil War. When peace returned, the feminist leaders, contending that women's war services had earned them the right, flooded Congress with petitions to obtain the vote at the same time as the freedmen. Their hopes were dashed, however, and in 1869 they proceeded, out of a difference of opinion as to tactics, to organize two suffrage associations: the National, which strove for the ballot through a federal amendment, and the American, which advocated state action. Not until 1890 did they join forces in the National American Woman Suffrage Association. Among prominent men to lend their pens and voices to the cause were George W. Curtis, Senator George F. Hoar, John Greenleaf Whittier, the poet-reformer, and Henry Ward Beecher, the eloquent Brooklyn clergyman. The Knights of Labor and the American Federation of Labor also rallied to the standard.

But if the outstanding suffragists hailed from the East, the chief gains occurred in the democratic West. Women were first given the ballot in certain matters of community concern, as in Great Britain and the Scandinavian countries during these years. Thus by 1895 seventeen commonwealths in all parts of the nation but the old Confederacy had granted the suffrage in school elections. In addition, several states, including Louisiana in 1898, permitted women to vote on local bond issues, taxation questions and the like. But full equality, the ultimate goal, eluded the feminists until Wyoming, which as a territory had allowed it since 1869, entered the Union in 1890. Colorado bravely emulated the example in 1893, and Utah and Idaho in 1896. Meanwhile pressure upon Congress for a constitutional amendment had led to several favorable reports by Congressional committees and an unsuccessful vote in the Senate in 1887, but to nothing more. The platforms of the great parties ignored the question, while the Prohibitionists may have hurt it by linking it with their unpopular cause. Most people continued to regard universal suffrage as an aberration of the wild and woolly West.

THE REORIENTATION OF RELIGION

These years also posed formidable problems for organized religion. One was a legacy of the Civil War. As early as 1844–1845 the Methodists and Baptists had split into Northern and Southern branches over the slavery question, and the onset of hostilities caused similar ruptures among the Presbyterians and some other denominations. The breach was widened by the seizure of Southern church properties in conquered areas by overzealous missionaries of some Northern sects. As though to rub salt into the wounds, certain churchmen after the war indulged in the clerical equivalent of waving the bloody shirt. Bishop Gilbert Haven of the Northern Methodists, for example, acclaimed the Carpetbaggers as the "true knight-errantry of the age" and advocated miscegenation for the good of both races. Under the circumstances it is not surprising that the sectional divisions among the Methodists and the Baptists persisted into the twentieth century.

The biggest challenge to religion, however, arose from the effects of the Economic Revolution on the living conditions of the urban masses. American Protestantism, traditionally rural and attuned to the comfortable middle class, could not easily adapt itself to the needs of hordes of native wage workers and slum-dwelling immigrants—and many congregations were frankly indifferent. In the twenty years after 1868, while two hundred thousand more people jammed into Manhattan below Fourteenth Street, seventeen Protestant churches moved out and only three Catholic and Jewish ones were added. When Jane

Addams founded Hull-House in Chicago, the neighborhood contained nine churches and missions as against two hundred and fifty-five saloons. In the meaner quarters of cities barrooms and brothels sometimes outnumbered houses of worship a hundredfold. The Y.M.C.A. and the Y.W.C.A., both dating from mid-century, provided countless young men and women with decent lodgings, gymnastic facilities and Christian surroundings, but these agencies, too, were middle-class institutions of little use to the poor. Even such spirited revivalists as Dwight L. Moody and Ira D. Sankey worked mostly with laggard members of existing congregations, hardly touching persons without church affiliations. The clergy's silence in the face of social injustice further antagonized the laboring class. The fact that wealthy Trinity Church in New York City derived some of its revenue from slum properties seemed proof positive that official Christianity rejected the teachings of Jesus.

Little wonder that the masses avoided churches and treated the Sabbath with disrespect. Other factors, however, also contributed to the latter attitude. After six days of grinding toil the workers naturally turned to pleasure on the seventh. In the cities, too, the immigrant influence was strong—the Germans with their liberal Continental Sabbath, the Irish and other aliens with their Catholic Sunday, the Jews with their religious observance of Saturday. In vain did the American Sabbath Union and similar bodies cry that Divine law had established the Lord's day "to be sacredly observed by all except the depraved and morally reckless." They proved more successful when they joined trade-unions in resisting employers' demands for Sunday labor.

Only gradually did the forces of Protestantism learn to cope with the new conditions. The success of the Catholic and Jewish faiths in attracting and holding the vast proportion of their communicants pouring in from Europe proved both an object lesson and a spur to action. Shortly after the Civil War the larger denominations began to increase religious missions in the needy districts of the cities. In 1879 the Salvation Army, an English importation, commenced its evangelistic labors on the street corners, preaching to "rumdom, slumdom and bumdom" the exciting gospel of repentance and reform. Ten years later it branched out into social service, maintaining cheap lodgings, employment agencies and rescue homes. Meanwhile Protestant congregations in many cities instituted systematic philanthropic and educational work for the poor, providing reading rooms, day nurseries, recreational facilities and manual-training courses along with spiritual instruction. The resulting growth of membership quickly justified the innovation, and by 1894 these 'institutional churches' were numerous enough to form a nation-wide union.

In harmony with the new tendencies clergymen here and there began to expound what became known as the social gospel. They insisted that Christianity no longer stand apart from life but be a part of life. Notable among the pioneers were Lyman Abbott, editor of the *Christian Union;* Josiah Strong, general secretary of the Evangelical Alliance; and Washington Gladden, Congregational minister in Springfield, Massachusetts, and later in Columbus, Ohio. Gladden, besides setting forth his views in books like *Applied Christianity* (1886) and *Tools and the Man: Property and Industry under the Christian Laws* (1893), upheld the "right and necessity of labor organizations" in actual disputes. He saw the ultimate solution in an "industrial partnership" in which the employees would receive a "fixed share in the profits of production." Condemning the ethics of Big Business, he scourged religious bodies for accepting donations from such sources, branding the contributions as "tainted money," defiling the recipient as well as the giver. Some Eastern clergymen went even further, and imitating an English example, joined the Reverend William D. P. Bliss of Boston in forming the Society of Christian Socialists in 1889 "to awaken members of Christian churches to the fact that the teachings of Jesus Christ lead directly to some specific form or forms of Socialism."

Within the Catholic fold Cardinal Gibbons led in furthering a more enlightened understanding of labor's position. By interceding at Rome in 1886 he saved the Knights of Labor from papal condemnation. Against opposition from his own ranks he also championed the right of Catholics to espouse Henry George's single tax. His bold course received high sanction in 1891 when an encyclical of Leo XIII, though denouncing socialism, asserted that the government's chief function should be to promote human welfare, approved of trade-unions and called for the application of Christian principles to the relations of capital and labor. But in all faiths such churchmen were the exception rather than the rule. Nevertheless their advent marked a definite turning toward an increased social emphasis in religion. Later years would yield a fuller fruition of their efforts.

As if the problem of social adjustment were not enough, organized religion also faced an intellectual crisis. To defenders of the old-time theology the validity of the Bible itself seemed challenged by new findings of science and scholarship. Religion, in other words, was confronted by one of those recurrent conflicts between orthodoxy and heterodoxy, between fundamentalism and modernism, which have constituted a law of its growth. Those who labored to socialize religious practice usually labored also to liberalize religious thought. One source of dissension was the theory of evolution, which had steadily won friends in America after it was set forth by Charles Darwin in *The Origin of Species* (1859). With a plenitude of scientific evidence the great English naturalist attributed the origin of plants and animals to a process of evolution from simple organisms to more complex and higher forms by means of natural selection or survival of the fittest. Since this apparently contradicted the Biblical account of creation, the clergy generally branded the Darwinian view as materialistic and atheistic. A growing number of American scientists, however, adopted it, and following in their train, progressive ecclesiastics like Abbott and Gladden contended that, at the most, the theory imperiled theology, not genuine religion. Indeed, they saw in evolution a new and grander revelation of the mysterious way God moves His wonders to perform. The process of acceptance, however, was slow, particularly in those denominations which stressed emotional above intellectual considerations. Another shock to orthodoxy came from the 'higher criticism,' originating with German scholars who had examined the books of the Bible as historical and literary records rather than as God's infallible word. To make matters worse, the knowledge of Buddhism and other Asian faiths, popularized by James Freeman Clarke's *Ten Great Religions* (1871), appeared to rob Christianity of its exclusive character.

As a result of these various factors, sharp divisions occurred among both clergy and laity, concluding sometimes in heresy trials and the expulsion of those upholding the newer views. Yet, as the years went by, a spirit of tolerance began to make itself felt. If clerics could not always agree on points of doctrine, they learned that in the interests of common spiritual service they could agree to disagree. Equally significant was the introduction by theological seminaries of courses on the higher criticism, comparative religion and the relations of science and religion. Hence, notwithstanding these and the other difficulties that beset religion, church membership grew both numerically and relatively. The notable gains of the Catholics, Lutherans and Jews rested principally upon immigrant accessions. Nor did the religious spirit exhaust itself on strictly church activities. On the contrary, it pervaded most of the philanthropic efforts of the time; a great majority of the social workers and other humanitarians were inspired by Christian principles. As though the religious landscape were not sufficiently varied, a new sect, Christian Science, appeared on the scene, basing its creed upon *Science and Health,* a book by Mary Baker Eddy in 1875. The latest of a long succession of New England cults, it rejected medicine as the science of health and substituted for it a belief in the supremacy of mind over matter. According to the founder, "disease is caused by mind alone." Christian Science appealed particularly to nerve-racked urban folk and spread rapidly from Boston to New York and cities of the Midwest.

THE PROBLEM OF RACIAL MINORITIES

While most of the crying injustices of these years stemmed from urban conditions, two major problems were largely rural in setting. Both involved minority groups, not in the European sense of oppressed peoples striving to cast off an alien yoke, but in the American sense of handicapped peoples seeking larger rights under the same flag. The Negro question concerned the South; the Indian question, the West. The one race had been in America nearly as long as the white man, the other far longer; but unlike the European immigrants, they were not usually regarded as eligible for a full and unrestricted participation in American life. Recently their situation, though for special reasons in each case, had become critical.

President Hayes's withdrawal of the last Southern garrisons in 1877 marked the end of federal intervention on behalf of the Negro. In effect, the North, having become absorbed in the problems of its emerging industrial order, turned the race question over to the South to solve. Even if the Republicans had wished, they could not have done differently, for during the next twelve years they at no time controlled both Congress and the presidency. The bulk of the Negroes continued to dwell in the section where slavery had planted them. Increasing from 4,000,000 in 1860 to 6,000,000 in 1880, they numbered 8,000,000 in 1900, a rate of growth considerably less than that of the Southern whites. Though their birth rate was higher, this was offset by greater infant mortality and by the inroads of diseases which the paternalistic life of the prewar plantation had held in check.

Deserted by their former Northern allies, the Negroes faced a long, harsh, unremitting struggle with ignorance and poverty. The statesman of this new emancipation was Booker T. Washington, himself a former slave, who in 1881 founded the Normal and Industrial Institute in the heart of the Lower South at Tuskegee, Alabama. Believing that his people should perfect the mechanical skills learned in slavery, he and his associates, aided by funds from the state legislature and Northern sources, provided instruction in the trades and occupations necessary for gaining a foothold in the South's economic life. "I would set no limits to the attainments of the Negro in arts, in letters or statesmanship," he said, "but I believe the surest way to reach those ends is by laying the foundation in the little things of life that lie immediately about one's door." Washington's doctrine of vocational training influenced Negro education throughout the South. The schools, however, labored under great difficulties because of the postwar poverty and particularly because of the wasteful system of teaching the two races separately, which involved inferior instruction for the blacks. Northern philanthropy did something to help out, notably the Peabody Fund established in 1867 and the John F. Slater Fund in 1882. Despite deterrent conditions Negro illiteracy dropped from 70 per cent in 1880 to 44 in 1900, when more than 1,500,000 children were in school. A number of Negro colleges and universities were also founded, such as Atlanta (1865), Fisk (1866) and Howard (1867) as well as four state colleges—in Virginia, Arkansas, Georgia and Delaware. By 1900 over 2000 Negroes had graduated from institutions of higher learning in the South or the North.

The mass of the people stayed on the land, eking out a livelihood from raising cotton or tobacco. Handicapped on the one hand by the shiftless habits learned in slavery and on the other by the sharecropper system that arose during Reconstruction, only the most ambitious managed to achieve farm ownership. By 1890 the Southern Negroes owned nearly a fifth of their homes. Ten years later about 200,000 tilled their own fields, while about 500,000 still labored as tenants. This progress was a substantial testimonial to a people who had been virtually landless in 1860. Others worked at domestic or personal service, mostly in the towns, where some also entered the skilled trades and even business and the professions.

Generally speaking, the Negro was unmolested by his white neighbors provided he 'knew his place.' That place the dominant race defined with increasing precision as the passage of years dimmed the Negro's memory of his former inferiority in slavery. The color line was drawn most sharply where racial association appeared to imply social or political equality. Besides the prohibition of mixed schools, a universal ban was placed on intermarriage. In 1875 Tennessee went further by permitting hotels, railroads and theaters to discriminate against "persons of color" and six years later required rail companies to provide separate cars or compartments for them. Other states followed this example of 'Jim Crow' legislation, and presently Negroes throughout the South found themselves compelled, by law, custom or the threat of physical harm, to accept special and usually poorer accommodations in public conveyances, hotels, restaurants and amusement places, when admitted at all, as well as to live in the worst quarters of the cities. Jim Crow became the white man's policeman of race relations.

Such actions seemed to violate a law which Congress had passed in 1875 to assure Negroes the same treatment as other citizens in hotels, trains and public resorts, but the Supreme Court came to the aid of the Southern whites in the Civil Rights cases (1883) by declaring the statute unconstitutional. "It would be running the slavery argument into the ground," the tribunal solemnly affirmed, "to make it apply to every act of discrimination which a person may see fit to make as to the guests he will entertain, or as to the people he will take into his coach or cab or car." No clearer evidence could have been afforded of the hands-off attitude of the rest of the nation. Violent racial antipathy sometimes broke out in the mob murder of individual Negroes. Between 1882 and 1903 inclusive, 1985 lynchings occurred in the Southern states, with Mississippi, Georgia and Louisiana as the worst offenders. Such lawless proceedings generally involved the worst elements of the two peoples. They tended to obscure the fact that in most respects race relations were peaceful.

The whites also stole away the political rights guaranteed by the Reconstruction state constitutions. Intimidation, violence and fraud gradually fell into disuse, however, as the ruling class invented legal means of minimizing the colored vote. Through ingenious methods of redistricting (gerrymandering) they reduced Negro membership in the legislatures, and by imposing the poll-tax requirement they lessened the number of Negro voters. Another device was to adopt intricate election regulations like those of South Carolina in 1882 which bewildered the illiterate black by requiring that each of the many ballots be deposited correctly in the eight or more boxes. In the next decade the dominant race went even further. The growth of agrarian unrest in the late eighties had split the white electorate into two factions, with the result that the potential balance of power often lay with the Negroes. To allay this threat to white supremacy, steps were taken to alter the suffrage provisions in the state constitutions, though with due care not to infringe the Fifteenth Amendment's prohibition against denying the franchise "on account of race, color, or previous condition of servitude."

The three commonwealths in which Negroes outnumbered the whites were the first to act. Mississippi set the pace in 1890 by limiting the ballot to paid-up taxpayers able to read a passage from the state constitution, or understand it when read to them, or give "a reasonable interpretation thereof." These alternatives were avowedly designed to enable election officials to disfranchise illiterate blacks without disfranchising illiterate whites. Five years later South Carolina adopted a somewhat similar provision. Then, in 1898, Louisiana found a means of exempting whites from the tax and educational tests through the so-called grandfather clause: over a period of several months she admitted permanently to the voting list all male applicants whose fathers or grandfathers had exercised the suffrage before 1867. Other states presently devised variants of these restrictions.[1] Under the new arrangements the proportion of colored voters continued to fall. Torn from his giddy heights of Reconstruction times, the Negro became a negligible factor in Southern politics.

It was a heavy price that the whites of the South paid for Jim Crowism and the color line. Not only did they deny the Negro the advantages of normal association with the more advanced people, of sharing in the joint enterprise of American civilization, but they contracted the habit of treating every public issue from the standpoint of how it would affect race relations. Political life tended more and more to fall into the hands of demagogues whose stock in trade was hatred of the depressed folk. Unwittingly the white man took on a slavery of his own.

The Indian problem, though involving fewer persons, was hardly

[1] Finally, in 1915, the Supreme Court declared the grandfather clause contrary to the Fifteenth Amendment, in cases arising from Maryland and Oklahoma; but the action did not help the Negro voter, though it probably reduced the number of illiterate white voters.

less perplexing. Reduced to a dependent status after a quarter-century of bloodshed, these aboriginal Americans, numbering about two hundred and sixty thousand in the mid-eighties, lived the ancestral life on government reservations, their health impaired by the white man's diseases and their self-reliance sapped by the annuities and rations of the 'Great White Father' in Washington. Moreover, they were victimized by dishonest officials and avaricious traders. Even their reservations were subject to encroachment, and the Washington authorities could not always be counted on to prevent it. Signs of a more responsible attitude on the government's part appeared in the 1870's when Congress, after aiding missionary schools for Indians for over half a century, began to assume direct obligation for their education. By 1881 the annual appropriation for this purpose was more than $200,000, and by 1887 it had risen to $1,225,000. The object was to train the young in agriculture, home economics and other practical pursuits to fit them for the white man's way of life. In 1887 over fourteen thousand children were attending two hundred and twenty-seven schools. Unhappily, the teachers were usually political appointees and the instruction was inferior. Besides, the environment of the tribal home, with its communal ownership of the soil and reliance upon government doles, canceled out the benefits of the meager education. For many years, however, Congress resisted repeated recommendations by the executive department to abolish the communal land system and introduce the right of private property.

Two influences finally brought about the desired change. One was a strong protest by Eastern humanitarians outraged by the wrongs inflicted on the once proud race—a sentiment finding passionate expression in Helen Hunt Jackson's widely read *A Century of Dishonor* (1881). The other was the growing Western demand, as free homesteads became scarcer, to break up the reservations for the sake of the whites. The Easterners sought rights for the Indian, the Westerners lands for themselves. President Cleveland, shocked by Mrs. Jackson's pathetic portrayal, pressed for action, and the upshot was the Dawes Severalty Act of 1887. It authorized the President to end the tribal government in any reservation whenever time and circumstances seemed appropriate and to allot the land to individuals. To protect the owners from white greed, they were forbidden to sell or mortgage their holdings for twenty-five years or, at the President's discretion, even longer. In all other respects they should be citizens with the same rights as white citizens, including that of voting. The land remaining after allotments were made might be bought by the government, all money to be held as a fund for educating and civilizing those concerned.

The law was widely hailed as the 'Emancipation Act of the Indians.' In the first score of years over 21,000,000 acres passed into the hands of 150,000 red men, while the government acquired some 53,000,000 acres for sale to settlers or for forest reserves. But experience revealed flaws in the plan. The reformers, discounting the fact that the institution of private property reversed traditional Indian practice, had supposed that the parceling of land would magically cause the owner to develop a sense of responsibility, build a home and acquire other possessions. Unfortunately, too, the government neglected to furnish adequate instruction in the efficient use of the tracts. Some individuals, of course, surmounted all difficulties, but most found themselves at the end of the probationary period sadly unprepared to compete successfully with their white neighbors. As voters, moreover, they were apt to be preyed upon by corrupt white politicians.

To cure these faults Congress in 1906 passed the Burke Act. It annulled the twenty-five-year provision and instructed the executive branch henceforth to bestow full property title upon deserving persons whenever satisfied of their fitness. At the same time it withheld citizenship prior to full ownership, thereby helping to safeguard the sanctity of the ballot. But the Burke Act did not remove all the evils, for it proved difficult to know when particular Indians were ready to become independent landholders, with the result that many allotments were made prematurely. Furthermore, as before, the government did little to teach the red men how to make a living from the soil. The majority on acquiring full ownership sold their farms and squandered the proceeds. As a consequence they became social derelicts, cut off from their former tribal ties and forced to exist as best they could. As the twentieth century grew older, it became increasingly clear that the well-meant scheme fathered by the humanitarians of the 1880's had gone awry. A new direction of Indian policy awaited the coming to office of the second Roosevelt.

FULLER ACCOUNTS

Social Uplift in the Cities. Nevins, *Emergence of Modern America,* and Schlesinger, *Rise of the City,* treat this subject as well as most others in this chapter. Special works on the new charity include Watson, *Charity Organization Movement,* and Woods and Kennedy, *Settlement Horizon.* For the living quarters of the poor, see Ford and others, *Slums and Housing,* while playgrounds are a particular concern of Rainwater, *Play Movement.* Outstanding reformers are portrayed in Ware, *Jacob A. Riis;* Wise, *Jane Addams;* and Woods, *Robert A. Woods.* The standard study of penal methods is McKelvey, *American Prisons.* For preventive medicine, consult Ravenel, ed., *Half Century of Public Health,* and De Kruif, *Microbe Hunters.*

The Temperance Movement. Cherrington, *Evolution of Prohibition,* and Colvin, *Prohibition,* trace the developments from a temperance point of view, while Earhart, *Frances Willard,* pictures one of the leaders.

Woman's Expanding Sphere. Irwin, *Angels and Amazons,* is a general account, with special phases more thoroughly treated in Abbott, *Women in Industry;* Calhoun, *Social History of the American Family,* III; Woody, *History of Women's Education;* Croly, *Woman's Club Movement;* and Wilson, *Legal and Political Status of Women.* Outstanding feminists are treated in Blackwell, *Lucy Stone;* Harper, *Susan B. Anthony;* and Lutz, *Created Equal, a Biography of Elizabeth Cady Stanton.*

The Reorientation of Religion. Sweet, *Story of Religions,* offers general guidance from the colonial period onward, while Rowe, *History of Religion,* emphasizes interpretation, and Beardsley, *American Revivals,* and Loud, *Evangelized America,* stress emotional aspects. Abell, *Urban Impact on American Protestantism,* Garrison, *March of Faith,* Hopkins, *Rise of the Social Gospel,* and May, *Protestant Churches and Industrial America,* center on developments after 1865. Among the principal biographies are Will, *Cardinal Gibbons,* Bates and Dittemore, *Mary Baker Eddy,* and Powell, *Mary Baker Eddy.*

The Problem of Racial Minorities. Franklin, *From Slavery to Freedom,* Frazier, *Negro in the United States,* and Wesley, *Negro Labor,* discuss the postwar trials of their race. Other accounts include Cutler, *Lynch-Law,* Lewinson, *Race, Class, & Party,* which deals with Negro disfranchisement, and Mathews, *Booker T. Washington.* For Indian reform, turn to McNickle, *They Came Here First,* and particularly Priest, *Uncle Sam's Stepchildren.*

CHAPTER VI

THE CULTURAL RENEWAL

THE DIFFUSION OF KNOWLEDGE

THOUGH the city generated portentous social problems, it also was the dynamo of a virile intellectual life. As Josiah Strong said, "The city is the great center of influence, both good and bad. It contains that which is fairest and foulest in our civilization." The concentration of taxable property made it possible to spend more for educational facilities, libraries and the like than could rural localities, while many of the rich used their private means to supplement the municipal undertakings. In the urban communities were to be found not only the best schools and colleges, but also the best churches, the best newspapers and practically all the libraries, bookstores, art galleries, scientific and historical museums, theaters, concert halls and opera houses. Such an environment stimulated the gifted to creative work in letters and the arts; and since they could always find others with kindred interests, the mutual encouragement and criticism spurred them to their best efforts. At the same time the proximity of publishers, art dealers and well-to-do patrons afforded a market for their talent. It is not surprising that the great cultural advances came out of the city or that its influence penetrated to the farthest countryside.

Never before had private wealth contributed so much toward improving education and taste. From 1871 to the century's close no less than a third of a billion dollars was given for such purposes, half of it going to colleges and universities. Critics of the economic order cynically attributed this generosity to love of ostentation, eagerness for public approbation or, as the Reverend Washington Gladden would have said, an urge to drug an uneasy conscience. That there was also developing a sense of *richesse oblige* Andrew Carnegie made clear in discussing "The Gospel of Wealth" in the *North American Review* (1889). A successful capitalist's career, he wrote, should consist of two periods, first, that of acquiring money and, second, that of putting it to socially important uses. Whatever motives stirred the princely donors, the urban dwellers, who reaped most of the benefit, profited greatly.

The postwar years beheld a mighty advance in public education. Though elementary schools already existed throughout the North, much needed to be done to complete the system. One of the first additions was the kindergarten, where the very young were enticed by play activities to take the first steps in learning. The initial kindergartens were run privately—Mrs. Carl Schurz, a pupil of Froebel, conducted one for German children at her home in Watertown, Wisconsin, as early as 1855—but when St. Louis attached this feature to its schools in 1873, other cities followed until in 1900 there were nearly 3000 public kindergartens in the United States. In the rest of the school system methods of instruction showed constant improvement, partly through the use of better textbooks, and even more because an increasing number of states assumed the responsibility of teacher-training by establishing normal schools. At the same time the North made school attendance obligatory, thus registering the conviction that education was not merely an opportunity but a civic duty. Meanwhile high schools grew from about 500 in 1870 to 6000 in 1900. As home economics, manual training and other subjects demanded by the times crept into the curriculum, the typical secondary school lengthened its course from three to four years. In this way twelve years became the standard period of preparation for college.

The thinly populated country districts, however, lagged behind the towns and cities. Even in the North the rural schools generally remained ungraded, the terms short and the teachers ill trained and wretchedly paid. As a section predominantly rural the South was further hampered by the postwar unsettlement and poverty as well as by the heavy cost of maintaining two sets of schools, a burden borne chiefly by the whites. Moreover, having shared little in the earlier educational awakening of Horace Mann's time, the people had to build their system from the ground up. Despite such obstacles all the Southern states now provided for elementary instruction, though Alabama and North Carolina, for example, spent only fifty cents for each child in 1900 as compared with the national average (the South included) of $2.84. The principle of compulsory education was seldom applied, however, and the widespread establishment of high schools had to await the twentieth century.

In the United States as a whole the school enrollment rose from about 7,000,000 in 1870 to 15,500,000 in 1900. Although city children benefited principally, youngsters nearly everywhere were getting more schooling than their parents had obtained. Illiteracy declined in the three decades from 20 per cent to less than 11. The record would have been even better but for the mounting numbers of uneducated immigrants. Further improvement is revealed by the fact that the total amount of schooling received by the average American in his whole lifetime increased from about three and a third years in 1870 to a little more than five at the century's close. On a positive basis, however, this left much to be desired. Public education still faced gigantic labors in order to perform its proper role in a democratic society.

Though older folk stood outside the orbit of the school system, they nevertheless discovered their own means of offsetting the deficiencies of youthful training. Of these informal educational agencies none evinced so strikingly the popular thirst for knowledge as the Chautauqua movement. Beginning in the summer of 1874, great annual gatherings on the wooded shores of Lake Chautauqua, New York, heard outstanding authorities lecture on literary, scientific and political subjects, and many of the listeners were inspired to undertake a four-year course of home reading and study. Their friends often took advantage of the opportunity also, and by 1892 a total of a hundred thousand were enrolled in the Chautauqua Literary and Scientific Circle. Meanwhile other places blossomed with local Chautauquas, modest sprigs of the original, presented usually under a tent for a week or two during the hot season. In every such locality they furnished a stimulus to local intellectual activity.

In different fashion the spread of public libraries served a like purpose. Though circulating libraries for the use of subscribers had existed since Benjamin Franklin's time, the legislatures of New Hampshire, Massachusetts, Vermont and Maine in the mid-nineteenth century were the first to empower local communities to set up free tax-supported libraries. In the last year of the Civil War other states began to follow until the entire Union had fallen into line. Libraries with 1000 or more volumes increased from 2000 in 1875 to nearly 5400 in 1900. Conspicuous among philanthropists to aid the cause was the ironmaster Carnegie who in 1881 instituted the practice of presenting library buildings to towns that provided sites and pledged adequate maintenance. For this purpose he gave away $10,000,000 by the end of 1900 and $50,000,000 more before his death in 1919. Professional leadership in the movement fell to the American Library Association, formed in 1876, which promoted the adoption of expert methods of service and helped make American libraries the most efficient in the world.

Most people, however, kept abreast the changing world by reading newspapers and magazines. American journalism now entered a new epoch. The war had accustomed the press to lavish outlays of money and stimulated the readers' appetite for colorful and exciting news, and the fast tempo and high tension of city life reinforced the demand. Accordingly, newspapers began to fill their columns with items selected not because of their intrinsic importance but because of their human interest or sensational character. Charles A. Dana on becoming editor of the *New York Sun* in 1868 set the pattern, but his efforts were surpassed by Joseph Pulitzer, a journalist of Hungarian birth, who in 1878 took over the *St. Louis Post-Dispatch* and five years later the *New York World*. Pulitzer frankly directed his appeal to the increasing number of wage earners—the least literate section of the population—shrewdly tailoring the appearance and content of his paper to their mental capacity and tastes. Most of the elements of present-day journalism developed under his hand: startling headlines, political cartoons, thrilling 'stories' of scandal and crime, separate departments for sports, amusements and women's interests and, last but not least, the bulky Sunday edition, divided into many sections for the convenience of the family group and featuring pictures, special articles and colored comics.

Within a few years the *World* became the most profitable and widely imitated paper in the land. Pulitzer's example was responsible for bringing into the arena a young Californian, William Randolph Hearst, who acquired the *New York Morning Journal* in 1895 and quickly bested Pulitzer at his own game. The battle between these two masters of the craft—involving in part the rights to "The Yellow Kid," the first daily colored cartoon—gave rise to the term 'yellow journalism,' by which their brand of newspapering has ever since been known. Yet the influence of the yellow press was not wholly bad. Such sheets often attacked flagrant civic and social abuses and crusaded for their removal. James Bryce noted that in the war against municipal corruption "the newspapers of New York, Boston, Philadelphia, and Chicago have been among the most effective battalions."

It should also be remembered that journals of this type reached count-less numbers who in earlier times had read nothing at all.

A different trend was the transformation of the great metropolitan dailies into mammoth business enterprises, a development arising partly from the heavier costs of operation. Only rarely did newspapers express a dominant personality as in Horace Greeley's time. With the enormous growth of retail stores and nation-wide merchandising, the revenue from such sources exceeded the receipts from sales, and newspapers tended increasingly to become advertising sheets with a secondary attention to news. Gradually the control of policy shifted from the editorial sanctum to the office of the business manager, with a corresponding loss to the independence of the press. In William Dean Howells's *A Modern Instance* (1881) a newspaper publisher loudly asserts, "The press is a great moral engine," but hastily adds, "It ought to be run in the interest of the engineer."

The growing dependence of the average American upon his daily paper is shown by the increase of such journals from fewer than 600 in 1870 to nearly 2500 in 1900, as well as by the leap in total daily sales from 2,500,000 to more than 15,000,000. To meet the huge rise in circulation new mechanical short cuts and more efficient methods had to be adopted. Besides the introduction of faster presses and less expensive paper, the setting of type was converted into a machine process in 1885 when Ottmar Mergenthaler invented the linotype, which enabled the operator to cast solid lines of type from molten lead. To the reporter's aid came the typewriter, devised in 1868 by Christopher L. Sholes, a former editor of the *Milwaukee Sentinel,* and also the first practical fountain pen, invented in 1884 by Lewis E. Waterman. At the same time newspapers, in the interest of economy and efficiency, began to co-operate in gathering and dis-tributing news. Though the original Associated Press dated from before 1860, in the years after the war numerous competing news associations contested the field. In the last decade of the century the Western Associated Press under Melville E. Stone of Chicago gained the advantage, and in 1900 it was reorganized as the present-day Associated Press.

Though less widely read than newspapers, magazines also came to bulk larger in American life, with New York City as the chief publishing center. From 1860 to 1900 the number of monthlies rose from 280 to over 1800. Never before had they reached so high a plane of excellence or represented so well the varied interests of the public. Periodicals such as the *Atlantic,* dating from 1857, *Scribner's Monthly* (1870) which in 1881 became the *Century,* and *Scribner's Magazine* (1887) welcomed to their pages the new generation of authors and afforded them their principal source of income. Among journals appealing to special groups were *St. Nicholas* (1873) for children, *Outing* (1882) for sport lovers, and the *Ladies' Home Journal* (1883) for women.

It was particularly fortunate that in a period of the waning independence of the newspaper press certain weekly magazines were at hand to prick complacency and engage in fearless public criticism. Of these editors perhaps the most significant was the Irish-American, Edwin L. Godkin, who directed the *Nation* from 1865 to 1899 and deeply influenced the thinking of leaders of opinion. In *Harper's Weekly* the German-born Thomas Nast, whose cartoons helped to expose the Tweed Ring and other frauds, laid the foundations of modern American political caricature with the Republican elephant, the Democratic donkey and the Tammany tiger. The humorous possibilities of the American scene were more fully exploited by *Puck, Judge* and *Life,* three comic illustrated weeklies established between 1877 and 1883. The nineties brought the culminating development: a group of monthlies—*McClure's, Munsey's* and others—which without sacrificing good standards sold for ten or fifteen cents instead of the traditional twenty-five or thirty-five. Cheaper manufacturing processes, large-scale production and greater reliance on advertising revenues made them possible. The result was a vast increase in magazine readers.

THE INCREASE OF KNOWLEDGE

Not only did the general level of information and culture improve, but an ever growing proportion of youth attended the colleges and universities and an ever larger number of graduates made contributions to science and learning. Between 1860 and 1900 over 260 additional institutions of higher learning were founded. Some, like Vanderbilt (1873), Johns Hopkins (1876), Leland Stanford (1885), Clark (1889), the University of Chicago (1892) and the Armour Institute of Technology (1893), were the creation of philanthropists; others stemmed from denominational zeal; while, thanks to the federal land grants made available by the Morrill Act of 1862, twenty more state universities opened, mostly in the Middle and Far West. Everywhere the cause of higher education was quickened. Moreover, the need of the expanding industries and railways for technologists and the enhanced interest in social and economic problems turned educators to new fields of instruction, outmoding the narrow curriculum of earlier days. To give depth and direction to these trends there came to the fore a remarkable group of university presidents, including Andrew D. White of Cornell, James McCosh of Princeton, Charles W. Eliot of Harvard, James B. Angell of Michigan, Noah Porter of Yale, Daniel Coit Gilman of Johns Hopkins and William Rainey Harper of Chicago.

Under men of this caliber the traditional college curriculum, besides being enriched with many new subjects, was extended upward to include training for higher degrees. Since the 1860's increasing numbers of American college graduates had been attending German universities, where they drank of the learning of some of the world's greatest scholars and scientists. In the 1880's the exodus reached flood tide with over two thousand imbibing the Teutonic ideal of painstaking specialization. These eager young pilgrims returned home and, as President Eliot said, set about, each in his particular field, "to pierce, with his own little searchlight, if only by a hand's-breadth, the mysterious gloom which surrounds on every side the area of ascertained truth."

Johns Hopkins University, established primarily for graduate work, numbered among its faculty scarcely a professor without German training. Under its tonic influence other institutions expanded their advanced offerings. The total enrollment of nonprofessional graduate students soared from about 400 in 1875 to nearly 5700 in 1900, when a dozen universities offered as excellent opportunities for specialized training as could be found anywhere. It is worth noting that in this supposedly materialistic age a larger proportion of young Americans than ever before consecrated themselves to careers in which the financial rewards were scant. The zest for extending the bounds of knowledge reminded James Bryce of "the scholars of the Renaissance flinging themselves into the study of rediscovered philology." For the first time America's research workers began to hold their own with those of the Old World. In order to keep in touch with fellow investigators, specialists in the different branches banded together in great national organizations like the American Chemical Society

(1876), the Modern Language Association (1883) and the American Economic Association (1885). The federal government, too, turned actively to the promotion of research, not only by means of the agricultural experiment stations earlier noted, but also through such agencies as the Geological Survey and the Bureau of Ethnology, both established in 1879.

In nearly every field of inquiry the evolutionary hypothesis prompted new and significant findings by reason of its emphasis on origins, growth and interrelationships. Though some of the outstanding scientists like Louis Agassiz sided with leading theologians in rejecting the theory, far more typical was the course of two of his Harvard associates: Asa Gray, who lent it the weight of his prestige as a botanist, and John Fiske who, reaching a wider audience through his popular lectures and writings, taught that the evolutionary process explained man's social as well as his physical development.[1] While the Darwinian concept proved most important in the biological sciences, it also influenced such studies as economics, history, philosophy and philology. G. Stanley Hall, himself a contributor to the new subject of experimental psychology, called it "the greatest intellectual stimulus of the modern age."

The advance of knowledge rested on the minute investigations of myriad workers, but certain names stand out. Among the leaders in the natural sciences were Albert A. Michelson, who in 1879 began his epoch-making experiments in measuring the velocity of light; Othniel C. Marsh and Edward D. Cope, whose excavations of fossil beds of prehistoric beasts in the American West enlarged the world's knowledge of paleontology; and Simon Newcomb, world-famed for his recomputation of the elements of the solar system. As a fellow scientist said of Newcomb's work, "The sun and moon and planets have been weighed as exactly as sugar and tea at the grocer's and their paths measured as precisely as silks and woolens at the draper's." Outranking all of them, however, was J. Willard Gibbs, who laid the foundations of a new branch of research, physical chemistry, and is generally accounted the greatest scientist America has yet produced.

---

[1] Fiske formulated his views most completely in *Outlines of Cosmic Philosophy* (1874). Though deeply indebted to the contemporary English social philosopher Herbert Spencer, he differed from his master in insisting that evolution implied the working out of a Divine plan for the betterment of mankind.

Nor were the social sciences far behind. The major figures included Francis A. Walker and Richard T. Ely in economics; Lester F. Ward in sociology; Lewis H. Morgan in anthropology; John W. Burgess and Woodrow Wilson in political science; and John Bach McMaster, James Ford Rhodes and Henry Adams in history. During these years, too, Francis Parkman completed his masterly account of the early relations of France and England in North America. In 1893 Frederick J. Turner launched a new school of historical interpretation by stressing the profound influence that the frontier, then rapidly vanishing, had exerted upon American development from the first days of settlement. In psychology William James was a dominant force, as he also was in philosophy, where he developed the theory of method known as pragmatism, that is, the view that truth to be valid must be tested by its practical consequences. These men and their kind were as truly discoverers, explorers, pioneers, in the intellectual realm as were their forebears who had hewn a path through the physical wilderness of forest and mountain.

In their disinterested pursuit of knowledge, however, they sometimes offended the long-held beliefs of the society about them. Bryce noted the bitterness with which professional politicians denounced professors as "unpractical, visionary," and even "un-American," because "a considerable impulse towards the improvement of party methods, towards civil service reform, and towards tariff reform, has come from the universities, and been felt in the increased political activity of the better educated youth." Professors in denominational colleges who taught evolution were apt to occupy uneasy seats, while even in the larger universities scholars who dared condemn the ethics and practices of Big Business risked dismissal. In 1894, when critics tried to oust Professor Ely from the University of Wisconsin for alleged radical views, the board of regents responded: "We cannot for a moment believe that knowledge has reached its final goal, or that the present condition of society is perfect. We must therefore welcome from our teachers such discussions as shall suggest the means and prepare the way by which knowledge may be extended, present evils be removed and others prevented. . . . In all lines of academic investigation it is of the utmost importance that the investigator should be absolutely free to follow the indications of truth wherever they may lead." Although many institutions fell short of this ideal, it was only through freedom of inquiry that American scholars and scientists were able to contribute so vitally to the world's intellectual enlightenment.

LETTERS AND THE ARTS

No less fruitful were the forces at work in letters and the fine arts. In 1871 the poet Walt Whitman, publishing his most noteworthy prose volume *Democratic Vistas,* cried out for a literary culture springing from the common life, one begotten of the people, by the people, for the people. His challenge to the postwar era was like Ralph Waldo Emerson's *The American Scholar* to the generation of the thirties and forties. But where the Concord sage had pleaded for an aristocracy of literature—for the lone man thinking his own thoughts—Whitman pleaded for a democracy of literature, one "permeating the whole mass of American mentality, taste, belief, breathing into it a new breath of life." Know you not, he asked, that the people "may all know how to read and write, and may all possess the right to vote, and yet the main things may be entirely lacking?" Whitman carried out his own teachings. Beginning as early as 1855 *(Leaves of Grass),* he had shown how the poet, bursting the fetters of rhyme, meter and conventional imagery, might trumpet the glories of common folk and common things with a spacious and mystical enthusiasm previously unknown in American letters.

As if summoned by his clarion call, there trooped forth from every corner of the land young writers eager to record their varied impressions of a traditional rural civilization fast crumbling under the standardizing blows of urbanism and industrialism. Impatient with the bookishness and fastidious diction of their predecessors, they told their stories simply, often with unconscious idealization, and always with fidelity to dialect and local color. Never had American fiction so completely mirrored regional diversities. Edward Eggleston, drawing like all the others upon personal experience, depicted mid-century doings in rural Indiana in *The Hoosier Schoolmaster* (1871) and other novels. "Mark Twain" (Samuel L. Clemens) described humorously a boy's life along the Mississippi, producing his masterpiece in *The Adventures of Huckleberry Finn* (1884). With Bret Harte and the poet Joaquin Miller, he also made memorable the picturesque life of the Far West, while Helen Hunt Jackson in *Ramona* (1884) recalled the romance and drama of the passing of the old Spanish order in California. Nor was the West the only section heard from. There was a literary New South as well as a political and economic one. In delicately wrought sketches George W. Cable, Grace King and Kate Chopin introduced wondering readers to the exotic, orange-scented atmosphere of Creole life in Louisiana, while the chivalry of the old Virginia gentry lived again in the pages of Thomas Nelson Page and F. Hopkinson Smith. By contrast, "Charles Egbert Craddock" (Mary Noailles Murfree) in such stories as *In the Tennessee Mountains* (1884) pictured the humble folk dwelling amidst the grandeur of her native highlands, and Joel Chandler Harris immortalized Negro folklore in the whimsical tales of Uncle Remus. In authors like Sarah Orne Jewett and Mary E. Wilkins (Freeman), New England had its own regional spokesmen, but they painted not a colorful past but the drab present, portraying sympathetically the impact of New England's rural decline on the people.

Still other writers found their themes in the main stream rather than the backwaters of American life. In novels distinguished by such works as *The Rise of Silas Lapham* (1884) and *A Hazard of New Fortunes* (1889), William Dean Howells chronicled the trials and foibles of middle-class urban dwellers, with ever sharpening emphasis upon the "economic chance-world" that was new to America. Henry James, an expatriate living in England, dissected with consummate artistry the reactions of his unsophisticated countrymen to Old World culture in such studies as *Daisy Miller* (1876) and *The Portrait of a Lady* (1881). Brother of William James the psychologist, he in his different medium concentrated on exploring the human mind. Like Howells he strove for realism, and though both were influenced by contemporary authors in France and Russia, they revealed their innate Americanism by dwelling upon the normal rather than the abnormal in people. As a wit remarked, "The present realism in fiction is in France a discovery of the unclean, and in America a discovery of the unimportant." A grimmer temper, however, pervaded a younger group of writers, notably Hamlin Garland, whose *Main-Travelled Roads* (1891) stressed the harsh aspects of Midwestern rural life, and Stephen Crane, who in *Maggie, a Girl of the Streets* (1892) exposed one of the tragic failures of the vaunted urban civilization and in *The Red Badge of Courage* (1895) depicted the bewilderment and terror of a Civil War recruit under fire for the first time. Their work foreshadowed the active concern with social injustice and the common lot which would characterize twentieth-century novelists.

The 1880's marked the full bloom of the new literary growths, with the publication of a greater number of first-rate novels than in any previous decade. Yet the era was even more distinctive for the short story, "literature in small parcels," a form which this generation molded into a finished work of art. It was peculiarly suited to the taste of the hurrying, scurrying people who thronged the cities. Through the short story the United States has perhaps made its greatest contribution to letters. Literary men, however, were handicapped by the absence of an international copyright. This enabled publishers to reprint English books and sell them at lower prices than American ones, since no royalties had to be paid the foreign authors. For many years American writers had complained of this 'piracy,' and now, with the increasing demand for American works abroad, the publishers found that they were suffering from piracy in the reverse. Joining forces with the authors, they induced Congress in 1891 to pass the International Copyright Act protecting native and foreign writers on a reciprocal basis. Henceforth American authors were able to compete in a fair and free field.

Equally as significant as the literary revival was the record of accomplishment in the fine arts. Just as fledgling scholars and scientists were flocking to German universities, so fledgling painters, sculptors and architects were storming the studios of Paris, the Mecca of the world's artists. During the seventies, as they returned home in ever increasing numbers, their advent was like a fresh wind on a sultry day, clearing the atmosphere of muggy traditions and introducing breadth, freedom and vigor. In painting, the clash of schools was so sharp as to cause the 'Younger Men' in 1877 to form the Society of American Artists in opposition to the long-established National Academy of Design. Into their ranks they drew some of the more progressive older men like George Inness and John La Farge. The years that followed brought an epoch of creative achievement such as the country had never before known.

A few examples will suggest both the quality and variety of the product. In George Inness America discovered perhaps her greatest landscape painter, an artist with a poet's insight into Nature's vagrant moods. By contrast Winslow Homer earned fame with his boldly colored canvases of the sea, while Thomas Eakins exemplified a matter-of-fact realism that led him to portray President Hayes in shirt sleeves. James A. McNeill Whistler's genius appeared best in his nocturnes, which conveyed inimitably the hue and mystery and quiet of night. His famous picture, "The Artist's Portrait of His Mother," a study in grays, was bought in 1891 by the French government. Albert P. Ryder devoted his brush to legendary and poetic subjects, which he interpreted with great imaginative power. La Farge transformed American mural painting into a fine art, and through his invention of opalescent glass he revived the ancient splendor of medieval stained glass. In response to the mounting interest, art schools increased from under 40 in 1880 to nearly 120 at the century's close. The opening of great art museums in Washington, New York and Boston in the postwar decade helped to improve public taste and prompted other large cities to imitation. In a less obvious way the waxing popularity of the camera, especially after the simplifications introduced in the eighties by George Eastman of Rochester, awakened in many a latent aesthetic sense.

In the plastic arts men like Daniel Chester French, George Grey Barnard and Frederick W. MacMonnies wielded a profound influence for higher standards. MacMonnies, however, shocked staid Boston by his nude representation of "Bacchante" (1894), which had been ordered for the court of the newly constructed public library, and it had to find sanctuary in New York's Metropolitan Museum. The foremost sculptor was the Irish-born Augustus Saint-Gaudens, whose statue of Admiral Farragut (1881) in Madison Square Garden, New York, first revealed his genius. His symbolic figure, "The Peace of God," erected at the tomb of Mrs. Henry Adams in Washington in 1891, is generally considered the greatest sculpture America has yet produced. In no other branch of art had the national traditions been so poor. These men and their like raised the native performance to a plane comparable with the best in contemporary Europe.

The new influences made slower headway in architecture, partly because of the need of the swift-growing cities for quick construction and partly because people confused ostentation with good taste. Even many men of wealth and note lived in houses disfigured with towers, turrets, Moorish arches and fantastic frills in wood and iron. It was Henry Hobson Richardson who ushered in a better day. Employing the heavy Romanesque style of southern France, he taught the superiority of sturdiness, unity and restraint in design. His crowning achievement was Trinity Church (1877) in Boston, for which John La Farge supplied the murals and much of the stained glass. Before Richardson died in 1886, others had risen to foster the higher standards, and from plans appearing in magazines like the *Ladies' Home Journal* even the ordinary person could learn how to build an attractive, inexpensive house. The younger craftsmen wrought characteristically in the classic mode or some of its Renaissance derivatives. The Chicago World's Fair of 1893—largely the artistic creation of Daniel H. Burnham, Charles B. Atwood, Richard M. Hunt and the firm of McKim, Mead and White—marked the supreme attainment of the classic style. The effect was a poignant dream of loveliness reminiscent of the chaste perfection of late eighteenth and early nineteenth-century architecture in America.

The congested business quarters of large cities presented a special problem because of the necessity of saving ground area. The solution lay in taller buildings, but how was this to be accomplished without sacrificing much of the desirable space in the lower floors to huge masonry piers? The answer came in the 'skyscraper,' a structure riveted securely in a metal frame and using brick or stone merely to afford privacy and screen out the weather. Fortunately the recent introduction of fast elevators removed the main objection to such buildings. Less trammeled by tradition than Eastern cities, Chicago erected the original skyscraper, the Home Insurance Building (1885), which rose to what then seemed the dizzy eminence of ten stories. The most significant contributor to the new mode was Louis Sullivan, who strove to adapt exterior decoration and design to the greater heights. His contention that form should express function had its biggest influence, however, on the next generation. Meanwhile Chicago and New York, generally employing ornamentation and conceptions in the Roman style, pushed their buildings higher and higher until in 1898 the Ivins Syndicate Building in Manhattan reached twenty-nine floors, a mere hint of what the next century would bring. These "proud structures, defiant in their altitude," fittingly symbolized the titanic energy, the urge to experiment, the superb engineering competence, that characterized the age. Since historical research has denied Americans credit for the log cabin, the skyscraper stands as the nation's most striking architectural gift to the world.

If progress in musical composition was less brilliant, still the people began in a modest way to repay their debt for the rich stores of melody they had long received from Europe. The principal composers had all been trained in Germany. John Knowles Paine, George W. Chadwick and Horatio Parker won transatlantic recognition for their orchestral and choral scores, while Edward A. MacDowell composed piano selections distinguished by originality and haunting beauty. Perhaps more significant was the heartening growth of musical appreciation. Conservatories of music appeared in the larger cities; artists' recitals enjoyed profitable patronage; choral societies flourished, notably in German centers; and the founding of the New York Symphony Orchestra in 1878 and of the Boston Symphony Orchestra in 1881 signalized a new era in that branch. More than any other one person, the German-born Theodore Thomas furthered an intelligent popular interest in music, organizing music festivals, establishing and conducting orchestras in various cities, and training his players to standards of performance never before known in his adopted country. Grand opera, too, secured a firmer footing with the opening of New York's Metropolitan Opera House in 1883. Such evidences of public support and improving taste augured well for the future.

THE CHALLENGE OF LEISURE

All classes in the cities were confronted with the problem of using their increasing leisure. Even the wage earners had more free time than formerly, thanks to the gradual reduction of the workday. But life under pioneer conditions had taught the people how to work, not how to play, and hence they turned to pleasure with the same fierce energy that they devoted to making a living. In Bryce's contemporary phrase, they "make amusement into a business." Society life in the great cities was marked by frantic display, especially on the part of the newly rich anxious to vault into the ranks of the exclusive. The well-to-do merchants and planters of an earlier day with incomes of $10,000 or $20,000 a year had set modest standards; now their places were taken by industrial magnates with earnings of from $50,000 to $1,000,000. It was not hard to find ways and means of advancing the family socially. An avalanche of etiquette books instructed one in what to wear and how to behave, with blunt warnings not to use half-understood words, or to err like the returned matron from Europe who upon being asked whether she had seen the Dardanelles said, "Oh, yes; we dined with them several times!" Palatial mansions and extravagant entertaining masked the rise from humble origins; lavish subscriptions to fashionable charities smoothed the path; proper 'ancestors' were always obtainable from the 'right' genealogists. But the supreme goal was a brilliant international marriage. So successful were ambitious mothers in this quest that toward the end of the century it was estimated that over $200,000,000 had replenished the coffers of impoverished European nobility.

Such matters did not affect the average person except as he read about them in the society columns, but other leisure-time interests did. None made greater appeal than the opportunity to join one or more of the secret fraternal orders that sprang up as if by spontaneous generation. A product of urban conditions, these lodges not only supplied a substitute for the neighborliness of rural communities but, through their elaborate ceremonialism, enabled the members to recover a sense of self-importance lost in the anonymity of crowds. A further attraction consisted in the sickness and death benefits usually provided. Between 1865 and 1901 no fewer than 568 different fraternal organizations were founded. A writer in the *Century Magazine* characterized this development as the "great American safety-valve." In 1890 Boston, Chicago and St. Louis had three times as many lodges as churches. As the century closed, the United States had firmly established its title of a 'nation of joiners,' with over six million names on the rosters of its secret societies.

The multiplication of city dwellers also led to a vast expansion of popular entertainment. The serious drama probably has never been better presented than by such native actors as Edwin Booth, Clara Morris and Lawrence Barrett and by such foreign visitors as Sarah Bernhardt and Helena Modjeska. Bronson Howard, the major dramatist, wrote plays that held the boards for from one hundred and fifty to four hundred nights. More characteristic, however, was the enthusiasm for the minstrel show and the circus, while bloodcurdling melodramas regaled a public whose taste had been whetted by the sensational press. Yet no form of stage performance so well suited the restless urban spirit as vaudeville, which Tony Pastor, B. F. Keith and others made into a great success. Vaudeville, observed a contemporary, "belongs to the era of the department store and the short story." By the 1890's it accounted for perhaps half the theatergoers. Comic opera also came into favor on the wave of popularity created by "Pinafore" and other delightful concoctions of the Britons, Gilbert and Sullivan. Soon Americans such as Reginald de Koven and Victor Herbert entered the field, the former in 1890 composing "Robin Hood," one of the most popular and melodious operas in the history

STUDENT LIFE AT VASSAR, 1885
See page 113.

THE ADAMS MEMORIAL (1891) BY AUGUSTUS SAINT-GAUDENS
See page 139.

of the American theater. The tunes from such performances swiftly spread to every corner of the country, thanks to the 'talking machine' or phonograph. Invented by Edison in 1877–1878, the first crude instrument, consisting of a tin-foil cylinder record turned by hand, was presently improved by Edison and others through the adoption of flat waxlike disks operated by spring or electric motors. The phonograph promoted a rage for popular songs beyond anything ever known. In the single year 1900 nearly three million records were sold.

These years also saw the rise of organized sport. As rural life receded into the background, as normal outlets for physical exertion lessened, as more and more people slaved long hours in office and factory, some form of outdoor diversion became imperative. Unhappily, however, softened muscles did not encourage personal participation. Most people were content to pay others to take their exercise for them, an inclination warmly abetted by sport promoters, who coveted the gate receipts which professional contests made possible. The 'audience habit,' nurtured by the theater, thus came to infect sport lovers as well. Many of the games were imported from Great Britain, where an athletic revival had been under way since the mid-century. In the United States, however, they were deemed not a special perquisite of the upper classes, but something to be enjoyed by all. In the case of basketball, originated in 1891, Americans contributed a game of their own.

Of the older sports, thoroughbred racing enjoyed unparalleled popularity. Pugilism, though still viewed askance by the respectable, brought to the fore a succession of world's heavyweight champions, beginning in 1882 with John L. Sullivan. Baseball, which had long been a favorite amateur pastime, began to assume its aspect of America's national game when the Cincinnati Red Stockings in 1869 took the revolutionary step of paying the players. Soon professional baseball overran the country, leading to intercity leagues and in 1884 to the first "World Series" between the pennant-winning teams of the two major leagues. Football, a modification of the English game of Rugby, developed more slowly, being associated with the growth of college athletics. The first intercollegiate contest occurred between Princeton and Rutgers in 1869, with twenty-five men on each side. In the next score of years the game under constantly changing rules spread to nearly all colleges and most high schools. At Connecticut Wesleyan, Professor Woodrow Wilson helped coach a team which in 1889 beat Pennsylvania, Amherst, Williams, Rutgers and Trinity.

Of the newer sports, lawn tennis, golf and polo crossed the Atlantic from Britain in the 1870's, and skiing was a contribution of Minnesota Norwegians in the next decade. In these and other cases differences as to rules brought about national associations to establish uniform regulations and often also to conduct annual tournaments. In some manner or other, all classes joined in this new play life of the nation. The well-to-do showed their interest by organizing athletic clubs, country clubs and yacht clubs. Amidst his political activities Theodore Roosevelt took time to box, wrestle, fish, hunt and play polo, exemplifying in these early years his belief in the "strenuous life." President Hayes liked to shoot at a mark in Rock Creek Park, and his successors Arthur and Cleveland ranked among the country's most expert fishermen. The popular reaction is suggested by the fact that in 1892 a leading New York daily devoted one column to John Greenleaf Whittier's death and nearly a dozen to the prize fight in which the great John L. Sullivan lost his crown to 'Gentleman Jim' Corbett.

No sport, however, attracted so many participants as bicycling. At first this exercise was limited to riders who were undaunted by an occasional header from the giddy perch over the high front wheel. But in the 1880's the introduction of the 'safety' bicycle of two medium-sized wheels, the adoption of the drop frame for women and the use of pneumatic tires instead of solid rubber ones inaugurated a cycling craze which ramified to every part of the country. By 1893 a million bicycles were in use, and soon manufacturers were selling that many each year. Spurred by the League of American Wheelmen, over half the states passed laws to improve their highways, a movement which would later be accelerated by the advent of the automobile. For untold thousands the diversion renewed the forgotten pleasures of open road and countryside. It was recommended by physicians, and it also helped bring about more rational fashions for women. "It is safe to say," declared the Census Bureau in 1900, "that few articles ever used by man have created so great a revolution in social conditions." This generation little dreamed that the rattling, chugging 'horseless carriage,' which inventors in the nineties were hopefully trying to perfect, would presently spell the doom of the universally popular 'bike.'

FULLER ACCOUNTS

The Diffusion of Knowledge. Nevins, *Emergence of Modern America,* and Schlesinger, *Rise of the City,* in their respective periods cover the topics in this and the succeeding sections. Cubberley, *Public Education,* and Knight, *Public Education in the South,* are surveys; Beale discusses the *History of Freedom of Teaching;* Ditzion, *Arsenals of a Democratic Culture,* traces the public-library movement in the Northeast; and Hurlbut tells *The Story of Chautauqua.* Mott, *American Journalism,* should be supplemented by particular accounts like Andrews, *Pittsburgh's Post-Dispatch,* Baehr, *New York Tribune since the Civil War,* Gramling, *AP,* and Stone, *Dana and the Sun,* and by such biographical studies as Seitz, *Pulitzer,* and Winkler, *Hearst.* Mott, *History of American Magazines,* III, carries the story from 1865 to 1885.

The Increase of Knowledge. Commager, *American Mind,* and Curti, *Growth of American Thought,* provide general guidance along with comprehensive bibliographies, while Dorfman, *Economic Mind in American Civilization,* III, Gabriel, *American Democratic Thought,* Hofstadter, *Social Darwinism,* and Schneider, *History of American Philosophy,* consider special aspects, and Jaffe, *Men of Science,* Jordan, ed., *Leading American Men of Science,* and Odum, ed., *American Masters of Social Science,* adopt a biographical approach. For higher education, see Butts, *College Charts Its Course;* Ryan, *Early Graduate Education;* and Thwing, *American and German University.*

Letters and the Arts. Spiller and others, eds., *Literary History of the United States,* II, records the major developments. Other surveys of letters include Parrington, *Beginnings of Critical Realism,* and Pattee, *American Literature since 1870,* with Mott, *Golden Multitudes,* singling out best sellers. Among works on the fine arts are Barker, *American Painting;* Larkin, *Art and Life in America;* Isham, *History of American Painting;* Walker and James, *Great American Paintings;* Taft, *History of American Sculpture;* Tallmadge, *Story of American Architecture;* and Howard, *Our American Music.*

The Challenge of Leisure. Dulles, *America Learns to Play,* views the whole subject, while particular phases are treated in Wecter, *Saga of American Society;* Schlesinger, *Learning How to Behave;* Anderson, *American Theatre;* Mayorga, *Short History of the American Drama;* Coffin, *Vaudeville;* Krout, *Annals of American Sport;* Davis, *Football;* Spalding, *America's National Game;* and Johnston, *Ten—and Out!* (prize fighting).

CHAPTER VII

THE RURAL REVOLT

THE WIDENING BREACH BETWEEN COUNTRY AND CITY

As the post-Civil War years wore on, urban life moved farther and farther ahead of rural life. The Economic Revolution worked unevenly, favoring the city while by-passing or impoverishing the countryside. The large bankers and industrialists carried out their far-flung projects regardless of the farmer's welfare. Nor did the rural dweller reap any benefit from the many new mechanical inventions, such as the telephone, the electric light and the streetcar; and his wife had to manage without central heating, sanitary plumbing, gas burners and other housekeeping conveniences. To make matters worse, the farmer failed to obtain his share of the increasing national wealth. The value of agricultural land in 1880 just equaled that of urban real estate, whereas ten years later it was only half as much; and if other forms of property were included, country folk came off even more poorly. An economist fixed the average wealth of rural families at $3250 in 1890 as against more than $9000 for urban families.

Such disparities were thrown into sharper relief by the city's many social opportunities. Not the least was that of seeing and mingling with other people. In contrast to Europe, where the peasants lived together in pleasant villages with their fields adjoining, in America farm homes were widely scattered, with no more than four to the square mile under the Homestead Act of 1862. Isolation and loneliness were the almost inescapable price of existence in the newer West, a fact which worked a special hardship on womenfolk and the younger generation. Country folk also lacked other advantages of the city—opportunities for choosing among a variety of careers, for laboring shorter hours, for educational and cultural development, for pleasure and recreation. Hamlin Garland called his fictional indictment of rural life *Main-Travelled Roads* because, he said, the main road "is long and wearyful and has a dull town at one end and a home of toil at the other." Though many continued to prefer the

146

familiar life, the phenomenal exodus from the countryside suggests how differently their sons and neighbors felt. "The farm youth sees only the dazzling, gaudy side of city life," lamented one student of conditions. "He sees not that for every success there are scores, nay hundreds, who sink into darkness and misery." This growing sense of rural inferiority, this deepening conviction that the yeoman was losing his ancient heritage of economic independence and equal opportunity, needed only specific bread-and-butter grievances to touch off organized movements of protest.

Such grievances the eighties provided aplenty. The return of prosperity in 1879 after the long depression benefited chiefly the urban and industrial sections. Because of the enormous expansion of Western agriculture and of stiffer competition in the world's markets with the wheat of Russia, Australia, Canada and the Argentine, crop prices fell disastrously. The wheat grower who received eighty cents a bushel in the years 1882–1885 did well to get seventy-one in 1890. In Kansas at the latter date corn, selling for as little as ten cents a bushel, was commonly burned for fuel. The farmer, toiling "from daybreak to backbreak," scoffed at the notion of overproduction when millions of urban workingmen suffered from undernourishment. He blamed his ills, rather, on the undue profits of the middlemen, the heavy charges imposed by the railroads, and the unreasonable interest rates that his creditors (mostly Easterners) exacted. "There are three great crops raised in Nebraska," raged an agricultural editor. "One is a crop of corn, one a crop of freight rates, and one a crop of interest. One is produced by farmers who by sweat and toil farm the land. The other two are produced by men who sit in their offices and behind their bank counters and farm the farmers."

To add to the afflictions, an almost uninterrupted decade of drought and chinch bugs, starting in 1887, destroyed the plantings of countless settlers who had homesteaded in the subhumid zone embracing the western halves of Kansas, Nebraska and the Dakotas. It seemed as though the hand of both man and Nature was raised against the husbandman. By 1890 mortgages averaged one for every two persons in Kansas and North Dakota, one for every three in Nebraska, South Dakota and Minnesota. In some counties debts blanketed 90 per cent or more of the land. Meanwhile the Southern agriculturist complained of similar woes: low farm prices, high charges for what he bought, steep transportation costs, excessive taxes, grinding debts.

The market price of cotton, the principal staple, tumbled from fifteen cents in 1870–1873 to eight cents twenty years later. The crop-lien system, by which the farmer mortgaged his growing crop at extreme interest rates, enmeshed perhaps eight or nine out of every ten cotton growers, reducing them to a condition of 'debt-peonage.' Everywhere in the South, land tended to gravitate into the hands of moneylenders, loan companies and a few of the financially stronger planters. In the nation as a whole, agricultural indebtedness rose from $343,000,000 in 1880 to $586,000,000 in 1890.

As the 1880's advanced, signs of agrarian unrest multiplied. The farmers formed local and then state and regional organizations to discuss their wrongs and demand their rights, with the Northern Farmers' Alliance and the Southern Farmers' Alliance emerging as the dominant groups in the two sections. Taking a leaf from the experience of the Grangers, the aroused people launched co-operatives, setting up cotton yards, grain elevators, insurance companies and the like. But when these projects miscarried, as most of them did because of poor business direction or cutthroat competition, they turned to the government for help. In various parts of the South, men 'fresh from the soil,' like Ben Tillman in South Carolina and Jim Hogg in Texas, sprang into prominence. Inflaming the rural masses against the well-to-do and the towns, they captured the Democratic party in their states. In the strongly Republican commonwealths of the West the agrarians usually founded independent parties, sometimes through fusion with the Democratic minority. The ultimate goal, however, was the control of Congress, for thereby they hoped to secure their chief means of relief: currency inflation, a graduated income tax and the public ownership of railroads. Derided as 'hayseed socialists' by Easterners, the farmers in fact had no wish to overturn the capitalist system. Most of them owned land or expected to, and true to the American tradition they wanted merely to ensure better opportunities for themselves and their children. Like the urban wage earners they were capitalists on the make.

Of the several demands the one for currency inflation took first place. Although the greenback dream still lingered fondly in the minds of some, circumstances directed chief attention to 'free silver.' Until 1873 the country had been on a bimetallic standard, that is, the government stood ready to coin into dollars all the gold and silver that might be brought to the mint. Actually, no silver dollars had been known for forty years, for the metal was so scarce and valuable that it paid people to sell it to jewelers rather than to take it to the mint. Therefore Congress when reorganizing the monetary system in 1873 dropped the silver dollar as a domestic coin. No sooner was this done, however, than the fabulous finds in the Far West produced a huge leap in the world's stock of the ore, and about the same time several European governments, deciding to go on the gold standard, disposed of their larger silver coins, thus further augmenting the supply.[1] Though the demonetization of silver had excited little notice when adopted, it soon gained an ugly repute as the 'Crime of 1873,' and in the political discussions of the next quarter-century the action was ascribed to a sinister plot of Big Business and Wall Street.

With the nation floundering in the depression of the seventies, agrarian spokesmen, abetted by urban labor groups, demanded a return to free silver, in other words, to the earlier unlimited coinage of the silver dollar and at the same legal ratio with gold as had then existed (sixteen to one). By enlarging the volume of money the silverites believed the government would bring about higher prices for farm crops and better wages in industry and make it easier for the poor to pay their debts. But they reckoned without the waxing strength of the business classes who opposed any measure that might diminish the purchasing power of their incomes and enable debtors to discharge their obligations in 'cheap money.' To the aid of the inflationists, however, came the small but energetic group of silver-mine owners, who saw the market price of the bullion content of the old dollar toboggan from $1.02 in 1872 to eighty-two cents in 1885, with the downward trend unchecked. If the government could again be induced to buy all the ore brought to the mint, the mining interests reasoned that its market price and their profits would rise in response to the unlimited demand. The question did not become an issue between the parties for many years. Within each party, however, it caused jangling discord, the members from the rural West and South generally opposing those from the moneyed East and the manufacturing districts of the Midwest.

The first trial of strength occurred in 1877–1878 when the House

---

[1] Germany demonetized silver in 1871, Denmark, Sweden and Norway in 1873, while in the latter year the Latin Union of France, Italy, Belgium, Switzerland and Greece limited their silver coinage.

of Representatives under Western and Southern pressure passed a free-silver bill only to have the Senate tone it down. Even in its altered form President Hayes vetoed the measure as involving a partial repudiation of debts and hence a breach of contract; but Congress easily carried it over his objections. The Bland-Allison Act of 1878 directed the Treasury to buy from $2,000,000 to $4,000,000 of silver bullion each month for coinage. As a compromise settlement it allayed further agitation for several years, though both Arthur and Cleveland urged its repeal. The least amount of bullion permitted by the statute was purchased and coined, adding about $31,000,000 each year to the circulating medium. Then, toward the end of the eighties, the free-silver movement sprang to life again. The reasons were various. For one thing, the government, bent on reducing the surplus revenue, was buying up the outstanding war bonds, and since the volume of national bank notes varied with the amount of federal bonds, this caused these notes to shrink from $359,000,000 in 1882 to $186,-000,000 in 1890. The economic recession of 1884–1885 was another factor, while the admission of the six plains and mountain states in 1889 and 1890 further strengthened the silver demand, particularly in the Senate. Besides, the Farmers' Alliances now loomed big on the national political horizon. Observers were scarcely surprised when the fall elections of 1890 placed fifty-three 'Alliance men' in Congress.

When the question of a new monetary law was taken up early that year, it happened that, contrary to their previous attitudes, the Senate now favored free silver while the House opposed it. The silverites in the House, however, finally forced the majority to make concessions by threatening to vote against the McKinley tariff bill, then in course of passage. In July, 1890, the Sherman Silver Purchase Act went into effect. Though still not providing for free silver, it required the Treasury to buy 4,500,000 ounces of bullion each month (nearly twice as much as had been coined before), and to issue in payment therefor treasury notes of full legal-tender character, redeemable in either gold or silver at the government's option.

THE DEEPENING OF SOCIAL DISCONTENT

Unlike the Bland-Allison Act, the new law failed even momentarily to hush the outcry for free silver. Another downswing began in the prices of grain, livestock and cotton, the Department of Agriculture reporting in 1893 that the cost of raising wheat and corn exceeded the selling price. Between 1889 and 1893 more than eleven thousand mortgages were foreclosed in Kansas alone. In the single year 1891 no fewer than eighteen thousand covered wagons crossed from Nebraska to the Iowa side of the Missouri River in flight from the scene of disaster. Moreover, despite the government's greater absorption of silver, the bullion value of the dollar plunged from eighty-one cents to sixty in 1893. A wave of despair swept over the West and South. Hamlin Garland, who spoke from firsthand knowledge, declared in retrospect, "As ten-cent corn and ten per cent interest were troubling Kansas, so six-cent cotton was inflaming Georgia—and both were frankly sympathetic with Montana and Colorado whose miners were suffering from a drop in the price of silver." The new spirit was exemplified by Mrs. Mary E. Lease of Kansas who, exhorting the farmers to "raise less corn and more hell," screamed to huge audiences, "The great common people of this country are slaves. . . . The West and South are bound and prostrate before the manufacturing East. . . . Our laws are the output of a system which clothes rascals in robes and honesty in rags." The effect on conservative Easterners was revealed by the New York *Evening Post's* caustic comment: "We don't want any more states until we can civilize Kansas."

Flushed by their successes in the November elections of 1890, the Farmers' Alliances laid plans to bring city wage earners into the movement. In May, 1891, over fourteen hundred representatives of agrarian, labor and reform groups, meeting in Cincinnati, resolved to form the People's party, and in July, 1892, a second convention, in Omaha, made preparations for the presidential campaign. The platform, promising to restore the government to the "plain people," pledged such measures as free silver, a graduated income tax, government ownership of railways and telegraphs, a shorter day for urban laborers and the popular election of United States Senators. The platform excited a tornado of cheers and yells which, according to an onlooker, "raged without cessation for thirty-four minutes, during which women shrieked and wept, men embraced and kissed . . . and leaped upon tables and chairs in the ecstasy of their delirium." James B. Weaver of Iowa, veteran inflationist, who had headed the Greenback ticket in 1880, was named for President, with James G. Field of Virginia as his running mate. In the ensuing contest the

Populists amazed old-party leaders by polling twenty-two electoral votes, all in the plains and mountain states, and more than a million popular votes.

Nevertheless the Democrats, as has been seen, easily captured the election on the tariff issue, and it appeared likely that, if economic conditions improved, the Populist upsurge would quickly subside and the political stream resume its normal course. But no sooner did Cleveland enter the White House than the Panic of 1893 crashed upon the country. It was bred of a complication of causes. Over-investment in railways and industrial combinations, involving many of a highly speculative character, was a prime factor. A depression in Europe, beginning in France in 1889 and spreading to Great Britain and Germany in 1890, aggravated the situation by causing foreigners to withdraw some of the gold they had invested in American enterprises. An added, if not decisive, influence was the mounting fear of the business community that the flood of silver freed by the Sherman Silver Purchase Act would sweep the government off a gold basis and force a suspension of gold payments. Though that law permitted the government to redeem the new treasury notes in either gold or silver, gold was a popular symbol of the nation's financial integrity, and refusal to pay in the more precious metal would have wrecked public confidence. Yet no provision had been made in the Sherman Act for enlarging the gold reserve, which meant that the $100,000,000 fund, established under the Resumption Act of 1875 to protect the greenbacks, must now serve, in addition, to back up the treasury notes that were increasing at a rate of $50,000,000 a year. Moreover, since the gold reserve was not kept separate from other public funds, there was the further danger that the government under pressure of need might dip into it for current operating expenses.

Just such an emergency confronted Cleveland when he entered office. Because of lavish appropriations by Harrison's outgoing Congress and the scant revenue produced by the McKinley Tariff, the gold reserve fell within six weeks below the $100,000,000 mark, greatly to the alarm of the business and financial classes. People everywhere rushed to redeem their treasury notes and greenbacks in gold,[1] while foreign investors redoubled their efforts to settle their American

[1] Greenbacks to the amount of nearly $347,000,000 were in circulation. The 378,000,000 silver dollars issued under the Bland-Allison Act were not, however, redeemable in gold.

accounts in the only metal used in international trade. Even a sounder economic structure might not have withstood this shock to public confidence. As it was, hysteria gripped the business world. More than eight thousand commercial concerns failed between April 1 and October 1, 1893, with liabilities of nearly $285,000,000. Many banks also toppled, particularly in the West and South, and a hundred and fifty-six railways, including the Erie, the Northern Pacific and the Union Pacific, went into receivership. In the urban centers the unemployed reached the unparalleled number of four and a half million according to trade-union figures. As in 1873, private benevolence sprang into action, and many cities appropriated funds for both direct relief and work on emergency projects, such as the paving of streets and the building of sewers. Meanwhile the farmers sank deeper into adversity, with wheat selling for but forty-nine cents a bushel in 1894.

Cleveland, an Easterner and 'sound money' man, was determined at all hazards to maintain the gold standard. This he planned to do by two courses of action. In order to stop additional silver purchases and thus ease the strain upon the already overburdened gold reserve, he jammed through Congress in November, 1893, largely by using the whip of patronage, a bill repealing the Sherman Act. As a second move he set about to borrow gold faster than it was drained from the Treasury. The trouble here was that paper currency presented for redemption had to be paid out again to defray the government's running expenses, and this money the recipients in turn exchanged for gold. Under the operation of what Cleveland called "an endless chain" the reserve dwindled from $95,000,000 at the end of June, 1893, to $65,000,000 a year later. When Congress, inspired in part by silver arguments, refused to authorize bond issues to replenish the fund, Cleveland, discovering authority in an earlier statute, twice sold $50,000,000 worth of bonds to the public for gold in 1894. The aim was partly defeated, however, by the fact that many of the purchasers bought the bonds with gold they had drawn out of the Treasury with paper. Cleveland then arranged with J. Pierpont Morgan and a financial syndicate early in 1895 to loan the government $65,000,000 worth of gold of which at least half should be obtained from abroad. The Populists and prosilver Democrats rapped the administration for allowing Wall Street bankers what seemed an excessive profit, but the transaction substantially relieved the situation. Normal conditions, however, did not return until the next year, when they were assisted in January, 1896, by a fourth bond sale—this time directly to the public—of $100,000,000, and also by a perceptible improvement of business.

While the government was struggling to balance its accounts, social discontent continued to grow. In the late summer of 1894 torrid winds blew over the Midwestern corn belt, searing the fields and reducing the crop to a quarter of its size the previous year. As the farmers sank deeper into woe, more urban workers lost their jobs or suffered disastrous pay cuts, outbreaks like the Pullman strike imperiled domestic order, and bands of the unemployed began a march on Washington. From Congress the jobless hoped to obtain a measure lending $500,000,000 in paper money to states and cities for work relief in the form of public improvements such as roads, schools and courthouses. These 'petitions in boots' moved slowly across the country, on foot and horseback, sometimes stealing trains for faster transit. They came from many points of the compass—Los Angeles, San Francisco, Seattle, St. Louis, Chicago, as well as from towns along the way and places in New England. The 'army' led by 'General' Jacob S. Coxey of Massillon, Ohio, though not the largest, excited most attention. With depleted ranks about 1200 of his men straggled into Washington from May to July, 1894, but there they were able to accomplish nothing. Although their basic idea of federal work relief was to be taken over by the New Deal in the Great Depression of the 1930's, the Senators of this time branded it as "socialism and populism and paternalism run riot." Coxey himself was arrested on the trivial charge of trespassing on the Capitol grounds, and his footsore comrades, facing starvation and harassed by the police, presently scattered for parts unknown. The failure of the movement, however, did not cure the conditions that had given it rise.

Those conditions were underscored by an article on "The Concentration of Wealth" in the scholarly *Political Science Quarterly* in December, 1893, which showed that 9 per cent of America's families owned nearly 71 per cent of the national wealth, figures which supplied potent ammunition for the Populists and other apostles of discontent. Suspicion of the overweening power of the moneyed interests seemed confirmed by the Senate's betrayal of Cleveland's tariff program in the Wilson-Gorman Act of 1894, and the attitude was reinforced by the Supreme Court's annulment of the income tax in 1895. This action

provoked the greatest outburst of wrath against that tribunal since the
Dred Scott decision. As Justice John M. Harlan, a member of the
Court, recalled in after years, "There was everywhere, among the
people generally, a deep feeling of unrest. The Nation had been rid
of human slavery . . . but the conviction was universal that the
country was in real danger from another kind of slavery, . . . the
slavery that would result from aggregations of capital in the hands of
a few."

In the fears, depressed spirits and lean purses of the times the doctrine of free silver found new soil for growth. It arrayed the West
and South against the East, debtor against creditor, country against
city. As the *Arena* magazine put it, the real meaning of the controversy "lies far deeper than any question of one metal or two for a
monetary base. It is a question of entrusting Federal power to men
in hearty sympathy with the great common people or to men in sympathy with Wall Street." The growing enthusiasm for unlimited coinage displayed many of the elements of a great religious revival, and
in 1894 appeared the Bible of the new faith—a cheaply printed tract,
Coin's Financial School by William H. Harvey. This little volume,
enlivened with caricatures and written for the common man, set forth
cogently the main silver arguments and skillfully played upon the
prejudices of the poor against the rich. Selling more than a hundred
thousand copies a month in 1895, it made numberless converts. In
schoolhouses throughout the West and the South the people assembled
to debate the burning question. All joined in. "The dragon's teeth
were sprouting in every corner of the land," wrote an observer.
"Women with skins tanned to parchment by the hot winds, with bony
hands of toil and clad in faded calico, could talk in meeting, and
could talk straight to the point." Organized labor also rallied to the
cause, the executive council of the American Federation of Labor
warmly endorsing free silver.

The old parties were badly frightened, but knew not what to do.
In their state conventions before the autumn elections of 1894 the
platforms of both Republicans and Democrats varied from ambiguous
generalities to forthright declarations for unlimited coinage. A significant demonstration among Western Democrats took place in June
at Omaha where, under the leadership of William Jennings Bryan of
Nebraska, a mammoth convention demanded the immediate adoption
of free silver. Handicapped by Cleveland's unpopularity, the Demo-

crats suffered severe losses at the polls. Though the Republicans were the chief gainers, the Populists elected six Senators and boosted their vote by nearly half over that of 1892.

THE SILVER CRUSADE

On the heels of the election the silver Democrats set about to cast off Eastern control of the party and commit the next national convention to their doctrine. In Chicago on July 7, 1896, they succeeded over bitter opposition. The platform acclaimed free silver as the question "paramount to all others," assailed the income-tax decision and, rebuking the party's own President for his actions in the Pullman strike, denounced federal intervention in labor conflicts. In the debate over the platform, William Jennings Bryan, speaking with a full-toned, richly modulated eloquence unmatched in his generation, presented the free-coinage issue as "a cause as holy as the cause of humanity." To its foes he thundered, "You tell us that the great cities are in favor of the gold standard; we reply that the great cities rest upon our broad and fertile prairies. Burn down your cities and leave our farms, and your cities will spring up again as if by magic; but destroy our farms and the grass will grow in the streets of every city in the country." His closing defiance to the gold adherents brought the vast audience in a frenzy to its feet: "You shall not press down upon the brow of labor this crown of thorns; you shall not crucify mankind upon a cross of gold." The 'Boy Orator of the Platte'—he was thirty-six years old—had made himself the man of the hour. Without strength before the convention met, he won the nomination on the fifth ballot, the second place going to Arthur Sewall, a Maine banker who shared Bryan's financial views. Most of the Eastern delegates abstained from voting.

When the Republicans gathered in St. Louis on June 16, their ranks were divided between advocates of the gold standard, those who preferred the customary policy of evasion, and a resolute minority from the Far West clamorous for free silver. William McKinley of Ohio, known chiefly as an ardent protectionist, was the leading candidate, thanks to the tireless endeavors of Marcus A. Hanna, a wealthy Cleveland industrialist. Hanna's efforts and money had facilitated his friend's election as governor in 1891, and when two years later McKinley became involved in heavy financial obligations, Hanna joined with Carnegie, Frick and others in supplying the $130,000 needed to save him from bankruptcy. In preparing the way for the presidential nomination Hanna spent not less than $100,000 in a campaign of publicity and personal canvass among the delegates. But the question of a monetary standard posed difficulties for McKinley, since until recently he had been a champion of free silver. Partly because of his earlier stand and partly because of his conciliatory nature and the fear that a gold pronouncement would "divide the party at the Mississippi River," he wanted the convention to straddle the issue in favor of the tariff.

Hanna, sinking the businessman in the politician, assented, but not so the powerful leaders from the industrial regions, who made a gold avowal the price of their support. The outcome was a shrewdly devised plank which read in part, "We are opposed to the free coinage of silver except by international agreement with the leading commercial nations of the world, which we pledge ourselves to promote, and until such agreement can be obtained the existing gold standard must be preserved." Taken literally, the platform declared for international free silver, but since various intergovernmental conferences had demonstrated European unwillingness to abandon the gold standard, the utterance was rightly construed by the silverites as a rejection of free coinage. Thirty-four delegates, with Colorado's Senator Henry M. Teller at their head, bolted the convention in protest. In the completed platform the money plank appeared inconspicuously in the middle, the first nine paragraphs being devoted to berating the Democrats and praising the protective system. McKinley was named on the first ballot, with Garret A. Hobart of New Jersey as his teammate.

The action of the two conventions caused a disruption of party loyalties comparable to the impact of the slavery issue on the voters of 1860. A gathering of old-school Democrats with Cleveland's approval reaffirmed the gold standard and nominated John M. Palmer of Illinois and Simon B. Buckner of Kentucky. Had McKinley's platform been less emphatic on the tariff, they might have come out for him. The Republican irreconcilables, calling themselves the National Silver Party, endorsed Bryan and Sewall, and, as was to be expected, the Populists also backed Bryan, though for Vice-President they chose one of their own group, Tom Watson of Georgia, in preference to the Maine capitalist. Even the Prohibitionists were affected by the all-absorbing issue and split into two parties with different platforms and tickets.

In the electioneering, the Republicans at first avoided the money question, putting all stress upon 'Bill McKinley and the McKinley Bill,' but Bryan forced their hand by going on an eighteen-thousand-mile tour, addressing nearly five million people in twenty-nine states, and everywhere preaching free silver and the gospel of discontent. Samuel Gompers and other labor leaders also spoke for the Democrats, while Homer Davenport in Hearst's *New York Journal* cartooned Mark Hanna, the Republican campaign manager, as a pot-bellied figure checkered with dollar marks, leading the child McKinley on a leash. For financial sinews the Democrats leaned upon the silver-mine owners, something like $500,000 being raised in all. But Hanna collected from the business and banking interests a sum nearly ten times as great—perhaps considerably more, since the exact amount is unknown—and with it he financed a vast number of rallies, parades, posters and pamphlets. In the last week he had eighteen thousand speakers on the stump. McKinley, pictured on billboards through-out the country as "The Advance Agent of Prosperity," remained quietly at home, delivering from his front porch in Canton, Ohio, carefully staged addresses to visiting delegations. Though Cleveland himself kept mum, the electorate witnessed the singular spectacle of all the members of his cabinet openly repudiating their party's choice.

As the contest drew toward an end, the excitement became intense. Manufacturers made contracts contingent upon McKinley's victory, and wage earners were told that otherwise the factories would close and their families starve. The Democratic national chairman charged that "with scarcely an exception" the great corporations were "engaged in a concerted effort to coerce their employees to vote against their convictions." By such newspapers as the *New York Tribune* Bryan was reviled as an "anarchist" and a "madman." The *New York Mail* declared, "No wild-eyed and rattle-brained horde of the red flag ever proclaimed a fiercer defiance of law, precedent, order, and government," while the *Evening Post* saw the struggle as one between "the great civilizing forces of the republic" and "the still surviving barbarism bred by slavery in the South and the reckless spirit of adventure in the mining camps of the West." One Republican spellbinder, commending the sobriquet 'Boy Orator of the

Platte,' asserted that that river was "six inches deep and six miles wide at the mouth." More to the point for the Republicans, however, was the fact that in the week before the election crop failures in Russia, the Argentine and elsewhere lifted the price of wheat from fifty-three cents a bushel in August to ninety-four, thus encouraging the farmers to return to their traditional allegiance.

The outcome was decisive. McKinley received 51 per cent of the popular ballots (7,112,000) to less than 47 per cent (6,733,000) for his opponent, the largest majority since Grant beat Greeley. His preponderance in the electoral college was far greater: 271 to 176. In general, the industrial and older grain-growing states supported McKinley as against the cotton, prairie and silver-mining states. As was to be expected, Bryan polled a considerably smaller proportion of the votes of the cities than of the rural sections, and for the first time the Republicans carried New York City. They also swept both houses of Congress. The farmers' attempt to beat back the urban and industrial civilization had turned to rout. "God's in his Heaven, all's right with the world," Hanna jubilantly wired the President-elect upon learning the returns. The future, however, was to disclose that dynamic new forces, never again to be stilled, had entered political life.

McKinley was a man of different stamp from his Democratic predecessor, suave where Cleveland had been blunt, resolved always to keep step with his party, and "wise," as William Allen White noted, "with the ancient lore of politics, crafty with the ways that win men and hold them." To obtain a seat for his benefactor Mark Hanna in the Senate he created a vacancy in that body by naming seventy-four-year-old John Sherman Secretary of State; but mental impairment caused Sherman to be replaced after a year by another Ohioan, William R. Day, and on the latter's retirement in August, 1898, John Hay, a third Ohioan, came into the office to serve eventually through the first term of McKinley's successor.[1]

Notwithstanding the apparent popular verdict against silver, McKinley chose to interpret his triumph as primarily a mandate for tariff protection, which, as has been seen, the party carried out in the

---

[1] The other members of the original cabinet were Lyman J. Gage of Illinois, Secretary of the Navy; Henry C. Wallace of Iowa, Secretary of Agriculture; and James of California, Attorney-General; James A. Gary of Maryland, Postmaster-General; John D. Long of Massachusetts, Secretary of the Navy; Cornelius N. Bliss of New York, Secretary of the Interior; and James Wilson of Iowa, Secretary of Agriculture.

Dingley Act of 1897. The fact was that the Republicans remained uncertain and divided on the money question despite their united front during the campaign; hence it seemed good political strategy to let well enough alone. However, in deference to the platform pledge, an official commission conferred with France and Great Britain in 1897 as to the possibility of establishing free silver by international agreement. Britain's anticipated refusal, followed presently by the distracting effects of the Spanish-American War, eased the path for the gold adherents. Other events worked to the same end. After 1896 a period of bewildering prosperity burst upon the country. It was accompanied by an immense increase in the gold supply, thanks to the new cyanide process of extracting the metal from low-content ores and to the discovery of fresh deposits in Alaska, Australia and South Africa. The world's annual output, which had averaged between 5,000,000 and 6,000,000 ounces from 1860 to 1890, climbed to nearly 11,500,000 in 1897 and to 22,000,000 in 1910. The volume of paper currency also grew because of the purchase by national banks of the government bonds issued during the war with Spain as well as a liberalization of the National Banking Act. With all reasonable fear of the scarcity of money removed, the argument for silver inflation collapsed.

Moreover, this time the agricultural regions shared in the good times. A recurrence of foreign crop failures in 1897 shot the price of wheat even higher than in the preceding season. As the farmers recovered a sense of material well-being, some of the worst psychological drawbacks of rural life were also lessened. The beginning of rural free delivery of mail in 1896, the spread of mutual telephone companies in farm communities after the expiration of the basic Bell patents in 1893, the advent of improved roads and interurban electric railways and an increase of country schools assured advantages which earlier had been confined to the city. These new conveniences of living—a mere earnest of what the future held in store—helped to dispel the solitude and loneliness and to relieve the feeling of rural inferiority.

In March, 1900, Congress took the long-awaited step. The Gold Standard Act declared other forms of money redeemable in gold on demand and enlarged the supporting fund to $150,000,000. In order to avoid the difficulties that had vexed the Cleveland administration, the law made the gold reserve a separate and distinct account, not to be drawn upon for current deficiencies in the revenue, and it provided further that, when paper notes were offered for redemption, they should not be paid out again except for gold. Thus the war of the standards closed, leaving the next generation to solve certain knotty problems arising from other imperfections of the circulating medium, notably its inelastic character.

FULLER ACCOUNTS

The Rural Revolt. Hicks, *Populist Revolt,* traces with impartial hand the history of the Farmers' Alliances, the People's party and the 1896 election, and his bibliography lists state, biographical and other studies, including Croly, *Hanna;* Fine, *Labor and Farmer Parties;* and Olcott, *McKinley.* Of additional works, Billington, *Westward Expansion,* Oberholtzer, *History,* V, Schlesinger, *Rise of the City,* Shannon, *Farmer's Last Frontier,* and Tarbell, *Nationalizing of Business,* shed light on the farmers' predicament, while Ellis, *Teller,* Nevins, *Cleveland,* Simkins, *Tillman,* Werner, *Bryan,* and Woodward, *Watson,* feature particular leaders. More specifically for the silver controversy, see Laughlin, *History of Bimetallism,* and Noyes, *Forty Years of American Finance,* and, for the business slump and its effects, Lauck, *Causes of the Panic of 1893,* Weberg, *Background of the Panic of 1893,* Feder, *Unemployment Relief,* and McMurry, *Coxey's Army.*

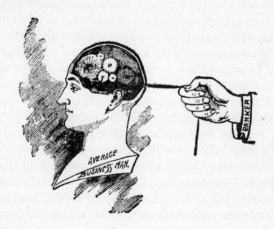

CHAPTER VIII

THE FLOWERING OF NATIONALITY

THE MORE PERFECT UNION

Between 1870 and 1900—the lifetime of a single generation—the federal system grew from thirty-eight states to forty-five, and the population nearly doubled, rising from 38,558,000 to 75,995,000. But despite this increase of extent and people the bonds of nationality became stronger rather than weaker. The 1896 campaign, for example, revealed deep antagonisms between sections of the country; yet, though the farmers' dilemma was no less real than had been that of the slaveholders, there were no threats of nullification or secession, no John C. Calhoun or Jefferson Davis sounding the tocsin of state sovereignty. Many things were responsible for the "more perfect union." The defeat of the Southern Confederacy had not only ensured the nation's geographic solidarity, but the awful expenditure of blood and treasure had infused the concept of nationality with a mystical quality. The adventure of settling the Far West heightened the sense of national accomplishment, while the Economic Revolution knitted the country together ever more tightly with strands of steel and ties of mutual interest, causing men to think in terms of the nation as a whole rather than of particular states. As James Bryce observed, "The South and the West need capital for their development, and are daily in closer business relations with the East. The produce of the West finds its way to the Atlantic through the ports of the East. Every produce market, every share market, vibrates in response to the Produce Exchange and Stock Exchange of New York."

Other influences—the increasing urbanization and standardizing of American life, the extension of public schools to all parts of the land, the universal appeal of the new literature, the widespread absorption in athletic sport—yielded a similar result. As the republic reached the centenary of its birth, pride of nationality begot a series of great patriotic celebrations, first observing the battles of Concord and Lexington and then going on year after year until the setting up

162

of the Supreme Court was duly commemorated in 1890. Responsive
to the nationalizing trend, innumerable country-wide voluntary associations sprang up—not only of capital and labor, but also, it will be
recalled, of scholars, scientists, artists, social and political reformers,
sport lovers and secret-society joiners. Andrew Carnegie, paying
grateful tribute to his adopted country in *Triumphant Democracy*
(1886), noted, "Groups of men with allied interests invariably have
an organization to watch over the common weal," a trait which he
attributed to the natural instincts of a "people trained to govern itself."
Whatever the cause, the effect in erasing local attachments and substituting larger loyalties was incalculable. In view of these various
factors it is little wonder that Edward A. Freeman, visiting America
in 1882, observed that "where the word 'federal' used to be used up
to the time of the civil war or later, the word 'national' is now used
all but invariably. It used to be 'federal capital,' 'federal army,' 'federal
revenue,' and so forth. Now the word 'national' is almost always used
instead." Yet only twenty years before, the Englishman had ominously
entitled one of his works *History of Federal Government from the
Foundation of the Achaian League to the Disruption of the United
States.*

No part of the country afforded clearer evidence of the resurgent
nationalism than the one which had recently tried to overturn the
government. Despite the folly of Republican politicians in waving
the bloody shirt, nearly every year brought fresh proof that the South
accepted its defeat not only in good faith but with increasing satisfaction. Even Jefferson Davis, writing in 1881 without apology for
the past, expressed the earnest hope that "there may be written on the
arch of the Union, *Esto perpetua.*" About the same time veterans'
organizations of the blue and the gray began to hold joint reunions in
order to compare wartime experiences in a spirit of amity and mutual
respect. The Virginian, John S. Wise, probably voiced the sentiment
of most who had fought on his side when he wrote in the 1890's,
"Through our tears, and without disloyalty to the dead, in the possession of freedom and union and liberty, true Confederates, viewing
it all in the clearer light of to-day, ought to thank God that slavery
died at Appomattox." Behind this change of attitude lay a multitude
of reasons, notably the South's recovery of home rule in race relations,
a better knowledge of the Northern people as a result of freer inter-
migration, Dixie's increasing identification with the national economic

order and, not of least importance, the healing balm of time and the oncoming of a new generation. Moreover, Southern local-color fiction, winning nation-wide acclaim, did much to restore sectional self-esteem while giving Northerners a mellow and romantic picture of Southern life and ideals to offset the old abolitionist exaggerations. All these tendencies reached a climax in the Spanish War of 1898. For the first time the former foemen were called upon to face a common enemy. The jubilant response stilled the last faint notes of ancient discord. Congress, for its part, now removed the remaining disabilities imposed on ex-Confederate leaders under the Fourteenth Amendment. None could doubt that the Union had become one in spirit as well as in name.

In national politics the centripetal tide swept parties and leaders before it. The Republicans as the heirs of Hamilton welcomed it; the Democrats, true to their Jeffersonian lineage, decried it; but even the Democrats when in power yielded to the current. The Republicans abetted federal centralization not only through the Thirteenth, Fourteenth and Fifteenth Amendments, but also through tariff protection and lavish grants for railroad, river and harbor development, while a Democratic House originated and a Democratic President signed the Interstate Commerce Act. The fact is that whether men sought to quicken or curb the mighty forces remaking the economic order, they turned to Washington, not to their legislatures, for decisive action. When Cleveland defied the state-rights interpretation of the Constitution by intervening in the Pullman strike, Governor Altgeld felt obliged to remind him that "the principle of local self-government is just as fundamental in our institutions as is that of Federal supremacy." Yet there was no time when Altgeld and others of progressive or radical views would not gladly have used federal authority to achieve ends they themselves wanted. Bryce acutely pointed out that the state, once a "self-sufficing commonwealth," was becoming "merely a part of a far grander whole, which seems to be slowly absorbing its functions and stunting its growth, as the great tree stunts the shrubs over which its spreading boughs have begun to cast their shade." The twentieth century was to bring an even greater expansion of national power.

The judiciary succumbed more reluctantly to the centripetal trend. The "convenient vagueness" of the first section of the Fourteenth Amendment admitted of a variety of interpretations, but the Supreme

Court's early decisions buttressed the authority of the states. "No State," reads the amendment, "shall make or enforce any law that shall abridge the privileges or immunities of citizens of the United States; nor shall any State deprive any person of life, liberty, or property, without due process of law; nor deny to any person within its jurisdiction the equal protection of the laws." In the Slaughterhouse cases (1873) certain butchers of New Orleans had asked the Supreme Court to annul the monopoly of slaughtering which a Carpetbag legislature had granted a local company for the city and its environs. They charged that the action abridged their "privileges and immunities" as "citizens of the United States" and, further, that it deprived "persons" of property "without due process of law" and withheld "the equal protection of the laws." The judges by a bare majority decided that there was a difference between state citizenship and national citizenship, and that since the privileges and immunities in dispute belonged to state citizenship, the complainants could obtain relief only from Louisiana. As for the other contentions, the Court denied that the statute in question involved a deprivation of property without due process of law and held that the provision for equal protection was intended for Negroes. Four years later the Court in the Granger cases again sided with the states by upholding the untrammeled right of Illinois to fix rates for businesses "clothed with a public interest" and rejecting the plea that property was being taken without due process.

But in the 1880's the judiciary shifted to a boldly national position, an outlook hastened by the appointment of younger judges to replace three of the older ones. In the case of Santa Clara County v. Southern Pacific Railroad (1886) the Court greatly broadened the scope of the Fourteenth Amendment by construing the word "person" to include artificial as well as natural persons, thus bringing corporations within the amendment's protection. The same year the Court held in the Wabash case, contrary to the Granger cases, that states could not regulate rates that affected interstate commerce. In the Minnesota Rate case (1890) the judges, going even further, rejected the state's uncontrolled right to fix rates of any kind, declaring in effect that under the due-process clause the Court was the final authority as to the reasonableness of charges. In these and other later decisions the tribunal arrogated to itself the power of reviewing most state and local legislation affecting private property. That its actions generally helped the great corporate interests is less important in the present connection than that the Court, sensitive at last to the centralizing impulse, assumed the high function of arbiter and censor of the whole economic order.

As so often in American history, the nationalizing process paralleled a similar one in Europe. After Italy, Austria-Hungary, the French Republic and the German Empire set up national states in the 1860's and early 1870's, the tendency everywhere was to strengthen the central organs of authority at the expense of local autonomy, thus enabling the government to exercise increasing control over economic and social life. Bismarck in Germany, Crispi in Italy and Witte in Russia typify the statesmen who guided and directed this consolidating trend. Thus the United States, though prompted by its own needs and compulsions, reflected a world movement.

THE CHANGING ATTITUDE TOWARD IMMIGRATION

The heightened sense of nationality also engendered a new attitude toward immigration. Since colonial times people from other lands had flocked to America without let or hindrance. The majority had been farmers and workingmen from Western and Northern Europe. Of the 6,680,000 foreign-born in 1880, the Germans numbered about 2,000,000, the Irish 1,855,000, the Canadians 717,000, the English 664,000 and the Scandinavians 440,000. These arrivals had generally taken up farming, and in 1880 a larger proportion of immigrants lived in the Upper Mississippi Valley than in any other section. They were easily assimilated, coming as they did from the stocks from which the Anglo-Saxon people had originally sprung, and so greatly were they desired that the newer states maintained official bureaus to attract them. The railroads also helped, in some instances arranging to teach them prairie agriculture and to provide schoolhouses and churches. With plenty of land for everyone, their advent caused no shock to the economic structure. America's traditional hospitality to Europe's needy was fittingly commemorated by the inscription of Emma Lazarus for the base of the Goddess of Liberty, that huge statue erected at the entrance of New York Harbor in 1886 by the generosity of the French people:

"Keep, ancient lands, your storied pomp!" cries she
With silent lips. "Give me your tired, your poor,

Your huddled masses yearning to breathe free,
The wretched refuse of your teeming shore.
Send those, the homeless, tempest-tost to me.
I lift my lamp beside the golden door."

But while the monument was still being completed, events were foreshadowing a less cordial attitude. The turning point came in 1882, the year when the influx from Western and Northern Europe reached its crest, noticeable numbers began to arrive from Eastern and Southern Europe, and Congress enacted the first important restrictive law. The hosts from Russia, Austria-Hungary, Italy and other Mediterranean countries increased as time went on until in 1896 they exceeded those of the older type. Many influences accounted for this 'new immigration,' notably the oppression of minorities in the home countries, the desire to escape military service, the opening of direct steamship connections between Mediterranean ports and the United States, and the opportunities of employment in the new mines and factories. Steamship companies aided by low rates for steerage passengers, while agents of American corporations offered to prepay the passage of laborers agreeing to work at wages that seemed to Europeans fantastically high but to Americans fantastically low.

The new immigrants did not fade so quickly into the American population as had the old. Poverty-stricken and hiving in the industrial centers, they established self-contained communities that clung tenaciously to Old World customs and languages and vastly complicated the problems of sanitation, health and housing for the city authorities. Moreover, since one out of every three planned to go back home after laying aside a little money, many were indifferent when not openly hostile to labor's efforts to improve working conditions. Poorly educated, if educated at all, most of them also lacked familiarity with democratic institutions and ideals. Though they were widely charged with responsibility for municipal misrule, this could hardly have been true when 'American' cities like Philadelphia and Portland, Oregon, were as badly governed as polyglot New York and Chicago. Individuals among them proved equal to the best that the older strains produced, while the bulk of these Slavs, Magyars, Poles, Russians, Italians, Greeks and others supplied the heavy labor upon which the Economic Revolution of these years rested.

The swelling tide from Eastern and Southern Europe hastened the adoption of a new national policy toward immigrants. The conviction was growing that, with the dwindling of free homesteads in the West and the formidable problems raised by the herding of aliens in cities,

Where the Old and New Immigrants Came From

the national interest called for some degree of selection. Organized labor urged the same course to safeguard its members against unfair competition, while persons whose patriotism had been kindled by the historical centennials joined in out of pride of ancestry, asking, "Who shall respect a people who do not respect their own blood?" Congress responded with legislation of increasing severity. The act of 1882 excluded lunatics, convicts and persons likely to become public charges. Three years later the Alien Labor Contract Law forbade employers to import workingmen under previous contract. Every few years brought further restrictions until by 1903 the prohibited classes embraced physical, mental and moral defectives of all kinds, contagious cases, professional beggars, assisted immigrants, polygamists and anarchists.

Since 35 per cent of the Southern and Eastern Europeans were illiterate as against only 3 per cent of those from the North and West, this afforded a way to discriminate against the new immigration in favor of the old. But the proposal of a literacy test ran into vigorous objections on the ground that ability to read gave evidence of youthful opportunity, not of mental capacity or social usefulness. President Cleveland, vetoing such a bill shortly before leaving office in 1897, dismissed the charges as to the inferiority of the later arrivals by saying, "The time is quite within recent memory when the same thing was said of immigrants who, with their descendants, are now numbered among our best citizens." A literacy test had to await another twenty years.

The sheer magnitude of the immigration is amazing. Between 1865 and 1900 no fewer than thirteen and a half million entered the United States—a total exceeding by more than a million the entire population in 1830—and the volume was to become larger. "During the last ten years," wrote Josiah Strong in 1891, "we have suffered a peaceful invasion by an army four times as vast as the estimated numbers of Goths and Vandals that swept over Southern Europe and overwhelmed Rome." The flooding stream changed the social composition of certain sections in startling ways. As *Donahoe's Magazine* pointed out in 1889, "Boston is no longer the Boston of the Endicotts and the Winthrops, but the Boston of the Collinses and the O'Briens." Greater New York was then the world's largest center of foreign-born, a veritable amalgam of nations, with half as many Italians as Naples, as many Germans as Hamburg, twice as many Irish as Dublin and two and a half times as many Jews as Warsaw. Chicago, hardly less cosmopolitan, possessed more Czechs, Poles and Canadians than New York, while the great agricultural empire to its northwest seemed about to be turning into a new Scandinavia.

Yet everywhere, even in the dense population centers and among foreigners of the new sort, the 'melting pot' was quietly at work. As James Bryce observed, "The intellectual and moral atmosphere into which the settlers from Europe come has more power to assimilate them than their race qualities have to change it." Sometimes, unusual business success or the liberalizing effect of belonging to a labor union hastened the process. More often, it was the democratic school system that carried the influences of the new land into the immigrant home. The American-born children were apt to intermarry with other national stocks and accept American ways and ideals so zealously as wholly to forget their ancestral culture.

Though the government raised the bars higher and higher against undesired individuals from Europe, it did not go so far as to proscribe whole peoples. This more drastic course, however, it adopted toward the Oriental influx on the Pacific Coast. In the fifties and sixties Chinese cheap labor had been in such demand in California that Leland Stanford and other captains of industry imported whole shiploads of coolies. While the total was still less than 60,000, the United States made the Burlingame Treaty of 1868 with China, which explicitly recognized the "inalienable right of man to change his home and allegiance, and also the mutual advantage of the free migration and emigration." Soon, however, local sentiment turned against the newcomers. In the next decade their number rose to over 100,000, and European immigrants, multiplying in California as the transcontinental railroads were completed, found themselves competing for jobs with a people content with a lower standard of living than the white man had ever known. As Robert Louis Stevenson, sojourning in California, wrote, "Hungry Europe and hungry China, each pouring from their gates in search of provender, had here come face to face." Racial differences and a belief in the unassimilability of the Orientals further sharpened the antagonism.

As early as 1871 twenty-one Chinese were killed in a riot in Los Angeles, and for the next ten years the question of the 'yellow peril' convulsed the state. A Workingmen's party adopted the slogan, 'The Chinese must go,' mobs attacked the 'Chinatowns' of San Francisco and other places, and the legislature passed discriminatory laws, though most of these were annulled by the courts. In time the violence of the agitation aroused national attention. In 1879 the Democratic House of Representatives, vying with the Republican Senate for the electoral vote of California, joined in a bill revoking the Burlingame Treaty and restricting Chinese immigration. But President Hayes, disapproving the method though not the purpose, vetoed it and instead negotiated a new pact with China. The Treaty of 1880 permitted the

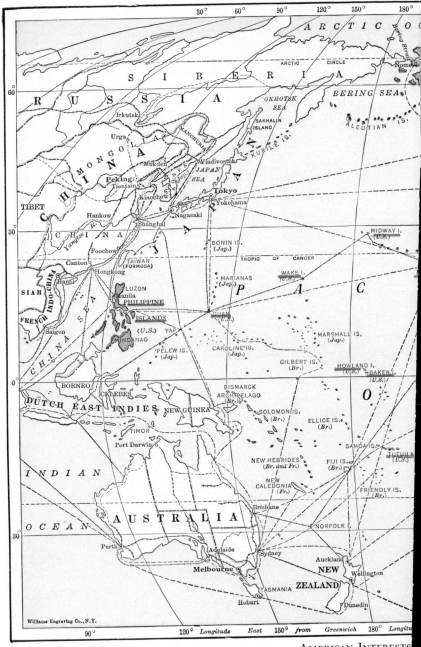

AMERICAN INTERESTS

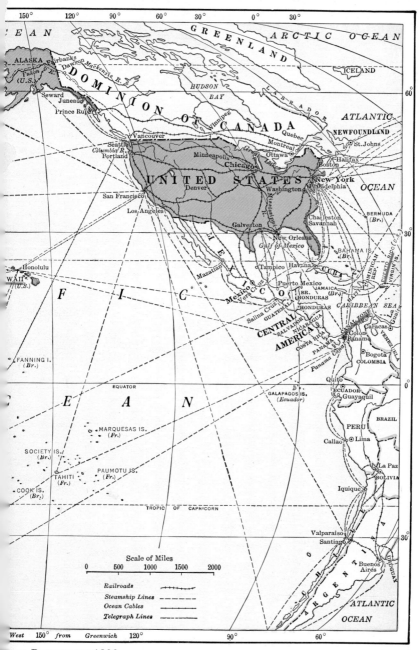

United States to "regulate, limit, or suspend" but "not absolutely prohibit" future coolie immigration, and two years later Congress passed a ten-year exclusion law. Subsequent acts renewed the suspension from time to time until Congress in 1902 made the ban indefinite. Though China in 1904 declined to lend the practice further treaty sanction, the United States continued the prohibition upon its own authority.

THE WANING OF ISOLATIONISM

With the enhanced nationalism at home came a new attitude in foreign affairs. Though avowals of isolationism and warnings against 'entangling alliances' continued to mark the utterances of statesmen, the march of events irresistibly loosed the nation from ancient moorings. As the Economic Revolution gained momentum, industrialists found they needed to look beyond the national borders to market their growing surplus of goods, and capitalists began to scan the globe for opportunities to supplement their domestic investments. Between 1870 and 1900 exports rose from a value of less than $393,000,000 to nearly $1,395,000,000, while American investments in other countries leaped from an unknown but trifling amount to $500,000,000. As the Bureau of Foreign Commerce noted in 1897, "The 'international isolation' of the United States so far as industry and commerce are concerned has, in fact, been made a thing of the past by the logic of the change in our economic requirements . . . now that we ourselves have become a competitor in the world-wide struggle for trade."

Other influences operated to the same end. Missionary activity, particularly in the Pacific islands and the Orient, had long been a feature of American life, and the advantages of carrying the blessings of Christianity to 'benighted heathen' living under the Stars and Stripes made a strong appeal. With some, this religious aspiration was blended with a deep conviction of the superiority of the Anglo-Saxon stock to all others. As the Reverend Josiah Strong told the countless readers of *Our Country* (1885), "This race of unequaled energy, with all the majesty of numbers and the might of wealth behind it—the representative, let us hope, of the largest liberty, the purest Christianity, the highest civilization— . . . will move down upon Mexico, down upon Central and South America, out upon the islands of the sea." Equally important was the fact that the national spirit of adventure and acquisition, now thwarted by the occupation of the last continental frontier, sought fresh channels for expression. "In our infancy we bordered upon the Atlantic only," wrote Captain Alfred T. Mahan in 1893 in a plea for greater sea power, "our youth carried our boundary to the Gulf of Mexico; to-day maturity sees us upon the Pacific. Have we no right or no call to progress farther in any direction?"

Obedient to the broadening outlook, the Navy Department throughout the 1880's urged a bigger and better navy. Other powers had gone over to steel ships, but the United States vessels still consisted of wood. Even some South American governments possessed warships which singlehandedly could have destroyed the entire American navy. In 1883 Congress under President Arthur made a start with four steel cruisers; Cleveland in his first term provided additional steel ships (including the ill-fated *Maine* of Spanish War fame), improvements in armament, stronger coast defenses and a naval ordnance plant; and Harrison built the initial first-class battleships, bringing the 'new navy' to a total of twenty-two modern vessels. By 1893 the United States had advanced from twelfth to fifth place as a sea power, and by 1900 to third.

Impelled by similar motives, the government departed increasingly from its hermitlike seclusion in world affairs. Against all earlier precedent the United States between 1865 and 1900 joined in fifteen collective treaties dealing with such subjects as submarine cables, patents, weights and measures, and the suppression of the African slave trade. Of the various commitments none aroused keener interest at home than the adherence to the Geneva Convention for establishing the International Red Cross Society. This agreement, formed originally by sixteen European nations in 1864, provided that in every country concerned there should be set up a civilian organization to co-operate in time of war with the army medical corps in caring for the sick and wounded. Long indifferent, the Washington government in 1882 was finally brought to act through the persistence of Clara Barton of Massachusetts, who as a nurse in the Franco-Prussian War had learned the superiority of the Red Cross to the United States Sanitary Commission in the Civil War. To her also belongs credit for the 'American Amendment' to the Geneva Convention in 1884, which extended the Red Cross's activities to peacetime humanitarian work during floods, earthquakes and other public disasters.

Meanwhile the Washington authorities awoke to the need of promoting trade and investments in two sections of the world where rich opportunities still beckoned: the Pacific area and Latin America. The former constituted, in the language of diplomacy, a 'backward region' subject to domination and seizure by 'more advanced' powers; the latter offered a market which American businessmen had hitherto done little to develop. The new policies were adopted hesitantly and without a predetermined program, but they quickly carried the United States to the edge of the powerful current of imperialism that late in the seventies had begun to overspread Europe. Far more than America, these nations felt the urge to obtain new markets and sources of raw materials, find fresh fields for the export of capital, enhance their national prestige and acquire territories in which to colonize their surplus populations. Before 1890 Great Britain, France and Germany had divided up most of Africa with portions for Italy and Belgium. Between 1870 and 1900 the British Empire grew by about 5,000,000 square miles exclusive of spheres of influence, while France picked up 3,500,000 and Germany 1,000,000. In the Pacific, as will be seen, the advancing outposts of Europe and America clashed, necessitating an adjustment of interests. In Latin America, however, Washington was able to play virtually a lone hand, thanks largely to the Monroe Doctrine, which kept Europe at arm's length. Not only economic interest but historical considerations and geographic proximity impelled the United States to seek dominance there.

THE ADVANCE INTO THE PACIFIC

For many reasons the Hawaiian Islands in the mid-Pacific were of special concern to America. They had long been a resort of traders and whalers. Lying halfway between California and the Asian mainland, the little archipelago was also well situated for a commercial coaling station, a naval base and a cable landing. Yankee missionaries had reduced the native language to writing and helped modernize the government; many of their children became landholders and sugar planters. In 1875 a treaty granted sugar and other Hawaiian products access to the United States duty free and in return pledged the insular king not to dispose of any territory to another country. This was followed in 1884 by the lease of Pearl Harbor, near Honolulu, as a naval station. By 1890 American cane plantations were valued at $25,000,000. But the McKinley Tariff in that year dealt the sugar growers a damaging blow. By putting all foreign sugar on the free list it took away Hawaii's favored position, and by providing bounties for United States producers it further handicapped the American planters in Hawaii. Annexation would, of course, cure these difficulties, and as a result sentiment for this step developed rapidly.

In January, 1893, the opportunity came. The illiberal queen was deposed by a revolt engineered by American residents who received moral support at least from United States marines landed for that purpose. The revolutionary government, made up of Americans and other foreigners, promptly negotiated a treaty of annexation, but Harrison's term expired before the Senate could act. President Cleveland, a stanch foe of imperialism, recalled the treaty from the Senate, and after an official inquiry disclosed the American Minister's complicity in the revolt, he denounced the whole transaction. Yet his action only delayed the inevitable. Japan cast hungry eyes on the tiny republic, and the British were also known to be interested. Hence when the Republicans returned to power and the Philippine operations of the Spanish-American War dramatized the naval advantages of ownership, Congress in July, 1898, acquired the islands by joint resolution. "Annexation," declared McKinley, "is not a change. It is a consummation."

Meanwhile another series of events was preparing a foothold for the United States far to the south. Four thousand miles from San Francisco, on the direct trade route to Sydney, Australia, lay the Samoan Islands. One of the group, Tutuila, possessed in Pago Pago the finest harbor of the South Pacific. In 1872 a treaty was negotiated for a naval station in Samoa, but the Senate let it die. Six years later, however, a new treaty accomplished the object, with the United States pledging in return its "good offices" to adjust difficulties between the native king and other nations. Great Britain and Germany also secured treaty rights in Samoa, and the islands soon became a miniature storm center of international intrigue and conflict. In 1886, to block German designs, the American consul proclaimed a protectorate, an act, however, which President Cleveland promptly disavowed. Germany continuing aggressive, all three powers hurried warships to the scene in March, 1889. A destructive hurricane swept away hostile feeling for the moment and led to a treaty guaranteeing Samoa's independence and neutrality under a tripartite protectorate. But this arrangement, indubitably an 'entangling alliance,' did not work well,

Playing Croquet, 1869

Bicycling on Riverside Drive, 1895
See pages 143–144.

A PERILOUS SITUATION.

THE PRODUCERS OF THE COUNTRY IN DANGER FROM SILVER DEMAGOGUES AND POPULISTS.

AN EASTERN VIEW OF FREE SILVER
See page 151.

and in 1899 the three countries agreed to partition the islands. The United States received Tutuila and several minor islands, Germany took the rest, and Great Britain was compensated with other Pacific possessions of Germany, including a part of the Solomon Islands.

Besides these more noteworthy accessions, the United States in the eighties and nineties asserted jurisdiction over more than fifty scattered small islands, mere specks on the face of the Pacific. Among the largest were Wake, Canton, Enderbury, Gallego, Starbuck, Penrhyn, Palmyra, Howland, Baker, Jarvis, Gardner, Morell and Marcus. It was not clear what national advantage accrued from these annexations, but it was supposed that some of the islands might prove useful as relay cable stations. In the next century they acquired an unsuspected importance as potential air bases and radio stations.

RELATIONS WITH LATIN AMERICA

In Latin America the United States sought leadership rather than dominion. Hitherto the government, concentrating upon the Monroe Doctrine, had been content merely to stand guard against possible military or political intervention by Europe. Now, determined on a more constructive role, it set about to ensure greater peace and stability among the chronically quarreling republics and to tighten Uncle Sam's commercial bonds with them. The State Department repeatedly offered to act as mediator in the controversies and achieved some success. In 1876, for example, the United States arbitrated a boundary dispute between Argentina and Paraguay, and in 1881 Secretary of State James G. Blaine helped to smooth over certain difficulties between Venezuela and France. He failed, however, to stop Chile from waging war in 1881 with Peru and Bolivia over the nitrate districts, Tacna and Arica.

This experience convinced Blaine of the need of general machinery for inter-American arbitration, and when he returned to the State Department under Harrison, he combined that idea with the twin objective of closer economic ties with the republics. The trouble here was that though Latin America sold immense quantities of raw materials to the United States, it bought the bulk of its manufactured goods from Europe. Never very large, America's export trade to the southern countries actually declined between 1860 and 1880. Thanks to Blaine's tireless advocacy, the first Pan American Congress met in Washington in October, 1889, under his chairmanship. Among the subjects considered were a comprehensive system of arbitration, a customs union, a monetary union, uniform patents and trademarks and improved railway and steamship connections. The sole tangible results were the appointment of a committee to report on an intercontinental railroad and the creation in Washington of what became known as the Pan American Union to serve as a permanent clearing house of information. Nevertheless the discussion of common problems did something to dispel mutual jealousies and suspicions and caused the congress to be the forerunner of similar ones in later years. It will also be recalled that Blaine's interest in Latin American trade led to the introduction of the short-lived reciprocity feature into the McKinley Tariff of 1890.

The tender plant of good will, however, received a sudden chill when Patrick Egan, the United States Minister at Santiago, displayed sympathy for the defeated party in the Chilean civil war of 1890–1891. Apparently this former Irish agitator could not bring himself to favor the same side as the English residents there. Other disturbing incidents followed, and finally, on October 16, 1891, a quarrel between seamen on shore leave from the United States ship *Baltimore* and some Chileans in a Valparaiso saloon developed into a riot that resulted in the killing of two Americans and the wounding of seventeen. The provisional Chilean government, regarding the affair as a sailors' brawl, failed to accord satisfaction; and President Harrison, ignoring Secretary Blaine's plea for less peremptory action, threatened to sever diplomatic relations. This move, together with the election of a new government in Chile, brought an apology and the ultimate payment of damages.

However harmful the effect of Harrison's conduct on Latin America, it was pretty much offset a few years later by President Cleveland's handling of Venezuela's boundary controversy with British Guiana. Like so many other South American frontiers this one had never been accurately determined. After years of tedious wrangling with Great Britain, Venezuela began to insist that the question be settled by arbitration, a course which the United States also urged but England rejected. To Washington it seemed as though Britain was seeking to enlarge her borders by bullying a weak and defenseless neighbor. When gold was discovered in the disputed area in 1888, the situation became increasingly critical, with hostile encounters during the next few years between British settlers and the Venezuela police.

Cleveland, whose knowledge of the trouble dated from his first administration, decided in 1895 to bring matters to an issue. In a dispatch of July 20, drafted by Secretary of State Olney, he apprised Great Britain that her failure to submit the quarrel to arbitration looked like an attempt to encroach upon the territory of a free American nation and accordingly fell within the purview of the Monroe Doctrine. If, encouraged by America's indifference, other powers should follow England's example, "it is not inconceivable that the struggle now going on for the acquisition of Africa might be transferred to South America." London was further told that "today the United States is practically sovereign on this continent" and its "infinite resources combined with its isolated position" made it "practically invulnerable against any or all other powers." This dispatch, blunt and provocative, elicited a long-delayed reply from Lord Salisbury, the British Foreign Minister, on November 26 to the effect that the Monroe Doctrine was not involved and that the United States had no warrant to interfere.

Cleveland now took the question out of diplomatic channels. Notifying Congress on December 17 that the Monroe Doctrine was in jeopardy, he requested authority to appoint a boundary commission whose findings the United States would, if need be, enforce against Great Britain. "In making these recommendations," he stated, "I am fully alive to the responsibility incurred and keenly realize all the consequences that may follow." Congress in a burst of patriotism unanimously voted funds for the commission's expenses. To the general public in both nations, unaware of the crisis, Cleveland's message came like a bolt from the blue. Evidences soon appeared on every hand that the two English-speaking peoples were resolved to avert the war which the rashness of their rulers had brought near. True, some Americans felt with the ebullient Teddy Roosevelt: "Let the fight come if it must; I don't care whether our seacoast cities are bombarded or not; we would take Canada." But much more characteristic was the outspoken protest of leading newspapers, church groups and peace societies. Business and financial interests also acted as a brake on the jingoism, the New York Chamber of Commerce sternly rebuking the "war craze" and J. P. Morgan condemning the "threatened disaster" to "relations of confidence" with "the money markets of Europe." In England prominent figures like the Prince of Wales and the Archbishop of Canterbury took a similar stand, and thirteen hundred British authors united in a plea for an amicable settlement.

Joseph Chamberlain, an influential cabinet member, voiced British official opinion when he declared in an address in January, 1896, "We do not covet one single inch of American territory. War between the two nations would be an absurdity as well as a crime. . . . The two nations are allied and more closely allied in sentiment and in interest than any other nations on the face of the earth." Indeed, with Continental Europe already dividing into hostile alliances, British statesmen realized the folly of needlessly antagonizing the principal non-European power.[1] An impending clash with the Boers in South Africa was another reason for avoiding a rupture with the United States. Accordingly, though the American boundary commission had already begun its work, Great Britain agreed to submit the question to international arbitration, and when a treaty for this purpose was drafted in February, 1897, the American commission ceased its labors. In 1899 the new tribunal, much to English satisfaction, awarded to British Guiana the larger part of the disputed area. Despite this outcome London's yielding did much to vindicate Cleveland's claim of America's primacy in the Western Hemisphere. In foreign eyes the Monroe Doctrine gained new prestige. The incident is also significant as marking the adoption of a systematic policy on Britain's part to cultivate closer ties between the two English-speaking powers. The results became increasingly evident in the international developments of the years ahead.

FULLER ACCOUNTS

The More Perfect Union. For the enhanced nationalism, see Curti, *Roots of American Loyalty,* and Gabriel, *American Democratic Thought;* for the upsurge of voluntary associations, Schlesinger, *Paths to the Present,* chap. 2, with bibliography; and for the *rapprochement* of North and South, Buck, *Road to Reunion.* The role of the Supreme Court is shown in Boudin, *Government by Judiciary,* II; Kelly and Harbison, *American Constitution;* and Warren, *Supreme Court in United States History,* II.

The Changing Attitude toward Immigration. Such general treatments as Garis, *Immigration Restriction,* and Wittke, *We Who Built America,* can be supplemented for the 'new immigration' by Balch, *Slavic Fellow Citizens,*

---

[1] The Triple Alliance, formed in 1882 by Germany, Austria and Italy, was renewed from time to time. Russia and France entered into the Dual Alliance in 1894. Great Britain, possessing interests apart from either coalition, held aloof until 1904 when she formed an Entente Cordiale with France and three years later with Russia.

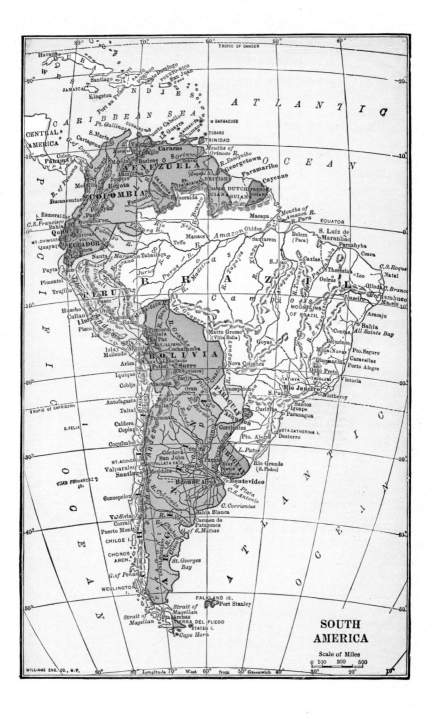

SOUTH
AMERICA

Scale of Miles
0   100   300   500

Burgess, *Greeks in America,* Foerster, *Italian Immigration,* and Joseph, *Jewish Immigration,* and for the Chinese by Coolidge, *Chinese Immigration,* McWilliams, *Brothers under the Skin,* and Sandmeyer, *Anti-Chinese Movement.*

The Waning of Isolationism. Coolidge, *United States as a World Power,* Faries, *Rise of Internationalism,* and Langer, *Diplomacy of Imperialism,* illuminate America's changing position in world affairs, while Pratt, *Expansionists of 1898,* and Weinberg, *Manifest Destiny,* clarify the ideology of expansion and navalism in the United States. The development of the 'new' navy' is traced in Mitchell, *Modern American Navy,* and Sprouts, *Rise of American Naval Power.* Dulles, *American Red Cross,* tells the story of that organization.

The United States in the Pacific and Latin America. Tyler, *Foreign Policy of James G. Blaine,* Dulebohn, *Principles of Foreign Policy under the Cleveland Administrations,* and Tansill, *Foreign Policy of Thomas F. Bayard,* elaborate the shorter accounts in the diplomatic histories by Bailey and Bemis. Special studies of Pacific relations include Dulles, *America in the Pacific;* Ryden, *Foreign Policy of the United States in Relation to Samoa;* Pratt, *Expansionists of 1898* (for Hawaii); and Leff, *Uncle Sam's Pacific Islets.* For Latin America as a separate theme, turn to Perkins, *Hands Off,* and Dennis, *Adventures in American Diplomacy* (for Venezuela). See also Gelder, *Rise of Anglo-American Friendship.* Expositions of leading figures include James, *Olney,* Muzzey, *Blaine,* and Nevins, *Cleveland.*

PART II

DEMOCRACY AND EMPIRE

The basic issue confronting the new generation was set forth by the Democratic platform of 1900: "We assert that no nation can long endure half republic and half empire." Yet, in the years that followed, neither political party was unalterably opposed to colonial adventures, and both did much to broaden democracy at home while condoning or furthering overseas dominion. These contradictory trends give the period its peculiar character. In the end the people, condemning Europe's imperialism and beginning to regret their own, joined in a crusade to extend the ideal of democracy to the whole world.

CHAPTER IX

AMERICA A WORLD POWER

THE CUBAN QUESTION

THE final years of the nineteenth century brought to fruition the new tendencies in foreign policy, establishing the United States as a world power with insular dependencies in two hemispheres and a potential voice in the affairs of Asia and Europe. The precipitating cause was America's intervention in the revolt of Cuba against Spain. This fertile island, about as large as Virginia and occupied by a people of whom two thirds were white and the rest black or mixed, was the sole remnant of Spain's once magnificent empire in the New World except for its smaller neighbor Puerto Rico. Cuba had interested Americans even before Democratic politicians in the midcentury had thirsted for it as a possible enlargement of slave territory. Its commanding position at the entrances of the Gulf of Mexico and the Caribbean Sea gave it strategic naval importance, and its economic penetration by American capital in recent years created concern for the maintenance of orderly conditions there.

Spain's despotic rule had engendered a rebellion in 1868 which harassed the island for ten years without yielding any real gains for the Cubans. At one point the United States itself came close to being involved. The Cuban-owned *Virginius,* unlawfully flying the American flag and bearing aid to the insurgents, was captured on the high seas by a Spanish gunboat in October, 1873, and fifty-three of those on board, including eight American citizens, were executed as pirates. The Washington government, though admitting the expedition's illegality, insisted on its exclusive right of action so long as the vessel was not in Cuban waters. The danger of war subsided, however, with Spain's apology and payment of reparations. The return of peace in 1878 inflicted even heavier taxation on the people, for they were now saddled with the whole cost of their luckless uprising. Unrest persisted until the smoldering wrath burst forth in February, 1895, in a new war for independence. This event was hastened by a depression in the cane industry caused by the Wilson-Gorman Act of 1894, which repealed the duty-free entry of sugar into the United States provided four years before by the McKinley Act. Atrocities and wanton destruction of property marked the hostilities. The insurgents' plan was to avoid open battle with the much superior Spanish army, but to fight incessant skirmishes and devastate the country in the hope either of exhausting Spain or of drawing the United States into the conflict. Unable to distinguish friend from foe, the Spaniards herded the inhabitants of insurrectionary areas into *reconcentración* (concentration) camps, which in the absence of proper sanitary precautions became pestholes filled with starving and diseased unfortunates. In the province of Havana alone over fifty thousand perished.

The United States watched these proceedings with growing concern. Apart from the traditional interest in Latin American struggles for freedom, American investments in Cuban plantations, mines and railways totaled $50,000,000, and trade with the island reached an annual $100,000,000. These profitable relations were now in jeopardy. Moreover, American humanitarianism was outraged by the ruthless warfare, particularly the plight of the *reconcentrados*. The yellow press, spearheaded by the *World* and *Journal* in New York, broke out in a rash of inch-high headlines and imaginative full-page pictures playing up alleged Spanish cruelties. "Blood on the roadsides, blood in the fields, blood on the doorsteps, blood, blood, blood!" shrieked Pulitzer's *World,* adding, "The old, the young, the weak, the crippled —all are butchered without mercy." In 1897 a party financed by Hearst's *Journal* actually effected the escape of Evangelina Cisneros, a Cuban girl imprisoned in Havana for treason. Such sheets ceaselessly churned the public's emotions, and Hearst's organ erred merely in claiming too much for one newspaper's prowess when it gloated after America's entry: "How do you like the *Journal's* war?" Early in 1898 the American Red Cross, responding to the call of humanity, began work among the sick and starving *reconcentrados* near Havana.

Notwithstanding the rising popular clamor President Cleveland, in office when the trouble began, kept a cool head, and his vigilance stopped nearly all the filibustering expeditions fitted out by Cuban agents in American ports. Yet even he warned Spain in a message to Congress three months before his term ended that the "senseless slaughter," if continued, would invite intervention. His successor McKinley also hoped for a peaceful solution; and partly in response to his urging, Spain in October, 1897, modified the policy of *recon-centratión* and offered the natives a large measure of self-government. Granted in time, this concession might have attained its object; but after all the suffering and bloodshed the revolutionists were willing to accept nothing short of complete freedom. Now occurred two incidents which inflamed American sentiment to fever pitch. Thanks to the *New York Journal,* the public learned on February 9, 1898, that Dupuy de Lôme, the Spanish Minister in Washington, had written to a friend that McKinley was a tricky politician and he had further admitted duplicity in certain trade negotiations then under way with the State Department. Spain refused to disavow the utterances and, instead of dismissing De Lôme, allowed him to resign. Of graver import was the sinking of the United States battleship *Maine* on February 15 in Havana Harbor with a loss of two hundred and sixty lives. An American court of naval officers ascribed the disaster to a submarine mine, but a similar board appointed by Spain laid it to an internal explosion. Though the American findings were afterward confirmed when the vessel was raised in 1911, it is still unknown whether the destruction was due to an overzealous Spanish underling, to a Cuban bent on provoking intervention, or to an accident.

The outburst of patriotic feeling surpassed anything since 1861. Goaded by the sensational press, public gatherings throughout the land echoed the slogan: "Remember the *Maine!*" Congress seethed with bellicose spirit, while even the churches, hitherto the mainstay of peace sentiment, saw good in a war "for humanity's sake." But President McKinley, who had asserted on taking office that "peace is preferable to war in almost every contingency," was still resolved to avert the eventuality if possible, an attitude in which he was ardently backed by Big Business and Wall Street. These men feared that war would undo the prosperity which the country was enjoying for the first time since 1893. But Roosevelt, then Assistant Secretary of the Navy, told McKinley's mentor, Mark Hanna, "We will have this war for the freedom of Cuba in spite of the timidity of the commercial interests." Only the small group of capitalists with a personal economic stake in Cuba sided with Roosevelt. McKinley, moving to compose the crisis by diplomatic means, asked Spain on March 27, 1898, to abandon *reconcentración,* grant an armistice and, if the two parties could not then arrange a peace, allow him to act as arbiter. The first demand was agreed to, but national pride and a fear of revolution at home delayed acceptance of the second. Nevertheless the United States Minister in Madrid cabled, "I believe the ministry are ready to go as far and as fast as they can and still save the dynasty here in Spain." Within six months, he promised, "I will get peace in Cuba, with justice to Cuba and protection to our great American interests." On April 7 the Washington representatives of Great Britain, Germany, France, Austria-Hungary, Russia and Italy united in an appeal to the President to continue negotiations, and two days later Madrid informed him that the queen, at the Pope's intercession, had consented to an armistice.

By this time, however, McKinley had suffered a change of heart. Perhaps he doubted Spain's good faith and felt that, after all, war was the only real solution. More likely, he was frightened by the din of the jingoes in Congress and the imminence of a split in his own party. At all events, on April 11, he sent a message to Congress which after scant mention of Spain's latest concession recommended armed intervention in the interests of common humanity and of the "commerce, trade, and business of our people." Eight days later the lawmakers authorized the President to employ force to establish Cuba's independence, and on motion of Senator Henry M. Teller they assured an incredulous world that the United States would claim no "sovereignty, jurisdiction, or control over said Island except for the pacification thereof." [1] Europe observed these developments with mixed emotions. In Germany, Austria-Hungary and France sentiment condemned the United States, and talk was rife of joint European action on Spain's behalf. British feeling was mirrored in a widely quoted statement of the London *Spectator* on April 19, 1898: "If America were really attacked by a great Continental coalition, England would be at her side in twenty-four hours." In reality, all the powers observed official neutrality, although at one juncture, shortly to be described, the United States feared a clash with the Germans in Far Eastern waters.

THE WAR WITH SPAIN

Blithely the American people took on a war that yielded martial glory for some, unexpected scandals for others and new and heavy

[1] Joseph Pulitzer, who in 1898 clamored for a "short and sharp" war, admitted in 1907, when criticizing President Roosevelt's proposal to send battleships into the Pacific to impress Japan, that "Spain had granted to Cuba all that we had demanded, but passion in Spain and here forced the hands of the government." "To his dying day

responsibilities for the nation. Sea power overshadowed land power in importance, and those who in the 1880's had nursed the 'new navy' into being now won vindication. For the instant readiness for action, however, credit belonged largely to Theodore Roosevelt, the vigorous Assistant Secretary of the Navy. One squadron guarded New York and New England, where the great seaports feared bombardment, while the main fleet maintained headquarters at Key West from which to conduct operations in the Caribbean and convoy troops to the war front. Throughout the brief struggle the United States enjoyed considerable naval superiority. In sad contrast was the army. Though it was increased from 29,000 regulars to 62,000, and though 200,000 volunteers (most of whom it proved unnecessary to send out of the country) were called to the colors, politics affected the appointment of officers; ammunition, rifles and storage facilities fell short of the need; and mismanagement, lack of plans and general confusion hindered mobilization and transport. To worsen matters, the men were sent to a tropical country in winter uniforms without suitable provision for a hot-weather diet and lacking adequate hospital facilities. A picturesque feature of the volunteer cavalry was a regiment of 'Rough Riders,' recruited from cowboys, ranchers, Indians and college athletes by Roosevelt, who became their colonel.

The actual fighting proved swift and decisive, lasting but four months. The chief sphere of activity was the West Indies, where Cuba was promptly placed under blockade in order to debar reinforcements and supplies from Spain. Nevertheless, on May 19 seven vessels under Admiral Pasqual Cervera succeeded in reaching Santiago, which had rail connections with Havana, the capital. Santiago was at once placed under close siege by Rear Admiral William T. Sampson, and in the ensuing weeks troops under General William R. Shafter assembled for a land attack. When they took El Caney and San Juan Hill, Santiago's outer defenses, the city was doomed. To avoid capture, Cervera's fleet two days later on July 3 made a gallant attempt to escape, but as the warships steamed out of the harbor, one by one they were engaged by the blockaders and either captured or destroyed. As Sampson was absent on an official errand, Commodore Winfield S. Schley was in actual command at the moment. The fall of Santiago followed on July 13. Shortly afterward, an army

Mr. Cleveland never believed that the war with Spain was necessary," wrote his personal friend George F. Parker in 1923.

under General Nelson A. Miles began the occupation of nearby Puerto Rico.

Meanwhile the Spaniards had been beaten on the other side of the globe. Upon the outbreak of war Commodore George Dewey, then

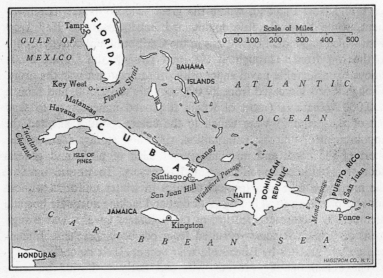

The Theater of War in the West Indies, 1898

at Hong Kong, had proceeded with his six cruisers to the Philippine Islands, a Spanish dependency, under orders to cripple the enemy fleet in Manila Bay for operations in American waters. Though his nearest base was seven thousand miles away, Dewey acted with boldness and dispatch. Before dawn on May 1 he ran the shore batteries, and by high noon he had destroyed the seven ill-equipped vessels without losing an American life. His main purpose accomplished, he established a blockade of Manila and its environs preparatory to a combined attack when land forces should arrive. As usual on such occasions, neutral men-of-war gathered to watch over their national interests. The German squadron under Otto von Diederichs was actually stronger than the United States fleet, and its commander, disputing Dewey's interpretation of international law, violated some of the blockade regulations. On one occasion Dewey, sorely tried, told Diederichs, "If Germany wants war, all right, we are ready." Despite

Dewey's suspicions and the lurid reports in the American press, we know now that Diederichs's purpose was not to help the Spanish, but rather to buttress Germany's claims to the Philippines in case the United States should not want them. During July and early August the reinforcements from America arrived, and the city was besieged with the aid of the Filipinos under Emilio Aguinaldo, who were fighting for independence. On August 13 after a joint sea and land assault Manila capitulated. Two months earlier a United States cruiser had bloodlessly taken over Guam and the other Mariana Islands, tiny Spanish possessions fifteen hundred miles east of the Philippines.

The war proved tremendously popular at home, partly perhaps as an emotional release from the economic pall that had so long shadowed the nation. A special bond issue of $200,000,000, offered in amounts as low as $20, was readily subscribed, while the government raised additional funds by a wide variety of internal taxes. The Red Cross, supported by the public with money and local volunteer workers, extended its activities to all parts of Cuba as well as to the mobilization camps in southern United States and eventually to the Philippines and Puerto Rico. By contrast, the almost criminal negligence of the War Department toward soldier health and welfare evoked widespread criticism. Malaria and typhoid fever assailed the unseasoned troops about Santiago, Shafter reporting on August 3 that three out of four were sick. Yellow fever was an even deadlier menace, and after his top officers joined in a plea to return the men to the United States, the government acquiesced. Thanks to this precaution and the recent progress of medicine, the proportion of deaths from disease proved to be only about three fifths that in the first year of the Civil War. An epochal by-product of this initial contact of American science with the tropics was the discovery in 1900 by an army medical board under Major Walter Reed that the yellow-fever germ was transmitted by the female *Stegomyia* mosquito. Perhaps rediscovery would be the better term, since the Cuban Dr. Carlos Juan Finlay had announced the same conclusion almost twenty years before. With this new knowledge the disease was banished from the island, and the way opened for ending it in other tropical regions.

After the fighting had been under way about three months Spain made overtures through France for peace, and an armistice on August 12, 1898, foreshadowed the final terms. At Paris, where the details were worked out, William R. Day headed the American delegation of five, of whom three were Senators. Since the United States had won an easy victory, the negotiations offered little difficulty. The treaty, signed on December 10, transferred Cuba to the United States for occupation preliminary to independence, and handed over Puerto Rico and Guam in lieu of a war indemnity and the Philippines for the sum of $20,000,000. The acquisition of nearby Puerto Rico was a logical fruit of the hostilities, while the annexation of distant Guam might be justified as a desirable Pacific coaling station. But the taking of the Philippines, whose very location McKinley had not known before the war, raised many doubts. Forming a part of the Asian coastline, these islands, about the size of Arizona, were not only remote for defense, but were inhabited by a people who, being alien in race, language and institutions, were unlikely ever to achieve statehood. Moreover, the Philippines could not be expected to accommodate a surplus American population, though it was hoped they might supply openings for trade and investment and serve as a springboard to the markets of China. Before the peace conference McKinley had been undecided about annexation, but strong pressure was brought to bear upon him by chambers of commerce and Protestant missionary bodies. There was, besides, a belief that, if America did not take the archipelago, Germany or Japan would. Germany in fact did purchase Spain's remaining colonies in the Pacific.

When the treaty came before the Senate, the Philippine provision was bitterly assailed. George C. Vest, a Missouri Democrat, denied that it was constitutional "to acquire territory to be held and governed permanently as colonies." George F. Hoar, an equally stanch Massachusetts Republican, stressed the point that, since the Filipinos had declared their independence, annexation would violate the precious American principle of "the consent of the governed." The supporters retorted by dwelling upon the economic advantages, national prestige and the infamy of 'hauling down the flag.' The nays failed by only two votes to prevent ratification. The Senate's action was accompanied by the McEnery resolution, which stated in effect that the treaty stipulation should not be deemed a final disposition of the question. Since the resolution received less than a two-thirds majority, however, it did not carry the same weight as the vote on the treaty.

In the light of earlier history the war was significant chiefly as marking Spain's final exit from the Western Hemisphere. From a prospective point of view, however, it signalized a momentous departure in American policy. The United States for the first time became a colonial power in the New World, and through acquiring the Spanish holdings in the Pacific together with Hawaii and Tutuila, it became a Far Eastern power as well. To render these far-strewn possessions safe from foreign aggression required a larger navy and army than the people seemed likely to maintain. There were also tough problems of internal administration. The nation took under its wing nearly a million subjects of Spanish and Negro blood in Puerto Rico. It shouldered certain as yet undefined responsibilities in Cuba. It was master and protector of seven and a half million people in the Philippines, ranging from the civilized Tagalogs of Manila to the head-hunting Igorots of northern Luzon. Like Europe, America had at last chosen the path of empire.

OPENING THE DOOR IN CHINA

This fateful decision embroiled the United States almost at once in grave international rivalries on the Asian mainland. Japan's success in wresting Formosa and other territory from China in the war of 1894–1895 had served as a signal to Europe to join in the spoils. In the next five years the leading powers bullied helpless China into granting naval bases, leased territories and spheres of influence. By these moves they gained not only a monopoly of trade for their citizens, but usually also exclusive privileges for the investment of capital in railways and mines. Thus in 1898, a record year, Germany obtained control of the Shantung Peninsula in North China; Russia secured Port Arthur, which dominated the sea approaches to Peiping (then Peking); Great Britain extended its power over the Yangtze Valley and established its rights to Wei-hai-wei, lying between the German and Russian holdings; and France acquired Kwangchow Bay in southeastern China. "The various powers," bewailed the Chinese empress dowager, "cast upon us looks of tigerlike voracity, hustling each other in their endeavors to seize upon our innermost territories."

From the standpoint of the United States, newly entrenched in the Philippines, this game of grab threatened the hopes of a vigorous trade with China. American industrialists, notably the textile manufacturers, were looking particularly to the markets of North China and Manchuria, the regions most affected by German and Russian imperialism. In its earlier diplomatic relations with Oriental countries the United States had always insisted that all nations receive identical commercial treatment. If this principle were now to be preserved, a bold course was necessary. The English were willing to lend aid, even

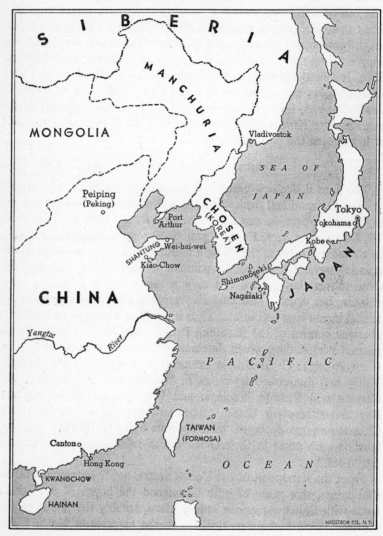

Foreign Encroachments on China

going so far in 1898 as to suggest an Anglo-American alliance for the purpose. In spite of Britain's aggression in China her commercial welfare demanded a policy that would admit her manufactures alike to all ports. But, as in the instance of the Monroe Doctrine in 1823, Washington preferred to pursue an independent course while relying upon England's support.

In September, 1899, Secretary of State John Hay addressed a note to the powers urging them to declare an 'open door' for all nations in China, that is, equality of trade—identical tariffs, harbor duties and railway charges—in the areas they controlled. The proposal, however dramatic, was only a part-way measure, since it said nothing about mining and railroad concessions or capital investment and asked no pledge against a further carving up of the country. Great Britain, Germany, France, Italy and Japan more or less agreed to Hay's note on condition that the others do likewise, while Russia returned a thinly disguised rejection. Hoping to clinch matters, Hay announced that he had received assurances which he regarded as "final and definitive." The future was to disclose, however, that many difficulties remained.

The year 1900 afforded opportunity for a further development of American policy. The Chinese, increasingly hedged in by encroachments from without, took affairs into their own hands and with the government's connivance struck out blindly against the 'foreign devils.' In June the insurgents, known as Boxers, seized Peiping and besieged the legations. To subdue the uprising an international relief expedition, including twenty-five hundred American soldiers, hurried to the scene. Secretary Hay, fearing that the presence of foreign troops would result in a naked dismemberment of the country, promptly notified the powers that the United States would object to any disturbance of China's territorial or administrative rights or any violation of the Open Door. Once the Boxer Rebellion was quelled, however, it required all his skill to carry through the American program and to protect China from crushing indemnities. That he succeeded as well as he did was due to the mutually distrustful attitude of the several countries. In October Great Britain and Germany signified adherence to the Open Door and the preservation of Chinese independence, and the others presently followed. Two months later the powers announced the basic terms of withdrawal: punishment of the rebel leaders, reparations to foreign individuals and governments, and preventive measures against future outbreaks. The details were embodied in a treaty of September, 1901.

Despite Hay's efforts the total indemnity was fixed at nearly twice as much as he deemed proper. Even the $24,500,000 awarded to the United States far exceeded the actual American losses. In 1908 nearly $11,000,000 was given back, and in 1924 an additional $6,-000,000. This investment in international good will bore noble returns, for China set aside the money as a fund for sending students to American colleges. Russia's retention of troops in Manchuria, contrary to the treaty, made it clear that China still had perils to face, and it caused Great Britain and Japan to form a defensive alliance in 1902 to protect their respective interests in Asia and the Pacific. Notwithstanding America's endeavors the Open Door still swung on shaky hinges.

THE PEOPLE'S VERDICT ON IMPERIALISM

Meanwhile the presidential campaign of 1900 enabled the electorate to pass judgment on the administration's program of foreign adventure and colonial aggrandizement. In Philadelphia on June 19 the Republicans expressed jubilation over the war with Spain, the insular accessions, the restored prosperity, and the effort to "obtain new markets" through "the policy of the open door." McKinley's renomination was a foregone conclusion, and for the vice-presidency the convention drafted Governor Theodore Roosevelt of New York, late of the Navy Department and hero of the Rough Riders. Teddy, as he was popularly known, had repeatedly said he would not run, but Boss Platt wished to rid his state of an energetic and self-willed executive, and the genuine enthusiasm of the Western delegates made refusal difficult. Hanna, who had resisted Roosevelt's nomination to the last, told McKinley, "We have done the best we could. Now it is up to you to live!"

The foes of overseas expansion rallied to the Democratic standard. The fact that since February the Filipinos had been fighting for independence from the United States aroused sympathy at home and put America in the position of forcing her rule upon an unwilling people. Moreover, American tobacco and beet-sugar growers disliked the thought of Philippine competition in the domestic market. When the Democrats assembled in Kansas City on July 4, they declared "the paramount issue" to be "imperialism," that is, "the seizing or purchasing of distant islands to be governed outside the Constitution and whose people can never become citizens." They also condemned America's entry into "world politics, including the diplomacy of Europe and the intrigue and land grabbing in Asia." William Jennings Bryan was unanimously renominated, and at his behest the platform contained also a brief plank for free silver. Adlai E. Stevenson of Illinois, Cleveland's Vice-President, was picked as his running mate.

As in 1896, Bryan was endorsed by the Populists and the Silver Republicans, and reverberations of the silver question served to confuse the main issue. Mark Hanna, once more McKinley's campaign strategist, attributed the return of good times to the Republican party, and everywhere appeared emblems and posters of the "Full Dinner-Pail." Roosevelt, delivering as many as thirteen talks in a day, bore the brunt of the speechmaking, extolling America's new role as a world power and gesticulating to vast audiences, "We are a nation of men, not a nation of weaklings." In spite of Bryan's eloquent assaults on imperialism the policy of overseas dominion seemed to strike most voters as a happy fulfillment of American destiny. In any case the abounding prosperity would have assured Republican victory. With fewer ballots cast than in the preceding election, McKinley received a larger proportion—51.6 per cent (7,200,000) to 45.5 per cent (6,360,000)—with the electoral results standing at 292 to 155. The Republicans also boosted their majorities in both branches of Congress.

McKinley did not long enjoy his triumph. On September 6, 1901, while attending an exposition in Buffalo held to symbolize Pan American unity, he was shot by an anarchist. Eight days later he died, and Roosevelt, whose succession Hanna had dreaded, stepped into his shoes. Impetuous and pugnacious, Teddy was the most dynamic and colorful figure in the White House since Andrew Jackson. His eyes were small and piercing behind thick lenses, his body was short and muscular, his voice rasping, and his prominent teeth were the delight of cartoonists. Scarcely forty-three years of age, he was the youngest man ever to assume the office.[1]

[1] Roosevelt retained McKinley's cabinet, consisting of John Hay, Secretary of State; Lyman J. Gage of Illinois, Secretary of the Treasury; Elihu Root of New York, Secretary of War; Philander C. Knox of Pennsylvania, Attorney-General; Charles E. Smith of Pennsylvania, Postmaster-General; John D. Long of Massachusetts, Secretary of the Navy; Ethan A. Hitchcock of Missouri, Secretary of the

LINKING THE ATLANTIC AND THE PACIFIC

Though Roosevelt devoted principal attention to domestic affairs, it fell to him to consolidate the new imperial edifice by building a canal through Central America. Such a waterway had long been an American dream, and as early as the mid-nineteenth century steps had been taken toward its realization. By a treaty of 1846 Colombia granted American citizens free right of passage across the Isthmus of Panama, and in return the United States guaranteed the "perfect neutrality" of the isthmus and Colombia's "rights of sovereignty and property" there. Four years later in the Clayton-Bulwer Treaty with England the Washington government agreed to the principle of an internationalized and unfortified canal. But the upsurge of nationalism after the Civil War changed America's attitude toward joint sponsorship. In 1880 President Hayes informed Congress, "The policy of this country is a canal under American control. The United States cannot consent to the surrender of this control to any European power or to any combination of European powers."

Britain, however, refused to alter the Clayton-Bulwer Treaty, and what seemed a new threat to America's plans arose when a private French company headed by Ferdinand de Lesseps, builder of the Suez Canal, started constructing a waterway with Colombia's consent. From 1881 to 1889 it spent $260,000,000 on the project, but gross financial irregularities and unforeseen engineering difficulties forced it into bankruptcy. Some Frenchmen then reorganized the concern in order to keep alive its franchises and salvage the canal equipment. Under a treaty of 1867 an American syndicate, the Maritime Canal Company, in 1890 began digging a rival waterway through Nicaragua, but the work was stopped by the Panic of 1893 and appeals to Congress for financial aid went unheeded. Despite favorable official reports for the Nicaraguan route in 1895 and 1897 the government was unwilling to go forward under the chafing Clayton-Bulwer restrictions.

Meanwhile interest in the matter grew apace. A canal would speed the economic development of the West Coast hampered by the steep freight charges of the transcontinental railroads, and it was rendered

---

Interior; and James Wilson of Iowa, Secretary of Agriculture. In 1903, when the Department of Commerce and Labor was created, George B. Cortelyou of New York was made its first Secretary. In 1904 William Howard Taft of Ohio became Secretary of War, and upon Hay's death in 1905 Root succeeded to his place. Numerous other changes also occurred.

imperative by the acquisition of a colonial empire in two hemispheres. As President Roosevelt told Congress, it would "greatly increase the efficiency of our navy" by abbreviating distances between the oceans. By the same token a canal would facilitate trade. Both political parties called for it in their 1900 platforms, and Britain, true to her new policy of courting America's favor, now shifted ground. In the Hay-Pauncefote Treaty in 1901 she conceded the exclusive right of the United States to control the passage and to maintain "military police" adequate for its protection, a provision which the American government construed as the right of fortification. The next step was to decide on a site. Should it be Panama, where the French company had worked, or Nicaragua, where the American company had made a start and where Lake Nicaragua and the San Juan River might serve as links? Roosevelt himself argued for the Panama route as shorter and cheaper to build, but there were dissenting views in Congress. After extended debate the Spooner Act in June, 1902, instructed him to undertake the Panama project if he could arrive at "reasonable" terms "within a reasonable time" with both the French company and Colombia; otherwise, to proceed with the Nicaraguan alternative.

The moribund French company, whose sole interest was to dispose of its rights before they expired in 1904, promptly sheared its former exorbitant figure of $109,000,000 to the acceptable one of $40,000,000. Dealings with Colombia, however, proved more difficult. By the Hay-Herrán Treaty in January, 1903, the United States was granted on indefinite lease a six-mile-wide belt of land across the isthmus in return for $10,000,000 and an annual rental of $250,-000. But in August the Colombian senate unanimously rejected the pact. The members felt that Colombia would surrender too much sovereignty in the canal strip and that, in any case, the compensation was niggardly as compared with what the French company was to get. This action enraged Roosevelt who, as he afterward said, "did not intend that any set of bandits should hold up Uncle Sam." Others shared his indignation. The people in Panama saw their chance of straddling one of the world's great crossroads of commerce blasted, while for the stockholders of the French company Colombia's decision meant an almost certain farewell to $40,000,000. Here were the combustibles for a conflagration.

The rapid march of events in November, 1903, bears eloquent testimony to the unity of purpose which actuated the several interested parties. On November 2 the United States cruiser *Nashville* arrived in the harbor of Colón on the Atlantic side of the isthmus. The next evening occurred a bloodless revolution in Panama City on the Pacific side. On the fourth, marines from the *Nashville* kept the Colombian troops in Colón from using the railroad to get to the seat of the trouble. Two days later Washington recognized the new Republic of Panama and on November 18 concluded a canal treaty with it. The United States received perpetual use and control of a zone ten miles wide across the isthmus in return for the payments which Colombia had spurned and for a guarantee of independence. Philippe Bunau-Varilla, former chief engineer of the French company, acted for the isthmian government in these negotiations.

In a message to Congress Roosevelt later brilliantly defended the part he had played. Denying that the American government had fomented the revolution, he claimed justification for its subsequent actions on three grounds: "First, our treaty rights; second, our national interests and safety; and, third, the interests of collective civilization." By barring the railway to the Colombian troops he asserted that the United States was merely executing its treaty pledge of 1846 to protect the "perfect neutrality" of the right of passage. He disposed of the related obligation—to protect Colombia's ownership of the isthmus—by insisting that this guarantee held only against external aggression. His further contentions—that transcendent interests of national and world import were involved in an interoceanic canal—no one could deny, but his critics did not fail to point out that a Nicaraguan waterway, the substitute proposal of the Spooner Act, would have served these purposes equally well. The final word was spoken in 1921 when, two years after Roosevelt's death, an administration of his own party made a treaty giving Colombia $25,-000,000 in payment for her recognition of Panama's independence.

In 1906 the War Department began excavating the canal. As an engineering feat it was comparable in this new age to the transcontinental railway of four decades earlier. Eight years were required to finish it. "It is," said James Bryce, "the greatest liberty Man has ever taken with Nature!" Formidable as were the engineering difficulties, the dearth of labor, problems of sanitation and the task of stamping out yellow fever and malaria proved almost as serious. The canal cost $275,000,000 to build and another $113,000,000 for military and naval defenses. It was completed at a timely moment—just at the beginning of World War I—shortening the distance between

New York and San Francisco by nearly seven thousand nautical miles. The greater mobility afforded the American navy was an important factor in safeguarding national security as that conflict developed.

FULLER ACCOUNTS

Democracy and Empire. The only large-scale singlehanded history of the period 1900–1919 is Sullivan, *Our Times,* intended for the general reader but containing much of value for the student. Volumes of the *American Nation, Chronicles of America Series* and *History of American Life* also cover these years.

The Cuban Question and the War with Spain. For this subject and other diplomatic and military developments, see the standard surveys of American foreign policy by Bailey and Bemis; Dennis, *Adventures in American Diplomacy;* Ganoe, *History of the United States Army;* Mitchell, *Modern American Navy;* Oberholtzer, *History,* V; and Pringle, *Roosevelt.* Among important special works are Chadwick, *Relations of the United States and Spain;* Flack, *Spanish-American Diplomatic Relations;* and Millis, *Martial Spirit.* For the European background, consult Ferrara, *Last Spanish War;* Keim, *German-American Political Relations;* and Reuter, *Anglo-American Relations;* and for popular sentiment in the United States, Pratt, *Expansionists of 1898;* Wilkerson, *Public Opinion and the Spanish-American War;* and Wisan, *Cuban Crisis as Reflected in the New York Press.*

Opening the Door in China. Langer, *Diplomacy of Imperialism,* gives the international setting, while America's role is set forth in Dennett, *Hay,* and his *Americans in Eastern Asia;* Dulles, *China and America;* Griswold, *Far Eastern Policy of the United States;* and Treat, *Relations between the United States and Japan,* III.

Linking the Atlantic and the Pacific. The biographies of Roosevelt and Hay by Pringle and Dennett are enlightening, while noteworthy special studies include Hill, *Roosevelt and the Caribbean;* Mack, *Land Divided;* Miner, *Fight for the Panama Route;* Padelford, *Panama Canal;* Parks, *Colombia and the United States;* and Williams, *Anglo-American Isthmian Diplomacy.*

CHAPTER X

THE PROGRESSIVE MOVEMENT

THE GROUND SWELL OF REFORM

ROOSEVELT'S elevation to the presidency marked a profound change in domestic as well as foreign affairs. As in the diplomatic field a long train of events was responsible. "For thirty years," William Howard Taft remarked in retrospect, "we had an enormous material expansion in this country, in which we all forgot ourselves in the enthusiasm of expanding our material resources and in making ourselves the richest nation on earth. We did this through the use of the principle of organization and combination, and through the development of our national resources. In the encouragement of the investment of capital we nearly transferred complete political power to those who controlled corporate wealth and we were in danger of a plutocracy." To many thoughtful people the danger seemed an actuality: in Henry Demarest Lloyd's phrase the initials U. S. A. had come to mean "United Syndicates of America." Organized wealth was active in municipal, state and national politics, the laws to restrain railways and trusts were openly flouted, and a spirit of unbridled materialism infected every branch of business and society. Roosevelt reported the rail magnate Edward H. Harriman as saying that "he could buy a sufficient number of Senators and Congressmen or State Legislators to protect his interests, and when necessary he could buy the Judiciary." The tocsin of revolt sounded in 1896 against Wall Street and Big Business had been hushed by the new and bewildering national interests arising from the Spanish War, and in 1900 predatory capital was more firmly entrenched than ever before.

As Big Business grew bigger, the ruling hand in the mergers was almost invariably some powerful banking concern which, as a condition of finding the huge sums required, imposed outside direction in lieu of control by those who had founded and built up the industry. As James J. Hill noted in 1902, this was generally "not for the purpose of manufacturing any particular commodity in the first place, but for the purpose of selling sheaves of printed securities which represent nothing more than good will and prospective profits to promoters." In this way 'finance capitalism' was rapidly usurping the role formerly played by creative business brains, with men trained in banking and governed by financial expediency dominating many branches of manufacturing and transportation. To such an extent did the Morgan, Rockefeller and similar groups initiate, control and exploit the processes of consolidation that the Pujo committee of the House of Representatives in 1913, after painstaking study, reported the existence of a "money trust" which "through stock holdings, interlocking directorates, and other forms of domination over banks, trust companies, railroads, public-service and industrial corporations" had brought about "a vast and growing concentration of control of money and credit in the hands of a comparatively few men." Four allied New York financial institutions run by the Morgan and Rockefeller interests held, according to the committee, 341 directorships in 112 banks, transportation, insurance and public-utility corporations with aggregate resources of $22,245,000,000—more than the assessed value of all property in the twenty-two states and territories west of the Mississippi.

In the latter years of the preceding century the farmers and the wage earners had pitted their strength against predatory capital, but had accomplished little. Now, as conditions worsened, the spirit of revolt spread to the urban middle class, notably the small businessmen and white-collar workers. The gathering storm owed much to the enterprise of *McClure's* and other low-priced magazines in publicizing the evils of Big Business. President Roosevelt, who bent to the rising wind to his great political profit, likened the more sensational writers to the Man with the Muckrake in *Pilgrim's Progress,* who was so absorbed in the filth on the floor that he refused a celestial crown; and it was as Muckrakers that the whole group became known.

One of the most famous exposés was Ida M. Tarbell's "History of the Standard Oil Company" in *McClure's* (1902–1903), based upon a three-year study of government investigations and court testimony. Thomas W. Lawson, a notorious Boston stockmarket operator, pilloried the Amalgamated Copper Company in "Frenzied Finance" (1904–1905), telling the readers of *Everybody's* of the inner workings of a gigantic financial system which he said menaced the nation's economic and political life. The fulminations against trust-controlled government reached their climax in David Graham Phillips's series, "The Treason of the Senate," in the *Cosmopolitan* (1906–1907). The Senators were considered one by one, with the startling conclusion that seventy-five of the ninety served the railways, the Beef and Sugar Trusts, the Standard Oil and the steel interests. Meanwhile Samuel Hopkins Adams in *Collier's* revealed the fraudulent claims and dangerous ingredients of patent medicines, while other targets of the Muckrakers were the railroads, banking and insurance companies and municipal and state corruption. Sometimes they sugarcoated the pill as fiction, the outstanding instance being Upton Sinclair's *The Jungle* (1906), which described the filthy Chicago packing houses where everything was saved but "the squeal of the pig and the health of the laborer." For the most part the crusaders named names and made their accusations specific, and their disclosures prompted legal prosecutions and new legislation to correct some of the worst abuses.

This agitation graphically spelled out for the average citizen the gross failures of laissez faire and caused increasing numbers to demand that government assume an active responsibility for economic justice, that democracy as a concept and practice be enlarged to include conditions of living and the earning of a livelihood. This point of view was most cogently expressed in Herbert Croly's thoughtful work *The Promise of American Life* (1909). Observing that social progress was no longer a matter of "automatic fulfillment," he declared that a deliberate and sustained effort was required to restore the promise of American life. To cure "chaotic individualism," government must use its powers to "strike, not at the symptoms of the evil, but at its roots," and he constantly underscored the thought: "The problem belongs to the American national democracy, and its solution must be attempted chiefly by official national action." This plea to employ Hamiltonian means for Jeffersonian ends gave further impulse to tendencies already at work.

The first battles for reform were waged in the local and state arenas. In some cities the aroused people chose mayors like 'Golden Rule' (Samuel M.) Jones and Brand Whitlock in Toledo and Thomas L. Johnson and Newton D. Baker in Cleveland, who ended crookedness and boss rule and speeded municipal ownership of public utilities. In other places, like Minneapolis in 1902, a grand jury bared the misdeeds of a corrupt machine and broke its power. The principal advance, however, was the introduction of the commission plan of government to replace the clumsy mayor-and-council type, which imitated the checks and balances of the state and federal governments. First devised by the citizens of Galveston, Texas, in 1900 to meet a dire flood emergency, it was later modified by other cities to include a city manager, a feature which made it resemble the streamlined structure of a business corporation, with the commission corresponding to the board of directors and the city manager to the president or general manager appointed by the board to conduct detailed affairs. This mode of government minimized partisan politics and stressed training and expertness as the prime requisites for the chief executive official. By 1912 the commission plan in some form or other had spread to over two hundred localities and was still growing in favor. Though a good form of government could not ensure good government, it made that goal easier to reach.

In state affairs the chief reforms struck at the power of the party convention and the legislature, in both of which machine politics reigned almost unchallenged. In place of the convention method of naming candidates, the progressives advocated direct nominations by general vote of the party membership. Wisconsin instituted the first state-wide primary in 1903, with seven other commonwealths acting in 1907. From these beginnings the practice spread through most of the Union. As a curb on the legislature after election, the progressives championed the initiative and referendum, a dual system long known in democratic Switzerland. By means of the initiative the electorate could themselves propose laws either for action by the legislature or submission to popular vote, and by the referendum they could pass on measures which the legislature had already approved. South Dakota and Oregon set the example in 1898 and 1902, the next decade saw fifteen other states follow, and presently half the Union had the system in part or whole. This unceasing warfare with entrenched privilege served as a training ground for leaders who subsequently took up the fight on the national stage—men like Robert M. La Follette of Wisconsin, Hiram Johnson of California and, somewhat later, Woodrow Wilson of New Jersey, all of whom had first been governors of their states. Both parties were involved. In many a contest Republican and Democratic progressives battled shoulder to shoulder against those in the same parties whom Mark

Hanna meant to compliment with the name "standpatters." This fact lent increasing unreality to party labels.

The deep-seated distrust of the United States Senate as a 'rich man's club' revived the old Populist demand that the members be chosen directly by the people, instead of by the legislatures as the Constitution then provided. On several occasions the Senate rejected the House's proposal of an amendment for that purpose, but the democratic torrent could not be so easily stayed. Beginning with Nevada in 1899, various states passed laws which pledged candidates for the legislature to support for Senator the man who won endorsement in a state-wide primary election. By 1912 three fourths of the Union had some modification of this plan. It was only a matter of time until the Senate should consent to incorporating the principle of popular election in the Constitution. As a further move against the undue power of wealth in politics thirty-five states by 1911 enacted legislation against lavish and corrupt expenditures in elections. Most of the states also established public-utility commissions to regulate the rates and practices of railroad, telephone and electrical companies.

In spite of constant agitation by feminists most of the reformers at first brushed aside the demand for equal suffrage. As it became increasingly clear, however, that women might prove valuable allies in the political struggle, the cause sprang to life again. In 1910 and 1911 Washington and California gave them the franchise, and by the end of 1914 they enjoyed full voting rights in eleven states, all west of the Mississippi. Not much longer could the major parties afford to ignore the demand. As time went on, the progressives also concerned themselves more and more with social legislation. Thanks to their efforts, over half the states improved and extended their child-labor acts and shortened the workday for women; a few even adopted minimum-wage legislation for women and provided pensions for destitute mothers. Men benefited chiefly from the establishment of an eight-hour day on public works by more than half the states and most of the larger cities. However, they shared with women the advantages arising from employers' liability (workingmen's compensation) laws. These acts, contrary to the old common-law doctrine, made employers responsible for injuries sustained by employees in the course of work. Maryland led the way in 1902, and by 1917 all but ten legislatures had set up insurance systems, optional or compulsory, for this purpose. More welfare legislation was passed in the first fifteen years of the century than in all previous American history.

This body of laws conflicted with the laissez-faire doctrine that had generally guided legislatures and courts in the past. Accordingly the judiciary at first rejected many of the acts as violating the Fourteenth Amendment, alleging either that the employers were being deprived of "property without due process of law," or that the wage earners were being denied the "liberty" to work under any conditions they pleased. Such decisions rubbed public opinion on the raw, and in time the bench came to display greater liberality. It began to sustain the laws on the ground that a state, under that vague authority known as the police power, could correct social injustices despite infringements on freedom of contract or property values. The trend is strikingly shown in the instance of the federal Supreme Court. In the Lochner case (1905) it annulled a New York ten-hour statute for bakers, finding "no reasonable foundation for holding this to be necessary or appropriate as a health law," but twelve years later, after many changes in the Court's personnel, it upheld in Bunting v. Oregon a ten-hour act for all Oregon factory workers as falling within a justifiable exercise of the police power. This gradual yielding of the laissez-faire attitude to the concept of social responsibility marked perhaps the most distinctive advance made by this generation.

The American quest for social justice coincided with a similar but more vigorous trend abroad. William Jennings Bryan returning from a world trip in 1906 declared, "In all the countries which I have visited there is a demand that the government be brought nearer to the people." In Great Britain during these years Parliament set minimum wages in industry, provided for health and unemployment insurance, established old-age pensions for the needy, instituted slum clearance and better housing for the poor, and levied heavy taxes on incomes and inheritances and (inspired in part by Henry George's writings) on the unearned increment of land. France took steps in the same direction, while Germany now rounded out the social legislation she had inaugurated in the 1880's. Thus it was in a world atmosphere of ferment and change that the American progressives carried on their crusade.

ROOSEVELT AND THE SQUARE DEAL

Against the background of social aspiration and constructive achievement in the states and cities occurred the stiff, uphill fight to render the general government more responsive to the popular will. Without federal co-operation and support many of the reforms could be only partial and ineffectual. As Herbert Croly emphasized in *The Promise of American Life,* the responsibility in final analysis rested with the "American national democracy." Yet Big Business and the great financial interests had a grip upon the federal government and the Republican organization that seemed unshakable. To Roosevelt fell the task of breaking this hold and liberalizing the party. Equipped by long experience in public life, he enjoyed the give-and-take of politics. With the nation in a mood to swing to the left, he readily adopted the progressive tenets, espousing them with a moral fervor that led an associate playfully to credit him with "an original discovery of the Ten Commandments." He had a rare talent for dramatizing his actions, and though an aristocrat by rearing, he possessed in unusual degree the common touch, inviting to the White House all sorts and conditions of men. More than any President since Thomas Jefferson, he was also the scholar in politics, having won distinction in such varied fields as natural history, literature and historical research. As a party man he never flinched from working with the bosses, and this fact, together with his frequent failure to fight through reforms to a finish, caused uncompromising progressives like Wisconsin's Senator La Follette to distrust him as an opportunist and charlatan. It is only fair to note, however, that neither Taft nor Wilson, his successors in the White House, faced such tenacious resistance in Congress, and also that Roosevelt's leadership grew in decision and independence after the voters in 1904 turned his accidental incumbency into an elective term.

Sending his first message to Congress in December, 1901, he used the occasion to expound his views on the principal questions of the day. Acclaiming business concentration as natural and desirable, he opposed the prohibition of large-scale enterprises and demanded legislation to eliminate their abuses while retaining their advantages. He also recommended broader powers for regulating railways and directed attention to the need of conserving natural resources. Law-abiding labor unions received his approval, and he advocated protective legislation for women and children in all industries carried on directly or indirectly for the federal government. Though the program evoked widespread popular favor, it aroused no answering chord in Congress, where stolid conservatism reigned under Speaker Joe Cannon's

CASTLE GARDEN, IMMIGRANT RECEIVING CENTER IN NEW YORK

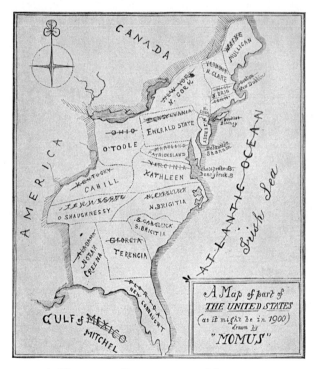

A HUMOROUS PREDICTION OF MIDCENTURY
See page 166.

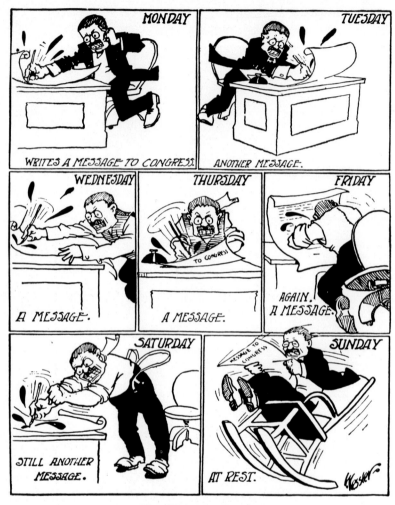

THE TIRELESS TEDDY

leadership in the House and that of Aldrich and Hanna in the Senate. During the summer and autumn of 1902 the President stumped New England and the Midwest, carrying his proposals directly to the people. Everywhere he urged the policy of federal regulation and preached a "square deal" for all—for labor, for capital and for the public.

A great labor outbreak in the Pennsylvania anthracite fields blatantly emphasized corporate selfishness and fortified the President's cause. The United Mine Workers asked a reduction of the ten-hour workday to nine for certain groups of workers and eight for others, also a 20-per-cent wage increase and recognition of the union; but the owners declined either to negotiate or to submit the issues to arbitration. The strike, beginning in May, 1902, involved nearly a hundred and fifty thousand men and ultimately a loss to employers and employed of almost $100,000,000. As winter approached and the East faced a coal famine, Roosevelt decided to intervene on behalf of the public whose interests, he held, transcended those of either of the contending parties. Early in October he urged the disputants to arbitrate their differences. When the owners, denying his right to interfere, still refused, he let it be known that, if necessary, the government would seize the railroads and operate them with troops and in the meantime he would appoint an arbitration board whose findings he expected Congress to back with legislation. J. P. Morgan and other New York financiers at once exerted strong pressure on the operators, and on October 23 the strike ended with an agreement that arbiters appointed by the President should settle the controversy. After four months' investigation this tribunal granted the men a 10-per-cent raise of pay and the shorter workday and made provision for adjusting future difficulties by a board of conciliation jointly representing labor and management. As a result, peace prevailed in the anthracite industry until the troubled years after World War I.

Goaded by an aroused public sentiment, Congress now made grudging concessions to Roosevelt's demands for extending government regulation. In February, 1903, it passed the Elkins Act to cure the rebate evil which the Interstate Commerce Law of 1887 had failed to stop. The statute forbade variations from the published rates and in cases of violation inflicted fines not only on the railroad and its officers but also on the shippers. It left the power of rate-fixing, however, with the companies as hitherto. A few days later Congress created a Department of Commerce and Labor, including a Bureau of Corporations empowered to investigate business practices. Its function was not to prosecute offenders, but to collect data for use of the Attorney-General and of Congress. Meanwhile Roosevelt pressed for stricter enforcement of the Sherman Antitrust Act. Earlier judicial decisions, it will be recalled, had narrowed its scope and rendered convictions difficult. Now the administration embarked upon a 'trust-busting' course, singling out businesses which in its judgment took unfair advantage of their bigness. In the case of the Northern Securities Company, a holding company formed by the Morgan and Hill interests to unite the management of two transcontinental railroads, the Supreme Court in 1904 by a bare majority dissolved the merger as a combination in restraint of trade. Encouraged by this friendlier attitude the Attorney-General pushed other prosecutions. In January, 1905, the tribunal handed down a decision against the Beef Trust. Altogether the Roosevelt regime in its seven and a half years secured twenty-five indictments.

By 1904 Teddy had become the idol of the Republican rank and file. Even children in the nursery loved to play with 'Teddy Bears.' His striking personality, his flaming espousal of the Square Deal, his trust busting, his brandishing of the 'big stick' in the Panama revolution, captured the imagination of the man on the street. Nor did the machine politicians, left leaderless by Hanna's death early in 1904, dare refuse him a second term. The national convention in Chicago on June 21 named him by acclamation, with Senator Charles W. Fairbanks of Indiana for Vice-President. The influence of the stand-patters, however, appeared in the platform, which was largely a eulogy of the party's historic achievements. On the trust question it declared simply that the combinations of capital and labor "are alike entitled to the protection of the laws . . . and neither can be permitted to break them." For the first time since 1892 Democrats of the Cleveland stamp dominated that party's convention in St. Louis on July 6. Against Bryan's wishes the nomination went on the first ballot to Alton B. Parker, a New York judge unknown to the nation, with ex-Senator Henry G. Davis of West Virginia for the second place. The platform called for the prohibition of industrial monopolies and for augmenting the powers of the Interstate Commerce Commission. It flayed Roosevelt for "executive usurpation of legislative and judicial functions" and condemned his whole course in office as "erratic, sensational, spectacular, and arbitrary."

'Rooseveltism,' rather than any of the President's specific policies, proved the decisive issue. Where the light is strong the shadows are deep; and like Andrew Jackson, Roosevelt had the faculty of exciting passionate enmity as well as fanatical devotion. Though Judge Parker represented better the conservative approach to public questions, the *New York Sun* spoke for its business-minded readers when it said, "We prefer the impulsive candidate of the party of conservatism to the conservative candidate of the party which the business interests regard as permanently and dangerously impulsive." Morgan, Harriman, the Standard Oil and other moneyed groups, knowing that Roosevelt would win in any case, contributed as usual to the Republican campaign chest, while progressive Democrats were drawn more to Teddy than to their own candidate, though Bryan himself gave Parker lukewarm support. The great prosperity was another influence for Republican success. The outcome was an extraordinary testimonial of confidence in the President. He received 56.4 per cent of the popular ballots (7,629,000) to 37.6 per cent (5,084,000) for Parker, and 336 electoral votes as compared with 140. Incidentally, the result vindicated the new-school Democrats, for in both 1896 and 1900 Bryan had polled over a million more votes than Parker in 1904. The Republicans also enlarged their majorities in Congress. When Roosevelt was notified of his victory, he stated, "The wise custom which limits the President to two terms regards the substance and not the form, and under no circumstances will I be a candidate for or accept another nomination."

Elated by his triumph, Roosevelt, now President in his own right, stepped up his reform program. One objective was a more drastic regulation of railroads. At his urging, the House passed a bill granting the Interstate Commerce Commission full power to fix interstate charges, but the standpatters in the Senate forced a compromise. The Hepburn Act in June, 1906, authorized the ICC to reduce unfair rates, its orders to become immediately effective unless challenged by the railroad in a federal court. Though the progressives got less than they wanted, the law marked an advance over the original act of 1887, since the burden of initiating litigation to test the validity of the Commission's orders now rested upon the railways, not upon the Commission as hitherto. The Hepburn Act also extended the ICC's authority to express and sleeping-car companies and pipe lines. Free passes, long an indirect source of political influence, were prohibited except under strict limitations. In addition, the Commission was empowered to prescribe methods of bookkeeping and accounting for the roads, a regulation prompted in part by the practice of certain companies of concealing corrupt expenditures through false book entries.

The year 1906 also saw the adoption of the Meat Inspection and Pure Food Acts, the one directly inspired by Upton Sinclair's *The Jungle* and the other by the disclosures of Samuel Hopkins Adams and like Muckrakers. The first required federal supervision of all meats sold in interstate trade, while the second forbade any "deleterious drug, chemical or preservative" in patent medicines, processed foods or liquors sold in interstate trade. A further curb on corporations followed in 1907 when they were forbidden to make campaign contributions in federal elections. Trust prosecutions also continued, one notorious case in 1907 bringing the conviction of several officers of the Sugar Trust and the recovery of over $4,000,000 of fraudulently withheld import duties. The same year the Standard Oil Company of Indiana, a subsidiary of the Standard of New Jersey, was indicted for secret rebates on its shipments over the Chicago and Alton Railroad. The altered temper of the times was reflected in the fine of $29,240,000 imposed by Federal District Judge K. M. Landis for 1462 separate offenses. Though the Circuit Court annulled the verdict, popular belief as to the defendant's guilt remained unchanged, and Roosevelt's private comment on the reversal was: "There is altogether too much power in the bench."

Next to corporation control, President Roosevelt devoted chief attention to the conservation of natural resources. Because of the policy of giving away land to all comers the country was now confronted with dire results. No nation in history had so wasted its physical assets or permitted such exploitation as the United States. Timber had been recklessly destroyed, mineral wealth had been depleted, soil fertility had been sapped, land had been allowed to become eroded and the precious top soil to be carried off by floods and winds—all under the banner of laissez faire. At the turn of the century it was reckoned that the forests would last about thirty years longer, anthracite coal fifty years, bituminous perhaps a century. As another phase of the problem, wide stretches of public domain, though looked upon as worthless, needed only proper attention to be fit for cultivation. In the nineties Congress had adopted some preliminary steps toward the husbanding of natural resources. A law of 1891 gave the President discretion to reserve from sale and settlement forested public lands. Three years later the Carey Act offered to cede arid tracts to states agreeing to irrigate them and open them to settlers at reasonable prices.

Upon these beginnings Roosevelt greatly enlarged. Starting with his first annual message in 1901, he lost no occasion to preach the doctrine of conservation until the masses came to understand the relationship between land policy and social welfare. In place of the heedless practices of the past he urged national planning, not for the immediate present but for the long future, and embracing both the guarding of irreplaceable resources and the restoring of renewable ones. His program had four main objectives: forests, unwanted lands, minerals and inland waterways. Where his predecessors had set aside 47,000,000 acres of woodland, Roosevelt over the protests of the Western lumbering and grazing interests added 148,000,000 more, and through Gifford Pinchot of the Division of Forestry he instituted systematic efforts to retimber denuded areas and prevent disastrous fires. The close of his regime saw most of the great forests on the public domain in the Pacific and Rocky Mountain states set apart to protect watersheds and power sites and for the permanent use of the nation.

Hardly less noteworthy was the progress in redeeming useless agricultural areas. Because the Carey Act had accomplished little, the Newlands Reclamation Law in 1902 provided that the proceeds of land sales in sixteen semiarid Western states and territories should constitute a revolving fund for the construction of irrigation works. Soon one important project after another was undertaken, large dams and reservoirs were built, and great thirsty tracts supplied with water. A year after Roosevelt left office it was estimated that more than 3,000,000 acres of farm land had been so improved as to yield an increased annual profit of $75,000,000. Steps were also taken to reclaim swamp or overflowed lands of an interstate character. In order to safeguard mineral wealth, Roosevelt withheld from sale a total of 85,000,000 acres containing oil, coal and other valuable deposits. The interest in waterways arose in part from the desire to relieve freight congestion on the railroads, and in part from the need

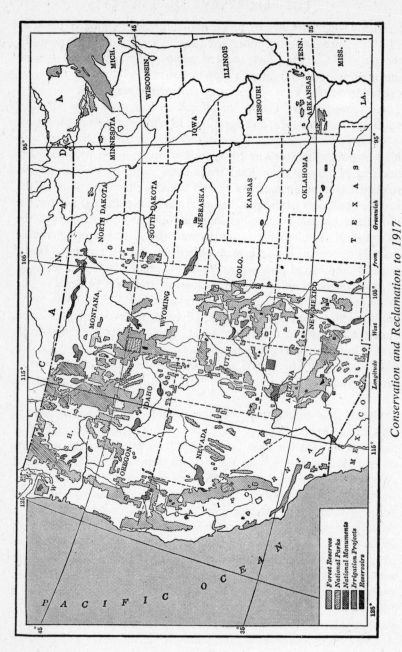

Conservation and Reclamation to 1917

Forest Reserves
National Parks
National Monuments
Irrigation Projects
Reservoirs

212

of preventing destructive floods on the rivers, especially the Mississippi. In 1907 Roosevelt appointed an Inland Waterways Commission to study the problem, and on the basis of its report appropriations began to be made for an orderly development of the nation's rivers, lakes and canals. Realizing that the success of conservation required co-operation by the states, the President set a precedent by summoning the governors to a conference on the subject in 1908. Within eighteen months forty-one state conservation commissions were at work. Roosevelt's efforts had the effect of making conservation a major national policy. Only at their peril would his successors fail to give it unstinted devotion.

As the campaign of 1908 drew near, the President was at the peak of his popularity. He had added new prestige and power to his office. Time and again he had taken his policies directly to the voters, winning their support and scaring laggard members of Congress into rallying to his side. Yet his great service to the country consisted less in specific additions to the statute book than in giving the people new faith in themselves. Furthermore, at a time when capital and labor were at each other's throats, his voice declared with ringing emphasis, "The corporation has come to stay just as the trade union has come to stay," and, he unfailingly added, both must bow to the popular will. This creed of the Square Deal for all was too radical for conservatives and too conservative for radicals. Deeply indebted to the agitation of the Muckrakers as well as to the progressives of the two parties in Congress, he strove to hold a balance between the contending forces in modern society, seeing the means in an enlargement of government control. He blazed a path along which his successors would move farther.

TAFT INHERITS THE PRESIDENCY

Teddy could easily have been nominated for a 'second elective term,' but recalling his statement of self-denial after his 1904 victory, he threw his support to his good friend William Howard Taft of Ohio, Secretary of War since 1904, who had faithfully advocated his policies in public and private and who knew the insular dependencies as no other American. Roosevelt's preference occasioned considerable surprise and, among progressive Republicans, misgivings, for Taft in his earlier career as federal judge had betrayed an antilabor outlook. However, they bowed to the judgment of their chief who, through use of the federal patronage and manipulation of the Southern delegates, had his way on the first roll call at the party convention in Chicago on June 16. James S. Sherman of New York was chosen for Vice-President. The platform eulogized Roosevelt for combating "the abuse of wealth and the tyranny of power," promised still ampler regulation of trusts, and acknowledged the growing demand for tariff reform by pledging a "revision" based on the difference between "the cost of production at home and abroad, with a reasonable profit to American industries."

In the Democratic convention at Denver on July 17 the progressive wing of that party, again on top as a result of Parker's stinging defeat in 1904, gleefully named William Jennings Bryan on the first ballot for his third run, with Indiana's John W. Kern as his teammate. "The overwhelming issue," declared the platform, is "Shall the people rule?" —an issue created by Roosevelt's designating his own successor, Speaker Cannon's "absolute domination" of the House and the alliance of corporate wealth with the party in power. Branding the Republican tariff plank as belated and insincere, the Democrats explicitly committed themselves to a "reduction" of protective duties. They also demanded the destruction of industrial monopolies and denounced the use of injunctions in labor disputes.

Both nominees made long speaking tours, with Teddy on the sidelines vainly entreating the tranquil Taft, "Hit them hard, old man!" Thanks to Roosevelt's reform activities, Bryan found himself somewhat in the position of a soldier whose ammunition had been stolen by the enemy. Partly for this reason, he bore down heavily on the tariff question and pressed his opponent so hard that Taft interpreted the Republican plank as meaning revision downward. Organized labor for the first time took part in a presidential fight when the American Federation of Labor endorsed the Democrats because of their stand on injunctions. In harmony with the new political ethics, Bryan's managers made public during the campaign all contributions above $100, and both parties issued postelection statements. Taft won easily with 321 electoral votes to 162 for Bryan and 51.6 per cent of the popular ballots (7,679,000) to 43 per cent (6,409,000). His popular plurality, however, was hardly a third of that polled by Roosevelt in 1904, while Bryan exceeded Parker's vote by more than a million. Afterward, in explaining his defeat, Bryan ruefully declared that the Republican party had enjoyed the unfair advantage of two candidates: Taft the progressive who carried the West, and Taft the conservative who carried the East. The Republicans also returned majorities to both branches of Congress.

While the campaign was under way, Roosevelt had written an English friend, "Always excepting Washington and Lincoln, I believe that Taft as President will rank with any other man who has ever been in the White House," and he added, "He and I view questions exactly alike." Events quickly revealed how badly he was mistaken. The new President did not have the temperament for strong executive leadership. Unlike the strenuous Teddy he was steeped in the law and hence shaped his course with legalistic caution. He would have been more at home in the Supreme Court, where indeed he was to end his career. It is significant of the bent of his mind that all his cabinet appointees but the two taken over from Roosevelt were lawyers.[1] Moreover, with his former chief now away on an African hunting trip, he tended to revert to his naturally conservative slant on public questions and, at any rate, felt that the country needed time and quiet to digest the gains that had been made. If Teddy was essentially a man of action, 'Big Bill' was essentially a man of reflection. In any case, the kindly nature and imperturbable good humor embodied in his three hundred and fifty pounds inclined him to conciliate the powerful party leaders whom his predecessor had often found it necessary to antagonize. Senator Jonathan P. Dolliver of Iowa reflected the opinion of other progressive Republicans in describing him as "an amiable island entirely surrounded by men who know exactly what they want."

The most urgent problem confronting the new administration was tariff revision, a question which Roosevelt had let sleep. A growing number of people had come to believe that the Dingley Act of 1897 was a veritable mother of trusts and the cause of the steepening cost of living. The center of the protest was the Midwest, the stronghold of the progressive movement. Summoning Congress in special session to deal with the matter, Taft induced the House to pass the Payne bill for lower rates, but the Senate under Aldrich's direction added

[1] The members were Philander C. Knox of Pennsylvania, Secretary of State; Franklin MacVeagh of Illinois, Secretary of the Treasury; Jacob M. Dickinson of Tennessee, Secretary of War; George W. Wickersham of New York, Attorney-General; Frank H. Hitchcock of Massachusetts, Postmaster-General; George von L. Meyer of Massachusetts, Secretary of the Navy; Richard A. Ballinger of Washington, Secretary of the Interior; James Wilson of Iowa, Secretary of Agriculture; and Charles Nagel of Missouri, Secretary of Commerce and Labor. Meyer and Wilson were the holdovers.

847 amendments undoing most of the reductions. The compromise Payne-Aldrich Act, adopted in August, 1909, actually imposed somewhat higher duties than its objectionable forerunner and empowered the President to hoist them further by as much as 25 per cent in the case of countries which discriminated against American trade. To assist in administering this latter provision it created a bipartisan Tariff Board. At every stage the increases had been fought by La Follette, Cummins, Dolliver and other Western Senators, who thereby won the name of Insurgents. The principal concession they obtained was a one-per-cent tax on the net earnings of corporations above $5000. "Schedule K," which dealt with wool and woolens, proved a particular abomination to the Insurgents, since it left the high duties virtually unchanged at a time when woolen manufacturers were declaring dividends up to 50 per cent. Even the President did not defend this feature of the act, though he indiscreetly pronounced the tariff as a whole "the best the country ever had."

The Payne-Aldrich Act was the first step in Taft's downfall. Hard on its heels two other events alienated Roosevelt's old followers. One appeared to involve the President's good faith toward the conservation of natural resources. In the summer of 1909 Gifford Pinchot, head of the Division of Forestry, accused his chief, Secretary of the Interior Ballinger, of lack of zeal in protecting water-power sites and coal lands and of conniving with groups seeking to plunder the public domain. Taft, believing the charges unjust, sided with Ballinger and dismissed Pinchot for insubordination. There ensued a bitter newspaper controversy, heightened by the fact that Pinchot was an intimate of Roosevelt. In the end, Ballinger, hoping to relieve the President of embarrassment, resigned. Reform sentiment was further inflamed by Taft's failure to aid the Western Republicans in their fight to unhorse Speaker Joseph G. Cannon. In the course of years the presiding officer of the House had come not only to appoint all committees, but, through domination of the Rules Committee, also to limit debate and direct the whole process of lawmaking. A confirmed standpatter, Cannon constantly used his authority to block the progressives. Consequently, on March 19, 1910, the House Insurgents led by George W. Norris of Nebraska combined with the Democratic minority to shear the Speaker's powers. Though permitted to retain his office, Cannon was denied the right to appoint the Rules Committee and be one of its members. When the Democrats came into control the next year, they went still further and made all committees elective.

The revolution in the House foreshadowed a greater one in the fall elections. On the issues of tariff reform and 'Cannonism' the voters transformed a Republican majority of 47 in the House into a Democratic majority of 63, and the Democrats also won many state elections. Even New Jersey, a boss-ridden Republican commonwealth hitherto the despair of reformers, placed in the governor's chair a progressive Democrat, Woodrow Wilson. The moral was not lost upon Taft. In an effort to appease antiprotectionist sentiment he recommended to Congress a reciprocity agreement with Canada providing for the reduction or abolition of duties on many Canadian food products and raw materials in return for similar concessions on American farm implements and certain other commodities. This proposal, which did not affect the principal Eastern manufactures, proved acceptable to the Republicans of that section, but it sowed a whirlwind of protest among the farming and lumbering interests of the Middle and Far West apprehensive of Canadian competition. The Democratic members took prompt advantage of this new breach in Republican ranks. Viewing Canadian reciprocity as an entering wedge for general tariff reduction, they helped the President carry it through Congress in July, 1911, though he won little credit for the achievement since Canada later rejected the terms. Then, to offset the displeasure of the Insurgents, the Democrats united with them to pass a number of bills for lowering the tariff on Eastern manufactures. These ran afoul of the President's veto, intensifying his unpopularity both within and without his party.

Yet, despite Taft's inept leadership and the growing revolt against him, the administration had done much in a quiet, untheatrical way to further reform. In 1910 Congress put new teeth into the Interstate Commerce Law by passing the Mann-Elkins Act, which extended the Commission's authority to cable, telegraph and telephone companies, and made the Commission's orders for lower rates effective even when a court investigation was being conducted into their reasonableness. Congress also tackled the question of campaign contributions, adopting legislation in 1910 and 1911 limiting the amount of money a candidate for the Senate or House might spend and requiring that all receipts and expenditures be published during and after both primaries and elections. Moreover, the dust raised by the Ballinger-Pinchot affair obscured the fact that Congress in 1911, at the President's urging, enlarged the scope of conservation by providing for the purchase of forest lands near the headwaters of navigable streams in the White Mountains and the southern Appalachians. The next year a Children's Bureau was set up to consider problems of child welfare, and a parcels-post law was enacted. The last days of Taft's presidency also saw the creation of a Department of Labor with membership in the cabinet.

Apart from this legislative record, the administration conducted nearly twice as many prosecutions against business consolidations as had the Roosevelt regime. In 1911 the Supreme Court ordered the dissolution of the Standard Oil Company of New Jersey and also of the American Tobacco Company. The immediate rise in the value of Standard stock, however, indicated how little the decision affected the actual conduct of the industry. More important was the fact that the tribunal in these cases set its face against indiscriminate attempts to break up large-scale enterprises. This appeared in a new construction of the Sherman Antitrust Act. Where that statute had outlawed "every" contract or combination in restraint of trade, the Court now interpreted the prohibition as applying only to undue or unreasonable restraints of trade.

Most noteworthy of all was the initiating of two new amendments to the Constitution, the first since Reconstruction days. The controversy begun by the Supreme Court's judgment against the income tax in 1895 was solved once and for all when the Sixteenth Amendment, submitted to the states at Taft's suggestion in 1909, empowered Congress to levy an income tax without the necessity of apportioning it among the states according to population. The Seventeenth Amendment, proposed by Congress in 1912, climaxed the demand for a reconstitution of the Senate. It provided that Senators should be elected by popular vote of the state instead of by the legislature. The one change was ratified by the required number of states in 1913 shortly before Taft left office, the other three months later. It was significant of the altered temper of America that the Taft administration should clothe with constitutional sanction two reforms which the Populists had been the first to agitate.

Had Taft possessed his predecessor's gifts of showmanship, he might have capitalized these achievements to political advantage. As it was, the progressive Republicans began to lay plans as early as January, 1911, to head off his renomination. Deciding at first upon 'Fighting Bob' La Follette as their choice, they later shifted to the colorful Roosevelt as a more inspiring leader and surer vote-getter. In the contest for delegates Taft denounced his former friend's "explosive inconsistencies," while Roosevelt taunted Taft with betraying progressive principles and added with regard to their past relations, "It is a bad trait to bite the hand that feeds you." In the thirteen states with preferential primaries Roosevelt won 278 delegates to 68 for Taft, but elsewhere Taft came out on top through control of the local party machinery. At the national convention in Chicago on June 18, 1912, the President captured the prize on the first ballot, with Vice-President Sherman once more as his running mate. Three hundred and forty-four Roosevelt adherents—a third of the members—refused to vote, though critics unkindly pointed out that Teddy himself had rammed through Taft's nomination by similar methods four years before. The platform, while declaring for a "self-controlled representative democracy," carefully skirted questions provocative of factional bitterness. The chief planks called for a federal commission to regulate trusts, "readjustment" of the tariff with the aid of a board of experts, and reformation of the monetary system.

Roosevelt's supporters, charging that the convention had overridden the wishes of the rank and file, repudiated the Republican party. In a gathering in Chicago on August 5 described by the *New York Times* as "a Methodist camp meeting done over in political terms," they launched the Progressive party with Roosevelt and Governor Hiram Johnson of California as their standard-bearers. The platform, the most unusual yet framed by a party with reasonable hopes of success, championed not only such political reforms as woman suffrage and the initiative and referendum, but also a referendum on court decisions that annulled state laws. As economic reforms it advocated a federal commission to regulate combinations, tariff revision along protective lines through an expert commission, and an overhauling of the banking and currency laws. In addition, it endorsed a wide range of measures for "social and industrial justice," including the eight-hour day, a "living wage," and safeguards against industrial accidents and occupational diseases.

Because of the Republican schism the Democrats for the first time in many years had a real chance for victory. As a result, the conservative and liberal wings both battled to dictate the convention's choice in Baltimore on June 25. Thanks largely to the generalship of William Jennings Bryan, a Nebraska delegate and for once not himself an aspirant, the nomination went on the forty-sixth ballot to Woodrow Wilson who as governor of New Jersey had shown himself a militant reformer. Governor Thomas R. Marshall of Indiana was chosen for the second position. The platform blamed the high cost of living on the Republican tariff, pledged "immediate downward revision," repeated the anti-injunction plank of 1908, promised to restore the Sherman Act to its original vigor and demanded reconstruction of the banking and currency laws.

In view of its dramatic prelude the campaign proved surprisingly quiet. Teddy was inevitably the central figure, and his followers, glorying in the nickname 'Bull Moosers' because of an exuberant remark of Roosevelt's that he felt "as fit as a bull moose," made the welkin ring with his praises. His opponents, digging up his declaration in 1904 against a third term, flayed him for unseemly ambition and boundless egotism. Though the Progressive platform was widely condemned as 'socialistic,' the ticket had the warm support of certain well-known capitalists who saw in the elaborate provisions for government control of industrial conditions the promise of an efficient and contented labor force. It is significant that Samuel Gompers, as in 1908, called on organized labor to back the Democrats. Wilson summarized his program in the slogan "the new freedom," by which he meant the use of federal power to prevent monopolies from restraining free competition. Though not differing essentially in purpose from either of his rivals, he phrased his thought in dignified and well-chosen words which convinced people that he stood midway between candidates of extreme tendencies—'a progressive with the brakes on.' In any event, the divided opposition ensured Democratic success. Wilson mustered 435 electoral votes, Roosevelt 88, Taft 8. But the popular ballots mirrored the situation more accurately, Wilson winning 41.8 per cent (6,286,000), Roosevelt 27.4 per cent (4,126,000), and Taft 23.2 (3,484,000). The victor polled one and a third million votes fewer than the total for his two rivals. The Democrats also carried both houses of Congress. The remarkable showing made by the Progressive party promised to give it a permanent place in American politics if indeed its strength represented anything more than devotion to a brilliant chief.

WILSON AND THE NEW FREEDOM

The new chief executive embodied the finest traditions of his party. A Virginian by birth, Wilson knew the North from having spent his mature years there as professor and then president of Princeton University. Like Jefferson, who had fathered the Democratic party, he was a student and philosopher of political institutions; and like

Jackson, who had made it responsive to the common man, he understood intuitively the unspoken hopes of the masses. His obstinate courage, reminiscent of his Scotch Presbyterian forebears, recalled a still later Democratic President, Grover Cleveland, whose neighbor he had been in Princeton. But more than any of these except perhaps Jefferson, Wilson surveyed the world with singular mental detachment, with the eyes of a scholar accustomed to probe beneath the immediate flux of events for timeless principles. His high forehead, angular face and aggressive jaw suggested the special qualities of his leadership. His hold on the people rested on their growing confidence in his penetrating intelligence rather than on devotion to the man, though he was deeply loved by his intimates. Not the least of his gifts was a literary style that made his public utterances a tapestry woven of noble and luminous phrases. His intellectual aloofness and stubborn independence proved a constant irritant to political foes and often to his own party leaders and in the end contributed to his defeat in the last great battle of his career, that over ratification of the League of Nations.

The election of 1912 was a victory for progressivism if not for the Progressives. Wilson showed no disposition to evade or straddle any of the urgent questions of the day. He felt a solemn mission to commit the Democrats unalterably to reform, and he rendered his position clear from the start by making Bryan his Secretary of State.[1] In any case, this was the course of political wisdom, for the President might thereby hope to undermine the new Progressive party and win for the Democrats the majority support that had been wanting in the election. Though the Democrats controlled both branches of Congress, the party, long out of power, lacked cohesion and responsible leaders. To Wilson this was a challenge rather than a deterrent. For many years as a professional student of political science he had maintained that the chief magistrate should not be a mere chairman of the government, but an aggressive director of public policy, bearing a relationship to his party and the people like that of Britain's Prime Minister. In *Constitutional Government in the United States* (1907) he had written, "The President is at liberty, both in law and con-

[1] The other cabinet members were William McAdoo of New York, Secretary of the Treasury; Lindley M. Garrison of New Jersey, Secretary of War; James C. McReynolds of Tennessee, Attorney-General; Albert S. Burleson of Texas, Postmaster-General; Josephus Daniels of North Carolina, Secretary of the Navy; Franklin K. Lane of California, Secretary of the Interior; David F. Houston of Missouri, Secretary of Agriculture; William C. Redfield of New York, Secretary of Commerce; and William B. Wilson of Pennsylvania, Secretary of Labor.

science, to be as big a man as he can. His capacity will set the limit." Accordingly he frankly assumed the reins of leadership, revived the custom which Jefferson had abandoned of reading his messages to Congress, and in other ways outstripped even Roosevelt in building up the office. In accounting for his legislative achievements, however, it is well to remember that his regime was the beneficiary of all the agitation for democratic reform that had occurred since the opening of the century.

The new Congress, summoned in special session, carried through a program which was outstanding in American history. The first task was tariff revision. "We must abolish everything," declared the President, "that bears even the semblance of special privilege or of any kind of artificial advantage, and put our businessmen and producers under the stimulation of a constant necessity to be efficient, economical, and enterprising." To rout the powerful manufacturers' lobby which always assembled on such occasions, he called in the newsmen and exposed the "astute men" who were striving by hook or crook to "overcome the interests of the public for their private profit." Thanks to such tactics, the Underwood-Simmons Act, passed in October, 1913, was the most revolutionary tariff since 1846. It slashed the rates on important raw materials and foodstuffs, cotton and woolen goods, iron, steel and other commodities, and removed the duties from more than a hundred articles. Although the act retained many protective features, a real attempt had been made to lower the cost of living. To offset the expected loss of revenue, advantage was taken of the recent Sixteenth Amendment to include a graduated tax (ranging from one to seven per cent) on incomes; and a somewhat stiffer tax than before was levied on corporate earnings. The fiscal effects of the act were never fairly tested, however, for the outbreak of World War I in 1914 caused a decline of dutiable imports and customs revenue. The law discontinued the Tariff Board of 1909, but agitation for such a body presently became so strong that in 1916 Congress created a bipartisan Tariff Commission with somewhat similar powers.

The second objective of the New Freedom was a revision of the banking and currency system. The act of 1900 establishing the gold standard had left unaltered another serious defect of the monetary system: its lack of elasticity. The currency—a hodgepodge of greenbacks, treasury notes, national bank notes, gold and silver arising from fortuitous historical conditions—was ill adapted to meet the normal ebb and flow of business. There was no way to expand or contract the amount according to fluctuating need. This and other faults had been dramatically projected on the public consciousness by a financial panic, lasting from November, 1907, to January, 1908, which had caused widespread failures of banks and business concerns. If the banks had been able temporarily to enlarge the volume of their currency, or if the stronger institutions had felt it safe to help out banks in momentary difficulty, much of the trouble would have been avoided. Shocked into action, Congress in 1908 adopted a stop-gap plan to enable national banks in times of emergency to issue additional bank notes, and then, looking to a permanent remedy, it created a National Monetary Commission to investigate the question and make recommendations. In 1912 the Commission finished its work, and though its proposals left too much power in the hands of private banking interests to suit the Democrats, the report in other respects formed the basis of the Federal Reserve Act which Congress passed in December, 1913.

This law aimed to cure the three glaring flaws which experience had revealed: (1) lack of co-operation among banks during crises; (2) inelasticity of the money supply; and (3) concentration of control in a few financial magnates. As machinery for accomplishing these purposes the act set up a Federal Reserve Bank in each of twelve districts or regions of the country. These institutions were to serve as depositories for the cash reserves of national banks and of such state banks and trust companies as might join the system. Their primary function, in other words, was to act as a bank for banks. To achieve the first of the three aims, a method was provided whereby the funds thus accumulated might be used to assist individual banks at times of temporary distress. To attain the second object, provision was made for issuing federal reserve notes to meet changing business demands. Local banks might deposit with the Federal Reserve Banks approved commercial paper (for example, promissory notes of reliable business concerns), receiving in exchange federal reserve notes for use during the period of need. Finally, to curb the power of large private bankers, management of the system was entrusted to the direct oversight of the boards of the regional Reserve Banks, a third of whose members were named by the government, and to the general supervision of a Federal Reserve Board, consisting wholly of federal appointees.[1] The new scheme was a landmark in American banking history comparable to Hamilton's financial plan and the national banking system established during the Civil War. Though its passage had been bitterly opposed by the private banking interests, and though it went into effect under the abnormal conditions created by the onset of World War I, it quickly demonstrated its utility. Nevertheless, many evils remained in the banking system, as the Great Depression of 1929 was to disclose.

The next goal of the New Freedom was trust regulation. Experience suggested a method of control like that of the Interstate Commerce Commission over the railways, but it required Wilson's most vigorous efforts to bring it about. The results appeared in two laws of 1914. One abolished the Bureau of Corporations, dating from 1903, and transferred its functions to a new and more powerful agency, the Federal Trade Commission. In addition to investigating corporate abuses, the FTC could order businesses in interstate trade to cease "unfair methods of competition," and it could seek aid from the courts to enforce its decrees. The second enactment, the Clayton Antitrust Act, forbade many business practices that had thus far escaped specific condemnation by federal statute, such as interlocking directorates, the acquisition by one corporation of stock in others to the extent of substantially lessening competition or creating a monopoly, and price discriminations of a similar monopolistic tendency. This law also granted important safeguards to labor. It exempted from antitrust prosecution all labor and agricultural organizations "lawfully carrying out the legitimate objects thereto," and it declared that strikes, peaceful picketing and boycotting did not violate federal law. Finally, it prohibited injunctions in disputes over conditions of employment "unless necessary to prevent irreparable injury to property," and required jury trial for contempt of court except when the offense was committed in the judge's presence. These last provisions harked back to troubles connected with the Pullman strike of 1894.

The public at large greeted the new trust legislation with high satisfaction. In trade-union circles the elation was unexampled. Decisions of the Supreme Court, however, tended to chip away many of the benefits of the labor clauses and to rob the workers of immunities which they believed the law had conferred. In one notable case

[1] The act discontinued the subtreasury system, a Democratic reform of the forties, by requiring the government's funds to be deposited in the Federal Reserve Banks. Provision was also made for replacing national bank notes with federal reserve bank notes.

(Duplex Printing Press Company v. Deering, 1921), the bench upheld an injunction issued by a lower court to prevent the national membership of a union from boycotting a local employer. The judges asserted that the exemptions of the Clayton Act applied only to the employees directly involved, not to members of their union throughout the country who joined in the boycott. Again, in the case of United Mine Workers v. Coronado Coal Company (1922), the Court held that unions, being incorporated, were liable like business corporations for damages, including triple damages under the Sherman Antitrust Act.

The fall elections of 1914 enabled the voters to pass judgment on the accomplishments of the New Freedom. Though the Democratic majority in the House was cut, the administration nevertheless had reason to rejoice, since it had maintained control of Congress in what was essentially a two-party contest. With the Progressives displaying startling weaknesses all along the line, it was evident that many of them had deserted to the President.

Notwithstanding the growing importance of foreign affairs in the next two years the Democrats proceeded to enact further reform legislation. In 1916 a Rural Credits Law gave farmers credit facilities comparable to those granted by the Federal Reserve System to manufacturers and merchants. Under general administration of a Federal Farm Loan Board they were enabled to borrow from Federal Land Banks on farm-mortgage security over long periods of time at a lower rate of interest than a commercial bank would charge. Congress also attacked the thorny problem of child labor. Though most of the states had legislation on the subject, the laws were often poorly enforced, while in other states the evil flourished unchecked. But how could the general government act when the Constitution was silent on the point? The Democrats resolved to test the issue with the judiciary. Stretching to the utmost its power to regulate interstate commerce, Congress in 1916 excluded from interstate transportation the products of establishments employing workers under fourteen years. In Hammer v. Dagenhart (1918) the Supreme Court, however, by a vote of five to four annulled the law. In 1919, during Wilson's second term, Congress tried a different method. Under its power "to lay and collect taxes" it imposed a 10-per-cent tax on the net profits of companies hiring children under the age of fourteen. Again the judicial lightning struck, this time in the case of Bailey v. Drexel Furniture Company (1922). There the matter rested for the time.

FULLER ACCOUNTS

The Ground Swell of Reform. Allen, *Lords of Creation,* Cochran and Miller, *Age of Enterprise,* Edwards, *Finance Capitalism,* and Moody, *Truth about the Trusts,* trace the changes in Big Business; Brandeis, *Other People's Money,* discusses the findings of the Pujo committee; while Regier describes *The Era of the Muckrakers.* For municipal and state reforms, turn to Faulkner, *Quest for Social Justice,* which deals also with other topics in this chapter.

Roosevelt and the Square Deal. The general accounts include Josephson, *President Makers;* Mowry, *Roosevelt and the Progressive Movement;* Ogg, *National Progress;* Rhodes, *McKinley and Roosevelt Administrations;* and Sullivan, *Our Times,* I–III, with major actors treated in Bowers, *Beveridge and the Progressive Era;* Pringle, *Roosevelt;* and Stephenson, *Aldrich.* For railroad regulation, consult James, *Principles of Railway Transportation,* and, for the conservation movement, Hibbard, *Public Land Policies,* and Robbins, *Our Landed Heritage.*

Taft Inherits the Presidency. Most of the foregoing continue into the Taft and Wilson regimes, and in the case of the Taft administration they should be supplemented by Hechler, *Insurgency,* Pringle, *Taft,* and Taussig, *Tariff History.*

Wilson and the New Freedom. See particularly Paxson, *American Democracy and World War,* I, and, for special phases, Frankfurter and Greene, *Labor Injunction;* Henderson, *Federal Trade Commission;* Knauth, *Policy of the United States toward Industrial Monopoly;* Ratner, *American Taxation;* Taussig, *Tariff History;* and Willis, *Federal Reserve System.* Baker, *Wilson,* is an encyclopedic biography; Bell, *Wilson and the People,* and Cranston, *Woodrow Wilson,* are shorter and more recent studies.

CHAPTER XI

SOCIAL AND CULTURAL FERMENT

THE MARCH OF LABOR

SOCIETY'S increasing willingness to grant legislative protection to wage earners was a tardy recognition of labor's basic role in the American economy as well as of the rising strength of trade-unions. The United States Industrial Commission, reporting to Congress in 1902, ascribed past improvements in working conditions to the initiative of the employees and stressed particularly the value of unions with national memberships. It also justified labor's goal of a closed shop—that only union members be hired. In similar spirit another official board, the Commission of Industrial Relations, urged eleven years later that "every means should be used to extend and strengthen organizations throughout the industrial field." The progress made came in the face of many difficulties. After the return of business prosperity in 1897 and throughout the period, labor pressed its demands on a scale hitherto unknown, with more work stoppages in the years 1901–1905 than in the entire preceding decade. Against the bitter opposition of the National Association of Manufacturers and other employers' groups, wages were increased and the workday was shortened until eight hours prevailed in most skilled occupations. Ten hours continued to be the rule on the railroads, however, and the great steel industry balked any unionization. The practice of trade agreements also became more general. This acceptance of the principle of a joint partnership in fixing terms of employment afforded heartening evidence of saner relations between management and labor.

The American Federation of Labor rose from 550,000 members in 1900 to 2,371,000 in 1917 exclusive of unaffiliated bodies such as the Railway Brotherhoods. As earlier, it flinched from launching a separate political party, and it viewed with dislike the increasing strength of the Socialists, who in 1912 polled nearly 900,000 votes. Nevertheless, as has been seen, the Federation in 1908 began the practice of endorsing the major candidate whose platform leaned toward labor. How effective was this policy of "Reward your friends and punish your enemies" is uncertain, since traditional party loyalties made it hard for wage earners, as with other citizens, to switch their votes as occasion demanded. The Wilson regime, however, bestirred itself to justify the AFL's support. The appointment of William B. Wilson of the United Mine Workers to the new post of Secretary of Labor in 1913 was one indication, while Congress's legislative program supplied even clearer evidence, President Gompers of the Federation going so far as to acclaim the Clayton Act as "Labor's Magna Charta."

As a further gesture the Newlands Act in 1913 created a permanent board of mediation and conciliation to assist, when asked, in settling railway labor difficulties. Already by October, 1916, it had helped to adjust sixty-one disputes. Yet in March, 1916, when the four Railway Brotherhoods demanded a basic eight-hour day, they declined to refer the matter to the board and, instead, threatened a country-wide strike unless the companies conceded the shorter day at the same pay as for ten hours, with time-and-a-half for overtime. To avert a disastrous tie-up of transportation, President Wilson went before Congress on August 29 and urged the immediate enactment of legislation granting ten hours' pay for the first eight hours of work, with a proportionate additional wage for overtime. In defending his unprecedented action he declared that "the eight-hour day now undoubtedly has the sanction of the judgment of society." Within exactly one hundred hours the Adamson Law containing his proposals was passed. Critics of the administration believed the government's 'surrender' to be a precedent fraught with dangerous consequences.

The American Federation, though greatly increasing in size, continued to ignore the ill-paid, unskilled, immigrant toilers in the mills as well as the migratory workers in the Great West who followed the harvest or cut the timber. To represent their interests a new organization, the Industrial Workers of the World, sprang up in 1905 under 'Big Bill' (William D.) Haywood, a fighter trained in the savage industrial warfare of Colorado's Cripple Creek mining district. Like the old Knights of Labor, the I. W. W. proposed to unite all workingmen regardless of trade or skill in 'one big union,' but to this program it added two significant features. One was to continue the struggle against capital until the wage earners "take possession of the earth and the machinery of production and abolish the wage system." The other was to employ as the means 'direct action' (the general strike, violence and sabotage). The 'Wobblies' were a catchall for socialists, anarchists, opportunists and malcontents of many varieties. Probably at no time did they exceed sixty thousand; but for nearly ten years they kept the Pacific Northwest in turmoil, and in 1912 and 1913 they reached eastward to conduct desperate strikes among the sweated textile workers in Lawrence, Massachusetts, Paterson, New Jersey, and Little Falls, New York. Only the Lawrence effort succeeded. Their violence alarmed a public used to the more orderly methods of trade-unions and in some instances provoked lawless or extralegal reprisals. In 1917 I. W. W. opposition to America's entry into the European war arrayed the government against the organization and hastened its collapse. Yet its brief and stormy career led the American Federation for a time to pay more heed to unskilled and unorganized wage earners.

It is less surprising that the I. W. W. arose than that it did not make a greater appeal, considering the mounting deluge of foreign-born workers unfamiliar with the American way of life. From 1900 to 1917 nearly fourteen and a third million men, women and children entered the United States from Europe. President Roosevelt, informing Congress in 1905 that over a million had arrived in twelve months, added, "In the single year that has just elapsed there came to this country a greater number of people than came here during the one hundred and sixty-nine years of our Colonial life which intervened between the first landing at Jamestown and the Declaration of Independence." Though so high an annual figure had never before been reached, it was surpassed on five later occasions during this period. The influx from Southern and Eastern Europe, consisting predominantly of illiterates, formed the greater part of the flood, accounting for three quarters of those entering in the year World War I began. All the earlier fears of the nation's power to digest these strangers deepened, while organized labor became clamorous on the subject of unfair competition. As a result, Congress in 1913 revived the idea of a literacy test, passing a bill to require of immigrants a reading knowledge of English or some other language. But Taft vetoed the measure, as did also Wilson when faced with a similar one two years later. Both men maintained that illiteracy implied not absence of natural capacity but lack of youthful opportunity. In 1917, however, shortly before America entered the war, Congress won out over Wilson's continuing opposition.

The question of Oriental immigration also arose but now in a different form. Though the Chinese were effectively curbed, growing numbers of Japanese appeared on the Pacific Coast in the early years of the century. Thrifty, hard-working, inured to a bare subsistence, they began to displace white workers, notably in truck gardening. Talk soon became rife of a new 'yellow peril,' organized labor demanded exclusion, and the people of California generally gave hearty support. Yet their fears looked to the future rather than to the present, for in 1910 the newcomers numbered only 2 per cent of the state's population. It was also true that a federal statute of 1875 barred Japanese and other Asians from naturalization, though, of course, their American-born offspring acquired citizenship under the Fourteenth Amendment. In 1906 the antagonism flared up in an order of the San Francisco board of education to segregate Japanese children in a separate building, this despite the fact that there were but ninety-three in the schools out of a total of twenty-five thousand pupils. Japan promptly protested the action as violating its treaty with the United States. Though the Washington authorities had no jurisdiction whatsoever over school affairs in San Francisco, President Roosevelt induced the board to withdraw its decree and took steps to bring about an understanding between the two countries in regard to the larger issue. By the 'Gentlemen's Agreement' in 1907 Japan engaged on its own initiative to prevent the future emigration of laborers to the United States.

Anti-Japanese feeling in California persisted, however, and in 1913 the legislature, over President Wilson's protest, adopted the Webb Act which forbade aliens ineligible to citizenship to own agricultural land thereafter. But the Japanese found legal means of evasion by taking out the title in the name of their American-born children, or by leasing rather than buying the land. To plug up these and other holes the legislature in 1920 expressly forbade such practices. Tokyo continued to remonstrate, but the American government, insisting that no actual treaty rights were denied, proposed to leave the question to the United States Supreme Court. In 1923 the judges affirmed the constitutionality of the Webb Act and of a similar one of the state of Washington. In 1924, as we shall see, Congress superseded the

Gentlemen's Agreement with a statute banning all Japanese immigration. This needless offense to Nippon's dignity became a disturbing factor in the future relations of the two powers.

THE PROGRESS OF SOCIAL REFORM

In the nation's urban communities the pioneer work of the humanitarians in the 1880's and 1890's bore fruit in wide-flung efforts to relieve poverty and distress. The conservation of human resources, no less than of natural resources, became a goal of the age, one actively promoted by the fast-growing profession of social workers. Charity-organization societies and social settlements now spread to many of the smaller cities and extended westward and southward until the whole nation was covered. At the same time the slum evil was attacked with fresh zeal. In 1901 the New York legislature, confronted with housing conditions on Manhattan Island that were the worst in the world, enacted a tenement-house code for the state which in most respects was a model of its kind. As the price of passage, however, the statute did not include slum clearance and thus left for continued occupancy sixty-four thousand of New York City's filthy 'old-law' tenements. Nevertheless, the legislation lifted standards throughout the state and inspired commonwealths like Pennsylvania, New Jersey and Connecticut, as well as many cities, to enact similar regulations.

All such measures, directly or indirectly, betrayed a renewed concern for children's rights. Further evidence appeared in municipal ordinances safeguarding the quality of milk, in the creation of separate courts for juvenile delinquents and in the multiplication of community playgrounds. Playgrounds increased at such a rate that by 1910 they existed in a hundred and fifty cities, and by 1917 in well over four hundred. By supplying outlets for children's energies they were designed on the one hand to promote health and pleasure and on the other to check juvenile tendencies to crime. The introduction of the Boy Scouts from England in 1910 and the establishment two years later of the Girl Scouts and the Campfire Girls represented yet other efforts to turn the gang spirit natural to youth into wholesome channels.

New gains also came to the temperance movement. The widening reach of the social settlements and the increase of urban recreational facilities steadily undermined the saloon as the 'poor man's club,' while the pecuniary advantage of sober employees was driven home to industrialists by the workingmen's compensation laws. Though nearly every religious denomination had its temperance committee or teetotal society, the brunt of the attack was borne by the W. C. T. U., the Temperance Society of the Methodist Church and a relatively new and markedly militant body, the Anti-Saloon League of America. These groups left little undone to arouse public opinion against the liquor traffic and to agitate for restrictive measures. As the century opened, only Kansas, North Dakota, Maine, New Hampshire and Vermont—all agricultural states—had state-wide prohibition, and the last two reverted to local option in 1903. In other directions, however, the growth of dry territory was startling. For the first time the South, spurred by the desire to keep strong drink from the Negroes, adopted state-wide bans, eight commonwealths doing so between 1907 and 1915. In 1915 and 1916 the movement swung into the Far West, scoring victories in Arizona, Oregon, Washington, Colorado and Idaho. Meanwhile Iowa joined the procession, and local option had largely dried up other rural parts of America. Nearly everywhere, however, there were difficulties of enforcement, and in 1913 the temperance forces induced Congress to pass the Webb-Kenyon Act to protect dry areas against liquor shipments from outside the state. The cities continued to be the citadels of wet sentiment, and in order to bring them to heel, the prohibitionists determined to secure a federal constitutional amendment. The unusual conditions created by America's entrance into World War I were to give them their opportunity.

At all points the quest for community betterment received support from persons affiliated with churches and, to a growing extent, from the churches themselves. Building on the social gospel of the 1880's and 1890's, organized religion showed an ever greater disposition to further the progressive ideals in city, state and nation. During the first decade and a half of the century most of the leading Protestant denominations set up social-service commissions and issued declarations of social purpose. Institutional churches increased; ministers' conferences sent fraternal delegates to city trade assemblies; congregations co-operated with welfare agencies. Not all religious groups advanced with equal pace, but few failed to devote greater attention to the social teachings of Jesus. In 1908 came a collective expression when the Federal Council of Churches, representing thirty-three Protestant sects, framed a social creed which in a sense anticipated and outstripped the Progressive platform of 1912. It declared labor's right to organize; advocated a living wage with shorter hours, a six-day week and old-age insurance; denounced child labor and the sweating system; and demanded "the most equitable division of the product of industry that can ultimately be devised." The Federal Council's function, however, was not so much to accomplish results itself as to stimulate other religious bodies to greater activity and to correlate their efforts. To that end it diligently fostered the formation of state and local interchurch federations. Meanwhile the Catholic Church, strong in organization, alert to its opportunities, enlarged its welfare activities and strove to conserve the gains that accrued from the swelling immigration from the Catholic parts of Europe.

Increasing attention was also focused on the problem of rural communities. Drained of much of their best blood by the exodus to the cities, such places were apt to be overstocked with Protestant churches whose listless spiritual life was galvanized occasionally by temporary revivals. Improvement began to appear, however, as the people buried ancient doctrinal differences and joined in federated or union churches. Theological seminaries assisted by providing special courses for training country clergymen. As a result, abler men were attracted into the ministry and rural Christianity took on new vitality.

INTELLECTUAL AND ARTISTIC CURRENTS

In the newspapers and magazines the bulk of the people found their mirror of the times. Though the number of dailies rose only from 2190 to 2410 between 1900 and 1917, their circulation doubled. The business of co-operative news gathering grew in comprehensiveness and efficiency as rivals of the Associated Press appeared in the International News Service (1906) and the United Press (1907), the former sired by William Randolph Hearst. The tendency toward the standardizing of news was strengthened further by the formation of newspaper chains under single control, an application to journalism of a familiar principle in the business world. The Scripps-McRae (later Scripps-Howard) League, founded in 1895 with four dailies in the Midwest, had acquired twenty-two in many parts of the land by 1910. By the latter date thirteen chains were active, with the number increasing.

As prodders of the public conscience, however, the low-priced magazines surpassed the newspaper press. It was from their pages that the Muckrakers discharged their principal volleys. While Thomas W. Lawson's "Frenzied Finance" was running in *Everybody's,* the circulation leaped from 150,000 to more than 750,000. These periodicals also proved a training ground for some of the ablest literary men, such as Theodore Dreiser, Jack London, William S. Porter ("O. Henry") and David Graham Phillips. Never had the monthlies attracted so large and interested an audience. Of the weeklies, the *Nation* after a temporary eclipse resumed its role as fearless critic, and in 1914 it was joined by the *New Republic,* founded by Herbert Croly and a group of progressive-minded associates. Yet the giant among the weekly journals was of a different kind, being less concerned with social and economic criticism than with expressing the traditional ideals of the comfortable. This was the *Saturday Evening Post,* for which Cyrus H. K. Curtis had paid $1000 in 1897 and which within a decade mustered nearly a million buyers. Through its stories and articles and even its advertising, the *Post* appealed to such rooted middle-class traits as optimism, nationalistic feeling, the gospel of hustle and glorification of material success.

The rebellious mood of the generation pervaded much of the literature. Under the spell of the Spanish-American War there was a temporary flurry of interest in historical novels, with books like Paul Leicester Ford's *Janice Meredith* (1899), Mary Johnston's *To Have and To Hold* (1900) and Winston Churchill's *The Crisis* (1901) enjoying an enormous vogue. As the rumblings of insurgency became louder, however, fiction writers tended to desert the glamorous past for the grim present. In *The Octopus* (1901) Frank Norris pictured the struggle between California wheat farmers and a rail monopoly. The socialist Jack London, after penning adventure stories about the Arctic, heralded an impending social revolution in *The Iron Heel* (1907). David Graham Phillips added *The Plum Tree* (1905), *Light-Fingered Gentry* (1907) and a host of other novels exposing the flaws and injustices of a money-mad society, and Theodore Dreiser, using the traction magnate Charles T. Yerkes as his model, portrayed the rise of an unscrupulous capitalist in *The Financier* (1912) and *The Titan* (1914). Churchill contributed *Coniston* (1906), a tale of the railroads in politics, while Upton Sinclair and many others brewed a similar mixture of love interest and social propaganda. It was as a relief from such fare that readers turned to O. Henry's scintillating short stories of metropolitan life. But even his writings were not awarded the crown of a million or more sales. This distinction fell to Edward N. Westcott's *David Harum* (1900), Owen Wister's *The Virginian* (1902), Kate Douglas Wiggins's *Rebecca of Sunnybrook Farm* (1903), Jack London's *The Call of the Wild* (1903), John Fox's *The Little Shepherd of Kingdom Come* (1903), Harold Bell Wright's *The Winning of Barbara Worth* (1911) and Eleanor H. Porter's *Pollyanna* (1913) as well as four novels by Gene Stratton Porter. Not many of these, however, survived their ephemeral fame.

Poetry, which since Walt Whitman's heyday had been the poor relation of American letters, now came into its own as it rediscovered average humanity. Such writings as Vachel Lindsay's *General William Booth Enters into Heaven, and Other Poems* (1913), Edgar Lee Master's *Spoon River Anthology* (1915) and Carl Sandburg's *Chicago Poems* (1916) were tinged with social protest. The verse, though often crude in form, was ore fresh from the mine, not metal smoothed and dulled by incessant use. Of greater lasting value perhaps was the work of Edwin Arlington Robinson and Robert Frost in a more conventional tradition. The one, a bleak spare writer of gray moods, dealt with the Arthurian past as well as the New England present; the other portrayed unforgettably the integrity and reticence of the Yankee farmer.

The legitimate drama went through somewhat the same cycle as fiction. Content at first with stage versions of historical novels and with society plays like those of Clyde Fitch and Augustus Thomas, the public soon expressed its preference for shows that dealt trenchantly with contemporary social problems. Among the more popular offerings were Charles Klein's "The Lion and the Mouse" (1906), inspired by Ida M. Tarbell's *History of the Standard Oil Company;* Charles Rann Kennedy's "The Servant in the House" (1908), which revealed how far the practice of Christianity fell short of the theory; Charles Kenyon's "Kindling" (1911), a play of slum life; and Edward Sheldon's "The Boss" (1911), which dealt with the struggle between capital and labor. Players like Minnie Maddern Fiske, John Drew, Richard Mansfield, Otis Skinner, Julia Marlowe and E. H. Sothern did much to sustain the high standards of acting inherited from the previous generation.

Meanwhile the schools quietly carried on their work of banishing illiteracy and handing on the torch of knowledge. The task became constantly greater with the increasing numbers of immigrant children, but public and private funds streamed into the educational system as never before. The total expenditures more than trebled between 1900 and 1917, while the total enrollment grew from 15,500,000 to around 20,500,000, embracing a larger proportion of American youth than ever before. Though the cities continued to set the pace, notable progress was also made in rural education. Aided by the good-roads movement and the introduction of the motorbus, country folk began to abandon the scattered 'little red schoolhouses' and to pool their resources in centrally located 'consolidated schools,' where better instruction, modern equipment and separate grades could be provided. Especially noteworthy was the advance in the South. Throughout the section compulsory-attendance laws were now enacted, public appropriations were enlarged, school terms lengthened, and high schools added to cap the system, though the South still lagged behind the rest of the country and the Negro schools continued to be inferior to those for the whites. Despite the impressive gains nearly everywhere in the nation, the total schooling of the average person in his entire lifetime increased only from a bit over five years in 1900 to six and a half in 1916. Much remained for the future to accomplish.

Sensitive to the political aspirations of the day, outstanding educational leaders strove to remodel the school into a vital adjunct of democracy. Professor John Dewey, the most outspoken critic of the older pedagogy, maintained that social utility, not mere knowledge, should be the aim of instruction. In such works as *The School and Society* (1899) and *Democracy and Education* (1916) he taught that "the primary business of the school is to train children in co-operative and mutually helpful living," and that the school should "reproduce on the child's level the typical doings and occupations of the larger, maturer society into which he is finally to go forth." In tune with his ideas a committee of the National Education Association declared in 1918 that education should "develop in each individual the knowledge, interests, ideals, habits, and powers whereby he will find his place and use that place to shape both himself and society toward ever nobler ideals." Dewey's conception of 'progressive education' served gradually to modify purposes and procedures of instruction not only in the United States but in other countries as well.

Though the public schools increasingly stressed preparation for life above preparation for college, university enrollments nevertheless trebled from 1900 to 1917. The chief divergence from earlier educational practice was the junior college limited to the freshman and sophomore years, of which a hundred and thirty-two existed in 1917. First successfully launched with public funds in 1902 at Joliet, Illinois, the innovation rapidly spread through the Middle and Far West. Sometimes the two years would be added to the regular school system; sometimes private colleges with dwindling incomes would eliminate the junior and senior years; sometimes the institutions would be created independently. Whatever the method, the junior college usually afforded opportunity for advanced study nearer the student's home and also supplied a shorter unit of training for those who could not complete a four-year course.

The din of the political conflict echoed in academic halls, heightening the interest of students in the social sciences and causing professors to play an increasing role as consultants on social and economic reforms in city, state and nation. 'Fighting Bob' La Follette, for example, worked closely with members of the University of Wisconsin faculty, obtaining expert advice and constant encouragement in his labors for progressive principles. The universities steadily drifted closer to the main currents of American life. The nation did not hesitate to make Woodrow Wilson, a former college president, its chief magistrate, nor was it surprised when his predecessor retired from the White House to a chair of law at Yale. Even scholarly work showed the impress of the times. Roscoe Pound of the Harvard Law School taught the doctrine of "sociological jurisprudence" in an effort to gear legal principles to the current needs of society. Thorstein Veblen of Chicago, Leland Stanford and Missouri, applying the razor of his intelligence to orthodox economics, exposed the antisocial effects of the profit system, absentee ownership and predatory business. In like fashion Charles A. Beard injected fresh realism into the study of history and political science, emphasizing the working of social forces behind political forms and subjecting even the sacrosanct Constitution to a rigorous economic interpretation. His Columbia colleague James Harvey Robinson added to the illumination by calling for a "new history," a scrutiny of the past which should go beyond the traditional precincts of politics, war and diplomacy to embrace all that man has thought and done. Contributions of this character helped to give point and direction to a mass of scholarly production exceeding anything the nation had before known.

In a quite different way science played an ever larger part in the daily life of society. Chemists manifested their wizardry by showing how familiar products might be concocted synthetically. Coal tar, for instance, was turned into commodities ranging all the way from coloring matter for cake frosting to high explosives. Scientists also made important discoveries as to food constituents, thereby leading the public to give greater attention to calories and vitamins as elements of diet and arming medical men for a fresh attack on scurvy, rickets and other ills arising from improper eating. Equally important advances were made in other phases of the healing art. Besides the discovery of the transmitting source of yellow fever, already noted, Dr. Howard T. Ricketts of the University of Chicago found that Rocky Mountain spotted fever was a tick disease, and with Russell M. Wilder he proved that typhus was carried by body lice. This latter knowledge proved of immense help in combating typhus epidemics in World War I. Meanwhile the annexation of Puerto Rico had prompted a scientific inquiry under Major Bailey K. Ashford into the cause of anaemia which held nine out of ten of the islanders in its grip. The discovery that a tiny intestinal parasite called the hookworm was responsible led Dr. Charles W. Stiles to identify the species as one which was also prevalent in the rural South, where its ravages helped explain the backwardness of the poor-white class. Financed by John D. Rockefeller, a campaign was begun in 1908 to stamp out the malady. After nineteen years the International Health Board was able to report, "At the present time it is fair to say that hookworm disease has almost disappeared from the United States, and is rapidly coming under control in many parts of the world."

In these and like instances the findings as to the causation of disease equipped medical scientists with better means of prevention, control and cure and greatly strengthened the effectiveness of the public-health agencies that had been increasing since the Civil War. Between 1900 and 1920 the expectation of life at birth lengthened from about fifty years to a little over fifty-six. Decline in the death rate was particularly notable in such sicknesses as typhoid, diphtheria, croup, tuberculosis and scarlet fever. The enlarging American contribution to world science thrice won signal recognition during these

CORTLANDT STREET, NEW YORK

APPROACHES TO GATUN LOCK, PANAMA CANAL

TWO ETCHINGS BY JOSEPH PENNELL

REMAKING HIGHWAYS IN THE PHILIPPINES

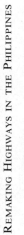

SLUM CLEARANCE IN PUERTO RICO

See pages 251 and 249

years when the coveted Nobel Prize was awarded in 1907 to the physicist, Professor Albert A. Michelson of the University of Chicago; in 1912 to the surgeon, Dr. Alexis Carrel of the Rockefeller Institute for Medical Research; and in 1914 to the Harvard chemist, Professor Thomas W. Richards.

Progress in the fine arts stemmed from the new beginnings in the eighties and nineties. Many of the master figures of those years now reached the zenith of their power, while younger men introduced fresh vigor and originality. In painting, the bent toward realism, exemplified earlier by the seascapes of Winslow Homer, found bolder expression in the work of Robert Henri, William J. Glackens, George W. Bellows and George Luks. Bellows, for example, painted prize fights, while Glackens and Luks derived their subjects from the tenements, saloons and streets of New York. In a different way Joseph Pennell's etchings of skyscrapers, the great locks of the Panama Canal and other feats of the new technology tingled with the life of the age. The masses, however, obtained their principal knowledge of art from the magazines, where illustrators like Charles Dana Gibson and Howard Chandler Christy portrayed idealized types of American girls and men which excited untold thousands in real life to imitation. Nevertheless, even the ordinary person had a better opportunity than ever before to learn of the more significant achievements through the multiplying art museums.

As a further influence for better standards of taste, the parks and public squares of the cities became studded with statuary fashioned by sculptors whose work ranked with the best of contemporary Europe. These compositions usually commemorated warriors and statesmen, but, more and more, themes typifying a broader national achievement crept in. Solon H. Borglum, drawing on his youthful experiences as a rancher, executed such works as "Burial on the Plains" and "The Blizzard." Among other notable creations were George Grey Barnard's "Hewer" (1902) at Cairo, Illinois; Charles H. Niehaus's "The Driller" (1902), erected by the Standard Oil Company at Titusville, Pennsylvania; and Lorado Taft's grand plan of sculptured decoration for Chicago, with "The Spirit of the Lakes" (1913) as the first unit.

Architecture expressed itself most strikingly in huge urban edifices: apartment houses which grew in number and height to accommodate the increasing army of 'cliff dwellers'; monumental passenger terminals such as Washington's Union Station (1907), New York's Pennsylvania Station (1910) and the Kansas City Union Station (1914); and steel-framed office buildings which dwarfed the skyscrapers of the 1890's. Manhattan's Singer and Woolworth Buildings (1908 and 1913), soaring respectively forty-one and fifty-one stories, revealed possibilities of the skyscraper's majestic beauty which the future would further unfold. A new note was also struck in domestic architecture, notably by Louis Sullivan's pupil Frank Lloyd Wright who, scorning mere decorative convention, endeavored to develop the natural qualities of the materials used and to set his structure in "the embrace of rock and tree and shrub." Generally speaking, the traditional regional types of construction tended to fade before the styles popularized by the cities. A hotel or schoolhouse or bank in Atlanta might just as well have been in Philadelphia or Minneapolis. Even in domestic architecture the contagious spread of the New England Georgian style and the Midwestern bungalow to all parts of America served to make residential and suburban districts everywhere look more or less alike. Yet, whatever its drawbacks, the standardization of architecture usually meant better architectural standards, a net gain for the average citizen.

OTHER CHANGES IN LIVING AND LEISURE

Notwithstanding the rising cost of living, which figured so prominently as a political issue, the mass of the people, especially in the towns and cities, enjoyed many advantages their fathers and grandfathers had not known. This was due in part to welfare enterprises which state and local governments undertook on an ever increasing scale—schools, parks, playgrounds, paved streets, sewerage, public-health safeguards, etc. Such undertakings, involving constantly higher taxes, diverted into socially useful channels some of the augmenting private wealth. Still more striking, because not equaled or even approached in any other country, was the voluntary financing by rich men of long-range projects for social improvement. The usual means was a foundation governed by a self-perpetuating board of trustees who employed a staff of experts to advise as to the spending of the funds. Rockefeller, whose benefactions for such purposes reached $400,000,000 by 1921, endowed the Rockefeller Institute for Medical Research (1901), the General Education Board (1903), the Rockefeller Foundation (1913) and the Laura Spelman Rockefeller Memorial Foundation (1918), the latter two with a broad mandate to promote the public good through fundamental investigations. Andrew Carnegie between 1902 and 1911 created the Carnegie Institution to encourage "research and discovery and the application of knowledge to the improvement of mankind," the Carnegie Foundation for the Advancement of Teaching, the Carnegie Endowment for International Peace, and the Carnegie Corporation with an undefined program to better society. By 1920 over a hundred such agencies existed to assist humanitarian enterprises, cultural development and scientific research, and by 1931 the number had grown to more than three hundred and fifty. Critics did not fail to flay an economic system that allowed the few to amass enormous wealth and then dole it back to the many, but the fact remained that such private accumulations, instead of being hoarded, found their way increasingly into channels of general usefulness.

More directly, the pleasantness of living was enhanced by many new mechanical inventions. To the aid of the housewife came countless labor-saving contrivances powered by electricity, such as vacuum cleaners and automatic refrigerators. Applied science also invaded the field of amusement, scoring its greatest triumph in the motion picture. Crude animated films had been projected on screens as early as the mid-nineties, but not till 1905, when Edison set up the first studio for indoor production, did they begin to attain a satisfactory technical perfection. To an even greater extent the movie's artistic development was indebted to David W. Griffith who in filming "The Birth of a Nation" (1915) went far toward freeing the screen from the physical restrictions of the stage. He was the first director to move his cameras about, obtaining close-ups, distant views, fade-outs and angle shots, and he also introduced the device of the flashback. Where Griffith led others followed. Though the film was not yet wedded to the phonograph and the performances were all in pantomime, the movie quickly established itself as a major form of entertainment, reaching multitudes who seldom if ever attended the regular theater. Such performers as the young English-born comedian Charlie Chaplin and Mary Pickford ('America's Sweetheart') commanded a devoted following not only in the United States but also abroad.

The stage showed as yet no signs of suffering from the competition. Particularly popular were the musical comedies—not delightfully satirical operas of the Gilbert and Sullivan type, but usually hodge-podges compounded of expensive scenery, an aimless plot, vaude-ville stunts, a few high-paid principals and a large prancing chorus. Victor Herbert, however, upheld the older standards, providing the musical setting for such successful shows as "Babes in Toyland" (1903), "The Red Mill" (1906) and "Naughty Marietta" (1910). Abetted by the ubiquitous phonograph, a kind of syncopated melody called ragtime laid its spell upon the masses, symbolizing as it did the increasing tempo and tension of American life. The best-known of such composers perhaps was Irving Berlin, a young Russian-Jewish immigrant in New York, whose greatest hit was "Alexander's Rag-time Band" (1912). At the same time the more serious forms of music evoked a growing patronage. This interest, which arose in part from the activities of the National Federation of Musical Clubs, formed in 1898, fostered the organization of symphony orchestras, hitherto restricted to a few leading centers, in cities as far removed as Minneapolis, New Orleans and Seattle.

Meanwhile outdoor recreation attained new proportions. The trend toward the professionalization of sports grew continually stronger, attracting tremendous crowds who were content to take their exer-cise passively instead of actively. In similar fashion college athletics, notably football, became so hedged about with highly paid coaches and so dominated by gate receipts as to render it more of a business than a pleasure even for the players. Signs of a reaction appeared in the increasing popularity of golf, which hitherto had been a fad of the wealthy. As late as the fall of 1908 Theodore Roosevelt warned Taft that his addiction to the aristocratic game was hurting his chances as a presidential candidate: "I have received literally hundreds of letters from the West protesting about it." But in the older parts of the country golf was already becoming a sport for the many as inex-pensive courses began to be laid out and even municipalities pro-vided facilities for their citizens.

The chief transforming influence in open-air life, however, was a new mechanical marvel, the self-propelling vehicle. As far back as 1893 ingenious young mechanics—Charles E. Duryea at Chicopee, Massachusetts, Henry Ford in Detroit, Ransom E. Olds in Lansing—had devised crude gasoline-driven cars, but European inventors had anticipated them, and for over a decade France and England produced more and better cars than did the United States. As American manufacturers made progress in standardizing the processes, however, and resorted increasingly to mass production, the price fell until it was within reach of the average purse, and the automobile swung into an immense popularity. The number in use rose from 300 in 1895 to 78,000 in 1905 and to 3,513,000 in 1916. The motorcar ceased being a luxury of the rich—of the "automobility," as a wag put it— and became a normal appurtenance of American life. The social effects were incalculable. Not only did it restore the forgotten delights of the open country to urban dwellers, not only did it help break down provincial barriers and mitigate rural isolation, but it begot a whole new brood of industries giving employment to millions. It also speeded the good-roads movement, accelerated the growth of suburbs and in countless ways heightened the momentum of American civilization. The introduction of the self-starting device in 1913 and 1914 ensured that the future would see women as well as men at the steering wheel.

Even more spectacular was the progress in navigating the heavens. Long an aspiration of mankind and vainly attempted by numberless inventors, heavier-than-air machines were made practicable by Orville and Wilbur Wright, two bicycle mechanics in Dayton, Ohio.[1] Familiar with what other experimenters had done, they finally succeeded in contriving a gasoline-motored plane which on December 17, 1903, remained aloft for a trial flight of 852 feet at Kitty Hawk, North Carolina. The secret of the eagle was now within grasp. In the years that followed, they and other inventors, notably in France, introduced changes and greatly improved the mechanism of flying; but it was not until World War I revealed its military possibilities that aviation really came into its own.

Significant as was the new role of gasoline in American life, it was outdistanced by the multiplied uses of electricity—its increasing application to the work of home and factory, to lighting, heating, traction and communication. The generating capacity of power companies rose nearly tenfold from 1902 to 1917, the number of customers from fewer than 600,000 to more than 7,000,000. Particularly noteworthy was the spread of hydroelectric plants until one or more were to be found in every state. Water-power sites assumed an

---

[1] Samuel P. Langley, secretary of the Smithsonian Institution in Washington, had devised a small steam-propelled model that flew 3000 feet in 1896, but his later experiments with a man-carrying, gasoline-driven craft in 1903 proved unsuccessful because of difficulties in launching it.

enormous importance and, except for those on the surviving public domain, were acquired by private corporations usually without adequate safeguards to assure good service and cheap rates for the public. As in other branches of industry, the urge for economical operation and the itch for bigger profits led to consolidation of ownership and to the weaving of a network of transmitting cables over great areas. An ampler public regulation of power companies was one of the problems which this generation, hardly appreciating its importance, bequeathed to its successors.

Into every phase of living the machine extended its sway. Historically Americans had always displayed mechanical ingenuity and a flair for tinkering; the twentieth century with its flowering of technology seemed the realization of a long-cherished dream. The environment of the people became to a surprising degree made up of machinery, much as the environment of wild animals is composed of fauna and flora. No one could doubt the beneficial results. The machine age freed mankind from an immeasurable amount of backbreaking toil. It pointed the way to shorter working hours without loss of productive capacity. It turned out more and cheaper goods. It conferred a degree of material comfort such as no nation had ever enjoyed. It widened horizons, created new pleasures for the many, enlarged their range of activity and added color and variety to everyday life. Moreover, through curtailing distances, it linked all parts of the land in closer comradeship and forged stronger bonds of nationality.

As the century advanced, however, thoughtful persons began to ask whether these gains did not come at too high a price, whether man's servant was not usurping the role of master. The deadly monotony of machine tending in the mill, the tremendous speeding up of industry, the displacement of faithful workers by new inventions, the depletion of natural resources through mass processes, the loss of individual craftsmanship in the making of standardized commodities, the growing dependence of people upon mechanical appliances for utilizing their leisure instead of relying upon their inner resources—all these bulked large on the debit side of the ledger. Yet no bold voice cried out for a return to a machineless age. The fault indeed lay not in machinery but in man's attitude toward it. Sooner or later, if he would achieve a more wholesome life, he must learn how to conserve the benefits of his extraordinary power over Nature and to combat its evils.

FULLER ACCOUNTS

The March of Labor. Faulkner, *Quest for Social Justice,* offers the best general treatment of this and other topics in this chapter. Commons and others, *History of Labor,* III–IV, is a detailed survey, with Dulles, *Labor in America,* and Harris, *American Labor,* offering shorter accounts. Lorwin, *American Federation of Labor,* and Brissenden, *I. W. W.,* single out the two major combinations of wage earners. Garis, *Immigration Restriction,* and Wittke, *We Who Built America,* include the newer population elements, while Jenks and Lauck, *Immigration Problem,* summarizes the findings of the Immigration Commission in 1911. For the new Oriental influx, see Bailey, *Roosevelt and the Japanese-American Crisis;* Buell, *Japanese Immigration;* and McWilliams, *Prejudice.*

The Progress of Social Reform. Watson, *Charity Organization Movement,* Woods and Kennedy, *Settlement Horizon,* and Rainwater, *Play Movement,* sketch the leading developments, with Ford and others, *Slums and Housing,* focusing on New York City. Asbury, *Great Illusion,* should be supplemented by Odegard, *Pressure Politics,* and Steuart, *Wayne Wheeler, Dry Boss,* for the temperance movement. Main trends in religion are set forth in Garrison, *March of Faith;* Macfarland, *Progress of Church Federation;* and Rowe, *History of Religion.*

Intellectual and Artistic Currents. Besides the references at the close of Chapter VI, the student should turn to Kazin, *On Native Grounds;* Morris, *Postscript to Yesterday;* Pattee, *New American Literature;* Hart, *The Popular Book;* Lee, *Daily Newspaper in America;* Meyer, *Education in the Twentieth Century;* Curti, *Growth of American Thought;* White, *Social Thought in America;* Slosson, *Creative Chemistry;* and Stieglitz, *Chemistry and Recent Progress in Medicine.*

Other Changes in Living and Leisure. Burlingame, *Engines of Democracy,* and Kaempffert, ed., *Popular History of American Invention,* discuss the principal technological advances. Morris, *Not So Long Ago,* tells about the motorcar and the movies, while special studies include Barber, *Story of the Automobile;* Lubschez, *Story of the Motion Picture;* Kelly, *Wright Brothers,* and Lougheed, *Vehicles of the Air.* For music, the theater and popular recreation, consult the works cited at the end of Chapter VI.

CHAPTER XII

IMPERIALISM IN PRACTICE

GEARING AN EMPIRE TO A REPUBLIC

PROGRESSIVISM put its stamp on the constitutions of the new states admitted to the Union in the early twentieth century: Oklahoma (including Indian Territory) in 1907 and New Mexico and Arizona in 1912. Arizona went so far as to provide for the popular recall of judges; but this proved too much for Congress which, at President Taft's urging, withheld approval of the constitution until the innovation should be rescinded. Arizona, having no choice, acceded only to restore the provision as soon as statehood was achieved. The addition of these three commonwealths rounded out the continental mass of the republic.

Progressivism at home contrasted greatly with the policies of the Roosevelt, Taft and Wilson regimes toward the insular possessions. The Constitution had never contemplated a colonial empire and, besides, such a course clearly violated the spirit and letter of the Declaration of Independence. This troubled the national conscience and led the government by way of expiation to promote the welfare, self-development and self-government of the native populations to a degree unknown in the case of European powers. In the end, however, the United States came to repent of its flier in imperialism, though it took the Great Depression of 1929 to spell out the lesson so that all might read.

The new acquisitions contained peoples of diverse races and religions at every level of political, economic and cultural progress. The United States therefore had to decide whether to allow them the large measure of autonomy which territories on the mainland had always enjoyed; to treat them as permanent dependencies beyond the pale of statehood; or to adopt some intermediate course. To this problem publicists and statesmen gave anxious thought. The solution was inevitably conditioned by motives of expediency as well as considerations rooted in time-honored ideals, and the policy or policies

246

agreed upon had to conform with what the Supreme Court conceived to be constitutional. Hence it fell to the judiciary to answer the question: 'Does the Constitution follow the flag?' In the Insular cases the high tribunal answered yes and no. The Constitution was held to consist of two kinds of provisions, "fundamental" and "formal," only the former of which applied to the annexations. The Court intimated that, from time to time as specific cases arose, it would say which clauses possessed this fundamental character. The cases at hand enabled the judges, however, to settle at once some of the most important issues.[1] They ruled that the inhabitants of these far-flung possessions were not to be United States citizens unless and until Congress should expressly so declare. The constitutional guarantees of citizens, such as indictment by grand jury and trial by jury, did not belong to them unless and until Congress should so say. In regard to tariff laws, duties might be freely imposed on their commerce with the United States. As Secretary of War Root neatly phrased it, "The Constitution follows the flag but doesn't quite catch up with it."

In other words, the government was for all practical purposes left free to administer the dependencies as it saw fit. Accordingly, it evolved a colonial program in which diversity, rather than uniformity, was the guiding principle. In each instance an effort was made to meet the needs of the people as indicated by their particular stage of political and social development. As the system gradually assumed shape, it came more and more to resemble the structure of the British Empire. Attached to the self-governing homeland were the outlying organized territories inhabited by alien nationalities with a large share of self-rule. Whether or not they might expect ultimate statehood remained unsettled. On the next plane below them were the possessions comparable to Britain's Crown Colonies, under Washington's direct tutelage with few if any rights of self-government. Nor did the similarity stop here. The imperial edifice was given its final touch by a fringe of political and economic protectorates in the Caribbean.

In accordance with historic practice the status of organized territory, with an elective legislature and a Washington-appointed governor, was bestowed on peoples who seemed ripe for the responsibility. Hawaii attained this rank under the Organic Act of 1900,

---

[1] Downes v. Bidwell (1900), De Lima v. Bidwell (1900), Dooley v. United States (1901), Pepke v. United States (1901), Hawaii v. Mankichi (1901) and Dorr v. United States (1904).

which declared the inhabitants to be American citizens and enfranchised all adult males who could read, write and speak either Hawaiian or English. The new territory, half the size of Maryland, progressed economically as additional American capital furthered the culture of sugar and the growing and canning of pineapples. The population, numbering 154,000 at the time of annexation, sprang from divers origins, over a third being Japanese, with strong infusions of Filipinos, Portuguese, Chinese and Americans. The total reached 255,912 by 1920. The pure native stock formed a dwindling minority, partly because of intermarriage with other strains. To offset the ethnic diversity there was established an excellent school system capped by the tax-supported University of Hawaii. With these advances occurred also a rising standard of living.

The next territory to be erected was Alaska, a much older dependency once belonging to Russia. More than twice the size of Texas, Alaska had for many years lived up to its reputation as 'Seward's Ice-Box.' Its chief springs of wealth were the fur-seal industry and the fisheries, but these had been developed by outsiders rather than by the native Eskimos and Indians. Though the 1867 treaty of annexation had granted American citizenship to the inhabitants (the uncivilized tribes excepted), it was not till 1884 that Alaska was given an appointive civil government. In the ensuing years white penetration of the interior gradually laid bare its dowry of natural resources. The finding of gold on Klondike Creek in 1896, on the Canadian side of the border, precipitated a rush from all parts of the world, which soon disclosed valuable deposits also on the American side—along the Yukon, near the head of Cook Inlet, and in the neighborhood of Nome. Before 1921 this treasure-trove yielded $320,000,000 in gold from Alaskan sources alone. Few of the Argonauts, however, became permanent settlers. Increasing knowledge of Alaska's resources made the question of safeguarding this reservoir of potential riches loom large in Roosevelt's conservation program. The best timberlands were set aside as national preserves, and efforts were made to protect coal and other mineral wealth from unlawful encroachment. With the gradual increase of white inhabitants, Congress in 1912 granted Alaska territorial status. Poor transportation facilities continued to hamper its development, however, and in default of other means Congress in 1914 provided for a government-owned and operated railroad which eventually stretched some five hundred miles from Seward to Fairbanks. But the population remained small, reaching only 55,000 by 1920, with the whites forming less than a majority. Despite many difficulties yet to overcome, there could be no doubt that Alaska would turn out to be one of America's most profitable acquisitions.

Five years after Alaska became a territory, Puerto Rico followed. Freed from military rule in April, 1900, this sunny island, half again as big as Delaware and inhabited largely by whites of Spanish descent, obtained at first only partial control of its affairs. Congress in 1900, though authorizing the adult males to elect the lower house of the legislature, had the President appoint the governor and the upper house, and it did not make the natives American citizens. American dominion greatly improved social and economic life. In the score of years after 1899 the highways lengthened from 430 miles to more than 1900, while school buildings increased from none at all to well over 500, with illiteracy declining from 80 per cent to 55. Public-health measures, including sewerage, quarantine regulations and hospitals, were introduced, and such scourges as yellow fever, smallpox and anaemia almost completely banished. Economic progress was quite as marked, sugar-cane culture outstripping coffee growing as the chief occupation, with tobacco ranking third. While the Puerto Ricans assisted wholeheartedly in these advances, they were discontented because they had not achieved American citizenship or a larger autonomy. In 1914 President Wilson reconstructed the upper house so as to give the natives a majority of the appointments, and three years later their demands were more nearly met by the Jones Act, which conferred United States citizenship and the right to elect the entire legislature. Nevertheless restiveness continued, partly because of the growing concentration of land in relatively few hands and a corresponding increase of farm tenancy. A rising sentiment favored statehood or some equivalent status, so that the people might enjoy greater freedom to deal with their problems in their own way.

Other parts of the overseas empire had to remain content with simpler and less democratic forms of government. In the Panama Canal Zone all political authority was vested in a resident official of the War Department, while Guam and American Samoa were similarly ruled by governors designated by the Navy Department. As for the multitude of other Pacific islands—Midway, Wake, Howland,

Baker and the rest—they contained few or no inhabitants and were given no local government at all. The purchase of the Virgin Islands (Danish West Indies), sixty miles east of Puerto Rico, under a treaty of 1916 with Denmark necessitated, however, some sort of political provision. Earlier efforts had been made to buy them, once in 1867 when the Senate had rejected Secretary Seward's treaty for that purpose, and again in 1902 when the Danish upper chamber stood in the way. The desire to obtain the islands grew steadily, however, because of their strategic position in relation to the Panama Canal and the belief that Germany, engaged after 1914 in World War I, coveted them. The third attempt succeeded, though the cost to the United States was $25,000,000, a sum wholly disproportionate to their intrinsic worth. The people, mostly Negroes, were placed under a presidential-appointed governor with a locally chosen legislature, and in 1927 they were made United States citizens. Unlike most of the other annexations, this one made only slight economic and social progress.

AMERICA IN THE PHILIPPINES

The Philippines occupied a special niche in the imperial structure, being partly in and partly outside it. As the McEnery resolution at the time of the peace with Spain had indicated, the United States was uncertain about permanent ownership and wished to do nothing to bolt the door against ultimate independence. Spain's relinquishment of the islands had not prevented the natives from resuming their fight for freedom against their new master, but they had no chance against the better trained and equipped Americans. Repeatedly routed in pitched engagements, they resorted to guerrilla tactics, laying waste fields and surprising and massacring small troop detachments. The United States soldiers, angered by the torturing of captive comrades, sometimes inflicted reprisals in kind. Finally, in March, 1901, a daring party under Brigadier General Frederick Funston seized Emilio Aguinaldo, the insurgent chieftain. It was not, however, until July 4, 1902—an unhappily chosen date—that President Roosevelt officially declared the rebellion crushed. Even afterward, sporadic outbreaks occurred, notably among the Moros and other wild tribes. The subjugation cost the United States $170,000,000, more than eight times the purchase price.

Under American tutelage the people were inducted by gradual

stages into the practice of self-rule. In July, 1901, when the military regime ceased, a governor-general (William Howard Taft) appointed from Washington took charge with the assistance of a commission of Filipinos and Americans. They promptly set about to reorganize the local governments, and for this purpose the suffrage was granted to all men of twenty-three or over who were taxpayers or who could speak, read and write English or Spanish. Then, a year later, Congress made more permanent provision for the islands. The Organic Act of July 1, 1902, declared the inhabitants "citizens of the Philippine Islands, and as such entitled to the protection of the United States." Most of the constitutional guarantees of life, liberty and property were extended to them except trial by jury, which could not easily be grafted onto the old Spanish legal system. Though the governor-general and the commission were continued in sole control for the time, the statute provided for the eventual creation of a legislature. In 1907 this pledge was fulfilled, the commission then becoming the upper house and the lower being chosen by the voters.

Meanwhile the islands awakened from their tropical sleep to a new interest in the bustling life of the modern world. One long-festering grievance had been the ownership of 410,000 acres of the best land by three Catholic orders. The Filipinos hated the friars so bitterly that during the revolt they had expelled them with great cruelty. When the religious orders, upon the establishment of American rule, insisted on their legal rights, Governor-General Taft took up the matter in person with the papal authorities in Rome, with the result that a payment by the United States of $7,239,000 in 1903 ended the dispute. With this and other difficulties removed, agriculture, aided by American capital, made rapid headway, notably the growing of sugar, coconuts, hemp and tobacco. Public order was assured through a native constabulary, and prison administration was reorganized. In addition, a currency system was instituted, and a public-works program was carried on, including highways, bridges, port improvements, lighthouses and irrigation projects.

Public education, unknown under Spain, also made astonishing progress. To start the schools hundreds of young American men and women went to the islands as teachers. With two hundred thousand pupils enrolled in 1902 the total more than trebled by 1917, and as the number of high-school graduates increased, the tax-supported University of the Philippines was established in 1909 to afford further training. English was added to Spanish as an official language, but sentiment grew among the people for adopting one of the many native dialects as the universal speech. This finally came about in 1937 when Tagalog, the language most widely spoken, was chosen as the basis for a national tongue, though the teaching of English in the schools continued to be compulsory. The population, which numbered less than seven million under Spain, exceeded ten in 1917.

In these reforms the islanders warmly co-operated. Keenly aware of their political inexperience, they sought to learn what they could from this intimate contact with a progressive Western people. In return, the American officials placed Filipinos in positions of trust and responsibility as rapidly as conditions seemed to justify. The people, however, never forgot their aspirations for independence. After the first few years every Philippine political party unfurled the banner of immediate freedom. In America the Democrats wanted to speed the consummation, and President Wilson upon entering office ensured full native control of the insular legislature by appointing Filipinos to a majority of the seats in the upper house. Three years later, in 1916, Congress in the Jones Act granted the islands what was in many respects territorial status: both legislative houses were made elective, with an appointive governor-general as before. It also trebled the electorate by extending the suffrage to all men of twenty-one or over who could read and write a native dialect. American citizenship was withheld, however, since the Jones Act stated Congress's purpose to recognize the independence of the islands "as soon as a stable government can be established therein." Almost at once the Filipinos were confronted with a severe test of their political capacity due to the financial and economic effects of World War I. Hostile critics saw evidences of governmental incompetence on every hand. Nonetheless, President Wilson informed Congress in December, 1920, that the people, having "succeeded in maintaining a stable government," were ready for independence. But the accession of the Republicans a few months later held up action for more than a decade. Added to their earlier reluctance to part with the Philippines was the fear that, if America let go, Japan would seize them. In this state matters remained until the Great Depression forced a reconsideration of the problem. By that time the United States was experiencing a revulsion from its imperialistic adventures in the Western Hemisphere as well as in Asia.

THE CARIBBEAN SPHERE OF INFLUENCE

In the meantime events had caused America to supplement her colonial holdings with a chain of protectorates in the Caribbean. The first impulse in this direction arose from the responsibilities which the government had assumed toward Cuba under the peace treaty of 1898. When the American military administration took charge on January 1, 1899, the people were poverty-stricken, disease-ridden, overwhelmingly illiterate and in political chaos. Under Major General John R. Brooke and his successor, Major General Leonard Wood, emergency relief was afforded the destitute, order was established, far-reaching sanitary reforms were introduced, the legal system was reorganized, and an extensive program of highway construction begun. Likewise, church and state were separated, and the public educational system was revived and greatly extended. On Wood's initiative a convention assembled at Havana in November, 1900, and drafted a constitution for the new republic modeled on that of the United States. Despite his urging, however, the instrument said nothing about future relations with the United States. Congress met the situation in the Platt Amendment to the Army Appropriation Act of March, 1901, which instructed the President to continue military control until certain specified provisions should be inserted in the constitution: Cuba must make no treaty that would impair her independence; she must never go into debt beyond her capacity to pay; she must allow America to intervene, with force if necessary, to preserve orderly government; and she must permit the United States to acquire naval bases.[1] Reluctantly the convention acceded. Two years later the stipulations were inserted in a "permanent" treaty.

In May, 1902, the government of independent Cuba was formally installed. Handicapped by a bad political heritage, the people were slow to value the ballot over the bullet in settling public issues. Corruption was also developed into a fine art; at some elections the number of votes far exceeded the number of voters. Civil disorders arising from the 1906 presidential election led to the first application of the Platt Amendment, the intervention lasting from September of that year to January, 1909. Again in 1912 marines were landed for several weeks near Santiago to protect American-owned mines and sugar plantations

[1] Naval stations were presently leased at Bahia Honda and Guantanamo, but the former was relinquished in 1913.

during a Negro uprising. Five years later a revolt, provoked by a disputed election of 1916, caused forces to be sent to Santiago and elsewhere, one detachment remaining until 1922. To prevent a recurrence of such disturbances a new electoral code, drafted with the assistance of United States General Enoch H. Crowder, was adopted by the insular legislature in 1919. But Cuba had not yet mastered the lesson of self-government, and other troubles lay ahead. On no later occasion, however, did Washington resort to armed intervention. In fact, in every earlier instance the government had acted with extreme reluctance despite the clamor in certain circles in the United States that the Gordian knot be cut by annexation. Since this large neighboring island, quite apart from economic considerations, was strategically vital to America's security, the forbearance exhibited a self-denial unknown to European powers in similar circumstances.

America's material stake in the island increased rapidly, the investment of capital rising from $80,000,000 in 1901 to $220,-000,000 at the outbreak of World War I—by far the largest amount in any Latin American country but Mexico. Preferential tariffs in the United States proved a special stimulus to cane growers, making Cuba the 'sugar bowl of the world,' with almost its whole output going to America. Real estate, railways, banks, government bonds, public utilities, mines, manufacturing and tobacco represented other ramifications of the economic penetration. To some Cubans it seemed that they had won independence from Spain only to turn over the country to Yankee business interests; but there could be no doubt that this relationship, plus the political balance wheel of the Platt Amendment, gave the island a measure of prosperity, and even of governmental stability, that it could not otherwise have achieved.

Shortly after Cuba unwillingly accepted the Platt Amendment, a second protectorate came into being under circumstances quite as natural. The Panama revolution put the infant republic in need of a defender against Colombia at a time when the United States sought a controlling hand in the territory bordering on the Canal Zone. Accordingly, the Washington government agreed in the treaty of November 18, 1903, to guarantee Panama's independence in return for the privilege of being allowed to use armed force whenever necessary "for the safety or protection of the Canal" or its auxiliary works. Under this arrangement the United States intervened five times between 1908 and 1921.

Even before this new protectorate was set up, a dramatic incident foreshadowed further and unexpected applications of the Platt Amendment principle. In December, 1902, Great Britain, Germany and Italy undertook a blockade of Venezuela, on the south shore of the Caribbean, in order to compel payment of long-standing debts to their citizens. The presence of a hostile European fleet boded ill for a weak Latin American country, and the State Department succeeded in having the blockade lifted and the claims referred to arbitration. To President Roosevelt the moral of the episode seemed clear. He informed Congress in December, 1904: "Chronic wrongdoing . . . may in America, as elsewhere, ultimately require intervention by some civilized nation, and in the Western Hemisphere, the adherence of the United States to the Monroe Doctrine may force the United States, however reluctantly, in flagrant cases of such wrongdoing or impotence, to the exercise of an international police power." In other words, the Monroe Doctrine imposed a duty on the Washington government to safeguard defaulting republics against possible foreign intervention by itself assuming responsibility for their financial good faith. By the 'Roosevelt Corollary' a doctrine of noninterference by Europe in the affairs of the New World thus became a doctrine of unmistakable interference by the United States.

If the Washington authorities originally entered upon the policy of protectorates somewhat casually, the desire to prevent new European outposts within striking distance of the Panama Canal quickened the process. Still another influence was the flow of American capital into the region. By the eve of the outbreak of World War I these investments amounted to $269,000,000 and by 1929 to $1,745,000,000. Commerce with the United States also grew, from $195,000,000 in 1900 to $272,000,000 in 1913. As a result of these various factors the circle of protectorates steadily widened, and the Caribbean Sea acquired the character of an American Mediterranean.

The Dominican Republic, occupying the eastern part of the island of Santo Domingo, was the first country to which the Roosevelt Corollary was applied. In order to avert probable action by European powers to collect debts long overdue, President Roosevelt in 1905, with the insular government's consent, placed an American financial expert in charge of its revenues, with authority to arrange for the gradual payment of the foreign bondholders. Two years later the stipulations were incorporated in a treaty giving the United States the right to extend "such protection" to the general receiver of customs and his staff as might "be requisite for the performance of their duties." Under this elastic clause American representatives supervised the Dominican elections of 1913, and three years later marines were landed to quell a revolt. The intervention grew into a complete military occupation, with the American officials restoring peace, enforcing sanitary measures, reorganizing the school system and undertaking an elaborate program of good roads and other public works. Angry at outside intrusion in their affairs, the native leaders insisted again and again that the occupation be ended. In June, 1921, Washington announced that withdrawal would occur only when the Dominican government entered into a treaty ratifying the acts of the military regime and amplifying the powers of the general receiver of the customs. These terms, though deeply resented, were eventually accepted. American evacuation took place in the summer of 1924, with the customs receivership, however, continuing.

The Negro republic of Haiti, occupying the remainder of the same island, was subjected to similar supervision. Following a revolutionary outbreak early in 1915 United States marines took possession of the chief towns. Then a treaty in September established America's management of Haitian finances, provided for a constabulary officered by Americans, and empowered the United States to intervene when necessary to ensure an orderly government. The American administration with characteristic efficiency carried through extensive sanitary, fiscal and governmental reforms and stabilized economic conditions. As will be seen, the marines did not leave until 1934.

Efforts were also made to extend the protectorate policy to Central America. In 1911 President Taft, following Roosevelt's example, negotiated treaties for fiscal receiverships in Honduras and Nicaragua, but these were rejected by the Senate. Nevertheless Nicaragua, with the State Department's approval, put her customs in charge of an American financial expert as the price of securing a loan from certain New York banking houses. In 1912 marines were landed to allay civil disorders, staying on until 1925. Meanwhile the United States by a treaty of 1914 obtained certain naval bases and the exclusive right to build a canal through Nicaragua, paying $3,000,000 for these privileges. Once more in December, 1926, the marines entered the country and eventually remained until 1933, fighting rebels and bandits and supervising elections. Thus, without express treaty sanc-

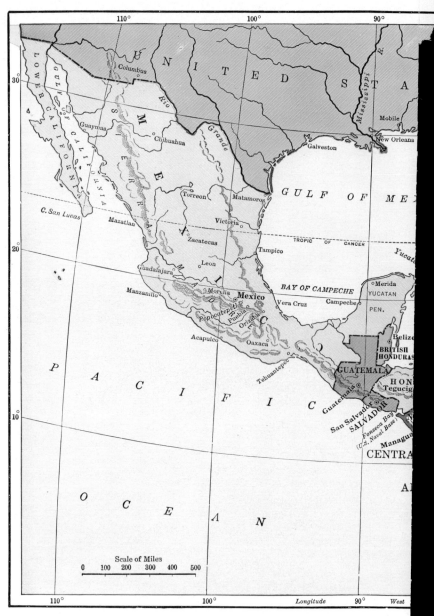

MEXICO, THE CARI

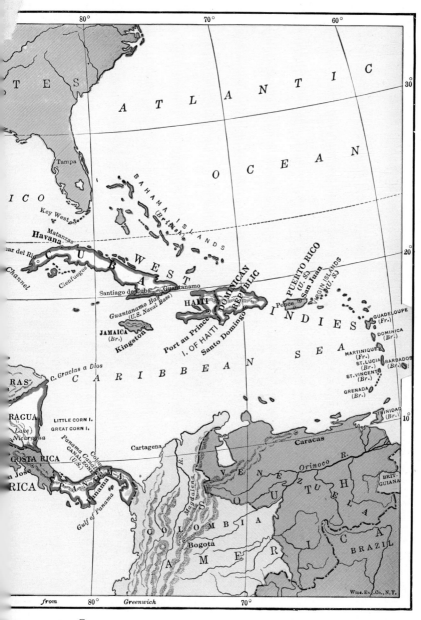

tion, Nicaragua found herself, in fact if not in law, a protectorate. In 1922 El Salvador placed herself in a similar position, accepting an American customs receiver in order to secure a loan from Wall Street bankers.

This whole course of policy was variously regarded in the United States as an altruistic assumption of what Rudyard Kipling called the "white man's burden," as an ungrateful task imposed by considerations of military security and as an ugly manifestation of 'dollar diplomacy' or economic and financial imperialism. Doubtless all these elements entered into the program. Nothing more clearly evinced the limited objectives of the progressive movement than the failure of these crusaders for democracy at home to insist on letting the Caribbean countries work out their own destinies. Even Woodrow Wilson, foe of Wall Street and ardent apostle of the New Freedom, subordinated his deep-grained belief in the right of national self-determination to the strategic needs of defense, especially with reference to America's lifeline, the Panama Canal. Only in the case of Mexico, which will next be considered, did he give his democratic instincts free rein.

TURMOIL IN MEXICO

Though the United States made no move to establish protectorates beyond Central America and the Caribbean, the outward thrust of Yankee dominion created uneasiness throughout Latin America. If, as Theodore Roosevelt asserted, the southward advance was warranted by the Monroe Doctrine, then it looked as though a policy originally forged as a defensive weapon had turned into an instrument of imperialistic aggrandizement. Resentment against 'Monroeism' burned especially fiercely in Argentina, Brazil and Chile, the so-called ABC powers, who felt that their political stability and cultural progress entitled them to freedom from alien tutelage. In these circles sentiment developed for a Pan American Doctrine which would substitute cooperative action for sole action by the United States in interpreting and enforcing the principles of the Monroe Doctrine. A Pan American Doctrine, of course, would be a curb on the 'Colossus of the North' as well as on Europe.

To allay Latin American fears aroused by his cavalier treatment of Colombia during the Panama revolt, President Roosevelt solemnly avowed to Congress in December, 1905, that "under no circumstances will the United States use the Monroe Doctrine as a cloak for territorial aggression." To the Latin Americans, however, the difference between actually annexing territory and controlling it under the guise of a protectorate seemed immaterial. Hence his assurance and that of President Taft in his turn did little to restore confidence. However, Wilson's course during a prolonged reign of anarchy in Mexico served somewhat to clear the atmosphere. In 1911, when the troubles began, United States citizens held Mexican investments, mostly in railways, mines, ranches and oil lands, totaling $1,000,-000,000. Forty or fifty thousand of them carried on business there, and the bulk of Mexico's trade lay with her northern neighbor. Notwithstanding these intimate economic ties President Wilson made it plain from the outset that the administration's policy would not be controlled by selfish considerations. "We have seen material interests threaten constitutional freedom in the United States," he declared in a speech at Mobile in 1913. "Therefore we will now know how to sympathize with those in the rest of America who have to contend with such powers, not only within their borders but from outside their borders also." As his program assumed form, he took the unprecedented step of inviting Latin American nations to co-operate in the settlement of Mexico's difficulties. Though his example was not followed by any of his immediate successors, it foreshadowed the much fuller collaboration of New World republics achieved by the Good Neighbor policy of Franklin D. Roosevelt.

Since 1877 Mexico had been almost continuously under the iron rule of Porfirio Díaz, nominally president but actually dictator. Constitutional government existed in form only, and the agrarian masses, mostly of Indian blood, were overwhelmingly illiterate, landless and tied to the soil by a system of peonage. But peace and order prevailed, foreign capital was welcomed, and the country experienced a great material transformation. In time, however, native dissatisfaction increased to so dangerous a pitch that the eighth 'election' of Díaz in 1910 precipitated a popular uprising. In 1911, when the aged ruler fled to Europe, Francisco Madero, the leader of the revolt, became his successor. The tide of lawlessness, however, still ran strong. In February, 1913, the reactionary General Victoriano Huerta, supported by the old Díaz faction, overturned the new government, and Madero and his vice-president were murdered. Once more Mexico was plunged into anarchy, with Venustiano Carranza directing the insurgents as Madero's political heir.

Though European powers promptly recognized Huerta according to accepted international practice, President Wilson declined to follow suit on the highly moral ground that the regime rested on force and assassination. "My ideal," he told a newsman, "is an orderly and righteous government in Mexico; but my passion is for the submerged eighty-five per cent of the people of that Republic who are now struggling toward liberty." Convinced that he could unseat Huerta by withholding recognition and preventing him from securing American loans, he opened the way for the Carranza forces to obtain munitions in the United States while he himself adopted a policy of "watchful waiting." Meanwhile the destruction of life and property continued, and American interests bent on armed intervention savagely denounced him as an impractical idealist. Even the President found the game of waiting arduous. When Huerta failed to make what Wilson considered a proper apology for the temporary arrest of some American marines at Tampico, United States forces bombarded and occupied the port of Vera Cruz in April, 1914, to head off an arms shipment to Huerta due to arrive in a German vessel. Wilson then accepted an offer of the ABC governments to mediate the difficulties. This move, however, had little practical effect, since Huerta, overwhelmed by his enemies, fled Mexico almost at once. Carranza then succeeded to his place, and in November the American forces evacuated Vera Cruz.

With the popular party once more in control, the situation assumed a new aspect as the victors fell to fighting among themselves, with Francisco Villa, a former bandit chieftain, the main disturbing element. Wilson, his patience sorely taxed, once more turned to Latin America for counsel. A joint conference of Bolivia, Uruguay, Guatemala, the ABC powers and the United States decided in October, 1915, to recognize Carranza as the true head of Mexico. This action strengthened Carranza's hold, but Villa managed to prolong his stormy career for over a year. Venting his rage against the United States, he raided across the border in March, 1916, killing seventeen persons in Columbus, New Mexico. A punitive expedition under General John J. Pershing went in pursuit, dispersing many lawless bands and quelling Villa once and for all. Meanwhile Wilson called out a hundred and fifty thousand state militiamen to patrol the international boundary. Not till January, 1917, were the troops withdrawn.

A few months later Mexico adopted a constitution incorporating the reforms of the revolutionary era. Besides ending the union of church and state and improving the lot of industrial workers, the new basic law provided for breaking up the huge landed estates and asserted national ownership of all oil and other mineral resources. The provision (Article 27) in regard to property rights vitally affected American investments and provoked sharp protests from Washington. Finally, Mexico in 1923 gave assurance that it would not be so applied as to confiscate American mineral rights acquired under the previous constitution, and agreed further to compensate American citizens whose estates had been expropriated. Other difficulties remained, but with Mexico now enjoying a stable government, their solution was assured through the normal channels of diplomacy.

AMERICA AND INTERNATIONAL PEACE

The swelling tide of democracy throughout the world, the new value placed upon the welfare of the common man, the tightening network of financial and commercial relations across frontiers, the staggering cost of national armaments—influences like these smoothed the way for the growth of an impressive peace movement in the early twentieth century. To an increasing number of people in all countries war seemed a relic of barbarism certain to disappear in the not distant future. To hasten that day the United States assumed an active role. No nation in the past had done more to further international arbitration, and America's new position as a world power enhanced the interest. The foreign investments of American citizens multiplied seven times from 1900 to 1914—from $500,000,000 to more than $3,500,000,000—and the growth of economic ties is further indicated by the fact that the United States Steel Corporation in these years established 268 agencies in some sixty countries and the International Harvester Company 53. Business on a global scale could be best served by a peaceful mankind.

It was, however, at the call of the Czar of Russia that twenty-six governments, meeting at The Hague in 1899, took collective action toward that goal, establishing a Permanent Court of Arbitration at The Hague and drafting certain regulations to govern the conduct of hostilities. A second conference in 1907 of forty-four countries, this time at President Roosevelt's prompting, adopted additional rules to mitigate the horrors of war and endorsed the principle that the debts of one country to the citizens of another should not be collected by force. The Hague Court comprised a panel of judges selected by the several countries, from which special tribunals were constituted from time to time to sit on specific disputes. Though the submission of cases was purely voluntary and the machinery of adjustment proved somewhat clumsy, the Court settled seventeen controversies between 1902 and 1917. To four of these the United States was a party, the most notable one involving the long-standing question of fishing rights off Newfoundland and Labrador. The decision, rendered in 1910, favored America.

Unofficial endeavors reinforced official ones. Where idealists and humanitarians had earlier backed the peace cause, solid men of affairs now also lent support. Thanks to the benefactions of Andrew Carnegie and Edwin Ginn, foundations were set up to investigate the causes and cure of war. In addition, Carnegie, whose wealth arose in part from the profits of selling armor plate, paid for constructing the Pan American Union building in Washington as well as the Peace Palace at The Hague. Peace societies multiplied, their literature was widely distributed, and the larger universities aided by creating international exchange professorships. These exertions did not go unopposed. The Navy League, formed in 1903 and dominated by retired naval officers and munitions manufacturers, urged bigger and better armaments. Nor did the increasing investments abroad always nourish a pacific spirit. Not only did they foster undeclared wars in the Caribbean, but American bankers found it profitable to supply the financial sinews for other nations' conflicts. In 1900 and 1901, for example, the British government, acting through J. P. Morgan and Company, borrowed $223,000,000, one fifth of the cost of the Boer War; and a few years later loans floated in the United States helped Japan, against Russia's resistance, to extend her sway into southern Manchuria.

Notwithstanding, Roosevelt struck a responsive chord when he assumed leadership in an effort to enlarge the authority of the Hague Court beyond the limits set. In 1904 he submitted to the Senate a sheaf of treaties which, departing from the existing voluntary arrangement, obligated the United States and the other signatory powers to submit to the Hague tribunal all their disputes save those involving vital interests, independence or national honor. An unhappy quarrel between the President and the Senate prevented ratification in a form acceptable to him, and the matter hung fire until 1908–1909 when the United States entered into twenty-two agreements of this kind.

As a promoter of peace, however, Roosevelt did not subscribe to many of the tenets of the professional pacifists. Even his arbitration treaties by excluding certain large subjects left the gate wide open for a resort to force. He held that heavy armaments were, after all, the best preventive of war. Nor did he hesitate to plunge into the hurly-burly of international politics to further general peace. In 1906, when war threatened in Europe because of a Franco-German controversy affecting Morocco, America united with ten other governments in a conference at Algeciras, Spain, for composing the differences. The Senate in ratifying the agreement cautiously disclaimed any "purpose to depart from the traditional American foreign policy which forbids participation . . . in the settlement of political questions which are entirely European in their scope." Meanwhile, in the Far East, a bloody conflict between Japan and Russia in 1904–1905 stirred Roosevelt to action. The President's sympathies, like those of the American public, lay with the smaller country, but he feared that a complete triumph by either would unsettle the balance of power in the Orient and endanger the Open Door. As Japan drew near the end of her resources, he persuaded the belligerents to join in a peace conference at Portsmouth, New Hampshire, from which Japan, the victorious combatant, issued with less than she wanted but with considerable territorial gains, including Russia's lease of Port Arthur in China. In recognition of his varied services Roosevelt was awarded the Nobel Peace Prize in 1906.

In the years thereafter the gravest threat to American peace from afar proved to be the growing friction with the Tokyo government. Roosevelt's pressure on Japan's delegates at Portsmouth not to insist upon extreme demands, coupled with the discriminations against her subjects on the Pacific Coast and America's increasing role in the Far East, steadily fed the flames of Nipponese resentment. The United States for its part suspected the island empire of designs on China's freedom and the Open Door as well as on the Philippines. As has been seen, the question of Japanese immigration was set at rest in 1907, and in 1908 a move was made to dispose of the more fundamental problem. The Root-Takahira Agreement pledged the two powers, "uninfluenced by any aggressive tendencies," to respect each other's territorial possessions in the Pacific and to support "by all pacific means" Chinese independence and the Open Door. As now defined, the Open Door went beyond John Hay's original formulation to include equal rights for all nations in industrial development as well as in trade. In the Lansing-Ishii Agreement in 1917 the two powers reaffirmed these assurances, with the imprudent admission by America that "territorial propinquity" gave Japan "special interests" in China. Innocently intended by Secretary of State Lansing, the phrase was construed by Japan to sanction aggressive action.

In the meantime President Taft had bent his efforts to create larger opportunities for the export of capital to China. From 1900 to 1914 American investments there rose from $17,500,000 to $42,000,000. To accelerate the process his administration encouraged American financiers to unite with bankers of other countries in joint loans to the Chinese government for railway construction and similar purposes. In this manner a four-power consortium with British, French and German bankers was formed in 1911, but a six-power consortium two years later was blocked by Woodrow Wilson when he came on the scene. Disapproving certain of the terms and particularly the "implications" of government backing, he withdrew official support, with the result that the American participants dropped out. Several years later, however, he saw the problem from a different angle—as a means of checking Japan's economic advance into China. Hence American bankers, with the government's full blessing, took the lead in arranging a four-power consortium in 1920.

The advent of the Democrats led to the arbitration principle being extended far beyond the scope of the Roosevelt treaties. Long before becoming Secretary of State, Bryan had advocated referring every sort of dispute, even those involving national honor or vital interests, to special boards of inquiry. In April, 1913, with Wilson's approval, he invited other governments to resort to this procedure in controversies "of whatever kind" with the United States and in each instance to agree to refrain from hostilities until after the investigating commission had reported its findings. By allowing time for bellicose passions to subside he believed most wars could be averted. Thirty countries agreed to sign 'cooling-off' treaties and twenty-two ratifications were eventually exchanged. Germany, Austria and Turkey were among those to remain aloof. A new era of international brotherhood seemed to be dawning when suddenly, almost without warning, the great European war of 1914 shattered the illusion.

FULLER ACCOUNTS

Gearing an Empire to a Republic. For an over-all account, consult Pratt, *America's Colonial Experiment,* and, in regard to particular areas, Kuykendall and Day, *Hawaii;* Nichols, *Alaska;* White, *Puerto Rico;* Tansill, *Purchase of Danish West Indies;* and Westergaard, *Danish West Indies.*

America in the Philippines. Forbes, *Philippine Islands,* Hayden, *Philippines,* and LeRoy, *Americans in the Philippines,* are comprehensive accounts.

The Caribbean Sphere of Influence. Bemis, *Latin American Policy,* and Munro, *Latin American Republics,* are helpful for this and the next section. More particularly, Callcott, *Caribbean Policy,* Munro, *United States and the Caribbean Area,* and Rippy, *Caribbean Danger Zone,* trace the American advance into the West Indies and Central America, while Perkins, *Hands Off,* illuminates the relation of the Monroe Doctrine to the situation and Hill, *Roosevelt and the Caribbean,* punctures a widely accepted earlier version of the Venezuelan incident. Individual protectorates are treated in Chapman, *History of the Cuban Republic;* Fitzgibbon, *Cuba and the United States;* Knight, *Americans in Santo Domingo;* Montague, *Haiti and the United States;* and Cox, *Nicaragua and the United States.*

Turmoil in Mexico. Callcott, *Liberalism in Mexico,* and Gruening, *Mexico and Its Heritage,* clarify internal conditions, while relations with the United States receive special attention in Callahan, *American Foreign Policy in Mexican Relations;* Dunn, *Diplomatic Protection of Americans in Mexico;* Hackett, *Mexican Revolution and the United States;* and Rippy, *United States and Mexico.*

America and International Peace. Significant phases are discussed in Curti, *Peace or War;* Scott, *The Hague Peace Conferences;* and Tate, *Disarmament Illusion.* For Far Eastern relations, see Dennett, *Roosevelt and the Russo-Japanese War;* Griswold, *Far Eastern Policy;* Treat, *Diplomatic Relations between the United States and Japan;* and Tupper and McReynolds, *Japan in American Public Opinion.*

CHAPTER XIII

AMERICA AND WORLD WAR I

TRIALS OF A NEUTRAL

THE seeds of the European struggle were sown as early as the Franco-Prussian War of 1870–1871 when the Germans imposed a harsh peace on their beaten foe. The soil was fertilized by the intensified nationalisms which in the years following sent European powers on a world-wide scramble for territory, spheres of influence, raw materials, markets and trade routes. The principal governments, both from motives of aggression and from dread of one another, undertook an exhausting competition in armaments leading to ever bigger armies and navies. After a while those countries with common interests or fears formed alliances and secret understandings to combat the supposed designs of rival nations. In this way Europe divided into two armed camps, with Great Britain, France and Russia composing one coalition, and Germany and Austria-Hungary heading the other. From the time of the Venezuela boundary dispute Britain also wooed the friendship of the greatest transatlantic nation. Through this system of balance of power it was hoped that a destructive war, which neither side wanted, might be indefinitely avoided.

By 1914 the Old World had become a powder magazine which a careless match might explode. This spark fell on June 28 when a youth belonging to one of the many subject peoples of the Austro-Hungarian Empire assassinated the heir-apparent. Austria-Hungary, suspecting Serbia's complicity, charged that government with instigating the crime and, after making certain of the German Kaiser's support, declared war on Serbia a month later. Though Austria-Hungary and her ally hoped to keep the struggle a local affair, such was the tenseness of feeling and the obligation of alliances that soon all the Great Powers plunged into the conflict, with the Central Empires (Germany and Austria-Hungary) captaining one set of belligerents,

265

and the Entente Allies (Russia, France and Great Britain) the other.[1] At bottom, the war was a product of long-time imperialistic rivalries, with Germany considering herself a 'have-not' nation because of her lateness in getting into the race. The balance-of-power system, so long successful in maintaining peace, now embroiled Europe in the most frightful conflict it had yet known.

The American people were stunned, for the international-peace movement preceding the war had nourished hopes of a perpetual reign of law and justice in the world. On August 4, when five countries had taken up arms, President Wilson issued a proclamation of neutrality, and two weeks later he appealed to his countrymen to be "impartial in thought as well as in action." The one move accorded with a century and a quarter of practice, but the other, however desirable, was impossible of fulfillment. From the outset a predominant sentiment favored the Allies. Of the hundred million Americans nearly half were of British or Canadian extraction, and even the descendants of other nationalities had unconsciously imbibed Anglo-Saxon traditions and ideals from their surroundings. Through Shakespeare, Dickens, Scott, Tennyson and countless other authors the people shared a common cultural heritage with England, and they were further bound by ties of language, law and custom. This basic sympathy was strengthened by the attitude of the Eastern business classes, who had long enjoyed close relations with London and who disliked and feared German commercial methods.

The Teutonic powers, of course, did not lack friends. A fifth of the American stock derived from Germany and Austria-Hungary, and many persons of this blood, especially the recent immigrants, instinctively sided with their ancestral homelands. Another source of support came from the Irish-Americans, who for their own reasons generally joined the Germans in hating England. Finally, the 'ancient grudge' against Britain, nourished by school histories, rendered a goodly number of old-stock Americans skeptical of the merits of the Allied cause. With still other European groups represented in the population, it is not surprising that, as the conflict developed, it stirred emotions

[1] Between July 28 and November 5 Austria-Hungary, Germany and Turkey entered the war on the one side, Serbia, Russia, France, Belgium, Great Britain (including Canada, Australia, New Zealand and South Africa), Montenegro and Japan on the other. Italy, after carefully calculating the advantages, abandoned her alliance with Germany to join Germany's enemies in May, 1915. Smaller European countries followed in 1916.

born of national attachments, family relationships and rekindled patriotisms. Despite this clash of sympathies, however, most people backed the President's position of official neutrality, viewing the Old World's resort to bloodshed as something horrible and unclean. "Peace-loving citizens of this country," asserted the *Chicago Herald,* "will now rise up and tender a hearty vote of thanks to Columbus for having discovered America." Of 367 editors polled by the *Literary Digest* in November, 1914, 105 favored the Allies, 20 the Central Empires, and 242 professed indifference to the outcome. The stronghold of isolationist feeling was the Midwest, hitherto the breeding ground of progressivism.

The holocaust placed America in somewhat the same position as a century before during the Napoleonic wars. With German shipping swept from the ocean and a large part of Britain's merchant marine devoted to war uses, the United States became the chief carrier of the world's trade. The derangement of European industry and agriculture and the avid demand for munitions, metal products, foodstuffs and raw materials poured a flood of gold into America, especially from the Allied countries which had no difficulty in buying, unlike Germany which was deterred by the British blockade. The value of explosives exported leaped from $6,300,000 in 1914 to $803,000,000 in 1917; iron and steel from $252,000,000 to $1,134,-000,000; wheat from $88,000,000 to $298,000,000. As a Senate investigation conducted in 1934–1936 by Gerald P. Nye of North Dakota was to reveal, immense profits accrued to American bankers and manufacturers. The J. P. Morgan firm made $30,000,000 as financial agent of the British and French governments, the Du Pont company (which manufactured 40 per cent of all the munitions used by the Allies during the war) reaped over $265,000,000 between 1914 and 1918, while other large financial and industrial concerns throve proportionately.

The country's shipping proved unequal to the zooming demand. For this reason Congress in August, 1914, facilitated the purchase of merchantmen built in neutral nations by admitting such vessels to immediate registry without the customary five-year wait. A few weeks later it created a Bureau of War Risk Insurance to keep down marine insurance charges. These moves, however, failed to reach the heart of the difficulty: the need for more newly built craft. To solve this problem Wilson proposed that the government itself undertake the construction. Congress, slow to act through fear of possible foreign complications as well as from dislike of government ownership, waited until September, 1916, when it set up the United States Shipping Board with authority to build, buy or lease merchantmen and to operate them until five years after the war. The Board was also granted permanent powers to regulate private vessels in interstate or foreign commerce, which gave it a legal footing comparable to that of the Interstate Commerce Commission and the Federal Trade Commission. Unfortunately the law came too late to be of much use before America entered the war, but thereafter the Board was given virtual control of the entire shipbuilding resources of the nation and in that capacity performed indispensable service.

Although the initial impact of the conflict disrupted normal trade and created fears of a deepening depression, the war boom soon ushered in an era of great prosperity whose benefits ramified to all classes. Since the abnormal expansion of industry occurred at a time of sharply declining immigration, organized labor was in a position to demand higher wages and other concessions which employers found it simple to pass on to the public in the form of higher prices. The war also stimulated an extraordinary export of private capital to embattled Europe. At first the administration, influenced by Secretary Bryan who held that loans to belligerents violated the "true spirit of neutrality," set its face against the practice; but late in 1914, under pressure from the banking interests, the President relaxed the policy and sanctioned such credits. When the United States finally joined the struggle, Americans had purchased nearly $2,300,000,000 of Allied securities and only $27,000,000 of German.

As in Napoleon's time, also, the tide of material prosperity brought grave threats to national security. Neither set of belligerents was willing to allow the interests of nonparticipants to endanger its chances of victory. Accordingly, America as the principal power not at war was obliged once more to assume her historic role as champion of neutral rights. Great Britain's infringements involved, mostly, arbitrary and vexatious interruptions of American trade with the neutral countries bordering on Germany. She freely intercepted cargoes of contraband in order to prevent them from finding a back door to the enemy, and she defined as contraband many articles, including foodstuffs, that had never hitherto been so classed, on the ground that they were potentially war materials. The United States, contending that commerce between neutral countries must not be interfered with except from "imperative necessity," denied that the need existed and denounced the interferences as unlawful; but the seizures nevertheless continued. Partly in the hope of obviating America's objections, Britain in March, 1915, adopted a policy that amounted to a long-distance blockade of the German coast and neighboring neutral ports. This likewise evoked a protest from Washington, emphasizing that under international law it was "illegal and indefensible" to blockade countries at peace. But the London authorities, again pleading the law of self-preservation, declined to yield.

Such practices, detrimental and unlawful as they were, inflicted property losses merely, and Washington, though keeping up a barrage of objections, avoided a showdown. Undoubtedly Wilson's own pro-English feeling, fortified by that of some of his advisers, including Ambassador Walter Hines Page in England, was partly responsible, but more important was the grosser nature of Germany's infractions. These, besides injuring trade, involved plots against America's domestic tranquillity as well as the killing of Americans. Since German success required that the Allied shortage in munitions should not be replenished from outside sources, Teutonic agents and adherents in the United States promoted a vigorous propaganda to induce Congress to embargo military supplies. The government, however, was not to be persuaded. Not only was the private munitions trade sanctioned by international law, but the Germans themselves had engaged in it in previous wars. Thwarted at this point, the Central Empires tried to gain their end through a campaign of sabotage. "It is my impression," the Austro-Hungarian Ambassador, Dr. Constantin Dumba, assured his government in August, 1915, "that we can disorganize and hold up for months, if not entirely prevent, the manufacture of munitions in Bethlehem and the Middle West." At the instigation of Teutonic agents and pro-German sympathizers, explosions and incendiary fires damaged or destroyed munition plants; bombs were concealed aboard vessels carrying cargoes to the Allies, and strikes were fomented among seamen and munitions workers. The federal authorities apprehended most of the culprits and soon managed to establish a linkage with the Teutonic embassies in Washington. In September, 1915, the President forced the recall of Dumba and three months later of two German naval and military attachés.

Along the sea lanes the Central Empires engaged in an even more desperate attempt to stop shipments to the Allies. Outmatched by the British on the ocean surface, Germany had developed undersea craft (U-boats) to a point of perfection never before known. By international law, however, submarines must not attack a merchant-man or passenger vessel unless, after being warned, it refused to allow visit and search, and they must not sink it without rescuing those on board. From Germany's unwillingness to abide by these regulations stemmed all the troubles that arose over submarine warfare. In justification she pleaded that U-boats could not accommodate addi-tional passengers and contended that, by rising to the surface to give warning, the frailty of the vessels exposed them to easy destruction from hostile gunfire. The United States, on its part, maintained that, if the weapon could not be used according to the rules, then the weapon must be scrapped, not the rules. Germany began her undersea operations by proclaiming that from February 18, 1915, she would destroy every enemy craft found in the waters about the British Isles without regard to the safety of those aboard and that even neutral ships might accidentally suffer a like fate. At once Wilson replied that, if this "unprecedented" action should occasion the loss of American vessels or lives, he would hold Berlin to "strict account-ability." Nevertheless, in March a United States citizen was drowned by the torpedoing of the British steamer *Falaba,* and on May 1 the *Gulflight,* an American tanker, was attacked.

Six days later occurred the most shocking incident of all: the unarmed British liner *Lusitania,* carrying some military supplies from New York, was sent unwarned to the bottom with a loss of nearly 1200, including 128 Americans. The United States blazed with resent-ment. "It is a deed for which a Hun would blush, a Turk be ashamed, and a Barbary pirate apologize," cried the New York *Nation,* adding, "The torpedo that sank the *Lusitania* also sank Germany in the opinion of mankind." With a less resolute friend of peace in the White House, war might easily have ensued. Instead, Wilson sternly demanded that the Berlin government cease its lawless practices and make all possible reparation for the damages inflicted. Even this move impressed Secretary Bryan as carrying the country dangerously near the brink of war. He took the position that citizens should travel on belligerent merchantmen at their own risk and argued that in any event the difficulties with Germany could best be composed by re-sorting to the principle of the 'cooling-off' treaties. He resigned in

PRESIDENT WILSON ENTERING PARIS WITH PRESIDENT POINCARÉ
See page 295.

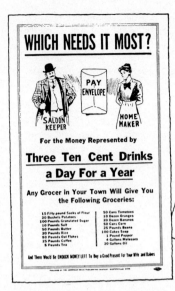

WORKING UP DRY SENTIMENT

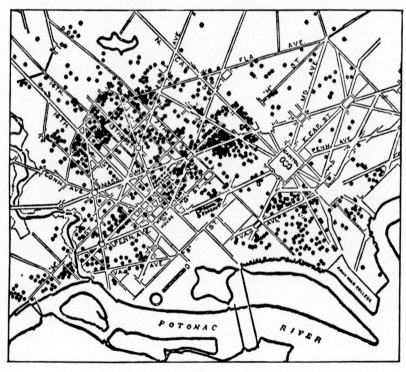

A 'SPEAKEASY' MAP OF WASHINGTON, D. C., 1930
See pages 308 and 329.

protest, making way in June for Robert Lansing of New York, an expert in international law who had been his chief legal adviser in the State Department.

Meanwhile the submarine depredations continued, culminating on August 19, 1915, in the sinking of the British liner *Arabic* and two more American deaths. Fearful of the consequences, Germany now definitely pledged that "Liners will not be sunk by our submarines without warning and without safety of the lives of noncombatants," and in October she offered apologies and indemnity for the *Arabic* disaster. Though Wilson had won a diplomatic victory, its edge was dulled by lack of confidence in Berlin's good faith, a feeling that seemed justified when the German authorities in February, 1916, though agreeing to pay for the lives lost in the destruction of the *Lusitania,* refused to admit its illegality. On March 24 American lives were once more put in jeopardy by the torpedoing without warning of the unarmed French channel steamer *Sussex.* Since this deed flagrantly violated the *Arabic* pledge, the President rejected the German excuse that the U-boat commander had merely made an unfortunate mistake. On April 18 he delivered an ultimatum to the effect that, unless such attacks ceased, the United States would sever diplomatic relations. Berlin, convinced at last of the aroused state of American opinion, now renewed her pledge, and for the next nine months the two countries were on better terms than at any time since hostilities had started.

FROM BYSTANDER TO BELLIGERENT

When the war began in 1914 it seemed remote from the ordinary concerns of Americans. But multiplying incidents, such as Britain's illegal restraints on trade, the German-inspired sabotage of American industry and the submarine depredations, gradually convinced the people that the conflict directly involved their own well-being and security. Their initial pro-Ally leanings became stronger, partly because of the greater enormity of the Teutonic infringements, and partly because Germany had commenced hostilities by invading little Belgium in glaring disregard of a treaty of neutrality three quarters of a century old. This event underscored Teutonic contempt for international commitments and led the American public to contribute generously to the relief work instituted among the suffering Belgians by Herbert C. Hoover, an American mining engineer, who thus first came to national attention. The rising anti-German sentiment was furthered by a well-oiled propaganda from London. Through their control of the cables the British censored all the news dispatches sent to the United States, and in addition they supplied the press with a weekly summary of the war, made personal contact with leaders of opinion and bombarded the country with lecturers and pamphlets. From such sources were disseminated appalling and frequently imaginary tales of Teutonic atrocities and barbarities. A growing number of people came to fear a triumphant Germany as a positive menace to their own country.

As the Teutonic cause lost ground, its advocates, spearheaded by the German-American Alliance and by the German-language press, waxed more and more strident. Many of the sympathizers, notably in the Midwest, gave support because, without being actively pro-German, they did not want the United States to be sucked into the maelstrom, while Irish-Americans, having their own ax to grind, commonly took the same side. The nation, as it were, turned into a vast debating society, with the President a somewhat lonely figure determined to avoid intervention save as a last resort. Increasingly he became a target for acrid criticism from 'hyphenated' Americans —both pro-Germans, who accused him of dealing too gingerly with Great Britain, and pro-Allies, who charged him with weakness toward Germany. Wilson's ill-timed statement shortly after the *Lusitania* disaster that "There is such a thing as a man being too proud to fight" was interpreted, not as the expression of a lofty ideal, as he intended, but as willingness to truckle to German might.

The President at first resisted pressure for military preparedness, believing with most of his countrymen that the demand represented hysteria. It was inspired principally by the National Security League, financed mainly by munitions manufacturers and international bankers, with powerful spokesmen in such figures as Theodore Roosevelt and General Leonard Wood. In time, however, the thickening dangers convinced Wilson himself of the need. In June, 1916, Congress at his behest augmented the regular army in five annual accretions, enlarged the state militia and placed it under federal control, established civilian training camps and introduced military instruction into the schools and colleges. Secretary of War Garrison, believing even this action insufficient, resigned in protest, to be replaced by Newton D. Baker of Ohio. In August, Congress, turning to the navy, adopted a three-year construction program. At the same time it authorized a Council of National Defense of six cabinet members to serve as a board of strategy for industrial mobilization if war should come.

With Wilson preparedness was a reluctant second thought. From the beginning of hostilities he had devoted his chief energies to meeting the crisis through the healing methods of diplomacy. Nor did he confine himself merely to safeguarding the rights of neutrals. On the contrary, he endeavored to attack the evil at its source by offers to the belligerents to help end the conflict. He made an even bolder gesture in February, 1916, while the opposing armies lay deadlocked on the western front. Through Colonel Edward M. House of Texas as his confidential agent he assured the British government that he stood ready to call and take part in a peace conference and that, if Germany would not co-operate, the United States "would probably enter the war against Germany." [1] This proposal the English leaders rejected, possibly because they hoped by prolonging the struggle to secure better terms, possibly because Walter Hines Page, the pro-Ally American Ambassador in London, cast doubt on Wilson's sincerity, and perhaps also because the word "probably" did actually leave the way open for Wilson to back down. At any rate, America's delay in entering the conflict, so bitterly criticized by Allied statesmen, may in some degree be laid at their own door.

But already the President was arriving at a new conception of peace aims. Deeply influenced by the League to Enforce Peace, an organization founded in 1915, he adopted as his own the notion of an international federation for the prevention of war. In such a plan he saw a substitute for the balance-of-power system that had brought Europe to disaster. As good may come out of evil, he thought the war might be made a war to end war. The idea also enlisted the support of ex-President Taft and of other public men regardless of party. In order to get the proposal before the belligerents Wilson on December 18, 1916, requested them to state "their respective views as to the terms upon which the war might be concluded, and the arrangements which would be deemed satisfactory as a guarantee against its renewal." On January 22, 1917, he reported the results to the Senate in an address keyed to the ears of the world. The Central Empires, he

[1] The President had in mind as peace terms "the restoration of Belgium, the transfer of Alsace and Lorraine to France, and the acquisition by Russia of an outlet to the sea," with compensation to Germany in "concessions to her in other places outside Europe."

said, had refused to define their purposes, while the Allies had indicated in broad terms their aims and expectations. As a neutral whose rights the struggle had put "in constant jeopardy," he asserted America's vital interest in a righteous and enduring peace—not "a victor's terms imposed upon the vanquished" and hence provocative of future bloodshed, but "a peace without victory." The settlement must embrace such principles as the right of self-determination, freedom of the seas, limitation of armaments and a league to guarantee "the permanence of peace." Through the President's efforts the United States was rapidly attaining the moral leadership of mankind. At home, however, the speech evoked fresh volleys of invective because of the expression "peace without victory," which his critics interpreted as blindness to the deeper issues involved.

Before the President sent his note to the warring powers the election of 1916 had taken place. On June 7 the Republicans and the Progressives held simultaneous conventions at Chicago in the hope of patching up their differences, but the outcome was two separate tickets: Charles E. Hughes of New York and Charles W. Fairbanks of Indiana for the Republicans, and Theodore Roosevelt and John M. Parker of Louisiana for the Progressives. Hughes had been chosen largely because as a member of the Supreme Court since 1910 he had kept free from partisan embroilments. The Republican platform stigmatized Wilson's foreign policy as one of "shifty expedients," endorsed thoroughgoing preparedness and promised "strict and honest neutrality between the belligerents." Roosevelt, who had no liking for lost causes, waited until the Progressive convention had adjourned and then declined to run, urging his supporters to follow him back into the Republican fold. The Democrats in St. Louis on June 14 renominated their ticket of 1912. For the first time in many years they could point to a record of actual achievement. After rehearsing the administration's epoch-making domestic accomplishments the platform condemned "hyphenism," pledged adequate preparedness and praised the President's skill in safeguarding neutrality.

The ensuing contest proved unusually exciting. The pro-Germans campaigned for Hughes, and until the last week he avoided saying anything that might alienate their support. In the words, "He kept us out of war," Democratic orators found an effective vote-getting slogan, especially in the case of women, who now wielded the ballot in eleven states. Wilson's own speeches, however, contained nothing to justify the expectation that peace would continue under any and all circumstances. The American Federation of Labor advocated his re-election, and as the weeks wore on, the independent voters began to turn to him, largely because of Hughes's lukewarm utterances on social and economic reforms. The result was so close as to be in doubt for several days. The President polled 277 electoral votes to 254 for his opponent, and 49.2 per cent of the popular ballots (9,130,000) to 46 per cent (8,538,000). He swept the South and the Far West, including nearly all the woman-suffrage states, and the Democrats also retained control of Congress. For the first time in almost fifty years, if the Hayes-Tilden contest be excepted, a candidate won without New York's electoral support.

The outcome was misunderstood in the Central Empires. "The Germans," later declared James W. Gerard, the American Ambassador at Berlin, "believed that President Wilson had been elected with a mandate to keep out of war at any cost, and that America could be insulted, flouted, and humiliated with impunity." Hence they redoubled the exertions already secretly begun for the most destructive submarine campaign within their resources. On January 31, 1917, Germany abruptly informed the United States that henceforth, in disregard of the *Sussex* pledge, she would sink on sight all ships, neutral as well as belligerent, in certain waters about the British Isles and in the Mediterranean. At once Wilson, faithful to his ultimatum on the earlier occasion, broke off diplomatic relations. Then, making another move to buttress America's neutral rights, he asked Congress on February 26 to empower him to arm merchant ships for self-defense. The House acted promptly, but in the Senate eleven Western and Southern members, including Robert M. La Follette and George W. Norris, filibustered the bill to death. The President, scourging the "little group of willful men" for rendering "the great Government of the United States helpless and contemptible," managed nevertheless to find the authority he needed in a century-old law against piracy.

Already Teutonic ruthlessness had begun to take its toll. By April 1 eight American vessels had been sent to the bottom with a loss of forty-eight lives. Armed neutrality was fast proving its futility when Wilson called a special session of Congress for April 2. Before that date two incidents helped to clarify further the nature of the crisis. Thanks to the British secret service, the American public learned on March 1 that Alfred Zimmermann, the Kaiser's Foreign Minister,

had instructed the German Minister in Mexico to offer that government financial help and "the lost territory of New Mexico, Texas
and Arizona" in return for supporting Germany if the United States
joined the struggle. The nation, outraged by the so-called Zimmermann note, found fresh reason to fear German militarism. The other
event was the news that a Russian revolution in March had set up a
republican regime. By the Czar's overthrow the principal European
Allies all became exponents of democratic government, leaving the
Teutonic powers and their partner, Turkey, as the last strongholds of
military autocracy.

When the special session assembled, President Wilson in words that
profoundly stirred the country asked Congress to recognize the
existence of a state of war with Germany. Reciting the submarine
depredations and the conspiracies against American security culminating in the Zimmermann note, he pictured these as the inevitable
actions of "autocratic governments backed by organized force." The
United States, he said, would fight "for the ultimate peace of the
world and for the liberation of its peoples, the German peoples included." And he added in a phrase that rang round the globe, "The
world must be made safe for democracy." On April 6 Congress acted
with resounding majorities. A declaration of war against Austria-
Hungary was withheld until December 7 in the vain hope that meanwhile she might be weaned from her ally.

Wilson's war message revealed that since his January address to the
Senate his mind had changed as to the fundamental issues at stake.
Then, he had proposed a "peace without victory," which meant, of
course, that neither side should win. Now, he envisaged the struggle
in ideological terms—as a conflict between two incompatible systems
of government. The Allied statesmen henceforth adopted similar
language, but with mental reservations as their conduct at the peace
table would show. Even in the United States other things affected the
situation, notably the sympathy of one English-speaking people for
another. To these factors should be added the extensive Allied propaganda and the alarm of the business and investing classes at the prospect of disastrous losses if Britain should fall. In postwar discussions
in America these last two influences came to assume a sinister aspect.
In fact, however, the propaganda had its principal effect merely in
heightening sentiments already existing. As to the economic motive,
the stake of bondholders, munitions makers and other exporting

interests was undoubtedly large—Ambassador Page wrote from London on March 5, 1917, that "Perhaps our going to war is the only way in which our present prominent trade position can be maintained and a panic averted"—but Wilson himself, who made the decision to intervene, had rendered it self-evident by his domestic program that he was neither an agent nor a dupe of Wall Street.

Whatever the complex of reasons, the plain truth is that after long and patient forbearance America fought because she was attacked. The die was cast in Berlin, not Washington—when Germany unleashed her submarines for what she expected to be a knockout blow against the Allies before the United States could throw its weight into the fight. For a full century the great New World republic had been content with Britain as mistress of the North Atlantic, America's historic safety zone, but the prospect of militaristic Germany in that position involved an intolerable threat to future security as well as a constant peril to the Monroe Doctrine. The President chose to place his case on the high ground of democratic principle, thereby tapping a fund of popular idealism going back to the Declaration of Independence and winning the nation's wholehearted support. America's entry set the example for other neutrals. The attitude of the republics of the Western Hemisphere was particularly significant because of the light it shed upon Pan American solidarity. Brazil, Cuba, Panama, Haiti, the Dominican Republic and all of Central America but El Salvador declared war on Germany, five other countries severed diplomatic relations, and the remaining seven observed neutrality.

THE HOME FRONT

When the United States unsheathed the sword hostilities had been raging for two years and eight months. At the outset the Germans had tried for a quick decision, but after fighting to within fifty miles of Paris they had been halted by the battle of the Marne. Since then, in spite of the Allies' best efforts, they had retained possession of most of Belgium and a large section of northeastern France. Besides the western front, the opposing forces also struggled on the Russo-Austrian border and after the spring of 1915 on the Austro-Italian frontier as well. On land the advantage lay everywhere with the Central Empires; but their commerce had been swept from the seas, nearly all the German colonies had been seized, and the Allied blockade had increasingly choked off essential supplies.

The conflict had developed unusual features. With millions of men involved, the open-field operations of earlier wars had given way to trench fighting on a vast scale. Moreover, peacetime achievements to promote human welfare had been converted into agencies of human destruction. Chief among these were the motorcar and the airplane. The former not only quickened the movement of men and materials but, in the form of the armored tank, became itself an engine of warfare. The latter, developed to new perfection, rendered indispensable service in scouting, combat and to some extent in bombing. Among other inventions, wireless telegraphy (devised in 1895 by Guglielmo Marconi, an Italian) proved valuable for keeping the many units of the gigantic armies in constant touch, while the beneficent discoveries of the world's chemists were used in the manufacture of hand grenades, bombs and poison gas. The new technology of warfare also gave unexpected importance to gasoline, which supplied motive power for conveyances on land, in the air and under the water and was even displacing coal on warships. "It is as necessary as blood in the battles of tomorrow," Georges Clemenceau, the French Premier, told President Wilson.

America's entry, occurring at a crucial moment for the Allies, placed at their disposal not only an unplumbed reservoir of man power, but also unlimited money, foodstuffs, minerals, manufactures, shipyards and material resources of every kind. Perhaps equally significant was the fresh enthusiasm and idealism the United States brought to the struggle, for war weariness and defeatism blanketed the Allied peoples. Official missions, hastening to Washington, explained their desperate plight and urged the greatest possible speed in sending troops. While the military preparations were getting under way during the rest of 1917, the United States lent Germany's foes $885,000,000, a mere earnest of the sums to follow. Though resolved to co-operate to the fullest extent, the government did not forget that it had joined the war for American, not European, reasons. Hence it officially regarded the Allies simply as "Associates" in a common effort.

In order to make up for its tardiness in preparing for war the administration now organized the nation with a thoroughness and on a scale hitherto unparalleled. Against fierce opposition from within his own party Wilson induced Congress on May 18, 1917, to adopt a Selective Service Act for conscripting men between the ages of twenty-one and thirty (the age range being enlarged a year later to those between eighteen and forty-five). Exemption or deferred classification was provided for public officials, clergymen, religious pacifists, workers in essential industries, men with dependents, and physical and mental defectives; but no one was permitted to purchase exemption or hire a substitute, as in the Civil War. Without loss of time the men of draft age were registered, and this, with the enrollment of youths later coming of age, eventually made available nearly 11,000,000. The act of May 18 also increased the regular army to 287,000 and incorporated the entire national guard in the federal service. With these additions the total military strength at the end of 1917 rose to 1,250,000 men and more than 100,000 officers.

The problem of assembling the elements of an army proved simpler than that of fashioning them into soldiers. Sixteen great tent-camps in the South accommodated the augmented national guard, while a similar number of cantonments in various parts of the country took care of the national or draft army. Swiftly constructed, these cantonments resembled full-fledged towns more than camps. There the men completed their training in an average of six months. Officers were supplied through separate camps, the best known at Plattsburg, New York. The curse of political appointments, which had marred earlier wars, was avoided by using a scientific rating system to ascertain ability. Even the colleges were utilized for military instruction, and ultimately about 170,000 youths in five hundred institutions joined the Students' Army Training Corps. Besides accomplishing the immediate purpose, this experience in mobilizing and making a vast citizens' army was to stand the country in good stead in a later world war as yet unforeseen.

Simultaneously, thoroughgoing steps were taken to mobilize the nation's material resources. "Under modern conditions," as Secretary of War Baker noted, "wars are not made by soldiers only, but by nations. . . . The army is merely the point of the sword." The Council of National Defense, authorized before America's entrance, assumed general charge, though much of the actual work was carried on through an Advisory Commission composed of seven men particularly informed as to the nation's industrial, professional and labor potentialities. Thus Daniel Willard, president of the Baltimore and Ohio Railroad, acted as expert in transportation, Julius Rosenwald, head of a Chicago mail-order concern, in clothing and similar supplies, and Samuel Gompers in labor matters. From this central group were generated from time to time numerous subcommittees and special technical boards. This elaborate federal organization was in many respects paralleled by the states. Every state had its own council of defense, and most of them networks of local agencies as well. Everywhere the people displayed that capacity for co-operation in face of an emergency which they had shown on earlier occasions.

Of the committees of the Council of National Defense, the one on munitions attained such importance that in July, 1917, it was reorganized as the War Industries Board. Under the vigorous direction of Bernard M. Baruch it regulated all businesses engaged in making war materials, developed new industries and sources of supply, eliminated waste, enforced efficiency and fixed prices. It purchased for the Allies as well as for the American government and determined priorities of production and delivery. The manufacture of some thirty thousand commodities came under its supervision. Of great assistance also was the War Finance Corporation which lent public funds to businesses lacking capital. Before peace came, the War Industries Board was credited with having boosted industrial output at least 20 per cent. The worst failures involved the production of heavy artillery, machine guns and aircraft, but this was a responsibility of the War and Navy Departments. For these essential weapons the American army had to rely largely upon the British and French. Even when the armistice was signed, only about twelve thousand aircraft had been completed in the United States, a third of them service planes.

The Food Administration derived its importance from a dangerous shortage of foodstuffs in the Allied countries as well as the need to amass supplies for the American forces. Under Herbert Hoover, famed as the organizer of Belgian relief, this agency acted vigorously to increase production and regulate civilian consumption. The problem centered largely in wheat, meat, sugar and fats. As one effective step, the government spurred farmers to enlarge their plantings with a guarantee of two dollars or more a bushel for all wheat raised. The crop soared from 690,000,000 bushels before 1914 to 921,000,000 in 1918. Even city dwellers converted their yards and nearby vacant lots into 'war gardens' and thus lessened the strain on the commercial supply of vegetables. To curtail consumption, the Food Administration restricted sales by wholesalers and retailers and appealed to the public to co-operate. The slogan, "Food Will Win the War," appeared on all the billboards of the country, and a new verb, 'to hooverize,' entered the popular vocabulary. Housewives hung cards in their windows to proclaim their fidelity to the regulations and showed patriotic zeal in the use of substitutes and the observance of 'meatless meals' and 'wheatless days.' The results amply justified the Food Administration's efforts. During the 1918 crop year America doubled the amount of food exported to Europe immediately before the war. By such means the United States was able not only to feed the Allied armies, but also to save their peoples (and later much of Central and Southeastern Europe) from starvation.

A Fuel Administration under Harry A. Garfield dealt similarly with the problem of an adequate coal supply. Miners and operators co-operated zealously in increasing output, while householders practiced domestic self-denial. Difficulties of shipment were heightened by the unprecedented rail congestion and by the cruelly cold winter of 1917–1918 which imprisoned coal barges in icebound harbors. At one juncture Garfield closed temporarily all factories east of the Mississippi except essential industries in order to divert coal to more vital uses. Oil production also received attention, and the public as its contribution reduced pleasure riding to the vanishing point and gladly heeded the request for 'gasless Sundays.'

Rail facilities were the real key to mobilization, being necessary not only for carrying coal but all military materials, as well as for the movement of troops. Because the railroads, burdened by the swollen traffic and hampered by long-established habits of competition, could not rise to the emergency, the President in the closing days of 1917 put them in charge of Secretary of the Treasury McAdoo, who proceeded to operate them as a single system. He cut passenger trains to a minimum, gave priority to war freight, used terminals and repair shops wherever they were available and did everything possible to clear the tracks for the government. His success was remarkable, but he found it necessary to raise wages by more than $600,000,000. Though he also increased freight and passenger rates, the roads operated at a deficit throughout the period of federal management. In July, 1918, Wilson confided the telegraph, telephone and cable lines to the oversight of the Postmaster-General, and in November he placed the express business under government control. By these multitudinous steps an administration which had tried desperately to keep the country at peace shouldered the responsibilities of total war.

FULLER ACCOUNTS

Trials of a Neutral. Fay, *Origins of the World War,* discusses the European background. Paxson, *American Democracy and the World War,* I, and Sullivan, *Our Times,* V, afford over-all treatments of America's difficulties, while among special studies are Morrissey, *American Defense of Neutral Rights;* Notter, *Origins of the Foreign Policy of Woodrow Wilson;* Seymour, *American Diplomacy during the World War;* and Tansill, *America Goes to War;* with shorter discussions in the diplomatic histories by Bailey and Bemis and in Perkins, *America and Two Wars.* For propaganda and the activities of foreign emissaries, turn to Jones and Hollister, *German Secret Service in America,* and Peterson, *Propaganda for War.* Biographies important for this and the succeeding sections include Baker, *Wilson,* V–VII; Cranston, *Wilson;* Hendrick, *Page;* Palmer, *Baker;* Pringle, *Theodore Roosevelt;* and Seymour, *Colonel House.*

From Bystander to Belligerent. Besides Paxson and Sullivan already cited, Squires deals particularly with *British Propaganda at Home and in the United States;* Child describes *German-Americans in Politics;* and Bartlett tells about *The League to Enforce Peace.* For an argument that World Wars I and II should be called World Wars VIII and IX, see Schlesinger, *Paths to the Present,* chap. viii.

The Home Front. Paxson, *American Democracy and the World War,* II, gives a circumstantial account, with major phases delineated at length in Clarkson, *Industrial America in the World War;* Crowell and Wilson, *How America Went to War;* Hines, *War History of American Railroads;* Powell, *Army behind the Army;* Van Hise, *Conservation and Regulation in the United States during the World War;* and Willoughby, *Government Organization in War Time and After.*

CHAPTER XIV

THE PATH TO PEACE

THE EUROPEAN FRONT

ALL of America's past major wars had been fought on home soil or close at hand, but World War I involved operations three thousand miles away, across an ocean infested with hostile U-boats. These craft had reached such a point of effectiveness that they were sinking Allied merchantmen faster than they could be replaced, and the English people faced imminent starvation. Under the circumstances the navy became the spearhead of the intervention. Its task was twofold: to help cripple the enemy's undersea power and to convoy the American Expeditionary Force. Within eighteen days after the beginning of hostilities six destroyers departed for the theater of war, where under Admiral William S. Sims they set about to aid the British in chasing and sinking submarines. Battleships and cruisers followed until ultimately there were abroad three hundred ships of all kinds with seventy-five thousand officers and men. To make this possible, the three-year construction program adopted in 1916 was accelerated and expanded; in the first nine months of 1918 no fewer than eighty-three new destroyers were launched. The government also commandeered private craft and took over more than a hundred interned German vessels, including the *Vaterland,* then the world's largest ship.

Among other notable exploits the navy, assisted by the British, planted a two-hundred-and-fifty-mile mine barrage in the North Sea from Norway to Scotland in order to stop U-boats from reaching the high seas. Also with British co-operation, it worked out an effective plan for protecting troopships against submarines in the Atlantic. One vital American contribution to this end was the invention of a sound detector for indicating the approximate location of the unseen craft. The results amply attested Anglo-American naval efficiency, since on the eastward voyage no transports were lost in spite of the fact

283

that over 2,000,000 soldiers eventually made the journey, and on the return trip only three empty ones were sunk.

Shortly after the declaration of war General John J. Pershing, fresh from his operations across the Mexican border, went to France to head the American Expeditionary Force. At France's urging, a division of regulars followed in June and July as a visible symbol of the hosts which were to come. These hosts, however, were still being trained, and by the end of 1917 only 195,000 soldiers had reached France. But then their numbers mounted rapidly. During the four months from May to August, 1918, more than 1,000,000 went over. To provide for their multifarious needs Pershing in February, 1918, organized the Services of Supply as a unit of the army, since the facilities and resources of France and Britain were already strained to the limit and nothing must be done to add to the burden. From its headquarters at Tours the S. O. S. assumed responsibility for assembling and distributing all the food, equipment and other stores required. Besides building gigantic docks at the ports, it constructed 1000 miles of railroad and more than 100,000 miles of telegraph and telephone and erected great hospitals and warehouses. Supplies of all kinds had to be conveyed from the United States—everything from bags of cement to monster locomotives ready to run from the vessel's hatch under their own steam. Before the armistice, 7,500,000 tons of materials, including more than 17,000 freight cars and 34,500 motor trucks, were transported. The fighting forces as they arrived usually underwent a month or so of further training before going to the front and then, brigaded with French or British troops, spent another month in a quiet part of the line. But in January, 1918, Pershing began to gather the scattered fragments of his command, though it was not until August that he established a separate American army.

While the United States was organizing its strength, the enemy, fearful of the might of the Western giant when fully aroused, tried to end the war with a series of terrific lunges. In October, 1917, the Austrians demoralized Italy with a crushing defeat at Caporetto. In March, 1918, war-weary Russia, now dominated by the Communists, concluded an inglorious peace with the Central Empires at Brest-Litovsk. Rumania, left in the lurch by the Soviet Union's defection, had little choice but to follow its example, which she did the same month. Free at last to concentrate on the western front, the Central

Empires under Erich von Ludendorff prepared for a knockout blow. In March, 1918, as the gigantic offensive got under way, the Allies under pressure from President Wilson buried their national jealousies and conferred supreme authority over the several armies on a single commander, the French Marshal Ferdinand Foch.

Though the Americans had hitherto done little beyond joining in nocturnal raids and occasional attacks, now, inured to the new conditions of warfare and eager to get into the fray on their own account, they played their full part. Of the United States participation certain phases stand out. On May 28, 1918, the First Division took Cantigny. Three days later the Third Division helped the French check the Teutonic advance at Château-Thierry on the Marne River, only forty miles from Paris. Nearby, enemy forces occupied a densely forested tract known as Belleau Wood. After six days of fighting marked by hand-to-hand encounters, the marines of the Second Division dislodged them on June 11. A new German assault on July 14 brought the Third Division into action again, and on the next day a Franco-American charge drove the foe back a mile and captured the villages of Chezy and Montlevon.

The Teutonic offensive was a gambler's last throw. The enemy not only failed to win a decision, but suffered irreplaceable losses in men, equipment and morale. Unexpectedly Marshal Foch in mid-July launched a massive counteroffensive. Once more the Yankees contributed to victory. On the 18th, in co-operation with picked French troops, they made a successful drive on Soissons. The following weeks found them repeatedly in action until on August 3 they assumed sole responsibility for about eighty-five miles of the front to the southeast of the British and French. This position threatened vital German communications and at the same time permitted men and supplies to be concentrated at a place which did not interfere with the movements of the British and French. Pershing now enlarged his operations. On September 12–16 he succeeded against feeble resistance in capturing the St. Mihiel salient, a triangle of enemy ground jutting into Allied territory. About 550,000 Americans fought in this battle—five and a half times as many as the Union troops at Gettysburg. But the most important attack in which they assisted was the Meuse-Argonne offensive. The goal was a four-track railroad behind the enemy's front which formed one of the crucial German supply lines. From September 20 the battle pro-

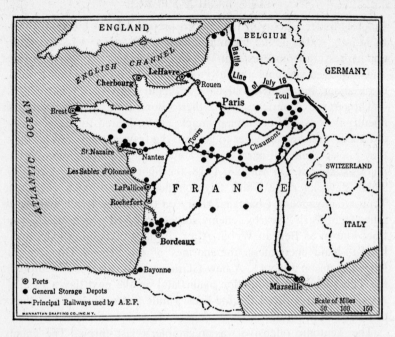

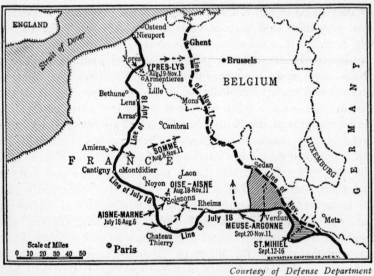

Courtesy of Defense Department

The American Army in France, 1918

ceeded with little abatement and increasing success for fifty-one days. A total of 1,200,000 Americans, besides 840 airplanes and 324 tanks, took part. At last, in the first week of November, a section of the coveted railway fell to the French and Americans. In Pershing's words, "We had cut the enemy's main line of communications, and nothing but surrender or an armistice could save his army from complete disaster."

AMERICA'S WAR EFFORT IN SUMMARY

Total number registered in draft	24,234,021
Total draft inductions	2,810,296
Graduates of officers' training schools	80,568
Total size of the army	4,000,000
Total armed forces, including army, navy, etc.	4,800,000
Men who went overseas	2,086,000
Men who fought in France	1,390,000
Battles fought by American troops	13
Months of participation in the war	19
American casualties in Meuse-Argonne battle	120,000
Cost of army to April 30, 1919	$13,930,000,000
Cost of war to April 30, 1919	$21,850,000,000

The heavy fighting lasted about two hundred days. The Americans captured around 44,000 prisoners and 1400 guns of all kinds, while Yankee aviators brought down 755 planes, themselves losing almost half that number. Nearly 50,000 perished from battle wounds. For every man killed in action six were injured without dying, and of these five were later returned to duty. Only 600 arms and 1700 legs had to be amputated, and some 700 men lost a hand or a foot. The soldier deaths from disease—far less proportionately than in any previous war—numbered 57,000. This record would have been still better but for a lethal epidemic of influenza-pneumonia which swept through the United States in the winter of 1918, taking its greatest toll in the crowded camps and cantonments. The improved conditions stemmed from the immense advance of medical science and the completeness of hospital accommodations. Into the army medical corps were drawn over 31,000 physicians and surgeons from civilian life, including some of the foremost leaders. They not only introduced the latest methods of prevention and cure, but themselves made discoveries of vast human benefit. Intestinal disorders, such as dysentery, typhus, cholera and typhoid which had ravaged armies in the past, were virtually banished as causes of death.

Though the military operations were confined chiefly to France, United States soldiers appeared on other fronts as well. At Italy's urgent call a regiment went to the Austro-Italian front in July, 1918. In October two divisions reinforced the French in Belgium. America also became involved in hostilities with the Soviet Union, although the two nations were officially at peace. The Allies refused to acknowledge Russia's treaty with Germany at Brest-Litovsk and were further angered by her cancellation of her foreign debt. Accordingly, they sent armed detachments to northern Russia to assist anticommunist movements and to safeguard large stores of military supplies. About 5000 Americans joined an Allied expedition which fought minor engagements in the vicinity of Archangel and Murmansk from September, 1918, until May, 1919, when their withdrawal began. Another force of about 10,000 took part in an Allied expedition to Vladivostok where they remained until January, 1920, one of the purposes being to prevent Japan from seizing eastern Siberia.

While World War I still raged, President Wilson renewed his efforts, begun as a neutral, to turn the greatest conflict yet known to man into an instrument for enduring peace. In his view victory was an opportunity not for vengeance, but for a "peace of justice" which would create lasting international good will. By tacit consent he became the spokesman of Germany's enemies. If they did not subscribe to all his idealism, they at least believed his utterances might weaken the hold of the military regime on the warworn Teutonic peoples and thus shorten the struggle. Addressing Congress on January 8, 1918, Wilson set forth his considered program of peace under Fourteen Points. The first group struck at four of the persistent causes of war: secret diplomacy, economic rivalry, militarism and imperialism. He demanded the ending of hidden international understandings; a guarantee of freedom of the seas with the removal of economic barriers among nations; a reduction of national armaments; and an adjustment of colonial claims with due regard to the interests of the inhabitants. Next followed a set of proposals for remaking the map of Europe in accordance with the principle of national self-determination and unhampered economic development. All German-occupied territories must be evacuated; the oppressed nationalities of Austria-Hungary must be liberated and the minorities in Turkey protected; an independent Poland should be formed out of German, Austrian and Russian territory; and the Franco-German and Austro-Italian frontiers should be readjusted along lines of nationality. For the final place, Point 14, he reserved the capstone of his arch: a system of collective security for peace instead of relying upon an uncertain balance of power. He urged the creation of a "general association of nations" to afford "mutual guarantees of political independence and territorial integrity to great and small states alike."

But it required Foch's great offensive of the summer of 1918 to convince Germany that the game was up. Her allies, hemmed in on every side, their morale shattered, were preparing to surrender with or without her consent. The German people were seething with revolution, and the Kaiser was about to abdicate and seek refuge in the Netherlands—"unwept, unhonored and unhung," in the words of the *Brooklyn Eagle*. On October 4 the government at Berlin asked Wilson to arrange for peace in accordance with the Fourteen Points. After assuring himself that the appeal came from representatives of the people rather than of the discredited military regime, the President referred it to the Allied leaders. The latter, reluctant to commit themselves officially to the Fourteen Points, hesitated until Colonel House, acting for Wilson, threatened that otherwise the President would have to consult Congress as to the advisability of continuing the fight for their special objectives. Thereupon the Allies acceded, subject to reservations as to freedom of the seas and to an explicit admission of German obligation for all damages to civilian life and property. On this basis the armistice was concluded on November 11. Germany's decision to capitulate before the war crossed her own frontiers saved her from the suffering and havoc which she had so freely visited on neighboring peoples. This may have made her readier to risk a second world conflict twenty years later.

THE WAR AND THE AMERICAN PUBLIC

The American public supported the national effort with tremendous enthusiasm. The war once joined became a holy crusade. Differences as to the relative merits of the European belligerents disappeared in the swelling tide of patriotism, and civilians everywhere gladly endured the wartime regimentation, rejoicing that a democracy could fight efficiently even if it involved a temporary sacrifice of traditional freedoms. Customary party lines vanished, though the Republicans naturally reserved the right to urge a more vigorous conduct of the war, and they grew increasingly resentful at what they called Wilson's 'dictatorial' methods. Even citizens of enemy stock almost without exception made America's cause their own. In Congress the President found them among his strongest adherents. The Provost Marshal General reported that "men of foreign and of native origin alike responded to the call to arms with a patriotic devotion that confounded the cynical plans of our archenemy and surpassed our own highest expectations." To keep the nation informed of the fortunes of the struggle and of America's aims and ideals, Wilson set up a Committee on Public Information almost at once. Under the journalist George Creel as chairman it supplied 20,000 columns of news a week to the press, withholding such as might aid the foe. It also published a daily newspaper, issued 75,000,000 leaflets and pamphlets, produced patriotic posters and films, directed speakers in over 5000 communities, established press agencies in Allied and neutral countries, and showered down propaganda from the skies on the enemy peoples.

Though no previous war had aroused such thoroughgoing response, the farmers of the Upper Mississippi Valley retained some of their earlier isolationism, and occasional individuals collided with the law. But the chief defiance came from the Socialists who, meeting in St. Louis on April 7, 1917, branded America's entry as a "crime" of the capitalist class to which they would offer "continuous, active and public opposition." Though the party had polled only 3 per cent of the popular vote in the recent presidential election and the Socialist stand was anticapitalist and antimilitarist rather than pro-German, Congress took alarm, and fearful lest the disaffection spread more widely, it passed a series of laws to stamp out every trace of dissent. The Espionage Act in June, 1917, imposed stringent penalties for willful attempts to obstruct recruiting or to incite insubordination or disloyalty in the armed forces, and instructed the Postmaster-General to bar from the mails any matter deemed seditious or treasonable. The Sedition Act of May, 1918, amplified the list of crimes, including among them abusive utterances about the government, the Constitution or the flag. A third statute, in October, empowered the Secretary of Labor to deport without jury trial aliens who "believe in or advocate" the forcible overthrow of government, or who sought the unlawful destruction of property, or who belonged to organizations holding such views. All three laws while in course of passage were assailed as infringing the constitutional rights of free speech and free press and as outdoing the Alien and Sedition Acts of 1798 in intolerance. Some of the states passed even more drastic legislation, while the veteran progressive Senator La Follette, censured by the Wisconsin legislature for voting against the war resolution, suffered nation-wide opprobrium despite the fact that he supported all the measures for waging the war.

As during the Civil War, the real or fancied rights of the individual were not permitted to thwart the majority will. Federal agents systematically prevented supposedly dangerous Socialist activities, censoring and suppressing their newspapers, raiding meetings and prosecuting speakers. Debs, four times Socialist candidate for President, was sent to prison for ten years, and the same sentence was meted out to another member of the party, Rose Pastor Stokes, for saying, "I am for the people, and the government is for the profiteers." Men were even jailed for excited remarks made in the heat of private argument. In all, about 1900 judicial proceedings were brought against Socialists and other suspects up to the middle of 1919, with about half the cases resulting in convictions. Higher courts, however, set aside a number of them including that of Mrs. Stokes. Oftentimes local communities 'took the law into their own hands,' mobbing persons failing to display the expected degree of patriotism, daubing yellow paint on their doors, boycotting their businesses and dismissing teachers from schools and colleges. In particular anything bearing a Teutonic label nourished the witch-hunting fever. Many schools dropped the teaching of German, bands and orchestras played German music at their peril, and families and even towns with German names hastened to Anglicize them to avoid trouble or to parade their loyalty.

Without an ardent support of the war it would have been harder to raise the unprecedented sums needed. From the first of April, 1917, through April, 1919, the United States spent more than $1,000,000 an hour on the struggle, or a total of $21,850,000,000. In addition, loans to the Allies amounted to nearly $500,000 an hour, totaling $8,850,000 in the same period. A third of the cost was raised by taxes—more than in any earlier war—and steps were taken to tax in accordance with ability to pay. Income rates were boosted at every level, rising finally to 77 per cent on personal earnings of $1,000,000 and over. In like fashion, corporation profits in excess of normal prewar standards were taxed on a progressive scale. Aside from these chief sources of funds, levies were placed upon inheritances, while internal-revenue duties were extended until they affected virtually all the luxuries and many of the necessities of life. To step up the borrowing of money, Congress authorized five great bond issues, the first four known as Liberty Loans and the last—after the armistice —as the Victory Loan. Publicity drives such as had never been known popularized the bonds, which could be bought in denominations as small as fifty dollars. In the fourth sale 21,000,000 subscribers responded, nearly one for every family in the nation. Though the government aimed to tap every available source of revenue, almost equally important was the desire to give a maximum number of people a financial stake in the war. These purposes were further served by selling War Savings Certificates in denominations of five dollars and Thrift Stamps as low as twenty-five cents. In the end, hardly a man, woman or child failed to contribute a 'silver bullet' toward victory.

At the same time Congress set a new standard in soldier welfare legislation. An act of October, 1917, required that fifteen dollars, or half the pay of a private, be sent home each month as an "allotment" for dependents, the government increasing the sum by an "allowance" which varied according to nearness of kin and the number involved. The maimed soldier was promised free vocational training in case he should be unable to resume his former employment. In addition, a war-risk insurance plan permitted the men at low cost to take out government insurance against death or disability. By 1919 over 4,500,000 policies had been written. It was hoped by these provisions to forestall a repetition of the pension abuses that had followed the Civil War.

Meanwhile private organizations to befriend the troops and bolster morale appeared on every hand. Outstanding was the American Red Cross, which now scaled new heights of service. Besides caring for needy soldiers' families, it took charge of sanitary conditions in the districts adjoining the camps, distributed comfort articles to the men at home and overseas and aided civilians fleeing the European war zone. It also recruited ambulance companies, trained and directed nurses and organized great base hospitals. Four months after the armistice Henry P. Davison, chairman of the Red Cross War Council, reported that since America's entry the people had donated $400,-000,000 in cash and materials—"by far the largest voluntary gifts of money, of hand and heart, ever contributed purely for the relief of human suffering." Scarcely less important were other agencies, notably the Y.M.C.A., the Y.W.C.A., the National Catholic War Council, the Jewish Welfare Board, the Salvation Army, the American Library Association and the War Camp Community Service. These groups carried on their work without class, racial or sectarian bias and, as in the case of the Red Cross, enjoyed generous financial support from the public.

Such support was facilitated by the widespread and dazzling prosperity which had climaxed the economic upsurge of the neutrality period. To the insistent call of the Allies for foodstuffs, manufactures and munitions was added the imperative need of the American army and navy for these supplies. To stimulate production, the banks freely lent money and the government added the bait of high prices. Thanks to the abnormal trade relations with Europe, sales abroad vastly exceeded purchases, changing the United States from a debtor to a creditor nation. As the passing months saw an increasing inflow of gold available for investment, every nerve of industry was galvanized. The farmer shared in the general well-being, obtaining prices beyond his wildest dreams of a few years before. The chief benefits, however, fell to businessmen, whose spiraling profits enabled them to keep far ahead of the climbing costs of operation. Some of the profiteering was unconscionable. From 1917 to 1920 the ranks of American millionaires grew from sixteen thousand to twenty.

As prices swung upward the cost of living rapidly advanced. To meet his heavier expenses the wage earner demanded higher pay and was in a good position to get it because Selective Service had reduced the number of workers and the sharp decline of immigration prevented any substantial replenishment. Moreover, the Wilson regime, unlike previous administrations, exerted constant pressure on employers to improve wages and conditions. To this end the American Federation of Labor was given representation not only on the Advisory Commission of the Council of National Defense, but also on the War Industries Board and other key agencies. A National War Labor Board, created by the President in April, 1918, listened to more than 1000 disputes, and a War Labor Policies Board declared for a basic eight-hour day, a living wage, equal pay for the sexes and the right to organize and bargain collectively. The years 1916 and 1917 had been unusually stormy ones in the labor world, with the latter bringing 4450 work stoppages; but in 1918, thanks to the new provision for mediation and the rising pay of rail, shipyard and munitions employees, the number dropped to 3350. Before the war closed, real wages had probably reached a higher level than ever before in America. Meanwhile 500,000 new members joined the AFL, raising the total at the end of 1918 to 2,726,000.

WILSON AND THE PEACE SETTLEMENT

Though Germany was defeated, President Wilson still faced the staggering task of obtaining the kind of peace that would accomplish his purposes. Unfortunately he no longer had a solid country behind him because the Republicans had captured the new Congress in November, 1918. In the electioneering, Wilson, to counter appeals by Senator Henry Cabot Lodge of Massachusetts and ex-President Roosevelt to repudiate him, had asked for a Democratic Congress; and the rebuff by the voters plus the ending of the war freed the Republicans for rough-and-tumble partisanship. Their majority in the Senate, while slender, enabled them to reorganize the Foreign Relations Committee with Lodge as chairman. Though this committee must pass upon the treaty when negotiated and Lodge was Wilson's personal enemy, the President believed that the greatness of the issues at stake would overcome pettier considerations. He proceeded with his plans to head the peace delegation in Paris in person, choosing as fellow members Secretary of State Lansing, Henry White, a retired diplomat, Colonel House and General Tasker H. Bliss. White, the only Republican, had long been inactive in the party, and the Senate was not represented, as it had been in the case of the Spanish-American War. Wilson's decision to be present occasioned surprise and criticism, since up to that time no chief executive had ever left North America or participated in peacemaking. As author of the Fourteen Points, however, he felt that no one else could fight for them so effectively. Assisting the delegation was a large group of legal, economic, historical, geographic and military experts who for months had been amassing pertinent data under Colonel House's general direction.

From the moment Wilson reached France in mid-December till the Peace Conference began on January 12, 1919, he enjoyed a triumphal progress through Western Europe such as no man had ever known. Everywhere the populace acclaimed him as the savior of humanity and showered him with gifts and honors. In Italy peasants put likenesses of the American President beside images of their saints.

In Poland men with glistening eyes greeted each other with the magic word: "Wilson!" But when the veteran Allied statesmen sat down with him to deliberate the peace provisions the scene changed. The very atmosphere of Paris reeked with fear and hatred of Germany. People could not forget the bitter conditions she had inflicted on Russia and Rumania only nine months before and knew full well that if the Germans had triumphed on the western front they would have been no less merciless. Moreover, the Allied governments had never in their hearts accepted Wilson's war aims, and since they had borne the brunt of the conflict and suffered most of the losses, they had no intention of letting him dictate the terms. Another stumbling block was that the broad principles enunciated in the Fourteen Points often lent themselves to differing or even conflicting interpretations in concrete instances, a fact of which the President's antagonists took prompt advantage.[1] Finally, despite Wilson's example and their own official approval of his program, the Allied leaders, recurring unashamedly to power politics, were resolved upon a division of territorial spoils. Some countries, notably England, France, Italy, Japan and Rumania, had driven advance bargains through secret agreements, and every nation had its own special necessities, jealousies and aspirations. The President knew of the secret treaties, but, as he had told Colonel House in July, 1917, he thought the powers concerned could be forced to "our way of thinking" because at the war's close "they will, among other things, be financially in our hands." In reality, however, he did not play this trump card at Paris.

Though twenty-seven governments figured in the proceedings, all the major decisions fell to the 'Big Four': Great Britain, France, the United States and Italy, with Japan raising her voice in Far Eastern affairs. The vanquished countries were denied representation until summoned to learn their fate. As the discussions proceeded behind closed doors, starvation spread over half the continent, communism was gaining new ground in Central Europe, and nearly a score of little fires, left over from the great one, still burned fiercely. As Prime Minister David Lloyd George afterward declared, "We had to . . . work crowded hours, long and late, because, while we were trying

[1] For example, the Poles demanded the application of Point 13 promising them "free and secure access to the sea," but in order to make this possible, it proved necessary to create the Polish Corridor dividing Germany into two parts and placing more than a million Germans under alien sovereignty, a disposition which violated the principle of self-determination found in others of the Fourteen Points.

to build, we saw in many lands the foundations of society crumbling into dust." And, resorting to metaphor, he added, "I am doubtful whether any body of men with a difficult task have worked under greater difficulties, with stones crackling on the roof and crashing through the window, and sometimes wild men screaming through the keyholes."

Wilson's chief adversary was the French Premier, Georges Clemenceau, grim, grizzled and cynical—an uncompromsing representative of power diplomacy. The more volatile Lloyd George usually sided with the President, but he could not be relied upon. Vittorio Orlando of Italy counted for less, though at one juncture the Italian claim to the Adriatic port of Fiume at Yugoslavia's expense led to an open clash with Wilson. The Italian delegates actually left the Conference temporarily, but later negotiated a compromise. As the weeks went by and the President felt obliged to make one concession after the other, many of the Fourteen Points suffered.[1] Yet, notwithstanding the inconsistencies and injustices that found lodgment in the treaty, its terms would have been far more punitive and imperialistic but for Wilson's watchfulness. At one crisis, his patience exhausted, he summoned the *George Washington* to take home the American delegation, a dramatic gesture which effected an immediate toning down of demands. Among other things, he resisted the Polish plea for East Prussia, he wrung from Japan a pledge not to retain indefinite political control of the German-leased territory of Shantung in China, and he prevented France from detaching the industrial Rhineland from Germany and taking permanently the Saar Basin. To obtain Clemenceau's compliance, however, Wilson had to accept a supplementary pact committing the United States and Britain to armed aid to France in the event of "unprovoked" attack by Germany—an agreement which the Senate Foreign Relations Committee later quietly pigeonholed.

Against all attempts to tamper with Point 14 the President stood like a rock. In an "association of nations" he saw an opportunity to repair the faults of the treaty as well as to ensure future world

[1] For example, the Conference's own proceedings violated Point 1 ("open covenants of peace openly arrived at"); Point 4 (pledging reduction of national armaments) was deferred for possible future action of the League of Nations; and Point 5 (regarding the disposition of colonies) was so interpreted as to give most of Germany's possessions to the British Empire under cover of the League's system of "mandatories." On the Continent itself the principle of self-determination was ignored not only in the case of the Polish Corridor, but also in the transfer of enemy territory to other newly created countries, including Germany's Sudetenland to Czechoslovakia.

peace. "This is the central object of our meeting," he told the delegates. "Settlements may be temporary, but the actions of the nations in the interests of peace and justice must be permanent. We can set up permanent processes. We may not be able to set up permanent decisions." On February 14 the body formally adopted a provisional Covenant or constitution of a League of Nations, and the next day Wilson sailed for the United States, where he took counsel with leading men of both parties in and out of Congress. Returning to Paris, he had the text altered to include an explicit recognition of the Monroe Doctrine and to meet certain other criticisms. By these changes he believed he had assured America's adherence, though while he was still at home thirty-nine Senators signed a manifesto, fathered by Henry Cabot Lodge, denouncing the Covenant.

The Covenant as finally inserted in the treaty provided for a three-fold organization at Geneva consisting of an Assembly in which each League member should have an equal voice; a Council representing the Five Great Powers with a few other countries elected from time to time by the Assembly; and a Secretariat or administrative division. Secret treaties were outlawed; a Permanent Court of International Justice was created; and the Council was empowered to propose plans for reducing national armaments. If any countries found it impossible to settle their disputes by diplomatic means, they agreed to resort to arbitration and in no event go to war before the end of a three-month 'cooling-off' period after the decision was rendered. Violation of this provision might subject the offender to economic sanctions (commercial boycott). If armed measures proved necessary, the Council should "recommend" what quotas each nation should furnish. The security-minded Clemenceau had advocated an international police force to back up the League's decisions, but Wilson and Lloyd George had been unwilling.

As a further makeweight for peace Article X of the Covenant, framed by Wilson, pledged the members "to respect and preserve as against external aggression the territorial integrity and existing political independence of all members of the League," with the Council to "advise upon the means by which this obligation shall be fulfilled." Another provision granted the League general supervision of the former enemy colonies, though these were to be confided directly to various powers acting as "mandatories." Finally, the League was charged with promoting international co-operation in certain matters of humanitarian concern, such as conditions of labor and the traffic

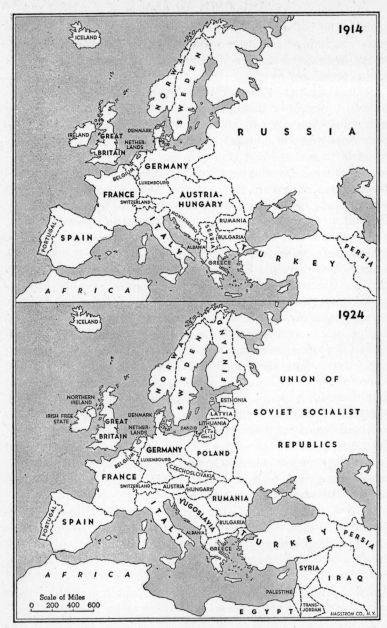

Europe and Asia Minor before and after World War I

in opium and other dangerous drugs. No important decisions could be made except unanimously by the Assembly and Council, and no amendment to the Covenant without the consent of all the governments in the Council.

On June 28, 1919, in the Hall of Mirrors of Louis XIV's famous palace at Versailles, representatives of the new German Republic signed the treaty, which they bitterly condemned as violating the Fourteen Points and intolerably harsh.[1] On July 10 President Wilson submitted it to the Senate for ratification. At once a storm that had been brewing for several months broke loose. The hostility stemmed from a variety of sources. Part of it was due to Wilson's aloofness and self-assurance, which had become intensified under wartime pressures. Part of it arose from liberal spokesmen who, hitherto friendly to the President, now accused him of betraying his own ideals of peace. More important politically was the attitude of Republican leaders, who perceived a strong party advantage in publicizing the treaty's flaws and their own efforts to 'Americanize' it. To their aid came various hyphenate groups, notably the Irish-Americans, who feared Article X would block Ireland's aspirations for independence, and the German-Americans, who disapproved the treaty's severity toward the old country. Beneath these springs of opposition, however, lay a deep-rooted and sincere hesitation of many citizens to depart from what they believed to be America's traditional policy of abstention from Europe's quarrels. The ancient warnings against "entangling alliances" were now resurrected. As someone noted, two of the treaty's most formidable foes were dead men, George Washington and Thomas Jefferson, who, though failing to keep the nation out of the war, were now keeping it out of the peace. On the other hand, the general opinion of the country appeared to be strongly for the League. A *Literary Digest* poll of editors indicated overwhelming press support, and thirty-two legislatures endorsed it, as did both the American Bankers Association and the American Federation of Labor.

[1] The Treaty of Versailles, a 264-page document, required Germany to admit guilt for the war, restored Alsace-Lorraine to France and otherwise sheared down Germany's boundaries in Europe, exacted military and naval disarmament, stripped away her overseas empire and imposed reparations of an indeterminate amount. Including the peace pacts with the other enemy powers, the Versailles settlement ushered into the world a group of new European sovereignties (Austria, Czechoslovakia, Hungary and Poland) and enlarged Serbia into Yugoslavia. The United States signed the treaties with Austria in September, Bulgaria in November, Hungary in June, 1920, and Turkey in August, 1920.

As the debate proceeded in the Senate the members divided into four fairly defined groups: those who like Wilson himself wanted to ratify with little or no change; those who were willing to concede a bit more if necessary; those led by Henry Cabot Lodge, who demanded amendments or strong reservations; and the irreconcilables or extreme isolationists who opposed ratification in any form. The irreconcilables, though but a handful, were fortunate in having as spokesmen such men as Hiram Johnson of California and Idaho's William E. Borah, long known as persistent champions of popular rights. The first two groups were predominantly Democratic, the latter two largely Republican. On September 10 Senator Lodge for the Foreign Relations Committee recommended ratification with a set of amendments and reservations. The principal attack was aimed at the Covenant, on the alleged ground that Article X guaranteed the territorial status quo throughout the world and committed the United States to send troops at the League's behest to defend even unjust boundaries. The Lodge resolutions expressly repudiated any such obligation except by specific vote of Congress when occasion should arise. Anticipating the committee's action, the President set forth on a Western stumping tour to arouse popular backing for unconditional ratification. But the effort proved too great for a physique worn by months of constant strain and responsibility. On September 26, while in Colorado, he suffered a paralytic stroke which ended the tour, confined him to the sickroom for nearly three months and left him permanently crippled. By this catastrophe the League forces lost their commanding general, and the way was cleared for their ultimate defeat.

The Senate discussions continued with increasing heat through the succeeding weeks. When the treaty came up for vote on November 19, 1919, it failed to muster a simple majority either with or without reservations. Had the rancor been less intense or President Wilson more tractable, it is possible that the requisite two thirds might even then have been secured through compromise. Senator Gilbert M. Hitchcock on behalf of the Democrats did indeed offer a series of reservations which differed from Lodge's chiefly in phraseology, but on the eve of a presidential election neither party was willing to yield to the other the credit for saving the peace. On March 19, 1920, the treaty with the Lodge reservations arose a second time, and once more ratification failed, though the vote stood 49 to 35 in favor. A switch of only seven nays would have put America into the League

and perhaps have changed the course of world history. The defeat
was administered by a union of the extremists of the opposing sides
—the irreconcilables and the President's thick-and-thin supporters.
The question of ratification was at a deadlock so far as the United
States was concerned. Further action waited an expression of the
popular will in the approaching election, which Wilson asked should
take "the form of a great and solemn referendum."

FULLER ACCOUNTS

The European Front. For this and the next section Paxson, *American
Democracy and the World War,* II, and Sullivan, *Our Times,* V, are useful.
Bell, *Wilson,* Davis, *Navy Second to None,* Mitchell, *Modern American Navy,*
and Spaulding, *United States Army in War and Peace,* offer short treatments,
while the following works go into greater detail: Baker, *Wilson,* VI–VII;
Beamish and March, *America's Part in the World War;* Frothingham, *American
Reinforcement in the World War;* Morison, *Admiral Sims and the Modern
American Navy;* and Palmer, *Newton D. Baker.*

The War and the American Public. Slosson, *Great Crusade and After,* pictures wartime civilian life, with special aspects receiving attention in Mock
and Larson, *Words That Won the War* (the Committee on Public Information); Chafee, *Free Speech in the United States;* Bogart, *War Costs and Their
Financing;* Clark, *Costs of the World War;* Davison, *American Red Cross;*
and Bing, *War-Time Strikes.*

Wilson and the Peace Settlement. For America's part in the Paris Conference,
see Bailey, *Wilson and the Lost Peace;* Baker, *Wilson and World Settlement;*
Birdsall, *Versailles Twenty Years After;* and Nevins, *Henry White.* On the
fight over ratification, read Bailey, *Wilson and the Great Betrayal,* and Fleming,
United States and the League of Nations.

DO NOT DISAPPOINT
THE WORLD'S HOPE
AMERICA MUST
KEEP THE
COVENANT
NO DRASTIC
RESERVATIONS
WRITE YOUR SENATORS:
"America Must Join
Whole-heartedly"

PART III

THE SEARCH FOR SECURITY

In the years following World War I the nation emphasized increasingly the search for security, whether against economic perils at home or armed aggression abroad. In simpler days this quest had had little importance. Blessed with ample economic opportunity men had enjoyed freedom from want, and remote from Europe's wars they had enjoyed freedom from fear. But now the onrush of history was rapidly changing the picture. Crises like the Great Depression, World War II and the Korean intervention showed tragically how these ancient safeguards had been weakened. So government and people, with much turmoil of spirit and nostalgia for the past, took steps to achieve social security within the country and collective security in global affairs. These two aims were not unrelated, for a peaceful international community afforded the best hope of strengthening and improving America's own way of life.

CHAPTER XV

THE REPUBLICANS AND WORLD AFFAIRS

POSTWAR DOMESTIC READJUSTMENTS

THE bitterness of the fight over the treaty reflected the widespread spirit of postwar intolerance and political bigotry. National sentiment, having been effectively mobilized for war, proved hard to demobilize. Though the German menace was quelled, people looked nervously about for other perils to America. "Property was in an agony of fear," wrote an English observer, "and the horrid name 'Radical' covered the most innocent departure from conventional thought." In particular, many took alarm at Soviet propaganda in the United States and seemed to see their suspicions confirmed when the left-wing Socialists in 1919 broke away from the party to form the Communist (or Workers) party, which aimed at a proletarian revolution. Attorney-General A. Mitchell Palmer and his aides fed the hysteria, suppressing unorthodox political and social opinions whether concerned with the war or not and frequently without regard to the individual's legal rights. Agitators suspected of Communist leanings received special attention. On one occasion, in 1919, the government deported 249 aliens to Russia in a single ship. The dynamiting of J. P. Morgan's Wall Street offices by unknown parties in September, 1920, heightened the popular uneasiness. Thirty-eight were killed and many injured, with a property loss of over $2,000,000.

State officials, abetted by local feeling, emulated the federal authorities. One incident excited international notice. In 1920 two Italian immigrants, Nicola Sacco and Bartolomeo Vanzetti, were tried and convicted for killing a factory paymaster and his guard near Boston. The testimony was flimsy and contradictory, but the proceedings brought out that the men were draft dodgers, atheists and philosophical anarchists. As in the instance of the Chicago Haymarket trial in 1886, these disclosures unleashed the passions of those who thought 'Reds' ought to be strung up on general principles. Unable to obtain a retrial in a higher court despite new evidence which further weakened the case against them, Sacco and Vanzetti were finally executed in 1927. During the long seven-year wait people throughout the nation and in other parts of the world became interested in the affair—not only radicals of various brands, but also conservatives who, disliking the men's opinions, nevertheless defended their constitutional right to a fair and impartial trial. Their execution occurred amidst demonstrations of protest all over the United States as well as in foreign countries.

While the red scare was still at its height, the New York legislature in April, 1920, expelled five of its members because they were Socialists. The incident challenged nation-wide attention. In vigorous disapproval, former Justice Charles E. Hughes of the Supreme Court asserted, "This is not, in my judgment, American government. . . . I count it a most serious mistake to proceed, not against individuals charged with violation of law, but against masses of our citizens combined for political action, by denying them the only resource of peaceful government; that is, action by the ballot box and through duly elected representatives in legislative bodies." Though the ousted members were not restored to their seats, Hughes's ringing plea for fair play may have deterred other legislatures from similar action.

Out of this soil of fear and anxiety arose a secret fanatical movement designed to establish its special conception of '100-per-cent Americanism' by eliminating all but white native-born Protestants from public life. Founded in Georgia in 1915 under the unoriginal name Ku Klux Klan, the organization had languished until the peace-troubled year of 1920 caused its rapid expansion, particularly in the South and Midwest. The white-robed, masked, night-riding Klansmen, lighting the countryside with fiery crosses, used such 100-per-cent un-American methods against their victims as threats, floggings and murder. In 1922 the Klan entered politics, backing friendly candidates of the old parties, carrying a number of local and state elections and wielding influence even in the 1924 Democratic national convention. Part of its strength was doubtless due to the inability of many Americans to resist joining another secret society. As time passed, it added to its initial hatred of immigrants, Negroes, Catholics and Jews an equal dislike of the advocates of such diverse causes as the League of Nations, prohibition repeal and birth control. Before entering on a decline the order in 1925 attained a membership of perhaps four or five million.

The cessation of hostilities also convulsed the labor world. Industry, freed from wartime restraints on conditions of employment, tried to recover lost ground, while the workers, harried by the ever ascending cost of living, fought back on every front. During 1919 more than 4,000,000 wage earners—nearly three and a half times as many as in 1918—engaged in work stoppages. One was a Boston police strike, the first of its kind in America; others provoked armed federal intervention; and many were 'outlaw' strikes, against the wishes of the national unions concerned. The greatest upheavals involved 125,000 men in the New York building trades in February, 250,000 railroad shop employees in August, 367,000 iron and steel workers in September, and 435,000 bituminous miners in November. In the case of the coal strike Attorney-General Palmer, taking advantage of the technicality that the United States had not yet made peace with Germany, secured two court injunctions ordering the United Mine Workers and "all persons whomsoever" to desist. Though resenting this reversal of the government's earlier friendliness toward labor, the union officials acquiesced. Through federal mediation the men eventually got a wage advance of 27 per cent instead of the 60 per cent they wanted, but no change in hours or conditions of labor. During the year the membership of the American Federation of Labor greatly increased, reaching 4,000,000 by 1920, twice the number in 1914.

The soaring prices were due to a prolonging of the wartime business boom. With Europe's industries still badly deranged, she continued in need of American exports, while at home the people, made gay by unwontedly fat purses and the sudden relaxing of the war strain, indulged in an orgy of extravagant buying and fast living. Overexpansion, speculation and swollen prices reached new extremes both in business and agriculture. But during 1920 the foreign demand began to fall off, the products of mill, mine and farm soon glutted the market, prices dropped, and a depression set in that lasted somewhat over two years in the industrial regions and much longer among the farmers. About 20,000 firms failed in 1921, 4,750,000 workingmen were rendered idle, and wages generally declined. Thanks to the efficient working of the Federal Reserve System, however, bank failures were kept to a minimum, and the deflation, though severe, did not reach the proportions of a nation-wide panic.

As steps toward restoring normal conditions Congress in 1920 enacted two important laws. The Esch-Cummins Act in February fixed the terms upon which the railways should be handed back to private management. Passed after much controversy, it embodied certain new principles growing out of the experience of government operation. The idea that competition must be enforced among the companies was abandoned. Pooling, hitherto forbidden, was legalized under supervision of the Interstate Commerce Commission, and plans were authorized for ultimately consolidating the lines into a limited number of systems. In addition, the ICC was empowered to set minimum as well as maximum rates, so that the roads would be assured a fair profit at the same time that they would be prevented from obtaining an excessive one. The statute also provided for special tribunals to handle railway labor disputes. The Merchant Marine Act in June, 1920, announced Congress's policy in regard to the fifteen hundred merchantmen which the United States Shipping Board had acquired during the war. The law ended further shipbuilding by the Board, but continued the experiment of government ownership and operation. The Board at its discretion, however, was empowered to sell the vessels from time to time to American citizens and to accumulate out of the profits a loan fund to assist private builders. By such means it was hoped—vainly, as the sequel was to show—that the United States might maintain its recently regained importance in the carrying trade.

Meanwhile the upheaval of war had brought about two changes in the nation's fundamental law. The first dealt with the long-agitated question of prohibition. By the time America entered the conflict thirty-two legislatures had outlawed the liquor traffic, while much of the remaining territory was dry under local option. In most of the country only the large cities and mill towns remained wet. Aside from other considerations, the increasing menace of drunken motorists had lent strength to the prohibition cause. The need for conserving grain and coal for war purposes caused Congress to add its bit in a law of August, 1917, barring the use of food products in making distilled beverages and authorizing the President to restrict the manufacture of beer, which he later did. Patriotism aroused further opposition to the drink traffic because so many of the breweries and distilleries were owned by persons of German stock. The outcome of these many factors was the Eighteenth Amendment, voted by Congress in December, 1917. This amendment, the first to seek to regulate a citizen's private habits, provided for banning the manufacture, transportation and sale of intoxicants one year after ratification. On January 29, 1919, it became a part of the Constitution. So great was the popular support that all but two states—Connecticut and Rhode Island—took favorable action. If the weather signs were to be believed, smooth sailing lay ahead for the prohibitionists.

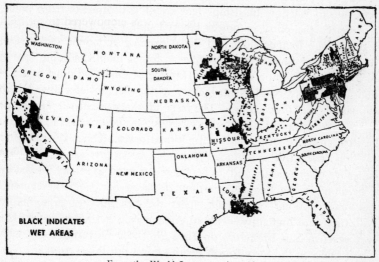

From the World League against Alcoholism, *Handbook for 1919*

Dry Territory on the Eve of National Prohibition

The other amendment granted the long-sought boon of universal equal suffrage. Its adoption, inevitable in any event, was prompted at this time by the public's heartfelt appreciation of the war services of the women. Not only had they helped conserve food and worked in Red Cross units and munitions plants, but thousands had accompanied the troops overseas, acting in a wide variety of capacities from ambulance drivers and nurses to office clerks and Y.M.C.A. entertainers. Wilson, earlier content with the slower process of extending the suffrage through state action, began after the outbreak of the war to champion a federal amendment. European countries were catching up and forging ahead of the United States in this respect, and he felt that democratic America could not afford to fall behind. After considerable delay Congress submitted the Nineteenth Amendment to the states in June, 1919, and it became a part of the Constitution on August 26, 1920, in time for the women to vote in the national election.

THE RETURN OF REPUBLICAN RULE

As the presidential campaign approached, the popular mood favored a change of rulers. All over the world a tide of accumulating resentment due to wartime hardships had swept governments from office. In America the party in power labored under the further handicap of the savage League fight and the deepening economic depression. At Chicago on June 8 the Republicans found their candidate on the tenth ballot in Senator Warren G. Harding of Ohio, a Lodge reservationist and party regular satisfactory to the Senatorial clique which dominated the proceedings. The second place went to Governor Calvin Coolidge of Massachusetts whose supposed firmness in quelling the Boston police strike had won national praise. The platform, after assailing "executive autocracy," promised economy, farm relief and the return of prosperity and, in language designed to satisfy all shades of opinion on the League question, declared for "such agreements with other nations" as would "meet the full duty of America to civilization and humanity" without endangering her sovereignty. The Democrats in San Francisco on June 28 chose Governor James M. Cox of Ohio on the forty-fourth ballot after a hot three-cornered contest in which Attorney-General Palmer and Wilson's son-in-law, former Secretary of the Treasury William G. McAdoo, were his chief rivals. Franklin D. Roosevelt of New York, Assistant Secretary of the Navy and a fifth cousin of the Republican Teddy, was picked for Vice-President. The platform lauded the administration's domestic and foreign policies, pledged farm betterment and urged immediate ratification of the peace treaty "without reservations which would impair its essential integrity."

The two presidential nominees were too little known to the country to arouse much enthusiasm, and one editor wryly suggested that the choice lay "between Debs and dubs," Debs having been named for a fourth time by the Socialists despite his custody in prison. The outcome, however, was never in doubt. The electorate was in a captious mood and eager to lay all its troubles at the door of the party in power. As for the League, the Republicans succeeded in befuddling the issue. Leading irreconcilables like Johnson and Borah maintained that Harding's triumph would mean the treaty's repudiation, while thirty-one Republican notables, including Hughes, Root and Hoover, declared in a joint statement that it was "the true course to bring America into an effective league." Harding's own speeches were sonorous and soothing, favoring something he called "an association of nations," but stressing "America's present need" as "not heroics but healing; not nostrums but normalcy." The term "normalcy" —defined by a wag as the desire that "everything should remain as it never was"—attracted a people tired of domestic reform and foreign war, and craving, as Harding went on to say, "not surgery but serenity." The unprecedented Republican plurality of over 7,000,000 was due in part to the new women voters. In the electoral college the returns stood 404 to 127, while Harding received 60.3 per cent (16,152,000) of the popular ballots to 34.2 per cent (9,147,000) for Cox. Even the Solid South was shaken, Tennessee deserting to the enemy for the first time since Reconstruction. The Republicans also won substantial majorities in Congress. They were back in office again, but there had not been the "great and solemn referendum" on the League for which Wilson had asked.

The new President had had a long but undistinguished career in Ohio politics, where he had always taken the conservative side. A handsome man with heavy features and a large frame, "this waxlike Adonis," as William Allen White called him, possessed the modesty and amiability of a Taft without Taft's brains or single-minded devotion to the public weal. Harding was better known for good fellowship than for statesmanship. As if to offset his own mediocre qualities, he placed in his cabinet three men of recognized ability: Charles E. Hughes as Secretary of State, Andrew W. Mellon, a Pittsburgh millionaire, as head of the Treasury, and Herbert Hoover as Secretary of Commerce. Some of his other and less happy choices stemmed from an undiscriminating personal friendship. Thus he made ex-Senator Albert B. Fall of New Mexico, a notorious anticonservationist, Secretary of the Interior, and Harry M. Daugherty, an Ohio machine politician, Attorney-General.[1] Several months after entering office Harding paid graceful tribute to the only living Republican ex-Presi-

---

[1] The remaining members were John W. Weeks of Massachusetts, Secretary of War; Will H. Hays of Indiana, Postmaster-General; Edwin Denby of Michigan, Secretary of the Navy; Henry C. Wallace of Iowa, Secretary of Agriculture; and James J. Davis of Pennsylvania, Secretary of Labor.

dent, William Howard Taft, by appointing him Chief Justice of the Supreme Court.

In dealing with the League issue the President yielded to the most vociferous element in his party and abandoned his own earlier stand as a Lodge reservationist. The strong upswing of nationalism marking the postwar years rendered this politically the safer course. Congress, summoned in special session, passed a joint resolution in July, 1921, which declared the war at an end, reserved the rights and advantages which the United States would have gained from the Treaty of Versailles, and provided that all enemy property seized during the conflict should be retained until Germany, Austria and Hungary agreed to satisfy America's war claims. In this manner the Republicans, concluding peace two years after the Allies, repudiated Woodrow Wilson's brain child—the most promising experiment in collective security the world had yet known. In August treaties with the enemy powers assented to these terms, and one year later Germany and America provided for a mixed commission to fix the losses from submarine depredations and other sources. Similar tribunals were subsequently arranged with Austria and Hungary.

Harding's election introduced a cycle of Republican supremacy that was to last for twelve years. The tapering off of the depression in 1922 ushered in a boom period which continued year after year and on which the party claimed an exclusive patent. Neither Harding nor his successor Coolidge possessed reform inclinations or the itch for leadership. The party's economic policies accorded with the desires of Big Business, and Mellon, one of the country's richest men, remained at the helm of the Treasury until 1932. Though at times sorely tried, the ordinary voter preferred to let well enough alone while he too nibbled at the fat ears of prosperity. The Democrats, on their part, seemed singularly lacking in cohesion, sacrificing through factionalism whatever chances they might have had to win in 1924 and 1928. As for the newly enfranchised women, the evidence indicates that those who were most active politically came from communities and states with strong Republican leanings, and hence during these years their votes merely increased the preponderance of the majority party.

But for these favoring conditions the Republican sway might not have outlasted the term for which Harding was elected. In domestic affairs he usually advised with a coterie of intimates, the so-called

Ohio Gang, who had hastened to Washington to be near him. The extent of the corruption in which they and their confederates involved his administration was not exposed until after the President's unexpected decease in San Francisco on August 2, 1923, while returning from a trip to Alaska. Though ugly rumors long persisted as to the cause of his death, probably the true reason was a stroke of apoplexy induced by worry over his criminal failure to safeguard the public interest and the certainty that his negligence would become known. In a moment of candor shortly before the end Harding told a friend, "I am not fit for this office and should never have been here." The disclosures stemmed from a series of Senate investigations, the unsavory record surpassing anything since President Grant's time. The first notable instance involved Charles R. Forbes's activities as director of the Veterans' Bureau, an agency which had taken over the functions of the Bureau of War Risk Insurance. In his two years in office the Senate committee found him guilty of "almost unparalleled waste, recklessness and misconduct" in the making of contracts for constructing hospitals and in the purchase and sale of supplies, with a loss to the government of over $200,000,000. He was indicted for conspiracy and fraud and given two years in Leavenworth prison and a $10,000 fine. For comparable offenses Thomas W. Miller, Alien Property Custodian, landed in jail for eighteen months with a $10,000 fine.

Revelations even more spectacular implicated members of the President's official family. In 1921 Navy Secretary Denby had with Harding's approval transferred to Secretary of the Interior Fall the administration of certain oil reserves which Taft and Wilson had set apart for the navy's exclusive use, and a year later Fall secretly leased Reserve No. 3 (Teapot Dome) in Wyoming to Harry F. Sinclair along with another and larger reserve in California to Edward L. Doheny. Though the government retained rights of royalty, these leases diverted the oil from defense purposes to private use and gain. However unwise, the transactions bore no sinister aspect until a Senate committee discovered that late in 1921 Doheny had lent Secretary Fall $100,000 without interest or security and that, after Fall's retirement from the cabinet in March, 1923, Sinclair had similarly given him $25,000. Government suits ultimately brought about a cancellation of the leases and a one-year prison sentence for Fall with a $100,000 fine. While the oil scandal was still under investigation, another committee unearthed shocking facts concerning Daugherty's actions as Attorney-General. The highly sensational testimony indicated that he had been working hand in glove with the most disreputable members of the Ohio Gang and that important decisions of the Justice Department had been corruptly influenced. Tried for conspiracy to "defraud the United States," he managed to escape conviction by a divided jury.

It was on the brink of these disclosures that Harding's death brought Calvin Coolidge to the presidency. Small and lanky, with a nasal twang reminiscent of his Vermont forebears, he was a shy matter-of-fact man who, in Dryden's celebrated phrase, had mastered the art of "saying much in little and often in silence." Though he possessed a moral sensitivity lacking in his predecessor, so completely negative a personality had probably never before occupied the White House. "All his physical tendencies were toward inertia," declared a long-time associate. Faced with the exposures of graft in high places, he displayed an unruffled calm; but in February, 1924, yielding at last to popular pressure, he accepted the resignation of Secretary Denby, whose chief fault had been negligence, and a month later he dismissed Daugherty. In the long run, his simplicity, Yankee caution and patent sincerity won him the firm confidence of a public unwilling in the midst of great prosperity to dwell long on the seamy aspects of government. A "Puritan in Babylon" a biographer called him. Coolidge's sentiment, "The business of America is business," showed that he was nonetheless attuned to the times.

Hoping to exploit the Harding scandals to their political advantage, the Democrats in high glee made preparations for the campaign of 1924. But the prospect of victory embroiled their New York convention on June 24 in a protracted fight between those who wanted to nominate New York's Governor Alfred E. Smith, a Catholic and wet, and the supporters of William G. McAdoo, a Protestant and dry, who was favored by the anti-Catholic, prohibitionist Ku Klux Klan. When neither faction could prevail, the exhausted delegates on the hundred and third ballot—an all-time record—turned to John W. Davis, a corporation lawyer connected with J. P. Morgan and Company, who had succeeded Walter Hines Page as Ambassador to England. To dilute the conservatism of the head of the ticket, Charles W. Bryan of Nebraska, brother of William Jennings Bryan, was chosen as his running mate. The Democrats denounced Republican corruption and incapacity, promised to restore rural prosperity and advocated a popular referendum on the League of Nations. Meanwhile the Republicans had nominated Coolidge without opposition in Cleveland on June 10, giving the second place to Charles G. Dawes, a Chicago banker. The platform took credit for the nation's economic recovery and praised the administration's success in promoting international peace without the entanglements of the League.

Discontented with the conservative outlook of both major nominees, some of the more radical trade-unions and farmers' organizations met with various middle-class reform groups in Cleveland on July 4 to found a new Progressive party. Senator La Follette of Wisconsin, veteran leader of the earlier progressive movement, and Burton K. Wheeler, Democratic Senator from Montana, headed the ticket on a platform assailing official corruption and private monopoly and pledging farm relief, public ownership of water power and railroads, and a constitutional amendment to enable Congress to override Supreme Court decisions. The party was endorsed by the Socialists, the American Federation of Labor and many national unions and state federations. But it evoked little response from the prosperity-drugged electorate, while Republican spellbinders took advantage of its existence to use it as a bogy. On every occasion they besought the public to "Keep Cool with Coolidge" and, in the President's words, insisted that the vital issue was "whether America will allow itself to be degraded into a Communistic and Socialistic state, or whether it will remain American." The wounds inflicted on Democratic unity by the convention rancors crippled the efforts for Davis. Assisted by a bulging campaign chest, Coolidge scored a decisive victory, winning 382 electoral votes to 136 for Davis and the 13 for La Follette from his own state of Wisconsin. Coolidge mustered 54 per cent (15,-725,000) of the popular ballots as compared with 28.7 per cent (8,386,000) and 16.5 per cent (4,823,000) respectively for his two rivals. The Republicans retained control of Congress by large majorities. The Progressives did not survive their first baptism of fire, though the name was to be revived under very different circumstances in the election of 1948. La Follette himself died in 1925, and his policies were inherited by his son 'Young Bob,' who succeeded him in the Senate.

Coolidge's good fortune attended him during his second administration.[1] As before, he favored the policies which business leaders favored and opposed those which they opposed; peace and plenty prevailed; and general contentment reigned. Had he been willing to run again, his party would have rejoiced, but this he chose not to do. At Kansas City on June 12, 1928, the Republican nomination went on the first ballot to Secretary of Commerce Hoover, with Senator Charles Curtis of Kansas next in line. The Democrats meeting in Houston, Texas, on June 26 faced as easy a choice. Since 1924 Al Smith had gained steadily in popularity in the country at large as well as in New York, where he was elected governor for the fourth time in 1926. He too was named on the first ballot, with Senator Joseph T. Robinson of Arkansas for the vice-presidency as a sop to the South. The two platforms offered few points of contrast, both promising agrarian relief, prohibition enforcement, reduction of armaments, labor welfare and care for war veterans. The Democrats even abandoned their traditional hostility to protection, pledging a tariff based on the "actual difference between the cost of production at home and abroad, with adequate safeguard for the wage of the American laborer."

Smith set the pace in the campaign. A colorful speaker, he departed from the party platform by demanding repeal of the Eighteenth Amendment, and he rapped the administration for what he deemed its veiled partnership with Big Business, especially the utility interests. But he faced insuperable odds. Hoover, stigmatizing his opponent's utterances on hydroelectric power and farm relief as "state socialism," dwelt fondly upon the country's phenomenal prosperity and foresaw the early day, if Republican rule be continued, "when poverty will be banished from this nation." Party orators echoed the sentiment by promising "a chicken in every pot and two cars in every garage." The Democratic nominee also suffered from other handicaps, especially in the rural South and West—his Catholicism, his Tammany connections, his occasionally ungrammatical speech and his opposition to temperance. Prosperity, prohibition and prejudice carried the day, giving Hoover a smashing victory. Forty of the forty-eight states cast their 444 electoral votes for him, leaving but 87 for Smith.

[1] In 1925 he made four cabinet changes, appointing Frank B. Kellogg of Minnesota, Secretary of State; Dwight F. Davis of Missouri, Secretary of War; John G. Sargent of Vermont, Attorney-General; and William M. Jardine of Kansas, Secretary of Agriculture.

The latter lost not only his own state but every border state and five of the former Confederacy. The popular ballots, however, were somewhat more evenly distributed, Hoover polling 58 per cent (21,-392,000) and Smith 40.7 per cent (15,016,000). The Republicans also continued their control of Congress.

The new President's past career seemed amply to justify the overwhelming endorsement. A mining engineer of international reputation and considerable wealth, Hoover had demonstrated during the war his constructive abilities, first as head of Belgian relief and then as federal food administrator. Moreover, he had fashioned the Department of Commerce into what the *Republican Campaign Text-Book* called "the world's most formidable engine of foreign trade conquest." Alarmed by what he considered state socialism, he believed that the government should guide and foster, not coerce and restrain, business, thus ensuring free play for "rugged individualism." His chubby face suggested geniality, but most of those who came in contact with him found his manner cold and indifferent. By promoting him to the White House the voters believed they had ended the Harding-Coolidge era of drift. Unhappily, Hoover despite his long public record had never held an elective office; he had dealt with subordinates, not with equals. It remained to be seen whether he could master the difficult art of party leadership and political accommodation.[1] And not far ahead loomed the clouds of the Great Depression.

PIECEMEAL STRIVINGS FOR COLLECTIVE SECURITY

The twelve-year lease of power enabled the Republicans to evolve a program of international peace in place of the one they had scuttled. President Harding in his inaugural address in 1921 enunciated the guiding principles: "We seek no part in directing the destinies of the world. . . . We are ready to associate ourselves with the nations of the world, great and small, for conference and counsel, for the suggestion of plans of mediation, conciliation, and arbitration; but every commitment must be made in the exercise of our national sovereignty." The Republican attitude was not one of isolationism

---

[1] His original cabinet consisted of Henry L. Stimson of New York, Secretary of State; Andrew W. Mellon of Pennsylvania, Secretary of the Treasury; James W. Good of Iowa, Secretary of War; William D. Mitchell of Minnesota, Attorney-General; Walter F. Brown of Ohio, Postmaster-General; Charles F. Adams of Massachusetts, Secretary of the Navy; Ray L. Wilbur of California, Secretary of the Interior; Arthur M. Hyde of Missouri, Secretary of Agriculture; James J. Davis of Pennsylvania, Secretary of Labor; and Robert P. Lamont of Illinois, Secretary of Commerce.

but rather of 'co-operation without entangling alliances,' and since they lacked a preconceived plan, they moved toward the goal haltingly step by step. In an era of easy optimism bred of the abounding prosperity it was believed that peace might be made everlasting with only the incidental collaboration of the United States.

Though the League had been rejected, it could not be ignored. Thriving without America's approval, it had speedily acquired fiftyfour members, including seventeen in the Western Hemisphere. Unavoidably, many of its activities and decisions involved matters in which the United States had a vital interest. Hence after six months, during which the State Department did not so much as answer League communications, the administration began hesitantly to send "observers" to conferences where questions of national concern were at stake. They were authorized to present the government's viewpoint but not to vote in determining the outcome. In this manner the United States attached observers to the League committees on health, the opium trade and the traffic in women and children. Private co-operation went much farther, for American experts in law, medicine and finance freely accepted important League assignments in their individual capacities. The ice having been broken, the government itself took a further step in 1924 by sending delegates to participate fully in League conferences when the national interest seemed to warrant. By March, 1930, they had taken part in twenty-two such gatherings. Before the end of another year the United States had adhered to a total of thirteen agreements sired by the League, maintained five permanent officials in Geneva and, under circumstances shortly to be related, even appointed a representative to sit with the League Council during the Manchurian crisis. Some people saw in this drift of events ultimate membership in the League, but Republican spokesmen continued to assert, in Harding's words, that the issue was "as dead as slavery."

Toward the World Court, however, Harding and his successors took a bolder attitude. This tribunal, officially termed by the League Covenant the Permanent Court of International Justice, had been set up at The Hague in January, 1922, following a plan which Elihu Root had helped draft. Unlike the pre-existing Permanent Court of Arbitration it had a fixed personnel, the judges being selected by the League Council and Assembly from nominations made by the older Hague body. The World Court had jurisdiction over "any dispute of an international character which the parties thereto submit to it." In addition, it might issue advisory opinions on application of the Council or Assembly. Both Harding and Coolidge recommended membership on certain conditions, and though the extreme isolationists delayed favorable action until 1926, the Senate then voted to join along the lines suggested. The principal reservation specified the right to veto requests for advisory opinions touching any question "in which the United States has or claims an interest." But the other countries would not agree, and the deadlock persisted until 1929 when Elihu Root, at the Council's invitation, devised an acceptable compromise. In essence, it provided that the judges must not, without America's consent, render an advisory opinion in any dispute to which she was a party; should cases arise in which she claimed merely "an interest," the Washington government might, if it thought proper, withdraw from the Court "without any imputation of unfriendliness." There the matter rested. The Senate failed to act on the Root proposal, though both political parties in the next presidential election declared for participation. The United States and Soviet Russia continued to be the only major powers outside the Court.

The American government meanwhile had launched a series of efforts to scale down national armaments. From the hindsight of World War II this action was condemned as a species of criminal folly because the victorious powers thereby reduced each other's military effectiveness, but this criticism overlooked the fact that the Versailles Treaty had already completely disarmed Germany. The greatest threat to peace at the time appeared to lie in the disturbed conditions and international rivalries of the Orient. With this in mind President Harding summoned a conference of nine nations—the five Great Powers plus the Netherlands, Portugal, Belgium and China—which met in Washington from November, 1921, to the following February. On the dramatic initiative of Secretary of State Hughes the Great Powers undertook to limit their relative strength in long-range offensive ships according to the ratio of 5:5:3 for the United States, the British Empire and Japan and 1:75 each for France and Italy, this 'naval holiday' to continue until the end of 1936. To offset her inferiority in battleships Japan induced Britain and the United State to agree not to fortify further their Pacific holdings (including in the case of America the Philippines, Guam, Samoa and the Aleutians but not Hawaii). The pact established a new balance of sea power, with the two English-speaking nations on an equality and jointly overtopping the other three. The five governments also agreed to limit their relative strength in aircraft carriers, and they joined in condemning unrestricted submarine warfare and the use of poisonous gas.

In order to remove the special Far Eastern incitements to war, Great Britain, Japan, France and America pledged themselves to respect each other's possessions in the Pacific and, if danger threatened from another power, to confer "as to the most efficient measures to be taken, jointly or separately." This Four-Power Treaty involved the abrogation of the Anglo-Japanese Alliance of 1902, which was unpopular in the United States, and at the same time quieted American fears as to Japan's designs against the Philippines. The Open Door policy, which the Japanese had flouted during the war by imposing oppressive demands on China, attained full international sanction in a Nine-Power Treaty to respect China's independence and maintain "the principle of equal opportunity for the commerce and industry of all nations." [1]

Important as were these moves for peace, the American government failed in its endeavors to apply the principle of restriction to smaller craft such as cruisers, destroyers and submarines. Competition in these vessels, particularly ten-thousand-ton cruisers, began at once. To check this new arms race President Coolidge called a conference at Geneva in 1927, but only Britain and Japan were willing to participate, and agreement proved impossible even among these three. In 1930, however, the English government at President Hoover's urging made a second and more successful attempt. At the London gathering the United States, Britain and Japan engaged to limit all their auxiliary naval ships until the end of 1936, the two English-speaking powers on a basis of parity and Japan at a more favorable ratio than that set at the Washington Conference. But neither Italy nor France—which was alarmed at Italy's rearming under the Fascist dictator Mussolini—would make any commitments. At both the Washington and London Conferences America was permitted a bigger navy than Congress chose to build. Encouraged by these signs of progress, the League assembled a World Disarmament Conference

[1] Other Far Eastern sources of irritation were also dealt with. Thus, a Nine-Power Pact established the principle of China's control over her own tariff; and in 1923, a year after the conference, Secretary Hughes induced Japan to cancel the troublesome Lansing-Ishii Agreement of 1917.

at Geneva in February, 1932, to consider plans for limiting the other two major branches of warfare, those of land and air. More than thirty nations attended, and many far-reaching proposals were offered, including America's to reduce all existing armaments by approximately one third. The sessions continued into 1933, but Japan's seizure of Manchuria and the threatening state of affairs elsewhere blocked any positive action.

Meanwhile Coolidge's Secretary of State, Frank B. Kellogg, had promoted a peace offensive of a different kind. At his instance a treaty was drawn up in Paris in 1928 to outlaw war "as an instrument of national policy" and to bind the nations to settle their "conflicts of whatever nature" solely by "pacific means." Within four years sixty-two of the sixty-four countries of the world had signed. To many persons the Pact of Paris seemed merely a pious gesture or, as Missouri's Senator James Reed put it, "an international kiss," for it provided no means of enforcement, and the State Department had said it did not preclude the "right of self-defense"—a pretext which had often been used to cloak aggression in the past. But others felt that this collective step possessed profound import as a moral commitment haling nations "not into a court of law, but into the forum of conscience." President Hoover went further in a joint statement with Ramsay MacDonald during the British Prime Minister's visit to America in October, 1929: "Both our Governments resolve to accept the Peace Pact not only as a declaration of good intentions, but as a positive obligation to direct national policy in accordance with its pledge."

Events in North China soon put the matter to a test. The invasion of Manchuria by Japan prompted the United States in October, 1931, to send a representative to sit with the League Council to consider a basis for common action under the Pact of Paris. Nippon, sternly reminded by the Council of her pledge to renounce war, nevertheless continued her career of conquest. In November Henry L. Stimson, Hoover's Secretary of State, further condemned Japan's course as a violation of the Nine-Power Treaty guaranteeing China's territorial integrity. The League despite its verbal protest balked at applying coercive measures because of the apathetic attitude of Britain, the chief European power in the Orient. This forbearance of the world organization was an object lesson not lost on Mussolini and Hitler in the years just ahead. When in spite of America's efforts Japan occupied all Manchuria, Secretary Stimson in January, 1932, formally notified her that the United States would not "recognize any situation, treaty, or agreement" which infringed the Paris Pact. Two months later the League Assembly (Japan and China not voting) unanimously endorsed this action. But Tokyo denied any culpability, advancing the plea of self-defense and setting up the "independent" state of Manchukuo in February as evidence that the Chinese in Manchuria remained free to exercise the right of self-determination. Smarting under the international rebuke, Japan in 1933 gave the required two-year notice of withdrawing from the League.

Other signs of the times indicated that the structure of peace so hopefully built in the 1920's was beginning to weaken. The war had put the Allied governments under heavy debt to the United States and left Germany with crushing obligations to the Allies. Of the $10,000,000,000 due the United States, more than 90 per cent was owing from Great Britain, France and Italy. America early assured the debtors of her willingness to take into account their financial capacity in arranging settlements, and between June, 1923, and May, 1930, seventeen governments—all but Russia, Nicaragua and Armenia —entered into agreements. Great Britain, for example, promised to repay over a period of sixty-two years at an interest rate averaging 3.3 per cent; France similarly at 1.6 per cent; and Italy at 0.4 per cent. For the means to defray these obligations the leading powers relied upon the reparation payments from Germany. This sum had not been fixed in the Versailles Treaty, but in 1921 a special commission had set the figure at $33,000,000,000. The burden, however, proved too heavy for Germany; and a revised plan in 1924 and another in 1929—named respectively after Charles G. Dawes and Owen D. Young, two Americans who helped frame them—provided for progressively smaller amounts and easier terms.

The Young Plan frankly coupled reparations and the intergovernmental debts by arranging for a still further reduction of German payments to the extent that America might in the future relax her demands on the Allies, a provision which gainsaid Washington's contention that the two transactions had no relationship. But when presently depression settled on the world and an overstrained Germany seemed on the point of financial collapse, President Hoover in the summer of 1931 negotiated a one-year moratorium or postponement of both debt and reparation payments. This action brought to a head a strong sentiment outside government circles for canceling or drastically revising the debts. Some argued that this would atone for America's delay in entering the war, while others pointed out that the debtor countries could not acquire the necessary gold because the high tariff curtailed their export sales in America. European resentment was represented by popular references to Uncle Sam as Uncle Shylock. The official attitude of the United States stemmed from the feeling that extremely generous terms had already been granted and that one third of the sum was not a war debt at all but a postarmistice loan. Germany never resumed her payments to the Allies, and in December, 1932, France, Belgium and four other governments stopped theirs to America. The next year all the remaining countries but Finland followed suit.

Despite the irritation engendered by the debt situation the period of Republican supremacy had beheld an impressive collective effort toward the goal of a warless world. America's part, though embarrassed by official rejection of the League, had nevertheless been substantial, and it had been abetted by an eager public opinion. The various peace societies again became active and new ones joined their ranks. A noteworthy indication of the revived interest appeared in a national poll of Protestant clergymen in 1931. Of the more than 19,000 responding, 12,000 (62 per cent) declared that the churches should refuse to support any future war, while over 10,000 (54 per cent) said that they personally would not take part in one. Though such sentiments were opposed by other elements in the population, notably veterans' groups and patriotic societies, yet the most significant scheme to strike at the evil through purely domestic action originated with the American Legion, the chief ex-soldiers' organization. At its prompting, Congress created a War Policies Commission including five cabinet officials. This body in 1932, after consulting with industrial and labor leaders, army officers and spokesmen for civilian groups, framed a plan to eliminate the profiteering motive as an incentive to war. It proposed legislation which in the event of hostilities would automatically subject individuals and corporations to a tax of 95 per cent on all earnings above the previous three-year average. But Congress took no action. At home its attention was absorbed in problems created by the deepening depression, while abroad Japan's lunge against China and the rising war temperature in Europe suggested the desirability of moving circumspectly.

FULLER ACCOUNTS

Postwar Domestic Adjustments. Paxson, *American Democracy and the World War,* III, and Slosson, *Great Crusade and After,* cover the main developments, with particular phases treated more fully in Mock and Thurber, *Report on Demobilization;* Samuelson and Hagen, *After the War;* Wecter, *When Johnny Comes Marching Home;* Oneal and Werner, *American Communism;* Bates, *This Land of Liberty;* Chafee, *Free Speech in the United States;* Joughin and Morgan, *Legacy of Sacco and Vanzetti;* Mecklin, *Ku Klux Klan;* Soule, *Prosperity Decade;* and Dulles, *Labor in America.*

The Return of Republican Rule. Allen, *Only Yesterday,* Faulkner, *From Versailles to New Deal,* Paxson, *American Democracy and the World War,* III (to 1923), and Sullivan, *Our Times,* VI (to 1925), are general accounts, while special treatments include Adams, *Incredible Era, the Life and Times of Warren Gamaliel Harding;* Fuess, *Coolidge;* Corey, *Truth about Hoover;* Johnson, *Borah;* and Jessup, *Root.*

Piecemeal Strivings for Collective Security. The comprehensive works include Fleming, *United States and World Organization;* Nevins, *United States in a Chaotic World;* Rappard, *Quest for Peace;* and Williams, *United States and Disarmament.* Particular developments concern Fleming, *United States and the World Court;* Buell, *Washington Conference;* Sprouts, *Toward a New Order of Sea Power;* Bryn-Jones, *Kellogg;* and Myers, *Paris Pact.* For the Manchurian crisis, see Griswold, *Far Eastern Policy,* and, for the debt question, Moulton and Pasvolsky, *War Debts and World Prosperity.*

CHAPTER XVI

FROM PROGRESS TO POVERTY

REPUBLICAN ECONOMICS

IN domestic affairs the three Republican Presidents furthered governmental thrift and economic nationalism. As an initial step toward the first goal, Congress in June, 1921, created the Bureau of the Budget as a watchdog of the Treasury, with authority under the President to examine and revise requests for funds before they were submitted to Congress. This system broke sharply with the traditional method of voting appropriations hit-and-miss and without due relation to the government's total income. Under Charles G. Dawes as first director the plan quickly demonstrated its utility. Next, the government, guided by Secretary of the Treasury Mellon, undertook the dual task of decreasing wartime taxes and the national debt. In both respects it was highly successful. Thanks to the amazing prosperity, it was able to lower the income and other taxes by stages and at the same time to cut the debt from $24,298,000,000 in 1920 to $16,-185,000,000 in 1930.

The principal obstacle to this course was the ceaseless propaganda of the American Legion and kindred organizations for additional compensation for ex-servicemen. Through the Veterans' Bureau the government was already providing medical and hospital care for the totally disabled, vocational training for the partly disabled and allowances for their dependents. It was also conducting a vast insurance business for the veterans and at the close of the war had granted them a discharge bonus totaling $256,000,000. Unsatisfied, the leaders insisted on a further bonus to help offset the wartime wages that the soldiers might have earned as civilians. In 1922 a bill for this purpose fell before Harding's veto, but a later one, in 1924, was carried over Coolidge's. It bestowed paid-up insurance policies averaging considerably more than $1000 for each man, with the principal to be discharged in 1945. When the country began to feel the pinch of unemployment in 1930, the men started an agitation for immediate redemption of the policies. Over Hoover's spirited veto Congress in February, 1931, went part way by permitting the holders to borrow on their policies up to half the amount of the insurance. Expenditures for World War I veterans, which had cost $402,000,000 in the year 1921, reached an annual outlay of over $860,000,000 in 1932.

The economy drive chimed in with the Republican doctrine that a paring of government costs and reducing of taxes—especially of those in the higher brackets—would spur investment, stimulate business and create more employment and higher wages. As a further lift to industry and business the party recurred to the protective tariff, eclipsing its own past efforts in this regard. The leaders saw no contradiction between aiding world peace through diplomacy and abetting economic nationalism through legislation. The Emergency Tariff Act of 1921 boosted duties on wool, sugar, meat, wheat and other farm commodities. The Fordney-McCumber Act of 1922 added manufactures, restoring many of the old Payne-Aldrich rates of 1909 and imposing prohibitive ones to encourage certain infant industries such as coal-tar products and dyestuffs. Since the underlying theory was to equalize the costs of production in the United States and other countries, the President was empowered to raise or lower duties on advice of the Tariff Commission by as much as 50 per cent. In practice this flexible clause almost invariably brought increases.

The higher duties on agricultural imports did not relieve the distressed farmers, and as the decade drew toward a close, Congress felt obliged to reopen the matter. But a powerful lobby of industrialists seized the occasion to secure more extortionate rates for themselves. Joseph R. Grundy, president of the Pennsylvania Manufacturers' Association, frankly told a Congressional committee that Big Business had largely financed Hoover's election and expected recompense; and as it happened, he was appointed to a vacancy in the Senate in time to help put his ideas into effect. The Hawley-Smoot Act of 1930 lifted the general level of duties by perhaps 20 per cent, the loftiest point in American history. In the case of automobiles and certain other items new duties were imposed even when a majority of the manufacturers did not want them. A thousand economists in colleges and universities besought Hoover to interpose his veto, but despite misgivings he refrained, hoping to be able to remedy the worst features through the flexible provision, which the bill retained. Angered by the unprecedented rates, foreign governments undertook reprisals. By the spring of 1932 more than twenty had raised their tariffs against the United States.

That America's international trade steadily grew from 1922 to 1929 despite the steep customs wall was due partly to Hoover's energy as Secretary of Commerce in making his Department "the world's most formidable engine of foreign trade conquest," a program which Congress promoted in 1927 by supplementing the regular consular service with a far-flung network of hustling special agents to search out openings for business and the export of capital. It was due further to the enormous sums loaned abroad, much of which was used to buy American commodities. The startling rise of foreign investments—from $8,500,000,000 in 1922 to over $12,000,000,000 in 1927—rested in part on the establishment of American-owned businesses abroad. The Washington government's negotiation of a moratorium in 1931 stemmed in large measure from fear lest Germany's plight imperil American holdings of nearly $2,000,000,000 in that country. America's high tariff made it hard for foreign nations to obtain goods in the United States because of the barriers against their own export trade. Hence, as a Yale economist pointed out in 1929, "substantial portions of our most highly developed and most profitable industries" found it expedient to migrate to alien lands, "carrying with them not only American organization and methods but also American talent, with all the resultant loss of purchasing of American domestic products and of the stimulus to American business in general." So American automobile plants were set up in Canada, cork factories in Spain, glove works in France, burlap mills in India.

To give freer reign to industrial enterprise at home the Sherman Antitrust Act was virtually suspended, and the Federal Trade Commission was filled with friends of the very businesses it was supposed to regulate. Partly as a result, more than six thousand manufacturing and mining companies disappeared between 1921 and 1930 either from being combined with or acquired by other companies. A portentous new development was the participation of giant corporations in foreign cartels, which engaged in such practices as exchanging patents, controlling sources of raw materials, restricting production, fixing prices and dividing up the world's markets. The result was another check on international trade and usually stiffer prices for the com-

modities in the United States. By this means also German manufacturers learned secret industrial processes that were to help Adolf
Hitler prepare for World War II. Among the products affected were
aluminum, magnesia, lead, copper, zinc, electric lamps, radio tubes
and matches.

Within the national borders the most conspicuous development
was the gigantic public-utilities holding company controlling actual
operating companies which might be scattered in many parts of the
country. These supermergers rose like a pyramid tier upon tier, holding company on top of holding company. Because of the intricacy of
their interlocking structures they lent themselves to stock watering,
speculation and dishonest accounting practices, and they were exempt
from regulation by state utility commissions since the judiciary had
ruled that they were not themselves public utilities. "A holding company," concluded America's favorite humorist Will Rogers, "is a thing
where you hand an accomplice the goods while the policeman searches
you." The full possibilities of the financial jugglery became known in
1932 with the collapse of the Insull group of utilities, which furnished
power, light and heat to nearly five thousand communities in thirty
states. The crash inflicted a staggering loss of nearly $700,000,000 on
the investing public. Samuel Insull, the architect of this glittering
empire, promptly fled to Greece and, when finally forced to return,
managed to escape punishment for lack of sufficient legal evidence.

Americans used as much electricity as all the rest of mankind combined, and this fact made water power, the largest potential generating
source, a matter of increasing public concern. Most men in political
life, however, did not yet class electric energy along with timber and
coal as falling properly under the program of conserving natural resources. Nevertheless Congress in 1920 under Wilson created a
Federal Power Commission to license hydroelectric enterprises in
public lands and on navigable waters. By 1930 it had authorized
nearly four hundred and fifty projects, chiefly in the West; but these
plants furnished only a sixteenth of the nation's total supply. An
unsettled question from wartime compelled the Republicans to give
the subject further attention. The point at issue was the disposition
of certain federal properties on the Tennessee River at the foot of
Muscle Shoals in northern Alabama. In 1918 President Wilson had
caused factories to be built there to make nitrates for explosives and
fertilizers, and he had also begun the construction of dams for gen-

erating electric power to run the plants. Led by Senator George W. Norris, the veteran Republican liberal of Nebraska, the progressive elements of both parties urged that the government own and operate these Tennessee Valley works in peacetime, whereas the Eastern industrialists insisted on turning them over to private companies. After prolonged and bitter controversy two bills framed to accomplish Norris's purpose—one in 1928 and the other in 1931—were killed by vetoes. Both Coolidge and Hoover, faithful to the creed of rugged individualism, decried the nation's entering into economic competition with its own citizens.

The progressives fared better, though, in the matter of erecting a dam to harness the Colorado River at the Arizona-Nevada border. Congress in 1928 authorized the Boulder Dam (now called Hoover Dam) for the triple purpose of irrigation, of flood control, and of supplying electric power to the seven Southwestern states. The law required that the undertaking be self-liquidating (the cost to be repaid over a period of fifty years by the users of water and power); that it be built by private contractors; and that when finished there be no competition with private enterprise. Actual construction, begun in 1930, was completed in six years. But a final disposal of the Tennessee Valley question awaited the coming of the New Deal.

LABOR AND THE IMMIGRATION QUESTION

While capital plucked the lush fruits of prosperity, labor also issued from the unsettled postwar years into easier times. Industrial relations had seldom been so quiet or wages so good. The number of work stoppages fell from 3400 in 1920 to 1100 in 1922 and to 600 in 1928, with the number of strikers dropping from nearly a million and a third in 1920 to less than a third of a million in 1928. For this unwonted peace many factors were responsible. On the one hand, employers resorted increasingly to court injunctions against strikes and at the same time introduced company unions in place of those belonging to national labor organizations. By 1928 some 1,500,-000 men belonged to company unions. On the other hand, management propitiated workers with such concessions as better pay, profit-sharing plans, recreational facilities, sickness and death benefits and retirement pensions. As the profits of industry kept climbing, businessmen not only strove to ensure a contented labor force, but many accepted the doctrine that high wages (and hence enhanced purchasing power) formed an essential element in the reigning prosperity. The American Federation of Labor, having little discontent on which to feed, dwindled from 4,000,000 members in 1920 to 2,900,000 in 1929.

The AFL, though a declining force in the industrial world, nevertheless left its mark on legislation. Besides bringing about the improvement of earlier labor laws, it induced seventeen states by 1930 to provide for old-age pension systems. It also helped prod Congress into submitting a constitutional amendment in 1924 to obtain the power, which the Supreme Court had said was lacking, "to limit, regulate, and prohibit the labor of persons under eighteen years of age." But this victory in the long fight against child labor proved barren because Southern employers of children, Northern investors in Southern mills and conservatives generally combined to block ratification. In 1937, when the last legislatures approved the proposal, eight states of the necessary thirty-six were still wanting. But labor's principal goal was federal action to protect workers against 'yellow-dog contracts' (binding them as a condition of employment not to join national trade-unions) and against the misuse of court injunctions in industrial disputes. After an extended struggle Congress took the desired step in 1932. The Norris-La Guardia Act declared yellow-dog contracts unenforceable in federal courts and expressly exempted "customary labor union effort short of fraud and violence" from injunctions. This immunity, furthermore, was extended to all persons "in the same industry, trade, or occupation," thus considerably broadening the benefits of the Clayton Act, which the Supreme Court had construed as applying only to the employees of the company immediately concerned.

Organized labor found it easier to marshal support for tightening the clamps on immigration. The intense nationalism bred by the war, the dread of a deluge of low-grade and perhaps radical newcomers from devastated Europe, the waxing power of the Ku Klux Klan—such influences impelled Congress to give ready ear to labor's fears of competition from hordes of destitute foreigners. A law of 1921 limited the annual quota from any European or African country to 3 per cent of the number of its immigrants in the United States in 1910. By this device Congress not only ensured a reduction in the sum total of arrivals, but also discriminated against those from Southern and Eastern Europe. But the door still stood too far open to suit public opinion. Hence the Johnson Act of 1924 cut the quota to 2 per cent and pushed the test year back to 1890. The earlier date meant even greater partiality for the old immigration from Northern and Western Europe. The act further stipulated that, as soon as the difficult calculations could be completed, the annual inflow should be kept to approximately a hundred and fifty thousand and that then the quota for each country should be determined in accordance with the proportion of Americans descended from the particular nationality. The national-origins provision, as it was called, went into effect in 1929.

IMMIGRATION BEFORE AND AFTER THE QUOTA LAWS

	Countries of Northern and Western Europe	Countries of Southern and Eastern Europe and Asia
Average annual number, 1907–1914	176,983	685,531
Quotas under act of 1921	198,082	158,367
Quotas under act of 1924	140,999	21,847
Under national-origins provision of 1929	132,323	20,251

This provision, however, was not applied to native-born residents of the Western Hemisphere, who could continue to enter without limit of numbers, nor did it apply to immigrants ineligible to citizenship, who were totally excluded. The exclusion clause was aimed primarily at Japan. The State Department had tried to keep it out of the bill in view of the Gentlemen's Agreement of 1907, which Tokyo had observed in good faith. If the same formula had been extended to the Japanese as to other nationalities, the number in any case would have been only 250. Japan, deeming Congress's action a gratuitous insult, entered a sharp protest. It should be added that the Chinese, who had been barred by earlier legislation as well as now by their ineligibility to citizenship, were eventually given different treatment, for in 1943 Congress, in recognition of China's resistance to the Japanese in World War II, authorized 105 admissions each year and opened the way for those already in the United States to become naturalized.

Even as the closing of the frontier in the 1880's had ended one great historic process, so this restrictive program ended another. No longer was America to be an open refuge for the peoples of the Old World. The nation had resolved to freeze the existing composition of the population, if possible, rather than leave it further to chance. That composition had become increasingly less British and more cosmopolitan since the republic was founded. In fact, English, Scotch, Scotch-Irish and Canadian blood did not now account for as much as half. Yet the freezing could only be approximate, for the various countries might not always fill their quotas and, in any event, the birth rate of different foreign groups already in the United States was likely to vary. Moreover, since the legislation did not affect the peoples of the Western Hemisphere, they might conceivably alter the balance by migrating in large numbers. From 1921 to 1931 the total from all parts of the world fell from 805,000 to 35,500. The arrivals in the latter year were scarcely more than a quarter of those legally admissible, an unexpected development for which the Great Depression was responsible.

PROHIBITION IN PRACTICE

While these events were taking place, the government embarked upon one of the boldest social experiments of all time: the attempt to change deep-rooted drinking habits of a continent-wide nation. The Volstead Act, which went into effect in January, 1920, prohibited as intoxicating any beverage having more than half of one per cent of alcohol. But it proved one thing to enact legislation and another to secure compliance. The federal authorities lacked both the experience and the prior organization to administer a law of this character; and as time went on and public opinion grew increasingly doubtful as to the wisdom of the wartime decision, difficulties of enforcement multiplied. A brisk smuggling trade along the Atlantic Coast and an overland traffic southward from Canada brought in much foreign liquor, while within the national borders illicit distilling and the illegal conversion of industrial alcohol formed an even greater source of supply.

Though Congress from time to time strengthened the machinery of enforcement, the task proved staggering because of the size of the country, the frequent failure of state and local officials to co-operate, and sometimes the venality of the federal agents themselves. From 1920 to 1932 nearly six hundred thousand cases were brought into the United States district courts. Compliance was most nearly attained in the rural sections and small towns, where a strong dry sentiment had traditionally prevailed. In the big cities, bribery of officials, 'racketeering,' 'hijacking' and other forms of organized criminality throve on the profits of furnishing supplies to 'bootleggers,' 'speakeasies' and 'roadhouses,' which in turn dispensed the liquor, good or bad, at fancy prices to consumers. Defiance of the Volstead Act by otherwise law-abiding citizens became in many circles almost a matter of pride. A Congressional committee in 1929 reported that three thousand bootleggers flourished in the national capital, and it was no secret that President Harding himself did not sacrifice his personal inclinations to the constitutional mandate. Particularly alarming was the seeming demoralization of young people, who found in carrying a hip flask the spice of adventure and sophistication.

Imperfect statistics suggest that the total consumption of intoxicants fell off under the Eighteenth Amendment, but both wets and drys testified to a change from the earlier preference for beer and light wines to hard drinks like whisky, rum and brandy. Prohibitionists, however, hopefully claimed credit for the increased savings deposits, the greater consumption of candy, milk and soft drinks and the generally improved condition of the poor. With characteristic timidity the major parties avoided making an issue of the question until Al Smith, true to his city upbringing, injected the demand for repeal of the Eighteenth Amendment into the campaign of 1928. The results of the election hardly seemed to warrant a repetition of his hardihood.

Yet, as the future was to disclose, the "experiment, noble in purpose"—President Hoover's phrase—could hardly have been tried at a less favorable time. Urban sentiment had always been the mainstay of the wet cause, and the 1920's saw the proportion of people living in cities of twenty-five thousand and upward increase from less than 36 per cent to over 40. Moreover, through the newspapers, magazines, movies and the radio, metropolitan notions and prejudices penetrated to the remotest corners of the land. Finally, the trial was made at a period when the recoil from wartime self-sacrifice brought a relaxation of morals in both personal behavior and public life, a tendency prolonged by the hectic living and easygoing standards of an era of extraordinary prosperity. But national prohibition lingered on until the advent of the Great Depression in 1929 provided new reasons for repeal. By restoring the liquor traffic it was argued that idle men would get jobs, farmers gain a market for their grain and sugar and the government recover a profitable source of revenue. The Democrats made it one of their campaign issues in 1932, but without waiting for them to assume office the outgoing Congress in

February, 1933, took the necessary constitutional step. The Eighteenth Amendment had required thirteen months for adoption; the Twenty-first was ratified in less than ten, becoming a part of the Constitution in December, 1933.

THE FARM PROBLEM

The prosperity that marked the 1920's had skipped the farmers. While the war was still on, they had brought their reserve power of production into play. Spurred by the unprecedented prices, they had greatly enlarged their holdings and rapidly mechanized their operations. Buying fewer than 28,000 tractors in the year 1916, they bought more than 136,000 in 1919. They also modernized their methods of marketing, with the Farmers' Nonpartisan League in the Upper Mississippi Valley going so far as to commit the North Dakota legislature to a program of state-owned flour mills, grain elevators and a bank. More typical was the spread of co-operatives, which in five years after 1914 increased from under 3000 to nearly 6000, the majority dealing in grain, dairy products, citrus fruits, vegetables and livestock. Unlike the nineteenth-century co-operatives, these were conducted with businesslike efficiency and bade fair to remain a permanent feature of farm marketing. The war period also witnessed a revival of the more familiar type of agrarian organizations—groups like the Farmers' National Council, the United Farmers of America and notably the American Farm Bureau Federation—which stood guard over agricultural interests and well-being.

From the giddy heights of boom times the postwar slump plunged the farmers into a slough of starvation prices, grinding debts and mortgage foreclosures. One cause was the sharp falling off of the European demand for American foodstuffs, which left the agriculturists with unsalable surpluses. Prompt readjustment to a shrinking world market was difficult if not impossible. Their plight was aggravated by the steep freight rates continuing from the war and the difficulty of borrowing money to tide over the bad times. Moreover, when conditions in the urban world returned to normal, the farmer's position remained as before except that he was obliged to pay higher prices for the goods he needed. Data collected by the Department of Agriculture in 1922 showed that the cost of growing wheat or oats exceeded the average selling price.

Under prod of the American Farm Bureau Federation with its

million members, a bipartisan farm bloc consisting mostly of Westerners was formed in Congress. This group, holding the balance of power between the two parties, forced the majority leadership to give heed to the agricultural situation. One series of laws aimed to ease rural credit facilities. An act of 1921 temporarily revived the War Finance Corporation to aid in subsidizing agricultural exports. Congress also increased the capacity of the Federal Land Banks to lend on farm mortgages, and a law of 1923 enabled farmers to borrow on livestock and crops on the way to the market. A second set of measures sought to narrow the gap between the low price paid the grower and the high price charged the public. An act of 1921 provided for government regulation of packing houses, stockyards and commission merchants with a view to correcting price manipulations and other unfair practices, and another in 1922 expressly exempted law-abiding co-operatives from antitrust prosecution.

Notwithstanding this legislation and the increased duties on agricultural imports in the successive tariffs, the total farm income melted from $15,500,000,000 in 1920 to $5,500,000,000 in 1932. Wheat selling for $1.82 a bushel in 1920 brought 38 cents in 1932, corn fell from 61 cents to 32, cotton from 16 cents a pound to 6. The trouble was that the government's efforts ignored the heart of the problem: overproduction. So long as more products were raised than could be sold profitably, agriculture could not be made to pay. Moreover, the farmers, widely scattered and traditionally individualistic, were not in the position of an industrial combination which could regulate output to boost prices.

As a way out, agrarian leaders advocated a federal loan fund to buy up the crop surplus and send it abroad for sale. From 1924 onward, this proposal became the subject of fierce controversy in Congress, the farm spokesmen insisting on their right to the same benevolent care that the industrialists had long received from tariff protection. As embodied in the McNary-Haugen bill, the plan provided that a federal farm board should purchase the annual surplus of certain crops, collecting from the growers of each an "equalization fee" to defray any losses to the government from an unfavorable difference between the domestic and foreign selling prices. Though the bill passed Congress in 1927 and again in 1928, each time it encountered Coolidge's veto. With unwonted heat he denounced the scheme as price-fixing, a grant of special favors and an incentive to overproduction. The question of farm relief figured in the election of 1928, as it had in the two preceding ones, and Hoover as President moved at once to put into execution the counterproposal he had offered during the campaign. An act of June, 1929, established a Federal Farm Board to stimulate the formation of co-operatives, encourage voluntary crop limitation and use its fund of $500,000,000 to stabilize agricultural prices. In this last effort it was instrumental in buying up 330,000,000 bushels of wheat and 1,320,000 bales of cotton. But these actions failed to stay the downward spiral of prices.

THE ONSET OF THE GREAT DEPRESSION

In point of fact the good times by-passed not only agriculture, but also shipbuilding, the railway-equipment business and the coal, textile and shoe industries. But in nearly every other respect the nation basked in the sunshine of unexampled opulence. A committee of economists in 1929 expressed amazement at the "outpouring of energy" which in seven years had "piled up skyscrapers in scores of cities; knit the 48 States together with 20,000 miles of airways; moved each year over railways and waterways more than a billion and a half tons of freight; thronged the highways with 25,000,000 motor cars; carried electricity to 17,000,000 homes" and "fed, clothed, housed, and amused the 120,000,000 persons who occupy our twentieth of the habitable area of the earth." Responsible public men and business leaders spoke of a 'New Economic Era'—a dream of good wages, high prices, inflated credits and fat profits from which there would be no awakening.

Little wonder that the ordinary citizen became dizzy with great expectations. Real-estate booms overspread the country. A fever of installment buying infected untold millions, causing them to spend beyond their means. Shopgirls and washerwomen, lucky in the stock market, acquired fur coats and drove to work in their own cars. At the same time state and municipal expenditures piled up beyond precedent. In 1928 and 1929 values in the stock market zoomed to heights out of all relationship to earnings present or prospective. A craze for speculation akin to that of the South Sea Bubble in eighteenth-century England bewitched the country. Banking houses, instead of giving clients conservative advice, became high-pressure salesmen for investments, domestic and foreign, of which they knew no more than what the roseate prospectuses told. People withdrew lifelong savings and even mortgaged their homes in the hope of doubling and trebling their money through the financial legerdemain. In vain did the Federal Reserve Board restrict bank credits to stem the flood of speculation. In late October, 1929, the crash came. Good securities and bad tumbled down like a house of cards. The Great Depression had begun.

Flashes and mutterings of the gathering storm might have fore-warned a people less befogged with the mirage of sudden wealth. Not only had the prosperity been unevenly distributed, but technological unemployment due to new labor-saving methods had idled something like two million men during the years 1920–1927. In the year before the crash, industry, overextended in many of its parts, showed signs of slowing down, with automobile sales off and the building boom and steel production slackening. Moreover, the government's postwar program of nursing foreign trade had largely ignored the interde-pendence of world commerce. Economic nationalism as expressed most strikingly in the mounting tariff wall inspired other countries to retaliatory measures; the intergovernmental debt situation hurt Ameri-can trade; and political and economic unrest in many lands endangered the unparalleled amount of American investments abroad. Added to these factors were certain others domestic in character: the reckless or fraudulent nature of many of the new business enterprises; the mountainous debts piled up by the state and municipal governments; and the wasteful living habits of all classes.

The United States had experienced bad depressions before—in 1837, in 1873, in 1893—but the country's situation had then been such that each time the evil had cured itself. Besides the opportunities afforded by the unsettled frontier, the foreign export market had aided recovery, as did also the advent of new industries and the rapid increase of consumers due to the high birth rate and free immigration. Now, all these avenues except the vague hope of developing new industries were blocked. Under the circumstances the economic crisis proved the worst America had ever known, spreading ruin deep and wide through every part of the country and every section of the popu-lation. In other lands, too, the creeping paralysis was at work, and in the summer of 1931 the debacle definitely became world-wide. The extent of the catastrophe in America became apparent as the year 1930 advanced. Prices shrank; business fell off; factories and mines shut down; agriculture lay prostrate. Commercial and bank failures during the year totaled nearly twenty-eight thousand with liabilities of more than $1,522,000,000. Winter found charitable agencies straining to keep even with the widening circle of want and woe. In all, nearly five million men were thrown out of work during this first year. Summer brought further suffering, for a prolonged drought, the severest in the nation's history, blighted the corn, hay and other crops in thirty states from Virginia to Montana and from Pennsylvania to Texas.

The chief executive, who as a candidate had promised that the Republicans would banish poverty from the land, could not believe the evidence of his own eyes. Repeatedly declaring that the difficulties would quickly pass, Hoover sought to hasten the event by providing temporary employment through speeding up the government's construction program. On his initiative, also, Congress lowered the income tax in the hope of stimulating business activity—a curtailment of revenues soon to be repented. As late as March, 1931, he vetoed a bill, introduced by Senator Robert F. Wagner of New York, which would have established a national employment system to co-ordinate and help finance state efforts to improve job opportunities.

Meanwhile new factors entered the situation, nerving Hoover to more positive action. In Congress the progressives of both parties were demanding direct federal subsidies to relieve distress, as well as other strong measures that enlisted growing outside support. In November, 1930, the discontented voters elected a Democratic majority to the House—the first Republican setback since Wilson's time. As 1930 drew to a close and the new year began, the depression instead of lifting worsened. Toward summer the Austrian and German financial systems collapsed, and England's abandonment of the gold standard in September served as a signal for thirteen other countries to follow before the year's end. In America during 1931 business failures rose to nearly 29,000 with liabilities of $736,000,000, while about 2300 bank suspensions entailed a further loss of $1,690,-000,000. Foreign trade reached its lowest point since 1914, the jobless totaled over 8,000,000, and the close of the fiscal year in June showed a federal deficit of more than $900,000,000, with a much larger one in sight.

When Congress met in December, Hoover submitted a sheaf of new proposals. A journalist compared him to "a man trying to plug a sieve, running from one place to another to stop up leaks which developed faster than he could run." None of the recommendations, however, met the popular outcry for financial help to the needy. Holding that the responsibility for unemployment relief belonged to the state and local authorities and charity agencies, he declared, "I am opposed to any direct or indirect Government dole." After vetoing one measure of the kind he disliked, he accepted a modified version in July, 1932, which authorized the lending (but not the giving) of $1,800,000,000 to states and cities for relief and for construction projects and provided $312,000,000 for federal public works to create additional jobs.

Hoover's own program, in accordance with Republican orthodoxy, aimed to bolster up the top of the economic pyramid in the belief that this would benefit the lower layers. At his behest Congress in January, 1932, created a Reconstruction Finance Corporation with a two-billion-dollar fund for making emergency loans to banks, life-insurance companies, savings institutions, farm-mortgage associations, railroads and the like. Other acts strengthened the Federal Land Banks, enlarged the credit facilities of the Federal Reserve System and set up a Home Loan Banking System to assist concerns that disbursed money for residential construction. The session was marked by increasing rancor between Hoover and the progressives of his own party, who now fought side by side with the newly victorious Democrats. A controversy almost as bitter as that over relief appropriations centered on new taxes for balancing the budget. Thanks to the opposition, the act as passed bore down heavily upon the bigger incomes, reaching as high as 55 per cent on those of $1,000,000 or more. As another way of making ends meet, Hoover pressed for reducing government costs, but the economies effected fell far short of the need. The deficit stood at $2,942,000,000 on June 30, 1932, and at $2,245,000,000 a year later.

Meanwhile the system of government lending went into effect. By October 1, 1932, the Reconstruction Finance Corporation had advanced funds to nearly six thousand financial institutions and railroads and had similarly made loans to thirty-seven states for public works and relief of the jobless. Nevertheless, banks and business houses continued to tumble, and the decline of state and local revenues necessitated shorter school terms and the slashing of teachers' pay. With 12,500,000 wage earners idle, many a city dump saw 'depression villages' spring up overnight bearing such resentful names as Hooverville and Hoover Heights. In rural America wheat plummeted to twenty-five cents, the lowest level on record, and farmers presently began to rally in armed bands to resist foreclosure sales. During mid-summer more than ten thousand unemployed ex-soldiers gathered in Washington to urge immediate cash payment of their insurance policies. There the 'Bonus Expeditionary Force' lingered to the annoyance of the administration until the authorities at last drove it out, unresisting, with army tanks and gas bombs.

As the party chieftains prepared for the 1932 election one thing was undeniably true: the people were in a sullen mood and disposed to lay all their troubles to the man in the White House, who they believed had failed them in foresight and leadership. Nevertheless the Republicans in Chicago on June 14 renominated Hoover and Curtis on the first ballot on a platform resounding with praise of the administration. In the same hall on June 27 the Democrats on the fourth ballot chose Governor Franklin D. Roosevelt of New York, with John N. Garner of Texas, Speaker of the House of Representatives, as his running mate. The platform pictured the hard times as the fruit of Republican postwar blundering, pledged a 25-per-cent cut in government costs, and promised "continuous responsibility of government for human welfare" through such measures as an "extension of federal credit" for relief needs, more public works, unemployment and old-age insurance, control of crop surpluses, regulation of stock exchanges and holding companies, revision of the banking system, the "use of the nation's water power in the public interest," and reciprocal trade agreements. As regards the Eighteenth Amendment the party, as has been seen, demanded prompt repeal, whereas the Republicans took the noncommittal position of promising to submit a repeal amendment without advising ratification.

Governor Roosevelt violated precedent by flying to Chicago to announce his immediate acceptance to the assembled delegates, declaring in ringing tones that his election would ensure "a new deal for the American people." In September he launched forth on an aggressive campaign that carried him into thirty-seven states. Everywhere he charged the Republicans with truckling to Big Business to the hurt of the "forgotten man," denounced their impotence in the face of the economic disaster and reiterated his pledge of a New Deal. His opponents in consternation sought to dismiss him as irresponsible and impractical or, as the columnist Walter Lippmann put it before moving over to Roosevelt's side, "a pleasant man who, without any important qualification for the office, would very much like to be President." Most voters, however, found in the fundamentals of public policy he set forth a tonic assurance of old-time Wilsonian liberalism.

Saddled with the blame for the depression, the Republicans faced a task rendered all the more hopeless by a bad split in their ranks, for most of the leading progressive Senators of the party—Hiram Johnson, 'Young Bob' La Follette, George W. Norris and others— declared for Roosevelt. In vain Republican spellbinders rang the changes on the theme, 'It might have been worse.' Hoover himself, stressing the international causes of the depression, cited sixteen different remedies he had applied to the nation's wounds and warned that under a Democratic tariff "The grass will grow in the streets of a hundred cities, a thousand towns." To his aid came many large employers of labor such as Henry Ford who posted bulletins in his numerous plants announcing, "To prevent times from getting worse and to help them to get better President Hoover must be elected." Roosevelt carried the country in a landslide comparable to that on which Hoover himself had ridden into office. He won 472 electoral votes—every state but six—to 59 for his rival and 57.4 per cent (22,800,000) of the popular ballots to 39.7 per cent (15,760,000). The Democrats also swept both branches of Congress.

Before the victors took over the reins the Twentieth Amendment was added to the nation's fundamental law. Championed by Senator Norris since 1923, and seven times approved by the Senate before the House accepted it early in 1932, the amendment abolished the so-called lame-duck session of Congress—that session of an outgoing Congress held from December to March 4 after a new membership had been chosen. The advocates of the change contended that the old system was undemocratic and that, furthermore, the lame ducks, being no longer subject to popular rebuke, often passed legislation against the public interest. Ratified in February, 1933, the amendment (which was to go into effect the following October) specified that, instead of March 4, Representatives and Senators should take office on January 3 following election and the President and Vice-President on January 20. Other sections dealt with certain contingencies overlooked by the Constitution, for example, that Congress should by law take care of the situation which would arise if both the President-elect and Vice-President-elect should die or be otherwise unable to qualify for the office. This latter provision assumed an unexpected importance when President-elect Roosevelt narrowly escaped being shot by a demented person on February 15 while in Miami, Florida.

FULLER ACCOUNTS

Republican Economics. For most of the topics in this chapter Allen, *Only Yesterday,* Beards, *America in Midpassage,* Faulkner, *From Versailles to New Deal,* Slosson, *Great Crusade and After,* and Soule, *Prosperity Decade,* are helpful. Two co-operative works of great value are Committee on Recent Economic Changes, *Recent Economic Changes in the United States,* and President's Research Committee on Social Trends, *Recent Social Trends in the United States,* while particular phases of economic development are discussed in Berge, *Cartels;* Berle and Means, *Modern Corporation;* Bonbright and Means, *Holding Company;* Hexner, *International Cartels;* Jones, *Tariff Retaliation;* Laidler, *Concentration of Control in American Industry;* Ratner, *American Taxation;* Simmons, *Boulder Dam;* and Williams, *Economic Foreign Policy of the United States.*

Labor and the Immigration Question. Commons and others, *History of Labor,* III–IV, Dulles, *Labor in America,* and Frankfurter and Greene, *Labor Injunction,* deal with the one subject, while the other receives attention in Garis, *Immigration Restriction,* and, with reference to the Japanese, in Griswold, *Far Eastern Policy.*

Prohibition in Practice. Asbury, *Great Illusion,* and Merz, *Dry Decade,* afford general accounts.

The Farm Problem. See particularly Capper, *Agricultural Bloc;* Forrester, *Large Scale Coöperative Marketing;* Nourse, *American Agriculture and the European Market;* and Williams, *Power on the Farm.* Saloutos and Hicks, *Agricultural Discontent in the Middle West,* surveys that subject from 1900 to 1939.

The Onset of the Great Depression. Consult Allen, *Since Yesterday;* Hirst, *Wall Street and Lombard Street;* Leonard, *Three Years Down;* Mitchell, *Depression Decade;* Wecter, *Age of the Great Depression;* and Wilbur and Hyde, *Hoover Policies.*

CHAPTER XVII

THE NEW DEAL

THE ROOSEVELT REVOLUTION

FRANKLIN D. ROOSEVELT more nearly resembled his famous kinsman Theodore than he did the outgoing President. Each Roosevelt came of colonial Dutch stock, and Franklin had married Teddy's niece Eleanor. Each had served successively in the New York legislature, the Navy Department and the governor's chair. The earlier Roosevelt, moreover, had defied the third-term tradition as the later one would also do. Though belonging to opposing political parties—which did not keep Franklin from casting his first presidential vote for Teddy— each symbolized the progressive ideals of his day. The difference in accomplishment stemmed doubtless from Franklin's later appearance on the scene and the opportunity afforded by the Great Depression to effectuate more sweeping reforms. By natural stages the Square Deal had evolved via Woodrow Wilson's New Freedom into the New Deal.

Both Roosevelts knew also how to dramatize public issues and to summarize vague human aspirations in an impelling phrase. Both, too, practiced the art of creating popular opinion in order to follow it. Franklin, however, enjoyed the incomparable advantage of the radio, which he used in his intimate 'fireside chats' with consummate effect to keep the electorate informed of his plans, difficulties, hopes and achievements. In disposition he was more urbane, less pugnacious, than Teddy, but his conciliatory manner, disarming to both friend and foe, was his way of yielding on minor points in order to win major ones—though he never flinched from a fight. His broad shoulders, buoyant spirit and tireless energy made people forget that in 1921, after his unsuccessful run for the Vice-Presidency, he had been stricken with infantile paralysis, which left him crippled from the waist down. By an amazing exercise of will power he had otherwise regained his health and had even learned to walk again with steel leg supports and a cane.

To head his cabinet he picked Tennessee's Senator Cordell Hull, a low-tariff Democrat and vehement foe of economic nationalism. Among the other members he included representatives of the diverse elements that had helped make his victory possible, notably three former Republicans—William H. Woodin of New York, Secretary of the Treasury, Harold L. Ickes of Illinois, Secretary of the Interior, and Henry A. Wallace of Iowa, Secretary of Agriculture—and he set a precedent by appointing a woman, Secretary of Labor Frances Perkins, who had served him in a similar capacity in New York.[1] For advice as to legislation, however, he usually relied upon a small group of private counselors, the so-called Brain Trust, which shifted in membership from time to time. With their help he worked out the details of the New Deal, communicating his proposals to Congress in short crisp messages that the man on the street might read, and usually accompanying the messages with bills ready for passage.

When Roosevelt delivered his inaugural address on March 4, 1933, 13,000,000 were out of work and a bank depositors' panic had shut the doors of nearly every financial house and stock exchange in the land. In vibrant tones the President summoned the people to face the future with confidence and courage. "The only thing we have to fear is fear itself," he asserted. Just as the Constitution had in the past "met every great stress of vast expansion of territory, of foreign wars, of bitter internal strife, of world relations," so it now would enable the government "to meet extraordinary needs by changes in emphasis and arrangement without loss of essential form." Matching his forceful language with equally forceful action, he issued two proclamations, one declaring a bank holiday throughout the land and the other calling Congress at once to Washington. In a session of one hundred days the legislators under the President's spur enacted a series of epochal laws with breath-taking speed. To meet the bank emergency they put all financial institutions under what was virtually a licensing system, permitting them to reopen only after satisfying the Treasury as to their soundness. Pursuant to this plan the great bulk quickly resumed operations. In an effort to balance the budget Congress increased taxes and empowered the President to effect drastic

---

[1] The remaining officers were George H. Dern of Utah, Secretary of War; Homer S. Cummings of Connecticut, Attorney-General; Claude A. Swanson of Virginia, Secretary of the Navy; James A. Farley of New York, Postmaster-General; and Daniel C. Roper of South Carolina, Secretary of Commerce. On Woodin's death late in 1933 Henry Morgenthau, Jr., succeeded to the Treasury. Other changes took place subsequently.

government economies. Under this warrant he slashed $125,000,000 from the federal pay roll and even reduced veterans' compensation by more than $300,000,000.

Other actions of the Hundred Days revealed more enduring aspects of the New Deal, which later legislation would further elaborate. Its features as regards unemployment relief, farm betterment, conservation and hydroelectric power had been anticipated by Roosevelt's accomplishments as governor of New York, and these policies were more fully outlined in his party's national platform. They represented a fruition of the earlier progressive movement, while the administrative means developed by the New Deal reflected President Wilson's wartime measures in mobilizing the nation's resources. Hugh S. Johnson, Bernard M. Baruch and others who came to play important roles in the Roosevelt revolution had been prominent under the last Democratic President, and Roosevelt himself had been in Wilson's regime as Assistant Secretary of the Navy. In many respects, too, the New Deal savored of the social and fiscal programs which England and other European governments had adopted earlier in the century, and in particular it was influenced by the world trend toward state intervention in economic life that characterized the 1930's. France under impact of the depression was restricting its wheat acreage, the Netherlands and Denmark were reducing their output of dairy products, and for a number of years the Soviet Union and Fascist Italy had engaged in comprehensive economic planning. Were there not leads here for America? Could not comparable means be employed to remedy the evils that had exploded in 1929, and could not these evils be avoided in the future by long-range preventive measures?

Unlike Russia and Italy, however, Roosevelt had no thought to work a cure at the cost of the people's liberties, nor did he wish to destroy the economic underpinnings of American society. His quarrel was not with capitalism but with the capitalists, whose reckless course had brought the world's richest nation to the verge of ruin. Broadly, his aim was to democratize and humanize the industrial system in order to preserve it. He had no pat solution for the nation's plight; he subscribed to no single school of economic thought; he listened to many advisers and placed his faith, as he had announced before election, in "bold, persistent experimentation." Under the circumstances he was constantly assailed by zealots to his left, who wanted him to move faster and farther, and by zealots to his right, who feared a descent into communism and chaos. After a time his scorching denunciations of industrial magnates enraged Big Business; but from the plain people, whose mute hopes he so accurately voiced, he won increasing trust. In particular, the President commanded the devotion of the "forgotten man" in factory and on farm. The labor and agrarian elements had formed rival interests in earlier administrations, but the Roosevelt program, made up in part of their own proposals, looked to their joint welfare.

The New Deal involved not only the greatest peacetime centralization of federal authority ever known, but also a vast extension of the power of the executive at the expense of the legislative. In many of the laws Congress merely laid down broad principles of action, leaving the President free to work out the details, to allocate the funds and to set up administrative tribunals as he saw fit. Soon a maze of commissions, boards and other agencies, generally known by their alphabetical designations, sprang up in Washington. Though some were designed merely for the emergency, others were permanent fixtures, and they were frequently given authority to issue rules and regulations that bore the effect of law though Congress had not expressly passed upon them. Thanks to this multiplication of administrative divisions, the ranks of the civil service increased in four years from 572,000 to 841,600. Since a growing proportion of the new appointees were not put under the merit plan, political foes accused the President of reviving the spoils system; but his defenders pointed to the need of a quick recruitment of personnel, and they took just pride in the fact that no earlier peacetime government had ever attracted into the public service, especially the higher ranks, so many disinterested, high-minded and well-trained persons. Scarcely a college or university failed to contribute one or more of its faculty for a time to some branch of the regime. Whatever the reasons, Roosevelt took no effective steps to remove the objections until his second term.

The ordinary citizen cared less about how the government was conducted than about what it strove to do. The New Deal, viewed analytically, set itself the threefold task of relief, recovery and reform. The immediate goal was to save the 13,000,000 unemployed from hunger and hopelessness; beyond this, the wheels of economic life must be made to turn again; and, finally, lasting solutions must be attempted for the evils that had bred the disaster. The business classes, though friendly to many of the measures for relief and recovery, angrily resisted the proposals for reform; they wished merely to re-establish the conditions that had existed before 1929. The 'three R's' were not always kept sharply separate and sometimes they clashed; but whatever the interrelations and inconsistencies, the triple object remained constant and was never long forgotten. Since most of the New Deal acts cost money, the initial emphasis on economy was soon abandoned, and in 1934 Congress over Roosevelt's veto restored all the cuts effected in the Hundred Days.

THE RELIEF PROGRAM

Unlike President Hoover, Franklin Roosevelt unhesitatingly pronounced it the federal government's duty to see that no one starved, and for that purpose he launched the most colossal program of relief ever undertaken anywhere. To allay immediate suffering, the New Deal spent millions in supplying food, clothing and shelter, but in the case of the able-bodied it arranged as soon as possible to convert direct relief—a form of charity or the dole—into self-respecting work relief. A variety of agencies were set up to administer the great sums which Congress made available. Under Harry L. Hopkins, who had served Roosevelt in a similar capacity in New York, the Federal Emergency Relief Administration, instituted in May, 1934, devoted chief attention to supplementing the depleted revenues of the states, leaving the local administrators free to use the money for direct or work relief as they chose and to aid both the physically fit and un-employables. During the first winter the Civil Works Administration, operating under close federal control, reinforced these efforts by providing stopgap work projects of its own, costing a total of nearly $845,000,000. In another attack on the problem the United States Employment Service, whose establishment Hoover had prevented but the Democrats now authorized, co-operated with state and local employment agencies to ferret out old jobs rather than to create new ones. By the close of 1934 over 5,000,000 families were relief recipients, and before the FERA came to an end it had disbursed more than $3,000,000,000.

Profiting by the experience so gained, the President in January, 1935, recommended certain changes in the program: to stop all direct relief as quickly as possible; to substitute socially valuable undertakings for the trivial tasks (such as raking leaves and picking up waste paper in parks) which had occupied many of the jobless; and to discontinue federal aid to the incapacitated. These unemployables, representing about 1,500,000 households, should be returned to the care of the state and local authorities, while the national government would furnish work for one breadwinner in each of the remaining 3,500,000 families. On this basis Congress in April voted an initial two-year appropriation of $4,880,000,000. The FERA was now replaced by the Works Progress Administration, also under Hopkins, and control of the program was centered in Washington, though the states and local communities were to share in the cost and responsibility of operation. The peak number of relief workers under the new arrangement reached 3,840,000 in March, 1936. Three months later Congress made an additional grant of $1,425,000,000.

From the first the relief exertions encountered a running fire of criticism. Hopkins and his aides, facing a situation without precedent in the federal government, could not rely upon an experienced, well-paid civil service, as Washington's regular departments did, and, moreover, they had to work against time. Hence politics, waste and incompetence entered into some of the undertakings. New Deal opponents applied the term 'boondoggling' to the trifling tasks to which the unemployed were sometimes assigned, but in any case the business classes preferred the dole to work relief on the ground that it would cost less. On the credit side of the ledger the gains were indubitable. Government-provided work not only saved people from starving, but it fostered their self-respect and enabled them to retain their occupational skills. Nor were manual and clerical workers the only ones helped, for as the program was expanded, it came to include writers, artists, teachers, architects, musicians and actors as well as specialists in the natural and social sciences. Moreover, as hastily conceived projects gave way to better-planned ones, public improvements of lasting value resulted in every part of the land. By the summer of 1936 over 6000 schoolhouses had been erected or repaired; numerous playgrounds, libraries, hospitals, bridges and airports had been constructed or improved; modernized sewerage had been installed in 5000 places; and about 128,000 miles of secondary roads had been built or repaired. Among the many white-collar projects, a series of comprehensive guidebooks was compiled for various states and local communities, and free concerts and inexpensive plays afforded entertainment and inner enrichment for vast numbers unaccustomed to such opportunities.

Though the relief authorities devoted principal attention to adults, they also attacked the worrisome problem created by the predicament of the growing generation. When Roosevelt took office, hordes of youths were roaming the country in vain search for employment— likely recruits for a criminal career. In order to throw them a life belt the Civilian Conservation Corps was promptly organized with a membership varying at different times from 250,000 to 500,000, mostly young unmarried men from destitute homes. Scattered in 2600 camps, paid wages they were required to share with their families, given opportunities for schooling in moments of leisure, they occupied themselves with protecting natural resources—draining marshes, building bridges and dams, planting trees, fighting forest fires and combating the ravages of insects and plant diseases. Probably no other New Deal undertaking enjoyed such unqualified popularity. By the middle of 1936 over 1,600,000 men had received CCC training. At the same time the government, in order to keep as many boys and girls as possible in school, assisted states whose educational revenues were insufficient and also paid small stipends to needy students for work after hours. So important did this latter aspect of relief become that in June, 1935, it was put under a special agency, the National Youth Administration. In its first year the NYA aided over 400,000 students at every level from the lower grades to the graduate school. The youth program in its various ramifications accomplished a treble purpose: it counteracted the corroding effects of enforced idleness; it trained the young people for future usefulness; and it delayed their entry into an already congested labor market.

THE RECOVERY PROGRAM

The business of relief did something to further the relief of business, for the huge expenditures provided the penniless with purchasing power, and the multitudinous work projects used a wide range of raw and manufactured products. But such effects were incidental. Hence the New Deal, in a more direct effort to promote recovery, undertook a series of measures to 'prime the pump' of business so that it might function again on its own motion. To this end the Reconstruction Finance Corporation, established under Hoover, proved important, especially after Congress in 1934 enlarged the RFC's scope to include industrial enterprises as well as financial institutions and railroads. By means of loans, and through the purchase of bonds and preferred stock in commercial and banking concerns, it exerted a steadying influence upon the country's basic economic structure. The RFC was also the channel through which funds for emergency purposes were disbursed to other federal agencies and to the states. From the beginning to October 1, 1936, it handled over $11,000,000,000, of which a considerable part was soon repaid.

Tackling the problem of recovery from another angle, the government embarked upon a far-reaching program of public construction— 'internal improvements' of an extent and variety which nineteenth-century America had never dreamed of. The Public Works Administration, set up under Secretary of the Interior Ickes in June, 1933, concentrated upon heavy projects, the work being performed by private firms which were not required to hire relief labor. The PWA sought, in other words, to restore the normal course of business by means of major undertakings of enduring public benefit. In addition, the Washington authorities aided state and municipal public works through loans and also through gifts varying in amount from 30 to 45 per cent of the total cost. Thanks to unceasing vigilance, politics and graft played practically no part, and the positive achievements were impressive. The nearly $2,500,000,000 spent by July 1, 1936, gave a tremendous stimulus to many segments of industry. The completed projects included about 1500 waterworks, 70 municipal power plants, 250 hospitals and educational structures, a great number of federal, state and municipal buildings, and an outlay of $8,000,000 for public-health work and of more than $250,000,000 for naval construction.

Since the building business held a position of central importance in the national economy, utilizing materials from myriad industries, the New Deal bent its energies to revive residential construction as well as to promote public works. The need was dire, for private building had nearly stopped during the depression, owners had neglected repairs, and when Roosevelt entered office homes were being sacrificed under the sheriff's hammer at the rate of a thousand a day. Congress in June, 1933, created a Home Owners' Loan Corporation to enable persons to recover their properties, or to pay off mortgages, by means of government loans over long periods at moderate interest rates. In this way more than a million dwellings were saved to their owners in the next three years. In addition, the Federal Housing Administration, established in 1934, facilitated the repair and modernization of residential and business properties by underwriting the repayment of a certain part of the money lent for such purposes by private agencies.

Various instrumentalities stimulated new construction. The Federal Housing Administration insured commercial loans to prospective builders up to as much as four fifths of the face value. With even greater boldness the government instituted housing projects for the poor. For this purpose the PWA assisted municipalities with loans and gifts, and by the summer of 1936 slum clearance and up-to-date multiple-dwelling units had been undertaken in twenty-seven cities. Moreover, the Resettlement Administration, created in 1935, constructed three "greenbelt" suburban communities where wage earners employed in nearby cities might eke out their earnings by raising some of their own food. Despite these efforts the total amount of private residential construction increased but slightly. As for the public housing projects, the program dragged because of obstacles raised by the courts, the excessive prices asked for the land, or the hostility of local real-estate interests. Furthermore, the government's zeal to provide model lodgings enhanced the cost of construction and put the rentals beyond the reach of the very poor. The benefits accrued mainly to members of the middle class.

Transportation was another nerve of business which the New Deal sought to galvanize. Even before the crash the railroads had felt the increasing competition of motor, water and air traffic. Then the years from 1929 to 1933 halved their revenues, throwing nearly a third of the total mileage into bankruptcy or receivership. But for the timely assistance of the Reconstruction Finance Corporation many of the roads would have suffered complete collapse, in which case they would have pulled down countless insurance companies and savings banks that had invested heavily in rail bonds. One decided betterment in their condition resulted from a reduction of passenger fares. After the Western companies showed a 50-per-cent gain of business by cutting their charges from 3.2 to 2 cents a mile, the Interstate Commerce Commission in June, 1936, imposed the new rate on all lines. Aided by government loans, the roads also installed improvements in service, including in some instances motor-driven, air-conditioned, streamlined trains. These and other steps to combat the rival modes of transportation promised a brighter day for the railroads. Congress in 1936 helped further by vesting the ICC with power to regulate motor busses and trucks in interstate trade and, three years later, water traffic as well. To offset these advantages, however, the government's vast expenditures for improved highways and waterways favored the railroads' competitors. Other difficulties also confronted the lines: huge debts, high taxes and, in some cases, overcapitalization and top-heavy financial structures. Nevertheless, the rail companies after four years of deficit began to show a profit in 1936, and despite all handicaps they continued to carry two thirds of the nation's freight.

In dealing with the railways the New Deal aimed at recovery by expanding their business through lower rates. In other branches of economic life it reversed the formula, seeking to assure profits through higher prices. This purpose governed the moves regarding the currency and those for rehabilitating industry and agriculture. No other emergency actions broke so sharply with tradition or provoked such heated controversy. By going off the gold standard in April, 1933, the administration planned to reduce the value of money and hence boost prices. Congress co-operated by canceling the gold clauses in public and private contracts, thus making all debts payable in paper money and silver. Other steps included the purchase of all available gold on the market at artificially advanced prices, which it was hoped would further cheapen the dollar in terms of gold. Similar action was taken in respect to silver bullion, but here the motive in part was to aid the Western mining industry and thereby stave off political clamor for free silver. Finally, in February, 1934, Roosevelt with Congressional authority cut the gold content of the dollar to 59 per cent of its former value. In the older sense, this was not a return to the gold standard, even a less valuable one, for no resumption of gold coinage was provided and there was no convertibility into gold on demand; but the result was much the same since Congress set up a special fund of $2,000,000,000 for regulating and stabilizing the devalued dollar in relation to other forms of currency. It is hard to say whether these measures had the desired inflationary effect. Though prices rose somewhat, the immense governmental expenditures and many other factors in the complex economic situation may have been responsible. Devaluation did, however, temporarily enlarge export trade because the fall of the dollar in international exchange made American products cheaper for foreign purchasers.

The far-reaching program of resuscitating industry and trade had the double goal of larger profits for the owners and of better wages for the employees who would thereby both improve their living standards and buy more. The method used was for each industry to adopt a "code of fair competition" which, after receiving the President's approval, should be carried into effect by a "code authority." In June, 1933, Congress created the National Recovery Administration as the over-all supervising agency under Hugh S. Johnson, an ex-general with wide experience in both government and business. A picturesque personality addicted to explosive speech, Johnson rallied popular enthusiasm behind the plan with fanfare and parades, and encouraged the public to boycott all employers who did not display a Blue Eagle, the symbol of compliance. Within less than two years seven hundred and fifty NRA code authorities, usually controlled by the biggest industrialists, were in operation. Practically all the codes specified a minimum pay of from $12 to $15 a week, a forty-hour week and the abolition of child labor under the age of sixteen. Under Section 7a of the governing statute all the codes also granted employees "the right to organize and bargain collectively through representatives of their own choosing" without "the interference, restraint, or coercion of employers."

The NRA's drastic making-over of business ran into numerous snags due to the complexity and wide distribution of American industry, the hurried nature of the code making and the fact that small local firms as well as large-scale ones were included. Moreover, the Ford Motor Company and some other key concerns would not participate, while those who joined the Blue Eagle all too often took advantage of the opportunity to revive monopolistic practices. Thus over half the codes provided for uniform prices, and many limited production and assigned quotas to particular factories. Such restrictions harmed the smaller producers and also in frequent cases caused the benefits of higher pay to the workers to be lessened by a rapid increase of prices. Besides, the minimum-wage requirements favored highly mechanized plants with few workers over those employing a greater number.

Though Roosevelt set up a National Labor Board to administer Section 7a, that provision for guaranteeing the right of collective bargaining quickly became a vortex of controversy. The large industrialists sought to turn it to their own advantage by forming company unions unconnected with national unions; the American Federation of Labor insisted upon the exclusive rights of its own affiliates; the NLB held that the decision in every case should be left to a majority vote of the employees; and the President, faced with a threatened shutdown in the important automobile industry in the spring of 1934, overruled his own Board by permitting both types of union with the stipulation that each should have proportionate representation in collective bargaining. Apparently he wished to placate Big Business in the hope of ensuring its support for other recovery measures. Efforts in Congress to outlaw company unions failed, but in June, 1934, the lawmakers made the NLB independent of the President, thus depriving him of the power to review its orders. By that time it had settled four fifths of the 3755 disputes referred to it, mediated 1300 strikes and averted nearly 500 others. Renamed the National Labor Relations Board and limited as before to the duration of the NRA, the agency was expressly empowered to conduct elections to determine the representation of workers, and Congress, to allay any doubt, explicitly affirmed labor's right to strike.

To that right labor had increasingly turned as the first bright hopes of Section 7a began to dim. A wave of industrial turmoil swept over the country, with 1700 work stoppages in 1933 (over twice as many as the year before), 1860 in 1934, and 2000 in 1935. The accompanying violence led to the calling out of the militia in sixteen states. One of the worst disorders involved 12,000 longshoremen in San Francisco who in May, 1934, demanded recognition of their union. Within two months the contest developed into a general strike crippling the business of the entire Bay district. It ended when the longshoremen agreed to submit the issue to a special federal arbitration board. September brought an even graver disturbance, this time a nation-wide walkout of 400,000 cotton textile workers caused by the owners' refusal to grant a shorter work week and to recognize the union. As in the case of the longshoremen, peace returned when Roosevelt induced the men to refer the dispute to federal arbitration.

The President, satisfied in most respects with the NRA, asked Congress in March, 1935, to ban price fixing and other monopolistic abuses that had developed. On the positive side he said that the NRA had increased collective bargaining, eliminated cutthroat methods of competition and abolished child labor, and that it had given jobs to 4,000,000 while raising total annual wages by $3,-000,000,000. But before the legislators could act to amend the law, the Supreme Court in May in the Schechter case ended the experiment by destroying its legal foundations. The judges held unanimously that Congress could not "delegate legislative power to the President to exercise an unfettered discretion" in code making and that, in the particular instance, the interstate-commerce clause could not possibly justify regulating the business of a local poultry dealer. The decision incensed Roosevelt, but his political foes hailed the bench as a modern St. George slaying the dragon of state socialism. Congress at the President's urging proceeded to salvage what it could from the wreckage. In July the Wagner Act gave the National Labor Relations Board permanent status. In August the Guffey Coal Act applied a form of code control to the bituminous industry, where chaotic conditions had long been chronic, but this law fell before a six-to-three decision of the Supreme Court in May, 1936 (Carter *v.* Carter Coal Co.). Not until his second term, when the judiciary was more favorably disposed, did Roosevelt move to recover more of the ground that had been lost.

New Deal efforts to succor industry and trade were paralleled by equally elaborate plans to revive agriculture, which had been ailing since World War I. When Roosevelt entered office two out of every five farms were under mortgage. Though the farmers themselves were the immediate sufferers, the inability of a quarter of the population to buy needed goods at a time of general business decline acted as a drag on recovery everywhere. Congress set about to restore their purchasing power through two sets of enactments, one to ease the crushing load of debt, the other to induce them by means of subsidies to undertake crop control. For the first purpose the lawmakers in 1933 and 1934 authorized the Federal Land Banks and other designated bodies—all acting under the newly created Farm Credit Administration—to refinance agricultural mortgages at substantially lower interest rates, and also to advance money for current operations and for buying back property that had been foreclosed. To facilitate the purchase of new farms a Resettlement Administration (later named the Farm Security Administration) made long-time loans on easy terms; and as a special move to aid submarginal agriculturists it bought about 17,000 farms, mostly in Montana, South Dakota and ten Southern states, to enable the penniless owners to make a fresh start on better land.

Along with this series of endeavors Congress also ventured upon what Roosevelt hailed as the "new and untrod path" of crop restriction. The Agricultural Adjustment Act in May, 1933, made it possible for farmers, under the Secretary of Agriculture's general supervision, to adjust supply to demand through voluntary collective action, just as industrial combinations had long been accustomed to do by illegal means. Growers who agreed to limit output were to receive benefit payments out of money raised from taxing processors (meat packers, flour millers, textile manufacturers and others who reworked farm products for the market). On the financial side the purpose was to enhance the agriculturists' buying power immediately without waiting for the higher crop prices expected from controlled production. The original law confined the plan to cotton, wheat, corn, hogs, rice, tobacco and dairy products, but after a year's trial Congress, acting partly under political pressure, extended the regulations to cattle, rye, barley, peanuts, flax, grain sorghums and sugar.

Under the Agricultural Adjustment Administration the program made rapid headway. To curtail production already started, the AAA induced the cotton farmers by cash payments to plow under a quarter to a half of their acreage, and also brought about the destruction of a part of the tobacco crop as well as the slaughter of several million pigs. Some of the butchered animals were converted into fertilizer and the rest distributed as food to persons on relief. Looking to the next planting season, the AAA made over 1,000,000 contracts with the cotton growers, which resulted in withdrawing 10,000,000 acres from cultivation. More than half a million wheat farmers entered into similar contracts for removing 7,500,000 acres from tillage, and agreements were also concluded with the producers of certain other commodities. But notwithstanding the reduction of cotton acreage the new crop equaled that of the preceding year. This was due partly to more intensive tillage and partly to unusually fine weather. To forestall a like outcome in the future the Bankhead Act in 1934 put a top limit on the total amount that might be raised. Somewhat similar restraints were applied to tobacco a few months later. Despite the refusal of some of the smaller producers to enter into restriction agreements and occasional evasion by farmers who did, the efforts were attended by a rapid rise of crop prices. But Nature was in part responsible, for a disastrous drought in 1934 cut production in the West and South below the AAA limits and caused widespread dust storms the following year, which had a like effect. But thanks to the higher prices and the benefit payments, the farmers' cash earnings rose from four and a third billion dollars in 1932 to over seven in 1935.

City folk, however, concerned with their own pocketbooks, felt aggrieved. The meat packers, cotton manufacturers and other processors, obliged to pay AAA taxes on their raw materials, passed on the added costs to consumers, and this fact, coupled with the higher prices resulting from crop curtailment, made urban dwellers pay more for foodstuffs and clothing, thereby removing some of the advantages of better wages. Behind such complaints, however, lay a deep-seated protest against an 'economy of scarcity,' involving an artificial shortage at a time when millions did not have enough to eat and wear. The President in some degree met this latter objection in October, 1933, by creating the Federal Surplus Commodities Corporation for buying excess farm products to distribute among the needy. It was through this channel, for example, that the pork and lard made from the swine slaughtered in 1933 reached persons on relief. Still other critics pointed out that crop limitation with the resulting higher prices served to decrease agricultural exports and spurred other countries, like Brazil in the case of cotton, to produce the commodities for themselves.

The Supreme Court, basing its disapproval on the Constitution, emasculated the law in January, 1936, in a decision growing out of the refusal of the Hoosac Mills in Massachusetts to pay processing taxes (United States v. Butler). By six to three it declared that such taxes were a "means to an unconstitutional end" since "a statutory plan to regulate and control agricultural production" violated the "reserved rights of the States." The pronouncement robbed the AAA of its basic method of operation: subsidies to farmers for crop restriction. The minority, however, censured this "tortured construction of the Constitution," and agrarian leaders cried out in incredulous surprise. By that time nearly $1,000,000,000 had been collected in processing taxes. Certain that the judiciary would also invalidate the special acts for cotton and tobacco control, Congress now repealed those laws and turned its attention to framing a statute that might aid the farmer in some other way. The outcome was the Soil Conservation and Domestic Allotment Act of February, 1936, which authorized benefit payments to co-operating farmers for such objects as retiring worn-out land, shifting crops for the sake of soil enrichment, and guarding against soil erosion. The AAA was given wide discretion in selecting the crops and making other arrangements. Out of deference to the Court's states-rights views it was provided that after 1937 the program should be administered by state agencies operating in conformity with federal standards. The new law, however, contained no effective means of preventing crop surpluses. Not until two years later, after the bench had undergone a change of heart toward the New Deal, did Congress repair this defect.

THE REFORM PROGRAM

While many of the recovery acts contained reform features, these were usually secondary and in most cases not designed to outlast the depression. From the first, however, Roosevelt envisaged the New Deal as a sword to destroy long-existing wrongs as well as to cut through temporary difficulties. Hence he directed a vigorous and versatile attack that met with cumulative success as time went on, despite stubborn resistance from conservative elements in and out of Congress. The principal achievements in his first term had to do with banking and finance, hydroelectric power, holding companies and social security.

The collapse of the banking system in the opening days of the administration dramatized the weaknesses that called for correction. From 1933 to 1936 Congress dealt repeatedly with the problem. It extended the Federal Reserve System to industrial and savings banks and also enlarged the Federal Reserve Board's power over credit regulation in order to curb speculation. One means adopted was to give the FRB discretion to raise the legal reserve requirements of the member banks; another was to reorganize the Board in such a way as to make certain henceforth of unified action by the twelve Regional Reserve Banks. As a further move to restore popular confidence Congress in 1933 set up a Federal Deposit Insurance Corporation to guarantee depositors' accounts up to $5000 (raised to $10,000 in 1950). Congress also forbade banks to engage in the investment business, a confusion of functions which in the past had often endangered deposits. Other acts afforded the public additional protection against injurious corporate practices. A law of 1933 imposed heavy penalties for failure to give full and accurate information concerning new securities sent through the mails or the channels of interstate commerce. In 1934 Congress transferred the administration of this requirement from the Federal Trade Commission to a new agency, the Securities and Exchange Commission, and empowered it to license stock exchanges and regulate their proceedings.

With even greater hardihood Roosevelt grappled with the question of hydroelectric power. Viewing this form of energy as a basic natural resource which had thoughtlessly been allowed to fall into the hands of avaricious private interests, New Dealers blamed the resulting high rates for the fact that only one in three American families used electricity from central power plants, and of farm homes only three in twenty. The Tennessee River basin, where Wilson had built two nitrate plants and a power station at Muscle Shoals for war purposes, afforded an opportunity to demonstrate the social value of a more democratic distribution of current as well as the advantages of regional planning. This turbulent stream, ramifying into seven Southern states, drains an area nearly as large as England, one that was rich in undeveloped physical and human assets. The Tennessee Valley Authority, established in May, 1933, overlooked no element of the problem. It undertook to harness the river by means of massive dams and reservoirs for the threefold purpose of preventing floods, improving navigation and generating electric power. It also promoted reforestation, withdrew marginal lands from cultivation, resettled the farmers so displaced, taught the people how to fertilize the soil and prevent erosion, and furthered public health and recreational facilities. In addition, the TVA built transmission lines and sold its electricity to towns, co-operatives and private power companies at rates so attractive as greatly to multiply the users. As time passed, an increasing number of Valley folk learned to banish much of their age-old drudgery, using electricity not merely to light their homes, but also to refrigerate their foodstuffs for the market and to perform innumerable household chores. When World War II came, TVA power was to contribute importantly to the making of heavy metals, airplanes, shells and other military materials.

From the beginning the undertaking had much more than local significance, for the rates charged were put forward as a 'yardstick' to measure those of private companies all over the country. The fairness of the comparison was challenged by the utility interests, who contended that the TVA enjoyed special advantages and employed misleading accounting methods; but whatever the merits of a dispute in which experts sharply disagreed, many private utilities now scaled

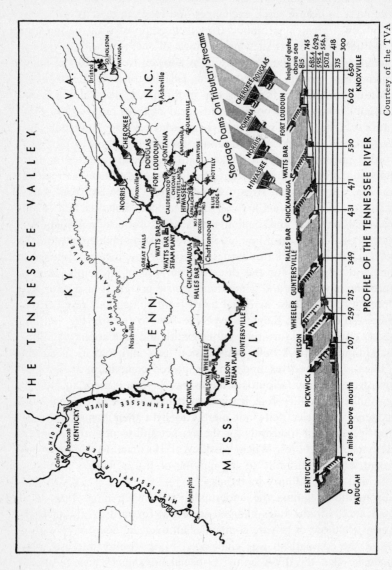

Transformation of the Tennessee Valley

Courtesy of the TVA

PROFILE OF THE TENNESSEE RIVER

down their charges. In June, 1935, the annual saving to consumers was reckoned at nearly $50,000,000. Even so, TVA current cost home users about half as much as the national average. Not content with a flank attack, the New Deal also encouraged local authorities everywhere to go into the business for themselves. The PWA helped municipalities with gifts and loans to erect or modernize publicly owned plants, and in 1935 the President climaxed these efforts by setting up the Rural Electrification Administration to lend government money for building power stations and transmission lines in the farming regions. Within five years a quarter-million miles of cable brought the boon of electricity to country dwellers in forty-three states. An even more ambitious undertaking was the constructing, principally at the cost of the PWA, of the great Bonneville and Grand Coulee Dams on the Columbia River, designed eventually to provide electricity as well as irrigation for millions of settlers in the Pacific Northwest. In the meantime Hoover Dam, initiated by the last Republican regime, had begun to sell power to a considerable number of publicly owned plants in the Southwest. These two regional projects, however, lacked the extensive program of social betterment that accompanied the TVA.

The utility interests, representing a $13,000,000,000 industry, bitterly resented government competition. They branded it as unfair, unwarranted and unconstitutional, and tried through incessant litigation to block the various ventures. Wendell L. Willkie, president of the Commonwealth and Southern Corporation, a holding company with operating concerns in Tennessee and ten other states, headed a vigorous campaign to alarm the business world against the TVA as "the entering wedge" for the "government ownership of all essential industries." In the end, however, he abandoned his Tennessee properties, selling them in 1939 to the TVA and a group of cities and rural co-operatives for $78,600,000.

Meanwhile Congress had moved to cure the evils that attended the formation of mammoth utility holding companies during the frantic 1920's. These companies sometimes stood on top of each other to a height of six or seven levels, the uppermost one dominating all those below with a minimum of capital—"a ninety-six-inch dog being wagged by a four-inch tail," as Roosevelt said. In the case of the Insull system one dollar invested in Middle West Utilities at the tip of the heap controlled $1750 in the Georgia Power Company at the base. The possibilities of financial chicanery were boundless, and in many cases the pyramiding united operating companies with no relation to geographic advantages or economy of management. To destroy these monopolistic growths the Wheeler-Rayburn Act in 1935 required the Securities and Exchange Commission as soon as possible after 1937 to limit electric and gas holding companies to natural regions, so that each would compose a "single integrated public utility system," and to eliminate all those which had more than one holding company intervening between them and the operating companies. The SEC and the Federal Power Commission were further authorized to police their financial practices. The utilities had vainly spent immense sums to arouse the public against this 'death sentence.'

Of all the New Deal reforms none dealt so comprehensively with the problem of the underprivileged as the Social Security Act. Passed in 1935 this measure had several objects. First, it provided unemployment insurance against future downturns of business by requiring employers of eight or more to pay a tax upon their pay rolls, to rise eventually to 3 per cent. The fund so collected was to be administered by state insurance systems, the payments to recipients depending upon the sum paid in. Second, for workers retiring at sixty-five the law provided old-age insurance from a fund in the Treasury created by contributions of employers and employees each of 1 (later $1\frac{1}{2}$) per cent of the wages. These retirement payments, scheduled to start in 1940, should not be less than $10 or more than $85 a month. Neither arrangement, however, applied to public employees, farm laborers, domestic servants, casual workers and employees in religious, charitable and nonprofit educational institutions. Finally, the act dealt with the welfare of three groups of unemployables: the aged, needy dependent children and the indigent blind. It instituted federal pensions up to $15 (later $20) a month for poor persons sixty-five or more on condition that their states add a like amount, pledged annual appropriations to assist the states to look after helpless children and the blind, and, in addition, assured funds for public-health work, maternity and infant care and vocational rehabilitation. General administration of the system was vested in a new federal agency, the Social Security Board (now the Social Security Administration).

The Social Security Act marked a considerable advance beyond the conception of national responsibility for relief merely in times of emergency. When it was adopted, only seven states had unemployment insurance, six of them having acted in the half year before, while pensions for the aged, a much older interest, existed in but thirty-five states. In both respects the United States had lagged behind Western Europe. The new law irked the business class because of the burdens put on industry, while at the other extreme it was criticized on the ground that the financial assistance was inadequate and did not extend to all groups of workers. Most people, however, felt the government had gone as far as it should in embarking on an experiment of such magnitude and intricacy. By the middle of 1939 nearly 27,500,000 wage earners were entitled to unemployment insurance and about 45,500,000 to retirement insurance. All but a handful of the states had also qualified to receive federal subsidies for the three classes of unemployables. As the *New York Times* remarked in 1940 on the fifth anniversary of the Social Security Act, "We have come a long way from the days when it was considered socially demoralizing to make provision against even some of the worst economic hazards that the individual encounters. Today millions of men and women are no longer haunted by the specter of poverty in old age, and even unemployment has lost much of its former terrors."

THE VOTERS PASS JUDGMENT

By the time of the presidential campaign of 1936 the New Deal's 'three R's' had evoked misgiving and alarm in conservative quarters but, as the outcome of the election was to show, overwhelming popular approval. The relief program, while costly and often wasteful, had not only fed and employed the jobless, but had restored the average man's faith in democratic government. Moreover, the work projects had enabled the state and local governments to carry on public improvements otherwise impossible. The recovery remedies presented a more confused picture because of their number, variety, expense and experimental nature. But if certain undertakings, notably the NRA, had created more difficulties than they solved, others like the RFC, PWA and AAA had helped materially to prime the economic pump. The depression touched bottom in March, 1933, and the months and years thereafter beheld an upturn with only an occasional setback. According to the Department of Commerce, the nation's output of goods and services, which had dropped from more than ninety-nine billion dollars in 1929 to less than fifty-five in 1933, rose to nearly sixty-four in 1934, about seventy-one in 1935 and almost eighty-two in 1936. This revival, however, rested in part upon continued federal spending, which meant that trouble lay ahead if private business should not take up the slack as the government reduced its support. It was also true that, though 5,500,000 or more persons had found work again, over 8,000,000 remained without regular jobs and about 3,500,000 were still on federal relief. Some of this unemployment was due to the half-million young people entering the labor market each year, and much of it was technological, since improved machinery enabled industry to produce more goods with fewer workers than in 1929.

A DECADE OF FEDERAL FINANCES

Fiscal Year	Expenditures	Deficit
1930–1931	$4,901,598,000	$ 901,959,000
1931–1932	4,947,776,000	2,942,051,000
1932–1933	4,325,149,000	2,245,452,000
1933–1934	6,370,947,000	3,255,393,000
1934–1935	7,583,433,000	3,782,966,000
1935–1936	9,068,885,000	4,952,928,000
1936–1937	8,546,379,000	3,252,539,000
1937–1938	7,691,287,108	1,449,625,000
1938–1939	9,268,338,000	3,600,514,000
1939–1940	9,537,000,000	3,612,000,000

As of July 1, 1933, Hoover had bequeathed Roosevelt a debt of $22,539,000,000. Four years later it stood at $36,425,000,000, and in 1940 at $42,967,000,000.

Federal expenditures had proceeded on a scale hitherto unknown, for the New Dealers believed that the country should spend as freely to defeat the depression as to defeat a foreign enemy. Most of the gigantic appropriations were for relief and recovery and, once the floodgates were opened, the President, even when he wished, could not always stay the tide. After he vetoed a bill in 1935 to pay off the World War I veterans' insurance policies without waiting for the expiration date in 1945, Congress the next year overrode his opposition at a cost of nearly $1,775,000,000. Though taxes were increased from time to time, the administration deliberately chose to finance the bulk of the expenditures through loans at low rates of interest. Roosevelt, unwilling to saddle heavy taxation on the people when they could least afford it, believed that debt reduction should await normal times. For the present he thought it more important to "balance the human budget." As a result each year saw a large deficit, rising to a total of over $13,000,000,000 from inauguration day to July

1, 1936, and swelling the aggregate national debt to $33,779,000,000
—the greatest up to that time in American history. Of this latter
amount, the deficits run by Hoover accounted for $4,488,000,000;
and of the remainder $4,000,000,000 represented outlays for which
the government expected ultimately to be reimbursed. New Deal
critics pictured the country on the brink of bankruptcy, but its friends
pointed out that in relation to national wealth the public debt remained
far below that of Great Britain or France.

The drive for reform—the third of the 'three R's'—probably made
the deepest impression upon the thoughtful voter, for these measures
sought to cleanse the future of the ugly blots of the past. No earlier
regime had done so much to subordinate private business to the
public weal, or devoted its energies so frankly to broad humanitarian
purposes. Though the President repeatedly urged social and economic
planning, few of the enactments fully realized the principle. Important
beginnings had been made, however, notably in the social-security
program, the AAA plan for agriculture, the Tennessee Valley and
Columbia River developments and other projects for conserving
natural resources. An example had been set which later administrations would ignore at their peril. If the average citizen could not keep
up with the dizzy pace of government, he nevertheless knew that he
himself—the "forgotten man"—was the constant object of its solici-
tude. No longer was Washington an impersonal power or something
to be feared. It was now his friend and protector, taking from the
rich to help the poor, keeping businesses afloat, creating jobs, strengthening trade-unions, guaranteeing bank deposits, subsidizing housing,
assisting farmers, providing social insurance, even sponsoring the
drama and the arts. Believers in rugged individualism raged against
'class rule,' 'bureaucratic meddling' and 'regimentation,' and charged
that the new conception of government was state socialism; but progressives saw the New Deal not as socialism but rather as an effort
to forestall it by timely inoculation.

The Republicans, disheartened by their rout in 1932 and further
demoralized by Democratic successes in the fall elections of 1934,
were unable to rally effectively against the New Deal. Hence this
task fell to outside groups. Some thundered at Roosevelt from the
left, others from the right, but though all were noisy, none carried
much weight. Of the leftist organizations, the Share-Our-Wealth
Society, captained by Senator Huey P. Long, political dictator of

Louisiana until his assassination in 1935, demanded that the federal government guarantee every family $5000 a year so as to make "Every Man a King." Another group gathered around Dr. Francis E. Townsend, a sexagenarian California physician, who urged monthly pensions of $200 for all the unemployed over the age of sixty who agreed to spend the money as fast as they got it. The idea was to stimulate business as well as to help the old. The National Union for Social Justice, headed by the Reverend Charles E. Coughlin, a Catholic priest of Detroit, put forth a rather vague program centering in the proposal that the government should own all the banks and natural resources and alone create currency and credit. Over the radio each week Father Coughlin reached a vast audience that included members of all religious faiths.

At the opposite pole stood the American Liberty League formed in 1934 to "combat radicalism, preserve property rights and uphold and preserve the Constitution." Heavily financed by the Du Ponts and other wealthy industrialists, it bombarded the New Deal through every channel of publicity, hoping to detach old-line Democrats from the President's following as well as to infuse new life into the moribund Republicans. The conservative elements gained more ground, however, from a series of Supreme Court decisions handed down in 1935 and early 1936. Of nine important New Deal acts the tribunal annulled seven. Since all the judgments but two were rendered by a divided bench, with three of the ablest members siding consistently with the administration, many sober people began to wonder whether the majority had not used specious legal technicalities to perpetuate what Roosevelt called "horse and buggy" ideas of government. Was the real difficulty, they asked, with the Constitution or with those who interpreted it? Even some who sympathized with the decisions were shocked when the Court on June 1, 1936, struck down a New York minimum-wage law for women in industry (Morehead v. New York ex rel. Tipaldo). By five to four the judges pronounced the act a deprivation of liberty and property without that due process of law guaranteed by the Fourteenth Amendment. But Justice Harlan F. Stone, speaking for the minority, ascribed the ruling to "personal economic predilections." Steeped in the laissez-faire philosophy, the majority declared in effect that neither the federal nor the state governments had authority to fix minimum wages. At the time such legislation existed in seventeen states.

PWA AND WPA PROJECTS
See pages 348 and 350.

Two of the Restored Buildings of Colonial Williamsburg, Virginia

The Williamsburg Housing Project in Brooklyn

AMERICA PONDERS TWO WILLIAMSBURGS

See pages 394 and 350.

While the reverberations of the Court's action still rang through the land, the political clans gathered for the impending election. In Cleveland on June 9 the Republicans, shelving their discredited older leaders, unanimously chose Governor Alfred M. Landon of Kansas and Frank Knox, a Chicago newspaper publisher. Landon was expected to attract Western voters, and as a colorless personality unknown nationally he seemed to offer a rallying point for anti-New Deal sentiment everywhere. The platform, while assailing Democratic extravagance and promising strict government economy, saw nothing inconsistent in guaranteeing further relief expenditures, more adequate social security and generous subsidies for the farmers. Before accepting the nomination Landon notified the convention that as President he would, if need be, propose a constitutional amendment to grant the states the authority that the Supreme Court had denied. The Democrats, meeting in jubilant mood at Philadelphia on June 23, unanimously renominated Roosevelt and Garner upon a platform eulogizing the New Deal and pledging more of the same. If the Supreme Court stood in the way, they would amend the Constitution to give Congress and the states full power "to regulate commerce, protect public health and safety and safeguard economic security." Before adjourning, the delegates abolished the two-thirds rule for nominations which had been the unbroken Democratic practice for over a century. As four years before, Roosevelt accepted the nomination on the spot. The Union party, a political newcomer, also put forward candidates on a patchwork platform designed to attract Coughlinites, Townsendites and the Share-Our-Wealth adherents.

At no time was the outcome in real doubt. Roosevelt, displaying his incomparable skill on the radio, blasted "economic royalists," reviewed the New Deal's achievements and asked the people to remember the heartbreaking days when he entered office. The Court question sank from sight probably because both parties viewed it so nearly alike. Landon's successive speeches revealed a steady drift toward the reactionaries in his party, and Republican spellbinders harped increasingly on the dangers of dictatorship and communism in the event of Democratic victory, provoking Roosevelt to retort, "I have not sought, I do not seek, I repudiate the support of any advocate of Communism." As the contest proceeded, party lines tended to blur. Two former Democratic presidential candidates, John W. Davis and Al Smith, worked with the American Liberty League to win over conservative Democrats to Landon, while Senators Norris and La Follette headed a National Progressive League to round up independent voters for Roosevelt. Organized labor helped similarly through the newly formed Labor's Nonpartisan League. Resolved to halt the adverse tide, the Republicans poured nearly $9,000,000 into the campaign as compared with the Democrats' $5,500,000. Landon was also backed by most of the nation's newspapers, including the Hearst press which lost no opportunity to castigate

> The Red New Deal with a Soviet seal
> Endorsed by a Moscow hand,
> The strange result of an alien cult
> In a liberty-loving land.

While the improved economic conditions aided the Democrats, perhaps more important was the people's confidence in the President's unwavering devotion to their welfare. Some millions who ordinarily stayed at home went to the polls on election day. Cynics attributed Roosevelt's landslide to the colossal expenditures for relief, but in reality the votes came from all income groups and from all sections of the country. He swept every state but Maine and Vermont, winning 523 electoral votes to 8 for Landon and 60.7 per cent (27,750,000) of the popular ballots to 36.4 per cent (16,680,000). It was the greatest triumph in the electoral college since Monroe's nearly unanimous election in 1820. Of the minor parties the Union party, polling 892,000 votes mostly in Ohio, Massachusetts and Illinois, did best. The Democrats also increased their control of Congress, capturing 333 seats out of 435 in the House and 75 out of 96 in the Senate.

EXTENDING THE NEW DEAL

On taking office the second time President Roosevelt was ready with a batch of proposals to amplify the New Deal. In his inaugural address on January 20—the new inauguration date set by the Twentieth Amendment—he declared, "The test of our progress is not whether we add more to the abundance of those who have much; it is whether we provide enough for those who have too little." But notwithstanding his immense majorities in Congress and what seemed a clear popular mandate, he ran into obstacles. These were due partly to circumstances beyond his control, partly to some of his own making. With economic recovery well advanced, the legislators no longer felt it necessary to act quickly and unitedly at his bidding. Moreover, many Democrats of the President's own way of thinking had come to resent his leadership for personal reasons, while others, mainly Southerners, who had never been more than reluctant New Dealers, welcomed the chance to block further reform adventures. Even the party's great preponderance in Congress proved a weakness, for the vastly expanded membership lacked cohesion and easily tended to disintegrate.

The spark which set off these combustibles was Roosevelt's plan to reorganize the judiciary. Early in February, 1937, he asked Congress to authorize him to enlarge the Supreme Court from nine members to a possible fifteen if judges reaching the age of seventy should decline to retire. He also advised certain less controversial changes in regard to the lower federal courts. Since Justice Louis D. Brandeis was the only confirmed liberal among the six septuagenarians on the high bench, the President hoped by this means to neutralize or replace anti-New Deal members. Considering the new conceptions of public policy Roosevelt had fathered, he had been singularly unfortunate in being the first chief executive since Andrew Jackson to fill no vacancies in the Court. The proposal precipitated a protracted struggle which soon also involved the general public in resounding debate. The plan was denounced as unconstitutional—which it was not—and as a reckless step toward greater centralization—on which opinions might honestly differ. When the President's foes accused him of wanting to 'pack' the Court, his supporters retorted that he sought only to 'unpack' it. Senator Wheeler, hitherto a zealous New Dealer but now leading the opposition forces, argued not that the Court had behaved well, but that any changes should come by constitutional amendment.

The high tribunal itself played the trump card by executing a timely about-face. In a chain of decisions from March 29 to May 24, 1937, it sustained four major New Deal innovations, including the National Labor Relations Board and the Social Security Act. Moreover, by upholding a minimum-wage act of the state of Washington, it ate its words of nine months before regarding the similar New York statute. A sardonic observer remarked, "A switch in time saves nine." Be that as it may, Roosevelt's chief reason for complaint against the judiciary had disappeared. Two further blows were inflicted when seventy-eight-year-old Justice Willis Van Devanter, one of the hide-bound conservatives, announced his impending retirement, and when Senator Joseph Robinson, leader of the anti-Court group in the upper house, suddenly died in mid-July. In August Roosevelt was obliged to accept a bill which ignored his cardinal proposal—a defeat administered by his own party. Nevertheless he had won the substance, if not the form, of what he desired, for the Supreme Court had at last swung round to the New Deal point of view; and, as it happened, a succession of vacancies in the years immediately ahead ensured that the conversion would be lasting. By the close of his second term he had replaced all but two of the original members, and eventually he was to appoint more Justices than any President since George Washington. In the circumstances the tribunal continued to approve important New Deal measures. As a legal writer remarked in 1941, "Never before in history has the Court so extensively altered so many basic principles in so short a time as in the years since February, 1937."

No sooner was the Court fight out of the way than an unexpected business recession turned attention again to problems of relief and recovery. The slump, beginning in August, 1937, struck bottom in June, 1938. The prime cause was probably the government's sharp retrenchment of expenditures during the period of returning prosperity in 1936–1937 or, to put it differently, the failure of private industry to expand as rapidly as the federal outlays diminished. Fortunately the nation's economic structure was far better able to withstand the shock than in 1929, for the new downswing had not been preceded by an orgy of speculation and overproduction. Moreover, the banking system was sound, credit was plentiful at low rates of interest, the farmers were in a stronger position, and unemployment insurance enabled twenty-five states to cushion the blow for nearly 2,000,000 of those rendered idle. Nonetheless the situation caused deep anxiety while it lasted. Congress adopted a new program of spending and lending, and the President made full use of the machinery that had pulled the country out of the earlier slough. The RFC lent funds to tide over businesses in temporary difficulty. The PWA stepped up construction projects. The WPA, which by September, 1937, had reduced the relief rolls to fewer than 1,500,000—the least since the agency had been created—widened its activities until by the early fall of 1938 it was caring for more than 3,000,000. The AAA and other alphabetical bodies also did their part. Thanks to these varied efforts better times began to return. The nation's output of goods and services, which had fallen to less than eighty-one billion dollars in 1938, reached a new high of eighty-eight in 1939.

Though the business slump redirected the government's energies to relief and recovery, it also helped the President's proposals for reform by accenting the economic maladjustments he wished to correct. In his second inaugural address he had pointed out that a third of the nation was "ill-housed, ill-clad, ill-nourished," and during the first half of 1938 he induced Congress to accept his principal recommendations for improvement. The lawmakers began with steps to assure better housing for the underprivileged. The earlier efforts had fallen short of the mark because the costs of construction had put the rents beyond the reach of those intended to be benefited. Even before the downturn became evident Congress had moved to repair this difficulty. The Wagner-Steagall Act of August, 1937, set up a United States Housing Authority empowered to make sixty-year loans to local public agencies for slum clearance and low-cost housing and also to grant subsidies for establishing the rents at a level which the poor could afford. Under shock of the recession Congress increased its funds early in 1938 from $500,000,000 to $800,000,000. By the end of 1940 the USHA had helped supply living quarters for about two hundred and forty thousand members of low-income families.

Roosevelt attained his second reform goal in a new Agricultural Adjustment Act, the most comprehensive yet known. The failure of the 1936 law to establish effectual means of crop control had led to new surpluses, and the resulting fall of prices had been hastened by the effects of the recession in reducing the urban demand for foodstuffs. In short, the farmer was faced again with that overwhelming plenty which had spelled ruin in the past. The act of February, 1938, combined most of the key features of earlier New Deal agricultural legislation with much that was novel. At the heart of the program was the provision to limit the wheat, corn, tobacco, cotton and rice crops. Under the supervision of the Secretary of Agriculture the AAA was given power not only to fix each season's acreage, but, if unusually good weather should produce a bumper crop, to recommend "marketing quotas" for restricting the sales. These quotas should become effective when two thirds of the farmers concerned expressed assent in a referendum. In bad seasons the growers were to get "parity payments" to offset the difference between the market price and the purchasing power the products would have commanded in the last years before World War I. In addition, a system of permissive crop insurance was set up for wheat farmers. Other sections of the act applied to all agriculturists. Benefit payments for soil-conserving purposes were continued but at a more generous rate. Finally, "commodity loans" were provided to enable farmers to store crop surpluses in good harvest years for sale in lean ones. This last arrangement—the "ever normal granary"—was designed to stabilize agricultural prices for the benefit of both producer and consumer.

The legislation was passed too late to have much effect in 1938, which turned out to be another year of teeming harvests. The AAA, however, brought its battery of devices into play as quickly as possible and did something to improve conditions. With a fuller operation in 1939 the results still fell short of expectations. The agricultural output proved the second highest on record, though the continued low farm prices were offset by payments of over $500,000,000 from the federal Treasury. The difficulties were due in part to overproduction in other countries as well as in the United States and to the many restrictions on international trade. To reduce cotton and wheat surpluses the government inaugurated a system of export subsidies for these crops. Though serious obstacles remained, it nevertheless seemed clear that the endeavor to substitute co-operative regulation for the traditional individualistic chaos was a move in the right direction.

The President won his third great victory with the adoption of the Fair Labor Standards Act in June, 1938. Ever since the Supreme Court's deathblow to the NRA three years before, he had resolved to find a way to restore its labor-welfare provisions. The new law, stubbornly resisted by Southern members who feared that the provisions would hamper Southern industry, fixed what Roosevelt called "a floor under wages and a ceiling over hours." The eventual object was a maximum 40-hour week and 40-cents-an-hour minimum pay in all businesses of an interstate character, but in order to ease the transition for small struggling concerns, this goal was to be approached by gradual steps. For the year beginning in October, 1938, the act forbade more than 44 hours or less than 25 cents. In subsequent years it specified further adjustments until the work week should be 40 hours by October, 1940, and the hourly wage 40 cents in 1945. At every stage overtime was to be paid at the rate of time and a half. Certain groups such as farm laborers, employees of retail stores, professional workers and seamen were, however, exempt from the regulations. Finally, the act smote the stubborn evil of child labor by banning from interstate commerce goods produced in concerns hiring persons under the age of sixteen or, in especially hazardous occupations such as mining, under eighteen.

The law aimed primarily to benefit the bulk of low-paid laborers who, not belonging to unions, had had to work on terms dictated by employers. It also protected industrialists who believed in decent labor standards from being undercut by unscrupulous competitors. Starting in the fall of 1938, higher earnings resulted for 300,000 adults and fewer hours for 1,300,000, while 200,000 children were freed from toil. A year later, with the minimum wage changing to 30 cents and the work week to 42 hours, 690,000 obtained pay increases and 1,650,000 shorter hours. In 1940, with the 40-hour limitation going into effect, 2,000,000 were the gainers, and in 1945 the 40-cent requirement bettered the wages of about 20,500,000.

In two respects Congress ignored Roosevelt's wishes. It buried his recommendation to extend the TVA idea to six other great natural regions, and the House declined to follow the Senate's lead in adopting his plan to organize the federal executive departments along more efficient lines. In the latter instance New Deal foes, still rankling from the President's effort to 'pack the Supreme Court,' made the welkin ring with cries of a 'dictatorship bill.' As the sequel was to show, this defeat was merely victory deferred. Other measures favored by the President were enacted, however. A statute of 1937 plugged up certain loopholes which the wealthy had discovered in the income-tax law, and a law of 1938 established stricter governmental standards for foods, drugs, patent medicines and cosmetics. A real advance over previous legislation, it prohibited both the misbranding of products and the use of false and misleading advertising. Another act in 1938 put 15,000 postmasters under the merit plan. When Roosevelt on his own motion added other categories of appointees, 300,000 out of the total number of 852,000 were still subject to political spoils.

In the fall elections of 1938 the Democrats enjoyed the advantage not only of an impressive legislative record, but of improved business conditions. Nevertheless, since the Republicans also professed now to believe in the New Deal's goals while condemning merely its inefficiency, the administration barely succeeded in retaining control of Congress. When the new group of lawmakers assembled, they turned again to Roosevelt's plan for revamping the administrative arm of the government. Every President since the first Roosevelt had urged simplification, and the New Deal's multiplying of agencies, often with overlapping powers, rendered the need critical. In March, 1939, Congress, oblivious of the earlier fears of 'dictatorship' now that the election was over, acceded to the White House's wishes with minor changes. The President was empowered to transfer, consolidate or abolish some sixty of the more than one hundred administrative boards and commissions. Accordingly he regrouped twenty-three agencies and departmental bureaus in three great units: the Federal Works Agency, the Federal Loan Agency and the Federal Security Agency. Congress also dealt with the related subject of "pernicious political activities" by federal officeholders. The Hatch Act of July, 1939, forbade appointees below the policy-making rank to use official favors to influence the outcome of a national election, or to solicit or accept contributions from relief workers, or to take "active part" in campaigns. A later Hatch Act, in 1940, extended these regulations to the three hundred thousand state and local employees who were paid partly or wholly from federal funds. In this second enactment Congress took occasion also to confine the annual expenditures of each political party to $3,000,000 and restricted single contributions to not more than $5000. Politicians, however, quickly discovered ways of evading these cramping limitations.

The President could not induce the legislators to embark upon a new seven-year spending program designed to ensure the country against another possible recession. Also because of the better times, they clipped the relief appropriations in June, 1939, to $1,775,-000,000, abolished the WPA theater project and placed restrictions upon other white-collar undertakings. Work relief had employed as many as 3,335,000 in November, 1938; the new arrangement cut the monthly average to 2,300,000. Incidentally, Congress now changed the name of the WPA from Works Progress Administration to Work Projects Administration. Though in these matters the lawmakers loudly preached economy, they voted the largest sums yet known to help agriculture and, because of the gathering war clouds abroad, boosted the expenditures for national defense. When the session ended in August, the total appropriations of over $13,000,000,000 marked a new peacetime record.

FULLER ACCOUNTS

The Roosevelt Revolution. General treatments of the New Deal include Allen, *Since Yesterday;* Beard and Smith, *Old Deal and the New;* Brogan, *Era of Franklin D. Roosevelt;* Mitchell, *Depression Decade;* Rauch, *History of the New Deal* (to 1938); and Wecter, *Age of the Great Depression.* For the bank crisis, read O'Connor, *Banking Crisis and Recovery,* and Pecora, *Wall Street under Oath.*

The Relief Program. Among special studies are Howard, *WPA and Federal Relief Policy;* Lane and Steegmuller, *America on Relief;* Lindleys, *New Deal for Youth;* Macmahon and others, *Administration of Federal Work Relief;* and Sherwood, *Roosevelt and Hopkins.*

The Recovery Program. Gayer, *Public Works,* Nourse and others, *Three Years of the Agricultural Adjustment Administration,* and Roos, *NRA Economic Planning,* deal with leading phases. See also Saloutos and Hicks, *Agricultural Discontent in the Middle West.*

The Reform Program. See especially Douglas, *Social Security;* Lilienthal, *TVA;* and Pritchett, *Tennessee Valley Authority.*

The Voters Pass Judgment. Burns and Watson, *Government Spending and Economic Expansion,* and Phillips and Garland, *Government Spending and Economic Recovery,* treat deficit financing; Eurich and Wilson, *In 1936,* reports the election, and McWilliams, *Southern California Country,* casts light on some of the fringe political movements.

Extending the New Deal. For the Court fight and its consequences, turn to Curtis, *Lions under the Throne;* Kelly and Harbison, *American Constitution;* Jackson, *Struggle for Judicial Supremacy;* and Pritchett, *Roosevelt Court.* Straus and Wegg, *Housing Comes of Age,* deals with federal activities in that important field.

CHAPTER XVIII

LIFE BETWEEN WARS

NEW DESIGN FOR LIVING

THE shift from the glittering 1920's to the shadowed 1930's left its mark on nearly every phase of American life. It even affected the growth of population, though here long-range causes were also at work. Down to 1890 the population had jumped a quarter or third every ten years, but thereafter the ratio began to decline, dropping to 16 per cent between 1920 and 1930 and to 7 per cent in the depression decade 1930–1940. The prime reason was the falling birth rate, due to more and more women pursuing full-time careers, to couples living in city apartments and to the desire of parents to give a few children advantages they could not give a larger number. A contributing factor was the new curbs on immigration after World War I. The foreign-born increased only slightly in the 1920's and, largely because of the Great Depression, actually decreased by 2,600,-000 in the 1930's. Of the number remaining in 1940—11,600,000—three out of five had become naturalized, the highest proportion on record. The undigested immigrant no longer imperiled the nation's powers of assimilation. On the other hand, the shrinking birth rate, if it persisted, meant that America faced a time—statisticians put it around the end of the century—when the population would cease expanding and might start contracting.

The character of the population was altering in other respects as well. Thanks to improved medical care and to better food and living conditions, the expectancy of life at birth lengthened from fifty-six years in 1920 to nearly sixty-three in 1940. The proportion of the elderly, in other words, was mounting, a trend accelerated by the declining birth rate. In 1900 only four in every hundred Americans had been as old as sixty-five, but by 1940 the number had risen to six or seven, and it was estimated that by 1980 or thereabouts it would be at least fifteen. Coming events were already casting their shadows before, for organized groups of the aged, captained by Dr.

Townsend and others of his kind, unsettled the political balance of power in many states in the 1930's and, as has been seen, helped shoulder Congress into passing the Social Security Act. Another change was the increasing ratio of women, who by 1940 almost equaled the number of men (65,608,000 to 66,062,000) and promised to be the dominant political force in the years ahead—if they hung together. Clearly these tendencies injected factors into the American situation with which not only politicians but also merchants, medical men, military authorities and others must reckon.

With the population growing from 106,000,000 in 1920 to 131,-670,000 in 1940, people continued to mass in urban localities. At the earlier date about twenty-five in every hundred lived in cities of 100,000 or more, but at the later over forty did, despite a temporary back-to-the-country movement when the depression was at its worst. Particularly significant was the rise of great metropolitan districts. These 'city states' had begun to form in the nineteenth century as swifter means of transportation and communication flung the inhabitants outward into the suburbs, but it was the coming of the automobile and motor truck and the extension of electricity and other modern conveniences into the surrounding territory that gave these supercommunities their enormous size. Increasingly the bedrooms of American cities were to be found in the outlying settlements, and many small retail businesses and factories followed. By 1930 one hundred and thirty-three metropolitan districts had emerged, by 1940 one hundred and forty, each composed of one or more central cities with dependent towns and rural areas. The district dominated by New York City contained two hundred and seventy-two towns and cities in four states. Within the regions the less congested and more lightly taxed urban and rural fringes tended to draw residents away from the core cities. So large was this centrifugal migration in the 1930's that Philadelphia, St. Louis, Pittsburgh and some other places had fewer people within their corporate limits in 1940 than ten years before. Since these districts were subdivided into independent municipalities, the citizens faced formidable difficulties in looking after such common governmental interests as policing, sewage disposal, public health and schooling. Some students of the problem, despairing of any other solution, proposed separate statehood for the major regions.

The civic renaissance begun earlier in the century continued into these years. The city-manager plan, unknown in America in 1900, had spread by 1940 to over four hundred and fifty localities, including places as large as Cincinnati, Rochester and Dallas. At the same time there occurred a wide adoption of the nonpartisan ballot, an extension of the merit system of appointment to four fifths of the nation's municipal employees, and a rise in the number of publicly owned waterworks and other utilities. The old-fashioned urban political boss, robbed of most of his traditional props of power, found the problem of survival increasingly tough. Along with these changes came the first sustained efforts at city planning. The purpose was to substitute intelligence for chance in determining a community's development and to ensure the citizens safer, more convenient and pleasanter surroundings. In 1905 Columbia, South Carolina, and San Francisco had set the example; by 1922 a hundred and eighty-five cities and towns had taken like action; and by 1940 the number had grown to eleven hundred. Even municipalities that did not go the whole way adopted zoning ordinances and building codes to improve conditions. As a result, urban life assumed an increasingly rural aspect. Parks, tree-lined boulevards and recreational centers multiplied far out of proportion to the growth of population, and the municipal authorities, notably with New Deal aid, devoted serious attention to slum clearance and better housing for the poor.

Both in city and country the people moved about with a celerity and ease denied to their fathers and grandfathers. As the automobile grew progressively cheaper and simpler to operate, it achieved a universality unknown in any other land. The number of vehicles in use mounted from 3,500,000 in 1916 to 10,500,000 in 1921 and to 31,104,000 in 1940. At the last date the American people owned 9,500,000 more motorcars than telephones. To meet the demand for long-distance journeys, the general government helped the states to build better highways. The motorist no longer had to fear getting stuck in the mud or to figure how to avoid 'taking the dust' of the driver ahead, for under the spur of federal subsidies hard-surfaced roads lengthened from 300,000 miles in 1916 to 1,200,000 in 1940. As further incentives to travel, service stations, wayside restaurants, overnight cabins and tourist camps sprang up in profusion. At any time after 1925 the whole population might have piled into cars and dashed off for parts unknown. The Americans had always been a migratory folk, and the auto permitted an independence of movement as well as cheapness of locomotion which the railroad had never afforded. If a man did not have his own car, public busses afforded an acceptable substitute; and if he lacked bus fare, he could join the army of hitchhikers who, in spite of adverse legislation, freely 'thumbed' rides to destinations far and near. Though vacation motoring had been confined at first to the warmer seasons, the use of closed cars and automobile heaters, reinforced by the snow-removal activities of state and local communities, tended to make it a year-round diversion. In the mid-thirties trailers began to appear on the road. These 'homes on wheels,' often having no permanent resting place, numbered 160,000 by 1937.

Flying also came into greater prominence, though few persons as yet had their own planes. Ninety per cent of the aircraft factories built during World War I had been scrapped, for the Washington authorities with strange blindness failed to appreciate the future importance of military aviation. The industry got its real start after Congress in 1925 authorized subsidies to commercial companies for carrying mail. The lush prosperity made ample private capital available, and Charles A. Lindbergh's dramatic solo flight across the Atlantic in May, 1927, added the fillip of popular enthusiasm. Soon regular routes linked the principal cities, and the number of passengers rose from 6000 in 1926 to 2,370,000 in 1940. In 1938 Congress created the Civil Aeronautics Authority (later Board) to regulate the economic aspects of the business, prescribe safety regulations and investigate accidents. By 1940 there were 2345 airports and landing fields, and flying connections had been established with South America, Europe and Asia. The plane was also turned to account for transporting freight, scattering insecticides to protect crops, fighting forest fires, and kindred purposes. Ahead lay its far-expanded uses in World War II.

LABOR IN UPHEAVAL

For reasons already described, the trade-union movement had languished during the 'New Economic Era' after World War I, the American Federation of Labor's membership dropping from 4,000,000 in 1920 to 2,700,000 in 1929 and to 2,317,000 in 1933. The New Deal, however, reversed the trend, first through the National Recovery Administration and then through the National Labor Relations Board. This agency, created by the Wagner Act in 1935, guaranteed workers the right to bargain collectively in unions of their own choosing and barred employers from giving financial or other aid to company unions. Total union strength (including groups outside the AFL) climbed from 2,973,000 in 1933 to an estimated 3,889,000 in 1935 and to around 9,000,000 in 1940.

Along with the upswing of membership, however, came increasing discord within labor's ranks. The principal clash concerned the question of craft versus industrial unions. Historically the Federation had consisted predominantly of craft unions—the 'aristocracy of labor'—enrolling only about one in every ten wage earners. With the unskilled and semiskilled mostly omitted, the workers in a given industry could not present a united front to management. Furthermore, so its critics charged, the AFL had lost touch with the problems of the bulk of toilers. Even some capitalists saw an advantage in dealing with a single large unit of all employees rather than with a host of petty groups urging special and sometimes conflicting demands. The foremost champion of industrial unionism was John L. Lewis, long a stormy petrel in the labor world. As president of the United Mine Workers in the coal field he headed an organization which embraced common laborers and the semiskilled as well as electricians, carpenters and other craftsmen. Lewis insisted that mass-production industries could be effectively organized in no other way. But the top men in the AFL were opposed. They foresaw as a result endless conflicts of jurisdiction with the old-line unions and feared that the latter might lose their dominant position.

Though the AFL made some cautious concessions to Lewis's demands, he forced the issue more decisively by forming a Committee for Industrial Organization in 1935 representing the eight industrial unions already in the Federation. President William Green, denouncing this "challenge to the supremacy" of the parent body, called upon the CIO to disband, and when it declined, the Federation in 1936 suspended the CIO unions for "insurrection." Thereupon open warfare broke out between the two factions, each invading the other's domain and seeking advantages at the other's expense. By the autumn of 1937 the CIO claimed 3,700,000 members (in thirty-two national unions) as compared with the 3,600,000 in the rival organization. If the two groups had joined forces, they would have formed the mightiest labor aggregation in the country's history. Moderates in both camps deplored the internecine strife, but could find no way of resolving the differences. Finally, in November, 1938, the CIO set up as an independent body with the name Congress of Industrial Organizations, under Lewis as president.

In carrying their program to the rank and file the CIO leaders directed their first blow at the unorganized automobile industry. The initial strike was waged against the General Motors Corporation. Though the storm center was Flint, Michigan, the disturbance laid off 135,000 men in fourteen states. The United Automobile Workers, a CIO union, demanded recognition as the sole bargaining agent for all General Motors employees; and to gain their point, the men resorted to the sitdown strike, remaining in the plants without working and forcibly resisting removal. After three months of turmoil the strikers in February, 1937, won the coveted recognition as well as a substantial improvement of conditions. Similar tactics got results from the Chrysler, Hudson and other companies. As the wave of sit-down strikes spread over the country, however, the public became increasingly antagonized by what some of the state and lower federal courts termed unlawful seizures of property—a view which the Supreme Court confirmed a few years later. President Green of the AFL also castigated such methods as illegal, though the contagion of example caused many of his own unions to use them. The United States Senate, too, condemned the sitdowns, but President Roosevelt himself maintained a hands-off policy.

The steel industry, hitherto immune to unionization, was the next target. The great United States Steel Corporation came to terms in March, 1937, without a strike, and other companies followed suit until over two hundred and sixty concerns employing nearly 360,000 men had signed up. Though 'Big Steel' yielded with surprising ease, 'Little Steel'—the Bethlehem, Republic, Inland and Youngstown Sheet & Tube companies—proved a tougher adversary. A walkout in the late spring started a conflagration throughout the steel belt from Chicago to western Pennsylvania, involving 90,000 workers and causing the militia to intervene in Ohio and Pennsylvania. In the end the Inland Company granted some of the demands, but the employees of the three other companies drifted back to their jobs during the summer without concessions. The National Labor Relations Board, reviewing the Republic's conduct before and during the troubles, found it guilty of employing spies, infringing civil liberties, terrorizing workers and fomenting bloodshed as well as of flouting the Wagner

Act in other ways. The officers were required to reinstate about 5000 strikers and to "cease and desist" henceforth from interfering with the self-organization of employees. Other corporations had used similar illegal methods, as a Senate committee under Robert M. La Follette, Jr., brought out in an extensive investigation.

Labor's new militancy, infecting the AFL as well as the CIO, produced 4470 strikes in 1937, more than twice as many as in 1936. The years 1938, 1939 and 1940, however, brought more normal conditions, with the work stoppages declining successively to 2770, 2615 and 2500. In 1940 the whole number of persons involved was between a third and a fourth of those three years before. Another outcome of the militancy was a more vigorous participation in politics, with the CIO leading the way. "Labor has gained more under President Roosevelt than under any president in memory," declared Lewis in 1936, adding, "Obviously it is the duty of labor to support Roosevelt 100 per cent." Hence the CIO in that year formed Labor's Nonpartisan League to re-elect the New Deal ticket, Lewis's United Mine Workers turning over $420,000 for the purpose. In New York the American Labor party, sponsored by the League, gave equally zealous help. But by 1940 Lewis, having meanwhile quarreled with Roosevelt and developed political ambitions of his own, appealed to the "men and women of labor" to switch to the Republicans, promising to resign as CIO head if Roosevelt won again. Many CIO leaders and unions, however, repudiated his action, as did numerous AFL officers and unions. Lewis kept his word after the election, and Philip Murray, who had organized the steelworkers, succeeded to his shoes. Labor's active intervention in politics alarmed conservatives, who deplored what they deemed class divisions at the polls and blamed the new departure on left-wing influences. Communists had in fact infiltrated the CIO, but though they dominated some of the unions, they at no time comprised more than a small fraction of the whole membership. Their presence, however, created a problem with which the national officers did not come to grips until the late 1940's.

Agricultural labor, traditionally unorganized, also benefited from the New Deal. Since Reconstruction days farm tenancy had constituted a growing social cancer in the cotton belt. In 1930 six or seven farms out of every ten were run by tenants, many of them occupying a position little better than peons. At the bottom tier was the sharecropper who, toiling in the field with his wife and children, eked out a bare existence in perpetual debt to the landowner, with whom he was required to divide his crop. During the depression nearly a million of these wretched, undernourished folk were thrown on relief. Driven to despair by the fierce drought of 1934, the share-croppers formed the Southern Tenant Farmers' Union. Conservative Southern sentiment, angered by this extension of the labor movement to agricultural workers, took further offense because its membership included both Negroes and whites. But the movement steadily gained strength and, most important of all, it helped arouse Congress to the need for action. The Bankhead-Jones Law in 1937 provided means by which this underprivileged group might climb to land ownership. It empowered the Farm Security Administration to lend government money to share-croppers and other tenants at low interest rates, with a possible period of forty years for repaying the principal. Out of its funds of $75,-000,000 the FSA in the first three years started nearly thirteen thousand families, mostly in the South, toward the goal of farm proprietorship.

Not unlike the share-cropper problem was that of displaced agricultural workers. Some of these had been set adrift by the introduction of tractors in the cotton belt; others were refugees from the wind-swept Dust Bowl embracing large sections of Oklahoma, Texas and Kansas. Eventually more than a hundred and fifty thousand families gravitated to the West Coast, where it was estimated only one job existed for every four applicants. Their predicament was brought to general attention in 1939 by John Steinbeck's novel *The Grapes of Wrath,* which portrayed their plight upon reaching California. Many of the fruit-growing corporations, taking advantage of their helplessness, treated them with great brutality, paying starvation wages, suppressing civil liberties and endeavoring to strangle all efforts at organization. In 1937, however, some of the workers formed a CIO union, which grew slowly. Meanwhile the wanderers took root wherever they could, usually settling in trailer camps or developing slums on the fringes of cities. To keep down the inflow the Farm Security Administration made small subsistence grants to several hundred thousand families in the Dust Bowl and the South. It also built camps on the Pacific Coast, which supplied decent living quarters for about thirty thousand families. The United States Department of Justice did its part by intervening to protect the migrants' civil freedoms. In the end, however, it was the outbreak of World War II that created the needed amount of additional employment.

NEW SOCIAL TRENDS

Though the Great Depression sapped the resources of charity organizations and the government assumed permanently many of their functions, these bodies continued to play an important role, if only to supplement official action. In the prosperous 1920's they had greatly increased their funds by making combined appeals to the public. Cleveland had instituted the first 'community chest' in 1913, but it was the joint money-raising drives of private civilian agencies during World War I that demonstrated the real efficiency of the method. From 12 chests in 1919 the number soared to 329 in 1929, and as the economic blight caused other localities to adopt the plan, the total reached 538 in 1940, embracing an aggregate of fifty million urban dwellers.

One ancient social problem entered a new phase when the Twenty-first Amendment in 1933 turned the liquor question back to the states. Either because the people had suffered an overdose of virtue, or because the prohibition forces were too battered by their defeat to be effective, the legislatures showed little inclination to resume the former restraints. Eighteen states followed the Canadian example of making liquor selling a government monopoly, while most of the other commonwealths adopted various types of licensing or permitted local option. With the relaxing of repressive regulations drinking became more general though the amount of drunkenness apparently did not increase. The availability of legal beverages also drove the bootlegger out of business and thus removed a fecund source of urban crime. Though the enforcement of local bans proved difficult, as had always been the case, there appeared no disposition to revive national prohibition.

A reconsideration of the Indian question brought about another change of public policy. Though the reformers of the 1880's believed they had started the tribesman on the path to civilization, the plan broke too sharply with his traditional way of life. Bred to a system of communal ownership, he failed to develop a sense of private property, with the result that he was easily swindled out of his holdings. Moreover, he drifted away from his own people and lost the cultural values that formed his natural heritage. He became a man without a country. In 1924 Congress bestowed citizenship on the race, but this was a legal formality which left their social and economic status unaltered and did not necessarily carry the right of suffrage. It was not till Franklin Roosevelt entered office that the government proposed a New Deal for the red man as well as for the white. By that time the Dawes Severalty Act of 1887 had whittled down the 139,000,000 acres of Indian domain to 49,000,000, much of it infertile. The Wheeler-Howard Act of 1934 forbade further allotments, provided for putting the landless back on the soil, subsidized vocational training, authorized a large measure of tribal self-rule and offered government aid for conservation and other economic undertakings. Though adoption of the plan was optional, 189 tribes out of 266 voted to accept it. The new purpose was to equip the Indians for responsible living in their own communities, with particular attention to safeguarding natural resources and reviving native arts and crafts. They were hampered by their long-time spiritual and economic demoralization, but it seemed clear that they had been placed at last upon the road to genuine self-help.

The much larger racial minority, the Negroes, also bettered their position in American life, though for reasons quite different. In the war period 1916–1919 perhaps four hundred thousand left the South for jobs in Northern factories and munition plants, and in the subsequent boom years others followed until a quarter of the colored people were packed in Northern industrial centers. By 1940 New York City, whose Harlem district had also attracted West Indian blacks, contained nearly as many Negroes as Arkansas, while Chicago had more than Kentucky or Missouri. Even in Dixie an increasing proportion shifted into the towns and cities. In 1940 fewer than one in every three throughout the country still worked on farms. Economically the effects were beneficial. The race forged ahead in business and the professions and also made notable contributions to literature, music and the drama. George W. Carver of Tuskegee, born in slavery, won international fame as an industrial chemist, extracting dyestuffs from Alabama's red clay and developing a hundred and sixty-five different products from the peanut and a hundred and seven from the sweet potato, greatly to the South's economic gain.

Yet the color line showed little sign of vanishing, and with the northward migration of Negroes, it was extended into some parts of that section. In the South, Jim-Crowism persisted in housing, educational facilities and all public accommodations, and the widespread poll-tax restriction denied the suffrage to some millions of dark-skinned citizens along with countless poor whites. This regulation required payment of one or two dollars some months in advance of an election plus usually the paying up of any back taxes. A further bar to political participation was exclusion from the Democratic primaries, which in this one-party section determined the outcome of the general elections. In the North sporadic mob violence revealed a growing race tension and, as earlier, the Railway Brotherhoods and a dozen or more AFL national unions ostracized Negroes, unlike the newer CIO which welcomed them. Unhappily, most whites continued to view the Negro with blinders, failing to distinguish between the educated and the ignorant, the worthy and the base, as in the case of their own race. Nonetheless a better day appeared to be dawning. Individual Southerners were joining with colored men in organizations to improve conditions; lynchings declined from 281 in the 1920's to 119 in the 1930's; the number of poll-tax states decreased from eleven to eight; and Northern Negroes were rapidly emerging into political life, with one a Congressman from Chicago. The race's varied achievements promised in the long run to efface the white man's inherited prejudices.

In most of the reform enterprises of the time women were active. Armed with the ballot in every state, they were able to urge their views far more tellingly than when they had been mere bystanders in politics. Upon ratification of the Nineteenth Amendment in 1920 the suffragists founded the nonpartisan League of Women Voters to study local and national problems and formulate solutions. In this manner they helped mold public opinion on such subjects as child welfare, housing, education and measures against injurious foods and medicines. More and more, too, women entered directly into government, holding positions of increasing prominence. By the twentieth anniversary of equal suffrage, as Secretary of Labor Frances Perkins noted, three had served as federal judges, twenty-eight as members of Congress, two as Ministers abroad and two as state governors. Their rising civic importance was further evidenced by President Roosevelt's wife. Deeply interested in social work before entering the White House, Eleanor Roosevelt broadened her horizon to include all efforts to aid distressed mankind. Reaching a nation-wide audience through her travels, daily syndicated column and radio appearances, she interpreted complex social abstractions in simple human terms and inspired people to fresh exertions against injustices.

Another factor in stirring the popular conscience was organized religion. As never before, church leaders strove to keep abreast the changing needs of society and advance the social gospel. As the Methodist bishops declared in 1919, "If Christianity is a driving force making for democracy . . . we must recognize the inevitability of the application of democracy to industry. While we rejoice in the adoption of such ameliorative measures as better housing and various forms of social insurance, we call for the more thoroughgoing emphasis on human freedom"; and the National Catholic War Council (later National Catholic Welfare Conference) agreed that the majority of workers "must somehow become owners, at least in part, of the instruments of production." As churchmen concerned themselves more and more with the world about them, the ancient theological differences among Protestants waned. Mergers of local congregations occurred with ever greater frequency, and between 1916 and 1926 eighteen national denominations took a like step, including three Lutheran sects which joined in the United Lutheran Church. Later years brought further amalgamations, notably the Christian Church and the Congregationalists in 1929; two Northern Methodist groups and the Methodist Episcopal Church, South, in 1939; and the Reformed Church and the Evangelical Synod of North America in 1940. On nearly every hand the portents indicated a determination to reduce the wastefulness of sectarian rivalries.

As doctrinal dissensions subsided, so also did fears of the menace of science to Christianity. Occasional rumblings of the earlier controversy over Darwinism could be heard, however, especially in quarters where the intellectual aspects of religion counted for less than the emotional. The 'Fundamentalists,' who upheld a literal interpretation of the Bible, succeeded in inducing three Southern legislatures to outlaw the teaching of evolution in tax-supported schools. The movement reached a climax in 1925 when in a dramatic trial a young Tennessee high-school teacher was found guilty of noncompliance. The state supreme court, though affirming the statute's constitutionality, reversed the decision, and subsequently the law fell quietly into disuse. Despite the increasing distractions of modern life and the reduced church revenues caused by the depression, religious membership lagged only a little behind the advance of population. From

1916 to 1936 the number of communicants rose from 42,000,000 to 55,800,000, with the Catholics forming the largest single group though less than a third of the whole.

INTELLECTUAL MAINSPRINGS

Never before had the American people found it so easy to keep informed about current affairs. Though the daily newspapers decreased from 2325 in 1920 to 2000 in 1940, their total circulation increased a third. The shrinkage in number of journals resulted partly from higher operating costs and partly from the growing competition of radio and movie. Among the New York papers affected were the *Herald* and *Tribune,* which were combined in 1924, and the *World* and *Telegram,* united in 1931. As a result of consolidations, cities which had earlier possessed five or more journals were forced to rely upon one or two, perhaps under identical ownership. Chicagoans, who during World War I could choose from among four morning papers, had only the *Tribune* twenty years later, though the *Sun,* a competitor, came on the scene in 1941. Newspaper chains acquired new importance as they grew from 31 in 1923 to 56 in 1940, when they accounted for a quarter of the country's daily circulation.

Everywhere the tendency was toward greater uniformity of presenting both news and views. The chain system, the news-gathering agencies and the syndication of 'features' helped to make the press more or less alike the country over. On the other hand readers benefited from a better coverage of national and world events. Generally, the editors pursued a policy of pleasing all and offending as few as possible; but dependent as the papers were for advertising and other support upon corporate business and being a form of corporate business themselves, they usually took a strong stand in defense of economic orthodoxy during political campaigns. Largely as a gesture toward greater journalistic independence, they opened their pages increasingly during the 1930's to columnists such as Walter Lippmann, Frank Kent and Drew Pearson, who commented on national and international affairs in widely syndicated articles. Individual journals printing these discussions could disclaim responsibility for the opinions expressed, but it usually happened that the political coloration of the columnist agreed with that of the newspaper.

The radio became a rival of the newspaper shortly after the first broadcasting station opened in Pittsburgh in time to announce the

1920 election returns. Broadcasting stations multiplied while the owners of radios increased even more rapidly. The annual sales leaped from 100,000 sets in 1922 to 11,800,000 in 1940, by which date the 51,000,000 receiving instruments in homes, offices, automobiles and schools far outnumbered the nation's bathtubs. In about twenty years the radio had attained the goal toward which print had been working for five hundred: access to the whole population. In 1926 the National Broadcasting Company, first of the great networks, was organized, to be followed in 1927 by the Columbia and later by others. Broadcasting did not become a government monopoly, as in most other countries, but after preliminary legislation in 1927, Congress established the Federal Communications Commission in 1934 to license stations, assign wave lengths and help improve the service technically. Since the stations and networks derived their profits from commercial sponsors, they strove to attract the largest possible number of listeners so as to make good as advertising mediums—an aim which tended to debase the quality of the programs.

The radio not only brought people within the country into closer communion but reached outward toward all corners of the globe. In 1929 the nation heard Commander Richard E. Byrd report from the Antarctic an account of his flight over the South Pole. In 1936 they listened to Edward VIII announce his abdication as King of England. With the outbreak of World War II in 1939, network commentators in European capitals kept Americans better advised of the developing hostilities than were the belligerent peoples. Progress was also made in other respects. As early as 1924 the Radio Corporation of America transmitted photographs across the Atlantic, and by the 1930's the method had been so perfected that newspapers were taking advantage of it. Ahead lay the miracle of television.

Meanwhile the movie learned to talk. In 1927 the Warner Brothers produced the first picture with synchronized sound effects. "The Jazz Singer," featuring the comedian Al Jolson, convincingly demonstrated the possibilities and soon helped to sweep silent films into the discard. Freed from the restrictions of pantomime, a galaxy of new stars arose in Hollywood, and the screen art made a fresh start. Although the motion picture was primarily a vehicle of entertainment, it also encroached on the domain of the newspaper in its newsreels and in special presentations like "The March of Time." After the early years, however, it did not seek to compete as an advertising medium, for the box-office receipts rendered unnecessary this supplementary source of revenue. By 1940 there were 19,500 picture houses with a weekly attendance estimated at over eighty million. As with the radio, the industry tended to gravitate into the hands of a few major producing companies, which also owned many of the theaters. Apart from its commercial uses, the movie proved an important handmaid to education, especially in the teaching of science. Every up-to-date school and college felt it needful to possess one or more projecting machines.

Compared with the radio and the movie, magazines wielded slight influence. Long since drained of their muckraking fervor, they were generally content to inform and amuse. The principal exception was the *American Mercury* edited by H. L. Mencken and George Jean Nathan from 1924. To the delight of sophisticates, Mencken alike bludgeoned reformers, professors, "Bible-belt Fundamentalists" and the "booboisie," but his devotion to the right of unfettered expression made him also crusade against all efforts at official or unofficial literary censorship. His cocky iconoclasm, his disdain for the clownish herd, suited the cynical mood of the postwar years but went amiss with the coming of the Great Depression. He gave up the *Mercury* in 1933. Other innovations in the periodical world proved more lasting. Outstanding examples were *Reader's Digest* (1922), a pocket-size monthly which compressed articles from other magazines for the busy reader; *Time* (1923), which condensed and spiced the week's news; the *New Yorker* (1925), whose weekly quips and cartoons modernized American humor; and *Life* (1936), *Look* (1937) and other pictorial weeklies, which exploited the new visual-mindedness of the public. Like the daily press and for much the same reason, most periodicals of wide circulation leaned to the conservative side of public questions, if expressing any views at all. During the booming 1920's magazine sales skyrocketed, but the hard times cut the number of monthlies from 2800 in 1929 to 2100 in 1937 before a slow recovery began. From this ill wind, however, certain weeklies profited, thanks to their low price. The *Saturday Evening Post, Collier's* and *Liberty,* devoted mainly to fiction, mustered circulations of from 2,500,000 to 3,000,000.

The novelists did more to jolt complacency. The 1920's brought to the fore a group of writers who viewed the American scene with a disillusion bred of revulsion against the moral wastes of war as well as of disgust with the meretricious tendencies in postwar life. Often experimental in their literary techniques, they further breached convention by treating sex with a frankness hitherto unknown in American letters. John Dos Passos's *Three Soldiers* (1921), E. E. Cumming's *The Enormous Room* (1922), William Faulkner's *Soldiers' Pay* (1926) and Ernest Hemingway's *A Farewell to Arms* (1929) stand out among the books which stressed the unheroic side of war. In criticizing ethical standards the novelists, unlike their predecessors of the muckraking era, were less concerned with assailing Big Business than with exposing the shabby ideals and misguided energies of the great middle class. In such works as *Main Street* (1920), *Babbitt* (1922) and *Arrowsmith* (1925) Sinclair Lewis satirized the cant and ostentation that usually passed for success. Sherwood Anderson in *Winesburg, Ohio* (1919) and *The Triumph of the Egg* (1921), collections of short stories, told of the cramping existence in small towns. With ponderous realism Theodore Dreiser in *An American Tragedy* (1925) unfolded the story of a weakling demoralized by the false values of a money-mad civilization. Unconcerned with the current scene, though perhaps of more enduring fame, were Willa Cather, who in *Death Comes for the Archbishop* (1927) wrote with warmth and insight of quiet heroism in early Mexico, and Thornton Wilder, whose *Bridge of San Luis Rey* (1927) tenderly recounted a tale of ancient Peru.

The Great Depression redirected fiction toward underlying economic realities. No longer censuring their countrymen for living by bread alone, the novelists in the 1930's focused on the plight of those who lacked bread. On every hand they discovered evidences of the "ill-housed, ill-clad, ill-nourished." Some of their books professed to be 'class-conscious' and 'proletarian,' but most belonged to the older tradition of social protest. Typical of the torrential flood were William Faulkner's *As I Lay Dying* (1930), Erskine Caldwell's *Tobacco Road* (1932), James T. Farrell's trilogy *Studs Lonigan* (1932–1935), Albert Halper's *Union Square* (1933), Jack Conroy's *The Disinherited* (1933), Robert Cantwell's *Land of Plenty* (1934), and John Steinbeck's *The Grapes of Wrath* (1939). As if to remind a disheartened public of its heritage of courage, there was also a resurgence of historical fiction. Neglecting great occasions and the merely picturesque, Walter D. Edmonds, Kenneth Roberts, James Boyd and others peopled the American past with believable men and women who succeeded in overcoming stubborn odds in spite of human frailties. Margaret Mitchell's *Gone with the Wind,* a novel of the Civil War and Reconstruction, was the publishing sensation of 1936. Many of the writers of these two decades commanded an audience abroad. Two of them—Sinclair Lewis and Pearl S. Buck, the latter a delineator of Chinese peasant life in *The Good Earth* (1931) and other novels —won the Nobel Prize in literature in 1930 and 1938, as did also the playwright Eugene O'Neill in 1936. They were the first American authors to gain the distinction.

The Great Depression hurt book publishing even more than it did magazine publishing. Though the enforced idleness created a large public demand, lack of purchasing power halved the sale of books between 1929 and 1933, the bleakest years. Instead, the jobless went to the public libraries, sometimes to browse or drowse, but more often to read something that might prove of future usefulness. The American Library Association in 1933 estimated an increase of three or four million borrowers. Much discussion occurred as to the effect of the radio on reading. Contrary to a general impression, several investigations indicated that it encouraged the habit by stimulating interest in subjects beyond the listener's ordinary ken. The movies may have exerted a similar influence. At any rate, Gallup polls in 1937–1939 revealed a popular concentration on books that had been previously filmed in Hollywood.

In formal education the 1920's saw a large increase of students, teachers and physical facilities. Public school enrollment grew from 21,580,000 in 1920 to 25,680,000 in 1930, while the total expenditures more than doubled. Educators, reflecting the laissez-faireism rampant in other phases of American life, experimented widely with 'progressive' methods and 'child-centered' instruction, much to the dismay of those parents who preferred to have the schools instill a sense of discipline and self-control. Professor John Dewey of Columbia was the principal inspiration of the new educational practices, but the master must often have winced at the excesses of his disciples. By curious contrast many legislatures required of teachers oaths of loyalty to the state and national constitutions and prescribed flag-saluting rituals for pupils. Though postwar hysteria was initially responsible, the movement persisted because of the fear that children might imbibe a critical attitude toward established institutions. Governor Al Smith of New York in vetoing a teachers' oath bill in 1920 declared, "If this law had been in force prior to the abolition of slavery, opposition to that institution which was protected by the Constitution and its laws would have been just cause for the disqualification of a teacher." Nevertheless by the end of 1935 twenty-one states, including New York itself, had adopted such legislation.

But for the New Deal the economic crisis would have paralyzed countless school systems from lack of local revenues. The PWA between 1933 and 1940 contributed $481,500,000 toward constructing and improving nearly 13,000 educational buildings, including those of colleges, and the NYA, as has been seen, did its part by helping needy students. Nevertheless, thanks to the falling birth rate, 250,000 fewer children were in school in 1940 than a decade before, though a record proportion—six out of seven of those eligible—were enrolled. Much remained to be done, however, for persons beyond school age, since among the population as a whole in 1940 over 10,000,000 adults had completed no more than four grades and 2,800,000 less than a year.

Like the schools, the colleges and universities issued from the sunshine of the twenties into the clouded thirties. Teaching suffered because of salary cuts, reduced staffs and diminished funds for libraries and laboratories. But after 1934, with New Deal subsidies and bettering times, enrollments, which had declined some eighty thousand since 1929, began to rise again, and by 1940 the full-time attendance reached nearly 1,500,000, which meant that one out of every six or seven eligibles was in college, a ratio unapproached in any other country. Throughout the university world the depression sharpened interest in social and economic questions. President Roosevelt's so-called Brain Trust was only a conspicuous instance of the greater activity of faculty members and college men in public life as speakers, technical advisers and officeholders. Undergraduates crowded the classes in economics, political science and sociology, and university authorities introduced systematic courses to train young men for government service.

Leading educators felt it necessary to defend the right of professors to interest themselves in controversial public issues. "The origin of the Constitution, for example, the functioning of the three branches of the Federal Government, the forces of modern capitalism," declared President James Bryant Conant at the Harvard Tercentenary in 1936, "must be dissected as fearlessly as the geologist examines the origin of rocks." But in many localities conservative trustees, prospective donors and influential businessmen, fearing professors even more than schoolmen, did not accept this principle. The oath laws commonly affected university instructors as well as other teachers; legislative investigations often had an intimidating effect; and according to a survey in 1936 of conditions since World War I, "More college professors have been dismissed or disciplined because of their views than in any other similar period in our history." Unwittingly, the repressive elements were seeking to enforce intellectual conformity by methods which the European dictators had developed to savage efficiency.

CREATIVE EFFORT AND THE USES OF LEISURE

Despite such deterrents the timeless search for truth continued to be a major function of higher education and on a greater scale than ever. The aggregate product cannot easily be summarized. According to an authority writing in 1940, American scientists had achieved world pre-eminence in astronomy, dentistry and neurosurgery and probably also in anatomy, physiology and certain branches of medicine. In medicine the greatest advance in the 1930's was the discovery of sulfa drugs, which worked miracles in dreaded infections like pneumonia, meningitis and trachoma. Though pioneered in Germany, these remedies were improved and applied to new uses in the United States. In physics some of the basic discoveries foreshadowed the practical utilization of atomic energy. The coveted Nobel Prize was bestowed on eleven American investigators in chemistry, physics, physiology and medicine between 1923 and 1939 as an international recognition of their contributions.

In the humanities and social sciences a series of large collaborative projects such as the *Dictionary of American Biography,* the *Encyclopaedia of the Social Sciences* and the *History of American Life* served to crystallize new points of view and stimulate students to fresh discoveries. The general public showed its interest by putting such historical works as Charles and Mary Beard's *Rise of American Civilization* (1927) and James Truslow Adams's *Epic of America* (1931) on the best-seller list. At the same time scholars in all parts of the country undertook investigations of American folklore, folk songs and folk speech, while historical societies intensified their efforts to exhibit the past to the present in museums, pageants and other displays, and the United States government made up for former negligence by establishing the National Archives in Washington in 1935 as a general depository for its official records. The government also restored numerous battlefield sites, ruined forts, famous houses and similar memorials of long ago. Between 1933 and 1940 the annual number of visitors at the national parks and shrines rose from 3,-000,000 to nearly 17,000,000. This varied and widespread interest was akin to a rediscovery of America.

Cutting across all branches of learning was a growing belief that minute specialization, notwithstanding its manifest advantages, was too often causing students to view their problems in limited terms, to blind them to the larger implications and interrelations. Research of the traditional kind was tending to breed mere technicians and fact-finders who, as the popular saying ran, were learning 'more and more about less and less.' To reverse the trend, the National Research Council, the American Council of Learned Societies and the Social Science Research Council were formed between 1916 and 1923. Backed by the nation's foremost scientists and scholars in the colleges and universities, these agencies set about to redirect intellectual ener-gies into broader channels and particularly to cultivate the borderlands between well-worked fields. The new emphasis was on the interde-pendence of knowledge. But not all original contributions emanated from academic centers. In the period between the wars the number of research workers in industrial laboratories grew fivefold, with upwards of $200,000,000 spent for this purpose in the single year 1940. Meanwhile the state and national governments increased their basic inquiries into matters affecting the general welfare, and the great edu-cational foundations, now rapidly multiplying, poured millions into exploring the unknown in many fields.

America's research effectiveness was further enhanced by gifted individuals driven from Europe by totalitarian tyranny. The first influx from Soviet Russia shortly after World War I was followed by a second from Fascist Italy in the mid-twenties and by a third and greater one from Nazi Germany and her conquered neighbors in the 1930's. These refugees included twelve Nobel Prize winners in science and other fields. As further evidence of their quality, over a hundred eventually attained admission to *Who's Who in America* and more than two hundred to *American Men of Science*. Along with research specialists, engineers, physicians, businessmen and lawyers came painters, sculptors, architects and musicians who, each in his own line, helped to fertilize the nation's cultural soil. Their homelands could ill afford this drain of talent which now redounded to America's advantage.

Notwithstanding these and other influences from abroad, the principal inspiration in the arts sprang from native sources. In every branch the practitioners strove to cast off threadbare conventions, experiment with fresh ways and impregnate their work with the meanings of American life. A keener aesthetic sense penetrated even the domain of industry as popular taste demanded that articles be beautiful as well as useful. The result appeared in a wide variety of wares—from motorcars, bathtubs and kitchen stoves to phonographs, book bindings and coffins. As another sign of the times the General Federation of Women's Clubs in 1927 persuaded a hundred and forty-seven national advertisers to stop the practice of defacing the landscape with billboards. The affluent twenties encouraged a lavish patronage of the fine arts—paintings, statuary and other art objects. Though the Great Depression abruptly altered the situation, the New Deal came to the aid of creative workers as well as of day laborers. The construction activities of the PWA and WPA afforded incidental employment to thousands of architects, sculptors and mural painters, and the Federal Arts Project, established in 1935, expressly extended the work-relief program to artists, musicians, actors and the like. Accordingly, artistic expression, instead of withering, blossomed in new soil with the accomplishments frequently perpetuated in schools, libraries, hospitals, post offices and other public buildings. Some fifteen hundred murals and thirty-five hundred sculptures were produced by WPA workers alone. The average man, even in remote rural towns, became aware of better aesthetic standards.

The outstanding leaders in the fine arts were more numerous in these two decades than ever before in the United States, and the work of high quality was also greater. In sculpture World War I produced a multitude of memorial monuments which in their chaste dignity and pictorial effectiveness made those of the Civil War appear stiff and stodgy. Typical of the American's liking for doing things on a large scale was Gutzon Borglum's colossal project, begun in 1927, of carving the heads of Washington, Jefferson, Lincoln and Theodore Roosevelt on the granite front of Mt. Rushmore in the Black Hills of South Dakota. In painting, a significant new source of support came from commercial concerns which employed artists to adorn their walls, as if to demonstrate that business had a soul above material gain. These murals, as in the Chicago Merchandise Market and the Groos Bank at San Antonio, portrayed historical developments culminating in recent economic progress. But the trends in painting were many. Under Europe's influence a predilection for primitivism seized some of the workers, who sought to reach behind externals of appearance to the essences of mass, color and design. Still others, revolting against this depersonalized 'abstract art,' chose to delineate their American surroundings with fidelity to simple everyday fact, an attitude exemplified by Charles R. Sheeler's technological studies, Thomas H. Benton's rural scenes and William Gropper's pictures of politicians, strikers and lynchers. Benton spoke for this large and growing school when he said, "American art can be found only in the life of the American people."

In architecture the principal innovation was the fashioning of the skyscraper into an object of impressive beauty. This came about by chance, as it were, when New York City, in order to save pedestrians from perpetual twilight, required tall buildings after 1916 to be constructed in tiers receding successively from the street as greater heights were reached. This 'setback' style quickly revealed artistic possibilities that caused other cities to copy it. The terraced or steplike effect was strangely reminiscent of Mayan architecture. Ironically enough, the highest building of all—New York's Empire State, soaring 102 stories—was completed in 1931 as the economic system was rapidly crumbling. In erecting its "Cathedral of Learning" the University of Pittsburgh adapted the skyscraper to educational uses, and Nebraska and Louisiana obeyed a like impulse in putting up their new capitols.

If musical composition lagged behind the other arts, musical appreciation attained dimensions hitherto unknown. This was due to several factors: an improvement of taste that had long been under way; the stimulus of free municipal concerts, which greatly increased in number during the 1920's; the WPA's sponsorship of orchestral and vocal performances in the 1930's; and, most of all, the influence of the radio. Though broadcasting stations at first confined themselves to popular tunes, they soon discovered an appetite for serious compositions. As early as 1926 the New York Symphony Orchestra occasionally went on the air; and its regular Sunday afternoon concerts, begun four years later, reached millions of listeners who seldom, if ever, had heard music of high quality. In 1931 the NBC went further by broadcasting the Metropolitan Grand Opera Company each week. So genuine was the public's interest that in 1940, when the Metropolitan needed $1,000,000 to keep going, the unseen audience contributed a third of the amount. In its first years the radio threatened the phonograph with virtual extinction; but as the popular education in music proceeded, more and more people responded to the phonograph companies' appeal to hear "what you want when you want it." The sale of records of the biggest concern multiplied six times between 1933 and 1938. Moreover, as Deems Taylor, music critic and composer, remarked in the latter year, "The staple moneymakers of the record dealer today, outside of his dance records, are albums—recordings of entire symphonies, suites, string quartets, even entire operas—a condition that was unthinkable fifteen years ago." As another indication of this trend, symphony orchestras increased from seventy-three in 1929 to two hundred and seventy in 1940.

Most of the music issuing from the radio and phonograph, however, was of a more ephemeral sort. Soon after the war the public's earlier addiction to ragtime gave way to jazz—which Paul Whiteman, one of its ablest exponents, termed the "folk music of the machine age" —and when jazz tended to lose its spontaneity, it was succeeded by a madder form of improvisation known as swing. If the extreme examples fell on older ears like a dissonant blare, the younger generation found in these innovations a release for their inhibitions, while the musicianly possibilities were developed in serious compositions like George Gershwin's "Rhapsody in Blue" and William Grant Still's "Afro-American Symphony." Light opera also exhibited fresh vitality, and in composers like Irving Berlin, Jerome Kern, Cole Porter and Sigmund Romberg the age found worthy successors to Reginald De Koven and Victor Herbert. Though musical comedies were of many kinds, the popular mood in the 1930's took particular delight in those that satirized the state of the nation. Gershwin's "Of Thee I Sing" and Richard Rodgers's "I'd Rather Be Right," two of the best, directed mocking shafts at Congressmen, cabinet officers, Supreme Court justices and other notables.

The legitimate stage had to learn to live with its two lusty rivals: the screen and the radio. The number of road companies fell off, and theatrical performances tended more and more to be restricted to metropolitan centers. The players, however, often found themselves in greater demand than before, for if Hollywood did not want them, the radio gave them an opening. Similarly, playwrights and musicians

REFUGEE CHILDREN FROM BELEAGUERED ENGLAND, JULY, 1940

See page 420.

Courtesy of Press Association, Inc.

IN THE WEST (WORLD WAR II)

Courtesy of Press Association, Inc.

IN THE EAST (WORLD WAR II)

GLOBAL WARFARE
See pages 447 and 452.

discovered new outlets for their talents. Though comedians were the chief beneficiaries, some of the ablest actors, including Helen Hayes, James Cagney and Paul Muni, took advantage of the triple opportunity. Katharine Cornell, the first lady of the theater, was one of the few to retain an undivided loyalty to the stage. In the depression years the WPA's Federal Theater Project provided work for thousands of performers in stock companies, historical pageants, vaudeville units, circuses and puppet shows traveling through every state. Between 1935 and its discontinuance in 1939 it presented over a thousand plays to a total audience of nearly forty million, and helped to develop actors and dramatists who later made good in the commercial theater.

The favorite themes of playwrights in these two decades closely paralleled those in fiction. In the 1920's the disillusionment with war found expression in such dramas as Laurence Stallings and Maxwell Anderson's "What Price Glory?" while a throng of plays, including Marc Connelly and George Kaufman's "To the Ladies," Sidney Howard's "They Knew What They Wanted" and George Kelly's "Craig's Wife," sniped away at smug conventions and the gospel of success. Eugene O'Neill, by contrast, ceaselessly experimented with dramatic forms and technical devices and usually built his plots about primitive or repressed individuals. If his reach often exceeded his grasp, "The Emperor Jones," "Anna Christie," "Desire under the Elms" and other efforts of his were accounted among the best plays of the decade. In the 1930's the dramatists occupied themselves with the grim problems posed by the depression, thrusting their flashlights into the sunless crevices of society, and reporting the results in plays like Elmer Rice's "Street Scene," Clifford Odets's "Waiting for Lefty" and Maxwell Anderson's "Winterset." "Tobacco Road," dramatized by Jack Kirkland from Erskine Caldwell's novel of a depraved Southern tenant family, achieved the longest consecutive run yet known in the American theater. Also as in literature and doubtless for the same reason, history had its innings. Maxwell Anderson's "Valley Forge" and Robert Sherwood's "Abe Lincoln in Illinois" were notable among the offerings that recalled the valiant past.

In so far as the screen dealt with serious themes, it tended to follow the drifts of interest in the theater. This was not so apparent in the 1920's when the Hollywood magnates lavished millions on gaudy shows featuring adventure and sex, but even in that gilded age film plays like "What Price Glory?" (adapted from the stage) mirrored the unsentimental attitude toward war, while a host of other productions such as "The Covered Wagon" and "The Iron Horse" afforded veracious glimpses of bygone frontier days. In the next decade Hollywood, registering the change in popular mood, turned increasingly to social and economic problems, treating such subjects as prison abuses, miscarriages of justice, political knavery and the violation of civil liberties. Many of the pictures were based upon novels and stage plays, and it may be surmised that the movie versions of "Winterset," "The Grapes of Wrath" and the like heightened the social consciousness of countless persons who were neither book readers nor theatergoers. At the same time the emphasis in historical films changed from heroic episodes to famous men, with the Great Emancipator scoring three times in the "Abraham Lincoln" of Walter Huston, the "Young Mr. Lincoln" of Henry Fonda and the "Abe Lincoln in Illinois" of Raymond Massey. As an art form the motion picture steadily grew in stature. The occasional use of technicolor added to the sense of reality, but the principal innovation was Walt Disney's imaginative achievement in endowing animated cartoons with the semblance of life. Mickey Mouse, Donald Duck and Disney's other creations vied with flesh-and-blood stars for public favor.

Physical recreation also entrenched itself more firmly in American life. Though professional baseball and similar spectacles continued to draw immense crowds, more significant was the increased participation of the rank and file in outdoor sports. In many parts of the land municipalities provided athletic fields, golf courses, bathing beaches and other facilities for their citizens, and a growing number of communities employed trained persons to plan and direct recreational activities. The Great Depression vastly expanded the nation's equipment for play. At a time when more people were idle than ever before, the New Deal spent millions on parks, beaches, tennis courts, baseball diamonds, swimming pools and the like. In a new sense the country awakened to the value of sport, for sport itself was becoming democratized.

FULLER ACCOUNTS

New Design for Living. Most of the topics in this chapter are treated in President's Research Committee, *Recent Social Trends,* and in such historical accounts as Allen, *Only Yesterday* and *Since Yesterday;* Beards, *America in Midpassage;* Slosson, *Great Crusade and After;* and Wecter, *Age of the Great Depression;* while Carskadon and Modley, *U. S. A.,* resorts to graphic presentation, and Rogers and Allen, eds., *I Remember Distinctly,* affords a pictorial review. For urban development, see Adams, *Town and City Planning;* McKenzie, *Metropolitan Community;* Odum and Moore, *American Regionalism;* and Stone and others, *City Manager Government;* and, for modes of travel, Burlingame, *Engines of Democracy;* Morris, *Not So Long Ago;* and Smith, *Airways.*

Labor in Upheaval. Supplementing Dulles's general survey in *Labor in America* are Brooks, *Unions of Their Own Choosing,* and Harris, *Labor's Civil War,* and, in respect to agricultural workers, Raper and Reid, *Sharecroppers All,* and McWilliams, *Factories in the Field.*

New Social Trends. Asbury, *Great Illusion,* and Harrison and Laine, *After Repeal,* summarize the new restrictions on the liquor traffic. La Farge, ed., deals with *The Changing Indian;* Embree, *American Negroes,* Frazier, *Negro in the United States,* Key, *Southern Politics,* and Myrdal, *American Dilemma,* fill out Franklin's briefer discussion in *From Slavery to Freedom;* while McWilliams, *Brothers under the Skin,* covers both races. For religious tendencies, consult Garrison, *March of Faith,* and Sperry, *Religion in America.*

Intellectual Mainsprings. Ernst, *First Freedom,* Lee, *Daily Newspaper in America,* and Mott, *American Journalism,* describe journalistic trends. Morris, *Not So Long Ago,* includes a discussion of the radio and the motion picture, with fuller treatments available in White, *American Radio;* Inglis, *Freedom of the Movies;* Jacobs, *Rise of the American Film;* and Thorp, *America at the Movies.* For literary development, turn to Beach, *American Fiction;* Kazin, *On Native Grounds;* Mott, *Golden Multitudes;* and Spiller and others, eds., *Literary History of the United States,* II; and, for further insights into the American mentality, Butts, *The College Charts Its Course;* Curti, *Growth of American Thought;* Meyer, *Development of Education in the Twentieth Century;* and Morris, *Postscript to Yesterday.*

Creative Effort and the Uses of Leisure. Gray portrays *The Advancing Front of Science,* and Davie pictures the role of *Refugees in America,* principally those from Nazi Germany. Among accounts of the New Deal's cultural activities are Baker, *Government Aid to Professional, Technical and Other Service Workers;* Overmyer, *Government and the Arts;* and Whitman, *Bread and Circuses* (the Federal Theater). Other works concerned with cultural interests are Duffus and Keppel, *Arts in American Life;* Howard, *Our American Music;* Krutch, *American Drama since 1918;* Larson, *Art and Life in America;* and Morehouse, *Matinee Tomorrow;* while Dulles, *America Learns to Play,* is good for sports and amusements.

CHAPTER XIX

GOOD NEIGHBORS AND BAD

THE RETREAT FROM IMPERIALISM

THE New Deal involved a changed outlook in external as well as internal affairs. "In the field of world policy," Franklin D. Roosevelt declared in his first inaugural, "I would dedicate this nation to the policy of the good neighbor." This statement evidenced something more than the traditional attachment to peaceful international relations. It reflected the President's conviction that a stable world was vital to the success of his domestic measures for reform, and it foreshadowed a departure from the economic nationalism of his Republican predecessors. Unhappily for mankind, however, the year of Roosevelt's accession to office also saw Adolf Hitler's rise to power in Germany with diametrically opposed hopes and plans.

The Good Neighbor policy registered its greatest triumphs in the Western Hemisphere, where fears of Uncle Sam had long engendered distrust. For various reasons the administration's program toward this part of the globe won strong support both in and out of Congress. Mounting doubts as to the wisdom of America's earlier imperialistic ventures had come to a head with the Great Depression. Experience had shown that the recurrent interventions in the Caribbean and adjoining regions heightened the national tax load with advantages for no one save a few interested business and banking groups. Added to this, the intense concern with domestic problems made the country flinch from more distant responsibilities. The conviction crystallized that colonies and protectorates yielded more trouble and financial loss than profit or glory. The whole policy, moreover, violated the principles which had once caused the American people to seek independence from England. It seemed evident too that the ill will aroused in the Latin American republics by the actions of the 'Colossus of the North' had hampered trade. Better relations were desirable also because of America's increasing suspicions of Nazi designs on Latin America.

The retreat from imperialism began even before Roosevelt entered the White House. It scored its first signal success in the case of the Philippines, the former Spanish dependency off the Asian mainland. For years the feeling had been growing that this acquisition had been a mistake. The policy of the 'white man's burden' had conferred many blessings on the Filipinos, but it had not paid off in dollars and cents from the standpoint of the United States, and it had saddled Washington with a formidable problem of naval and military defense. After Wilson's Congress in 1916 had promised the people eventual liberation, the insular legislature yearly reminded the world of this fact by unanimously asking for immediate separation. President Coolidge in rejecting one of these resolutions in 1927 said that the best case for freedom was "not the argument that it would benefit the Filipinos"—which he denied—"but that it would be of advantage to the United States." In particular, American sugar growers had long objected to Philippine competition, and until 1913 had succeeded in maintaining restrictions on sugar imports from the islands into the United States. In like fashion American dairy producers found duty-free coconut oil interfering with their sales, while organized labor took alarm as the number of low-paid Filipino workers on the West Coast increased to forty-five thousand in 1930.

The advent of the depression gave the disgruntled elements just the leverage they needed for swinging Congress into line to execute President Wilson's pledge. In January, 1933, a Republican Senate and Democratic House passed over Hoover's veto a bill which set forth a specific plan of separation. These conditions, subject to the insular legislature's approval, involved the creation of a transitional "Commonwealth of the Philippines" to facilitate the adjustment of the islands' economic life to a status outside America's tariff walls. This stopgap government, popularly elected except for an American high commissioner, would forfeit by gradual stages the right to send duty-exempt sugar, coconut oil and hemp products to the United States. It must also limit emigration to an annual quota of fifty and allow America to manage its armed forces and foreign affairs. When independence should be attained in 1946, the United States was to be permitted to keep certain defense bases. Though the economic provisions entailed serious hardships for the islanders, the Philippine legislature rejected Congress's offer because of the proposed military controls. To remove this objection, the Tydings-McDuffie Act, passed by Roosevelt's Congress in 1934, agreed to surrender all army stations and to leave the question of naval ones to future negotiation. On May 1, thirty-six years to a day after Dewey's memorable victory at Manila Bay, the Philippine government unanimously accepted the revised terms. When Manuel Quezon was inaugurated president of the Commonwealth in November, 1935, he declared, "We are witnessing the final state of fulfillment of the noblest undertaking ever attempted by any nation in its dealings with a subject people." Unsuspected troubles loomed ahead, however. Unhappily, the Filipinos were to suffer temporary conquest by the Japanese before achieving their promised freedom.

Progress was also made in the Western Hemisphere in cleansing the United States of the stigma of imperialism. In 1930 the Hoover administration disavowed the Roosevelt Corollary—the earlier Roosevelt's claim that the Monroe Doctrine justified the Washington government in acting as a collecting agency for foreign creditors. The same year President Hoover began a six-year process of withdrawing the marines from Haiti, where they had been since 1915. In one of his last moves before leaving office he also recalled the marines who had been in Nicaragua since 1926. President Roosevelt greatly widened such efforts. Announcing that "The definite policy of the United States from now on is one opposed to armed intervention," he not only took all the marines out of Haiti by 1934, but he made a treaty with Cuba that year canceling the Platt Amendment and another with Panama in 1936 relinquishing the right of intervening in that country. In 1940 he also ended the American customs receivership of the Dominican Republic after thirty-five years.

Besides renouncing the protectorates, steps were taken to grant larger rights of self-government to America's Caribbean colonies. In 1936 Congress conferred the suffrage on all Virgin Islanders who could read and write English and increased the powers of the legislative assembly while retaining the American-appointed governor. This former Danish possession had lost population since its acquisition in 1917, largely because of the attractions of employment in the United States. President Hoover after a visit in 1931 had called it "an effective poorhouse." It continued important, however, as a link in the naval defenses of the Panama Canal. In the case of Puerto Rico, where the people since 1917 had elected their legislature, Congress in 1947 under President Truman bestowed the further right of electing the governor. Puerto Rico still fell short of statehood, however, since the islanders were allowed no voting members in Congress.

Toward Mexico, a perennially troublesome neighbor, the Roosevelt administration adopted a policy of forbearance, resisting pressure at home to deal sternly with that government for having expropriated many million dollars' worth of American-owned property. Under the constitution of 1917 Mexico had broken up the great agricultural estates and taken over foreign oil concessions. As a result, diplomatic relations from time to time underwent great strain. Washington did not deny Mexico's legal right so to act, but, in Secretary Hull's words, insisted on "prompt and just compensation" for the American owners. Finally, in 1938, the two countries set up a joint commission to decide the amount due for the agricultural lands, and an adjustment of the oil claims followed three years later.

The Good Neighbor policy was given still broader application through the extension of economic and other aid to the republics and through a series of collective treaties for closer political co-operation. Since 1926 the United States had furthered the interchange of military missions, and in 1937 it went so far as to lease some of its old war-ships to Brazil. The following year Congress provided for a cultural-exchange program and the sending to Latin America of experts in agriculture, engineering, library administration and other fields. In like manner the Export-Import Bank, originally set up during the depression to revive overseas trade, made loans to the southern countries between 1935 and 1939 totaling over $115,000,000.

The multilateral treaties, concluded between 1933 and 1938, aimed to prevent political and financial imperialism in the New World and to create a solid front against the dangers presented by the rise of totalitarianism abroad. In the case of the Buenos Aires conference in 1936 Roosevelt voyaged the twelve thousand miles to open the proceedings in person. The commitments went far. The nations pledged themselves to abstain from aggression and armed intervention in each other's affairs; to refuse to recognize any territorial advantages so gained; to refrain from the forcible collection of debts; to promote the principle of reciprocal-trade agreements which Secretary Hull was fostering in his own country; and to consult on a united course of action in case of war outside the hemisphere. The deeper import of these pacts lay in their bearing upon the historic policy of the United States toward Latin America. In effect, Uncle Sam after more than a century abdicated as sole interpreter and enforcer of the Monroe Doctrine. The Pan American Doctrine, to which Wilson had accorded partial recognition but which had slumbered during the 1920's, now sprang into full life. Henceforth the twenty-one nations of the New World stood on a plane of legal equality and assumed common obligations. The Good Neighbor policy had rewritten the Monroe Doctrine into something like a hemispheric doctrine of collective security. As the sequel was to show, this move for inter-American collaboration came just in time to raise a shield against an Old World once more convulsed with war.

THE ISOLATIONIST OFFENSIVE

While the idea of collective security flowered in the Western Hemisphere, it rapidly withered elsewhere before the chill blasts of international distrust and mutual antagonisms. In trying to bolster the wider system Roosevelt ran into insuperable obstacles at home because of the fear of becoming entangled in the mesh of Old World hatreds. In one respect, however, Congress backed his policy of improving world relations. It supported Secretary Hull's efforts to increase foreign trade, for these were expected also to contribute to domestic betterment. An act of 1934 authorized the President to alter tariff duties by as much as 50 per cent in return for reciprocal concessions from other countries. The object was to stimulate America's external commerce and at the same time lessen the causes of war by promoting a freer flow of goods among nations. The President was given the power to change rates, rather than Congress, in order to avoid the usual lobbying by pressure groups. Before the close of 1939 he had concluded executive agreements for cutting duties with twenty-one governments, including Great Britain and Canada, America's largest customers, as well as eleven Latin American republics. To broaden the effects of the agreements, the act stipulated that in every instance the benefits should extend to all other countries that did not discriminate against the United States. The reciprocal-trade policy excited criticism, especially among the farmers, but it justified itself in an expanding commerce. In the peace years from 1934 to 1939 American exports to nations in the program rose 63 per cent as against 32 per cent in the case of those not participating.

When Roosevelt proposed a bolder commitment in behalf of world peace, however, the result was different. Early in January, 1933, the outgoing Hoover administration had asked Congress for power to impose an arms embargo on aggressor nations and to make arms available to the victims as well as to countries joining in the sanctions. Roosevelt upon entering office urgently renewed the request. Though disclaiming any intention of becoming a member of the League of Nations, he wished nevertheless to bring about the closest possible co-operation with that body in the interests of peace. The House of Representatives acted favorably in April, 1933, but the Senate turned a deaf ear.

As kinsman of the first Roosevelt as well as political heir of Woodrow Wilson, the President desired to play a large role on the international stage, and seeing farther ahead than most of his countrymen, he sensed the growing perils that threatened the maintenance of peace. Since 1922 Benito Mussolini had been consolidating his power as Fascist dictator of Italy, abolishing self-government, annulling civil liberties and building up the army. Beginning in 1933 Adolf Hitler in Nazi Germany pursued a similar course with even greater ruthlessness. He not only destroyed the republic, but he persecuted Jews and Catholics, terrorized, killed or expelled political foes, and rearmed his people on a scale which boded ill for his peaceful neighbors. Both men had profited from the social despair which postwar hardships and the Great Depression had brought to their countries and, by turning industry to preparations for future war, found a means of beguiling the people with work and food. Each proclaimed undying hatred of free institutions while declaring the mission of totalitarian militarism to spread over all the earth. "The struggle between the two worlds," Mussolini shouted, "can permit no compromise." America, Hitler told an intimate, represented "the last disgusting death rattle of a corrupt and outworn system," her chance for greatness having been lost when the South's defeat in the Civil War prevented a "real master class" from sweeping away "the falsities of liberty and equality." The 'Rome-Berlin Axis,' formed in 1936, locked the Fascist and Nazi powers in firm embrace. On the other side of the globe Japan, jubilant over her conquest of Manchuria and nursing fresh designs against China, drew steadily closer to the Axis.

In the face of these developments the pillars reared in the 1920's to support the structure of international peace began to topple one by one. The League's failure to halt Japan's invasion of North China in 1931, followed by Italy's subjugation of Ethiopia in 1935, revealed the hollow pretensions of that body as a guarantor of peace. The fault lay partly at America's own door, for by failing to join the Geneva organization she could not exert her influence as the greatest non-European power to prevent little disputes from becoming big ones, nor could the League count on her co-operation in applying economic sanctions against aggressors. As for the Pact of Paris, that solemn pledge to outlaw war won ironic deference from predatory powers by causing them to wage war without declaring it. Another landmark collapsed when Japan declined to renew the Washington and London Naval Limitation Treaties, due to expire at the close of 1936. Hoping to save something from the wreckage, Great Britain, France and the United States made a treaty in 1936 imposing uniform restrictions on the size of their naval vessels and guns, but placing no top limits on the fleets and leaving the signers free to ignore any or all the provisions if necessary to meet competition by other countries. This agreement meant little because of the nonadherence of Japan and Italy, both already guilty of aggression.

The people of the United States observed this train of events with more distaste than dismay. It confirmed their feeling that the Old World was past reforming and that America should mind her own affairs. Moreover, the sharp decline in immigration had decreased the elements in the population who retained a direct and excitable interest in the doings of their homelands. Isolationist sentiment was intensified by doubts as to whether the country should have fought in 1917. The people, haunted by fears of economic insecurity, were in a mood of disillusion; and writers who absolved Germany of the sole or main guilt for the war found a sympathetic hearing, which was increased by the revelations of the Nye senatorial investigation in the mid-1930's that bankers, munitions makers and other 'merchants of death' had reaped immense profits from the conflict. To the thoughtful the disclosures fell far short of accounting for America's intervention, but the effect on the popular mind was profound. When a Gallup poll in April, 1937, just twenty years after the declaration of war, canvassed a cross-section of sentiment as to the wisdom of the nation's entry, 70 per cent pronounced it a mistake. Resentment against America's former comrades-at-arms was further deepened by their continued failure to make payments on their war debts to the United States. Though this default stemmed largely from the high tariffs which Congress had erected against foreign imports, the ordinary person did not perceive the connection and noted only the ability of the governments concerned to spend money on armaments.

As a result of these various factors, extreme isolationism seized the reins in Congress. Only in desiring to enlarge the navy within the limits allowed by the Washington and London treaties did the White House and the legislators see eye to eye. Beginning with the Vinson Act in 1934, Congress in the next few years voted the largest peacetime naval appropriations in the nation's history. The Johnson Act, also adopted in 1934, forbade the debt-defaulting governments to market securities in the United States until their obligations should be met. In 1935 the Senate, rejecting Roosevelt's plea "to throw its weight into the scale in favor of peace," refused to join the World Court. America's adherence had been repeatedly pledged by both political parties, but the Senate's favorable vote of 52 to 36 fell seven short of the treaty-ratifying majority.

With strange obtuseness to the deeper issues involved in the gathering storm abroad, the lawmakers next twisted the President's proposal to forbid the sale of munitions to an aggressor into legislation to apply the ban to the attacked as well as the attacker. They saw no national advantage in favoring one set of belligerents over another, but only the danger of embroilment. To accomplish their aim a series of laws in 1935–1937 reversed America's historic position as to neutral rights. The basic provision required that, whenever the chief executive should proclaim a "state of war," all shipments of arms, ammunition and implements of war to the combatants should cease. Certain restraints were also placed upon other trade and, in addition, citizens were forbidden to travel on belligerent merchant vessels or to make loans to the warring governments. This legislation was designed to avert the provocations which it was believed had thrust the United States into the war in 1917. In order, however, not to bar America's continued support of the Monroe Doctrine, the terms did not apply to hostilities between a Latin American republic and other countries. Though the regulations were originally restricted to international wars, Congress early in 1937 extended them to civil wars because of a Spanish insurrection which had broken out the preceding July.

Roosevelt signed the neutrality legislation but with mental reservations, as his course on the occasion of a new crisis in the Far East was to reveal. Before that time, however, he invoked the provisions in October, 1935, against both aggressor and victim when Italy undertook the conquest of Ethiopia. This, however, did more harm to Italy, who had ships and money with which to obtain arms from the United States, than it did to Ethiopia, who had neither. In May, 1937, he took a like stand in regard to the civil war in Spain, where the Loyalist government with some Russian help was waging a losing fight against Francisco Franco's rebel army, which was heavily reinforced from Axis sources. The denial of munitions to the duly elected republican regime brought protests from American liberals, who also pointed out that Franco's victory would provide Hitler and Mussolini with a friend. The administration's action may have sprung from fear of the voting strength of the American Catholics, who were generally pro-Franco; but, if so, no comparable domestic influence hampered the President when Japan in July, 1937, launched a new invasion of China.

Taking refuge in the fact that neither country had officially declared hostilities, Roosevelt declined to proclaim a "state of war" and thus sidestepped an application of the neutrality regulations. By so doing he was, in effect, favoring the Chinese, who had to import most of their munitions, over the Japanese, who made most of theirs. As the struggle assumed ever bloodier proportions, the President's mind turned more and more to the desirability of collective action by the powers against Japan. Speaking in Chicago in October, 1937, he declared that, in the face of "those violations of treaties and those ignorings of humane instincts," "mere isolation or neutrality" was helpless. He compared the "state of international anarchy" to an epidemic of disease which only a quarantine could stop, and he asked peace-loving countries to act accordingly. On the next day the League of Nations formally pronounced Japan an aggressor and treaty breaker and summoned a conference to deliberate on appropriate measures. The only step upon which America and the eighteen other governments gathered at Brussels in November could agree was to reassert Japan's guilt as a violator of the Nine-Power Treaty and the Pact of Paris. A more decisive course was precluded both by Roosevelt's vagueness as to how far the United States would cooperate in a "quarantine" in view of the isolationist sentiment at home and by the unwillingness of England and France to let their energies be diverted from the lurking dangers in Europe.

As the Japanese, undeterred, continued on their career of conquest, Washington found increasing occasion for protest because of the infringement of American rights in China. Bombings with the loss of life and property, interferences with trade, and treaty infractions occurred time and again. An air attack on the United States gunboat *Panay* near Nanking in December, 1937—one of the more flagrant incidents—led Tokyo to apologize and pay an indemnity. In November, 1938, Japan exposed more of her hand by stating in effect that she would no longer recognize the Open Door in trade and industry, though, as Secretary Hull vigorously pointed out, she was bound by treaty to do so. Already in July the State Department had requested aircraft manufacturers to cease selling to the Japanese, and in 1939 this policy of 'moral embargo' was extended to materials essential for the making of planes. As another mark of displeasure, the United States in July, 1939, gave the required six months' notice for abrogating the treaty of 1911, which guaranteed "reciprocal freedom of commerce" between the two nations; but when the expiration date came, the President did not act. On further thought he feared the cancellation might provoke Tokyo into seizing the defenseless Dutch (or Netherlands) East Indies, which the United States was not prepared to prevent. Moreover, in the meantime a great conflagration had flamed up across the Atlantic, and as a result America was for the moment confronted with more pressing problems. Nippon, biding her time, hoped that Europe's misfortune might mean additional spoils for herself in the Orient.

WORLD WAR AGAIN

Roosevelt's Chicago speech in 1937, while aimed directly at Japan, referred unmistakably also to Hitler's menacing course on the other side of the globe. "The peace, the freedom and the security of ninety per cent of the world," the President said, "is being jeopardized by the remaining ten per cent, who are threatening a breakdown of all international order and law." Germany as well as Japan declined to attend the Brussels conference, and in the next two years the Nazi Fuehrer proceeded systematically to devour his helpless and unoffending neighbors. At first announcing the intention merely of uniting all Germans in a common country, he soon surrendered to the sheer lust for conquest. In March, 1938, he annexed Austria. In September, with England and France assenting to what in any case they felt powerless to prevent, he seized Sudetenland, the German-inhabited section of democratic Czechoslovakia. In March, 1939, he

HITLER'S RISE TO POWER

1933

Jan. 30, Hitler is appointed Chancellor by President Paul von Hindenburg.

Feb. 27, a fire (attributed by many to the Nazis) burns the Reichstag building. A reign of terror against Communists, Jews and liberal political parties follows.

March 5, elections give Hitler an overwhelming majority in the Reichstag.

April 1, he orders a nation-wide boycott against the Jews.

Oct. 14, he withdraws from the World Disarmament Conference.

Oct. 21, he takes Germany out of the League of Nations.

1934

Jan. 26, Hitler signs a ten-year non-aggression pact with Poland.

June 30, he stages a 'blood purge,' executing many Nazis and anti-Nazis.

Aug. 2, President Hindenburg dies and Hitler combines the posts of Chancellor and President.

1935

March 16, Hitler denounces the Versailles Treaty and reintroduces compulsory military service.

June 18, he signs a treaty with Britain limiting the German navy to 35 per cent of Britain's surface craft and to 45 per cent of her submarines.

1936

March 7, German troops enter the demilitarized Rhineland.

Oct. 23, the Rome-Berlin Axis is formed.

Nov. 25, Germany and Japan sign an anti-Comintern pact.

1937

Oct. 13, Hitler pledges Germany to respect Belgian neutrality.

Nov. 6, Italy joins the anti-Comintern pact.

1938

Feb. 20, Hitler in a speech demands self-determination for the Germans of Austria and Czechoslovakia.

March 12, he takes over Austria.

Sept. 15, Prime Minister Chamberlain flies to Germany for the first of three meetings with Hitler during the Czechoslovakian crisis.

Sept. 30, Hitler wins the Sudeten area of Czechoslovakia at Munich, and he and Chamberlain announce the "desire of our two peoples never to go to war with one another again."

1939

March 14, Hitler annexes the rest of Czechoslovakia.

March 22, Lithuania surrenders Memel to him.

April 28, he denounces the Polish nonaggression pact and the British naval pact.

May 22, he signs a ten-year military alliance with Italy.

Aug. 23, he signs a nonaggression pact with Soviet Russia.

Sept. 1, he orders the invasion of Poland.

completed the rape of Czechoslovakia and intimidated Lithuania into ceding the city of Memel. Five months later he made a nonaggression pact with Soviet Russia, whose ideology he had hitherto denounced with even greater venom than he had that of the democracies. As events were to show, this was a marriage of convenience whereby the Germans ensured themselves against having to fight simultaneously in east and west, and the Russians gained time for building up their military strength. With whetted appetite Hitler now turned upon Poland, demanding Danzig and the Corridor, Poland's outlet to the sea. This last action finally convinced the British and French governments that their policy of 'appeasement'—of trying to placate Hitler through repeated concessions—was a failure. On September 3, 1939, two days after the Nazi armies crossed the Polish border, Great Britain and France declared war. Within a few weeks, before the Allies could get into action, Poland lay prostrate. Germany divided the country with the Soviet Union, which obtained the eastern half as pay for joining in the onslaught.

World War II found the American people better informed than in 1914. By means of the radio, the news films and the press they had followed Hitler's truculent career with gruesome fascination. They had listened to him thunder over the air waves against liberalism and representative government and vaunt his own despotic rule. They had sent money to bring in many Jews and other refugees whom the Fuehrer's barbarous treatment had driven from the fatherland. Along with other citizens, the vast bulk of Americans of Teutonic stock viewed the totalitarian regime with abhorrence and alarm. As the war had drawn closer, the President had repeatedly tried to stave it off by appeals to the Nazi and Fascist dictators against further acts of aggression. He saw the impending conflict as a catastrophe for all mankind, his own country as well as others. "When peace is broken anywhere," he declared, "it is threatened everywhere." During the Czechoslovakian crisis he informed Hitler, "I am persuaded that there is no problem so difficult or so pressing for solution that it cannot be justly solved by the resort to reason rather than by the resort to force."

Such pleas, however, had no effect, and Roosevelt began to consider other ways of making America's influence felt. In January, 1939, he told Congress, "There are many methods short of war, but stronger and more effective than mere words, of bringing home to aggressor governments the aggregate sentiments of our own people." A Gallup poll the next month indicated that 69 per cent of the country—more than two to one—favored supporting Britain and France by every means short of war. Thus the onset of the European conflict found American sentiment strongly behind the two powers which stood forth as the chief bastions of freedom in the Old World. As Roosevelt put the matter, "This nation will remain a neutral nation, but I cannot ask that every American remain neutral in thought as well. . . . Even a neutral cannot be asked to close his mind or his conscience."

The government took certain emergency steps. Ships were sped to Europe to bring home nearly a hundred thousand citizens who were stranded in the danger zone. Roosevelt next called Congress in special session to repeal the arms embargo, whose principal effect had been to convince Germany that Britain and France when at war would be unable to get military supplies from the United States. Notwithstanding stubborn and protracted opposition by the isolationists, mostly Republicans, he finally carried the day. The act of November 3, 1939, permitted sales of munitions and weapons to all nations paying cash and carrying them away in their own ships. As was intended, geographical proximity made this relaxation beneficial only to the Allies. Congress continued the earlier prohibitions against traveling on belligerent craft and lending to warring governments, and it also barred American vessels and travelers from areas of probable naval hostilities.

Meanwhile Roosevelt had brought about an inter-American conference to act jointly in face of the crisis. The Good Neighbor policy now yielded rich fruit. Assembling in Panama City late in September, 1939, the twenty-one republics established a 'safety zone' surrounding the Americas south of Canada and reaching 250 to 1250 miles out to sea, within which the warring powers were warned to refrain from hostile acts. This move, unprecedented in international law, depended for its effectiveness more on the combatants' willingness to respect the collective pronouncement than on the ability of its authors to enforce it. The belligerents, however, refused to admit its legality and declared that in any case they could not heed it because their enemies wouldn't. Within a few months several clashes occurred between Allied and German craft inside the area. The New World governments, speaking through the President of Panama, vehemently protested. In general, it was the British navy which kept Nazi activity in these waters to a minimum prior to America's own entrance into the conflict.

Economically the first effect of the struggle was to accelerate the upswing of business which had followed the recession of 1937–1938. Stocks advanced, production increased and prices rose. Events in the next few months, however, showed that the benefits were unevenly distributed. In the first half year of the war exports jumped a third over a year before, but the gains accrued to the producers of military materials, notably cotton, metals, aircraft, chemicals and metal-working machinery. Foreign orders for grains, fruits, tobacco and passenger cars, on the other hand, dropped sharply. It was not until some months later, when the United States began its own active defense preparations, that business generally started to boom.

After Hitler's initial Blitzkrieg against Poland the conflict entered a lull that lasted through the winter of 1939–1940. On the sea Britain tightened her blockade in order to keep essential materials from the enemy, and on land the fighting seemed a stalemate, with the armies facing each other behind massive fortified lines on the western front. Only Soviet Russia braved the winter by launching an unprovoked assault against the neighboring Finns, who presently succumbed after heroic resistance. In this period of what an isolationist Senator called the "phony war" American public opinion began to crystallize into three fairly defined attitudes.

The extreme isolationists, seeing no issue at stake either of national security or of ideology, wanted to 'sit out' the contest. They scoffed at the possibility of Nazi designs against the United States or the Western Hemisphere, branded their opponents 'warmongers,' and argued that in any event the invaders could best be repelled at the water's edge. In Charles A. Lindbergh, the former transatlantic aviator, they had an effective popular advocate, and they further extended their influence through the Hearst press, the *Chicago Tribune,* the *Saturday Evening Post* and the well-financed America First Committee, of which Robert E. Wood, a Chicago businessman and veteran of World War I, was chairman. In Congress they had spokesmen in men like Representative Hamilton Fish of New York and Senators Gerald P. Nye of North Dakota and Robert A. Taft of Ohio, who mustered unsuccessful Republican majorities against the President's measures "short of war." Here and there knots of recent German and Italian immigrants, some in secret conspiratorial bands, also lent aid to the isolationist cause, while the self-styled Christian Front, organized by Father Coughlin, added its mite out of admiration for Hitler's anti-Semitism. The Communists and their sympathizers, adopting the Moscow party line, likewise stridently condemned the 'imperialist' war and instigated strikes in defense plants.

At the opposite pole stood the interventionists who, judging the Axis dictators by both word and deed, saw the struggle as a world revolution of totalitarian despotism against the free way of life. They demanded immediate participation while Britain and France were still able to resist the Nazi juggernaut, rather than wait until America, fighting alone, might herself fall a victim. Most vocal along the Atlantic Seaboard, which felt keenly the importance of keeping the ocean safe against aggressors, they also had adherents in many other parts of the nation, notably the South.

Midway between these groups was the dominant sentiment of the country spearheaded by the White House. With every desire to stay out of the fray, Roosevelt nevertheless was bent on stretching neutrality to the utmost limits to befriend the democratic powers and on rearming the nation meanwhile against possible involvement. Like the interventionists he had no doubts as to the irrepressible conflict of ideologies; and unlike Woodrow Wilson, his predecessor in the similar period during World War I, he believed that a peace without victory for the Allies would be a victory without peace. Since his "quarantine" speech in 1937 he had repeatedly expounded the dangers of totalitarian aggression to world peace and human welfare. Addressing Congress in January, 1941, he eloquently summed up the case against the "new order of tyranny" in democracy's ideal of the Four Freedoms: freedom of speech, freedom of worship, freedom from want and freedom from fear. Headed by William Allen White, nationally known progressive Republican editor of Emporia, Kansas, a Committee to Defend America by Aiding the Allies carried on a widespread campaign to support the President's program.

Early in the spring of 1940 unexpected developments on the fighting front deeply affected American opinion and brought the chief executive fresh accretions of strength. The German Fuehrer, turning with lightning swiftness upon his weak neutral neighbors, caught the Allied high command unawares and began crashing his way toward France. Assisted by fifth-columnists in the invaded lands, the Nazi war machine pounded ahead with parachute troops, tanks, bombing planes and motorized infantry, overwhelming Denmark and Norway in April, the Netherlands, Luxemburg and Belgium in May. Then, unleashing his fury against France, Hitler quickly brought that nation to its knees. He garrisoned Paris and the northern part of the country, permitting the French elsewhere to organize a nominal government at Vichy and to retain control of their fleet. On June 10, just a week before France's surrender, Mussolini, hitherto a bystander, attacked that country from the southeast in order to qualify for a share in the spoils. The hard-pressed British, evacuating their troops from Dunkirk with terrific losses of men and equipment, were the next Nazi target, but Hitler, unprepared for a cross-Channel invasion, delayed following up his advantage. At this desperate moment England dropped the timorous Neville Chamberlain as Prime Minister for a great and strong leader, Winston S. Churchill, who grimly offered his countrymen "blood, toil, tears and sweat" as the price of victory. As the summer advanced and winter came, German aerial assaults on Britain, which began in force about six weeks after the collapse of France, mounted in intensity and ruthlessness, with the enfeebled Royal Air Force unable to reply effectively. Meanwhile Italy proceeded to threaten Britain's possessions in the Mediterranean and Red Sea areas.

THE ARSENAL OF DEMOCRACY

With a crippled Britain alone protecting the Atlantic against Axis domination, President Roosevelt undertook a series of bold steps "short of war," in most instances against the persisting opposition of a majority of the Republicans in Congress. Public-opinion polls, however, showed that despite isolationist clamor he enjoyed at every stage widespread popular support.

One set of measures looked to sealing the Western Hemisphere against the aggressors, since the Nazi conquests opened the way for taking over the New World possessions of France and other subject countries. Congress promptly resolved that the United States "would not recognize any transfer, and would not acquiesce in any attempt to transfer, any geographic region of this hemisphere from one non-American power to another non-American power"; and a conference of the twenty-one republics at Havana in mid-July, 1940, took similar action. As further insurance, the British with consent of the refugee Netherlands government in London occupied the Dutch West Indies; in 1941 the United States and Brazil with like authorization assumed protection of Dutch Guiana (Surinam) on the South American mainland; and at about the same time the United States alone, with approval of the Nazi-disowned Danish Minister in Washington, did the same for Greenland. The delegates at the Havana conference also agreed to suppress totalitarian propaganda and fifth-column activities in their countries, and in order to offset the loss of peace-

GREENLAND

CANADA

NEWFOUND-
LAND

★ St.
John's

Portsmouth
Boston
New York
Philadelphia

NOVA SCOTIA
Halifax (Br.)

U. S   Norfolk

Charleston

★ Bermuda

BAHAMA IS.
(Br.)

★ Mariguana I.

CUBA

San Juan (P.R.)
St. Thomas (V.I.)

Jamaica

HAITI

PUERTO
RICO

★ Antigua
● Martinique (Fr.)
★ St. Lucia

Panama
Canal
Coco Solo

Balboa

★ Trinidad

Georgetown

SOUTH

AMERICA

★ Naval and Air Bases leased
     September, 1940
◐ Major Naval Bases
● Naval Bases

time markets in Continental Europe they made plans for disposing of surplus foodstuffs and raw materials through closer commercial relations with one another. In September, 1940, the United States Congress followed up these actions by empowering the Export-Import Bank to lend $500,000,-000 to Latin American nations for the acquisition of strategic supplies and the expansion of defense industries; and early the next year the government effected a coordinated program of defense with Mexico, including airports and naval bases.

Even more important was the possible plight of Canada should England go under. As far back as 1938 Roosevelt had promised in a speech at Kingston, Ontario, "The people of the United States will not stand idly by if domination of Canadian soil is threatened by any other empire." In August, 1940, he united with the Canadian Prime Minister in setting up a Permanent Joint Board to plan defenses for the northern half of North America. In September came an even more daring stroke, dictated by Britain's dire need to combat the submarine peril: the transfer to that country of fifty old-model destroyers in exchange for ninety-nine-year leases on eight naval and air bases strewn all the way from Newfoundland to British Guiana. As part of the deal Churchill pledged his government not to sink or surrender its navy if Germany should win. The President, who had acted without Congress's knowledge, stated that he considered the acquisition of these "outposts of security" the most important addition to the national defenses since the Louisiana Purchase. The public accorded wholehearted approval. As a further shield against possible Nazi attack Roosevelt in July, 1941, arranged with the government of Iceland to take over the defense of that island from the British during the emergency.

The transfer of the destroyers was only part of the government's plan to fortify England's powers of resistance. During Hitler's frightening sweep through the Low Countries the administration by indirect sale had released to the Allies substantial stores of weapons—rifles, airplanes, heavy guns and trench mortars—left over from the last war. In November, 1940, Roosevelt announced that henceforth Britain would be allotted half the nation's production of military implements. The United States, as he put it later, must be the "arsenal of democracy."

All this had to be done while girding America herself for full participation should the contingency arise. To give the program a bipartisan character, Roosevelt in June, 1940, called two leading Republicans into his official family. Henry L. Stimson, a veteran of the Taft and Hoover cabinets, took over the War Department, while Frank Knox, Landon's teammate in the recent election, became Secretary of the Navy. By early November Congress had voted a total of nearly $18,000,000,000 for rearmament since the first of the year. Part of the money was for building a two-ocean navy, one powerful enough to meet the heightening dangers in the Pacific as well as the Atlantic. The bulk was for assembling an army of 1,200,000, expanding air strength to 35,000 planes, speeding up the manufacture of war supplies and enlarging the number of G-men to look after fifth-columnists.

In order to avoid the delay involved in recruiting volunteers, the Burke-Wadsworth Law in September, 1940, established compulsory selective service. The first peacetime conscription act in American history, it provided for registering all men between the ages of twenty-one and thirty-six, of whom eight hundred thousand should be annually chosen by lot for twelve months' training. A year later the limit on the number was removed, and the age span lengthened to take in everyone from twenty to forty-five. In November, 1942, after America's entry had emphasized the need, youths of eighteen and nineteen were added. Somewhat as in World War I, exemption or deferment was granted to important public officials, ministers, conscientious objectors, the physically and mentally unfit, men with dependents and those in occupations "necessary to the national health, safety or interest." To protect the men against undue economic hardship after their discharge, employers were required to rehire them without reduction of pay or loss of seniority standing.

As steps to expedite industrial mobilization the President, finding authority in Wilson's statute of 1916, created an Advisory Commission on National Defense of seven members familiar with the country's business, agricultural and labor resources; and Congress granted the government power to finance, lease, commandeer or build plants engaged in making war materials. To discourage profiteering on defense contracts, Congress imposed a tax of 25 to 50 per cent on excess corporate profits. Meanwhile on the humanitarian front the American Red Cross took the lead in European relief activities, sending vast quantities of medical supplies, ambulances, clothing, food and the like to the war-stricken countries. The public contributed generously to these efforts, and in July, 1940, Congress added $50,000,000. Especially noteworthy was the opening of American homes to English children whose parents wished to remove them from the widening area of death and destruction.

At this point matters stood when the voters went to the polls in November, 1940, for the national election. Meeting in Philadelphia on June 24, the Republicans had found their standard-bearer in Wendell L. Willkie, a Wall Street public-utilities lawyer and until recently a Democrat. Though an archenemy of the various New Deal electrification projects, he had as vigorously supported the administration's foreign policy, and this fact had evoked such enthusiasm among the Republican rank and file that, despite opposition from the old-line politicians, he won on the sixth ballot over District Attorney Thomas E. Dewey of New York, Ohio's Senator Robert A. Taft and Michigan's Senator Arthur H. Vandenberg, all of them more or less in the isolationist camp. Senator Charles L. McNary of Oregon, a farm spokesman, was named for Vice-President. Shattering precedent in a different way, the Democrats in Chicago on July 15 renominated Roosevelt for a third term on the first ballot, giving the second position to Henry A. Wallace of Iowa, the Secretary of Agriculture. Even more than in 1936, the rival platforms occupied common ground. Both declared for keeping America out of the war, for aiding Britain short of armed participation and for rendering the Western Hemisphere impregnable against attack. Regarding domestic matters, each promised to expand the government's social and economic services, though the Republicans engaged to do so while at the same time avoiding regimentation, a larger public debt or interference with private enterprise. The Republican platform concluded by advocating a constitutional amendment against a third term.

Willkie quickly gave the contest a whirlwind character, surpassing Bryan's record in 1896 by delivering nearly five hundred and fifty speeches in thirty-four states and talking constantly over national hookups. He criticized the administration's handling of defense, flailed the New Deal for bungling praiseworthy objectives and, as time went on, pounded increasingly on the dangers of a third term. If the people rejected that sacred custom, he cried, "our democratic system will not outlast another four years." The *Saturday Evening Post,* of a similar mind, warned the voters that they were deciding "the fate of free government." The President, contrary to his original intention, felt obliged to leave the White House in order to meet the Republican offensive blow for blow, and to that end he repeatedly reminded his hearers that most of the Republicans in Congress had fought both his reforms and his rearmament proposals. As in the last election, there was much crossing of party lines, marked by the activity of such groups as the No-Third-Term Democrats and the Republicans-for-Roosevelt. To add to the confusion, William Green of the American Federation of Labor and many other labor leaders came out for the President, while CIO's John L. Lewis, now Roosevelt's bitter personal foe, declared for Willkie. Both parties dodged the $3,000,000 limit upon expenditures fixed by the Hatch Act by having the state committees assume obligations hitherto borne by the national committees. According to a later Senate investigation, the Republicans spent about $15,000,000 and the Democrats $6,-000,000. Nearly 50,000,000 citizens, the most yet known, cast their ballots. Roosevelt won the 449 electoral votes of thirty-eight states, leaving Willkie with 82 from ten states. Of the popular ballots the President polled 54.7 per cent (27,243,000) to 44.8 per cent (22,-305,000), and the Democrats retained control of Congress. Not even the third-term tradition could prevail against the voters' conviction that, with the nation's security in peril, it was unwise to 'swap horses while crossing the stream.' Undoubtedly the Democrats were helped also by the general economic upturn caused largely by the flooding rearmament orders; by election day factory employment approached the peak of 1929.

Fortified by the popular endorsement, Roosevelt devised a plan to open still wider the "arsenal of democracy." The cost of the war had been so colossal that Britain was rapidly exhausting her funds for buying American military equipment. To repair this difficulty Congress, overcoming isolationist opposition both in and out of its doors, passed the Lend-Lease Act by decisive majorities in March, 1941. It authorized the chief executive to "sell, transfer title, exchange, lease, lend or otherwise dispose of" materials to "any country whose defense the President deems vital to the defense of the United States," and to permit these governments to refit their vessels in American ports. Congress made an initial appropriation of $7,000,000,000 to furnish ships, planes, tanks, ordnance, manufacturing facilities and industrial and agricultural products. Over the radio Roosevelt announced that "immediate, all-out aid" would be provided for Britain, Greece and China and for "all the governments in exile whose homelands are temporarily occupied by the aggressors." The lend-lease enactment by providing for direct government financing quietly bypassed the Johnson Act of 1934, which forbade private loans to the debt-defaulting countries of World War I, as well as the loan ban of the Neutrality Law of 1939. It aimed further to forestall a repetition of the debt difficulties that had followed the previous war.

Soon America had a new and unexpected applicant for lend-lease help. In June Hitler, with Hungary, Rumania and Finland as allies, loosed a surprise assault upon his Soviet partner. He had come to view Russia's military might as a huge sham and, having fiercely castigated Communism up to the time of the Berlin-Moscow Pact, he now returned to his earlier convictions. He believed that he could easily crush the Reds, acquire vast resources of oil and wheat and then give all his attention to the war in the west. The invasion progressed with astonishing speed, and since a Nazi triumph would have been disadvantageous to Britain and the United States, those governments had no choice but to bolster up the enemy of their enemy with all possible material aid. In America the Communists and their fellow travelers at once changed their tune, becoming now the most militant of interventionists. More important was the fact that they ceased to foment strikes and sabotage in defense industries.

It was partly to canvass this new turn of affairs that Roosevelt and Churchill met secretly in mid-ocean to hold the first of what was to prove a succession of personal conferences. There, off the shores of Newfoundland under a protective screen of airplanes, they examined the plans for lend-lease and framed a joint statement of principles concerning the peace. The Atlantic Charter, made public on August 14, set forth the following goals: no aggrandizement, territorial or otherwise; the right of all peoples to retain their traditional boundaries and choose their forms of government; the fullest possible co-operation among nations to assure equal access to trade and raw materials and to bring about improved living standards and "freedom from fear and want"; an unhindered use of the seas; the disarming of the aggressor powers; and the creation of a "permanent system of general security" to replace force in international relations. The declaration, if somewhat less specific than Wilson's Fourteen Points, recalled that historic pronouncement; but in the manner of promulgation there were two significant differences. Roosevelt took his stand before, rather than after, entering the war; and he avoided another of his predecessor's blunders by committing Britain in advance to the same purposes. Within six weeks the Soviet Union and nine governments in exile added their signatures.

Meanwhile the lend-lease shipments had been encountering difficulties because of the submarine menace. The principal supply route ran near Greenland and Iceland, and it was partly for this reason that the United States had occupied these islands. A naval patrol also helped to protect the 'bridge of ships' as far as Iceland, where British warships took over for the rest of the way. Nevertheless, American-owned freighters, some under the flag of Panama because of the Neutrality Law, began to be torpedoed and sunk without provision for the safety of those aboard, and early in September, 1941, the mail-carrying destroyer *Greer* was unsuccessfully attacked on its way to Iceland. Reporting these "acts of international lawlessness" to Congress a few days later, Roosevelt declared that henceforth naval vessels and planes

would shoot on sight. But the assaults continued on both merchantmen and naval craft, the destroyer *Kearny* being damaged with the
death of eleven sailors in October and another, the *Reuben James,*
sent to the bottom two weeks later. Hence in mid-November Congress,
at the President's urging, sanctioned the arming of merchant ships
and authorized them to carry cargoes to belligerent ports in combat
zones. This series of precautions ensured the delivery of the bulk of
the materials.

THE WAR ENGULFS AMERICA

Many of these moves were sufficiently unneutral to have caused
Hitler to declare war; but the Nazi Fuehrer had himself trampled
upon too many neutral rights to be sensitive on the point, and in
any event, with Britain and Russia putting up a far stiffer resistance
than had been expected, he had nothing to gain and much to lose by
taking on a new war. Instead, the Axis governments tried to confuse
American opinion and obstruct action by assisting isolationist and
appeasement propaganda. In June, 1941, the President wiped out the
principal sources of contagion by closing the Nazi and Fascist con-
sulates, deporting their personnel, and freezing all German and
Italian assets in the United States. Hitler's other great hope lay in
diverting America's energies by a war in the Pacific. For this undertaking he had a willing confederate in the Tokyo government, which
had its own vaulting ambitions to satisfy.

Though the Japanese after three years of fighting were still far
from subduing the Chinese, Hitler's European conquests offered
Nippon new opportunities for aggression by orphaning the Dutch and
French possessions in the Far East. Even before the Nazi seizure of
the Netherlands the Tokyo authorities had raised questions about the
future of the Dutch East Indies to which their country was "economically bound by an intimate relationship." These islands, half the size
of Europe and including Java, Sumatra and large sections of Borneo
and New Guinea, had been in Dutch hands for three centuries and
were the source from which the United States drew its principal supplies of rubber and tin, so essential for the nation's industries and
defense. On April 17, 1940, Secretary Hull countered Japan's overtures by bluntly asserting that a forcible change of ownership would
jeopardize the "stability, peace and security" of the entire Pacific area.
Again in May, after the motherland's downfall, Japan raised the point,

and again he reminded her of her pledge in the Four-Power Treaty of 1922 not to disturb the colonial status quo. Japan, unimpressed, announced in June what her Foreign Minister called a "Japanese Monroe Doctrine" for East Asia and the South Seas, declaring this region a single economic sphere under Tokyo's "stabilizing power."

The White House on the pretext of defense needs now took the long-delayed step of placing restrictions on the shipment of high-grade aviation gasoline and certain kinds of scrap iron and steel outside the Western Hemisphere. Toward the end of September, as Tokyo began putting its intentions into effect by sending troops into French Indo-China with the extorted consent of the Vichy government, Roosevelt clamped down a complete embargo, effective October 16, on all scrap iron and steel to Japan. The island empire had obtained 90 per cent of these vital military materials from America in 1939. As a further rebuke the United States lent $25,000,000 to China, bringing the total of such loans since 1938 to about $69,000,000. On September 27, 1940, Tokyo met this increasing pressure by making a ten-year military alliance with Germany and Italy, which recognized Japan's hegemony in "Greater East Asia" and pledged united action against any country (other than Russia, then still an ally of Hitler's) that might attack any of them. It was a gun pointed at America. By forming the Rome-Berlin-Tokyo Axis, Nippon hoped to gain her ends either by frightening Washington into concessions, or by making sure that, if this did not work, the United States would be hampered by having to fight a European as well as an Asian war. Hull promptly warned American citizens in Japan to hasten home; and the government, guarding against a future deprivation of rubber and tin, proceeded to increase the stocks on hand and to try to develop additional sources of supply in both the United States and South America.

The new year saw a steady worsening of relations. Exchanges between Tokyo and Washington showed that the viewpoints of the two governments were poles apart and impossible to reconcile. Nippon would not relinquish her predatory designs, and the United States could not assent to her violation of collective treaties and to her contention that might makes right. In July, 1941, Roosevelt froze all Japanese assets in the United States. In August, after Japan had acquired a springboard for fresh conquests by occupying all French Indo-China, he informed her that any further acts of aggression would compel him to take "any and all steps" necessary for protecting American rights and "insuring the safety and security of the United States." A few days later Prime Minister Churchill told the House of Commons that, if the President's warning went unheeded, "we shall, of course, range ourselves at the side of the United States." In November, Tokyo made a last pretense of preserving good relations by sending a special envoy to Washington in the person of Saburo Kurusu. On November 10, a week after he left the homeland, the Japanese task force to demolish the great naval base at Pearl Harbor in Hawaii set forth secretly by way of the Kurile Islands. While Kurusu and the Japanese Ambassador were closeted with Secretary Hull on Sunday afternoon, December 7, the news arrived of the early morning attack by bombing planes from offshore carriers. The United States contingents, caught tragically napping, lost most of their aircraft on the ground, along with the destruction or disabling of eight battleships and other vessels in the harbor and the killing or wounding of nearly forty-six hundred men. The foe had struck treacherously, swiftly and decisively. The same day other enemy forces assaulted the Philippines, Guam and Wake and Midway islands as well as Britain's colonies of Hong Kong and Malaya. By crippling America's naval power in the Pacific, Tokyo believed it had cleared the way for realizing its dream of a Japan-dominated Asia.

In tense excitement Congress the next day listened to the President denounce the "unprovoked and dastardly attack"—a "date which will live in infamy"—and then with a single dissenting vote declared that war existed with Japan. On December 11 her two European partners declared war on the United States, and Congress responded unanimously. Public opinion reflected almost equal unity. Those whom the iron logic of distant events had failed to convince were now confronted by aggression against their own territory and people. In previous world conflicts America had fought to safeguard the Atlantic against predatory powers; this time she faced formidable dangers on both oceans. Moreover, the ideological challenge was more brazen than at any earlier time. To Prussian militarism, against which President Wilson had taken up arms, was added totalitarian tyranny which, in Asia as well as Europe, demanded the extinction of free institutions: self-government, equal opportunity, political and social diversity, and the right to live at peace. It was clear that in a world reduced by science and technology to the dimensions of a neighborhood no nation was safe unless all were safe.

A second conference of Roosevelt and Churchill, this time in the White House, brought about a joint declaration by the Axis-resisting powers on January 1, 1942, under the name of the United Nations. The twenty-six governments endorsed the Atlantic Charter, pledged full co-operation in waging hostilities and agreed not to make a separate armistice or peace. Three other countries added their signatures later in the year. Two weeks after the cementing of the wartime coalition a gathering at Rio de Janeiro of the foreign ministers of the twenty-one American republics subscribed to the Atlantic Charter and advised a severance of all diplomatic and economic relations with the enemy powers. The nine Caribbean and Central American countries already in the United Nations had declared war immediately after Pearl Harbor, and Mexico and Brazil followed suit by the middle of the year. All the other countries save Chile and Argentina speedily broke off diplomatic relations. Even these two granted the United States navy special rights in their ports and in the end also severed relations with the Axis, Chile in January, 1943, and Argentina a year later. Before the close of the conflict, however, all Latin America was officially in the fight, although Argentina, where anti-Yankee feeling combined with domestic Fascist tendencies to delay action, did not take the step until March, 1945, when the struggle was all but over. In general, those countries most easily defended by American sea power were the quickest to act.

FULLER ACCOUNTS

The Retreat from Imperialism. For the Philippines, see Hayden, *Philippines,* and for the Western Hemisphere, Bemis, *Latin American Policy of the United States,* and Guerrant, *Roosevelt's Good Neighbor Policy.*

The Isolationist Offensive. Beckett reviews *The Reciprocal Trade Agreement Program,* while America's diplomatic moves in regard to the developing war situation abroad are discussed from various angles in Perkins, *America and Two Wars;* Feis, *Road to Pearl Harbor;* Borchard and Lage, *Neutrality for the United States;* and Davis, *A Navy Second to None.*

World War Again. Haines and Hoffman, *Origins and Background of the Second World War,* Langsam, *The World since 1914,* Quigley, *Far Eastern War,* Nevins, *New Deal and World Affairs,* and Nevins and Hacker, eds., *United States and Its Place in World Affairs,* provide a general setting. For the differing American attitudes toward the war, consult Lavine and Wechsler, *War Propaganda and the United States;* Johnson, *Battle against Isolation;* Myers, *Bigotry in the United States;* Derounian, *Under Cover;* Sayers and Kahn, *Sabotage!;* and Oneal and Werner, *American Communism.*

The Arsenal of Democracy. Rauch, *Roosevelt from Munich to Pearl Harbor,* a systematic account, should be supplemented by Sherwood, *Roosevelt and Hopkins,* and Gunther, *Roosevelt in Retrospect.*

The War Engulfs America. Besides many of the references already cited, Millis, *This is Pearl!,* traces the final steps of involvement.

Freedom of Speech   *Freedom of Religion*

CHAPTER XX

AMERICA IN WORLD WAR II

THE WAR AND THE PEOPLE

THE American people faced the struggle grimly. The older generation had fought World War I only to be disappointed in their dream of a durable peace. The younger generation, just beginning to find their feet after the ordeal of the Great Depression, saw the conflict simply as an unwelcome necessity. There was none of the glamour or exhilaration attaching to earlier wars. The issues at stake, however, fused all classes and sections into unexampled unity and prepared them for the utmost sacrifices. The pattern of total war set by the Axis surpassed that in the previous world conflict and meant that civilians as well as soldiers must become cogs in a well-oiled, high-powered, centrally run machine to a degree hitherto unknown in American history.

Thanks to the upsurge of patriotism, the authorities found little need to invoke the drastic penalties against sedition which Congress had adopted at the time of the fall of France. The so-called Alien Registration Act of 1940, dealing only incidentally with the registering of aliens, forbade all Americans to incite disaffection in the armed forces, or to teach or advocate the forcible overthrow of "any government in the United States," or to belong to an organization which taught or advocated the overturning of government. This last clause involved the doctrine of guilt by association in defiance of the ancient principle of Anglo-American law that guilt must be personal. There was, however, no hysteria or witch-hunting by the authorities or the public during the period of hostilities, such as had occurred during World War I. This was due partly to the fact that no political group, like the Socialists in 1917, took an extreme antiwar line, but it was due even more to the self-restraint of the Department of Justice and its agents, who allowed obstructive critics the largest possible scope. Open discussion of all aspects of national policy proceeded practically unmolested, though the Postmaster-General found it necessary to withhold mailing privileges from some periodicals of a subversive tendency, including *Social Justice,* Father Coughlin's organ. The American Civil Liberties Union, whose director had been jailed as a conscientious objector in the earlier conflict, rejoiced that "our democracy can fight even the greatest of all wars and still maintain the essentials of liberty."

Moreover, enemy aliens gave little trouble. As a precautionary measure the government dissolved the German-American Bund, an organization subsidized by Nazi funds, and deprived some of its foreign-born members of citizenship. But of over 300,000 unnaturalized Germans it proved necessary to intern only 1715; and of nearly 700,000 unnaturalized Italians, only 242. Acts of spying and sabotage were few and insignificant. The most sensational incident was the arrest and conviction of eight trained German saboteurs in 1942 shortly after two submarines had secretly landed them on the Atlantic Coast. The Japanese posed a special problem, not because of active treachery but because of the supposed risks due to their concentration in the Pacific Coast military zone. Some 110,000, of whom more than two out of three were native-born citizens, were herded into relocation centers outside the prohibited area—an emergency action the harshness of which was later somewhat softened by permitting those of proved loyalty to remove to other parts of the country and even to join the armed forces. After the war, in 1948, Congress established a claims commission to settle the losses suffered by the evacués. In the strategic outpost of Hawaii, where a still greater number of persons of Japanese stock were to be found, they were subjected to relatively few restraints and in general justified this confidence in their trustworthiness.

Immediately after hostilities began, the President appointed Byron Price, an Associated Press executive, as Director of Censorship to pass upon all mail, radio and other communications going overseas. The task was enormous, busying some ten thousand employees who deleted references to military and naval movements, details of industrial production, air-raid precautions and even the state of the weather. At home the press and radio undertook a voluntary self-censorship in co-operation with the government. At first the function of divulging official war news was divided among a group of agencies, but in June, 1942, it was centered in the Office of War Information, headed by

Elmer Davis, a widely respected radio commentator. As part of its activities the OWI broadcast twenty-fours hours a day in twenty-four languages to Europe, Africa and Asia, and prepared printed matter for foreign distribution. This phase of the program was of the nature of 'psychological warfare,' designed to impair enemy morale, keep alive resistance movements in Nazi-conquered lands and counteract Axis efforts to sow dissension among the Allied peoples.

Congress, spurred by the disaster at Pearl Harbor and the demands of global warfare, voted stupendous sums for the struggle. In the peace years 1935–1938 military appropriations had approximated $3,000,000,000; in the three years after July 1, 1940, they jumped to $110,000,000,000. By June, 1943, the monthly outgo was $7,700,-000,000—nearly twice the entire cost of the Civil War to the federal government. In the first half year of 1944 the disbursements (almost $42,000,000,000) exceeded the entire cost of World War I by $17,-000,000,000. Though taxes of all kinds were hoisted from time to time and the number of persons paying income taxes was enlarged from four million in 1939 to seventeen in 1941, nearly three fifths of the money came from borrowing. For this purpose bonds were sold in denominations as low as $25 and savings stamps for as little as ten cents. Seven special drives, all oversubscribed, helped to swell the sales.

Thanks to peacetime conscription, the army was already expanding rapidly when hostilities commenced. By October, 1942, it numbered 4,250,000, and by May, 1945, at the time of Germany's surrender, 8,300,000, two thirds being then overseas. To prepare for the job ahead, camps, airfields, ordnance depots and other training centers thickly dotted the land. At such places the men took a twelve-to-seventeen weeks' basic course, after which those especially qualified were given more specialized instruction, some in officer candidate schools. The amazing improvement in prewar educational facilities was reflected in the fact that 14 per cent of the soldiers were college men and 43 per cent had attended high school, as compared with 5 and 15 respectively in General Pershing's army. Both the War and Navy Departments also used the colleges and universities for advanced training. About 140,000 soldier students and 76,000 navy men were taking such courses on more than two hundred campuses in 1943, thereby incidentally enabling the institutions to offset some of the financial losses from declining civilian enrollments. Because of the pressing need on the various fighting fronts, however, most of the army students were withdrawn in the spring of 1944.

The navy, which at first relied solely upon volunteers, began to make use of the Selective Service System late in 1942 in order to meet the accelerated demand due to the completion of new ships. The personnel increased from 325,000 at the time of Pearl Harbor to 3,389,000 at the war's close, while the number of vessels rose from 4500 (including 346 combat ships) to 91,209 (including 1171 combat ships). Among the newer types of boat were the LCI (landing craft for infantry), the LCT (landing craft for tanks) and the carrier or 'flat top,' which served as a floating base for warplanes. Meanwhile the number of aircraft grew from a mere 8000 to about 120,000. The famous B-29 had a wing spread of 141 feet and could fly round trips of 3600 miles with ten tons of bombs. The United States by a Herculean effort thus attained the mightiest sea and air strength yet known. Scarcely a community in the land but had daily reminders of the gigantic exertions: sons and husbands departing for camp, planes roaring overhead, uniformed men on the streets, the rumbling of troop trains, the distant thunder of artillery practice and, presently, the lengthening casualty lists in the newspapers.

Science was also mobilized as never before, telescoping into a few years achievements that would otherwise have taken decades. The Office of Scientific Research and Development, headed by Vannevar Bush of the Carnegie Institution and working with scientists all over the land, furthered the contriving of such crucial military devices as radar (for discovering and locating the approach of unseen airplanes and similar uses), submarine-detecting mechanisms, long-range navigational aids, the flame thrower, and the radio proximity fuse (which guided a shell and exploded it on its target). Among the OSRD's services in military medicine was the quantity production of penicillin to cure infected wounds as well as a wide range of other destructive diseases; of the insecticide DDT to combat the mosquito-borne malaria (particularly important in the Pacific and Italian campaigns); and of dried plasma to replenish the blood supply and hasten recovery of the injured. To meet the sharply rising need for plasma, the Red Cross established blood-donor centers throughout the country, where civilians supplied an amount growing from 50,000 pints in 1941 to 5,000,000 in 1944. The plasma treatment, more than any other single factor, accounted for the remarkable reduction of mortality from wounds. The OSRD's most sensational and awe-inspiring feat, however, was the production of the atomic bomb in the expiring months of the war. This was the joint accomplishment of a group of scientists, including Britons and Canadians brought to the United States for the purpose and Nazi exiles. It required an out-lay of nearly $2,000,000,000 for the experimental work. In spite of great ingenuity by the Nazis and their occasional important innova-tions, such as the robot rocket bombs (V-1 and V-2) with which they pounded London in 1944, American scientific superiority short-ened the struggle by many months.

Women aided the national cause not only by thronging into offices and factories, but also by joining the armed forces for the first time in American history. Known according to the branch of service by such names as the WACs (Women's Army Corps), the navy WAVES (Women Accepted for Volunteer Emergency Service) and the SPARs (derived from the marines' motto *Semper Paratus* and its translation "Always Ready"), they performed noncombatant duties that freed the men for more active assignments. The number so engaged stood at about 150,000 in the spring of 1944. Meanwhile in numerous localities, especially those near the coasts, many stay-at-homes of both sexes assumed semimilitary functions, generally under direction of the Office of Civilian Defense. The fear of bombing attacks in the early stages of the conflict caused cities to observe dimout and black-out regulations and led the people to volunteer as airplane spotters, air-raid wardens, nurses' aides and auxiliary firemen and police. Such duties at one period occupied 5,500,000 persons.

To brighten and improve the off-duty hours of the GIs (a name which the men in uniform humorously adopted as standing for "Gov-ernment Issue"), six public-spirited agencies—the Y.M.C.A., the Y.W.C.A., the National Catholic Community Service, the National Jewish Welfare Board, the Salvation Army and the Travelers Aid Association—combined their efforts for greater effectiveness, forming the United Service Organizations in February, 1941. This body, with the help of countless volunteers and a total of approximately $200,-000,000 from the public, operated recreational centers wherever soldiers and sailors gathered, not only in the United States but also in Latin America and the Philippines. In addition, professional enter-tainers from stage, screen and radio gave nearly 275,000 performances under the USO in forty-one countries around the world, sometimes so near the firing line as to endanger their lives. As in the two preceding wars, the Red Cross also rendered humanitarian and medical service at home and abroad. With the USO it distributed over 10,000,000 books among the fighting men. It also carried on welfare work among the GIs and their families in local communities, sponsored social clubs, mobile units and rest homes for the men in Europe and the Orient, and assisted in hospitals. For these and like purposes it expended more than $700,000,000 from 1941 to 1946.

As a further lift to morale, Congress in 1942 more than doubled the pay of servicemen and increased dependency allowances for their wives and children. In 1944, to cushion the shock of return to civilian life, it adopted the measure popularly known as the GI Bill of Rights. This, among other things, provided a year's unemployment compensation for discharged veterans at $20 a week, guaranteed 50 per cent of loans up to $2000 (later $4000) in the case of those buying homes or starting businesses, and subsidized postwar educational training in accordance with the length of time spent in the armed services, including $500 a year for tuition and books and an additional sum for living expenses. No government had ever dealt so generously with its defenders.

THE BATTLE OF PRODUCTION

Probably the greatest civilian contribution to victory consisted in speeding the manufacture of military essentials. The problem of production was fourfold: to create additional plant capacity; to convert existing facilities wherever possible to war uses; to allot scarce materials to factories in such a way as to avoid 'bottlenecks' and ensure a maximum over-all output; and to accomplish these objects while continuing to meet basic civilian requirements. In going about the job the President, heedless in many instances of the precedents of World War I, tried out various types of organization, setting up new war agencies (which often clashed because of vague or overlapping jurisdictions) and making frequent changes of personnel. His administrative methods led a friendly critic to say that he liked to "shoot from the hip." In time, however, an effective co-ordination of effort took form. Thus the crucial Advisory Commission on National Defense, appointed in May, 1940, was succeeded in January, 1941, by the double-headed Office of Production Management, only to give way a year later to the War Production Board which endured for the rest of the hostilities. Congress kept a constant scrutiny of the defense agencies, notably through a special Senate committee under Harry S. Truman of Missouri, who thus first came to national notice. His committee exposed instances of fraud and profiteering in government contracts as well as of failure to meet production schedules, and offered constructive criticism for greater speed and efficiency.

The War Production Board under Donald M. Nelson, a Chicago business executive, exercised far-reaching centralized authority over procurement, priorities and manufacturing, somewhat as the War Industries Board had done in the previous conflict. Working closely with the WPB, the Defense Plant Corporation, a subsidiary of the Reconstruction Finance Corporation, released government funds for industrial construction and conversion. By October, 1943, it had lent over $9,000,000,000 for these and like purposes, including the laying of six pipe lines for the long-distance conveyance of oil. Simultaneously, peacetime factories were shifted to war work as fast as they could be retooled. In this way farm-implement companies began making tanks and ordnance, refrigerator concerns turned out binoculars and machine guns, while automobile plants produced such essentials as airplane engines, jeeps, trucks and tanks.

Because of the voracious demand, shortages quickly appeared in vital materials, notably steel, aluminum, magnesium, copper, lead, zinc and chemicals. Through an elaborate system of priorities the government allocated the available supplies where most needed, and at the same time it took steps to increase the stocks in order to forestall future deficiencies. Besides subsidizing new production, it made use of substitutes when possible (for example, plywood instead of metal in training planes) and collected scrap iron, tin, aluminum and the like from housewives. A special branch of the WPB dealt with the rubber crisis arising from the Japanese seizure of Malaya and the Dutch East Indies. Without rubber all motor transport would stop, to say nothing of the harm to the electrical industry. To conserve the existing supply, tires were rationed to civilians and, partly for the same reason, gasoline was later rationed, while in regions of gas scarcity all pleasure driving was banned. On the positive side, fifty-one plants for making synthetic rubber were built. By the end of 1944 they were producing more annually than the total yearly imports of natural rubber in prewar times.

Notwithstanding the delays and confusion in carrying through this complicated program, a huge expansion of output resulted. Before the end of 1942 the over-all amount had caught up with the three Axis powers combined, and by 1944 it was twice as great. To put it differently, America's total production doubled between 1939 and 1945. In particular items like aluminum, fabricated metals, machine tools and artificial rubber the gain was even more remarkable. To help bring this about, factories mushroomed in the rural South and multiplied in the Pacific Coast states. Meanwhile the yield in agriculture increased a third despite a surplus of farm staples in 1939 when the war began. In World War I, rail congestion had caused the government to take over the lines, but now the roads under private management, co-operating with the Office of Defense Transportation under Joseph B. Eastman, efficiently moved troops and munitions, besides shouldering the added burden resulting from the decline of coastwise shipping and civilian motor transport.

The surging productive effort affected civilian life at many points. As industries were diverted to military uses, and as the armed forces and lend-lease shipments absorbed an ever greater quantity of foodstuffs, clothing and the like, thousands of commodities became scarce or disappeared altogether from the market. In order to stretch the limited supplies as far as possible, the WPB, acting through the Office of Price Administration, embarked on systematic rationing. Even before the OPA, restrictions had been put on the buying of motorcars, typewriters and other articles. In May, 1942, housewives registered for the purchase of sugar, and rationing was presently extended to a wide variety of products, including fuel oil, shoes, meat, butter and coffee. To supplement the commercial stock of provisions, people planted vegetables in back yards and vacant lots and canned much of the crop for winter use.

The administration also acted to combat the rise of prices, due to the public having more money to spend and fewer things to buy. If living costs should spiral upward as in World War I, labor would demand constantly higher wages, farmers stiffer prices, and the mounting inflation would render it hard for persons with fixed incomes to make ends meet. It was partly to siphon off some of this excess purchasing power that the government imposed heavy taxation and conducted high-pressure bond drives. Tackling the problem more directly, the Office of Price Administration began in 1941 to regulate certain prices with the voluntary co-operation of business. But stronger methods proved necessary, and in 1942 Congress granted adequate power to curb all prices except those of raw foodstuffs which, thanks to the farm bloc, were not to be cut below a specified minimum. Late in the year the President set up the Office of Economic Stabilization under former Supreme Court Justice James F. Byrnes, which reinforced the OPA's efforts. Under the 1942 legislation ceilings were clamped upon the wholesale and retail prices of numerous commodities as well as upon rentals in defense areas. A cardinal aim of both rationing and price controls was to ensure equitable distribution— to see that all citizens were treated alike, the well-to-do no better than the poor. Though there was some evasion of these restrictions through the patronage of 'black markets,' where goods were sold clandestinely, this did not become a major problem.

Considering the manifold difficulties of enforcement in a country of continental dimensions, prices were kept well in check. From Pearl Harbor to the end of 1944 wholesale prices advanced around 35 per cent and living costs 25—about a quarter as much as during the far shorter period of World War I. The rise of uncontrolled prices was far greater. The steepest increases occurred in the case of some agricultural products. To relieve the consumer, the government in 1943 began subsidizing the production of meat, butter and certain other staples in order to enable the farmers to sell them more cheaply without loss of profit. Price curbs, besides saving the public billions of dollars for civilian goods, saved the government immensely more in the cost of war materials.

The question of an ample labor force presented another troublesome hurdle. With industry expanding at breath-taking speed, a critical demand for man power had to be filled at the very time Selective Service was curtailing the supply. Occupational deferments partly met the shortage, a longer workday (with overtime pay) also helped, while fresh reservoirs of labor were tapped by drawing on employees in nonessential occupations, boys under draft age, oldsters, the partially disabled and women who had never before worked outside the home. Combining humane with practical considerations, the President also set up a wartime Fair Employment Practice Committee which, though not wholly successful, helped open jobs in defense industries and the government for perhaps 1,000,000 additional Negroes. As a result, the number of civilian wage earners rose from

44,200,000 in 1939 (including those in the WPA and CCC) to 54,-000,000 in 1944 (with these depression-born agencies no longer in existence). As the conflicting needs of army and industry sharpened, Roosevelt in April, 1942, created a War Manpower Commission in order "to assure the most effective mobilization and maximum utilization of the nation's manpower," and in December he subordinated Selective Service to the WMC, an action which Congress, however, revoked after a year's trial.

As soon as America took up arms, William Green of the AFL and Philip Murray of the CIO joined with the Railway Brotherhoods to proclaim a no-strike policy. The prewar year 1941, then ending, had seen some serious stoppages in defense industries. Federal troops had been used to reopen strike-bound aviation plants at Englewood, California, and Bendix, New Jersey, while navy authorities had taken over a shipbuilding concern in Kearny, New Jersey, until the owners accepted a prolabor ruling of the government. In November a bituminous-coal strike of John L. Lewis's United Mine Workers, starting in the 'captive mines' that served the great Pittsburgh steel companies, had spread to other areas until 253,000 men were laid off. Early in December they won their demand for a closed shop, thanks to federal arbitration. To assist labor's no-strike pledge, President Roosevelt in January, 1942, established a National War Labor Board with authority to pass on wages and adjust all union controversies affecting the military effort. In July the NWLB in the 'Little Steel formula' laid down the principle of a 15-per-cent raise of pay to offset the advance of living costs since January 1, 1941; and in October, 1942, the White House with Congressional sanction empowered the Board to stabilize the compensation of all employees, whether in defense industries or otherwise, at approximately the levels then existing.

Enforcement, however, did not prove easy, for wage earners continued to fume over living costs. In the spring of 1943 a walkout of 530,000 bituminous and anthracite workers under Lewis, who spurned the NWLB's jurisdiction in the pay dispute, concluded in the government's taking over and operating some three thousand mines in twenty-six states. An angry Congress in June passed over the President's veto the Smith-Connally Act which set forth elaborate regulations for taking strike votes, made it a criminal offense to promote a work stoppage in a government-seized plant and forbade unions to contribute to political campaigns. On October 31, after the mines were returned to the owners, the men again quit work and the government again took possession. But the new crisis passed within less than a week when the miners, with the NWLB's consent and in indirect violation of the Little Steel formula, won a higher rate of pay by agreeing to a longer workday. In December trouble arose with the Railway Brotherhoods and associated rail unions, causing the government temporarily to administer the roads until the wage differences were adjusted at a compromise figure. The year 1944, though, brought a turn for the better, with the man-hours lost declining from 13,500,000 to 8,720,000. Throughout the war period, strikes and threats of strikes created much concern. Many of the interruptions, however, were local 'wild-cat' or unauthorized outbreaks, and in fact labor's record on the whole was extraordinarily good, since all the stoppages amounted actually to considerably less than one per cent of the total working time. The organized movement also doubled its size, with 14,000,000 members in 1944.

The nation's colossal economic effort had to meet not only its own compelling needs, but also the dire wants of the Allies, for the lend-lease program, begun in March, 1941, committed America to assisting all enemies of the Axis. Starting with Great Britain, China and Soviet Russia, arrangements for this purpose were made with country after country, the matter of repayment if any being left to future adjustment on easy terms. Munitions and ships made up about half the supplies, followed by industrial materials and then by foodstuffs. Among other things the expenditures included the repair of Allied vessels in American ports and the training of foreign air forces in the United States. In all, lend-lease cost the country about $43,000,000,000, the British Empire getting more than two thirds of the total and the Soviet Union nearly a quarter. Beleaguered China obtained a pitifully small share because Japan held the seaports and had closed the Burma Road, the principal inland route from India. Everywhere, even in China, where most of the meager aid was flown in 'over the hump' of the Himalayas, the succor proved indispensable. Lend-lease tanks and artillery helped the British throw back the Axis legions from Egypt, Yankee planes and tanks reinforced Russian resistance to the Nazi invaders, and comparable equipment bolstered the defenses of Australia, India and other places. The United States received return benefits in such forms as ocean and land transportation for its overseas troops and the construction of hospitals and warehouses. The total amount of 'lend-lease in reverse' came to $5,600,000,000.

As in World War I, the branch of the army known as the Services of Supply transported and distributed munitions, gasoline, tires, food, wearing apparel, medical supplies and other stores to America's own forces in Europe, besides building camps, maintenance depots, lines of transportation and communication and the like. The task proved far heavier than in the previous struggle, however, because of the greater number of the fighters, the bulkier equipment, the enemy's control of the Continent's main ports, as well as the war's longer duration. Nearly six times as much matériel was needed per man as in the last war. The vast job was executed with an efficiency and dispatch that contributed vitally to ultimate victory. In another way, the Office of Strategic Services, a civilian body, aided overseas operations by assembling data of military value through research at home and espionage abroad.

In order to co-ordinate Anglo-American operations behind the lines, Roosevelt and Prime Minister Churchill in January, 1942, set up three commissions: a Combined Shipping Adjustment Board, a Munitions Assignment Board and a Combined Raw Materials Board. On its own account the United States established the Economic Defense Board (later called the Board, then Office, of Economic Warfare), which sought to prevent Nazi economic penetration of neutral countries and to acquire from them scarce metals and fibers for war industries. As another American overseas undertaking, the Office of Foreign Relief and Rehabilitation Operations was created late in 1942 to plan for meeting the civilian wants of peoples as they were liberated from the Axis yoke. Finally, in September, 1943, these latter two bodies were joined with the Lend-Lease Administration in a single Office of Foreign Economic Administration. The object was to centralize and unify all economic aspects of wartime international policy. With a similar purpose the Office of War Mobilization, instituted in May, 1943, tied more closely together the various agencies engaged in administering the nation's domestic economic activities. James F. Byrnes, its director, became a sort of deputy President with the special function of streamlining these exertions. Never before had the country been so thoroughly organized, both inwardly and outwardly, to meet a national peril.

THE GLOBAL FIGHTING FRONT

When Japan's assault on Pearl Harbor catapulted America into the war, the titanic struggle had been raging for two years and three months. A smashing Axis triumph seemed unavoidable and close.

Germany had vanquished all Western Europe except Great Britain, Spain, where the dictator Franco was a sly collaborator, and Eire, Portugal, Switzerland and Sweden, whose neutrality Hitler had not cared to violate. His armies also held the Ukraine, Soviet Russia's major farming and industrial area, and were approaching the gates of the great cities of Moscow and Leningrad. As subsequent events were to show, the onslaught on Russia—which had been accounted an easy prey—was a crucial blunder, since the opening of an eastern front divided Germany's forces and hastened her eventual defeat. England, having escaped invasion after Dunkirk, still stood intact despite aerial bombardments and the tightening noose of the submarine blockade. Her control of the Mediterranean, the life line of her Empire, was gravely endangered, however, by the Axis conquest of Yugoslavia, Greece and the other Balkan countries and the persistent attacks on Malta and Egypt. In the Mediterranean operations Mussolini's army, though taking part, had proved a frail support unless or until reinforced by Nazi troops and leadership. Where the Italians fought alone, as in Ethiopia, the British had succeeded in forcing their surrender.

It was at this critical juncture that the conflagration spread to the United States. To assure unity of action in the global campaigns ahead, America and Britain promptly organized the Combined Chiefs of Staff with headquarters in Washington. The United States members were General of the Army George C. Marshall, Fleet Admiral Ernest J. King, General Henry H. Arnold of the army air force and Fleet Admiral William D. Leahy, the President's chief of staff, with four British associates of equal distinction. This group planned the high strategy, and their advice guided the military decisions made by Roosevelt and Churchill. As the war developed, the same principle of co-ordination was applied wherever the Americans and British operated, a commander in chief in each theater being given responsibility for all Allied forces, land, sea and air. But despite the greatest advance preparations the nation had ever made, the United States could do no more at first than fight delaying engagements. As General Marshall later put it, "Approximately eight months were required by this country, acting in collaboration with its Allies, to accumulate the munitions, train the initial forces and then transport them to where they could be employed in offensive action against the enemy."

While the giant was mustering his strength, pygmy Japan, having maimed the United States fleet at Pearl Harbor, swept triumphantly through the Far East. By New Year's Day, 1942, Guam, Wake Island and England's dependencies of Hong Kong and North Borneo had fallen. Other British holdings soon followed: Malaya and the great naval base of Singapore in February; Burma in May; and, to the north and northeast of Australia, New Britain Island, the Solomon

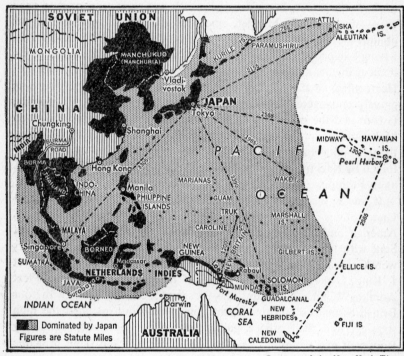

Courtesy of the *New York Times*

The Flood Tide of Japanese Conquest

group and the northern coast of Dutch as well as British New Guinea. Simultaneously the Japanese lunged against the other Dutch East Indies, seizing island after island, and at the end of February, 1942, they fought a costly but victorious three-day naval battle in Macassar Straits against a hastily assembled fleet of Dutch, American, British and Australian vessels. In March they overran Java, key island of the group. From these hapless lands they now threatened Australia. But early in May a five-day battle in the Coral Sea, northeast of Australia, halted the foe. In one of the strangest engagements in naval history the blows were inflicted not by the opposing warships, which never came in sight of each other, but by airplanes. The enemy lost two of their carriers to one for the Anglo-American fleet, and though suffering a lighter loss in cruisers and destroyers, never again ventured in strength so close to Australia.

The Japanese, however, experienced delay in grabbing the Philippines, against which they had loosed an attack on the same day as Pearl Harbor. General Douglas MacArthur's outnumbered and underequipped army of Americans and natives put up a heroic resistance, first on the jungle-clad mountainous Bataan Peninsula, which the 37,000 survivors finally surrendered on April 9, 1942, and then on the fortified, rock-tunneled island of Corregidor four miles away in Manila Bay, where 11,500 of the starving, wounded and diseased defenders managed to hang on for another month. Early in June greater success attended the United States arms when land and carrier-based planes decisively repulsed a heavy assault on the Midway Islands in a fight lasting two days. It was the biggest disaster the Japanese navy had ever suffered, though worse ones were to come. Had it triumphed, the next target would have been Hawaii. A week later, however, the Nipponese stole a march on the Americans in the North Pacific by landing troops at Attu, Agattu and Kiska at the extreme end of the fog-bound Aleutian Islands off Alaska. Here their presence constituted a threat to Alaska, Canada and America's West Coast. The victorious foe now stood astride an area of more than 1,300,000 square miles abounding in rubber, oil, hemp, rice, quinine and other military and civilian essentials. At the edges of this vast domain the Allies took up positions in India and Australia. To the latter country General MacArthur, at the President's behest, had escaped by motor boat and submarine before the fall of Bataan in order to take command of the Allied forces in the Southwest Pacific. American GIs had begun arriving in Australia in March.

Nor did the Allied cause fare much better in other parts of the world. In Russia the Reds continued to battle furiously against tremendous odds, regaining some territory adjoining Leningrad and Moscow, but losing vital industrial centers and important agricultural and mineral areas in the vicinity of the lower Volga and the Black Sea. Upon the ocean the submarine menace grew ever graver as the Nazis, hunting in packs and wreaking destruction even in the Caribbean and the Gulf of St. Lawrence, sank Allied merchant craft faster than they could be replaced. In North Africa the Axis army under the Nazi Marshal Erwin Rommel drove the British, invading westward from Italian Libya, back into Egypt with immense losses in men and equipment, and then pressed on as far east as El Alamein, seventy miles from the great seaport of Alexandria and dangerously near Britain's Suez Canal. About the only ray of cheer in the dismal picture was the mounting series of English air assaults upon armament plants, docks and railroads in Germany, France and other Nazi-held countries. In this warfare American fliers began to take part on Independence Day.

VICTORY IN EUROPE

These disheartening months of Allied weakness and affliction came to an end in August, 1942. By this time the contending forces stood more evenly matched, with the Allies beginning to excel in military might. The preparations for America's unlimited participation, of which General Marshall spoke, were at last complete. By the close of 1942 the United States armed services overseas totaled 1,700,000, and in the next twelve months 3,800,000. They went to every theater of war, east and west, except Russia. As quickly as possible the Allies everywhere now shifted from the defensive to the offensive. In a crucial decision of strategy the Combined Chiefs of Staff determined to deal the heaviest blows first against the European Axis. Not only was Germany the strongest and closest adversary, with England as a nearby base for invasion and Russia menacing Germany's other flank, but Hitler's defeat would ensure the finishing off of Japan, whereas Japan's defeat would not do the same for Hitler.

From the summer of 1942 onward the Russians, fortified with lend-lease equipment, attained increasing success against the Nazi invaders. The stubborn Soviet defense of the important industrial city of Stalingrad on the Volga in the autumn gave the Germans their first great setback. For nearly ninety days the Reds fought off the besieging hosts. They ended by killing and capturing 100,000, and then unexpectedly in November they launched a savage counteroffensive. Along a two-thousand-mile front hostilities raged almost continuously with huge losses on both sides. By November, 1943, Marshal Joseph Stalin's legions had regained two thirds of the 537,000 square miles which the Nazis had occupied at the crest of their conquest. By the spring of 1944 they had pushed back the enemy at some points beyond the old Polish frontier, penetrated into Czechoslovakia and also deep into Rumania, a major source of German oil. The foe, however, still held strong positions in Finland and the other Baltic states as well as elsewhere, and had a precarious hold on the Crimean Peninsula in the Black Sea.

Meanwhile Anglo-American efforts were throttling the submarine peril in the Atlantic. Planes, blimps, destroyer escorts, corvettes and smaller patrol boats drove the marauders away from North American waters, and similar means helped protect the convoy of cargo and troop ships. The number of Allied and neutral vessels destroyed fell from 585 in the first year after Pearl Harbor to 110 in the second. During the latter months of 1943 the Germans actually lost more U-boats than the Allies did merchant craft, and the swift construction of ships assured the Allies ever greater safety on the ocean. The submarine was thus extinguished as a significant factor in the war.

Simultaneously, overhead onslaughts on the enemy grew in magnitude, intensity and effect, amounting almost to a vertical blockade. For many months the major objective was the Ruhr, an area roughly forty miles square in the Rhineland, containing most of Germany's heavy industry as well as rich deposits of iron and coal. The British relied chiefly on giant nocturnal raids, while American daylight fliers supplemented the wholesale devastation by stabbing at particular targets. These attacks were on a larger scale and far more destructive than the worst Nazi bombings of Britain in 1940–1941. In other parts of Axis-occupied Europe this warfare of attrition also proceeded, blasting submarine bases, oil refineries, railways and dams, reducing key cities to smoking rubble, crippling the foe's economic sinews and impairing civilian morale. As the spring of 1944 approached, a sustained offensive was directed against aircraft factories and the Nazi combat force (Luftwaffe). On almost every operational day, from 700 to 1000 heavy bombers were out over Germany. By whittling Hitler's aerial strength the Allied high command ensured the weakening of his powers of resistance when the long-planned invasion of Western Europe should begin.

In North Africa, too, the fortunes of war favored the Allies. Late in October, 1942, General Sir Bernard L. Montgomery's British Eighth Army in Egypt, now reinforced and re-equipped, expelled the Italo-German invaders from El Alamein and began pursuing them westward. While this desert campaign was gaining tempo, Anglo-American troops landed early in November in French Morocco and Algeria fifteen hundred miles farther to the west, an operation which involved about 200,000 men and over 300 warships, transports and

The Mediterranean Theater of War

supply ships. This surprise move, under United States General Dwight D. Eisenhower, had been planned when Prime Minister Churchill visited the White House the preceding summer, and the great expedition reached its destination without losing a single ship or man to a submarine. Striking simultaneously at Casablanca, Oran and Algiers, the Allies met relatively little opposition, thanks to the co-operation of local French officials and to the timely aid of Admiral Jean Darlan, commander of all of France's forces, who now renounced his Vichy superiors. The Anglo-American army, assisted by Free French contingents, battled their way eastward against stiff resistance into the adjoining French protectorate of Tunisia. The struggle reached its climax at Bizerte in northern Tunisia when Montgomery's army, converging on the scene from Egypt, closed in on the Axis forces on the one side while Eisenhower's cohorts pummeled them on the other. On May 15, 1943, victory was complete. The enemy suffered a stunning defeat, with 266,000 taken prisoner.

This master stroke yielded several important advantages. By rendering secure the Mediterranean off the African shore it protected the Allies' life line through the Suez Canal to the Far East. Moreover, it not only drew the colonial French into the fray, but it helped ease Germany's military pressure on Russia and provided a springboard for assailing the 'soft underbelly' of Europe. In midsummer of 1943 an armada of some 160,000 American, British and Canadian troops, spearheaded by a cloud of bombers, descended upon Sicily, off the toe of Italy. Outwitting the defenders gathered at the west shore of the island, they landed on the southeastern tip on July 10, and in thirty-eight days of strenuous fighting over mountainous terrain they completed the conquest. The civilian population, weary of Fascist tyranny, welcomed the invaders with flowers and fruit. While these hostilities were still going on, popular discontent on the mainland caused Mussolini's downfall on July 25; and the new regime negotiated a secret armistice, made public five days later on September 8, for Italy's unconditional surrender. The principal immediate benefit was to deliver most of the Fascist navy into Allied hands and to free British sea power for action elsewhere, notably in the Pacific.

The Allies, at once crossing the two miles of water to the mainland, began an arduous and protracted campaign to dislodge the Nazi forces there, for Hitler ignored Italy's capitulation. The southernmost part of the peninsula put up the least resistance; but it took United States General Mark Clark's army, landing on the beaches of Salerno south of Naples, three hard weeks to capture that great seaport on September 30. Rome was the next objective. The Nazis in well-chosen mountain positions fiercely contested the advance into central Italy. By another amphibious operation Clark in January, 1944, seized the Anzio beach behind the German lines, just below Rome, but he did not succeed in taking the Italian capital till early June. Much fighting still lay ahead as the Allies battered their way stubbornly into the industrial region of northern Italy, with Florence, Bologna and other strongholds eventually to fall to their arms. The incessant hostilities had the useful effect of putting the Allies within closer bombing range of German-held Europe as well as of pinning down some of Hitler's best divisions, which might otherwise have been battling the Russians or have been available for repelling the Allied assault on the Atlantic side of the Continent.

At daybreak on June 6, 1944—'D-Day'—General Eisenhower unleashed his gigantic offensive across the English Channel, preceded by paratroopers and shielded by overwhelming air power and a huge naval force. Landing in Normandy on sixty miles of open beach heavily fortified against them, the Americans, British and Canadians made good their positions at heavy cost and in the weeks ahead drove the enemy inland in a ceaseless fury of fighting. Presently additional Allied forces invaded at other points, including Marseilles on the Mediterranean Coast. Outgeneraled, outnumbered, and outstripped in equipment, fire power and air strength, the Nazis, still stoutly resisting, retreated into Germany three months later on September 6. Besides losing all of France except some of the seaports, they lost Belgium with its great harbor of Antwerp, whose opening to the Allies simplified the critical problem of obtaining munitions and supplies.

Then came the battle of Germany and the knockout blow. The Nazis defended their homeland desperately against the closing vise of the Allies (including the French and other nationalities) on the west and the Russians on the east. Early in October, 1944, the American GIs began pounding Germany's supposedly impregnable Westwall, and a month later the Americans, British and Canadians started moving against the Cologne gateway of the industrial Ruhr. On December 16 the enemy, in a double gamble to regain Antwerp and isolate the northern prong of the invading hosts, suddenly counterattacked the Allied center in the snow-covered, wooded Ardennes on the Belgian-Luxemburg frontier. This engagement, known as the Battle of the

Bulge from the fifty-mile gap (at some points fifty miles deep) punched in the Allied front, ended a few weeks later as the Allied ground and air forces, perfectly handled, closed in on either side. Hitler had expended his last reserves, and from then on, the Allied war machine crashed inexorably forward. In March, 1945, after a

Courtesy of the Associated Press

pause at the Rhine, it forced its way across the river and trapped more than 100,000 of the Fuehrer's best remaining troops in the Ruhr, while the British and Canadians turned northward to seize the great ports of Hamburg and Wilhelmshafen.

April, 1945, swiftly brought the finish. The Russians, already in possession of Budapest, took Vienna and surged westward; an American army under General George S. Patton swept into Czechoslovakia; British forces broke into the plains of the Po in northern Italy; and the Russians after a twelve-day encircling siege captured Berlin. East and West stood united when the Americans and Russians met on April 26 on the banks of the Elbe. As a fitting accompaniment of this last gasp of the war, Mussolini, who had escaped to northern Italy after his overthrow, was killed by his own people, and Hitler died apparently by his own hand in the ruins of Berlin. On May 7, almost exactly eleven months after D-Day, the beaten foe signed terms of unconditional surrender at General Eisenhower's headquarters in Reims, France.

VICTORY IN ASIA

Though the United States hurled its main strength against the European Axis, it managed also to halt, turn back and finally crush the Asian enemy. No country had ever waged simultaneously two major conflicts so unlike. Not only were they separated by the width of the earth, but they were distinct strategically and required very different tactics. The Pacific struggle, besides being twice as far from the home base as the European, involved operations over immense distances within the war zone itself. Moreover, the men and materials usually had to be transported by water; the military objectives were jungle-clad, malarial islands; and the United States received only minor Allied help, chiefly from the Australians and, on the mainland, from the Chinese. The very extent of Japan's conquest, however, afforded an advantage, for it stretched her powers of defense to the utmost. America's over-all strategy was to seize one island with the overwhelming support of carrier-based planes, then, reinforced by land-based planes, press on to the next, repeating the process indefinitely. When key strongholds blocked the way, they were bypassed and cut off from effective contact with the Japanese homeland.

Despite the concentration on Europe, the United States in August, 1942, began turning to the offensive also in the Pacific. Action was vital to forestall a possible invasion of Australia, the indispensable base for future full-scale operations against Japan. American marines, unexpectedly landing in the Solomon Islands to the northeast of Australia, captured the menacing air bases on Guadalcanal and Tulagi against tough opposition; but offshore the Nipponese at first had the advantage, destroying three American and one Australian heavy cruisers. In a three-day naval engagement in mid-November, however, the American Admiral William F. Halsey, Jr., turned the tables, sink-

The Southwest Pacific Front

Courtesy of *Current History*

451

ing 24 enemy ships, including 12 troop-laden transports, while losing 2 cruisers and 7 destroyers himself. The land fighting persisted until February, 1943, when the surviving Japanese were cleaned out of Guadalcanal. Meanwhile the foe, ensconced in northern New Guinea, threatened Australia from a different quarter, their immediate objective being Australia's outpost of Port Moresby in Papua on New Guinea's southeastern coast. The American-Aussie forces, however, sent the attackers reeling back through the jungles. On March 2, 1943, MacArthur's airmen, sighting a Japanese fleet approaching New Guinea, bombed the 12 warships and transports with 3000 soldiers to the bottom of the Bismarck Sea in a four-day battle. By September the enemy after savagely resisting, frequently hand to hand, were rooted out of eastern New Guinea. The rest of the island yielded in the months just ahead, and Australia's safety was thereafter assured.

The year 1943 also saw the Allied subjugation of other Southwest Pacific islands, notably most of the remaining Solomons and some of the New Britain group, as well as the Gilbert Islands, where the marines in November won the gory four-day battle of Tarawa. Some months before, in the North Pacific, the Japanese had been harried out of Attu and Agattu in the Aleutians in May, and they had fled Kiska under cloak of fog in August. The enemy's lines of communication became steadily more precarious as American submarines and planes constantly attacked, sinking more tonnage than could be replaced. In the last three days of March, 1944, United States warships and carrier planes scored a spectacular victory in the western Carolines, demolishing 200 aircraft and 23 ships and disabling other vessels, with negligible losses in return. The way was now open to the Marshall Islands, the Marianas and the Philippines in the Central Pacific, nearer to Japan.

By August, 1944, the Marshall group, first attacked in January, were taken with the key atoll of Kwajalein, while the Marianas, invaded at Saipan in June, fell in mid-July. This victory assured America naval control of the Central Pacific. Incidental to these operations, United States arms recovered Wake Island in May and Guam in July. Late in November, B-29 Superfortresses, based on the Marianas and Guam, began blasting airfields and industries on the Japanese mainland, but meanwhile in October General MacArthur, with 600 ships convoying and transporting 250,000 GIs, landed at Leyte in the heart of the Philippines, precipitating hostilities on land and sea that raged until the whole archipelago was overrun in July, 1945. Manila, in ruins, was liberated in February. This campaign involved the greatest naval encounter in American history: the battle of Leyte Gulf on October 23–26, 1944. The conflict, ranging over thousands of miles in three simultaneous actions, cost the enemy some sixty ships, with relatively little damage to the American side. At its close Tokyo's sea power, in Admiral Halsey's words, was "beaten, routed and broken." The loss of the Philippines cut Japan off from the oil, rubber and tin of Malaya and the Dutch East Indies.

Time was now fast running out for Japan. In Europe her ally Germany was staggering toward utter collapse; in the Pacific the Americans were relentlessly closing in from every direction; and in China a new threat to the invaders was soon to appear as a result of Stalin's secret promise to Roosevelt and Churchill at a conference at Yalta in South Russia in February, 1945, to join the fray. Nonetheless the Nipponese continued to resist fanatically. In February, United States marines in a costly twenty-six-day battle captured Iwo Jima, a dot in the ocean only seven hundred and fifty miles south of Tokyo. In April a bloody eighty-two-day fight on land and sea and in the air, with British naval help, reduced Okinawa in the Ryukyus, Japan's last outpost, only three hundred and fifty miles from her shores. In July Admiral Halsey with further British assistance began hammering the homeland, smashing the remnants of the enemy fleet in Tokyo Bay itself. Overhead American fliers rained down the same destruction that had flattened Germany.

Then on August 6, 1945, a United States army plane wiped out the great military base of Hiroshima with the first atomic bomb ever used in warfare. Two days later Soviet Russia, declaring war on Japan, launched attacks from Siberia on Manchuria and by sea on Korea, and within twenty-four hours a second American A-bomb pulverized Nagasaki, an enemy naval base. The White House, warning of more such assaults to come, demanded unconditional surrender, and on August 14 Tokyo acceded. Japan asked only that Emperor Hirohito be not dethroned, and to this the Allies agreed with the proviso that he do the bidding of the Supreme Allied Commander during the occupation and that the ultimate form of government be left to the people. On September 2, less than four months after Germany's capitulation, Japan signed the terms of defeat aboard the battleship *Missouri* in Tokyo Bay with all America listening in over the radio. The greatest of wars had come to an end.

FULLER ACCOUNTS

The War and the People. Goodman, ed., *While You Were Gone,* affords a general view of civilian life. On particular phases, read McWilliams, *Prejudice,* and Grodzins, *Americans Betrayed,* for the Japanese-Americans; Baxter, *Scientists against Time,* and Andrus and others, eds., *Advances in Military Medicine,* for science's contributions to victory; Carson, *Home Away from Home,* for the United Service Organizations; and Dulles, *American Red Cross,* and Korson, *At His Side,* for the Red Cross.

The Battle of Production. Bureau of the Budget, *The United States at War,* describes the development and administration of the domestic military program, while Civilian Production Administration, *Industrial Mobilization for War,* Nelson, *Arsenal of Democracy,* and Mansfield and others, *Short History of OPA,* concentrate on the national economic effort. Dulles, *Labor in America,* covers labor's part; Stettinius treats *Lend-Lease, Weapon for Victory;* Leigh, *48 Million Tons to Eisenhower,* the Services of Supply; Alsop and Braden, *Sub Rosa,* the Office of Strategic Services; and Gordon and Dangerfield, *Hidden Weapon,* economic warfare.

The Global Fighting Front; Victory in Europe and in Asia. Hall, *Iron Out of Calvary,* Pratt, *War for the World,* and Shugg and DeWeerd, *World War II,* provide concise over-all accounts, while Brown shows *The War in Maps.* Fuller treatments, still in course of publication, include Morison, *United States Naval Operations in World War II,* and Department of the Army, Historical Division, *United States Army in World War II.* Among the rapidly increasing number of special studies are Roscoe, *United States Submarine Operations;* Clifford, *Conquest of North Africa;* Langer, *Vichy Gamble;* Cant, *Great Pacific Victory from the Solomons to Tokyo;* and Eichelberger and MacKaye, *Jungle Road to Tokyo.* Tourtellot has compiled *Life's Picture History of World War II.*

Freedom from Want   *Freedom from Fear*

CHAPTER XXI

POSTWAR PROBLEMS AT HOME

THE PRICE OF VICTORY

No earlier war had ever engulfed so much of the world or had such momentous consequences. The Western Allies took pardonable satisfaction in the knowledge that democracy, though requiring public discussion and legislative consent before action, had nevertheless surpassed dictatorship in the one field where an authoritarian regime was supposedly superior. The 'decadent' democracies had outfought the two most militaristic powers in history despite the enemies' long preliminary planning and preparation. Free institutions had nurtured nations which, though slow to draw the sword, were resolved at any cost to stay free. Nor, in America's case, would the advantage of vast natural wealth have availed without the creative vigor and moral stamina of a people dedicated to making that wealth spell survival. For the second time in the twentieth century events had shown that a truly democratic system with an intelligent, well-informed electorate offers the best bulwark against imperialistic aggression. In the years just ahead this belief was to hearten and sustain America and Western Europe when totalitarian Russia began to shake the pillars of peace.

The war, however, had been dearly won. In both Europe and Asia it had disrupted economic life, upset trade relations and wiped out billions of property of the victors as well as the vanquished, posing formidable problems of recovery. Only the United States, whose home soil had escaped the ruinous blows, emerged stronger and richer than ever. The wartime reliance of the Allies on America's natural and technological resources, added to her own urgencies, had built up an industrial machine of unprecedented size. Peace laid new demands on these facilities to meet both the pent-up domestic needs and those of the war-impoverished world. As a result, the nation's total output of goods and services, which had stood at about $160,000,000,000 in 1939, rose to nearly $248,000,000,000 in 1946 (the first full year after the hostilities) and to an annual rate of $267,000,000,000 in

1950 before the impact of the Korean War was felt. By the same token, civilian employment grew from 45,200,000 in 1939 to almost 61,500,000 by the middle of 1950. Though the conflict had cost the United States $350,000,000,000 from 1941 to 1945 and had boosted the national debt from $49,000,000,000 to $258,682,000,000, the extraordinary economic progress nevertheless made it possible for the country to spend billions on rebuilding Western Europe as a postwar rampart against Communism.

More serious than the material destruction or the financial cost was the war's toll in human lives. The number of killed, wounded and missing on the two sides, excluding the United States, was estimated at over 43,000,000, nearly a quarter of them civilians. America's armed forces of 15,494,000 men and women had suffered nearly 995,000 casualties. These losses, which included 325,000 deaths, were half again as large as in the Union army and navy during the Civil War and almost three times as large as in World War I. The greatest casualty of all was the civilian commander in chief, Franklin D. Roosevelt, who had died unexpectedly of a cerebral hemorrhage on April 12, 1945, at Warm Springs, Georgia, where he had gone for a brief rest. With Winston Churchill he had been the architect and inspiring leader of the war, and his life ended before he saw the fruit of his labors in either military victory or the formation of the postwar United Nations, though both goals were in sight.

Less than six months before, he had stood for a fourth election, having been overwhelmingly renominated on the first ballot by the Democratic convention in Chicago on July 19, 1944, with Senator Harry S. Truman of Missouri replacing Vice-President Henry A. Wallace (against that gentleman's desire) as second on the ticket. The Republicans on June 26 in Chicago picked Governor Thomas E. Dewey on the first ballot, with Ohio's Governor John W. Bricker as his teammate. As a New York district attorney Dewey had earlier made national headlines for jailing racketeers and grafting politicians, and as the only Republican to attain the governorship since 1920, he was expected to wrest the President's home state from the Democratic column. Both platforms pledged unstinted support of the war and the creation of an international body to safeguard future peace, but the Republicans warned against perpetuating a regime addicted to wasteful spending and hampering private industry, and they also renewed their promise of 1940 for a two-term constitutional amendment.

Dewey toured the country, rapping the administration for its "tired old men" and demanding new blood in Washington, while the Democrats retorted that the Republican party's latent isolationism unfitted it for governing in the difficult years ahead. Roosevelt, though making few speeches, displayed his old-time fire and, as before, he had the support of both the great labor groups. The CIO, finding a way around the Smith-Connally Act's ban against using official union funds in a campaign, formed a nation-wide Political Action Committee, which operated with voluntary contributions from members— an example which the AFL was to follow in 1948. The fact that the President was challenging the two-term tradition for the second time seemed to make slight impression on a public which feared that a change of regime might endanger the war's outcome. Though the Democrats and their supporting committees spent less than $7,500,000 in the campaign as compared with more than $13,000,000 by the Dewey cohorts, they carried both Congress and the White House, Roosevelt polling 432 electoral votes and 53.4 per cent of the popular votes (25,603,000) to 99 electoral votes and 45.8 per cent of the popular votes (22,007,000) for Dewey. The armed forces cast 2,-793,000 ballots. Labor's role in the outcome is suggested by the fact that the majorities in seven union strongholds—New York, Chicago, Philadelphia, Detroit, Baltimore, St. Louis and Jersey City—swung those states to the Democrats and prevented what would otherwise have been a national defeat.

TRUMAN'S SUCCESSION

Roosevelt's death within three months of his new inauguration shocked and benumbed not only the people of the United States but those of Allied lands. His vibrant courage and unwavering devotion to democratic ideals made men everywhere feel a sense of almost personal bereavement. The new chief executive promptly pledged himself to uphold like policies, but to most of his countrymen he was an unknown quantity. A farm boy with hardly more than a high-school education, a veteran of World War I, a failure in business, Truman had held various local political offices, and with the aid of Tom Pendergast, a notorious Kansas City boss, he had vaulted into the United States Senate in 1934. There he had unassumingly supported the New Deal, and in his second Senatorial term he had served ably as a watchdog over the country's industrial mobilization. Despite his early machine associations there was no doubt as to his personal integrity and civic devotion. It remained to be seen, however, whether he could rise to greater responsibilities. As he himself ruefully put it, "The whole weight of the moon and stars and all the planets fell on me." [1]

The most urgent task, as victory came in Europe and Asia, was to return the country to a peace footing. This involved demobilization of both men and materials. The GIs, instead of being discharged by military units as in past wars, were released as individuals according to their length of service, time overseas, decorations and number of dependents. By the close of 1945, 6,500,000 had been sent back to civil life, with the process continuing in the next year. Coming events were to disclose that more of the armed forces should have been kept intact, but America's antimilitaristic tradition plus a misplaced confidence in Soviet Russia's peaceable intentions made any other course at the time politically impossible. With even greater precipitancy President Truman upon Japan's defeat stopped the lend-lease program, an action which ignored the needs of the Allied peoples for postwar economic recovery. The administration, too, canceled $35,-000,000,000 worth of military contracts and arranged for the sale of surplus war materials. This latter undertaking entailed, among other things, the disposing of two hundred and fifty-two factories which had cost the government nearly $1,500,000,000. This hasty riddance

---

[1] The holdover cabinet consisted of Edward R. Stettinius, Jr., of Virginia, Secretary of State; Henry Morgenthau, Jr., of New York, Secretary of the Treasury; Henry L. Stimson of New York, Secretary of War; James V. Forrestal of New York, Secretary of the Navy; Francis Biddle of Pennsylvania, Attorney-General; Frank C. Walker of Pennsylvania, Postmaster-General; Harold L. Ickes of Illinois, Secretary of the Interior (continuing from Roosevelt's original cabinet); Claude R. Wickard of Indiana, Secretary of Agriculture; Henry A. Wallace of Iowa, appointed Secretary of Commerce in March, 1945, as a consolation prize for having been dropped as Vice-President; and Lewis B. Schwellenbach of Washington, Secretary of Labor. Before the end of the year, however, all but Forrestal, Ickes and Wallace had been replaced, and the latter two went out in 1946, Wallace being dismissed for having publicly advocated a milder policy toward Russia than the President stood for. Stettinius's successors were James F. Byrnes of South Carolina (1946), General George C. Marshall of Pennsylvania (1947–1948) and Dean G. Acheson of the District of Columbia in 1949. In July, 1949, Congress merged the Departments of War and the Navy under Forrestal as the first Secretary of Defense, whereupon the Secretary of War (renamed Secretary of the Army) and the Secretary of the Navy ceased being cabinet officers.

of supposedly unneeded military stores and facilities was also to be later regretted.

In September, 1945, Truman placed before Congress a comprehensive statement of the administration's social and economic goals. Besides asking for a temporary prolonging of the wartime price, rent and wage controls, he proposed a "substantial upward revision" of the forty-cent minimum wage, government planning for full employment, expansion of social security, a permanent fair-employment-practice act to prevent racial and religious discrimination in businesses in interstate commerce, a thoroughgoing housing and slum-clearance measure, adjustment of farm legislation to peace conditions and the regional development of the country's great river valleys. As steps for "the nation's long-range security," he recommended continuance of Selective Service to supplement volunteering, universal military training and legislation for the use and control of atomic energy. Though the Democrats ruled both branches of Congress, the President obtained little of his program. Conservative Southern members, many in key committee posts, joined the Republicans in open opposition, and Truman lacked his predecessor's skill and experience in fighting back. When the administration's foes could not bottle bills up or vote them down, they strove to denature them with amendments.

The full-employment proposal was a case in point. The huge wartime production, which had created jobs for all, persuaded Truman, as it had Roosevelt before him, that the federal authorities in peacetime could by proper guidance and aid bring about a like condition. The administration's bill placed upon the government the duty to maintain full employment with the assistance of a board of economists who would from time to time draft a national production and employment budget to show what government spending, if any, was needed to attain the object. The National Association of Manufacturers and the conservatives in both parties recoiled in horror, and the measure as passed in February, 1946, was a watered-down version. It provided for an annual report to the President on business conditions from a three-member Council of Economic Advisers and instructed the government to "co-ordinate and utilize all its plans, functions and resources" to attain "maximum" (not full) employment.

The need for additional housing, neglected during the war and now aggravated by soaring costs, could hardly be ignored, but again Congress did not go nearly so far as the White House desired. The Patman

Act in April, 1946, granted subsidies to makers of construction materials to keep charges down and guaranteed a government market for as many as 200,000 prefabricated dwellings. Another measure made army barracks, trailers and war housing available to veterans and their families. Many of these structures, removed to the vicinity of colleges and universities, soon served as lodgings for the men who resumed their education under the GI Bill of Rights. After weeks of pulling and hauling, Congress in July also agreed to an extension of Selective Service at the government's option, with more liberal exemptions than before, but the army was to be cut to 1,070,000 men by July, 1947, and the navy to 664,000. Truman's proposal for a system of universal military training went unheeded. Congress in August dealt with a related matter by setting up a permanent Joint Congressional Committee on Atomic Energy and an Atomic Energy Commission of five civilian members. The aim was threefold: to safeguard national security through rigorous provisions for secrecy; to promote research and development for both military and civilian uses; and to forestall the future growth of private monopoly in this field.

The question of price regulation occasioned further dissension. The issue did not involve rationing, for Truman on his own motion had ended the rationing of meats, butter and other foods in November, 1945, shortly after Japan surrendered. But the administration contended that, as long as the deferred demand for goods exceeded the supply, the Office of Price Administration should be retained to ensure fair prices to the public and prevent living costs from skyrocketing. On the other hand, the National Association of Manufacturers, as well as conservatives generally, argued that business, if allowed to go its own way, would expand production so rapidly that the shortages would be overcome and prices be brought down. With the OPA due to expire at the close of June, 1946, Congress at the last minute voted to continue it but under such hampering conditions that the President, branding the measure "a sure formula for inflation," vetoed it.

For three weeks, during which the OPA was left without legal power, the prices of twenty-eight basic commodities rose nearly 25 per cent. Then Truman accepted a bill which was not noticeably better than the one he had rejected. Prolonging the OPA another year, it required an adjustment of prices to afford manufacturers the same margin of profit they had enjoyed in 1940, created a special board to remove price ceilings at will and clap them on again, and preserved rent control. One provision also temporarily exempted meat and other staples from curbs. The resulting leap in meat prices caused that basic food to be subjected again to regulation, and the resentful producers retaliated by withholding their supplies from the market. Meat became difficult to buy at any cost. Truman, on the horns of a dilemma, now gave up the fight. In October, 1946, he not only terminated the meat restrictions, but announced the early abandonment of all other restraints except those on rents. With the relaxing of controls prices reached the highest peaks ever known in America. Rent regulations, however, lingered on, with later Congresses narrowing their scope from time to time and permitting greater local flexibility of adjustment.

Other troubles beset the administration because of the postwar militancy of organized labor, now some 14,000,000 strong. Thanks to longer hours, overtime pay and bonuses, the average factory worker took home twice as much money in 1945 as in 1939; and the unions, unwilling to forgo the added dollars, especially in view of the 33-percent jump in living costs since 1941, demanded equivalent wages for the standard forty-hour week. Labor, no longer bound by the wartime no-strike pledge, was free to assert itself. The President, for his part, declared "there is room in the existing price structure for business as a whole to grant increases in rates"—a view which industrialists hotly denied. The initial series of strikes, starting shortly after Japan's defeat, lasted from the autumn of 1945 to the spring of 1946, with nation-wide walkouts of more than 5,000,000 in the automobile, electrical-equipment, packing-house, railway, steel, coal and other industries. The steel strike alone idled 750,000 in 1200 plants in 250 cities and 25 states, besides shutting down many other businesses dependent upon steel as a basic material. In the case of the coal, meat and oil industries and the railroads, the government, acting under the wartime Smith-Connally Act (due to expire in June, 1947), had to take them over before settlements could be negotiated.

This first great round of work stoppages—others were to follow—effected a general wage advance of eighteen to twenty cents an hour, usually with collateral concessions, but the new price rises soon absorbed the pay increases. This disruption of businesses vital to the nation's welfare alarmed the public. President Truman, at the height of the rail strike (May, 1946), went so far as to ask Congress for temporary power to draft strikers into the armed forces in the case of industries seized by the government. The House immediately agreed but not so the Senate, where Taft was one of the objectors. When the two chambers presented a less stringent measure of their own (the Case bill), Truman rejected it on the ground that it was premature to adopt permanent legislation to deal with the problem. As on some earlier occasions, the President created an impression of not knowing his own mind.

REPUBLICAN REVIVAL

A chief executive in office after a great war always breasts stormy seas—recall Andrew Johnson and Woodrow Wilson. Perhaps Franklin Roosevelt, had he lived, could not have done better than his successor. As it was, Truman faced the mid-term elections in the fall of 1946 with most of his domestic program shelved or mangled by a Congress of his own party. According to the *New York Times* score, the legislators had rejected outright thirteen of his major recommendations, besides trimming down a number of others. His leadership had consisted of words rather than performance, and his occasional sudden shifts of attitude had even sown doubts as to whether he always meant the words. He had gained friends among neither conservatives nor liberals and, justly or not, he had incurred further blame because of the exorbitant price of meat and other necessities as well as the housing shortage. The Republicans, summarizing the popular reaction in a crisp slogan, asked the voters, "Had enough?" The country answered by rejecting the Democrats for the first time since 1930 and handing over both branches of Congress to the minority party. If almost unbroken precedent meant anything, the Republicans in two years more would take over the presidency.

In this spirit of overweening confidence the victors organized the new Congress, with Senator Taft as the chief policy maker in domestic matters and his colleague from Michigan, Arthur H. Vandenberg, calling the tune in foreign relations. The Republicans, as will appear in the next chapter, distinguished themselves in the international field where Senator Vandenberg, atoning for his prewar isolationism, cooperated wholeheartedly with the White House in putting through such crucial measures as the Truman Doctrine and the Marshall Plan. This course undeservedly won the party little credit, however, doubtless because the public had been accustomed by the war to expect bipartisan unity in facing the outside world. In domestic affairs the Republicans acted with equal boldness, but in doing so they not only went against the President but also stirred up antagonism in other quarters.

One of their first moves was to fulfill their anti-Roosevelt platform pledge of 1940 and 1944 to submit a constitutional amendment holding a President to two terms. The step was taken in March, 1947, a time limit of seven years was set for ratification, and by February 26, 1951, the requisite number of state legislatures had complied. The Republicans also tackled the problem of tax reduction, but it was not until 1948, after two trials, that they were able to frame a measure that could get by Truman's veto. Ignoring his continuing recommendation of universal military training, they also allowed Selective Service to expire in March, 1947. Then in June, 1948, upon the President's plea that "our badly depleted military strength is one of the nation's greatest dangers," they restored the system for youths from nineteen through twenty-five years of age for twenty-one months of service and set the total armed forces at 2,006,000 men.

Another law in 1948 provided for admitting from Europe over a two-year period 205,000 displaced persons whom the war had uprooted from their countries. Truman had asked that 400,000 of these unfortunates be received, and he further considered some of the conditions affixed for entry "flagrantly discriminatory." Nevertheless he felt he had no choice but to sign the measure. Turning to the perennial farm question, the Republicans in 1948 enacted the Hope-Aiken Law which assured basic commodities—wheat, corn, cotton, tobacco, rice and peanuts—of price supports at 90 per cent of parity (a figure intended to guarantee the same purchasing power as in a selected earlier period, generally just before World War I) and which announced a more flexible and less favorable formula, to go into effect after two years. On the whole the act involved less liberal government subsidies than before.

The most controversial piece of legislation was the Taft-Hartley Act, carried over the President's veto in June, 1947. The preceding fall a federal district judge had fined John L. Lewis $10,000 and his United Mine Workers $3,500,000 (later cut to $700,000) for ignoring a court order to end a work stoppage while the mines were under government operation; and the spring of 1947 had brought a second great round of wage disputes, with fewer actual strikes than before, but with eventual gains through collective bargaining averaging fifteen cents an hour. This renewal of disturbances deepened public anxiety about the growing power of the unions. To an increasing number of citizens it looked as though Big Labor was coming to dominate the country's economic order as ruthlessly as Big Business had once done. The new enactment passed Congress with a majority support of both parties.

The Taft-Hartley Act—in form an amendment of the Wagner Act and containing many features of the rejected Case bill—reaffirmed labor's right to organize and bargain collectively, but sought to bar certain practices detrimental to the public interest and to restrict others which management found objectionable. Where the earlier statute had condemned only unfair employer methods, the new one dealt also with unfair union methods. It made labor organizations liable for damages from such actions as secondary boycotts and jurisdictional strikes, forbade walkouts by federal employees, outlawed 'feather-bedding' (by which unions exacted payment for work that was unneeded or unperformed), prohibited the closed shop, and permitted the union shop only when an employer agreed after a majority of all his employees had so voted by secret ballot. It further imposed a sixty-day cooling-off period for strikes and lockouts and empowered the President to postpone an industry-wide shutdown for seventy-five or more days of additional negotiation if the national health or safety required. It also restored the wartime ban upon political contributions by unions in federal elections and required these organizations to make financial reports and to file affidavits that their officers were not Communists as a condition of submitting disputes to the National Labor Relations Board and of taking part in collective-bargaining elections. Lastly, the law clipped the powers of the NLRB itself by giving to a new official, its general counsel, the sole right to start prosecutions of unfair union practices.

Union leaders, castigating the measure as a 'slave-labor law,' did not deny the existence of abuses, but insisted that labor should have been allowed to clean its own house and should not have been penalized for the derelictions of a small minority. The curb on Communist officers, for example, had been inserted in the act to prevent strikes being waged for political rather than economic ends, as in the defense industries in 1940–1941 before Hitler's invasion of Russia, and as had sometimes occurred since the war's close. But the AFL had already dealt effectively with this situation, and the CIO, where the condition was at its worst, had moved in the same direction in its 1946 convention with a resolution condemning Communist-led unions. The Communists nevertheless continued to dominate perhaps a quarter of the CIO unions until 1949 when the CIO convention adopted a constitutional amendment ousting them from the organization. The leaders, however, denied any credit to the hated law for this action. President Murray happily reported to the 1950 convention that nearly three fourths of the 900,000 members in the expelled unions had by then repudiated their Communist officers and returned to the parent body.

Whatever the objections to the Taft-Hartley Act, it did not keep labor from obtaining a third round of wage boosts in the spring of 1948. The auto workers, for example, won another eleven cents an hour, the coal miners twelve and a half cents and the steelworkers fourteen. Lewis, continuing his tempestuous career as boss of the United Mine Workers, again defied a district-court injunction, and in April incurred a fine of $20,000 for himself and of $1,400,000 for his union—double the earlier penalties. But the total number of work stoppages, which had reached an all-time high of about 5000 in 1946, receded to 3420 in 1948, though the booming prosperity rather than the new law may have been chiefly responsible. At the same time union membership continued to rise to an estimated 15,600,000 in 1948. Moreover, President Truman made successful use of the legislation in intervening in several national-emergency strikes which might otherwise have crippled the nation's economy. Labor leaders, however, nursing their resentment, prepared to make repeal the major issue in the presidential campaign.

TRUMAN AND THE FAIR DEAL

The election of 1948 proved one of the most unusual on record. The Republicans in Philadelphia on June 21 renominated on the third ballot their 1944 choice, New York's Governor Thomas E. Dewey, over Senator Taft and former Governor Harold E. Stassen of Minnesota, and gave the second place to Governor Earl Warren of California. The platform endorsed the bipartisan policy in foreign affairs, justified the Taft-Hartley Act as a "sensible reform" and, plagiarizing the administration's own proposals, pledged effective action to reduce prices, encourage low-cost housing, broaden social security, and protect Negroes against lynching and Jim Crowism in voting and employment. The dispirited Democrats, meeting in the same city on July 12, reluctantly accepted Truman on the first ballot after efforts to replace him with the war hero Dwight D. Eisenhower —whose politics were unknown—encountered the ex-General's refusal. Senator Alben W. Barkley of Kentucky was named for Vice-President. The platform praised the administration's policies, promised repeal of the Taft-Hartley Act, and was so emphatic on Negro civil rights that thirty-one enraged Southern delegates bolted the gathering. President Truman, accepting his nomination on the convention floor in a rousing speech, dramatically summoned the Republican Congress into immediate session to make good on their party's platform avowals.

Two other groups, both new to the scene, also entered the arena. The States' Rights party or 'Dixiecrats,' organized by seceders from the Democratic convention, picked Governor J. Strom Thurmond of South Carolina and Mississippi's Governor Fielding L. Wright as their standard-bearers on a platform which denounced federal intervention on behalf of the Negro as flouting the Constitution and introducing totalitarianism. In their own states and in Louisiana and Alabama the two men ran as the regular Democratic candidates. The Progressive party, fathered by the Communist party which in due course endorsed the nominees, put forward former Vice-President Henry A. Wallace, lately of Truman's cabinet, and Democratic Senator Glen H. Taylor of Idaho on a platform which coupled a program of domestic reform with a pro-Russian line in foreign affairs featuring opposition to the Marshall Plan. The Progressives counted on widespread liberal and labor support, but in fact obtained little.

The Truman-called special session of Congress adjourned after thirteen days without practicing what the Republican platform had preached, but this apparently made slight dent on the electorate. In any event a Dewey triumph seemed assured by the Republican upsurge of two years before and by the lack of Democratic enthusiasm for Truman as well as by the advent of the two new parties, both aiming to nab Democratic votes. All the political commentators and pollsters forecast the President's defeat, and the Republican nominee, sharing this illusion, adopted a strategy which sidestepped specific issues for safe generalities. Truman, undaunted, stumped the country, blasting the "do-nothing Congress" as the tool of the "special interests" and pledging Taft-Hartley repeal and civil-rights legislation. To offset the lukewarmness of his own party he enjoyed an ardent labor support from the CIO's Political Action Committee and the AFL's newly formed Labor's League for Political Education, and he was also backed by the Americans for Democratic Action, a recently organized group of anti-Communist liberals.

Greatly to the country's astonishment, Truman won by 303 electoral votes to 189 for Dewey and 49.4 per cent of the popular returns (24,106,000) to 45 per cent (21,969,000)—this despite the fact that Thurmond with 1,169,000 popular ballots captured 39 electoral votes in five Southern states (South Carolina, Alabama, Mississippi, Louisiana and a lone electoral vote in Tennessee), and that Wallace's 1,156,000 popular ballots, though winning him none in the electoral college, turned the 74 electoral votes of New York, Maryland and Michigan over to Dewey. The Democrats also carried both chambers of Congress. The governing factors in the outcome were the general prosperity, the feeling of Midwestern farmers that the Republican Congress had not done enough for them, the well-organized labor support, the sympathy excited by Truman's spunky battle against apparently insurmountable odds, and Republican overconfidence. It may have been the supposed certainty of the result which drew a million fewer voters to the polls than in 1940.

Truman now was President in his own right, but this did not save him from further tribulations. Though the Democrats again controlled the lawmaking branch, many of them had been elected by larger majorities than the chief executive and hence felt free to oppose him when they wished. Moreover, 54 of the 96 Senators of both parties in the new Congress had favored the Taft-Hartley Act in the old, and the same was true of 224 of the 435 Representatives. And, as in Truman's first Congress, a coalition of the Republican minority and Republican-minded Southern Democrats could sabotage or defeat his measures. Nevertheless, as an elected instead of an accidental President, he felt more certain of his footing, and in an address to Congress on January 5, 1949, he provided a name and rallying cry for his reform program in the phrase "the fair deal," which he characterized as "the promise of equal rights and equal opportunities which the founders of our republic proclaimed to their countrymen and to the whole world."

The Fair Deal, as Truman outlined it more concretely in his speech, aimed to keep "our economy running at full speed" and to "see that every American has a chance to obtain his fair share of our increasing abundance." The means he proposed had a familiar look. They consisted largely of the unfinished business of his first term, including a national health program. Taken as a whole, the recommendations involved greater federal responsibility for social and economic welfare than had Roosevelt's New Deal. Truman even wanted the government to build steel plants "if action by private industry fails to meet our needs." According to Kenneth S. Wherry of Nebraska, the Senate minority leader, it was a "spendthrift, socialist program," while other Republicans were soon attacking the "welfare state," which the aged but still vocal ex-President Hoover called a "disguise for the totalitarian state." Despite important setbacks the President nevertheless gained a surprising number of his objectives.

On his two major pledges in the campaign he quickly went down to defeat. Five bills to outlaw the poll tax as a suffrage prerequisite (a practice surviving in seven Southern states) had passed the House since 1942, but in the Senate, where a majority also favored the reform, Southern filibusters or threats of one had kept it from coming to a vote. Both party platforms in 1948 had promised civil-rights legislation for Negroes, but the White House's efforts to facilitate action in the upper chamber through the adoption of a rule to make filibustering more difficult ended actually in a rule to make it easier. The result was that neither the anti-poll-tax nor a fair-employment-practice bill nor any of the other measures for aiding the Negro race could reach the floor. By contrast, eight Northern and Western states —Massachusetts, Rhode Island, Connecticut, New York, New Jersey, Washington, Oregon and New Mexico—with others to follow, had enacted legislation since the war to bar racial and religious bias in hiring workers. As for Taft-Hartley repeal, the other crucial issue in the election, both branches of Congress in 1949 opposed a substitute measure supported by the administration and labor, and a Senate-adopted bill to modify some of the law's particulars died in the House. The lawmakers likewise did nothing about compulsory health insurance and universal military training.

In other respects, though, the Fair Deal scored a real advance. One act in 1949 boosted the minimum wage from forty to seventy-five cents an hour, bettering the lot of about 1,500,000 workers, mostly in the lumber, fertilizer, tobacco and cotton-garment industries. Another in 1949 accomplished a threefold object, providing for

810,000 public-housing apartments in six years, to be subsidized by the government in order to cheapen the rents; for slum clearance over a five-year period, in financial co-operation with local authorities; and for loans and gifts to improve farm dwellings. As further help to agriculturists, a law in that year continued through 1950 price supports for the six basic commodities and bade the Secretary of Agriculture at his discretion to do likewise for others, after which time a flexible system, more generous than that in the Hope-Aiken Act, should go into effect.

A bipartisan achievement was a 1949 act empowering the President to reorganize the executive branch of the government, with the proviso that either the Senate or House could reject his proposals. The preceding Republican Congress had in 1947 authorized an advisory commission for this purpose, which under former President Hoover conducted elaborate studies. Upon these findings Truman based his recommendations, most of which Congress allowed to go into force. The President in 1950 repaired an earlier partial defeat by inducing the lawmakers to increase the total admissions of Europe's displaced persons in a four-year period to 415,000 and to remove the unfair restrictions previously imposed. In the same year he also secured a law to plug up a loophole in the Clayton Antitrust Act of 1914. The earlier statute had forbidden corporations to absorb rival corporations through the purchase of their stock when the effect was to reduce competition substantially, but it had left them free to accomplish the same object through purchasing the business assets of such concerns. Wide advantage had been taken of the oversight. The new enactment outlawed the practice.

Perhaps Truman's outstanding success, however, was the Social Security Act of 1950, the first major change in the system since it began under Roosevelt in 1935. It extended old-age-retirement insurance from 35,000,000 persons to an additional 9,700,000, including farm hands, domestic servants and with certain exceptions the self-employed. In view of the much higher cost of living since the original enactment, it also lifted the benefits by an average of 77 per cent, and to make this possible it required that after 1953 employer and employee should each contribute 2 (instead of 1½) per cent on the amount of pay, then by gradual stages a higher proportion until each would be giving 3½ per cent in 1970 and thereafter. In addition, the act increased federal subsidies to the states for the aged, the blind, the totally and permanently disabled, dependent children and maternal and child care. "This kind of progressive, forward-looking law," declared the President, "is the best possible way to prove that our democratic institutions can provide both freedom and security for all our citizens." Though he was not able to bring about a like modernization of the unemployment-insurance system, the Democrats, as the fall elections of 1950 approached, could point to a substantial record of performance.

FULLER ACCOUNTS

Postwar Problems at Home. This period is too recent to have received as yet much attention from historians. Dulles, *Labor in America,* however, covers the difficulties that confronted the unions, and Daniels, *Man of Independence,* presents a sympathetic view of President Truman. To fill out the picture of domestic developments, see such weeklies as *Life,* the *Nation,* the *New Republic, Newsweek,* the *New York Times Review of the Week, Time* and the *United States News and World Report;* the biweekly *Reporter* (since 1949); such monthlies as the *Congressional Digest, Current History* and the *Monthly Labor Review;* such quarterlies as the *Congressional Quarterly* (since 1945) and the *Yale Review;* and such annuals as the *Americana Annual,* the *American Year Book,* the *Information Please Almanac* (since 1947), the *New International Year Book* and the *World Almanac.*

"CAN'T HEAR A WORD YOU'RE SAYING"

CHAPTER XXII

WORLD LEADERSHIP

FORMING THE UNITED NATIONS

THE Truman administration will probably be longest remembered for what it did in international affairs. To the newly elevated executive fell the responsibility not only of upholding his predecessor's foreign policies, but also of devising fresh ones to meet fearfully changing conditions. The first of these tasks proved relatively simple, particularly as to its major objective. As Roosevelt had stated to his countrymen in his fourth inaugural in January, 1945, "We have learned to be citizens of the world, members of the human community." This sentiment, born of the common dangers of a mighty war, pervaded both political parties. Republicans as well as Democrats demanded that steps be taken to repair the ghastly mistake of 1919–1920 and defend the future peace of mankind. As far back as 1941 the Anglo-American Atlantic Charter, endorsed subsequently by all the Allies, declared for a "permanent system of security." In 1943 a Moscow conference of the Foreign Ministers of America, Britain and Russia joined with the Chinese government in further pledging such action, while at home the House by a vote of 360 to 29 and the Senate by 85 to 5 lent bipartisan approval. This augured that the proposed world organization would not suffer the fate of Wilson's League at the hands of Congress.

Other developments also set the stage for a new league. In 1943 a conference of forty-four nations at Hot Springs, Virginia, deliberated on the world's food resources and made plans for a permanent Food and Agriculture Organization as an international fact-finding and advisory agency to improve conditions. As a stopgap measure the United Nations Relief and Rehabilitation Administration, established the same year, carried emergency relief and other assistance to liberated areas with funds provided by the member governments in proportion to their national wealth. Before this project came to an end early in 1947, UNRRA under American leadership had spent nearly

471

$4,000,000,000 (mostly supplied by the United States) in thirty-nine countries of Europe and Asia. In July, 1944, a forty-four-nation conference at Bretton Woods in New Hampshire's White Mountains determined upon an International Bank for Reconstruction and Development and an International Monetary Fund. The one, known usually as the World Bank, was to lend money to war-stricken countries to help them get back on their feet; the other was to use its funds to stabilize the value of currencies as an aid to international trade. America in each case furnished a third of the capital. In November a gathering of fifty-four governments in Chicago set up a provisional organization to deal with matters of civil aviation.

Meanwhile in the summer and autumn of 1944 American, British, Soviet and Chinese delegates at Dumbarton Oaks, an estate in the District of Columbia, laid the groundwork for the over-all world body, subject to later revision and elaboration by a conference of all the nations concerned. At Yalta in the Crimea in February, 1945, Roosevelt, Churchill and Stalin advanced the cause a step further by settling tentatively the knotty question of special voting rights for the Big Five (America, Great Britain, Russia, France and China) in the projected Security Council. Later in the month an Inter-American Conference on Problems of Peace and War in Mexico City reaffirmed and strengthened earlier commitments for peace in the Western Hemisphere as part of the expected global system. The principal pledge, known as the Act of Chapultepec (March 3), stipulated that, while the Axis struggle continued, an attack on any of the countries would be deemed an attack on all and pledged them in such case to confer upon the "measures they think that it might be advisable to take" conformable to the regulations of the world organization when formed. This action was aimed particularly at Argentina, the lone absentee from the gathering, which because of pro-Germanism, native fascism and long-time jealousy of the United States had stayed out of the war. In the interests of hemispheric unity, however, Argentina was told that, by accepting the Act of Chapultepec and entering the conflict even at this late date, she would be eligible to attend the impending meeting to establish the global machinery of peace. She hastily complied.

Late in April, 1945, President Truman, newly in office and speaking from the White House by radio, opened the San Francisco Conference of forty-six (later fifty) governments. Argentina, not present at the beginning, was admitted only over the Soviet Union's strenuous opposition. Outstanding among the two hundred members of every race and clime were Britain's Foreign Secretary Anthony Eden, Russia's Vyacheslav M. Molotov and China's T. V. Soong. The aged Jan C. Smuts of South Africa, veteran of the Paris Peace Conference where he had effectively championed the League of Nations, was also present. The United States was represented at the gathering by a bipartisan delegation of seven led by Secretary of State Edward R. Stettinius, Jr., and including two members each of the Senate and House, ex-Governor Harold E. Stassen of Minnesota and a woman (Dean Virginia C. Gildersleeve of Barnard College). The Conference's most serious disputes arose over the distribution of authority between the General Assembly and the Security Council, with the smaller powers striving to buttress the former and weaken the latter.

The outcome of two months of discussion was the Charter of the United Nations, modeled broadly on the League Covenant and perpetuating the name of the victorious wartime coalition. The new body should by collective means "maintain international peace and security," bar "acts of aggression or other breaches of the peace," and promote the "fundamental freedoms" and "economic and social advancement of all peoples" regardless of race, sex, language or religion. Its principal organs are the General Assembly, composed of all the participating nations; the Security Council, with the Big Five as permanent members plus six others chosen for two-year terms by the General Assembly; the Economic and Social Council of eighteen, named for three-year terms by the General Assembly and empowered to make recommendations on economic, cultural, humanitarian and other matters affecting human rights; the International Court of Justice (essentially a carry-over of the old World Court), elected by the General Assembly and the Security Council; and the Secretariat or administrative division, headed by a Secretary General similarly appointed.

The General Assembly's chief function is to consider matters touching international peace and the other interests of the UN and to frame recommendations for action by the Security Council or by UN members. This last provision was to assume unforeseen significance during the Korean War. On important subjects a two-thirds majority is required, with each delegation voting on a basis of equality. The Security Council, the more powerful branch, has "primary responsibility" for the preservation of peace and security. It has authority to "call upon" the participating governments to impose economic sanctions against aggressors and can "take such action by air, sea or land forces as may be needed." For this purpose the UN members "undertake" to make armed assistance available to the Security Council. Seven of the eleven Council votes are required for affirmative actions, but any one of the Big Five can veto a majority decision except of a "procedural" or routine nature. The parties to a dispute, however, must abstain from voting.

The provision for the veto involved gross inequality of status, but it was justified by its proponents on the ground that, without unanimity among the great powers, the Charter could not work anyway. Stalin at Yalta had insisted on the arrangement; Roosevelt, recalling the Senate's objections to the League Covenant, had readily gone along; and Molotov at San Francisco was its most tenacious advocate. The smaller powers, however, succeeded in excluding two matters from the single-power veto: the election of World Court judges; and the calling of conferences to revise the Charter, though in the latter case one of the Big Five could still kill a proposed amendment. It was expected that the veto would be seldom used and then only as a last resort.

In addition to these organs, a Trusteeship Council exercises general supervision over politically immature colonial areas, whether acquired from the enemy powers or otherwise. Moreover, under the aegis of the Economic and Social Council there soon appeared, like satellites around a planet, a number of specialized agencies as contemplated by the Charter. Some, as we have seen, were in process before the UN was formed. The principal ones are the Food and Agriculture Organization, the World Bank, the International Monetary Fund, the Civil Aviation Organization, the World Health Organization, the International Labor Organization (surviving from the League) and the United Nations Educational, Scientific and Cultural Organization or UNESCO. The Charter also recognizes the "inherent right of individual or collective self-defense" by UN members against aggression until the Security Council takes appropriate action, and it authorizes "regional arrangements or agencies" for carrying out the UN's objectives, thus leaving scope for such agreements as those in the Western Hemisphere as well as for the later North Atlantic Defense Treaty. All members agree to "give the United Nations every assistance in any action" taken in accordance with the Charter and to "refrain from giving assistance to any state against which the United Nations is taking preventive or enforcement action."

On July 28, 1945, the Senate after six days of unruffled discussion ratified the Charter by a sweeping bipartisan vote of 89 to 2—a shining contrast to the eight months' violent debate that had slain the League Covenant. On October 29, when Soviet Russia, last of the Big Five and the twenty-ninth government to act, gave assent, the UN came into being. In December, Congress in the United Nations Participation Act committed itself further by authorizing the President to institute economic sanctions at the bidding of the Security Council and to negotiate an agreement with the Council for designating the armed forces subject to its call. Though Congress must approve the terms of this agreement, the President thereafter would be free to act in particular instances without further reference to the lawmaking branch. Late in 1946 the UN General Assembly voted to fix the world organization's permanent headquarters in New York City on a site presented by John D. Rockefeller, Jr. There could be no doubt of America's intent to make the new system of collective security succeed. Never in a single generation had a great nation undergone so complete a transformation of sentiment.

THE COLD WAR IN CENTRAL AND EASTERN EUROPE

The San Francisco Conference was held before the close of hostilities in order to separate the long-range task of international security from the immediate one of arriving at peace conditions for the Axis countries. These terms were foreshadowed by certain actions taken during the war by the chief Allied belligerents. The decisions affected both Europe and Asia, but for the present only those involving Europe will be considered.

At Moscow in October, 1943, after Italy's surrender, the Foreign Ministers of the United States, Britain and Russia had pledged the restoration of democratic regimes in Italy and Austria. At Yalta in February, 1945, Roosevelt, Churchill and Stalin, going farther, assured all Axis satellites and liberated peoples the right to "create democratic institutions of their own choice," and enjoined Poland, already liberated, to hold "free and unfettered elections on the basis of universal suffrage." At the same time they promised eastern Poland to the Soviet Union, with compensation to the Poles in the form of nearby German territory, subject to final determination in the peace treaty. These boundary changes, decreed without consulting the inhabitants concerned and hence breaching the Atlantic Charter, reflected a fear by the President and Prime Minister that Russia, despite her plighted word, might otherwise conclude a separate peace with Germany. They were not the last of such concessions to the Soviet Union. The conferees also agreed upon Germany's disarmament and her temporary occupation in distinct zones by the three powers plus France. As for reparations, Germany must make German labor available to the victors, relinquish ships and industrial equipment as well as all foreign investments and, for an unstated period, part with an annual share of current production.

By the time of the next Big Three conference in July, 1945, at Potsdam on the outskirts of Berlin, Germany had capitulated, Truman had succeeded to office, and Churchill was replaced during the sessions by Clement R. Attlee, the new Prime Minister thanks to a Labour victory in a British election. The defeated Nazi foe again received major attention. The Allied chiefs decided that Germany's leaders should be punished as war criminals, her political structure be decentralized and no general government be permitted for a while, but that pains should be taken at the local and provincial levels to revive political life on a democratic basis. Furthermore, Germany, though divided into military zones, should be treated during the occupation as a single economic unit; trusts and cartels—fountainheads of past armed aggression—should be broken up; and the country's economic life be reshaped to emphasize agriculture and peaceful industries. An Allied Control Council at Berlin would supervise these proceedings. Conditional upon the eventual settlement, Russia was now granted a further slice of territory, bordering on the Baltic Sea.

To clear the ground for the final settlement, the Potsdam conference authorized a Council of Foreign Ministers of the four great Western powers to draft treaties for Italy and the Axis satellites: Rumania, Bulgaria, Hungary and Finland. Similar action in the case of Germany was put off because of the lack of any government there as well as the desire to avoid the mistakes of haste that had marred the Treaty of Versailles. But already there were appearing the tensions and crises which, as they increased, came to be known as the 'cold war.' The Soviet Union, pleading considerations of security and acting singularly in the tradition of old-time Czarist imperialism, had sought systematically from early 1945 to expand its boundaries and extend the sway of Communism. On the other hand, the United States, commencing to regret the earlier concessions to Moscow, was beginning to consider how to hold Russia in check. With Britain in a precarious economic state because of the war, America had inherited the position of leadership in global affairs which the older country had so long and peaceably exercised. Just an hour before his death Roosevelt had written to Churchill regarding Moscow's increasing truculence, "We must be firm." When Secretary of State James F. Byrnes, in office from July, 1945, sought to reassure Russia in September, 1946, as to her security by proposing a forty-year guarantee of the major powers against future German aggression, Moscow turned a deaf ear.

Meanwhile Soviet obstructionism stalled the writing of the five peace treaties. Three meetings of the Foreign Ministers broke up in discord; a fourth did better only by postponing the more troublesome issues; and a twenty-one-nation conference in Paris to consider the proposals proved equally stormy. A subsequent meeting of the Council of Foreign Ministers in New York in December, 1946, however, concluded the drafting of the terms on the basis of mutual concessions. With the signing of the treaties in Paris in February, 1947, peace came formally to Italy and the satellites, with territorial losses, the imposition of reparations, and limitations on their armed strength. They were also required to protect the "fundamental freedoms" of their peoples, including liberty of the ballot, of the press and of political opinion. How little these latter provisions meant to some of these countries was soon to appear.

The question of Austria, which Hitler had forcibly annexed in 1938, proved harder to solve. When the fighting stopped, the country was split into four zones after the German model, with occupation troops in each and an Allied Council in Vienna. Russia vainly tried to get a Communist-controlled regime recognized, and in November, 1945, a non-Communist federal republic was set up following a free election. The peace treaty was delayed, however, mainly by Moscow's greed for reparations, with other difficulties due to Yugoslavia's territorial demands on Austria. In June, 1949, the Council of Foreign Ministers compromised the Russian claims and prepared once more to work out final terms, but without success. Moscow evidently hoped that time would work on its behalf and in October, 1950,

Courtesy of the *New York Times*

fomented a series of political strikes and disorders in Vienna and elsewhere. But the authorities quickly quelled the commotions, and America and Britain informed the Austrian government that, should Soviet-backed disturbances recur, they would lend it "full support." Two months later, when the deputies of the Foreign Ministers held their two-hundred-and-fifty-eighth meeting on the peace question, the prospects seemed as remote as ever.

Prostrate Germany provided the principal focus of the Cold War in this area of the world. The Western democracies, for their part, aimed to revive normal living and working conditions as fast as possible and thereby forestall a resurgence of dictatorship as well as restore Europe's economic balance. The Soviet Union, on the contrary, hoped by blocking these efforts to win the despairing masses to Communism. Endless disputes occurred, notably over Russia's excessive reparations levies, her refusal to carry out the Potsdam pledge for Germany's economic unification and her opposition to currency reform as an aid to recovery. Great Britain and the United States nevertheless merged their zones economically in December, 1946, France added hers a few months later, and the three powers in 1948 introduced a sound legal tender in their areas. On their initiative, too, a federal republic for West Germany was created on the basis of free elections in May, 1949, with its headquarters at Bonn. It embraced the three Western zones—two thirds of the whole country—and the rest of Germany was given a standing invitation to join. The military occupation continued, however, and the three nations retained for the time a veto over all acts of the regime.

The Soviet Union replied to these proceedings by organizing a puppet government in its own area which promulgated a pro-Communist constitution for all Germany and had its capital at Berlin in the heart of the Russian zone. As a more defiant step, it shut off land and water traffic between Berlin (where all four powers occupied sectors) and the Western zones. By this daring move Moscow intended to starve the non-Communist Berliners into submission, force the democratic powers to leave, and so gain prestige and support for Communism throughout Germany. The blockade, lasting from June, 1948, to May, 1949, utterly failed because the Americans and British countered with a gigantic 'airlift,' which flew in food, coal and other stores on a round-the-clock schedule. The 60,000 men who took part carried 1,600,000 tons at a cost (exclusive of the supplies) of $175,000,000 to the United States and $50,000,000 to Britain.

Anticipating further designs by Russia on the weak West German republic, the Foreign Ministers of America, Britain and France at a meeting in New York in September, 1950, served warning that an act of aggression against the new state or the non-Communist sectors of Berlin would be considered an attack on their own countries. Besides, they authorized the Bonn government to enlarge greatly its police force for internal security and to augment steel production to a point that would facilitate the defense of Western Europe. In addition, they agreed to relax certain other political and economic controls. Several months later, in March, 1951, Bonn was permitted to establish direct diplomatic relations with foreign governments, subject to some limitations as to the agreements that might be reached. But the outlook for a general peace treaty with Germany remained dim.

Meanwhile, elsewhere in Central and Eastern Europe, the Soviet Union registered notable gains, with one country after another disappearing behind the 'Iron Curtain.' In less than three years of peace Russia by political infiltration and secret subversion won a great deal more territory for Communism than her armies had overrun during the war.[1] Yugoslavia, Albania, Rumania and Bulgaria came out of the conflict with Communists in power; Poland and Hungary were taken over in short order by Red minorities; and Czechoslovakia succumbed in February, 1948. Of these states only Yugoslavia, in 1948, repudiated Russia's control of her affairs—much to the Kremlin's fury. Jossip B. Tito, the Yugoslav dictator, did not repudiate Communism as an ideology, however, and in international relations he only reluctantly deserted the Moscow line. All these countries were one-party states, substituting the secret police for the secret ballot and ruthlessly suppressing basic human freedoms and political dissent. In the case of Poland and the three former Axis satellites (Rumania, Bulgaria and Hungary) these actions brazenly violated the conditions of their re-establishment as independent governments. In 1949 and again in 1950 the UN General Assembly vainly denounced the satellites for "willful refusal" to discharge their treaty obligations.

Communism, reflecting another ancient aspiration of the Czars, also probed southward toward the shores of the Mediterranean.

[1] Moscow's technique of taking over a foreign country became gradually clear to the outside world. First, Soviet agents or adherents organized secret groups ('cells') in labor unions and among discontented elements. Next, these groups formed a 'popular front' by allying themselves with liberals and socialists of various shades of opinion. As Stalin says in *Foundations of Leninism,* "The revolutionary will accept a reform in order to use it as a screen behind which his illegal activities for the revolutionary preparation of the masses for the overthrow of the bourgeoisie may be intensified." On obtaining political office the Communist leaders sought such key positions as Minister of the Interior (in order to control the police) and Minister of Public Instruction (in order to control the press and radio). Then they proceeded to extend their sway over all other branches of the government. Finally, they purged the non-Communist liberals who had innocently helped them rise to power. By this devious process they arrived at what Karl Marx called the "dictatorship of the proletariat."

Guerrilla forces crossing into Greece from Yugoslavia, Albania and Bulgaria aided a bloody insurrection against the duly elected royalist regime, while the Soviet Union itself sought by menaces to frighten Turkey into conceding joint control of the Dardanelles as well as surrendering some territory. Until March, 1947, Britain furnished military and economic help to the Greek government, but then financial troubles at home brought this to an end, and President Truman stepped vigorously into the breach with reference to both Greece and Turkey. "It must be the policy of the United States," he told Congress, "to support free peoples who are resisting attempted subjugation by armed minorities or by outside pressures" and so give "effect to the principles of the Charter of the United Nations." Pointing out that "The seeds of totalitarian regimes are nurtured by misery and want," he particularly stressed material and technical assistance. In response, Congress in May backed up the 'Truman Doctrine' with smashing majorities, voting an initial $400,000,000 to strengthen Greece and Turkey economically and militarily, but providing at Senator Vandenberg's suggestion for suspending the aid whenever the Security Council should find it "unnecessary or undesirable." This proviso brought the action formally under the UN without, however, exposing the undertaking to the possibility of a Soviet veto. Though the fighting in Greece went on into 1949, the government forces eventually prevailed and, for the time at least, Communist imperialism in that direction was halted.

THE COLD WAR IN WESTERN EUROPE

The Truman Doctrine became the touchstone of America's later moves in the Cold War. Its central principle—the right of a people to protection against aggression—harked back to the original Monroe Doctrine; it had been evoked again in the Open Door policy on behalf of China; and now the United States, as a champion of the United Nations Charter and the most powerful of the Western democracies, reasserted it with reference to other parts of the world. The object was not to destroy Communist totalitarianism where it already existed, however hateful its practices, but to prevent its spread elsewhere by illegal and violent means. In short, the policy was one of 'containment' to safeguard both global stability and America's own security. In the President's words to Congress, "If we falter in our leadership, we may endanger the peace of the world—and we shall surely endanger the welfare of our own nation."

The next application of the principle was to Western Europe. There the Communists, coached from Moscow and capitalizing upon the postwar prostration of business and agriculture, had developed strong parties, notably in France and Italy, where they also staged political strikes and engaged in terrorist and other disruptive activities. From time to time the United States had made loans to various governments to better economic conditions—the largest, of $3,750,-000,000, to Britain in July, 1946—but these sums had been spent mostly for immediate purposes and without reference to a considered program of general European recovery. To correct this situation, Secretary of State George C. Marshall, who had succeeded Byrnes several months before, speaking at Harvard University in June, 1947, invited all Europe to work out a long-range co-ordinated plan which the United States would help to finance. "Our policy," he observed, "is directed not against any country or doctrine but against hunger, poverty, desperation and chaos" so as to "permit the emergence of political and social conditions in which free institutions can exist."

The 'Marshall Plan' to help the Old World help itself was curtly rejected by the Soviet Union, where free institutions were anathema. Molotov termed the offer an "imperialist plot to enslave Europe," and the Communist satellites had no choice but to parrot him. If the proposal had first been submitted to the Security Council, Russia's veto would have killed it. But sixteen other nations, meeting in Paris in July, 1947, gladly accepted it, and in April, 1948, Congress by massive majorities voted $5,055,000,000 as the first annual installment on a tapering four-year European Recovery Program affecting the sixteen countries with their overseas dependencies as well as the Western occupation zones of Germany. "Search back as one may through the annals of the United States or of any other Power," declared the London *Economist,* "there is no record of a comparable act of inspired and generous diplomacy." The expenditures, mostly in gifts, partly in loans, were supervised for America by an Economic Co-operation Administration initially under Paul G. Hoffman, a former automobile manufacturer, and the total amount available was increased by the requirement that each country match with its own currency ("counterpart funds") the sums given outright by the United States. For the first three years Congress's appropriations amounted to $11,000,000,000.

The projects thus instituted included such undertakings as factories, up-to-date machinery, technical assistance, hydroelectric plants,

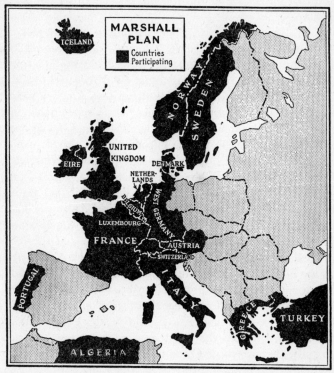

Courtesy of the *New York Times*

railroads, highways, bridges, public housing, the reclamation of farm land and the reduction of national debts. By 1950, halfway through the four-year span, Western Europe's industrial production had been brought above the prewar level, agricultural production was approaching it, and the emphasis was turning toward finding markets for the enlarged output in freer trade relations in Europe and with the rest of the world. In fact, Great Britain in the final days of the year announced that conditions were so satisfactory that she would forgo future Marshall Plan aid. Moreover, the Communist tide had been reversed in France and Italy, and a powerful impetus been given toward creating a closer union, both economically and politically, among the ancient countries of Western Europe, so long divided by historical feuds, business rivalries and national ambitions. Congress in making the second annual appropriation had indeed specifically declared that one of its objects was "to encourage the unification of Europe."

As a further move against "hunger, misery and despair" President Truman in his inaugural in January, 1949, recommended a "bold new program" for the underdeveloped areas of the globe—a proposal which became known as 'Point Four' because of the order of its presentation in his address. He urged that America share with backward peoples her vast technological knowledge in manufacturing, road building, agriculture and other fields and, in co-operation with other free nations, foster the introduction of private capital for such purposes. "The old imperialism—exploitation for foreign profit —has no place in our plans," he said. "What we envisage is a program of development based on the concepts of democratic fair dealing."

The underlying idea was not new. Technical assistance had long been provided by the State Department for Latin America and had more recently entered into the Truman Doctrine and the Marshall Plan. It had also played a modest role in the work of UN agencies such as the Food and Agriculture Organization and the World Health Organization. Truman now proposed to broaden such activities into a continuing large-scale effort to benefit other peoples as well, notably in Africa and the Near and Far East. By raising the standard of living in retarded regions the Point Four program was expected not only to spike the growth of Communism but to create new markets for sustaining European recovery. The UN Economic and Security Council and the General Assembly eagerly approved the idea, and a conference of fifty-four nations in 1950 laid plans for its financing. In August of that year Congress for its part voted $34,500,000 as a starter, though the Senate refused to go along with the House in providing a guarantee of $250,000,000 for private American investments under the plan. The long-range effects of the undertaking belong to the future. Among the Washington government's initial projects were rural-welfare programs in Liberia and Iran (formerly Persia) and a survey of Paraguay's natural resources and technological needs.

While Point Four was still under consideration, the United States made an even greater breach with the past by forming a peacetime military alliance with Europe. In September, 1947, Washington and the Latin American republics, acting within the framework of the UN Charter, had signed a treaty at Rio de Janeiro, Brazil, to make permanent the wartime pledge in the Act of Chapultepec for collective measures against attacks on any of them. The pact authorized the Foreign Ministers of these governments to decide by a two-thirds vote upon the appropriate means, with the proviso that no country would be required to use armed force without its consent. On the basis of this accomplishment in the Western Hemisphere, the United States Senate in June, 1948, on Vandenberg's motion, invited a group of Europe's non-Communist governments to take a like step. The upshot was the North Atlantic Defense Treaty in April, 1949, largely the handiwork of Dean G. Acheson, an experienced official in the State Department who had succeeded General Marshall as Secretary in January.

Twelve nations—the United States and Canada in North America, Iceland in mid-ocean, and Great Britain, Norway, Denmark, the Netherlands, Belgium, Luxemburg, France (including Algeria), Portugal and Italy in Europe—bound themselves to resist an assault on any of them as an assault on all of them, with each government free to determine, individually or in concert with others, the measures to be employed. After twenty years any of the participants might withdraw upon a year's notification. Resting on the principle of the interdependence of independence in a world imperiled by Soviet imperialism, the pact served notice that America would not again stand neutral while Europe was being overrun: the aggressor would face a solid Western phalanx. It replaced the old pacifist doctrine of peace through weakness with the bitterly learned lesson of peace through strength. In July, 1949, the Senate ratified the treaty by more than six to one (82 to 13), with Taft in the minority voting against Vandenberg and the bulk of his own party. In October Congress, to put teeth into the action, enacted the Mutual Defense Assistance Program giving America's partners weapons and other armament—$1,000,-000,000 worth for the first year.

In addition, America, resolved to counter Soviet propaganda around the world, moved vigorously into the area of psychological warfare. The State Department staffed United States embassies with public-information officers and cultural attachés and stepped up the distribution of printed matter. Through the "Voice of America" on the radio it endeavored to pierce the Iron Curtain and enlighten the peoples there as to the differences between democracy and Communism. It also subsidized the exchange of teachers and students with other nations by means of funds realized through the sale of surplus war

Courtesy of the *New York Times*

materials left in those countries. Unofficial efforts paralleled official ones. For example, a World Federation of Trade Unions was established, and when this fell under Communist control, it was replaced in 1949 by the International Confederation of Free Trade Unions.

RUSSIA AND THE UNITED NATIONS

As this chain of events disclosed, mankind instead of working together as One World—the fond expectation of the statesmen at San Francisco—was again divided into two hostile camps. Repercussions of the Cold War constantly hampered the effectiveness of the United

Nations. Yet the organization quietly accomplished much good. Thus it put a stop to bloodshed and paved the way for establishing the new Republic of Israel in Palestine. For his services as UN mediator in this undertaking Ralph J. Bunche of the United States, grandson of an American slave, was awarded the Nobel Peace Prize in 1950. Farther to the east, the UN helped compose dangerous disputes in Iran, in Indonesia (the former Dutch East Indies) and between the two new states of India and Pakistan. In Africa it disposed of two problems left unsettled in the Italian peace treaty by granting independence to Libya from 1952 and to Somaliland from 1960, with Italy acting as UN trustee for the latter until that time. In the Near East it organized a program of public works to give employment to homeless Arab refugees from Palestine.

It also adopted an impressive Declaration of Human Rights to serve as an economic as well as political standard for all peoples—a special endeavor of Mrs. Franklin D. Roosevelt who headed the drafting committee. In like fashion the many UN specialized agencies furnished assistance where need called. In 1948, for example, the International Monetary Fund made loans to ten nations to keep their currencies in order, the World Bank lent more than $500,000,000 to five countries for reconstruction projects, while the World Health Organization aided in immunizing 15,000,000 European children against tuberculosis. In the first four years the UN and its branches sponsored some eleven hundred meetings of one sort or another in the effort to promote lasting peace through mutual helpfulness.

On the other hand, Soviet recalcitrance prevented more decisive measures for global stability. That government, judged by its performance, strove to advance its own security by making the free nations feel insecure. Vaunting its totalitarian system as "democracy," it unfailingly used the UN as an ideological soapbox for condemning America's "warmongering" and "capitalistic imperialism." It blocked all attempts at effective international control of atomic energy—an action that took on new meaning when it became known in September, 1949, that Russia had mastered the secret of the bomb. Likewise it barred the regulation of other weapons and of armed strength, and it sabotaged the provision of the UN Charter for earmarking military contingents and facilities of the member nations as a police force to execute the Security Council's decisions. By the end of 1950 it had cast forty-seven vetoes in the Security Council in pursuit of its various objects, as compared with two by France and none by America, Britain and China. In addition, it refused to join or support any of the new UN specialized agencies except, briefly, the World Health Organization.

Because of this record of non-co-operation some persons in the United States and elsewhere urged that the United Nations be reorganized without Russia. But it was the considered judgment of Trygve Lie of Norway after four years as Secretary General that "our troubles would have been much worse if the United Nations had not been established," and President Truman cautioned Congress in May, 1950, "We cannot expect from the United Nations immediate solutions of problems as large and complex as many that are before it. . . . We, for our part, will continue to negotiate and to examine every proposal in our unending effort to achieve security."

Within the United States, Russia's wanton course kindled new fears of Communism at home. As a political party the Communists had polled only 48,600 votes out of 48,820,000 in 1940, and they had not attempted a ticket of their own in either 1944 or 1948. But even with negligible numbers the danger existed of an infiltration of spies into branches of the government, such as the State and Defense Departments, whence vital information might be relayed to Moscow. The instance of Alger Hiss, who was convicted of perjury early in 1950 for denying that he had transmitted secret State Department documents to Soviet agents in 1937–1938, was paralleled by other cases involving, for example, the betrayal of technical data relating to the atom bomb. To guard against more such incidents, the administration in March, 1947, devised machinery for subjecting all federal employees to a continuing loyalty check with the help of the FBI. This screening involved not merely the men's personal opinions and conduct, but also their membership in organizations listed by the Attorney-General as subversive—thus applying the principle of guilt by association. In three and a half years it proved necessary to dismiss only 280 of the 13,000 persons examined as security risks, with others resigning during the inquiry. When Senator Joseph R. McCarthy, Wisconsin Republican, accused the State Department in 1950 of harboring from 205 to 57 Communists—he kept altering the number—the special Senate committee which sifted the charges pronounced them "a fraud and a hoax." Nonetheless, in the prevailing state of panic and alarm, McCarthy's allegations were not without political effect.

Communism outside the government also came under increasing fire. The labor movement, as has been seen, expelled pro-Soviet officials and unions, and without similar justification about half the states imposed anti-Communist oaths on teachers. In a direct blow at the Communist party the Department of Justice in October, 1948, after a disorderly nine-month trial, secured the conviction of eleven of the national leaders for advocating or teaching the overthrow of the government in violation of the Smith Act of 1940. In Congress agitation mounted for still stiffer legislation. The outcome was the Internal Security Act of September, 1950, popularly called the McCarran Act. It required all Communist and Communist-front organizations to register with the Justice Department with statements of their receipts and expenditures. It denied the members foreign passports, barred Communists from working for the government or defense plants, and forbade Communist and front groups to use the mails or broadcast over the radio unless their words were labeled as Communist-inspired. It provided further that in the event of war or insurrection Communists and others who might engage in sabotage or espionage be lodged in concentration camps. Additional sections of the law tightened existing regulations as to sabotage, espionage, immigration, naturalization and deportation.

The President, pronouncing many features of the enactment unconstitutional, unworkable or unwise, vetoed it. He called the registration clause "about as practical as requiring thieves to register with the sheriff," and declared that by putting government officials into the "thought-control business" the measure would enable them to "harass all of our citizens in the exercise of their right of free speech." Congress, unconvinced, repassed the bill over his veto by bipartisan majorities—286 to 48 in the House, 57 to 10 in the Senate.

THE COLD WAR IN ASIA

Russia cast her shadow over Asia as well as Europe. In that huge continent and its myriad islands dwelt a majority of the world's inhabitants, largely agricultural, economically backward, wretchedly poor, and long exploited by foreign governments or native feudal regimes. There, too, the struggle with Japan had fueled nationalist aspirations, and since the war-spent imperialistic powers could put up little resistance, this augured the speedy cessation of alien colonial rule. In addition, the war had created special problems for particular countries such as Japan and China. The Soviet Union, fishing in

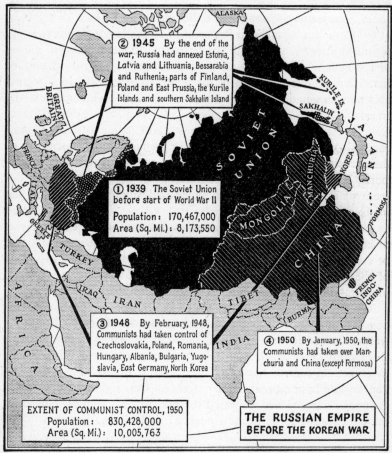

② **1945** By the end of the war, Russia had annexed Estonia, Latvia and Lithuania, Bessarabia and Ruthenia; parts of Finland, Poland and East Prussia; the Kurile Islands and southern Sakhalin Island

① **1939** The Soviet Union before start of World War II

Population: 170,467,000
Area (Sq. Mi.): 8,173,550

③ **1948** By February, 1948, Communists had taken control of Czechoslovakia, Poland, Romania, Hungary, Albania, Bulgaria, Yugoslavia, East Germany, North Korea

④ **1950** By January, 1950, the Communists had taken over Manchuria and China (except Formosa)

EXTENT OF COMMUNIST CONTROL, 1950
Population: 830,428,000
Area (Sq. Mi.): 10,005,763

THE RUSSIAN EMPIRE BEFORE THE KOREAN WAR

Courtesy of the *New York Times*

troubled waters, posed whenever possible as the friend of the discontented and disinherited, hoping by fair words, if not fair deeds, to acquire new bastions for Communism.

In bringing colonialism to an end the United States set Europe an example on America's own Independence Day, July 4, 1946, by freeing the Philippines, as had been scheduled in 1934. To give the new nation a favorable economic start, Congress turned over $520,000,000 for war damages and postwar rehabilitation plus $100,000,000 worth of surplus military materials, and it also authorized free trade with the United States until 1954, after which full duties should gradually be restored over a span of two decades. The constitution of the fledgling republic at first allowed only natives the future right to develop natural resources and public utilities, but an amendment in 1947 extended it for half a century to American citizens. In the same year the Manila government leased to the United States for ninety-nine years twenty-three military, naval and air bases, to be available as well to the Security Council. This evidenced that notwithstanding the political divorce Washington still stood committed to protecting the islands. Despite the careful training for self-rule under American tutelage the Filipinos made a poor start at governing themselves. Inept leadership and the demoralizing effects of the long Japanese occupation led to the wastage and corrupt use of much of the financial aid, as well as to other malpractices. To repair the situation, Washington in November, 1950, agreed to provide up to $250,000,000 in closely supervised loans and gifts over a period of five years on condition that the Manila authorities carry out basic economic, fiscal and land reforms.

The United States sought likewise to improve the status of Pacific lands continuing under the American flag. In 1950 Congress made the people of Guam, hitherto lacking self-government, American citizens with an elective legislature and a presidential-appointed governor. At President Truman's urging, the House of Representatives in 1950 also voted to admit Hawaii and Alaska as states, but the Senate delayed taking action.

In 1947 and 1948 the English government, foreseeing the inevitable, granted independence to Burma and a comparable status to Ceylon, India and Pakistan, though these remained nominally under the British Crown. In Malaya it also made concessions, setting up the Malayan Federation in 1948, with Britain's influence confined to military matters and foreign affairs. The Netherlands acted more reluctantly. Loath to loosen its profitable ties with Indonesia, it did so only after bloody fighting with the natives and intervention by the UN Security Council. The United States of Indonesia resulted late in 1949, officially under the Dutch Crown but otherwise master of its

own fate and equal partner with the home country in all things of
joint concern. Meanwhile France bestowed limited autonomy on the
several provinces of Indo-China and at the end of 1949 sponsored
the creation of Viet Nam ("Southern Land"), a federal system for

the country under Bao Dai as Chief of State. But the French retained
certain economic rights and the control of defense and foreign affairs;
and this fact, coupled with the weaknesses of Bao Dai's government,
fed the growth of Communism.

In all these lands Communist elements took advantage of the unsettled conditions to stir up trouble. In Burma, Malaya, Indonesia
and the Philippines (where the Communist-led peasant insurgents
were known as the Hukbalahaps or 'Huks') they staged repeated
uprisings. In Indo-China the Reds, largely trained and armed by the
Chinese Communists, were a standing threat to the Bao Dai regime,
and they would almost certainly have crushed it but for the prowess
of the French military. Calling themselves the Viet Minh ("Light of
the Land"), they obtained the Soviet Union's recognition as the lawful government. Russia's hand appeared even more boldly in countries
nearer her borders. In China, as we shall see, her problem was simpli-

fied by the long existence of a vigorous Communist movement, but in Iran and Korea she took a strong initiative.

In Iran, where rich oil deposits existed, a Moscow-incited revolt shortly after the war's close took over an important northwest province (Azerbaijan), and to preserve this foothold Russia declined to evacuate her wartime occupation troops on March 2, 1946, as she had agreed by treaty to do. The Iranian government promptly protested to the Security Council; the Council, against the Soviet delegate's bitter protests, kept close watch over the situation; and President Truman in a speech in Chicago on April 6 pledged military support of any UN actions to prevent the "coercion or penetration" of Iran. Yielding to pressure, Russia recalled her forces on May 6 upon an Iranian promise of oil concessions—which that nation's Parliament later repudiated.

In the case of Korea, on the North Pacific side of Asia, Moscow pursued different tactics. This country, a peninsula half again as large as Florida, had been an unwilling Japanese dependency before the war. Upon the conclusion of hostilities Soviet troops occupied it north of the 38th parallel and the United States south of the line in accordance with a plan to quiet conditions preparatory to national independence. Russia, however, on innumerable pretexts balked the culminating step; and when the UN General Assembly at America's suggestion authorized an election to set up an all-Korean government in May, 1948, the Soviet authorities not only kept their zone from taking part, but proclaimed a Russian-model all-Korean government of their own. Moscow's veto power precluded the Security Council from intervening with enforcement measures, but the General Assembly recognized the southern regime as the legal government of Korea, and the United States released $140,000,000 of Economic Co-operation Administration funds to it. These funds made it possible to achieve a food surplus and to double manufacturing output within a year. President Syngman Rhee also induced the legislature early in 1950 to undertake extensive land reforms. Though a majority of the countries in the UN followed the General Assembly's example in recognizing the new republic, the Soviet Union's veto blocked its admission to membership. The Russians, after equipping and training a strong North Korean army, departed late in 1948, while some of the American forces stayed on at the Korean government's request until the following June. In contrast to the Iranian adventure, Moscow had this time made good its defiance of the world organization and had, in addition, gained a new outpost for expanding Communism, the consequences of which would soon appear.

As regards Japan, a more crucial objective, Russia was able to make no headway. She was only one of a large number of governments (the others: America, Britain, China, France, the Netherlands, Canada, Australia, New Zealand, the Philippines, India and, later, Pakistan and Burma) on the Far Eastern Commission in Washington, which formulated the broad policies of the occupation. True, she, like America, Britain and China, had a veto over its acts, but this counted for little, for the effective authority resided in General Douglas MacArthur, the Allies' choice as Supreme Commander and the man on the ground. Though the Soviet Union also sat with the United States, China and the British Commonwealth of Nations on the resident Allied Council for Japan, this too availed little since that body was restricted mainly to offering advice to the Supreme Commander.

MacArthur in his new post worked as vigorously for peace as he had earlier for war. Heading occupation troops largely American, he disarmed and demobilized the Nipponese army, prohibited all aircraft construction, released political prisoners, disbanded the secret police, restored civil liberties, and saw to the trial and punishment of war criminals. He also supervised the collection of provisional reparations—Japanese foreign assets and a part of the island's industrial equipment—broke up the powerful financial and economic monopolies (the *Zaibatsu* or "Treasure Clans"), which had abetted imperialistic aggression, and obtained legislation to distribute land on easy terms to tenant farmers. At the same time the United States poured some two billion dollars into the country, at first for relief and then to provide raw materials for rebuilding the national economy. By these and like measures MacArthur aimed to clip the wings of the prewar militarists, business magnates and large landlords while strengthening democratic sentiments among the masses. And as a long-run assurance of peace he sponsored a new constitution for Japan which forever banned war and armed forces, declared the people's "right to life, liberty and the pursuit of happiness" to be the "supreme consideration in legislation," and demoted the once 'divine' Emperor to a mere figurehead in a representative parliamentary system like England's.

In July, 1947, the United States, satisfied with the progress that was being made, recommended that the nations in the Far Eastern Commission proceed to the drafting of a peace treaty; but the Soviet government, badly outnumbered in that body, insisted that this function belonged to the Foreign Ministers of Russia, America, Britain and China, with each power retaining a veto. As a result nothing was done. In fact, however, certain features of the settlement were predetermined by wartime agreements, most of which had already been put into effect. At a conference in Cairo in November, 1943, Roosevelt, Churchill and China's Generalissimo Chiang Kai-shek had decided on stripping Japan of Manchuria, Korea, Formosa and all other conquests since her war with China in 1895. At Yalta in 1945 the President and the Prime Minister, in order to draw the Soviet forces stationed on the Siberian-Manchurian frontier into the Asian fight, had secretly promised Stalin the Kurile Islands, Southern Sakhalin and special privileges in Manchuria as well as in Dairen and Port Arthur on the Yellow Sea. Still later, in 1947, the Security Council at Washington's request designated the United States as the UN trustee for the Marshalls, the Carolines and the Marianas (except Guam, already in America's hands). These had been German possessions before World War I, which Japan, administering as mandates under the League of Nations, had illegally fortified and used against the Americans in the recent war. The three groups comprise fourteen hundred islands, many mere coral reefs, and the total land area is less than that of Rhode Island. The United States was further granted permission to fortify the islands.

Because of Russia's continued intransigence, the United States informed her in December, 1950, that it could not admit that "any nation has a perpetual power to veto the conclusion by others of peace with Japan." Conferring separately with the various interested parties, Washington worked out a provisional settlement, and in July joined Britain in calling the well-disposed governments to a conference in San Francisco in September, 1951, to take final action. The terms limited Japan to her four home islands but, in view of the Soviet menace, allowed her to rearm for self-defense. At the same time America signed a pact with Australia and New Zealand declaring that an attack on any one of them in the Pacific would be deemed an attack on all of them. A bilateral agreement with Tokyo, to follow the peace treaty, provided for the retention of American troops and bases in Japan.

China, the greatest prize in the Asian Cold War, fell to the Soviet orbit largely as a result of internal anarchy. For many years Chinese Communist armies had been warring on the lawful government, Chiang Kai-shek's Kuomintang or Nationalist regime. Chiang's failure to carry through agrarian reforms and other welfare projects for the impoverished masses combined with administrative incompetence, repressive methods and widespread graft to discredit the Nationalists and further the Red cause. Even during the Japanese invasion, from 1937 onward, the contending forces did not altogether cease fighting each other while resisting the common foe. The Communist strongholds were North China and Manchuria. At the San Francisco Conference the strife-plagued country was made one of the five permanent members of the Security Council in the belief that it would soon solve its difficulties, and with the close of the Pacific war the United States tried repeatedly to end the civil convulsions by throwing its weight in the scales for a coalition government representing all factions. Throughout 1946, for example, General Marshall, not yet Secretary of State, was in China on a special mission for this purpose. Washington also continually urged on the Kuomintang the necessity of land redistribution to the peasants as well as other progressive measures. These efforts failed; but America nevertheless supported the Nationalists with funds, transport facilities and military stores as the lesser of the evils in a thoroughly unsatisfactory situation.

The Communists, beginning their march to victory in the autumn of 1948 and aided by American-supplied weapons captured from the Nationalists, harried the government forces successively out of Peiping, Nanking (the Kuomintang capital), Hankow and Canton. By December, 1949, Chiang had no alternative but to abandon the mainland and transfer his remaining troops to the island of Formosa, one hundred miles off shore. Though the Reds under Mao Tse-tung now held practically all of China, and though London as well as Moscow and other capitals formally recognized the new regime, the United States refrained; and the Security Council, for its part, declined to expel the Nationalist delegate. The Soviet Union, branding this proceeding illegal, withdrew from the Council in January, 1950, until a representative from Communist China should be given the seat.

Russia was soon bitterly to regret this move, however, for her absence made it impossible to exercise a veto when the Council some months later intervened in the Korean conflict. Jacob A. Malik, the Soviet delegate, eventually returned to the Council in August after the damage was done.

FULLER ACCOUNTS

World Leadership. Bailey, *Diplomatic History,* and Bemis, *Diplomatic History,* cover most of the developments, while more specific treatments include Dean, *Four Cornerstones of Peace,* on the genesis of the UN; Chase, *United Nations in Action;* Hurewitz, *Struggle for Palestine;* Bailey, *America Faces Russia,* which touches on the Cold War; and Reischauer, *United States and Japan,* which considers the American occupation of Japan. For subversive activities and anti-Communist restraints in the United States, see Barth, *Loyalty of Free Men,* and Weyl, *Treason.* For additional information on the international scene the student should consult the periodical publications cited at the end of the preceding chapter and also the quarterly *Foreign Affairs,* as well as the following annual surveys: Brookings Institution, *Major Problems of United States Foreign Policy* (from 1947); Council on Foreign Relations, *United States in World Affairs; Newsweek's History of Our Times* (from 1950); and *Yearbook of the United Nations.*

CHAPTER XXIII

THE KOREAN CRISIS

AGGRESSION BY NORTH KOREA

THE Korean War, though involving a small and far-off country, was to test America's capacity for global leadership and the UN's fidelity to the principle of collective security at the awful risk of a third world war. At dawn on Sunday, June 25, 1950, the North Korean Reds, equipped with Soviet-made weapons and tanks, swept across the 38th parallel into South Korea in overwhelming force, driving the ill-armed and demoralized defenders before them. This unprovoked assault of the Moscow-blessed regime on the UN-sponsored republic took the free nations by surprise. The aggression, however, had perhaps been unintentionally invited by a remark of Secretary of State Acheson before the National Press Club in Washington in January, 1950, that the United States did not consider Korea vital to national security. This may have created the impression that neither America nor the United Nations would come to its defense. Russia, though officially disclaiming any complicity in the invasion, hoped by this action of her puppet to establish Communism throughout the peninsula and so to gain a commanding position at the entrance of the Yellow Sea as well as to point a pistol at nearby Japan. It was also to her interest, if the unexpected should happen and the free nations did intervene, to bog them down in a distant conflict which would weaken their resistance to her own further aggressions in Europe.

The Security Council, called together at President Truman's request some hours after the invasion, and unhampered by the Soviet Union's presence, promptly branded the onslaught a "breach of the peace," bade the invaders withdraw, and asked the countries in the UN to "render every assistance" to that end. The victorious North Koreans, however, ignored the Council's action, and on the 27th Truman, under his constitutional authority as commander in chief, ordered United States air and sea forces into the fray. He also announced that the American Seventh Fleet would guard Formosa,

Chiang Kai-shek's last stronghold, against Red China and, further-more, that he would speed up military supplies to the Philippines and Indo-China. These supplementary steps he justified as necessary to localize the conflict and forestall a backfire of wars which would hinder the Korean operations. That evening the Security Council called upon all UN members "to repel the armed attack and to restore international peace and security in the area." Since Soviet objections long before the crisis had prevented military power from being placed at the Council's disposal, the Council could merely rec-ommend that the separate governments voluntarily take enforcement measures. At once the Russian newspaper *Pravda,* which spoke for the Kremlin, charged the United States (not the United Nations) with a "direct act of aggression" against North Korea. In words soon to be repeated again and again on the floor of the UN, it denied the Council's legal right to act, because of Russia's absence from its ranks—a self-imposed exile—and also Communist China's.

The events of June 27 mark a milestone in history. Never before had a world organization resorted to military sanctions, and never before had an American President unsheathed the sword on behalf of collective security before his own country was assailed. "The action was taken," in Truman's words, "as a matter of basic moral prin-ciple." He did not ask Congress for a declaration of war, since the intervention was an act of the United Nations to repulse aggression, not a conflict between the United States and another country. Fifty-three of the fifty-nine governments in the UN quickly accorded ap-proval of the Council's course, and thirty pledged assistance of one kind or another. At the Council's instance the United States desig-nated General MacArthur, who was heading the military occupation of Japan, as commander in chief of the UN forces under the UN flag.

The North Koreans at first had everything their own way. Greatly outnumbering the defenders, they also possessed superior weapons and knew how to take advantage of the hilly, scrub-coated, rain-soaked terrain. Moreover, many of them were battle-hardened vet-erans who had campaigned earlier with the Chinese Communists against Chiang Kai-shek, and who with their comrades now received munitions and other supplies from Red China and the Soviet Union. The brunt of the resistance fell on the Americans and South Koreans, with Lieutenant General Walton H. Walker in field command until his death from a motorcar accident in December caused him to be

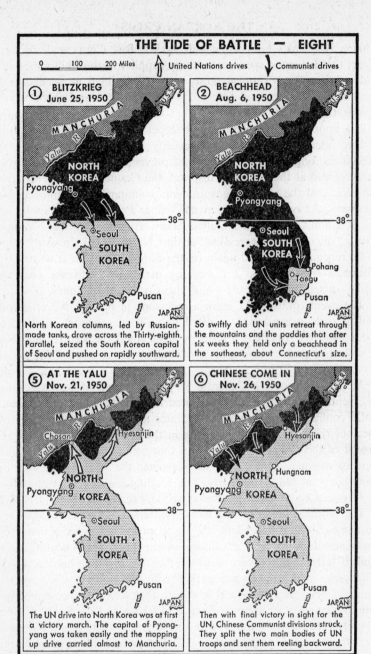

THE TIDE OF BATTLE — EIGHT

0 100 200 Miles ⇧ United Nations drives ⬇ Communist drives

**① BLITZKRIEG
June 25, 1950**

MANCHURIA

Yalu R.

U.S.S.R.

NORTH
KOREA

Pyongyang

38°

Seoul

SOUTH
KOREA

Pusan

JAPAN

North Korean columns, led by Russian-made tanks, drove across the Thirty-eighth. Parallel, seized the South Korean capital of Seoul and pushed on rapidly southward.

**② BEACHHEAD
Aug. 6, 1950**

MANCHURIA

Yalu R.

U.S.S.R.

NORTH
KOREA

Pyongyang

38°

Seoul

SOUTH
KOREA

Pohang

Taegu

Pusan

JAPAN

So swiftly did UN units retreat through the mountains and the paddies that after six weeks they held only a beachhead in the southeast, about Connecticut's size.

**⑤ AT THE YALU
Nov. 21, 1950**

MANCHURIA

Yalu R.

U.S.S.R.

Chosan

Hyesanjin

NORTH
KOREA

Pyongyang

38°

Seoul

SOUTH
KOREA

Pusan

JAPAN

The UN drive into North Korea was at first a victory march. The capital of Pyongyang was taken easily and the mopping up drive carried almost to Manchuria.

**⑥ CHINESE COME IN
Nov. 26, 1950**

MANCHURIA

Yalu R.

U.S.S.R.

Hyesanjin

NORTH
KOREA

Hungnam

Pyongyang

38°

Seoul

SOUTH
KOREA

Pusan

JAPAN

Then with final victory in sight for the UN, Chinese Communist divisions struck. They split the two main bodies of UN troops and sent them reeling backward.

STAGES IN THE KOREAN FIGHTING

▨ United Nations-held areas ■ Communist-held areas of Korea

③ COUNTERATTACK
Sept. 15, 1950

For another six weeks the UN withstood repeated attacks on its defense arc. Then its armies began a big push with an amphibious landing at Inchon on the west coast.

④ CROSSING THE 38TH
Oct. 2, 1950

The Inchon landing was followed by a break out of the beachhead. The North Koreans fell back in disorder and the reconquest of South Korea was quickly made.

⑦ CHINESE PUSH
Jan. 14, 1951

UN forces in the west fell back to new defenses below Parallel 38. Those in the east were evacuated by sea and brought south to take up positions in the line.

⑧ ATTRITION
June 25, 1951

After stabilizing its line, the UN began a slow, punishing advance. The strategy was to make the war so costly for the Chinese that they would accept a settlement.

Courtesy of the *New York Times*

replaced by Lieutenant General Matthew B. Ridgway. The other UN countries were slow in sending troops. Since the GIs found it hard to distinguish between friend and foe, it was simple for the North Koreans to infiltrate the lines and launch murderous attacks from unexpected quarters. The outmatched UN forces had no choice but to yield ground repeatedly until they were flung back into an area in the extreme southeast, about half the size of New Jersey, which guarded the vital supply port of Pusan. It was the old story of American unpreparedness. Despite this series of defeats, however, the United States navy tightly blockaded the coasts with help from the British Commonwealth, and American aircraft with similar support bombed industrial and military objectives and communication lines. Though the fliers met slight opposition they had no easy task. "The enemy," reported General MacArthur, "shuns exposure by day, concealing his supplies and reserves in homes, in schools and other public buildings. He drives his tanks and trucks through walls of simple peasant shelters that he might avoid daylight detection."

By mid-September, however, the disheartening period of retreat and defense came to a halt. The UN army, reinforced and re-equipped, loosed a powerful counteroffensive starting with an amphibious landing at Inchon on the west coast, a hundred and fifty miles behind the enemy's front, and soon they hurled the foe back across the 38th parallel. This restored the situation existing before the invasion, but it still left the peninsula divided politically, and if no further action were taken, it would free the North Koreans to reorganize at leisure for a new onslaught. Hence the UN General Assembly on October 7 voted that "all appropriate steps" be adopted to establish "stability throughout Korea," with the troops remaining no longer than necessary for creating a "unified, independent and democratic government." Red China at once warned that it would "not supinely tolerate" any crossing of the parallel by the UN forces, and in the ensuing weeks increasing numbers of Chinese soldiers—serving on an independent and volunteer basis, as the Peiping regime blandly announced—fought alongside the North Koreans. Nevertheless the UN troops in subzero weather and against bitter resistance drove stubbornly on over mountainous, forested country toward the Yalu River at the Manchurian border. This point some South Korean elements reached on October 26, and several weeks later General MacArthur unleashed a grand assault to wind up the war. Victory seemed well in hand when, as we shall see, the whole character of the conflict was transformed by an unexpected massive counterthrust of the Chinese from Manchuria.

At home the initial successes of the North Korean aggressors dazed the public, for Congress since the beginning of 1946 had spent $48,-440,000,000 on defense. Why, then, had the nation been caught napping? The answer lay largely in the fact that the government had stressed preparations for a possible atomic showdown with Russia to the relative neglect of other forms of armament and of a balanced military program. The United States was readier for a great war than a small one—a war, moreover, which, if it came, was expected to explode in Europe rather than in Asia. Though the total armed forces stood at 1,450,000 when the hostilities began, the ground troops, so important in the Korean fight, had been allowed to fall to 596,000, with many doing police duty in Germany, Austria, Japan and elsewhere. Others, to be sure, were in the Reserves or in training under Selective Service, but few of these were available for instant combat. Finally, the Defense Department was confronted with the giant task of transporting the bulk of the men, equipment and supplies to a battlefield seven thousand miles from the homeland. The build-up of strength even under more favorable conditions would have been necessarily slow.

To redress past miscalculations the White House and Congress now acted vigorously. They were spurred not only by the existing emergency, but by fear that Korea-type incidents would erupt in other parts of the earth and so dissipate America's resources further to Russia's advantage. The reaction outside government circles was indicated by a Gallup poll reporting seven out of ten people (68 per cent) as opposed to Soviet expansion in Asia and Europe even at the cost of a general war; in 1940–1941 a similar majority had condemned Nazi aggression. Congress promptly removed the statutory limit on the nation's armed strength, and on July 7, 1950, the President, announcing a goal of at least 3,000,000 for the army, navy and air force, appealed for more volunteers, stepped up inductions under Selective Service and ordered other additions from the Reserves and the National Guard. In September he replaced Defense Secretary Louis A. Johnson, whose economy program had contributed to the unpreparedness, with George C. Marshall, who brought to the office the prestige of having been Chief of Staff during the Axis war as well as an able Secretary of State under Truman. As financial sinews for the military speed-up, Congress in September voted an additional $11,600,000,000 (totaling $25,600,000,000 for the year), besides $4,000,000,000 more for rearming Western Europe (making $5,225,-000,000 for the year). To help defray the expenditures it boosted taxes all along the line. Then, following the pattern set in World War II, it passed the Defense Production Act the same month, which conferred on the President extraordinary economic powers—to requisition plants and materials, to allocate essential supplies, and to combat inflation with wage, price and credit controls and rationing.

The November elections of 1950 renewed Democratic control of Congress but with reduced majorities. The Republicans had helped to increase their strength by accusing the administration of coddling Communists in government posts and of blundering into an avoidable war in Korea, but the UN military successes combined with the Fair Deal's domestic program to blunt these charges. The role of domestic issues is suggested by the fact that the American Medical Association spent over $1,000,000 on newspaper, magazine and radio advertising to discredit the President's health-insurance proposal. Moreover, in Ohio, where the national labor organizations strove to defeat Senator Taft for re-election because of the Taft-Hartley Act, he won by the biggest vote ever cast for a Senatorial candidate in that state. With the White House mustering only slim margins in the new Congress (2 in the Senate and 34 in the House), a coalition of conservatives—Southern Democrats and Northern Republicans— was in a position to wield the whip hand. The importance of this, however, was lessened by the fact that the intervention of Communist China in the Korean War a few weeks later united all factions, at least for the time, in measures to confront the new crisis.

AGGRESSION BY RED CHINA

Though more and more Chinese 'volunteers' had been reinforcing and stiffening the demoralized North Koreans, General MacArthur told President Truman, who flew to Wake Island to confer with him in mid-October, 1950, that he did not expect Red China to stage a full-scale offensive. A month later MacArthur was still so confident of the restricted nature of the war that he promised his men they would be home by Christmas. He had not reckoned sufficiently, however, with the growing alarm of the Communist authorities in both Peiping and Moscow as the UN arms approached nearer their frontiers and endangered the great hydroelectric plants on the south side of the Yalu River, which supplied power for Manchuria's industries. Indeed, to reassure the Chinese ruler Mao Tse-tung on this score, MacArthur had carefully refrained from bombing these plants. In the belief that he could quell the remaining enemy resistance at will, he now overextended his lines, outrunning his supplies, scattering his units and exposing their flanks.

Unexpectedly on November 26, two days after his offensive to end the war began, the Chinese Reds, overtopping the UN forces by an estimated two or three to one, counterattacked across the Yalu from Manchuria, routing the South Korean contingents, stalling MacArthur's advance and presently splitting his command into two parts. The UN troops in the northwest reeled back in the cruel winter cold to establish a defense line near the 38th parallel. Those in the northeast escaped almost certain destruction by being evacuated from the port of Hungnam in a remarkable amphibious operation under a curtain of protective fire from offshore ships. With clocklike precision the United States navy between December 12 and 24 lifted the 105,-000 trapped men, their equipment and 91,000 Korean civilians from the beachhead and conveyed them southward, where the troops resumed the fight.

By mid-January, 1951, the foe had penetrated as far as seventy-five miles below the 38th parallel, returning the seesaw war to about where it had been a half year before, shortly after the original invasion began. But the UN forces, now reorganized and in a much stronger defensive position, were determined to retreat no farther, and within three months of incessant fighting they succeeded in thrusting the enemy back across the parallel in some places. The new aim, however, was less to recapture lost territory than to expel the aggressors from South Korea and to convince Mao by decimating his man power that the game wasn't worth the candle. The UN side also enjoyed the advantage of controlling 85 per cent of Korea's rice-producing area, the major domestic source of food. The lion's share of the fighting continued to be borne by the Americans and South Koreans —140,000 of the former and 100,000 of the latter at the end of 1950—but they had been joined by infantry units totaling some 20,-

000 men from ten other nations. In addition, twelve countries, including most of those sending foot soldiers, had contributed air, naval and medical contingents and equipment.[1]

In repelling the Chinese invaders the UN command had been gravely handicapped by instructions not to bomb the enemy's bases and supply routes in what General MacArthur bitterly called the "privileged sanctuary" of Manchuria. By this restriction the UN participants in the struggle hoped to prevent the limited Korean War from becoming an unlimited one involving Russia as well as the whole of China, and Western Europe as well as Asia. MacArthur chafed at this restraint and wished further to blockade China's coast and to free Chiang's forces on Formosa to attack the Reds on the mainland. He did not believe that these actions would draw the Soviet Union, Peiping's ally, into the conflict. When he sought to arouse popular sentiment at home by expressing such views publicly, the President in April, 1951, dismissed him for insubordination, transferring MacArthur's responsibilities in Korea and Japan to Lieutenant General Ridgway and turning over the field operations in Korea to Lieutenant General James A. Van Fleet. Truman saw the controversy as one involving the supremacy of the civilian over the military authority in a democracy. The American public divided violently over the dismissal, with the Republicans generally siding with MacArthur. The returned hero eloquently presented his case before a joint session of Congress; but a prolonged Senatorial inquiry, which probed into all aspects of America's Far Eastern policy, disclosed that Defense Secretary Marshall, the Joint Chiefs of Staff, Secretary of State Acheson and other high officials backed the President not only in the recall of MacArthur but also in the measures to guard against a third world war.

Meanwhile Peiping's armed intervention in Korea had posed the question of what steps the global organization in New York should take to compel the Chinese to withdraw from the contest. Counsels in the UN were divided, for it was one thing to have dealt vigorously with a little country like North Korea and another to intimidate strong

---

[1] By mid-February the UN announced that twelve countries besides the United States had ground troops in Korea (Australia, Belgium, Canada, France, Great Britain, Greece, Luxemburg, the Netherlands, New Zealand, the Philippines, Thailand and Turkey) and that the following had sent naval or air units: Australia, Belgium, Canada, Colombia, Great Britain, Greece, the Netherlands, the Union of South Africa, New Zealand and Thailand.

and populous China. Moreover Russia's veto meant a paralysis of action in the Security Council. The United States government, however, was not daunted, for the whole principle of collective security hung in the balance. Hence Warren R. Austin, America's spokesman in the Security Council, demanded stern measures against Red China and bluntly accused Moscow of secretly instigating the troubles. Indeed, as early as September 6, 1950, the Soviet delegate had vetoed a resolution asking all nations to refrain from actions that might spread the conflict beyond Korea. The Russian representative in replying to Austin denounced the United States as the real aggressor, and on November 30 he negatived a Council resolution calling upon Peiping to take out its invading hosts.

But the General Assembly had already cleared the way for acting in the crisis on its own authority. At Secretary of State Acheson's initiative that body on November 3, 1950, enacted a "United Action for Peace" plan which provided that, whenever a veto tied the Council's hands, the Assembly itself could make "appropriate recommendations to members for collective measures." For this purpose the member governments should set aside armed contingents (which would also be at the disposition of the Security Council), and a Peace Observation Commission was established to render firsthand reports on critical international situations when they arose. In making this move the Assembly stretched its powers under the UN Charter to the utmost, and the efficacy of its "recommendations" for enforcing peace rested in final analysis on the willingness of the separate nations to go along. Actually, however, as has been seen, the Security Council in its proceedings against North Korea on June 27 had also been obliged to rely upon recommendations. The "United Action for Peace" plan was one which aggressors alone could have reason to fear. The Soviet bloc (Russia, Byelorussia, the Ukraine, Poland and Czechoslovakia) cast the only votes against it.

Though the means now lay at hand, the General Assembly nevertheless postponed further steps against the Peiping regime. As in the case of General MacArthur's military proposals, the countries of Western Europe, just emerging from the ashes of war, dreaded doing anything which might ignite another global conflagration. India, bordering on Communist China, was even more determined to avoid a provocative course. Accordingly the Assembly, with Washington's unenthusiastic backing, tried three different times to get Peiping to accept a cease-fire arrangement. China, however, set too steep a price: the recall of the UN forces from Korea and of the American fleet from Formosa together with the Red government's admission to the Security Council in place of Nationalist China. To have acceded to these demands would have been to reward the criminal for his crime and renounce the UN's principal reason for being.

The American public demanded more resolute action, and toward the close of January, 1951, the House and Senate by thumping bipartisan majorities asked the United Nations forthwith to label Peiping an aggressor. On February 1 the General Assembly did so. By a vote of 44 to 7 (India, Burma and the Soviet bloc), with 9 other countries abstaining, it formally declared that China's invasion and warring on UN troops in Korea constituted aggression, and it authorized a committee to "consider additional measures" to meet the situation. Several months passed without further action in the hope that the Allied successes in the field would have the effect of bringing the enemy to terms. When this expectation failed, the United States Congress on May 15 again took the lead, unanimously requesting the Assembly to embargo the sending of war materials to Red China.

Three days later the Assembly, with the approval of its committee on "additional measures," recommended that the UN governments ban all such shipments to China and North Korea. The vote was 47 to 0, with eight nations abstaining and the five members of the Soviet bloc not participating. To put teeth into the embargo recommendation as well as to widen its application, Congress on May 21 prohibited American economic or financial aid to nations which knowingly permitted the export of strategic products to the proscribed countries or to Russia and her European satellites. The President, however, was empowered to make exceptions in the interests of national security. Behind these various measures of economic pressure lay the fact that, though the United States and many other free nations had earlier stopped their trade in munitions to the Soviet bloc—with America in December, 1950, extending her boycott to include Red China as well—the flow of military commodities to China had greatly risen during the Korean War, notably through British Hong Kong and the nearby Portuguese island of Macao. The UN and the United States now sought to plug these holes. By July, Russia saw no further advantage in continuing the war; and at her suggestion the North Koreans and their Chinese allies entered into negotiations with the UN command for a cease-fire agreement preliminary to peace discussions.

The spreading crisis in Asia, added to the threatening Soviet shadow over Western Europe, had made it imperative that the free nations of Europe rearm as swiftly as possible. Fortunately the situation was favorable. The Marshall Plan had by now restored their economic production; the North Atlantic Treaty had given them new hope of survival; and Congress under the Mutual Defense Assistance Program was rapidly re-equipping them militarily. The next step was to create a unified armed force of the North Atlantic Treaty countries. To bring this about the North Atlantic Council, established under the pact, unanimously appointed General Eisenhower in December, 1950, to the post of Supreme Commander. Eisenhower, who since the Axis war had been serving as president of Columbia University, donned his uniform again, this time to prevent a general war rather than to end one.

DOMESTIC REPERCUSSIONS

While the UN troops were battling in Korea and the General Assembly was turning the screws on Red China, America had been striving against time to rebuild her strength at home. Under the legislation of July, 1950, training centers were reopened all over the country; President Truman on December 17 proclaimed a national emergency of indefinite duration; and by March, 1951, the fighting forces reached 2,900,000—double the number when the war began —with 3,500,000 as the announced goal. This feat had been accomplished twice as fast as in the days of the Axis peril. In March Congress also greatly enlarged the navy, voting to build 173 warships and modernize 291 others. Thanks to the speed in expanding the armed services, however, the lawmakers proved cool to Truman's proposal—which they had always shelved in the past—to institute a system of universal military training as a continuing reservoir of man power ready at need. Though the Senate complied, the House refused; and the compromise act as passed in June merely lowered the Selective Service age from nineteen to eighteen and a half, extended the draft period from 21 to 24 months, and then authorized the preparation of a plan of universal training for later consideration. Meanwhile, in January, Congress provided for a Federal Civil Defense Administration to co-ordinate the activities of states and cities against the danger of enemy attack. Among other things, the government undertook to install warning devices and assist in financing the construction of air-raid shelters. To help meet the spiraling costs of preparedness, Congress voted additional funds and new taxes, starting in January with a $16,845,000,000 appropriation which included a billion for atomic weapons and nearly two billion for the stocking of strategic materials. To distribute the financial burden more equitably, it levied a 77-per-cent tax on excess corporate profits arising from the rearming.

Industrial mobilization, authorized by the Defense Production Act of September, 1950, also proceeded apace. The alphabetical designations characteristic of World War II now reappeared in the nation's capital as President Truman set up one administrative body after another to reorganize the country's economy for the emergency. By January, 1951, the new organs included the ODM (Office of Defense Mobilization, the DMB (Defense Mobilization Board), the NPA (National Production Authority), the DTA (Defense Transportation Administration), the ODM (Office of Defense Manpower), as well as the ESA (Economic Stabilization Agency) which had as special branches the OPS (Office of Price Stabilization) and the WSB (Wage Stabilization Board). The Office of Defense Mobilization, the key agency, was under Charles E. Wilson who till then had been president of the General Electric Company. Acting with advice from the Defense Mobilization Board made up of cabinet members and other high officials, the ODM had over-all responsibility for the defense effort. It thus resembled the Office of War Mobilization in World War II.

The system of controls, though potentially as complete as during the Axis struggle, was designed for a protracted crisis rather than an existing all-out war. Hence the regulations were imposed more gradually and with less shock to the nation's economy than on the earlier occasion. The first and most pressing need was to step up defense production. For this purpose the government required manufacturers to give priority to its orders, helped finance new plants and additional output, and banned the construction of theaters and similar buildings. It also placed restrictions upon the civilian use of lumber, tin, zinc, natural rubber and other basic defense materials. Beginning in April, 1951, for example, the steel, copper and aluminum in such products as passenger automobiles, refrigerators and utensils were reduced by 20 to 35 per cent, with further cuts announced for later in the year. Meanwhile factories, as during World War II, diverted their facilities to turning out tanks, aircraft, weapons and the like. Full production was planned for 1952. Thanks to the country's enormous manufacturing capacity, however, these developments did little as yet to interfere with the normal flow of civilian goods.

Civilians, however, suffered from the rising cost of living. The higher prices were due to a sharpened demand for commodities springing partly from fear of future shortages, partly from the increasing needs of the defense industries and partly from the greater earnings of the employees. By the end of January, 1951, farm prices were 21 per cent more than when the hostilities began; textiles had climbed 32 per cent, aluminum 78, tin 138. The mounting inflation not only hurt the ordinary citizen but also raised the cost of the defense effort to the nation. The government used various means to stay the trend. The heavier taxation was designed in part to hold down prices by absorbing some of the public's purchasing power. With a similar object Congress in December, 1950, re-enacted the system of rent control, though on the existing basis of local option. The situation, however, called for more stringent action. Hence the Office of Price Stabilization on January 26, 1951, issued a blanket order freezing all prices, except of farm produce, at their highest levels in the period since the preceding December 19. To correct the inevitable injustices of so sweeping a mandate the OPS a month later fixed the margin of profit which merchants could earn in the case of some 200,-000 articles. These included clothing, footwear, dry goods and furniture. In March the agency applied a similar margin-of-profit regulation to most grocery items (to be effective May 1) and to restaurant charges (effective August 1).

In curbing farm prices the OPS was hampered by a provision in the Defense Production Act which forbade price ceilings when agricultural products were selling for less than during the month before the Korean War or below "parity" (a level intended to assure the farmer a fair return in relation to what he bought). Meat, however, was selling above such limits, and the OPS against strong opposition from producers moved to bring it under control. To forestall black markets in this basic article of consumption the agency in February, 1951, required all commercial slaughterers to register with the government and to confine their output to 1950 totals. A little later it put price restrictions on beef all the way from the stockyard to the retail dealer. This order, effective in May, was designed to reduce the cost to the consumer to a point somewhat higher than it had been before the Korean crisis. Comparable rollbacks were planned for other kinds of meat. The net effect of the OPS's various measures by the summer of 1951 was to slow down or reverse the upward trend of prices and so effect substantial savings for both householders and the government.

The blanket order of January 26, 1951, aimed to stabilize wages as well as prices, since the two were closely interrelated. In anticipation of this, many of the unions, spurred by the advancing living costs, had secured pay raises after the outbreak of the war, in most cases without striking. Employers made the concessions because, with skilled labor already in great demand and certain to be in greater as industrial mobilization proceeded, they wished to hold on to experienced workers. General Motors (the country's largest automobile concern), Chrysler and Ford set the pace, and it was difficult for other branches of business not to follow. Chrysler, for example, boosted hourly wages by 10 and 15 cents for various classes of employees, while the steel industry averaged increases of 16 cents.

Strikes nevertheless occurred, and a threatened one on the railroads, where a wage-and-hour dispute involving the trainmen and conductors had been hanging fire for seventeen months, would have gravely hampered the defense effort. To avert a nation-wide tie-up, the President late in August, 1950, acting under a 1916 statute for the seizure of rail facilities in wartime, put the army in charge of the roads. In December, however, an outlaw strike by the switchmen (members of the Brotherhood of Railroad Trainmen) broke out only to end after a few days at Truman's demand. To play safe, the Justice Department obtained a court restraining order against such incidents in the future. Government-sponsored negotiations later in the month appeared to have effected a compromise settlement, but the brotherhoods subsequently rejected the terms, and on January 30, 1951, the switchmen began deserting their posts all over the country, this time on the pretext of sickness. Their action crippled freight and passenger traffic, restricted the movement of mails and stopped most of the trains between East and West. By the same token it idled steel mills, automobile plants, coal mines and other industries vital to the production program. The situation was getting out of hand when the army authorities at President Truman's bidding brought the walkout to an end on February 8 by ordering the switchmen to report for duty in forty-eight hours on pain of being discharged. At the same time the government granted pay increases which were half as much as provided for in the attempted compromise agreement, but which were subject to further negotiation between the men and the rail companies. In federal court proceedings after the strike the Brotherhood of Railroad Trainmen pleaded guilty to violating the judicial restraining order and incurred a fine of $75,000. A final settlement, more favorable to the men than the government's terms, was reached in May.

Meanwhile the general wage freeze had gone into effect on January 26. It established pay ceilings at the levels then prevailing but left them open to later modification with the consent of the Wage Stabilization Board. A certain flexibility was necessary because many union contracts contained 'escalator clauses' for periodically readjusting wages to the cost of living, and also because in other cases, like that of the railroad switchmen, the pay rates had not recently been scaled upward and gross inequalities would result. To take care of such situations the WSB a month later ratified existing escalator agreements and authorized employers at their own discretion to grant increases up to 10 per cent above the amounts paid in January, 1950. In instances regarded as involving unusual hardships the Board itself approved of even larger advances. In May, 1951, for example, it sanctioned a nine-cent hourly raise for 220,000 workers in meat-packing plants, though this meant a total increase of 14 per cent since January, 1950. By June the Board was receiving requests to exceed the 10-per-cent limit at the rate of a hundred a day. Its continuing problem was to balance the rightful claims of labor against the national need to curb prices and to accelerate production.

Under impact of the prolonged Korean crisis the nation was thus rapidly putting itself on a semiwar footing. The expansion of armed forces, the precautions for civilian defense, the huge expenditures and taxes, the gigantic industrial mobilization, the regimentation of prices and wages—all these recalled the beleaguered America of World War II. There was, however, this basic difference. The preparations now under way looked less to an immediate danger than to an indefinite period of threatening conflict and watchful waiting. No one knew when or where or by what direct or indirect means the Soviet enemy would strike next, and it was devoutly hoped that, if the United States and the other democratic powers made themselves strong enough, peace might in the long run be assured and the principles of the United Nations be vindicated.

The stakes were high, for, as President Truman observed in his proclamation of a national emergency, "If the goal of Communist imperialism were to be achieved, the people of this country would no longer enjoy the full and rich life they have with God's help built for themselves and their children; they would no longer enjoy the blessings of the freedom of worshiping as they severally choose, the freedom of reading and listening to what they choose, the right of free speech including the right to criticize their Government, the right to engage freely in collective bargaining, the right to engage freely in their own business enterprises, and the many other freedoms and rights which are a part of our way of life." Those freedoms and rights a people schooled in the maxims of the Declaration of Independence and dedicated to the political ideals of Jefferson, Lincoln, Wilson and Franklin Roosevelt would never willingly surrender.

FULLER ACCOUNTS

The Korean Crisis. Oliver, *Why War Came in Korea,* provides background material. For subsequent developments, consult the magazines and yearbooks listed for the two preceding chapters. Rovere and Schlesinger, Jr., *The General and the President,* deals with the MacArthur controversy.

APPENDIX

CONSTITUTION OF THE UNITED STATES

WE THE PEOPLE of the United States, in Order to form a more perfect Union, establish Justice, insure domestic Tranquillity, provide for the common defence, promote the general Welfare, and secure the Blessings of Liberty to ourselves and our Posterity, do ordain and establish this CONSTITUTION for the United States of America.

ARTICLE I

Section 1. All legislative Powers herein granted shall be vested in a Congress of the United States, which shall consist of a Senate and a House of Representatives.

Section 2. The House of Representatives shall be composed of Members chosen every second Year by the People of the several States, and the Electors in each State shall have the Qualifications requisite for Electors of the most numerous Branch of the State Legislature.

No Person shall be a Representative who shall not have attained to the Age of twenty-five Years, and been seven Years a Citizen of the United States, and who shall not, when elected, be an Inhabitant of that State in which he shall be chosen.

Representatives and direct Taxes shall be apportioned among the several States which may be included within this Union, according to their respective Numbers, which shall be determined by adding to the whole Number of free Persons, including those bound to Service for a Term of Years, and excluding Indians not taxed, three fifths of all other Persons. The actual Enumeration shall be made within three Years after the first Meeting of the Congress of the United States, and within every subsequent Term of ten Years, in such Manner as they shall by Law direct. The Number of Representatives shall not exceed one for every thirty Thousand, but each State shall have at Least one Representative; and until such enumeration shall be made, the State of New Hampshire shall be entitled to chuse three, Massachusetts eight, Rhode-Island and Providence Plantations one, Connecticut five, New-York six, New Jersey four, Pennsylvania eight, Delaware one, Maryland six, Virginia ten, North Carolina five, South Carolina five, and Georgia three.

When vacancies happen in the Representation from any State, the Executive Authority thereof shall issue Writs of Election to fill such Vacancies.

The House of Representatives shall chuse their Speaker and other Officers; and shall have the sole Power of Impeachment.

Section 3. The Senate of the United States shall be composed of two Senators from each State, chosen by the Legislature thereof, for six Years, and each Senator shall have one Vote.

Immediately after they shall be assembled in Consequence of the first Election, they shall be divided as equally as may be into three Classes. The Seats of the Senators of the first Class shall be vacated at the Expiration of the second Year, of the second Class at the Expiration of the fourth Year, and of the third Class at the Expiration of the sixth Year, so that one-third may be chosen every second Year; and if Vacancies happen by Resignation, or otherwise, during the Recess of the Legislature of any State, the Executive thereof may make temporary Appointments until the next Meeting of the Legislature, which shall then fill such Vacancies.

No Person shall be a Senator who shall not have attained to the Age of thirty Years, and been nine Years a Citizen of the United States, and who shall not, when elected, be an Inhabitant of that State for which he shall be chosen.

The Vice President of the United States shall be President of the Senate, but shall have no Vote, unless they be equally divided.

The Senate shall chuse their other Officers, and also a President pro tempore, in the Absence of the Vice President, or when he shall exercise the Office of President of the United States.

The Senate shall have the sole Power to try all Impeachments. When sitting for that Purpose, they shall be on Oath or Affirmation. When the President of the United States is tried, the Chief Justice shall preside: And no Person shall be convicted without the Concurrence of two thirds of the Members present.

Judgment in Cases of Impeachment shall not extend further than to removal from Office, and disqualification to hold and enjoy any Office of honor, Trust or Profit under the United States: but the Party convicted shall nevertheless be liable and subject to Indictment, Trial, Judgment and Punishment, according to Law.

Section 4. The Times, Places and Manner of holding Elections for Senators and Representatives, shall be prescribed in each State by the Legislature thereof; but the Congress may at any time by Law make or alter such Regulations, except as to Places of chusing Senators.

The Congress shall assemble at least once in every Year, and such Meeting shall be on the first Monday in December, unless they shall by Law appoint a different Day.

Section 5. Each House shall be the Judge of the Elections, Returns and Qualifications of its own Members, and a Majority of each shall constitute a Quorum to do Business; but a smaller Number may adjourn from day to day, and may be authorized to compel the Attendance of absent Members, in such Manner, and under such Penalties as each House may provide.

Each House may determine the Rules of its Proceedings, punish its Members for disorderly Behavior, and, with the Concurrence of two thirds, expel a Member.

Each House shall keep a Journal of its Proceedings, and from time to time publish the same, excepting such Parts as may in their Judgment require

Secrecy; and the Yeas and Nays of the Members of either House on any question shall, at the Desire of one fifth of those present, be entered on the Journal.

Neither House, during the Session of Congress, shall, without the Consent of the other, adjourn for more than three days, nor to any other Place than that in which the two Houses shall be sitting.

Section 6. The Senators and Representatives shall receive a Compensation for their Services, to be ascertained by Law, and paid out of the Treasury of the United States. They shall in all Cases, except Treason, Felony and Breach of the Peace, be privileged from Arrest during their Attendance at the Session of their respective Houses, and in going to and returning from the same; and for any Speech or Debate in either House, they shall not be questioned in any other Place.

No Senator or Representative shall, during the Time for which he was elected, be appointed to any civil Office under the Authority of the United States, which shall have been created, or the Emoluments whereof shall have been encreased during such time; and no Person holding any Office under the United States, shall be a Member of either House during his Continuance in Office.

Section 7. All Bills for raising Revenue shall originate in the House of Representatives; but the Senate may propose or concur with Amendments as on other Bills.

Every Bill which shall have passed the House of Representatives and the Senate, shall, before it become a Law, be presented to the President of the United States; If he approve he shall sign it, but if not he shall return it, with his Objections to that House in which it shall have originated, who shall enter the Objections at large on their Journal, and proceed to reconsider it. If after such Reconsideration two thirds of that House shall agree to pass the Bill, it shall be sent, together with the Objections, to the other House, by which it shall likewise be reconsidered, and if approved by two thirds of that House, it shall become a Law. But in all such Cases the Votes of both Houses shall be determined by Yeas and Nays, and the Names of the Persons voting for and against the Bill shall be entered on the Journal of each House respectively. If any Bill shall not be returned by the President within ten Days (Sundays excepted) after it shall have been presented to him, the Same shall be a Law, in like Manner as if he had signed it, unless the Congress by their Adjournment prevent its Return, in which Case it shall not be a Law.

Every Order, Resolution, or Vote to which the Concurrence of the Senate and House of Representatives may be necessary (except on a question of Adjournment) shall be presented to the President of the United States; and before the Same shall take Effect, shall be approved by him, or being disapproved by him, shall be repassed by two thirds of the Senate and House of Representatives, according to the Rules and Limitations prescribed in the Case of a Bill.

Section 8. The Congress shall have Power To lay and collect Taxes, Duties, Imposts and Excises, to pay the Debts and provide for the common Defence and general Welfare of the United States; but all Duties, Imposts and Excises shall be uniform throughout the United States;

To borrow Money on the credit of the United States;

To regulate Commerce with foreign Nations, and among the several States, and with the Indian Tribes;

To establish an uniform Rule of Naturalization, and uniform Laws on the subject of Bankruptcies throughout the United States;

To coin Money, regulate the Value thereof, and of foreign Coin, and fix the Standard of Weights and Measures;

To provide for the Punishment of counterfeiting the Securities and current Coin of the United States;

To establish Post Offices and post Roads;

To promote the Progress of Science and useful Arts, by securing for limited Times to Authors and Inventors the exclusive Right to their respective Writings and Discoveries;

To constitute Tribunals inferior to the supreme Court;

To define and punish Piracies and Felonies committed on the high Seas, and Offences against the Law of Nations;

To declare War, grant Letters of Marque and Reprisal, and make Rules concerning Captures on Land and Water;

To raise and support Armies, but no Appropriation of Money to that Use shall be for a longer Term than two Years;

To provide and maintain a Navy;

To make Rules for the Government and Regulation of the land and naval Forces;

To provide for calling forth the Militia to execute the Laws of the Union, suppress Insurrections and repel Invasions;

To provide for organizing, arming, and disciplining the Militia, and for governing such Part of them as may be employed in the Service of the United States, reserving to the States respectively, the Appointment of the Officers, and the Authority of training the Militia according to the discipline prescribed by Congress;

To exercise exclusive Legislation in all Cases whatsoever, over such District (not exceeding ten Miles square) as may, by Cession of particular States, and the Acceptance of Congress, become the Seat of the Government of the United States, and to exercise like Authority over all Places purchased by the Consent of the Legislature of the State in which the Same shall be, for the Erection of Forts, Magazines, Arsenals, dock-Yards, and other needful Buildings;—And

To make all Laws which shall be necessary and proper for carrying into Execution the foregoing Powers, and all other Powers vested by this Constitution in the Government of the United States, or in any Department or Officer thereof.

Section 9. The Migration or Importation of such Persons as any of the States now existing shall think proper to admit, shall not be prohibited by the Congress prior to the Year one thousand eight hundred and eight, but a Tax or duty may be imposed on such Importation, not exceeding ten dollars for each Person.

The Privilege of the Writ of Habeas Corpus shall not be suspended, unless when in Cases of Rebellion or Invasion the public Safety may require it.

No Bill of Attainder or ex post facto Law shall be passed.

No Capitation, or other direct, tax shall be laid, unless in Proportion to the Census or Enumeration herein before directed to be taken.

No Tax or Duty shall be laid on Articles exported from any State.

No Preference shall be given by any Regulation of Commerce or Revenue to the Ports of one State over those of another: nor shall Vessels bound to, or from, one State, be obliged to enter, clear, or pay Duties in another.

No Money shall be drawn from the Treasury, but in Consequence of Appropriations made by Law; and a regular Statement and Account of the Receipts and Expenditures of all public Money shall be published from time to time.

No Title of Nobility shall be granted by the United States: And no Person holding any Office of Profit or Trust under them, shall, without the Consent of the Congress, accept of any present, Emolument, Office, or Title, of any kind whatever, from any King, Prince, or foreign State.

Section 10. No State shall enter into any Treaty, Alliance, or Confederation; grant Letters of Marque and Reprisal; coin Money; emit Bills of Credit; make any Thing but gold and silver Coin a Tender in Payment of Debts; pass any Bill of Attainder, ex post facto Law, or Law impairing the Obligation of Contracts, or grant any Title of Nobility.

No State shall, without the Consent of the Congress, lay any Imposts or Duties on Imports or Exports, except what may be absolutely necessary for executing its inspection Laws: and the net Produce of all Duties and Imposts, laid by any State on Imports or Exports, shall be for the Use of the Treasury of the United States; and all such Laws shall be subject to the Revision and Control of the Congress.

No State shall, without the Consent of Congress, lay any Duty of Tonnage, keep Troops, or Ships of War in time of Peace, enter into any Agreement or Compact with another State, or with a foreign Power, or engage in War, unless actually invaded, or in such imminent Danger as will not admit of delay.

ARTICLE II

Section 1. The executive Power shall be vested in a President of the United States of America. He shall hold his Office during the Term of four Years, and, together with the Vice President, chosen for the same Term, be elected, as follows:

Each State shall appoint, in such Manner as the Legislature thereof may direct, a Number of Electors, equal to the whole Number of Senators and Representatives to which the State may be entitled in the Congress: but no Senator or Representative, or Person holding an Office of Trust or Profit under the United States, shall be appointed an Elector.

The Electors shall meet in their respective States, and vote by Ballot for two Persons, of whom one at least shall not be an Inhabitant of the same State with themselves. And they shall make a List of all the Persons voted for, and of the Number of Votes for each; which List they shall sign and certify, and transmit sealed to the Seat of the Government of the United States, directed to the President of the Senate. The President of the Senate shall, in the Presence of the Senate and House of Representatives, open all the Certificates, and the Votes shall then be counted. The Person having the greatest Number of Votes shall be the President, if such Number be a Majority of the whole Number of Electors appointed; and if there be more than one who have such Majority, and have an equal Number of Votes, then the House of Representatives shall immediately chuse by Ballot one of them for President; and if no Person have a Majority, then from the five highest on the List the said House shall in like Manner chuse the President. But in chusing the President, the Votes shall be taken by States, the Representation from each State having one Vote; A quorum for this Purpose shall consist of a Member or Members from two thirds of the States, and a Majority of all the States shall be necessary to a Choice. In every Case, after the Choice of the President, the Person having the greatest Number of Votes of the Electors shall be the Vice President. But if there should remain two or more who have equal Votes, the Senate shall chuse from them by Ballot the Vice President.

The Congress may determine the Time of chusing the Electors, and the Day on which they shall give their Votes; which Day shall be the same throughout the United States.

No Person except a natural born Citizen, or a Citizen of the United States, at the time of the Adoption of this Constitution, shall be eligible to the Office of President; neither shall any Person be eligible to that Office who shall not have attained to the Age of thirty-five Years, and been fourteen Years a Resident within the United States.

In Case of the Removal of the President from Office, or of his Death, Resignation or Inability to discharge the Powers and Duties of the said Office, the same shall devolve on the Vice President, and the Congress may by Law provide for the Case of Removal, Death, Resignation or Inability, both of the President and Vice President, declaring what Officer shall then act as President, and such Officer shall act accordingly, until the Disability be removed, or a President shall be elected.

The President shall, at stated Times, receive for his Services, a Compensation, which shall neither be encreased nor diminished during the Period for which he shall have been elected, and he shall not receive within that Period any other Emolument from the United States, or any of them.

Before he enter on the Execution of his Office, he shall take the following Oath or Affirmation:—"I do solemnly swear (or affirm) that I will faithfully execute the Office of President of the United States, and will to the best of my Ability, preserve, protect and defend the Constitution of the United States."

Section 2. The President shall be Commander in Chief of the Army and Navy of the United States, and of the Militia of the several States, when called into the actual Service of the United States; he may require the Opinion, in writing, of the principal Officer in each of the executive Departments, upon any Subject relating to the Duties of their respective Offices, and he shall have Power to grant Reprieves and Pardons for Offences against the United States, except in Cases of Impeachment.

He shall have Power, by and with the Advice and Consent of the Senate, to make Treaties, provided two thirds of the Senators present concur; and he shall nominate, and by and with the Advice and Consent of the Senate, shall appoint Ambassadors, other public Ministers and Consuls, Judges of the supreme Court, and all other Officers of the United States, whose Appointments are not herein otherwise provided for, and which shall be established by Law: but the Congress may by Law vest the Appointment of such inferior Officers, as they think proper, in the President alone, in the Courts of Law, or in the Heads of Departments.

The President shall have Power to fill up all Vacancies that may happen during the Recess of the Senate, by granting Commissions which shall expire at the End of their next Session.

Section 3. He shall from time to time give to the Congress Information of the State of the Union, and recommend to their Consideration such Measures as he shall judge necessary and expedient; he may, on extraordinary Occasions, convene both Houses, or either of them, and, in Case of Disagreement between them, with Respect to the Time of Adjournment, he may adjourn them to such Time as he shall think proper; he shall receive Ambassadors and other public Ministers; he shall take Care that the Laws be faithfully executed, and shall Commission all the Officers of the United States.

Section 4. The President, Vice President and all civil Officers of the United States, shall be removed from Office on Impeachment for, and Conviction of, Treason, Bribery, or other high Crimes and Misdemeanors.

ARTICLE III

Section 1. The judicial Power of the United States, shall be vested in one supreme Court, and in such inferior Courts as the Congress may from time to time ordain and establish. The Judges, both of the supreme and inferior Courts, shall hold their Offices during good Behaviour, and shall, at stated Times, receive for their Services, a Compensation, which shall not be diminished during their Continuance in Office.

Section 2. The judicial Power shall extend to all Cases, in Law and Equity, arising under this Constitution, the Laws of the United States, and Treaties made, or which shall be made, under their Authority;—to all Cases affecting Ambassadors, other public Ministers and Consuls;—to all Cases of admiralty and maritime Jurisdiction;—to Controversies to which the United States shall be a Party;—to Controversies between two or more States;—between a State and Citizens of another State;—between Citizens of different States;—between Citizens of the same State claiming Lands under Grants of different States, and between a State, or the Citizens thereof, and foreign States, Citizens or Subjects.

In all Cases affecting Ambassadors, other public Ministers and Consuls, and those in which a State shall be Party, the supreme Court shall have original Jurisdiction. In all the other Cases before mentioned, the supreme Court shall have appellate Jurisdiction, both as to Law and Fact, with such Exceptions, and under such Regulations as the Congress shall make.

The Trial of all Crimes, except in Cases of Impeachment, shall be by Jury; and such Trial shall be held in the State where the said Crimes shall have been committed; but when not committed within any State, the Trial shall be at such Place or Places as the Congress may by Law have directed.

Section 3. Treason against the United States, shall consist only in levying War against them, or in adhering to their Enemies, giving them Aid and Comfort. No Person shall be convicted of Treason unless on the Testimony of two Witnesses to the same overt Act, or on Confession in open Court.

The Congress shall have Power to declare the Punishment of Treason, but no Attainder of Treason shall work Corruption of Blood, or Forfeiture except during the Life of the Person attainted.

ARTICLE IV

Section 1. Full Faith and Credit shall be given in each State to the public Acts, Records, and judicial Proceedings of every other State. And the Congress may by general Laws prescribe the Manner in which such Acts, Records and Proceedings shall be proved, and the Effect thereof.

Section 2. The Citizens of each State shall be entitled to all Privileges and Immunities of Citizens in the several States.

A person charged in any State with Treason, Felony, or other Crime, who shall flee from Justice, and be found in another State, shall on Demand of the executive Authority of the State from which he fled, be delivered up to be removed to the State having Jurisdiction of the Crime.

No Person held to Service or Labour in one State, under the Laws thereof, escaping into another, shall, in Consequence of any Law or Regulation therein, be discharged from such Service or Labour, but shall be delivered up on Claim of the Party to whom such Service or Labour may be due.

Section 3. New States may be admitted by the Congress into this Union; but no new State shall be formed or erected within the Jurisdiction of any other State; nor any State be formed by the Junction of two or more States, or Parts of States, without the Consent of the Legislatures of the States concerned as well as of the Congress.

The Congress shall have Power to dispose of and make all needful Rules and Regulations respecting the Territory or other Property belonging to the United States; and nothing in this Constitution shall be so construed as to Prejudice any Claims of the United States, or of any particular State.

Section 4. The United States shall guarantee to every State in this Union a Republican Form of Government, and shall protect each of them against Invasion; and on Application of the Legislature, or of the Executive (when the Legislature cannot be convened) against domestic Violence.

ARTICLE V

The Congress, whenever two thirds of both Houses shall deem it necessary, shall propose Amendments to this Constitution, or, on the Application of the Legislatures of two thirds of the several States, shall call a Convention for proposing Amendments, which, in either Case, shall be valid to all Intents and Purposes, as Part of this Constitution, when ratified by the Legislatures of three fourths of the several States, or by Conventions in three fourths thereof, as the one or the other Mode of Ratification may be proposed by the Congress; Provided that no Amendment which may be made prior to the Year One thousand eight hundred and eight shall in any Manner affect the first and fourth Clauses in the Ninth Section of the first Article; and that no State, without its Consent, shall be deprived of its equal Suffrage in the Senate.

ARTICLE VI

All Debts contracted and Engagements entered into, before the Adoption of this Constitution, shall be as valid against the United States under this Constitution, as under the Confederation.

This Constitution, and the Laws of the United States which shall be made in Pursuance thereof; and all Treaties made, or which shall be made, under the Authority of the United States, shall be the supreme Law of the Land; and the Judges in every State shall be bound thereby, any Thing in the Constitution or Laws of any State to the Contrary notwithstanding.

The Senators and Representatives before mentioned, and the Members of the several State Legislatures, and all executive and judicial Officers, both of the United States and of the several States, shall be bound by Oath or Affirmation, to support this Constitution; but no religious Test shall ever be required as a Qualification to any Office or public Trust under the United States.

ARTICLE VII

The Ratification of the Conventions of nine States, shall be sufficient for the Establishment of this Constitution between the States so ratifying the Same.

DONE in Convention by the Unanimous Consent of the States present the Seventeenth Day of September in the Year of our Lord one thousand seven hundred and Eighty seven, and of the Independence of the United States of America the Twelfth.

ARTICLES IN ADDITION TO, AND AMENDMENT OF, THE CONSTITUTION OF THE UNITED STATES OF AMERICA, PROPOSED BY CONGRESS, AND RATIFIED BY THE SEVERAL STATES PURSUANT TO THE FIFTH ARTICLE OF THE ORIGINAL CONSTITUTION.

· ARTICLE I

(The first ten Articles, in force December 15, 1791)

Congress shall make no law respecting an establishment of religion, or prohibiting the free exercise thereof; or abridging the freedom of speech, or of the press; or the right of the people peaceably to assemble, and to petition the Government for a redress of grievances.

ARTICLE II

A well regulated Militia, being necessary to the security of a free State, the right of the people to keep and bear Arms, shall not be infringed.

ARTICLE III

No Soldier shall, in time of peace, be quartered in any house, without the consent of the Owner, nor in time of war, but in a manner to be prescribed by law.

ARTICLE IV

The right of the people to be secure in their persons, houses, papers, and effects, against unreasonable searches and seizures, shall not be violated, and no Warrants shall issue, but upon probable cause, supported by Oath or affirmation, and particularly describing the place to be searched, and the persons or things to be seized.

ARTICLE V

No person shall be held to answer for a capital, or otherwise infamous crime, unless on a presentment or indictment of a Grand Jury, except in cases arising in the land or naval forces, or in the Militia, when in actual service in time of War or public danger; nor shall any person be subject for the same offence to be twice put in jeopardy of life or limb; nor shall be compelled in any Criminal Case to be a witness against himself, nor be deprived of life, liberty, or property, without due process of law; nor shall private property be taken for public use, without just compensation.

ARTICLE VI

In all criminal prosecutions, the accused shall enjoy the right to a speedy and public trial, by an impartial jury of the State and district wherein the crime shall have been committed, which district shall have been previously ascertained by law, and to be informed of the nature and cause of the accusation; to be confronted with the witnesses against him; to have compulsory process for obtaining Witnesses in his favor, and to have the Assistance of Counsel for his defence.

ARTICLE VII

In suits at common law, where the value in controversy shall exceed twenty dollars, the right of trial by jury shall be preserved, and no fact tried by a jury shall be otherwise re-examined in any Court of the United States, than according to the rules of the common law.

ARTICLE VIII

Excessive bail shall not be required, nor excessive fines imposed, nor cruel and unusual punishments inflicted.

ARTICLE IX

The enumeration in the Constitution, of certain rights, shall not be construed to deny or disparage others retained by the people.

ARTICLE X

The powers not delegated to the United States by the Constitution, nor prohibited by it to the States, are reserved to the States respectively, or to the people.

ARTICLE XI
(January 8, 1798)

The Judicial power of the United States shall not be construed to extend to any suit in law or equity, commenced or prosecuted against one of the United States by Citizens of another State, or by Citizens or Subjects of any Foreign State.

ARTICLE XII
(September 25, 1804)

The Electors shall meet in their respective states, and vote by ballot for President and Vice-President, one of whom, at least, shall not be an inhabitant of the same state with themselves; they shall name in their ballots the person voted for as President, and in distinct ballots the person voted for as Vice-President, and they shall make distinct lists of all persons voted for as President, and of all persons voted for as Vice-President, and of the number of votes for each, which lists they shall sign and certify, and transmit sealed to the seat of the Government of the United States, directed to the President of the Senate;—The President of the Senate shall, in the presence of the Senate and House of Representatives, open all the certificates and the votes shall then be counted;—The person having the greatest number of votes for President, shall be the President, if such number be a majority of the whole number of Electors appointed; and if no person have such majority, then from the persons having the highest numbers not exceeding three on the list of those voted for as President, the House of Representatives shall choose immediately, by ballot, the President. But in choosing the President, the votes shall be taken by states, the representation from each state having one vote; a quorum for this purpose shall consist of a member or members from two-thirds of the states, and a majority of all the states shall be necessary to a choice. And if the House of Representatives shall not choose a President whenever the right of choice shall devolve upon them, before the fourth day of March next following, then the Vice-President shall act as President, as in the case of the death or other constitutional disability of the President. The person having the greatest number of votes as Vice-President, shall be the Vice-President, if such number be a majority of the whole number of Electors appointed, and if no person have a majority, then from the two highest numbers on the list, the Senate shall choose the Vice-President; a quorum for the purpose shall consist of two-thirds of the whole number of Senators, and a majority of the whole number shall be necessary to a choice. But no person constitutionally ineligible to the office of President shall be eligible to that of Vice-President of the United States.

ARTICLE XIII
(December 18, 1865)

Section 1. Neither slavery nor involuntary servitude, except as a punishment for crime whereof the party shall have been duly convicted, shall exist within the United States, or any place subject to their jurisdiction.

Section 2. Congress shall have power to enforce this article by appropriate legislation.

ARTICLE XIV
(July 28, 1868)

Section 1. All persons born or naturalized in the United States, and subject to the jurisdiction thereof, are citizens of the United States and of the State wherein they reside. No State shall make or enforce any law which shall abridge the privileges or immunities of citizens of the United States; nor shall any State deprive any person of life, liberty, or property, without due process of law; nor deny to any person within its jurisdiction the equal protection of the laws.

Section 2. Representatives shall be apportioned among the several States according to their respective numbers, counting the whole number of persons in each State, excluding Indians not taxed. But when the right to vote at any election for the choice of electors for President and Vice-President of the United States, Representatives in Congress, the Executive and Judicial officers of a State, or the members of the Legislature thereof, is denied to any of the male inhabitants of such State, being twenty-one years of age, and citizens of the United States, or in any way abridged, except for participation in rebellion, or other crime, the basis of representation therein shall be reduced in the proportion which the number of such male citizens shall bear to the whole number of male citizens twenty-one years of age in such State.

Section 3. No person shall be a Senator or Representative in Congress, or elector of President and Vice-President, or hold any office, civil, or military, under the United States, or under any State, who, having previously taken an oath, as a member of Congress, or as an officer of the United States, or as a member of any State legislature, or as an executive or judicial officer of any State, to support the Constitution of the United States, shall have engaged in insurrection or rebellion against the same, or given aid or comfort to the enemies thereof. But Congress may by a vote of two-thirds of each House, remove such disability.

Section 4. The validity of the public debt of the United States, authorized by law, including debts incurred for payment of pensions and bounties for services in suppressing insurrection or rebellion, shall not be questioned. But neither the United States nor any State shall assume or pay any debt or obligation incurred in aid of insurrection or rebellion against the United States, or any claim for the loss or emancipation of any slave; but all such debts, obligations and claims shall be held illegal and void.

Section 5. The Congress shall have power to enforce, by appropriate legislation, the provisions of this article.

ARTICLE XV
(March 30, 1870)

Section 1. The right of citizens of the United States to vote shall not be denied or abridged by the United States or by any State on account of race, color, or previous condition of servitude.

Section 2. The Congress shall have power to enforce this article by appropriate legislation.

ARTICLE XVI
(February 25, 1913)

The Congress shall have power to lay and collect taxes on incomes, from whatever source derived, without apportionment among the several States, and without regard to any census or enumeration.

ARTICLE XVII
(May 31, 1913)

The Senate of the United States shall be composed of two Senators from each State, elected by the people thereof, for six years; and each Senator shall have one vote. The electors in each State shall have the qualifications requisite for electors of the most numerous branch of the State legislature.

When vacancies happen in the representation of any State in the Senate, the executive authority of such State shall issue writs of election to fill such vacancies: *Provided,* That the legislature of any State may empower the executive thereof to make temporary appointments until the people fill the vacancies by election as the legislature may direct.

This amendment shall not be so construed as to affect the election or term of any Senator chosen before it becomes valid as part of the Constitution.

ARTICLE XVIII
(January 29, 1919)

After one year from the ratification of this article, the manufacture, sale, or transportation of intoxicating liquors within, the importation thereof into, or the exportation thereof from the United States and all territory subject to the jurisdiction thereof for beverage purposes is hereby prohibited.

The Congress and the several States shall have concurrent power to enforce this article by appropriate legislation.

This article shall be inoperative unless it shall have been ratified as an amendment to the Constitution by the legislatures of the several States, as provided in the Constitution, within seven years from the date of the submission hereof to the States by the Congress.

ARTICLE XIX
(August 26, 1920)

The right of citizens of the United States to vote shall not be denied or abridged by the United States or by any States on account of sex.

The Congress shall have power by appropriate legislation to enforce the provisions of this article.

ARTICLE XX
(February 6, 1933)

Section 1. The terms of the President and Vice-President shall end at noon on the twentieth day of January, and the terms of Senators and Representatives at noon on the third day of January, of the years in which such terms would have ended if this article had not been ratified; and the terms of their successors shall then begin.

Section 2. The Congress shall assemble at least once in every year, and such meeting shall begin at noon on the third day of January, unless they shall by law appoint a different day.

Section 3. If, at the time fixed for the beginning of the term of the President, the President-elect shall have died, the Vice-President-elect shall become President. If a President shall not have been chosen before the time fixed for the beginning of his term, or if the President-elect shall have failed to qualify, then the Vice-President-elect shall act as President until a President shall have qualified; and the Congress may by law provide for the case wherein neither a President-elect nor a Vice-President-elect shall have qualified, declaring who shall then act as President, or the manner in which one who is to act shall be selected, and such person shall act accordingly until a President or Vice-President shall have qualified.

Section 4. The Congress may by law provide for the case of the death of any of the persons from whom the House of Representatives may choose a President whenever the right of choice shall have devolved upon them, and for the case of the death of any of the persons from whom the Senate may choose a Vice-President whenever the right of choice shall have devolved upon them.

Section 5. Sections 1 and 2 shall take effect on the 15th day of October following the ratification of this article.

Section 6. This article shall be inoperative unless it shall have been ratified as an amendment to the Constitution by the legislatures of three-fourths of the several States within seven years from the date of its submission.

ARTICLE XXI
(December 5, 1933)

Section 1. The eighteenth article of amendment to the Constitution of the United States is hereby repealed.

Section 2. The transportation or importation into any State, Territory or possession of the United States for delivery or use therein of intoxicating liquors, in violation of the laws thereof, is hereby prohibited.

Section 3. This article shall be inoperative unless it shall have been ratified as an amendment to the Constitution by conventions in the several States, as provided in the Constitution, within seven years from the date of the submission hereof to the States by the Congress.

ARTICLE XXII
(February 26, 1951)

Section 1. No person shall be elected to the office of the President more than twice, and no person who has held the office of President, or acted as President, for more than two years of a term for which some other person was elected President shall be elected to the office of the President more than once. But this Article shall not apply to any person holding the office of President when this Article was proposed by the Congress, and shall not prevent any person who may be holding the office of President, or acting as President, during the term within which this Article becomes operative from holding the office of President or acting as President during the remainder of such term.

Section 2. This article shall be inoperative unless it shall have been ratified as an amendment to the Constitution by the legislatures of three fourths of the several States within seven years from the date of its submission to the States by the Congress.

GENERAL BIBLIOGRAPHY

ABBOTT, EDITH, *Women in Industry*. New York, 1910.

ABELL, A. I., *The Urban Impact on American Protestantism, 1865–1900 (Harvard Historical Studies, LIV)*. Cambridge, 1943.

ADAMS, J. T., ed., *Album of American History*. 5 v. New York, 1944–1949.

ADAMS, S. H., *Incredible Era, the Life and Times of Warren Gamaliel Harding*. Boston, 1939.

ADAMS, THOMAS, *Outline of Town and City Planning*. New York, 1935.

ALLEN, F. L., *The Lords of Creation*. New York, 1935.

——, *Only Yesterday*. New York, 1931.

——, *Since Yesterday*. New York, 1940.

ALLEN, RUTH A., *The Great Southwest Strike*. Austin, 1942.

ALSOP, STEWART, and THOMAS BRADEN, *Sub Rosa: the O. S. S. and American Espionage*. New York, 1946.

American Nation, The. See Hart, A. B., ed.

American Political Leaders. See Nevins, Allan, ed.

American Statesmen. See Morse, J. T., Jr., ed.

——, 2d ser. 7 v. Boston, 1905–1916.

ANDERSON, JOHN, *The American Theatre*. New York, 1938.

ANDREWS, J. C., *Pittsburgh's Post-Gazette*. Boston, 1936.

ANDRUS, E. D., and others, eds., *Advances in Military Medicine (Science in World II Series)*. 2 v. Boston, 1948.

ARMES, ETHEL M., *The Story of Coal and Iron in Alabama*. Birmingham, 1910.

ASBURY, HERBERT, *The Great Illusion*. Garden City, 1950.

BAEHR, H. W., JR., *The New York Tribune since the Civil War*. New York, 1936.

BAILEY, T. A., *America Faces Russia*. Ithaca, 1950.

——, *A Diplomatic History of the American People*. Rev. ed. New York, 1950.

——, *Theodore Roosevelt and the Japanese-American Crises*. Stanford University, 1934.

——, *Woodrow Wilson and the Great Betrayal*. New York, 1945.

——, *Woodrow Wilson and the Lost Peace*. New York, 1944.

BAKER, JACOB, *Government Aid during the Depression to Professional, Technical and Other Service Workers*. Washington, 1936.

BAKER, R. S., *Woodrow Wilson*. 8 v. Garden City, 1927–1939.

——, *Woodrow Wilson and World Settlement*. 3 v. Garden City, 1922.

BALCH, EMILY G., *Our Slavic Fellow Citizens*. New York, 1910.

BARBER, H. L., *The Story of the Automobile*. Chicago, 1927.

BARKER, VIRGIL, *American Painting*. New York, 1950.

BARRETT, D. C., *The Greenbacks and Resumption of Specie Payments, 1862–1879 (Harvard Economic Studies, XXXVI)*. Cambridge, 1931.

BARTH, ALAN, *The Loyalty of Free Men*. New York, 1951.

BARTLETT, R. J., *The League to Enforce Peace*. Chapel Hill, 1944.

BATES, E. S., *This Land of Liberty*. New York, 1930.

——, and J. V. DITTEMORE, *Mary Baker Eddy*. New York, 1932.

BAXTER, J. P., 3d., *Scientists against Time*. Boston, 1946.

BEACH, J. W., *American Fiction, 1920–1940*. New York, 1941.

BEALE, H. K., *A History of Freedom of Teaching in American Schools* (Commission on the Social Studies, *Report*, XVI). New York, 1941.

BEAMISH, R. J., and F. A. MARCH, *America's Part in the World War*. Philadelphia, 1919.

BEARD, C. A. and MARY R., *America in Midpassage (The Rise of American Civilization*, III). New York, 1939.

BEARD, C. A., and G. H. E. SMITH, *The Old Deal and the New*. New York, 1940.

BEARDSLEY, F. G., *A History of American Revivals*. New York, 1912.

BECKETT, GRACE, *The Reciprocal Trade Agreements Program*. New York, 1941.

BELL, H. C. F., *Woodrow Wilson and the People*. New York, 1945.

BEMIS, S. F., *A Diplomatic History of the United States*. Rev. ed. New York, 1950.

——, *The Latin American Policy of the United States*. New York, 1943.

BERGE, WENDELL, *Cartels*. Washington, 1944.

BERGLUND, ABRAHAM, *The United States Steel Corporation* (Columbia University, *Studies*, XXVII, no. 2). New York, 1907.

BERLE, A. A., JR., and G. C. MEANS, *The Modern Corporation and Private Property*. New York, 1933.

BERMAN, EDWARD, *Labor Disputes and the President of the United States* (Columbia University, *Studies*, CXI, no. 2). New York, 1924.

BILLINGTON, R. A., *Westward Expansion*. New York, 1949.

BING, ALEXANDER, *War-Time Strikes and Their Adjustment*. New York, 1921.

BINKLEY, W. E., *American Political Parties, Their Natural History*. New York, 1943.

BIRDSALL, PAUL, *Versailles Twenty Years After*. New York, 1941.

BLACKWELL, ALICE STONE, *Lucy Stone*. Boston, 1930.

BOGART, E. L., *War Costs and Their Financing*. New York, 1921.

BONBRIGHT, J. C., and G. C. MEANS, *The Holding Company*. New York, 1932.

BOUDIN, L. B., *Government by Judiciary*. 2 v. New York, 1932.

BOWERS, C. G., *Beveridge and the Progressive Era*. Boston, 1932.

BRANCH, E. D., *The Hunting of the Buffalo*. New York, 1929.

BRANDEIS, L. D., *Other People's Money*. New York, 1914.

BRIGGS, H. E., *Frontiers of the Northwest*. New York, 1940.

BRISSENDEN, P. F., *The I. W. W.: a Study of American Syndicalism* (Columbia University, *Studies*, LXXXIII). New York, 1919.

BROGAN, D. W., *The Era of Franklin D. Roosevelt (The Chronicles of America Series*, LII). New Haven, 1950.

BROOKS, R. R. R., *Unions of Their Own Choosing*. New Haven, 1939.

BROWN, FRANCIS, comp., *The War in Maps*. New York, 1942.

BRUCE, P. A., *The Rise of the New South* (G. C. Lee, ed., *The History of North America*, XVII). Philadelphia, 1905.

BRYN-JONES, DAVID, *Frank B. Kellogg*. New York, 1937.

BUCK, P. H., *The Road to Reunion, 1865–1900.* Boston, 1937.

BUCK, S. J., *The Agrarian Crusade* (*The Chronicles of American Series,* XLV). New Haven, 1920.

———, *The Granger Movement* (*Harvard Historical Studies,* XIX). Cambridge, 1913.

BUELL, R. L., *Japanese Immigration* (World Peace Foundation, *Pamphlets,* VII, nos. 5–6). Boston, 1924.

———, *The Washington Conference.* New York, 1922.

BUREAU OF THE BUDGET, WAR RECORDS SECTION, *The United States at War* (*Historical Reports on War Administration: Bureau of the Budget,* I). Washington, 1946.

BURGESS, THOMAS, *Greeks in America.* Boston, 1913.

BURLINGAME, ROGER, *Engines of Democracy.* New York, 1940.

BURNS, A. E., and D. S. WATSON, *Government Spending and Economic Expansion.* Washington, 1940.

BURTON, T. E., *Financial Crises and Periods of Industrial and Commercial Depression.* New York, 1902.

BUTTERFIELD, ROGER, ed., *The American Past.* New York, 1947.

BUTTS, R. F., *The College Charts Its Course.* New York, 1939.

CALHOUN, A. W., *A Social History of the American Family.* 3 v. Cleveland, 1917–1919.

CALLAHAN, J. M., *American Foreign Policy in Mexican Relations.* New York, 1932.

CALLCOTT, W. H., *The Caribbean Policy of the United States, 1890–1920.* Baltimore, 1942.

———, *Liberalism in Mexico, 1857–1929.* Stanford University, 1931.

CANT, GILBERT, *The Great Pacific Victory from the Solomons to Tokyo.* New York, 1946.

CAPPER, ARTHUR, *The Agricultural Bloc.* New York, 1922.

CARSKADON, T. R., and RUDOLF MODLEY, *U. S. A.: Measure of a Nation. A Graphic Presentation of America's Needs and Resources.* New York, 1949.

CARSON, JULIA M. H., *Home Away from Home, the Story of the U.S.O.* New York, 1949.

CASSON, H. N., *The History of the Telephone.* Chicago, 1910.

CHADWICK, F. E., *The Relations of the United States and Spain.* 3 v. New York, 1909–1911.

CHAFEE, ZECHARIAH, JR., *Free Speech in the United States.* Cambridge, 1941.

CHAPMAN, C. E., *A History of the Cuban Republic.* New York, 1927.

CHASE, E. P., *The United Nations in Action.* New York, 1951.

CHERRINGTON, E. H., *The Evolution of Prohibition in the United States of America.* Westerville, 1920.

CHIDSEY, D. B., *The Gentleman from New York: a Life of Roscoe Conkling.* New Haven, 1935.

CHILD, C. J., *The German-Americans in Politics, 1914–1917.* Madison, 1939.

Chronicles of America Series, The. See Johnson, Allen, ed.

CIVILIAN PRODUCTION ADMINISTRATION, *Industrial Mobilization for War* (*His-*

torical Reports on War Administration: War Production Board, I). Washington, 1947.

CLARK, J. M., *The Costs of the World War to the American People* (J. T. Shotwell, ed., *Economic and Social History of the World War*). New Haven, 1931.

CLARK, V. S., *History of Manufactures in the United States* (Carnegie Institution, *Contributions to American Economic History*). Rev. ed. 3 v. New York, 1929.

CLARKSON, G. B., *Industrial America in the World War*. Boston, 1923.

CLEMEN, R. A., *The American Livestock and Meat Industry*. New York, 1923.

CLIFFORD, A. G., *The Conquest of North Africa*. New York, 1943.

COCHRAN, T. C., and WILLIAM MILLER, *The Age of Enterprise*. New York, 1942.

COFFIN, CAROLINE, *Vaudeville*. New York, 1914.

COLE, A. H., *The American Wool Manufacture*. 2 v. Cambridge, 1926.

COLEMAN, C. H., *The Election of 1868* (Columbia University, *Studies*, CCCXCII). New York, 1933.

COLEMAN, J. W., *Labor Disturbances in Pennsylvania, 1850–1880*. Washington, 1936.

COLVIN, D. L., *Prohibition in the United States*. New York, 1926.

COMMAGER, H. S., *The American Mind*. New York, 1950.

COMMITTEE ON RECENT ECONOMIC CHANGES, *Recent Economic Changes in the United States*. 2 v. New York, 1929.

COMMONS, J. R., and others, *History of Labour [Labor] in the United States*. 4 v. New York, 1918–1935.

COOLIDGE, A. C., *The United States as a World Power*. New York, 1908.

COOLIDGE, MARY R., *Chinese Immigration*. New York, 1909.

COON, HORACE, *American Tel. & Tel. The Story of a Great Monopoly*. New York, 1939.

COPELAND, M. T., *The Cotton Manufacturing Industry of the United States* (*Harvard Economic Studies*, VIII). Cambridge, 1912.

COREY, HERBERT, *The Truth about Hoover*. Boston, 1932.

COREY, LEWIS, *The House of Morgan*. New York, 1930.

COX, I. J., *Nicaragua and the United States, 1909–1927* (World Peace Foundation, *Pamphlets*, X, no. 7). Boston, 1927.

CRANSTON, RUTH, *The Story of Woodrow Wilson*. New York, 1945.

CROLY, HERBERT, *Marcus Alonzo Hanna*. New York, 1912.

CROLY, JANE C., *The History of the Woman's Club Movement in America*. New York, 1898.

CROWELL, BENEDICT, and R. F. WILSON, *How America Went to War*. 6 v. New Haven, 1921.

CUBBERLEY, E. P., *Public Education in the United States*. Rev. ed. Boston, 1934.

CURRENT, R. N., *Old Thad Stevens*. Madison, 1942.

CURTI, MERLE, *The Growth of American Thought*. Rev. ed. New York, 1951.

——, *Peace or War; the American Struggle, 1636–1936*. New York, 1936.

——, *The Roots of American Loyalty*. New York, 1946.

CURTIS, C. P., JR., *Lions under the Throne*. Boston, 1947.

CUTLER, J. E., *Lynch-Law*. New York, 1905.

DAGGETT, STUART, *Railroad Reorganization* (*Harvard Economic Studies*, IV). Cambridge, 1908.

DALE, E. E., *The Range Cattle Industry*. Norman, 1930.

DANIELS, JONATHAN, *The Man of Independence*. Philadelphia, 1950.

DAVID, HENRY, *The History of the Haymarket Affair*. New York, 1936.

——, and others, eds., *The Economic History of the United States*. 9 v., in progress. New York, 1945– .

DAVIE, M. R., *Refugees in America*. New York, 1947.

DAVIS, G. T., *A Navy Second to None*. New York, 1940.

DAVIS, P. H., *Football, the Intercollegiate Game*. New York, 1911.

DAVISON, H. P., *The American Red Cross in the Great War*. New York, 1919.

DEAN, VERA M., *The Four Cornerstones of Peace*. New York, 1946.

DENNETT, TYLER, *Americans in Eastern Asia*. New York, 1922.

——, *John Hay* (*American Political Leaders*). New York, 1933.

——, *Theodore Roosevelt and the Russo-Japanese War*. Garden City, 1925.

DENNIS, A. L. P., *Adventures in American Diplomacy, 1896–1906*. New York, 1928.

DEPARTMENT OF THE ARMY, HISTORICAL DIVISION, *United States Army in World War II*. 4 v. Washington, 1947–1950. In progress.

DEROUNIAN, ARTHUR ("John Roy Carlson"), *Under Cover*. New York, 1943.

DEWEY, D. R., *Financial History of the United States* (A. B. Hart, ed., *American Citizen Series*). Rev. ed. New York, 1931.

——, *National Problems* (*The American Nation*, XXIV). New York, 1907.

DEWITT, D. M., *The Impeachment and Trial of Andrew Johnson*. New York, 1903.

DICK, EVERETT, *The Sod-House Frontier, 1854–1890*. New York, 1937.

——, *Vanguards of the Frontier*. New York, 1941.

Dictionary of American Biography. See Johnson, Allen, and Dumas Malone, eds.

DITZION, S. H., *Arsenals of a Democratic Culture, a Social History of the American Public Library Movement in New England and the Middle States from 1850 to 1900*. Chicago, 1947.

DOBIE, J. F., *The Longhorns*. Boston, 1941.

DORFMAN, JOSEPH, *The Economic Mind in American Civilization*. 3 v. New York, 1946–1949.

DOUGLAS, P. H., *Social Security in the United States*. Rev. ed. New York, 1939.

DUFFUS, R. L., and F. P. KEPPEL, *The Arts in American Life*. New York, 1932.

DULEBOHN, G. R., *Principles of Foreign Policy under the Cleveland Administrations*. Philadelphia, 1941.

DULLES, F. R., *America in the Pacific*. Boston, 1932.

——, *America Learns to Play, a History of Popular Recreation, 1607–1940*. New York, 1940.

——, *The American Red Cross, a History*. New York, 1950.

——, *China and America*. Princeton, 1946.

DULLES, F. R., *Labor in America*. New York, 1949.

DUNNING, W. A., *Reconstruction Political and Economic* (*The American Nation*, XXII). New York, 1907.

DYER, F. L., and T. C. MARTIN, *Edison*. Rev. ed. 2 v. New York, 1929.

EARHART, MARY, *Frances Willard*. Chicago, 1944.

EDWARDS, G. W., *The Evolution of Finance Capitalism*. New York, 1938.

EICHELBERGER, R. L., and MILTON MacKAYE, *Our Jungle Road to Tokyo*. New York, 1950.

ELLIS, ELMER, *Henry Moore Teller*. Caldwell, 1941.

EMBREE, E. R., *American Negroes*. New York, 1942.

ERNST, M. L., *The First Freedom*. New York, 1946.

EURICH, A. C., and E. C. WILSON, *In 1936*. New York, 1937.

FARIES, J. C., *The Rise of Internationalism*. New York, 1915.

FARRAR, V. J., *The Annexation of Russian America to the United States*. Washington, 1937.

FAULKNER, H. U., *American Economic History* (G. S. Ford, ed., *Harper's Historical Series*). Rev. ed. New York, 1949.

——, *From Versailles to the New Deal* (*The Chronicles of America Series*, LI). New Haven, 1950.

——, *The Quest for Social Justice* (*A History of American Life*, XI). New York, 1931.

FAY, S. B., *The Origins of the World War*. Rev. ed. 2 v. New York, 1934.

FEDER, LEAH H., *Unemployment Relief in Periods of Depression*. New York, 1936.

FEIS, HERBERT, *The Road to Pearl Harbor*. Princeton, 1950.

FERLEGER, H. R., *David A. Wells and the American Revenue System, 1865–1870*. Ann Arbor, 1942.

FERRARA, ORESTES, *The Last Spanish War* (W. E. Shea, tr.). New York, 1937.

FINE, NATHAN, *Labor and Farmer Parties in the United States, 1828–1928*. New York, 1928.

FISH, C. R., *The Civil Service and the Patronage* (*Harvard Historical Studies*, XI). Cambridge, 1905.

FITZGIBBON, R. H., *Cuba and the United States, 1900–1935*. Menasha, 1935.

FLACK, H. E., *Spanish-American Diplomatic Relations Preceding the War of 1898* (Johns Hopkins University, *Studies*, XXIV, nos. 1–2). Baltimore, 1906.

FLEMING, D. F., *The United States and the League of Nations*. New York, 1932.

——, *The United States and the World Court*. New York, 1945.

——, *The United States and World Organization, 1920–1933*. New York, 1938.

FLICK, A. C., *Samuel Jones Tilden* (*American Political Leaders*). New York, 1939.

FOERSTER, R. F., *The Italian Emigration of Our Times* (*Harvard Economic Studies*, XX). Cambridge, 1919.

FORBES, W. C., *The Philippine Islands*. 2 v. Boston, 1928.

FORD, JAMES, and others, *Slums and Housing with Special Reference to New York City*. 2 v. Cambridge, 1936.

FORRESTER, R. B., *Report on Large Scale Coöperative Marketing in the United States*. London, 1925.

FRANKFURTER, FELIX, and NATHAN GREENE, *The Labor Injunction*. New York, 1930.

FRANKLIN, J. H., *From Slavery to Freedom: a History of American Negroes*. New York, 1947.

FRAZIER, E. F., *The Negro in the United States*. New York, 1949.

FROTHINGHAM, T. G., *The American Reinforcement in the World War*. Garden City, 1927.

FUESS, C. M., *Calvin Coolidge*. Boston, 1940.

——, *Carl Schurz (American Political Leaders)*. New York, 1932.

GABRIEL, R. H., *The Course of American Democratic Thought*. New York, 1940.

——, ed., *The Pageant of America*. 15 v. New Haven, 1925–1929.

GANOE, W. A., *The History of the United States Army*. New York, 1942.

GARIS, R. L., *Immigration Restriction*. New York, 1927.

GARRISON, W. E., *The March of Faith*. New York, 1933.

GAYER, A. D., *Public Works in Prosperity and Depression*. New York, 1935.

GELDER, L. M., *The Rise of Anglo-American Friendship*. London, 1938.

GIDDENS, P. H., *The Birth of the Oil Industry*. New York, 1938.

——, *Early Days of Oil, a Pictorial History of the Beginnings of the Industry in Pennsylvania*. Princeton, 1948.

GINGER, RAY, *The Bending Cross, a Biography of Eugene Victor Debs*. New Brunswick, 1949.

GITTINGER, ROY, *The Formation of the State of Oklahoma, 1803–1906*. Rev. ed. Norman, 1939.

GOODMAN, JACK, ed., *While You Were Gone. A Report on Wartime Life in the United States*. New York, 1946.

GORDON, D. L., and ROYDEN DANGERFIELD, *The Hidden Weapon, the Story of Economic Warfare*. New York, 1947.

GRAMLING, OLIVER, *AP, the Story of News*. New York, 1940.

GRAY, G. W., *The Advancing Front of Science*. New York, 1937.

GRISWOLD, A. W., *The Far Eastern Policy of the United States, 1898–1938*. New York, 1938.

GRODZINS, MORTON, *Americans Betrayed*. Chicago, 1949.

GRUENING, E. H., *Mexico and Its Heritage*. New York, 1928.

GUERRANT, E. D., *Roosevelt's Good Neighbor Policy* (University of New Mexico, *Inter-American Series,* V). Albuquerque, 1950.

GUNTHER, JOHN, *Roosevelt in Retrospect*. New York, 1950.

HACKETT, C. W., *The Mexican Revolution and the United States* (World Peace Foundation, *Pamphlets,* IX, no. 5). Boston, 1926.

HAINES, C. G., and R. J. S. HOFFMAN, *The Origins and Background of the Second World War*. New York, 1943.

HALL, W. P., *Iron Out of Calvary*. New York, 1946.

HAMMOND, M. B., *The Cotton Industry* (American Economic Association, *Publications,* n.s., no. 1). New York, 1897.

538 THE RISE OF MODERN AMERICA

HANEY, L. H., *A Congressional History of Railways in the United States, 1850–1887* (University of Wisconsin, *Bulletin*, no. 342). Madison, 1910.

HARPER, IDA H., *The Life and Work of Susan B. Anthony.* 3 v. Indianapolis, 1898–1908.

HARRIS, HERBERT, *American Labor.* New Haven, 1938.

——, *Labor's Civil War.* New York, 1940.

HARRISON, L. V., and ELIZABETH LAINE, *After Repeal.* New York, 1936.

HART, A. B., ed., *The American Nation: a History.* 28 v. New York, 1904–1918.

HARVEY, GEORGE, *Henry Clay Frick.* New York, 1928.

HAWORTH, P. L., *The Hayes-Tilden Disputed Presidential Election of 1876.* Cleveland, 1906.

HAYDEN, J. R., *The Philippines.* New York, 1942.

HAYNES, G. H., *Charles Sumner* (E. P. Oberholtzer, ed., *American Crisis Biographies*). Philadelphia, 1909.

HECHLER, K. W., *Insurgency: Personalities and Politics of the Taft Era* (Columbia University, *Studies,* no. 470). New York, 1940.

HEDGES, J. B., *Henry Villard and the Railways of the Northwest.* New York, 1930.

HENDERSON, G. C., *The Federal Trade Commission.* New Haven, 1924.

HENDRICK, B. J., *The Age of Big Business* (*The Chronicles of America Series,* XXXIX). New Haven, 1919.

——, *The Life and Letters of Walter H. Page.* 3 v. Garden City, 1922–1925.

——, *The Life of Andrew Carnegie.* 2 v. Garden City, 1932.

HENRY, R. S., *The Story of Reconstruction.* Indianapolis, 1938.

HESSELTINE, W. B., *The Rise and Fall of Third Parties: from Anti-Masonry to Wallace.* Washington, 1948.

——, *Ulysses S. Grant (American Political Leaders).* New York, 1935.

HEXNER, IRVIN, *International Cartels.* Chapel Hill, 1945.

HIBBARD, B. H., *A History of the Public Land Policies* (R. T. Ely, ed., *Land Economic Series*). New York, 1924.

HICKS, J. D., *The Populist Revolt.* Minneapolis, 1931.

HILL, H. C., *Roosevelt and the Caribbean.* Chicago, 1927.

HILLQUIT, MORRIS, *History of Socialism in the United States.* Rev. ed. New York, 1910.

HINES, W. D., *War History of American Railroads* (J. T. Shotwell, ed., *Economic and Social History of the World War*). New Haven, 1928.

HIRSCH, M. D., *William C. Whitney: Modern Warwick (American Political Leaders).* New York, 1948.

HIRST, F. W., *Wall Street and Lombard Street.* New York, 1931.

History of American Life, A. See Schlesinger, A. M., and D. R. Fox, eds.

HOCKETT, H. C., *The Constitutional History of the United States.* 2 v. New York, 1939.

HOFSTADTER, RICHARD, *Social Darwinism.* Philadelphia, 1945.

HOPKINS, C. H., *The Rise of the Social Gospel in American Protestantism* (*Yale Studies in Religious Education,* XIV). New Haven, 1940.

HORN, S. F., *Invisible Empire; the Story of the Ku Klux Klan, 1866–1871.* Boston, 1939.

HOWARD, D. S., *The WPA and Federal Relief Policy.* New York, 1943.

HOWARD, J. T., *Our American Music: Three Hundred Years of It.* Rev. ed. New York, 1946.

HOWE, G. F., *Chester A. Arthur (American Political Leaders).* New York, 1934.

HUREWITZ, J. C., *The Struggle for Palestine.* New York, 1950.

HURLBUT, J. L., *The Story of Chautauqua.* New York, 1921.

HUSBAND, JOSEPH, *The Story of the Pullman Car.* Chicago, 1917.

INGLIS, RUTH A., *Freedom of the Movies* (Commission on Freedom of the Press, *Publications,* III). Chicago, 1947.

IRWIN, INEZ H., *Angels and Amazons.* New York, 1933.

ISHAM, SAMUEL, *The History of American Painting* (J. C. Van Dyke, ed., *The History of American Art,* III). Rev. ed. New York, 1927.

JACKSON, R. H., *The Struggle for Judicial Supremacy.* New York, 1941.

JACOBS, LEWIS, *The Rise of the American Film.* New York, 1939.

JAFFE, BERNARD, *Men of Science in America.* New York, 1944.

JAMES, HENRY, *Richard Olney and His Public Service.* Boston, 1923.

JENKS, J. W., and W. J. LAUCK, *The Immigration Problem.* 6th ed. New York, 1926.

JESSUP, P. C., *Elihu Root.* 2 v. New York, 1938.

JOHNSON, ALLEN, ed., *The Chronicles of America Series.* 50 v. New Haven, 1918–1921, with 5 supplementary volumes ed. by Allan Nevins, New Haven, 1950.

——, and Dumas Malone, eds., *Dictionary of American Biography.* 21 v. New York, 1928–1937, with a supplement edited by H. E. Starr, 1944.

JOHNSON, C. O., *Borah of Idaho.* New York, 1936.

JOHNSON, WALTER, *The Battle against Isolation.* Chicago, 1944.

JOHNSTON, ALEXANDER, *Ten—and Out!* New York, 1936.

JONES, ELIOT, *The Anthracite Coal Combination in the United States* (*Harvard Economic Studies,* XI). Cambridge, 1914.

——, *Principles of Railway Transportation.* New York, 1924.

JONES, J. M., JR., *Tariff Retaliation.* Philadelphia, 1934.

JONES, J. P., and P. M. HOLLISTER, *The German Secret Service in America.* Boston, 1918.

JORDAN, D. S., ed., *Leading American Men of Science* (W. P. Trent, ed., *Biographies of Leading Americans*). New York, 1910.

JOSEPH, SAMUEL, *Jewish Immigration to the United States* (Columbia University, *Studies,* LIX, no. 4). New York, 1914.

JOSEPHSON, MATTHEW, *The Politicos, 1865–1900.* New York, 1938.

——, *The President Makers.* New York, 1940.

——, *The Robber Barons.* New York, 1935.

JOUGHIN, G. L., and E. M. MORGAN, *The Legacy of Sacco and Vanzetti.* New York, 1948.

KAEMPFFERT, WALDEMAR, ed., *A Popular History of American Invention.* 2 v. New York, 1924.

KAZIN, ALFRED, *On Native Grounds.* New York, 1942.

KEIM, JEANNETTE, *Forty Years of German-American Political Relations.* Philadelphia, 1919.

KELLY, A. H., and W. A. HARBISON, *The American Constitution: Its Origins and Development*. New York, 1948.

KELLY, F. C., *The Wright Brothers*. Rev. ed. New York, 1951.

KENNAN, GEORGE, *E. H. Harriman*. 2 v. Boston, 1922.

KEY, V. O., *Southern Politics*. New York, 1949.

KIRKLAND, E. C., *Men, Cities, and Transportation*. 2 v. Cambridge, 1949.

KNAUTH, O. W., *The Policy of the United States toward Industrial Monopoly* (Columbia University, *Studies*, LVI, no. 2). New York, 1914.

KNIGHT, E. W., *Public Education in the South*. Boston, 1922.

KNIGHT, M. M., *The Americans in Santo Domingo*. New York, 1928.

KNOLES, G. H., *Presidential Campaign and Election of 1892*. Stanford University, 1942.

KORSON, G. G., *At His Side, the Story of the American Red Cross Overseas in World War II*. New York, 1945.

KOUWENHOVEN, J. A., ed., *Adventures of America, 1857–1900*. New York, 1938.

KROUT, J. A., *Annals of American Sport* (*The Pageant of America*, XV). New Haven, 1929.

KRUIF, PAUL DE, *Microbe Hunters*. New York, 1926.

KRUTCH, J. W., *The American Drama since 1918*. New York, 1940.

KUHLMANN, C. B., *The Development of the Flour-Milling Industry in the United States*. Boston, 1929.

KUYKENDALL, R. S., and A. G. DAY, *Hawaii: a History*. New York, 1948.

LA FARGE, OLIVER, ed., *The Changing Indian*. Norman, 1942.

LAIDLER, H. W., *Concentration of Control in American Industry*. New York, 1931.

LANE, MARIE D., and FRANCIS STEEGMULLER, *America on Relief*. New York, 1938.

LANE, W. J., *Commodore Vanderbilt*. New York, 1942.

LANGER, W. L., *The Diplomacy of Imperialism, 1890–1902*. Rev. ed. 2 v. New York, 1951.

——, *Our Vichy Gamble*. New York, 1947.

LANGSAM, W. C., *The World since 1914*. Rev. ed. New York, 1943.

LARKIN, O. W., *Art and Life in America*. New York, 1949.

LARSON, HENRIETTA M., *Jay Cooke, Private Banker*. Cambridge, 1936.

LAUCK, W. J., *The Causes of the Panic of 1893*. Boston, 1907.

LAUGHLIN, J. L., *The History of Bimetallism in the United States*. Rev. ed. New York, 1910.

LAVINE, HAROLD, and JAMES WECHSLER, *War Propaganda and the United States*. New Haven, 1940.

LEE, A. M., *The Daily Newspaper in America*. New York, 1937.

LEECH, HARPER, and J. C. CARROLL, *Armour and His Times*. New York, 1938.

LEFF, D. N., *Uncle Sam's Pacific Islets*. Stanford University, 1940.

LEIGH, RANDOLPH, *48 Million Tons to Eisenhower*. Washington, 1945.

LEONARD, J. N., *Three Years Down*. New York, 1939.

LEROY, J. A., *The Americans in the Philippines*. 2 v. Boston, 1914.

LEWINSON, PAUL, *Race, Class, & Party*. London, 1932.

LEWIS, E. R., *A History of American Political Thought from the Civil War to the World War*. New York, 1937.

LILIENTHAL, DAVID, *TVA, Democracy on the March*. New York, 1944.

LINDLEY, BETTY and E. K., *A New Deal for Youth*. New York, 1938.

LINDSEY, ALMONT, *The Pullman Strike*. Chicago, 1942.

LORWIN, L. L., *The American Federation of Labor: History, Policies and Prospects*. Washington, 1933.

LOUD, G. C., *Evangelized America*. New York, 1928.

LOUGHEED, VICTOR, *Vehicles of the Air*. Chicago, 1919.

LUBSCHEZ, B. J., *The Story of the Motion Picture*. New York, 1920.

LUTZ, ALMA, *Created Equal, a Biography of Elizabeth Cady Stanton, 1815–1902*. New York, 1940.

LYMAN, G. D., *The Saga of the Comstock Lode*. New York, 1934.

LYNCH, D. T., *"Boss" Tweed*. New York, 1927.

McCALEB, W. F., *History of the Brotherhood of Railroad Trainmen*. New York, 1936.

MACFARLAND, C. S., *The Progress of Church Federation*. New York, 1917.

MACK, GERSTLE, *The Land Divided*. New York, 1944.

McKELVEY, BLAKE, *American Prisons* (University of Chicago, *Social Service Series*). Chicago, 1936.

MACKENZIE, CATHERINE, *Alexander Graham Bell*. Boston, 1928.

McKENZIE, R. D., *The Metropolitan Community (Recent Social Trends Monographs)*. New York, 1933.

MACMAHON, A. W., and others, *The Administration of Federal Work Relief* (Social Science Research Council, *Studies in Administration*). Chicago, 1941.

McMURRY, D. L., *Coxey's Army*. Boston, 1929.

McNICKLE, D'ARCY, *They Came Here First*. Philadelphia, 1949.

McWILLIAMS, CAREY, *Brothers under the Skin*. Rev. ed. Boston, 1951.

——, *Factories in the Field*. Boston, 1939.

——, *Prejudice, Japanese-Americans: Symbol of Racial Intolerance*. Boston, 1944.

——, *Southern California Country* (Erskine Caldwell, ed., *American Folkways*). New York, 1946.

MANSFIELD, H. C., and others, *A Short History of OPA* (*Historical Reports on War Administration: Office of Price Administration, XV*). Washington, 1947.

MARSHALL, JAMES, *Santa Fé*. New York, 1946.

MATHEWS, BASIL, *Booker T. Washington, Educator and Interracial Interpreter*. Cambridge, 1948.

MAY, H. F., *Protestant Churches and Industrial America*. New York, 1949.

MAYORGA, MARGARET G., *A Short History of the American Drama*. New York, 1932.

MECKLIN, J. M., *The Ku Klux Klan*. New York, 1924.

MERZ, CHARLES, *The Dry Decade*. New York, 1931.

MEYER, A. E., *The Development of Education in the Twentieth Century*. New York, 1939.

MILLIS, WALTER, *The Martial Spirit*. Boston, 1931.

——. *This Is Pearl! The United States and Japan—1941*. New York, 1947.

MILTON, G. F., *The Age of Hate*. New York, 1930.

MINER, D. C., *The Fight for the Panama Route*. New York, 1940.

MITCHELL, BROADUS, *Depression Decade* (*The Economic History of the United States*, IX). New York, 1947.

——, *The Rise of Cotton Mills in the South* (Johns Hopkins University, *Studies*, XXXIX, no. 2). Baltimore, 1921.

MITCHELL, D. W., *History of the Modern American Navy*. New York, 1946.

MITCHELL, W. C., *A History of the Greenbacks* (Chicago University, *Decennial Publications*, 2d ser., IX). Chicago, 1903.

MOCK, J. R., and EVANGELINE THURBER, *Report on Demobilization*. Stillwater, 1944.

MOCK, J. R., and CEDRIC LARSON, *Words That Won the War; the Story of the Committee on Public Information, 1917–1919*. Princeton, 1939.

MONTAGUE, L. L., *Haiti and the United States, 1714–1938*. Durham, 1940.

MOODY, JOHN, *The Masters of Capital* (*The Chronicles of America Series*, XLI). New Haven, 1919.

——, *The Railroad Builders* (*The Chronicles of America Series*, XXXVIII). New Haven, 1919.

——, *The Truth about the Trusts*. New York, 1904.

MOREHOUSE, WARD, *Matinee Tomorrow, Fifty Years of Our Theatre*. New York, 1949.

MORGAN, A. E., *Edward Bellamy*. New York, 1944.

MORISON, E. E., *Admiral Sims and the Modern American Navy*. Boston, 1942.

MORISON, S. E., *History of United States Naval Operations in World War II*. 7 out of 14 v. completed. Boston, 1947–1951.

MORRIS, LLOYD, *Not So Long Ago*. New York, 1949.

——, *Postscript to Yesterday, America: the Last Fifty Years*. New York, 1947.

MORRISSEY, ALICE M., *The American Defense of Neutral Rights, 1914–1917*. Cambridge, 1939.

MORSE, J. T., Jr., ed., *American Statesmen*. Rev. ed. 32 v. Boston, 1898–1900.

MOTT, F. L., *American Journalism*. Rev. ed. New York, 1950.

——, *Golden Multitudes, the Story of Best Sellers in the United States*. New York, 1947.

——, *A History of American Magazines*. 3 v. New York and Cambridge, 1930–1938.

MOULTON, H. G., and LEO PASVOLSKY, *War Debts and World Prosperity*. New York, 1932.

MOWRY, G. M., *Theodore Roosevelt and the Progressive Movement*. Madison, 1946.

MUNRO, D. G., *The Latin American Republics, a History*. Rev. ed. New York, 1950.

——, *The United States and the Caribbean Area*. Boston, 1934.

MUSSEY, H. R., *Combination in the Mining Industry* (Columbia University, *Studies*, XXIII, no. 3). New York, 1905.

MUZZEY, D. S., *James G. Blaine (American Political Leaders)*. New York, 1934.

MYERS, D. P., *Origin and Conclusion of the Paris Pact* (World Peace Foundation, *Pamphlets*, XII, no. 2). Boston, 1929.

MYERS, GUSTAVUS, *History of Bigotry in the United States.* New York, 1943.

——, *History of the Great American Fortunes.* Rev. ed. New York, 1936.

MYRDAL, GUNNAR, *An American Dilemma.* 2 v. New York, 1944.

NELSON, D. M., *Arsenal of Democracy, the Story of American War Production.* New York, 1946.

NEVINS, ALLAN, ed., *American Political Leaders.* New York, 1930. In progress.

——, *The Emergence of Modern America* (*A History of American Life,* VIII). New York, 1927.

——, *Grover Cleveland (American Political Leaders).* New York, 1932.

——, *Hamilton Fish (American Political Leaders).* New York, 1936.

——, *Henry White: Thirty Years of American Diplomacy.* New York, 1930.

——, *John D. Rockefeller.* 2 v. New York, 1940.

——, *The New Deal and World Affairs* (*The Chronicles of America Series,* LVI). New Haven, 1950.

——, *The United States in a Chaotic World* (*The Chronicles of America Series,* LV). New Haven, 1950.

——, and L. M. HACKER, eds., *The United States and Its Place in World Affairs, 1918–1943.* Boston, 1943.

NICHOLS, JEANNETTE P., *Alaska.* Cleveland, 1924.

NOTTER, HARLEY, *The Origins of the Foreign Policy of Woodrow Wilson.* Baltimore, 1937.

NOURSE, E. G., *American Agriculture and the European Market.* New York, 1924.

——, and others, *Three Years of the Agricultural Adjustment Administration.* Washington, 1937.

NOYES, A. D., *Forty Years of American Finance.* Rev. ed. New York, 1909.

OBERHOLTZER, E. P., *A History of the United States since the Civil War.* 5 v. New York, 1917–1937.

O'CONNOR, J. F. T., *The Banking Crisis and Recovery under the Roosevelt Administration.* Chicago, 1938.

ODEGARD, P. H., *Pressure Politics.* New York, 1928.

ODUM, H. W., ed., *American Masters of Social Science* (same ed., *American Social Science Series*). New York, 1927.

——, and H. E. MOORE, *American Regionalism.* New York, 1938.

OGDEN, ROLLO, *Life and Letters of Edwin Lawrence Godkin.* 2 v. New York, 1907.

OGG, F. A., *National Progress* (*The American Nation,* XXVII). New York, 1918.

OLCOTT, C. S., *The Life of William McKinley* (*American Statesmen,* 2d ser., VII). 2 v. Boston, 1916.

OLIVER, J. W., *History of the Civil War Military Pensions, 1861–1885* (University of Wisconsin, *Bulletin,* no. 844). Madison, 1917.

OLIVER, R. T., *Why War Came in Korea.* New York, 1950.

ONEAL, JAMES, and G. A. WERNER, *American Communism.* Rev. ed. New York, 1947.

OSGOOD, E. S., *The Day of the Cattleman.* Minneapolis, 1929.

OVERMYER, GRACE, *Government and the Arts.* New York, 1939.

OVERTON, R. C., *Burlington West*. Cambridge, 1941.

PADELFORD, N. J., *The Panama Canal in Peace and War*. New York, 1942.

PALMER, FREDERICK, *Newton D. Baker*. 2 v. New York, 1931.

PARKS, E. T., *Colombia and the United States, 1765–1934*. Durham, 1935.

PARRINGTON, V. L., *The Beginnings of Critical Realism in America* (*Main Currents in American Thought*, III). New York, 1930.

PARRINGTON, V. L., JR., *American Dreams. A Study of American Utopias*. Providence, 1948.

PARTRIDGE, BELLAMY, and OTTO BETTMANN, eds., *As We Were, Family Life in America, 1850–1900*. New York, 1946.

PATTEE, F. L., *A History of American Literature since 1870*. New York, 1915.

——, *The New American Literature*. New York, 1930.

PATTON, C. W., *The Battle for Municipal Reform*. Washington, 1940.

PAXSON, F. L., *American Democracy and the World War*. 3 v. Boston and Berkeley, 1936–1948.

——, *The Last American Frontier*. New York, 1910.

PECORA, FERDINAND, *Wall Street under Oath*. New York, 1939.

PEIRCE, P. S., *The Freedmen's Bureau* (University of Iowa, *Studies*, III, no. 1). Iowa City, 1904.

PERKINS, DEXTER, *America and Two Wars*. Boston, 1944.

——, *Hands Off, a History of the Monroe Doctrine*. Boston, 1941.

——, *The Monroe Doctrine, 1826–1867*. Baltimore, 1933.

PETERSON, FLORENCE, *Strikes in the United States, 1880–1936* (United States Department of Labor, *Bulletin*, no. 651). Washington, 1938.

PETERSON, H. C., *Propaganda for War: the Campaign against American Neutrality, 1914–1917*. Norman, 1939.

PHILLIPS, C. F., and J. V. GARLAND, *Government Spending and Economic Recovery*. New York, 1938.

POWELL, E. A., *The Army behind the Army*. New York, 1919.

POWELL, L. P., *Mary Baker Eddy*. New York, 1930.

PRATT, FLETCHER, *War for the World* (*The Chronicles of America Series*, LIV). New Haven, 1950.

PRATT, J. W., *America's Colonial Experiment*. New York, 1950.

——, *Expansionists of 1898*. Baltimore, 1936.

PRESBREY, FRANK, *The History and Development of Advertising*. Garden City, 1929.

PRESIDENT'S RESEARCH COMMITTEE ON SOCIAL TRENDS, *Recent Social Trends in the United States*. 2 v. New York, 1933.

PRIEST, L. B., *Uncle Sam's Stepchildren*. New Brunswick, 1942.

PRINGLE, H. F., *The Life and Times of William Howard Taft*. 2 v. New York, 1939.

——, *Theodore Roosevelt*. New York, 1931.

PRITCHETT, C. H., *The Roosevelt Court*. New York, 1948.

——, *The Tennessee Valley Authority*. Chapel Hill, 1943.

PROUT, H. G., *A Life of George Westinghouse*. New York, 1921.

PYLE, J. G., *The Life of James J. Hill*. 2 v. Garden City, 1917.

QUIGLEY, H. S., *Far Eastern War, 1937–1941*. Boston, 1942.

RAINWATER, C. E., *The Play Movement in the United States.* Chicago, 1921.

RANDALL, J. G., *The Civil War and Reconstruction.* Boston, 1937.

RAPER, A. F., and I. DEA. REID, *Sharecroppers All.* Chapel Hill, 1941.

RAPPARD, W. E., *The Quest for Peace.* Cambridge, 1940.

RATNER, SIDNEY, *American Taxation.* New York, 1942.

RAUCH, BASIL, *The History of the New Deal, 1933–1938.* New York, 1944.

——, *Roosevelt from Munich to Pearl Harbor.* New York, 1950.

RAVENEL, M. P., ed., *A Half Century of Public Health.* New York, 1921.

REGIER, C. C., *The Era of the Muckrakers.* Chapel Hill, 1932.

REISCHAUER, E. O., *The United States and Japan* (Sumner Welles, ed., *The American Foreign Policy Library*). Cambridge, 1950.

RHODES, J. F., *History of the United States from the Compromise of 1850 to the McKinley-Bryan Campaign of 1896.* 8 v. New York, 1892–1919.

——, *The McKinley and Roosevelt Administrations.* New York, 1922.

RICHARDSON, R. N., and C. C. RISTER, *The Greater Southwest.* Glendale, 1935.

RICKARD, T. A., *A History of American Mining.* New York, 1932.

RIEGEL, R. E., *The Story of the Western Railroads.* New York, 1926.

RIPLEY, W. Z., *Railroads: Rates and Regulation.* New York, 1912.

RIPPY, J. F., *The Caribbean Danger Zone.* New York, 1940.

——, *The United States and Mexico.* Rev. ed. New York, 1931.

RISTER, C. C., *Southern Plainsmen.* Norman, 1938.

ROBBINS, E. C., *Railway Conductors: a Study in Organized Labor* (Columbia University, *Studies,* LXI, no. 1). New York, 1914.

ROBBINS, R. M., *Our Landed Heritage, the Public Domain, 1776–1936.* Princeton, 1942.

ROBERT, J. C., *The Story of Tobacco in America.* New York, 1949.

ROBINSON, J. S., *The Amalgamated Association of Iron, Steel and Tin Workers* (Johns Hopkins University, *Studies,* XXXVIII, no. 2). Baltimore, 1920.

ROGERS, AGNES, and F. L. ALLEN, eds., *The American Procession.* New York, 1933.

——, eds., *I Remember Distinctly.* New York, 1947.

ROOS, C. F., *NRA Economic Planning.* Bloomington, 1937.

ROSCOE, THEODORE, *United States Submarine Operations in World War II.* Annapolis, 1949.

ROSS, E. D., *Democracy's College, the Land-Grant Movement in Its Formative Stage.* Ames, 1942.

——, *The Liberal Republican Movement.* New York, 1919.

ROVERE, R. H., and A. M. SCHLESINGER, JR., *The General and the President.* New York, 1951.

ROWE, H. K., *The History of Religion in the United States.* New York, 1924.

RYAN, W. C., *Studies in Early Graduate Education* (Carnegie Foundation for the Advancement of Teaching, *Bulletin,* no. 30). New York, 1930.

RYDEN, G. H., *The Foreign Policy of the United States in Relation to Samoa.* New Haven, 1933.

SABIN, E. L., *Building the Pacific Railway.* Philadelphia, 1919.

SAGESER, A. B., *The First Two Decades of the Pendleton Act* (University of Nebraska, *Studies,* XXXIV–XXXV). Lincoln, 1935.

SALOUTOS, THEODORE, and J. D. HICKS, *Agricultural Discontent in the Middle West, 1900–1939.* Madison, 1951.

SAMUELSON, P. A., and E. E. HAGEN, *After the War, 1918–1920.* Washington, 1943.

SANDMEYER, E. C., *The Anti-Chinese Movement in California* (University of Illinois, *Studies,* XXIV, no. 3). Urbana, 1939.

SAYERS, MICHAEL, and A. E. KAHN, *Sabotage!* New York, 1942.

SCHLESINGER, A. M., *Learning How to Behave, a Historical Study of American Etiquette Books.* New York, 1947.

——, *Paths to the Present.* New York, 1949.

——, *The Rise of the City* (*A History of American Life,* X). New York, 1933.

——, and D. R. FOX, eds., *A History of American Life.* 13 v. New York, 1927–1948.

SCHNEIDER, H. W., *A History of American Philosophy* (*Columbia Studies in American Culture,* XVIII). New York, 1946.

SCHOULER, JAMES, *History of the United States of America, under the Constitution.* Rev. ed. 7 v. New York, 1894–1913.

SCHUSTER, EUNICE M., *Native American Anarchism* (Smith College, *Studies,* XVII). Northampton, 1931–1932.

SCHUYLER, HAMILTON, *The Roeblings.* Princeton, 1931.

SCOTT, J. B., *The Hague Peace Conferences of 1899 and 1907.* 2 v. Baltimore, 1909.

SCOTT, W. A., *The Repudiation of State Debts.* New York, 1893.

SEITZ, D. C., *Joseph Pulitzer.* New York, 1924.

SEYMOUR, CHARLES, *American Diplomacy during the World War.* Baltimore, 1934.

——, *The Intimate Papers of Colonel House.* 4 v. Boston, 1926–1928.

SHANNON, F. A., *The Farmer's Last Frontier, Agriculture, 1860–1897* (*The Economic History of the United States,* V). New York, 1945.

——, *America's Economic Growth.* Rev. ed. New York, 1951.

SHERWOOD, R. E., *Roosevelt and Hopkins.* Rev. ed. New York, 1950.

SHIPPEE, L. B., *Canadian-American Relations, 1849–1874* (J. T. Shotwell, gen. ed., *The Relations of Canada and the United States*). New Haven, 1939.

SHUGG, R. W., and H. A. DEWEERD, *World War II, a Concise History.* Washington, 1946.

SIMKINS, F. B., *Pitchfork Ben Tillman, South Carolinian.* Baton Rouge, 1944.

——, *The South Old and New: a History, 1820–1947.* New York, 1947.

SIMMONS, R. B., *Boulder Dam and the Great Southwest.* Los Angeles, 1936.

SLOSSON, E. E., *Creative Chemistry.* New York, 1919.

SLOSSON, P. W., *The Great Crusade and After* (*A History of American Life,* XII). New York, 1930.

SMITH, GOLDWIN, *The Treaty of Washington, 1871: a Study in Imperial History.* Ithaca, 1941.

SMITH, H. L., *Airways.* New York, 1942.

SMITH, J. P., *The Republican Expansionists of the Early Reconstruction Era.* Chicago, 1933.

SMITH, J. R., *The Story of Iron and Steel (The Library of Useful Stories)*. New York, 1908.

SMITH, T. C., *The Life and Letters of James Abram Garfield*. 2 v. New Haven, 1925.

SOULE, GEORGE, *Prosperity Decade, from War to Depression: 1917–1929 (The Economic History of the United States*, VIII). New York, 1947.

SPALDING, A. G., *America's National Game*. New York, 1911.

SPARKS, E. E., *National Development (The American Nation*, XXIII). New York, 1907.

SPAULDING, O. L., *The United States Army in War and Peace*. New York, 1937.

SPERRY, W. L., *Religion in America* (E. A. Benians, ed., *American Life and Institutions*). Cambridge, 1946.

SPILLER, R. E., WILLARD THORP, T. H. JOHNSON and H. S. CANBY, eds., *Literary History of the United States*. 3 v. New York, 1948.

SPROUT, HAROLD and MARGARET, *The Rise of American Naval Power*. Princeton, 1939.

——, *Toward a New Order of Sea Power*. Princeton, 1940.

SQUIRES, J. D., *British Propaganda at Home and in the United States from 1914 to 1917 (Harvard Historical Monographs*, VI). Cambridge, 1935.

STANWOOD, EDWARD, *American Tariff Controversies in the Nineteenth Century*. 2 v. Boston, 1903.

——, *A History of the Presidency*. 2 v. Boston, 1916.

STEDMAN, M. S., JR., and SUSAN W., *Discontent at the Polls*. New York, 1950.

STEPHENSON, N. W., *Nelson W. Aldrich*. New York, 1930.

STETTINIUS, E. R., JR., *Lend-Lease, Weapon for Victory*. New York, 1944.

STEUART, JUSTIN, *Wayne Wheeler, Dry Boss*. New York, 1928.

STIEGLITZ, JULIUS, *Chemistry and Recent Progress in Medicine*. Baltimore, 1924.

STONE, CANDACE, *Dana and the Sun*. New York, 1938.

STONE, H. A., D. K. PRICE and KATHRYN H. STONE, *City Manager Government in the United States*. Chicago, 1940.

STRAUS, M. W., and TALBOT WEGG, *Housing Comes of Age*. New York, 1938.

STREETER, F. B., *Prairie Trails & Cow Towns*. Boston, 1936.

SULLIVAN, MARK, *Our Times: the United States, 1900–1925*. 6 v. New York, 1926–1935.

SWEET, W. W., *The Story of Religion in America*. Rev. ed. New York, 1939.

SWISHER, C. B., *American Constitutional Development*. Boston, 1943.

TALLMADGE, T. E., *The Story of American Architecture*. New York, 1927.

TANSILL, C. C., *America Goes to War*. Boston, 1938.

——, *The Foreign Policy of Thomas F. Bayard, 1885–1897*. New York, 1940.

——, *The Purchase of the Danish West Indies*. Baltimore, 1932.

——, *The United States and Santo Domingo, 1798–1873*. Baltimore, 1938.

TARBELL, IDA M., *The History of the Standard Oil Company*. 2 v. New York, 1904.

——, *The Nationalizing of Business, 1878–1898 (A History of American Life*, IX). New York, 1936.

——, *The Tariff in Our Times*. New York, 1911.

TATE, MERZE, *The Disarmament Illusion: the Movement for a Limitation of Armaments to 1907*. New York, 1942.

TAUSSIG, F. W., *The Tariff History of the United States*. Rev. ed. New York, 1931.

TAYLOR, W. F., *The Economic Novel in America*. Chapel Hill, 1942.

THOMAS, B. P., *Russo-American Relations, 1815–1867* (Johns Hopkins University, *Studies*, XLVIII, no. 2). Baltimore, 1930.

THOMAS, H. C., *The Return of the Democratic Party to Power in 1884* (Columbia University, *Studies*, LXXXIX, no. 2). New York, 1919.

THOMPSON, HOLLAND, *The New South* (*The Chronicles of America Series*, XLII). New Haven, 1919.

THORP, MARGARET, *America at the Movies*. New York, 1940.

THWING, C. F., *The American and the German University*. New York, 1928.

TOURTELLOT, A. B., and others, eds., *Life's Picture History of World War II*. New York, 1950.

TREAT, P. J., *Diplomatic Relations between the United States and Japan, 1853–1905*. 3 v. Stanford University, 1932–1938.

TRIMBLE, W. J., *The Mining Advance into the Inland Empire* (University of Wisconsin, *Bulletin*, no. 638). Madison, 1914.

TUPPER, ELEANOR, and G. E. McREYNOLDS, *Japan in American Public Opinion*. New York, 1937.

TYLER, ALICE F., *The Foreign Policy of James G. Blaine*. Minneapolis, 1927.

VAN HISE, C. R., *Conservation and Regulation in the United States during the World War*. Washington, 1917.

WALKER, JOHN, and MACGILL JAMES, *Great American Paintings, 1729–1924*. New York, 1943.

WARE, LOUISE, *Jacob A. Riis*. New York, 1938.

WARE, N. J., *The Labor Movement in the United States, 1860–1895*. New York, 1929.

WARREN, CHARLES, *The Supreme Court in United States History*. Rev. ed. 2 v. Boston, 1926.

WATSON, F. D., *The Charity Organization Movement in the United States*. New York, 1922.

WEBB, W. P., *The Great Plains*. Boston, 1931.

WEBER, A. F., *The Growth of Cities in the Nineteenth Century* (Columbia University, *Studies*, XI). New York, 1899.

WEBERG, F. P., *The Background of the Panic of 1893*. Washington, 1929.

WECTER, DIXON, *The Age of the Great Depression, 1929–1941* (*A History of American Life*, XIII). New York, 1948.

——, *The Saga of American Society*. New York, 1937.

——, *When Johnny Comes Marching Home*. Boston, 1944.

WEINBERG, A. K., *Manifest Destiny*. Baltimore, 1935.

WELLMAN, P. I., *Death on Horseback, Seventy Years of War for the American West*. Philadelphia, 1947.

——, *The Trampling Herd*. New York, 1939.

WERNER, M. R., *Bryan*. New York, 1929.

WESLEY, C. H., *Negro Labor in the United States, 1850–1925*. New York, 1927.

WESTERGAARD, W. C., *The Danish West Indies*. New York, 1917.

WEYL, NATHANIEL, *Treason: the Story of Disloyalty and Betrayal in American History*. Washington, 1950.

WHITE, LLEWELLYN, *The American Radio* (Commission on Freedom of the Press, *Publications*, IV). Chicago, 1947.

WHITE, M. G., *Social Thought in America*. New York, 1949.

WHITE, TRUMBULL, *Puerto Rico and Its People*. New York, 1938.

WHITMAN, WILLSON, *Bread and Circuses*. New York, 1937.

WILBUR, R. L., and A. M. HYDE, *The Hoover Policies*. New York, 1937.

WILKERSON, M. M., *Public Opinion and the Spanish-American War* (Louisiana State University, *Studies*, no. 8). Baton Rouge, 1932.

WILL, A. S., *Life of Cardinal Gibbons*. 2 v. New York, 1922.

WILLIAMS, ARTHUR, *Power on the Farm*. New York, 1927.

WILLIAMS, B. H., *Economic Foreign Policy of the United States*. New York, 1929.

——, *The United States and Disarmament*. New York, 1931.

WILLIAMS, C. R., *The Life of Rutherford Birchard Hayes*. 2 v. Boston, 1914.

WILLIAMS, MARY W., *Anglo-American Isthmian Diplomacy, 1815–1915*. Washington, 1916.

WILLIS, H. P., *The Federal Reserve System*. New York, 1923.

WILLOUGHBY, W. F., *Government Organization in War Time and After*. New York, 1919.

WILSON, H. F., *The Hill Country of Northern New England, Its Social and Economic History, 1790–1930* (Columbia University, *Studies in the History of American Agriculture*, III). New York, 1936.

WILSON, JENNIE L., *The Legal and Political Status of Women in the United States*. Cedar Rapids, 1912.

WINKLER, J. K., *The Du Pont Dynasty*. New York, 1935.

——, *W. R. Hearst*. New York, 1928.

WINSTON, R. W., *Andrew Johnson*. New York, 1928.

WINTHER, O. O., *The Great Northwest*. New York, 1947.

WISAN, J. E., *The Cuban Crisis as Reflected in the New York Press, 1895–1898* (Columbia University, *Studies*, no. 403). New York, 1934.

WISE, WINIFRED E., *Jane Addams of Hull-House*. New York, 1935.

WITTKE, CARL, *We Who Built America*. New York, 1939.

WOLMAN, LEO, *The Growth of American Trade Unions, 1880–1923*. New York, 1924.

WOODS, ELEANOR H., *Robert A. Woods*. Boston, 1929.

WOODS, R. A., and A. J. KENNEDY, *The Settlement Horizon*. New York, 1922.

WOODWARD, C. V., *Tom Watson, Agrarian Rebel*. New York, 1938.

——, *Reunion and Reaction, the Compromise of 1877 and the End of Reconstruction*. Boston, 1951.

WOODWORTH, J. V., *American Tool Making and Interchangeable Manufacturing*. New York, 1911.

WOODY, THOMAS, *A History of Women's Education in the United States* (J. M. Cattell, ed., *Science and Education*, IV). 2 v. New York, 1929.

WRIGHT, C. W., *Economic History of the United States*. Rev. ed. New York, 1949.

YELLEN, SAMUEL, *American Labor Struggles*. New York, 1936.

YOUNG, A. N., *The Single Tax Movement in the United States*. Princeton, 1916.

ZINK, HAROLD, *City Bosses in the United States*. Durham, 1930.

INDEX

AAA. *See* Agricultural Adjustment Administration.

ABC powers, and Monroe Doctrine, 257; and Mexican imbroglio, 259.

A. E. F. *See* American Expeditionary Force.

Abbott, Lyman, and social gospel, 118; and evolution, 119.

Academic freedom, upheld, 135; restricted, 387, 392–393, 393–394; and anti-Communist oaths, 489.

Acheson, D. G., Secretary of State, 458 *n.*, 485; and North Atlantic Treaty, 485; on Korea, 498; backs Truman against MacArthur, 506; and United Action for Peace plan, 507.

Act of Chapultepec, 472, 485.

Actors and actresses, nineteenth-century, 142; early twentieth-century, 235; of 1920's and '30's, 399–400; entertain soldiers, 433–444.

Adams, C. F., Secretary of Navy, 317 *n.*

Adams, Henry, on Grant's administration, 53; on R. B. Hayes, 61; historian, 135.

Adams, J. T., historian, 394.

Adams, S. H., exposes patent medicines, 202, 210.

Adamson Law, passed, 228.

Addams, Jane, founds Hull-House, 108, 116–117.

Advertising, newspaper, 82, 131; billboard, 82, 396; magazine, 234; New Deal forbids misleading, 373; radio, 389; movie, 389; of American Medical Association, 504.

Advisory Commission on National Defense, created, 420; replaced, 434.

Africa, struggle for, 173, 177, 178; in World War II, 443–444, 445–447; and Point Four program, 484; UN mediates in, 487.

Agassiz, Louis, against evolution, 134.

Agattu Island, Japan seizes, 443; Japan abandons, 452.

Agricultural Adjustment Act, provisions, 355–356; new, 371.

Agricultural Adjustment Administration, curtails production, 356; protest against, 357; Supreme Court decision on, 357; made continuing agency, 358; accomplishments, 363, 365, 370–371; under new Agricultural Adjustment Act, 371–372.

Agriculture, post-Civil War, 4, 21–22, 45, 56; Economic Revolution in, 37–38; growth of scientific, 38, 134, 334; and tariff, 73, 77, 335; depression in 1880's, 147–148; and conservation, 211; during World War I, 280–281, 334; postwar depression in, 334; federal legislation for (1920's), 335–336; overproduction in, 335–336; Great Depression affects, 340; under New Deal, 355–357, 371–372, 382–383; production in World War II, 436; and price supports, 463, 469; and price control in Cold War, 511. *See also* Crop limitation, Farmers, Farms.

Aguinaldo, Emilio, and Spanish-American War, 189; captured, 250.

Air brake, invented, 42.

Air force, in World War I, 278, 287; in World War II, 416, 417, 419, 432, 442; in Korean War, 502.

Airplane. *See* Aviation.

Alabama, reconstructed, 14; postwar taxes, 18; redeemed, 20; manufacturing, 41; education, 128.

Alabama claims, 23, 24, 52.

Alaska, purchased, 24; as American possession, 248; gold, 248; threatened in World War II, 442; statehood proposed for, 491.

Hitler, Adolf, 321, 410; U. S.
industrial secrets aid, 328; rises to
power, 402, 407, 411, 412; on
America, 407; annexes territory,
411–413; makes pact with Russia,
412; American opinion against,
413; smashes toward France, 416–
417, 419; attacks Russia, 422;
counters U. S. acts, 424; Allied
bombing weakens, 445; ignores
Italy's capitulation, 447; expends
last reserves, 449; dies, 450.

Hoar, E. R., Attorney-General, 52.

Hoar, G. F., on political corruption,
56; for woman suffrage, 115; on
annexation of Philippines, 190.

Hobart, G. A., named for Vice-President, 157.

Hoffman, P. G., heads Marshall Plan,
482.

Hogg, James, agrarian, 148.

Holding companies, formed, 91–92;
decision against, 208; Clayton
Antitrust Act seeks to regulate, 224;
growth of, 328; against TVA, 361;
federal regulation of, 361–362.

Home Insurance Building, as skyscraper, 140.

Home Owners' Loan Corporation,
work of, 350.

Homer, Winslow, artist, 138, 239.

Homestead Act, provisions and purpose, 30–31; in operation, 37,
146.

Homestead strike, 78, 97, 102.

Homesteads, Southern nonrepresentation in Congress affects, 28; growth
of, 39–40; scarce, 124, 168. See also
Homestead Act.

Hong Kong, Japan attacks, 426; Japan
conquers, 442.

Hoover, Herbert, heads Belgian relief,
271–272; heads Food Administration, 280; and 1920 campaign, 311;
Secretary of Commerce, 311, 327;
elected President, 316–317; characterized, 317; cabinet, 317 n., 419;
backs London naval conference,
320; on Pact of Paris, 321;
negotiates moratorium, 322–323;
vetoes bonus bill, 326; and Big
Business, 326; tariff under, 326–

327; against federal control of industry, 329; on prohibition, 333;
agriculture under, 336; and Great
Depression, 338–341, 347; finance
under, 339, 364–365; fails of reelection, 340–341; against U. S.
Employment Service, 347; and RFC,
349; and Philippines, 403; antiimperialistic attitude of, 404; visits
Virgin Islands, 404; on welfare state,
468; urges reorganization of executive branch, 469.

Hoover Dam, constructed, 329; in
operation, 361.

Hope-Aiken Law, passed, 463; replaced, 469.

Hopkins, H. L., directs FERA, 347;
directs WPA, 348.

Hospitals, for contagious diseases, 111;
in Puerto Rico, 249; in World War
I, 284, 287, 292; New Deal aids,
350.

Hours of labor, increased in nineteenth century, 92, 100; shortened
for women, 204; Supreme Court
decisions on, 205; strikers demand
shorter, 207; shortened in 1900's,
227; the church for shorter, 233;
War Labor Policies Board fixes,
293; under NRA, 353; under Fair
Labor Standards Act, 372–373. See
also Eight-hour day.

House, E. M., peace envoy, 273, 289;
at Peace Conference, 294; Wilson
and, 295.

Housing, attempts to reform city,
108–109; reform in England, 205;
early twentieth-century, 239–240;
New Deal, 350–351, 371; cities improve, 378; Truman improves,
459–460; prefabricated, 460; government, 468–469. See also Slums.

How the Other Half Lives, influence
of, 108–109.

Howard, Bronson, dramatist, 142.

Howard, O. O., heads Freedmen's
Bureau, 6.

Howard, Sidney, dramatist, 399.

Howard University, founded, 121.

Howells, W. D., on Haymarket riot,
102; on newspapers, 131; as author,
137.

Yale University, Porter at, 133; Taft at, 237.

Yalta conference, Stalin promises to war on Japan at, 453; determines voting rights, 472; concessions to Stalin at, 474, 475–476, 495; declares for democratic institutions, 475.

Yellow-dog contracts, unenforceable, 330.

Yellow fever, in 1878–79, 110; controlled, 189, 238, 249; hampers building of Panama Canal, 198.

Yellow journalism, origin of term, 130; and war in Cuba, 184.

Yellow Kid, The, cartoon, 130.

Young, O. D., reparations plan, 322.

Young Men's Christian Association, Wanamaker aids, 74; work of, 117; in World War I, 293, 309; in World War II, 433.

Young Women's Christian Association, work of, 117; in World War I, 293; in World War II, 433.

Yugoslavia, in World War I peace negotiations, 296, 299 *n.;* Axis conquers, 441; in World War II peace negotiations, 477; disavows Russian control, 480.

Zimmermann note, made public, 275–276.